Principles *of* Microeconomics

Principles *of* Microeconomics
The Way We Live

Susan K. Feigenbaum
University of Missouri – St. Louis

R. W. Hafer
Southern Illinois University Edwardsville

Worth Publishers

Senior Vice President, Editorial and Production: Catherine Woods
Publisher: Charles Linsmeier
Executive Marketing Manager: Scott Guile
Marketing Assistant: Julie Tompkins
Developmental Editors: Marie McHale/Amy Ray
Senior Media Editor: Marie McHale
Associate Managing Editor: Lisa Kinne
Supplements Production Manager: Stacey Alexander
Supplements Project Editor: Edgar Bonilla
Assistant Editor: Mary Melis
Photo Editor: Bianca Moscatelli
Production Manager: Barbara Anne Seixas
Composition: MPS Limited
Printing and Binding: Quad/Graphics
Cover Art: Steven Miric/istockphoto; Roberto Gennaro/istockphoto;
Stephan Hoerold/istockphoto; traveler1116/istockphoto

ISBN-13: 978-1-4292-2021-7
ISBN-10: 1-4292-2021-X

Library of Congress Control Number: 2011943551

© 2012 by Worth Publishers

Printed in the United States of America

First printing 2012

Worth Publishers
41 Madison Avenue
New York, NY 10010
www.worthpublishers.com

To Professors Anne Carter, Barney Schwalberg, Ronald Teeples, and Burton Weisbrod for treating me like an economist long before I knew I was one. And to my husband, Jay Pepose, and our children, David, Max, Sam, and Morissa, who bore much of the opportunity cost of my writing this book. — S. K. F.

To Gail and Cait for the unending patience, support, and help they provided me during the writing of this book. — R. W. H.

ABOUT THE AUTHORS

Susan K. Feigenbaum is Professor and former Chair of the Department of Economics at the University of Missouri in St. Louis. She has been the recipient of several National Science Foundation research and curriculum innovation grants and has received both the Governor's and Chancellor's Awards for Teaching Excellence. She has published extensively in such areas as public versus private provision of goods and services; the economics of science; and the economics of health care finance.

R.W. Hafer is the Distinguished Research Professor of Economics and Finance in the Department of Economics and Finance at Southern Illinois University Edwardsville. Prior to joining the SIUE faculty he worked as an economist with the Federal Reserve Bank of St. Louis. In addition to SIUE, he has taught at Washington University in St. Louis and at Erasmus University in Rotterdam, the Netherlands. He has published widely on monetary policy and financial markets in academic and non-academic publications, including the *Journal of Monetary Economics*, the *Journal of Finance*, and the *Wall Street Journal*.

BRIEF CONTENTS

Part 5: Winners and Losers in a Competitive World: Are Free Markets Unfair?

CONTENTS

Part 2: From Individual Choices to Market Outcomes

Part 3: Comparative Advantage, Specialization, and Trade

Part 5: Winners and Losers in a Competitive World: Are Free Markets Unfair?

FOREWORD

The impetus for *Principles of Microeconomics: The Way We Live* came on a warm spring day during a visit to the Strand Bookstore in New York City. There in the dusty basement, tucked among the shelves of pre-owned economics books was a book written by Professor Victor Fuchs, a preeminent economist at Stanford University. The book, entitled *How We Live,* provided "An Economic Perspective on Americans from Birth to Death." With a smattering of data and graphs and no math whatsoever, Professor Fuchs offered a "lifecycle" perspective on the economic and demographic factors affecting the choices we make at every phase of our lives: from birth and infancy through young adulthood and, finally, old age. Anyone who has read the book would not be surprised that it won a National Book Award in 1983.

What serendipity! I had stopped in New York City on my way home from a reviewers' meeting of grant proposals submitted to the National Science Foundation's Undergraduate Course and Curriculum Development Program (UCCD). In the social science division, there were only a few proposals submitted by economists and even fewer that were worthy of funding. In contrast, the sociologists dominated with innovative, well-thought-out proposals with robust evaluation modules. I knew my economics colleagues and I could do better.

The Way We Live provided a unique framework within which my University of Missouri–St. Louis colleagues—Professors Tom Ireland, Sharon Levin, and Anne Winkler—and I could integrate more technical aspects of the microeconomics principles course, while preserving the accessibility of the material. By providing an experiential-based learning environment, we believed that we could better serve our increasingly diverse student body.

We were successful the first time we submitted our proposal to the UCCD review panel. Reviewers commented on its originality and the way in which economic theory and numeracy skills were integrated in nonthreatening ways. We were one of only two economics proposals funded that cycle, out of more than 90 funded projects. For the next several years, Myles Boylan, our National Science Foundation project officer, served as our conscientious steward. He prodded us to widely disseminate the materials we were developing and seek feedback on the feasibility of integrating them into the principles curriculum.

When the grant ended, I chose to continue with the project while my colleagues returned full-time to their research agendas. Nevertheless, the end product reflects a great deal of their creativity and efforts, for which I am truly grateful. I have also benefited from students in the dozen or so principles classes that have used versions of the manuscript as their course textbook. By and large, the students enjoyed participating in the creation of a textbook; their contributions ranged from correcting punctuation errors to questioning my reasoning and demanding more "proof" to support my conclusions. Although space precludes me from naming all of these students, I would be remiss if I did not mention those who made significant contributions. My deepest thanks go to Brian Regula, Dave Sanders, Emily Trevathan, Jason Buol, Neil Wiggins, Allison Levin, Kathleen Early, and Dave Rifkin.

Several economics colleagues provided ongoing support, especially when it was unclear whether anyone would adopt a principles book that tried to tell stories about the world without getting bogged down prematurely in technical analyses or unrealistic assumptions. I am deeply indebted to W. Lee Hansen, Bob Tollison, Janet Johnson, and Michael T. Allison for cheering me on to the finish line. And my warmest thanks go to Gloria Axe, who began the process of translating the course materials into a textbook, and Tania Michalicek, who gave me the gift of time that I needed to complete this project.

Finally, I am grateful that my colleague and friend, Professor Rik Hafer, accepted my invitation to assume primary responsibility for the macroeconomic materials in the book. He was once described to me as "a person who doesn't suffer fools lightly," and for that I am very grateful. Rik has improved the quality of both the microeconomics and macroeconomics sections of the book immensely as has his wife, Professor Gail Heyne Hafer, who prepared the instructors' materials that accompany the book. Rik and Gail share my vision of a future when introductory economics courses are no longer considered "the hardest, dullest, most boring classes" that students ever took. After all, Professor Fuchs put it best when he said that economics is really just about "how we live."

Susan K. Feigenbaum
March 2012

PREFACE

Our experiences in the classroom and our many years of talking with students and colleagues alike provided a catalyst for writing this book. Many principles texts introduce students to economics as if it were a foreign language—one that they have never encountered before. In reality, economic principles aren't foreign to anyone: day in and day out, we all make decisions that are in harmony with these principles, and these choices often have significant effects on our overall well-being.

In *Principles of Microeconomics: The Way We Live*, our goal is to help students cultivate an appreciation for—and an ability to use—their economic "instincts." Unlike other books, our approach exploits common experiences to demonstrate to students how they already use economic reasoning, whether consciously or not. This serves two purposes. First, it demystifies economics by showing students that the way in which they weigh costs versus benefits, for example, provides the foundation for an economic model that can predict economic behavior. Second, it shows students that the same economic principles upon which their own decisions are based are the principles used to gauge the economic success of decisions made by politicians and policy makers. We achieve these goals by building up an economic framework: first we explore the economics of individual decision making; then we extend this approach to economic decision making within markets and the conditions for trade. After this is completed, we move on to people's decisions to trade off their well-being today (make an investment) for more well-being tomorrow and how investments in human capital are valued in the market. Only then do we expand our analysis to economywide relationships. Throughout this book, we exploit the natural linkage between microeconomics and macroeconomics that other texts sometimes fail to capitalize on.

As teachers with more than 60 years of classroom experience combined, we have also come to believe that the language of economics should enhance learning—not be an impediment to it. As a result, we have made a concerted effort not to bog students down with an unreasonable amount of terminology. Our approach is to offer an applied introduction to modern economic thinking that is extremely readable and uses everyday events to develop the theory. We are storytellers first—whether it is about an individual's choice to invest in education or the impact of changing government regulations on people's purchases of hybrid cars—before we generalize to predictive economic models. In this way, students are engaged by the experiential nature of the course and become personally invested in it. Students using this book quickly come to realize that the analytical tools they learn really do "work"—that is, they can be used to better understand the behavior of people and organizations that these students interact with on a daily basis, to increase awareness of broader microeconomic and macroeconomic phenomena, and to better appreciate the ramifications of government policies. By anchoring economic theory to real-world events and data, we emphasize the relevance of economics to our students' everyday lives.

What Makes This Book Different?

When you consider adopting a principles of economics text, do you find yourself asking some or all of the following questions?

- Is it my job to teach students an entirely new way of thinking, or can I successfully teach economic principles by building on the way students already approach their everyday decision making?

- Why is it that most books do not apply economics in a way that students find interesting and applicable to their everyday lives?

- Why do I cringe every time I ask my students to buy into assumptions that they—and I—know are unrealistic simplifications of the world around them?

- Have I grown irritated with the overwhelming amount of technical apparatus that I must cover with my students, promising them that "down the line" they will get to applications and appreciate the relevance of the material?

- Why doesn't my micro text include public policy, business, international, and macro examples rather than leaving them to a later chapter or course?

- How can I get to the chapters at the end of the textbook—covering such topics as externalities, public choice, property rights, and international economics—that I know would be the most fun for my students?

If you have asked yourself these questions, then this textbook is a good choice for you.

Early readers of this book, even in rough manuscript form, often described our approach as an "inverted" one. That is, the book tends to describe a real-life situation, propose an economic explanation for observed behavior, and only then broaden the example to a more generalized theoretical result. This approach contrasts with other books that approach economic topics by first presenting a seemingly obscure conceptual construct and then offering (sometimes) relevant examples. Our goal is to motivate students to want to use economic theory because it helps explain what is going on around them every day.

This framework enables us to include material that will engage a wide variety of principles students, whether they are enrolled in arts and sciences, public policy, or a business program. For example, income elasticity of demand has important consequences for the movement of specific stock prices over the business cycle. At the same time, it provides vital information on how nutritional intake in developing countries changes as these nations become wealthier. Likewise, the price elasticity of demand offers a benchmark for the success of corporate-branding campaigns while, at the same time, helping us understand how price increases in core goods such as gasoline affect people's well-being.

We have consciously adopted a writing style that involves the student in a dialogue. It strives to be both accessible and engaging. We have woven and re-woven certain themes throughout the book to reinforce student learning. One unifying concept is opportunity cost and, relatedly, the weighing of marginal costs versus marginal benefits. We believe that these are core principles in economics that deserve to be emphasized throughout the textbook. We spend time at the outset exploring the meaning of economic cost and economic benefit and how costs and benefits can vary over time with changes in the economic environment.

Throughout the text, we bring in international examples that help move students beyond a U.S- centric perspective. Moreover, unlike virtually any other introductory book, we recognize that the economy is comprised of far more producing organizations than simply for-profit firms. In this regard, we explore the resource-allocation decisions within households, private nonprofit organizations, and government entities. Once again, the goal is to broaden the discussion and, correspondingly, take maximum advantage of the experiential learning of our students.

How This Book Is Organized

This book is organized in a way that incorporates our approach throughout the book, from introductory chapters through to the last chapter. The following walk-through highlights the concepts and examples presented in each part of the book.

Part 1: Economic Costs and the Choices People Make

In Part 1, we develop a framework for predicting how individuals make economic decisions. Specifically, we suggest that people act *as if* they weigh the costs against the benefits of the opportunities they face. This approach leads to a number of questions: Exactly what kinds of costs and benefits factor into a person's decision process? How are these costs and benefits affected by changes in the economic environment? How do changes in costs and benefits affect an individual's decisions? And, what happens if people base their decisions only on the costs and benefits they themselves face, rather than on the costs and benefits that their choices generate for other individuals and for society at large?

Part 2: From Individual Choices to Market Outcomes

In Part 2, we show how people's decisions create a foundation for how markets operate. We derive the demand curve directly from the concept of net benefit developed in Part 1, using as a bridge the notion of willingness to pay. The supply curve is generated in much the same way, by focusing on the net benefit that producers get from supplying goods to a market. After we have developed the supply-and-demand apparatus and have distinguished between movements along and shifts in these curves, we predict the price at which a good is exchanged, the total amount of the good that is traded, and how changes in the economic environment are likely to affect these outcomes. These include changes in property rights, factor prices, prices of substitutes and complements, technology (knowledge), preferences, and so on. We determine the gains from trade for buyers and sellers and show how government policies—specifically price controls—can lead to unintentional and sometimes adverse market outcomes that ultimately reduce at least some people's economic well-being while improving the well-being of others.

Part 3: Comparative Advantage, Specialization, and Trade

In Part 3, we look at why gains from voluntary trade arise and how scarce resources can be directed to maximize the economic "pie." We begin by looking at how scarce resources within a household are deployed. Within this context, the concepts of absolute and comparative advantage are introduced, along with the production possibilities frontier (PPF). After this framework is established, we provide some insights into the bargaining process that ultimately determines the division of gains from trade within organizations such as the household. This offers an innovative way to introduce the basics of game theory. Finally, we consider the impact that government policies, specifically taxes and subsidies, have on the substitution of market-based goods and services for household-based production.

Part 3 concludes with a discussion about how households—and other producing organizations, for that matter—make decisions about investing some of their current resources to potentially improve their well-being in the future. How much, if anything, should they invest, and what should they invest in? What special considerations might be given to investing in one's own human capital and the human capital of others in the household? We also discuss the value that labor markets place on investments in education and related types of human capital, and why these investments typically yield higher wage rates. Finally, we examine the extent to which these higher wages contribute to the growing income inequality in the United States. An added feature in Part 3 is an Appendix to Chapter 10 that describes the changing composition of households and predicts the effect on household production, including investment in children.

Part 4: The Strategic Behavior of Firms: Surviving in the Marketplace

We begin Part 4 with an inquiry into why producing organizations might want to minimize their costs of production, regardless of whether they are profit maximizing or not. The short- and long-run minimizing mix of inputs into production is tied back to the findings in Part 3 about how wages are determined. We examine the objectives of diverse types of producing organizations and evaluate their behavior within the context of their different sources of revenue, types of goods produced, and ownership forms. The output decisions of price-taking, for-profit firms are examined, and the profit-maximizing "rule" is developed within the marginal benefit and marginal cost framework of economic decision making. After we explore the response of perfectly competitive firms and markets to changes in the economic environment, we move on to firms operating in imperfectly competitive markets. Monopolies, oligopolies, monopsonies, and monopolistically competitive firms are discussed. We apply game theory to better understand the interrelated behavior of household and market *rivals*. The concept of rivalry is an important one in that it more clearly distinguishes competition between the few from competition between the many.

Part 5: Winners and Losers in a Competitive World: Are Free Markets Unfair?

Part 5 contains the final chapter of the book. It focuses on the distributional consequences of market-based activities and market adjustments to changes in the economic environment. How do people perceive markets in terms of their fairness? Does having "skin in the game" matter? How do government policies try to mitigate some of the economic "pain" resulting from free markets? An important distinction is made between growing the total economic pie and the piece that each individual receives. That is, we address the question of how some people can be made worse off from market trade despite the fact that exchanges are voluntary and result in a bigger economic pie. Labor market dislocations and their impact on wage rates and unemployment are discussed. We also explore some of the unintended consequences of government attempts to redistribute income, including the impact these policies can have on the well-being of low-income consumers. Within this context, we consider the possibility that government redistribution programs can be captured by vested interests, leading to "corporate welfare" and a redistribution of income to higher-income members in the community. Finally, we conclude with a discussion of efforts to alleviate global poverty by redistributing income from richer to poorer nations, and how these efforts have fared in terms of achieving their goals.

Supplements and Media

For Instructors

Instructor's Resource Manual with Solutions Manual

The *Instructor's Resource Manual*, written by Professor Gail Heyne Hafer (St. Louis Community College, Meramec), is a resource that provides materials and tips to enhance the classroom experience. The *Instructor's Resource Manual* provides the following:

- Overview of each chapter
- Chapter-by-chapter learning objectives
- Chapter outlines
- Teaching notes
- Outline of the principle concepts students will learn in each chapter
- Activities that can be conducted in or out of the classroom
- Solutions manual with detailed answers to all of the end-of-chapter problems from the textbook

Printed Test Bank

The Test Bank provides a wide range of questions appropriate for assessing your students' comprehension, interpretation, analysis, and synthesis skills. The Test Bank offers questions designed for comprehensive coverage of the text concepts. Questions have been checked for continuity with the text content, overall usability, and accuracy.

The Test Bank features include the following:

- To aid instructors in building tests, each question has been categorized according to its general *degree of difficulty*. The three levels are easy, moderate, and difficult.
  - *Easy* questions require students to recognize concepts and definitions. These are questions that can be answered by direct reference to the textbook.
  - *Moderate* questions require some analysis on the student's part.
  - *Difficult* questions usually require more detailed analysis by the student.
- Each question has also been categorized according to a *skill descriptor*. These include fact-based, definitional, concept-based, critical-thinking, and analytical-thinking questions.
  - *Fact-based questions* require students to identify facts presented in the text.
  - *Definitional questions* require students to define an economic term or concept.
  - *Concept-based questions* require a straightforward knowledge of basic concepts.
  - *Critical-thinking questions* require the student to apply a concept to a particular situation.

- *Analytical-thinking questions* require another level of analysis to answer the question. Students must be able to apply a concept and use this knowledge for further analysis of a situation or scenario.

■ To further aid instructors in building tests, each question is conveniently cross-referenced to the appropriate topic heading in the textbook. Questions are presented in the order in which concepts are presented in the text.

■ Questions have been designed to correlate with the questions in the textbook.

Computerized Test Bank

The printed Test Bank is available in CD-ROM format for both Windows and Macintosh users. With the Diploma program, instructors can easily create and print tests and write and edit questions. Tests can be printed in a wide range of formats. The software's unique synthesis of flexible word-processing and database features creates a program that is extremely intuitive and capable.

Lecture PowerPoint Presentations

These presentations, created by Eric R. Nielsen (St. Louis Community College), consist of PowerPoint slides that provide graphs from the textbook, tables, and bulleted lists of key concepts suitable for lecture presentation. Key figures from the text are replicated and animated to enhance class lectures. These slides incorporate concept-based questions that may be used along with i>clicker. The slides may also be customized by instructors to suit their individual needs and can be accessed on the instructor's side of the Web site or on the Instructor's Resource CD-ROM.

Instructor's Resource CD-ROM

Using the Instructor's Resource CD-ROM, instructors can easily build classroom presentations or enhance online courses. This CD-ROM contains all text figures (in JPEG and PPT formats), PowerPoint lecture slides, and detailed solutions to all end-of-chapter problems. Instructors can choose from the various resources, and then edit and save them for use in the classroom. The Instructor's Resource CD-ROM includes the following:

■ **Instructor's Resource Manual** (PDF): An overview of each chapter, chapter-by-chapter learning objectives, chapter outlines, teaching notes, outlines of the principle concepts students will learn in each chapter, and notes on activities that can be conducted in or out of the classroom.

■ **Solutions Manual** (PDF): Detailed solutions to all of the end-of-chapter problems from the textbook.

■ **Lecture PowerPoint presentations** (PPT): PowerPoint slides, including graphs, data tables, and bulleted lists of key concepts suitable for lecture presentation.

■ **Images from the textbook** (JPEG): A complete set of textbook images in high-resolution and low-resolution JPEG formats.

■ **Illustration PowerPoint slides** (PPT): A complete set of figures and tables from the textbook in PPT format.

For Instructors and Students

Companion Web Site:

www.worthpublishers.com/feigenbaumhafer

The companion Web site is a virtual study guide for students and an excellent resource for instructors. The tools on the site include the following:

Student Resources

- **Quizzes:** Provides a set of quiz questions per chapter with appropriate feedback and page references to the textbook. All student answers are saved in an online gradebook that can be accessed by instructors.

- **Key term flashcards:** Students can test themselves on the key terms with these pop-up electronic flashcards.

Instructor Resources

- **Gradebook:** The site gives you the ability to track students' work by accessing an online gradebook.

- **Lecture PowerPoint presentations (PPT):** These PowerPoint slides are designed to assist instructors with lecture preparation and presentation by providing bulleted lecture outlines suitable for large lecture presentation. Instructors can customize these slides to suit their individual needs.

- **Images from the textbook** (JPEG): A complete set of textbook images in high-resolution and low-resolution JPEG formats.

- **Illustration PowerPoint slides** (PPT): A complete set of figures and tables from the textbook in PPT format.

- **Instructor's Resource Manual** (PDF): Files provide materials and tips to enhance the classroom experience.

- **Solutions Manual** (PDF): Files provide detailed solutions to all of the end-of-chapter problems from the textbook.

EconPortal

EconPortal marries our rich content and customizability with a user interface that proves that power and simplicity aren't mutually exclusive. The features include the following:

- **Clear, consistent interface:** The eBook, media, assessment tools, instructor materials, and other content are integrated and unified to a degree unparalleled by other online learning systems.

- **Everything is assignable:** All course materials are assignable and computer-gradable: eBook sections, videos, flashcards, discussion forums, as well as traditionally assignable items such as quizzes. Studies show that assigning activities and making them part of students' grades is the most effective way to make online learning activities translate into higher student performance.

- **Everything is customizable:** Instructors can rearrange chapters or sections of the eBook and/or supplement or delete questions from the premade quizzes and homework assignments that come prepackaged in EconPortal.

- **Easy course management integration:** EconPortal is simple to integrate with existing learning-management systems.

EconPortal provides a powerful, easy-to-use, completely customizable teaching and learning-management system complete with the following:

- **Robust, interactive eBook:** The eBook enables a range of note-sharing options, highlighting, graph and example enlargement, a fully searchable glossary, and a full text search.

- **LearningCurve—personalized, formative assessments:** Learning Curve incorporates adaptive question selection, personalized study plans, and state-of-the-art question–analysis reports in activities with a game-like feel that keeps students engaged with the material. Integrated eBook sections provide students with one-click access to additional exposure to the course text. An innovative scoring system ensures that students who need more help with the material spend more time quizzing themselves than students who are already proficient.

- **Powerful online quizzing and homework:** EconPortal includes a state-of-the-art online homework and testing system. Instructors can use precreated assignments for each chapter or create their own assignments. Assignments may be created from the following:

  - **Complete Test Bank for the textbook:** Provides a wide range of questions appropriate for assessing students.

  - **End-of-chapter problems from the textbook:** The end-of-chapter problems will be available in a self-graded format—perfect for quick in-class quizzes or homework assignments. The questions have been carefully edited to ensure that they maintain the integrity of the text's end-of-chapter problems.

  - **Graphing questions:** EconPortal provides electronically gradable graphing problems using a robust graphing engine. Students will be asked to draw their response to a question, and the software will automatically grade that response. These graphing questions are meant to replicate the pencil-and-paper experience of drawing graphs for students.

Blackboard and WebCT

These WebCT and Blackboard e-Packs enable you to create a thorough, interactive, and pedagogically sound online course or course Web site. The e-Packs, provided free, give you cutting-edge online materials that facilitate critical thinking and learning, including Test Bank content, preprogrammed quizzes, links, activities, animated graphs, and a whole array of other materials. Best of all, this material is preprogrammed and fully functional in the WebCT or Blackboard environment. Prebuilt materials eliminate hours of course-preparation work and offer significant support as you develop your online course. The result is an interactive, comprehensive online course that allows for effortless implementation, management, and use. The files can be easily downloaded from our Course Management System site directly onto your department server.

Further Resources Offered

Faculty Lounge

Faculty Lounge is an online community of economics instructors. At this unique forum, economics instructors can connect, interact, and collaborate with fellow teachers and economics researchers, sharing thoughts and teaching resources. Instructors can upload their own resources and search for peer-reviewed content to use in class. Faculty Lounge is a great place to connect with colleagues nationwide who face the same challenges in the classroom as you do. To learn more, ask your Worth representative or visit www.worthpublishers.com/facultylounge.

i>clicker

Developed by a team of University of Illinois physicists, i>clicker is the most flexible and reliable classroom response system available. It is the only solution created *for* educators, *by* educators—with continuous product improvements made through direct classroom testing and faculty feedback. You'll love i>clicker no matter your level of technical expertise because the focus is on *your* teaching, *not the technology*. To learn more about packaging i>clicker with this textbook, please contact your local sales rep or visit www.iclicker.com.

Financial Times Edition

For adopters of the textbook, Worth Publishers and the *Financial Times* are offering a 15-week subscription to students at a tremendous savings. Instructors also receive their own free *Financial Times* subscription for one year. Students and instructors may access research and archived information at www.ft.com.

Dismal Scientist

A high-powered business database and analysis service comes to the classroom! Dismal Scientist offers real-time monitoring of the global economy, produced locally by economists and professionals at Economy.com's London, Sydney, and West Chester offices. Dismal Scientist is *free* when packaged with the Feigenbaum-Hafer text. Please contact your local sales rep for more information or go to www.economy.com.

Acknowledgements

A book like this would not be possible without the assistance of many people, which we gratefully acknowledge. First, the renowned team at Worth has spared no effort in supporting this project; it was clear from the start that Worth was committed to producing the highest quality product possible. Worth's experience and skill in publishing economics textbooks were invaluable. Numerous individuals have been involved in this project: the project was initiated by Craig Bleyer and guided to completion by editors Charles Linsmeier and Sarah Dorger. Through it all, the manuscript was improved enormously by our development editors Marie McHale and Amy Ray. We are greatly in their debt. We would also like to thank Professor Sang Lee, at Southeastern Louisiana University, who did a heroic job ensuring that the text was accurate and provided solutions to all end-of-chapter problems. A special thank you also goes to Professor Janet Johnson, who was brave enough to teach from a much earlier manuscript version and provided invaluable feedback that has improved the text's quality immensely. A number of our colleagues were very helpful in providing their reviews of the text. We wish to thank the following reviewers:

Dean Baim
Pepperdine University

James Bathgate
Willamette University

Gerald Bialka
University of North Florida

Okmyung Bin
East Carolina University

Calvin Blackwell
College of Charleston

Jeanne Boeh
Augsburg College

Barbara Burnell
College of Wooster

Lisa Citron
Cascadia Community College

Antony Davies
Duquesne University

John Deskins
Creighton University

Eric Dodge
Hanover College

Harry Ellis, Jr.
University of North Texas

Mark Funk
University of Arkansas at Little Rock

Robert J. Gitter
Ohio Wesleyan University

Michael G. Goode
University of North Carolina — Charlotte

Brian Kench
University of Tampa

Christopher Klein
Middle Tennessee State University

Andrew Kohen
James Madison University

Sang Lee
Southeastern Louisiana University

Alan Lockard
St. Lawrence University

Heather Micelli
Mira Costa College

Eric Nielsen
St. Louis Community College

Laudo Massaharu Ogura
Grand Valley State University

Michael Podgursky
University of Missouri

Timothy Reynolds
Alvin Community College

Boone Turchi
University of North Carolina at Chapel Hill

Jennifer VanGilder
Ursinus College

Jonathan Warner
Quest University

Jim R. Wollscheid
Texas A&M University — Kingsville

Madeline Zavodny
Agnes Scott College

Susan K. Feigenbaum
R.W. Hafer
March 2012

PART 1

Economic Costs and the Choices People Make

Every day, we are confronted with economic choices that we must make. Whether it's our time or money, we must decide how to use our scarce resources to make ourselves as well off as possible. Spending time in school means less time spent earning money; buying designer clothing means fewer outfits than if we shopped at a discount-apparel store; and getting married means sharing our scarce resources with someone else and vice versa.

In Part 1, we develop a framework for predicting how individuals make economic decisions. Specifically, we suggest that people act as if they have weighed the costs against the benefits of the alternatives they face. This approach leads to a number of questions. Exactly what kinds of costs and benefits factor into a person's decision process? How are the costs and benefits of a choice affected by changes in the economic environment? How do changes in costs and benefits affect an individual's choices? And, finally, what happens if people base their decisions only on the costs and benefits they themselves face, rather than on the costs and benefits that their choices create for other people and society at large?

Throughout Part 1, you will find many examples that should resonate with your everyday life experiences. This should come as no surprise to you because economics is merely the study of how each of us pursues our unlimited desires given our limited means.

Economics as a Framework for Making Life's Decisions

I f you ask ten people what economics is about, you will probably get ten different answers. Most often, people immediately think of business, Wall Street, and how to make money. Others mention taxes, recessions, inflation, unemployment, or the weak dollar. Older respondents might recollect the "home economics" class that was offered in high school that focused on mastering such household tasks as cooking, sewing, and budgeting. Pushed further, people often embellish their answers with such adjectives as "complicated," "hard to understand," "complex," and even "mysterious." As we will see throughout this book, Mick Jagger (an economics major) aptly summarized what economics is really about—the choices we make when we can't get everything we want. The rest is commentary.

1.1 Exactly What Is Economics?

What is economics? The answer is simple. Economics is the study of the trade-offs we face in our lives. Because each decision we make requires us to choose between two or more options, we face **trade-offs** in just about everything we do.

TRADE-OFFS Opportunities we pass up when we make one choice versus another choice.

EXAMPLE When Mick Jagger decided to become a musician, he gave up the opportunity to become a professional economist.

EXAMPLE When you chose to take this economics class during this time slot, you gave up the opportunity to take another class at the same time.

We each owe our very existence to choices made by our adoptive or biological parents. Our parents could have chosen to spend their resources—their time and their money—on other opportunities rather than parenting. So, as we will soon see, even decisions as basic as whether to have children or not are economic in nature. By observing the choices that people make, we discover that individuals *act as if* they have weighed the trade-offs they face, whether it is deciding which movie to see or whether to have children and, if so, how many. The Nobel Laureate Friedrich von Hayek, an economist, put it this way:

> Many of the greatest things man has achieved are not the result of consciously directed thought, and still less the product of a deliberately coordinated effort of many individuals, but of a process in which the individual plays a part which he can never fully understand.

In other words, humans are "hardwired" to act—not just consciously but also subconsciously—according to economic fundamentals. In fact, brain scientists have recently identified networks of neurons in our brains that assess the costs and benefits of potential actions.[1] Whether this hardwiring is actually due to nature or nurture, we don't know. What we do know, however, is that economists and biologists have discovered a similar pattern of behavior in many other species as well.

If, in fact, people make choices that are consistent with economic principles, then we can predict with some accuracy what their decisions will be when they face certain opportunities. Economics also provides a framework to predict how people will adjust to changes in the trade-offs they face. Although it may take a crystal ball to predict which horse will win the Kentucky Derby, economics does quite well when it comes to predicting how people will typically respond to changes in the price of gasoline or college tuition.

SOLVED PROBLEM

Q **Are people's leisure activities consistent with economic principles?** During their working years, people tend to spend less time playing golf and bowling. Instead, they get their aerobic exercise by working out in gyms and running. Once retired, these same people return to playing golf and bowling. Is this behavior consistent with economic principles?

A **Yes.** We know that during someone's working years, the trade-off between time-consuming recreational activities and other uses of this time (such as earning a living) is different from when a person is in school or retired. The *value* of our time is greater when we have the opportunity to make money at work (which we can then spend on things that give us pleasure) or can use it to move up the career ladder. When we are in school or retired, the value of our time is often less, which permits us to engage in more time-consuming recreational activities, such as bowling or golf. Of course, we do see instances in which active CEOs play golf, but this is usually to solidify business relationships that are directly related to a company's future profitability.

1.2 Living in a World of Scarcity

Why do we face trade-offs when we make choices? Why must we choose between alternatives and be forced to forgo some opportunities? To answer these questions, we must appreciate the reality that we—as well as the world around us—are constantly in a state of **scarcity**.

• • • • • • •

[1]Carl Zimmer, "The Brain." *Discover* (March, 2011): 28–29.

SCARCITY The condition we find ourselves in when only limited resources are available to meet our unlimited wants.

EXAMPLE Seats to popular concerts are scarce, leading to ticket scalping.

EXAMPLE Seats in certain sections of a course are scarce, resulting in waiting lists.

EXAMPLE The talent required to land a job that pays $1 million-plus is scarce.

Because of scarcity, we can't "have it all." We have limited amounts of money to spend on a seemingly unlimited number of goods and services. We have limited amounts of time to work and enjoy such leisure activities as playing video games and watching television. Students who work and go to school or who are raising families and holding down jobs know just how scarce their time is. How often do we say to ourselves "I wish I had another 10 hours in a day" or "I wish I had an extra weekend?"

Time often feels increasingly scarce as we age, especially once we reach middle age and realize that more than half of our life has already been lived. In fact, the degree to which a resource is scarce can vary over time. For example, parking spots at commuter colleges are at their peak scarcity during early morning and evening hours: students are more apt to attend classes during these times so that they can also hold down jobs. At other times, such as mid-afternoon, parking spots may be relatively plentiful.

Our time has, in some sense, become more abundant over the past century due to the introduction of time-saving technologies. The microwave oven and washing machine, for example, have reduced household time demands and allowed the primary homemaker—traditionally a woman—to pursue other activities, including paid employment outside the home. Online shopping opportunities have eliminated some shopping trips and freed up more time for reading books and other leisure activities. The Internet enables students to do research on term papers 24 hours a day, rather than only when their campus libraries are open.

In effect, technology is a tool that can loosen the bonds of scarcity. Because of new technology, drinking water can now be produced from ocean water at relatively low cost. New technology has also increased crop yields, led to new energy supplies, and put recycled materials to new uses. But technology itself is scarce. We must decide how much of today's scarce resources we want to invest in the discovery process to develop technologies that may lessen the degree of scarcity we face in the future. Generally speaking, wealthier nations are in a better position to make this sacrifice, while poorer nations functioning closer to a subsistence level cannot. This is the reason that the pharmaceutical discoveries used to treat AIDS, river blindness, and smallpox have taken place in the United States and Europe, despite the huge benefits they bestow upon people living in poorer countries.

Are there any resources that aren't scarce? Is sunshine, for example, scarce? Ask people who live in one of the Great Lakes states in December. Clearly, sunshine is a scarce resource to them, as evidenced by all of the northern states' license plates that populate Phoenix and Sarasota in the winter. At various times and in various locations, people are willing to sacrifice something (such as buying a new smart phone) to purchase an airline ticket that will bring some sunshine into their lives.

Is air scarce? Certainly, clean air is scarce, as is air in pressurized cabins under the sea or in an airplane at 37,000 feet. "Air" is a scarce resource from a legal standpoint when it contains a panoramic view that a new house will have or a view that a new building will block. People are willing to devote their scarce time and money to acquire "air rights" to unimpeded views and access to nonsmoking buildings with clean indoor air.

Are opinions scarce? Certainly, good ones must be, given the amount of money people are willing to pay stock brokers, financial consultants, and TV commentators.

Are children a scarce good? You need only look at the amount of scarce resources that some couples spend on infertility treatments or adoption to answer this question.

To the extent that we are willing to give up our time or money to obtain something else, the object of our pursuit must be scarce. If it were not, we could gain access to it without having to sacrifice either our time or money. Put this way, it is difficult to think of many things in our world that are not subject to some degree of scarcity. Even love requires us to invest time, not to mention money, for dates and membership fees to Match.com and other matchmaking services.

We use our scarce resources in ways that improve our sense of **well-being.**

WELL-BEING A person's happiness, benefit, pleasure, or contentment.

EXAMPLE Saving money for a rainy day can increase a person's sense of well-being by reducing anxiety about the future.

EXAMPLE Seeing a student grasp a difficult concept often adds to a teacher's sense of well-being.

EXAMPLE Volunteering time as a Boy Scout leader can add to a person's sense of well-being.

We call any scarce resource, product, service, or other source of well-being an **economic good.**

ECONOMIC GOOD Any scarce resource, product, service, or other source of well-being.

EXAMPLE Household pets are economic goods for/to their owners.

EXAMPLE A good movie is an economic good for/to an audience member.

EXAMPLE Time spent hanging out with your best friends is an economic good.

By its very definition, if an economic good were offered free of charge to everyone, there would not be enough of the good to fulfill everyone's "wants." Some people would walk away empty-handed or with less than they wanted. Notice that we refer to what people "want" rather than "need." We make this distinction because "needs" are generally subjective in nature. Beyond the most basic needs to stay alive—oxygen, water, and basic sustenance—to what extent are our "needs" truly necessary?

The perceived needs of people living in the twenty-first century in the United States (think about indoor plumbing, central air conditioning, and cell phones, for example) are very different from their great-grandparents' needs of only a century ago. As a country's standard of living increases, so do the needs of its people. To avoid having to subjectively evaluate economic goods according to some "neediness" scale, we instead focus on people's "wants" when we talk about the decisions they make to enhance their own well-being.

If, as we have argued, the condition of scarcity applies to virtually everything in the world, then we can treat virtually everything as an economic good. This means that economic principles, which deal with decision making in the face of scarcity, must be relevant to nearly every aspect of your life. Perhaps this is why economists believe that practically anything people do—whether the time they spend brushing their teeth or their choice of a college major—can be better understood and predicted using a basic economics framework.

This is why economics is sometimes referred to as the "science of scarcity." That is, economics is the study of how people choose to use the scarce resources at their disposal. For this reason, economists are often cast as the realists in discussions about how a society should use its scarce resources. For example, economists remind policy makers that new health-insurance programs must be paid for by sacrificing resources that are currently being used in some other economic activity: new payroll taxes that will pay for medical care for the uninsured will reduce workers' paychecks and the amount they can spend on food, housing, and so on. Economists encourage business leaders to consider what they will sacrifice—in terms of potential clients—when they locate their retail operations in one place versus another. We are the persistent, nagging reminder to policy makers, business leaders, and individuals that "there is no such thing as a free lunch." Each and every choice costs something in terms of forgone opportunities.

1.3 Economic Resources: Physical and Human Capital

The two types of scarce economic resources that economists usually talk about are **human capital** and **physical capital**.

HUMAN CAPITAL People's time, skills, ideas, and talents; their physical endowments, education, health status, entrepreneurship, and risk tolerance.

EXAMPLE The *Guinness Book of World Records* is filled with people's extraordinary feats, which are, by their very nature, scarce talents cultivated by years of training (such as the ability to eat 53.5 hot dogs and buns in 12 minutes).

EXAMPLE Tiger Woods has become one of the all-time greatest golfers by building his human capital through years of rigorous training.

EXAMPLE Movie stars build their human capital not only by honing their acting skills, but also by perfecting their physical appearance through exercise, plastic surgery, and strict nutritional regimens.

PHYSICAL CAPITAL Land and other natural resources, machinery, and technology.

EXAMPLE The United States is blessed with many natural resources, including fertile agricultural land and oil reserves.

EXAMPLE France has spent a great deal of resources to develop its nuclear power industry.

EXAMPLE Kuwait, Israel, and Saudi Arabia depend heavily on sea water to satisfy their countries' water demands.

The word *capital* is used because we are referring to a *stock* of resources; that is, an accumulation that can be depleted over time or grown by investing scarce resources.

In modern-day societies, slavery has been outlawed. This means that our human capital is *inalienable:* it cannot be bought or sold. It is only the *flow* of services that our human capital generates—which we call work effort, or labor—that can be traded. In societies where private property ownership is the norm, people can buy and sell their physical-capital holdings, although these sales may come with restrictions. Land sales in the United States often come with zoning restrictions that limit what buyers can do with the land. For example, factories cannot be built in the middle of residential neighborhoods.

People differ in the amount of human and physical capital they possess. These differences arise partially because people's initial *endowments* (the amount they are born with) aren't the same. Someone who inherits thousands of acres of land from her parents has an initial endowment of physical capital that is substantially greater than what most of us have. Similarly, some people are born with genetic characteristics that substantially increase their odds of living to be 100 years old. Other differences in capital holdings arise because people have invested differently in the past to augment their initial endowments. Both Mozart and Beethoven were wonderfully gifted musicians, but many musicologists argue that Beethoven's works are far superior because he worked much harder than Mozart, who was often drunk.

Like people, geographical areas—states, regions, countries, and so on—enjoy different endowments of physical capital. California boasts beautiful coastlines and beaches but suffers from a limited amount of water and the threat of earthquakes. The Pacific Northwest is plentiful in timber and fish but is often lacking in sunshine. And, Saudi Arabia enjoys an abundance of crude oil but a limited amount of arable farmland. By investing in technology, the constraints that limited endowments place on people and geographical areas can be significantly lessened. For example, irrigation systems have turned central and southern California's arid land into one of the most productive agricultural regions in the nation.

A country's stock of human capital can be augmented by growing its population and by investing in the human capital of its residents. The quickest way to increase the population in desirable locations is through open, low-cost immigration policies. Both the United States and Australia initially populated their countries by offering immigrants free land and even paid passage to move. More recently, then-Senator Edward Kennedy led the fight to relax U.S. immigration quotas for foreigners with in-demand skills, such as computer programming, or with money to invest in new business enterprises.[2] And, on the international front, Germany and Austria have lifted restrictions on the immigration of Eastern Europeans to counteract the aging of their indigenous populations and their shortage of low-wage workers.[3]

Governments that invest in education, public highways, water- and sewage-treatment facilities, and medical care increase their residents' stock of human capital. People who are healthier and better educated tend to be more productive. And, investments in technology may not only increase a country's physical capital but its human capital as well. Striking examples of this relate to advances in computer technology and software applications. Both have made assembly-line equipment and

. . . .

[2]Linda Greenhouse, "Redefining the Boundaries: Who May Come In; Immigration Bill: Looking for Skills and Good English." *New York Times,* April 10, 1988.

[3]Judy Dempsey, "As Germany Booms, It Faces a Shortage of Workers." *New York Times,* February 4, 2011.

workers "smarter," thereby increasing the value of the human and physical capital in industries where such computers are used.

Virtually every economic good is produced using both human and physical capital. In some instances, one type of capital can be substituted for another: checkout scanners in grocery stores (physical capital) have replaced cashiers (human capital). Generally speaking, the mix of human and physical capital used in production depends on the methods of production that are currently available and their cost relative to one another. The success of oceanic shipping once depended on a captain's skill (human capital) in navigating by the stars and crude maps. However, the invention of the sextant and, much later, radar and GPS systems (physical capital) substantially devalued these once-scarce human capital skills.

1.4 Economics as a Predictive "Science"

Economists try to identify factors that systematically influence how a person allocates her scarce resources. To the extent we are successful, we can predict (1) the mix of economic goods that will be produced in a society, (2) the way in which these goods will be produced, (3) how these goods will be distributed among people, and (4) how changes in the **economic environment** will change these outcomes.

ECONOMIC ENVIRONMENT Prices, wages, income, laws, and social norms that serve as external constraints on the choices that we make; external factors that dictate the trade-offs we face.

EXAMPLE The price of gasoline in the United States is less than half the price in Europe. Therefore, the trade-off between driving an automobile and taking public transit is different in these two locales.

EXAMPLE Marijuana use is illegal in the United States, but alcohol consumption by people over the age of 21 is legal. Because the legal system treats these two types of intoxicants differently, the trade-off between drug use and drinking is affected.

How do declining interest rates affect home ownership? How does an increase in the minimum wage impact full-time college enrollments? How does the introduction of a particular piece of tax legislation change the way that people spend their time at work and at home? We can use an economic framework to predict how people will respond to these types of changes in their economic environment. We use the term "prediction" in a very specific way here. We are not predicting future unknowns such as who will win the lottery or who will live to be 105 years old. We focus solely on predicting people's typical responses to changes in the trade-offs they face.

The *Ceteris Paribus* Assumption

To simplify the task of making such predictions, we examine the impact of only one change in the economic environment at a time. We know, for example, that during the Great Recession of 2007–2009, people's purchasing decisions were affected by many things, including changes in the prices of particular goods, losses in wealth due to the precipitous fall in home prices, and lower incomes due to actual or threatened job loss. Our job is to "tease" apart the impact of each of these factors on a person's purchase of specific goods or services. We might examine the impact that falling income had during this time period on the purchase of luxury cars, *holding everything else unchanged.* Or, we might analyze the impact of falling housing prices on purchases of furniture and home appliances, *holding everything else unchanged.* Economists refer to this as "partial" analysis—where everything in the economic environment is held constant except for one thing. Partial analysis rests on the assumption that "all else remains unchanged" or what we call the **ceteris paribus** assumption.

> **CETERIS PARIBUS** A Latin phrase meaning "holding all else unchanged." Assuming this condition allows us to analyze the impact of one change, and one change alone, in the economic environment that affects a decision maker's choices.

> **EXAMPLE** When the price of airline tickets falls, more people fly to their vacation destinations, *ceteris paribus.*

> **EXAMPLE** When the price of gasoline skyrockets, fewer people take car vacations, *ceteris paribus.*

Prediction versus Explanation

The key to making predictions about how people are likely to respond to changes in their economic environment is to identify the trade-offs they face and then make sense of how they would choose between their opportunities. The difficulty that can arise is that one person's trade-offs may not be the same as another's. A person who is allergic to peanuts would never consider a peanut butter sandwich to be a reasonable alternative to a grilled cheese sandwich, even if the peanut butter sandwich was free, and the grilled cheese sandwich was not.

Economists have long debated whether economics is supposed to *predict* people's behavior or *explain* it. Indeed, even though we are able to accurately predict behavior much of the time, economists usually refrain from explaining exactly why people act the way they do—that is, why they have the preferences they do. For example, economists (and those who study population statistics) have predicted with great reliability that birthrates rise nine months after extended electrical blackouts. However, they have not explained why this is so; that is, beyond the obvious loss of electricity-based activities, why do people use their time during a blackout the way they do?

It turns out that predicting people's choices—as difficult as that may be—is a far easier task than explaining the complexities of human behavior. Therefore, economists evaluate the goodness of one economic model of choice versus another based on their ability to predict actual outcomes, rather than explain why they occur. As more information becomes available about our economic environment, new theories arise that improve our predictive abilities. The "explanation part" of human behavior is left to psychologists, philosophers, and sociologists.

This means that economic analysis starts with people's preferences *as given* and predicts how the choices they make will change in the face of changing trade-offs. This approach allows us to sidestep a detailed description of personal preferences. It also permits people to have *different* preferences that affect the choices they make. For example, a vegan will not eat a steak even if meat prices fall, whereas a "steak and potatoes" kind of person might not reduce his meat purchases much, even in the face of substantial increases in the price of meat. Our religious beliefs, education, and family upbringing can greatly influence our preferences. We often make different choices than others, even when we face the same economic environment. This is an important result that deserves emphasis: economic prediction does not require everyone to make the same choices when faced with the same opportunities.

Simplicity versus Complexity

Simple economic models of choice are often better than more complex models. As economists, we ignore the details that do not contribute to our ability to predict people's behavior. Instead, we indicate under what conditions our economic predictions will be valid.

To appreciate the benefits of keeping models simple, think about how you give someone directions to your house. Most likely, you focus on main streets and landmarks, not on every street and every traffic light. Similarly, economists strive to be minimalists. We rely only on the basic "landmarks" to achieve our goal of accurately predicting responses to changes in the economic environment. Depending on where you live, directions to your home can be complex, or they may require only a few simple instructions. Similarly, in economics, there are situations in which we can predict people's behavior based on a few simple economic principles, and there are other cases in which more details must be considered.

One simple economic principle that has tremendous predictive power is the following: *More of a good thing is better (than less of it).* In other words, you can reasonably predict that if a person were offered more of something he desires, free of charge, he will take it and feel he is better off than before. However, we must qualify this prediction. At some point, too much of a good thing can become a bad thing. For example, a moviegoer might refuse a fifth free bucket of popcorn on the grounds that it will make him violently ill.

In reality, our predictions about the choices people make are rarely 100 percent correct. After all, we are talking about people, not balls rolling down a slope in a frictionless state. For example, it's possible that predictions based on economic models are less than perfect because people sometimes make mistakes when they make decisions. Even if we are hardwired to assess the trade-offs we face before making a choice, we sometimes have only limited information about our alternatives, resulting in a choice that deviates from what economics would have predicted. Often, these are the decisions that we judge to be subpar *after the fact*. This is why economists prefer to talk about a person's *tendency* to make a specific choice when faced with a particular trade-off. In other words, we can think of our predictions as being accurate, *on average*. It is important to keep this caveat in mind because we will be making a lot of predictions throughout this book. For this reason, "hard" scientists (like the chemist who combines elements and gets the same chemical outcome every time) sometimes scoff when economics is referred to as a "science."

The Short Run versus the Long Run

Economists also know that no matter how good their predictions are, the outcomes they expect might not happen immediately. This delay in response can occur because people are sometimes committed for a while to the old choices they have made, even when the trade-offs they face change. In other words, a person's *short-run* decisions might not be what he would decide to do in the *long run*. A couple that is locked into a one-year apartment lease might find it too expensive to break the lease. As a result, they will postpone their purchase of a home—even if mortgage interest rates have fallen to their lowest level in a decade. When gasoline prices increase precipitously, a college student who commutes to school will not immediately transfer to a university closer to her home; she will first complete the semester or academic year. In other words, in the short run, these people are constrained by their previous decisions: they are "stuck." Even though we can predict what they will do in response to a change in interest rates or gasoline prices, it may take some time for them to do it. Thus, our predictions about people's choices tend to be more accurate in the long run as people are able to adapt to their changed circumstances.

Predictions tend to be more accurate over time for another reason: as we just discussed, people sometimes make mistakes in their decision process and only later correct these errors. Information is itself an economic good that is scarce and can be costly to obtain. Unfortunately, in some situations, making a "bad" decision is the lowest-cost way to get the information you need to avoid mistakes in the future. Suppose you find two new protein bars at a convenience store and wonder which one you should buy. You could go home and research the matter at www.epinions.com or spend time surveying your friends, but that would take more time than it's worth. Instead, you will probably go ahead and buy the cheaper bar: if it tastes bad, you won't make the mistake of buying it again even if it is less expensive.

So, sometimes we use our scarce resources in ways that we later regret. On the next go-round, we use our scarce resources differently. Such errors are called **intelligent mistakes** because we learn from them.[4]

INTELLIGENT MISTAKES Errors in decision making that we learn from.

EXAMPLE On the first day of a new job, you follow the driving directions to work that you got online from MapQuest. After sitting in traffic and taking almost two hours to get to work, you find out from a co-worker that there is a shorter route that avoids all of the congestion. From then on, that's the route you take to work.

EXAMPLE Teenagers sometimes assume that they cannot get pregnant the first time they have sex. When they or a friend do get pregnant, there is a realization that their initial assumption was incorrect and that they must consider the possibility of pregnancy even the first time they have sex.

As you can probably tell, accurately predicting the choices people make when they have only limited information about the alternatives they face is a challenge for economists and their theories.

1.5 Positive versus Normative Analysis

As we move forward in developing predictive models of economic behavior, it is important that we distinguish between **positive analysis** and **normative analysis.**

POSITIVE ANALYSIS Evaluation of economic decision making that is based on facts and theories, leading to testable implications and validation.

EXAMPLE When elementary school students eat breakfast, they perform significantly better, on average, on in-class tests given before lunch.

· · · · · · · ·

[4]Alina Tugend, "The Many Errors in Thinking about Mistakes." *New York Times,* November 24, 2007.

NORMATIVE ANALYSIS Evaluation of economic decision making that is based on a person's values, religious beliefs, and opinions.

EXAMPLE Parents should be responsible for feeding their kids breakfast, rather than depending on the school to feed them.

Consider the following situation. The federal government asks an economist to predict what would happen to the amount of money people would save if a national sales tax replaced the current income tax system. People would only pay taxes when they purchased something. In contrast, they currently have to pay income taxes any-time they earn money, regardless of whether they save it or not. If a national sales tax replaced the income tax, we would predict that people will buy fewer goods and save more money. This hypothesis is readily testable, perhaps based on information from countries that have made such a switch in their tax system. The following is a *positive statement* related to the situation: "When savings are not taxed, more income is saved." A positive statement can be analyzed and validated. Compare this to a normative statement: "We shouldn't let rich people pay less in taxes by switching to a national sales tax that will encourage them to save more." This statement does not lend itself to analysis; it is simply an opinion.

Normative statements are opinions about how the world *ought* to be or how people *ought* to act. Scientific analysis cannot validate these opinions. Economists can do no more to settle conflicting normative positions than other opinionated individuals. They can only speak to these issues as individuals, not as economists. After all, everyone is entitled to his or her own opinion, even an economist.

Let's now look at some positive statements economists *can* make: most economists agree that legalizing trade in human organs—permitting kidneys to be bought and sold, for example—would increase the number of organs available and thereby reduce the amount of time people have to wait for a transplant. Similarly, economists largely agree that legalizing trade in illicit drugs would reduce the street prices for these drugs and, consequently, the amount of street crime. These are *positive* predictions based on economic principles.

Economists differ, however, in their opinion about whether the buying and selling of human organs or illicit drugs *ought* to be legal. They do so because of differences in their personal views. Therefore, it shouldn't surprise you that economists often disagree about whether or not various government policies are necessary and ought to be adopted or repealed.

Many of the issues we discuss in this book can be, and often are, the subject of intense normative debate. However, it doesn't matter what an economist believes, for example, about how household chores *ought* to be divided between husbands and wives, or whether or not employers *should* hire job applicants with tattoos, or which applicants *should* be admitted to elite, private colleges. Instead, economic analysis takes a positive approach to these questions. Adopting a positive approach means that we can talk about what factors influence the division of household chores between household partners; the consequences of employment discrimination against appli-cants with tattoos; and the impact of federal law on how colleges fill their admission spots. In summary, economics can only predict the consequences of changes in the economic environment on individual decision making.

Finally, when we engage in positive analysis, by definition, we refrain from mak-ing any moral judgments about the choices people make. Economics has nothing to say about whether a particular choice is immoral or unethical. We leave that analysis to politicians, philosophers, theologians, and others. Our responsibility throughout this book is to focus solely on predicting people's choices in the face of changing trade-offs.

1.6 The Nature of Economic Man and Woman

Although economic analysis doesn't pass judgment on people's decisions, it does make the assumption that individuals make choices that they believe will advance their own well-being. That is, people exhibit **economic rationality**.

> **ECONOMIC RATIONALITY** People make choices that they believe will advance their own well-being.

> **EXAMPLE** A college student goes to a review session for the final exam because she thinks it may improve her test performance, even though she already feels comfortable with the material.

> **EXAMPLE** A person gives ten percent of his income to his church because he believes this will enhance his current and future well-being.

Economic rationality is often equated to the pursuit of one's *self-interest*. The term *self-interest* is, quite possibly, the most misunderstood term in economics. You might be tempted to think it's the same as selfishness, or greed, but it is not. There is a big difference between being self-interested and being selfish. As it turns out, economic theory predicts that self-interest often motivates people to behave charitably. Your parents may make charitable donations to the local food pantry or homeless shelter because they derive an immense amount of satisfaction, or well-being, from doing so. Sometimes this sense of well-being is even greater when the contribution is publicized (e.g., a building is named for its donor) or when the donation is tax-deductible. In any case, people engage in acts of kindness and charity because they believe this is in their *own* self-interest. To reiterate: self-interest—the drive to advance one's own well-being—underlies all of the decisions that we make. This is, however, not the same as selfishness.

ECONOMIC FALLACY   Economics is the science of greed.

False. Economics provides a systematic framework for predicting people's choices, irrespective of their preferences or economic environment. For example, using economic principles, we can predict who will stand in line the longest when goods are rationed on a "first-come, first-served" basis, which often happens in socialist economies such as Cuba. Economics can even make predictions about how politicians in various political systems will finance and distribute goods such as education and medical care.

ECONOMIC FALLACY   Capitalism is an economic system that rewards greed.

False. The biggest difference between capitalism and other economic systems—such as socialism—is that private entities own and control most, if not all, of the capital used in production, rather than the government or a community collective. Owners of human and physical capital are the ultimate decision makers when it comes to how their capital is used. This often includes pursuing charitable activities (e.g., the Rockefellers established the Rockefeller Foundation) and using one's income and wealth to support family members and community institutions. In capitalist societies, labor services and physical capital are predominantly allocated to alternative uses through voluntary, free trade in the market. In more centralized economies, governments set prices and direct resources to particular activities, for example, to food production, clock manufacturing, or commercial construction. Workers are also directed to various regions of the country or to various productive activities. In these ways, the government pursues its own self-interest, which may or may not be consistent with the well-being of its population.

1.7 Microeconomic versus Macroeconomic Analysis

When the term "micro" is used, it brings to mind something very small. Microbes and microchips are things that are so small that they are virtually invisible to the naked eye. **Microeconomics** is the study of how individuals, households, and producing organizations make decisions to maximize their own well-being. Each and every one of these decision makers is virtually invisible in the economy as a whole, but in aggregate, their choices dictate market outcomes, including the prices that goods sell for and the wages that workers are paid. And, when these decision makers react to changes in their economic environment, this can have a significant impact on market outcomes and resource allocation.

MICROECONOMICS The study of how individuals, households, and producing organizations make decisions to maximize their own well-being.

EXAMPLE Microeconomists are employed by telephone companies to analyze the cell-phone usage of customers and to create pricing plans that will increase the firm's profitability.

EXAMPLE Microeconomists are hired by the government to develop policies that will stimulate housing purchases and increase the hiring of the long-term unemployed.

In this way, microeconomics is the foundation for all economic analysis: it all begins with the individual decision maker.

Macroeconomics is, relatively speaking, a newer branch of economics that focuses on the study of economy-wide events that influence the overall growth rates of national economies. Macroeconomics tries to make sense of why the rate of inflation is 15 percent or 2 percent, and why recessions happen.

MACROECONOMICS The study of economy-wide events, such as economic growth, inflation, and business cycles.

EXAMPLE The Environmental Protection Agency hires macroeconomists to assess how policies to lessen industrial air pollution will impact economic growth and employment in the United States.

EXAMPLE Macroeconomists are asked to forecast the effect of an increase in interest rates on the value of the dollar.

The following examples emphasize the difference between these two fields of economic analysis. Whereas a microeconomist would evaluate the impact of gas price increases on new SUV purchases, a macroeconomist would be concerned about whether higher gas prices will lead to greater price inflation in the overall economy or even to a recession. A microeconomist would examine how increases in the minimum wage affect hiring in the fast-food industry, whereas a macroeconomist would study the impact of wage policies on the overall unemployment rate. Even though there is some overlap, macroeconomics is really focused on big-picture issues compared with microeconomics.

Whether we are discussing a micro or a macro issue, economists agree that core elements are common to any type of economic analysis. We identify these building blocks in the next few chapters.

1.8 What This Book Reveals about the Decisions You Make in Life

In a nutshell, this book gives you the tools to cultivate an extraordinary self-awareness about factors in the world around you that influence the decisions that you make. You already absorb and process changes in your economic environment, responding in such a way as to maximize your sense of well-being. When gas prices rise, you are likely to drive less and may even substitute online shopping for trips to the mall. When tuition rises, you may take fewer classes and become more serious about studying so you don't have to retake a class. When your household partner loses his job, you shift more of the household tasks to him. When the price of movies goes up, you stay home and watch DVDs more often.

This book is not meant to teach you to think like an economist *because you already think this way*. Instead, its goal is to provide you with a framework within which you can organize this decision process and identify key factors that influence how you will react to changes in the trade-offs you face. Perhaps of even greater importance is that this framework will enable you to make better predictions about how others who contribute in some way to your sense of well-being (e.g., your friends, parents, spouse, employer, employee, or doctor) will act in response to changes in their economic environment.

Along the way, you will hopefully better understand how remarkable your decision-making abilities are already. You will see why it makes perfect sense that college students like yourself *tend* to have children later in life than those who do not go on to college. And why sometimes two people in a household both go to work, but at other times, one person stays home. You will also appreciate why people who take big risks as investors or entrepreneurs are sometimes rewarded handsomely; and why online sellers of items such as new music CDs and brand-name electric guitars tend to price their goods the same (after shipping and handling fees are included).

You will likely encounter new terminology and analytical tools in this book. Sometimes we use words and other times graphs and mathematical equations to explain economic principles. (A review of these tools is provided in Appendix 1A.) Whatever we use, we are involved in a delicate balancing act: we're trying to capture all of the essential elements required to make accurate predictions while ignoring the extraneous complexities of life. Regardless of the tools and models we use, the economic principles you learn should "ring true" in terms of your life experiences and those of your friends and family. After all, economics is about the way *all* of us live.

WHAT YOU SHOULD HAVE LEARNED FROM CHAPTER 1

■ That economics is the study of the choices we make.

■ That trade-offs are the opportunities passed up when we make one choice versus another choice.

■ That we live in a world of scarcity because there are limited resources to satisfy unlimited wants.

■ That capital is more than just physical (land, machinery, technology); it is also human (our time, education, skills, and health).

■ That a positive statement is readily testable, whereas a normative statement is an opinion, or judgment, that cannot be scientifically validated. Economics focuses solely on the analysis of positive statements.

■ That economic analysis seeks to make predictions about the way people tend to respond to one change in their economic environment, holding all else constant.

■ That we make choices we believe are in our self-interest. Because we do not always have perfect information about the alternatives we face, we regret some of our decisions in hindsight and learn from them. We call these decisions "intelligent mistakes."

■ That self-interest is not the same as selfishness.

■ That microeconomics deals with the decisions of individuals and producing organizations, whereas macroeconomics is concerned with big-picture economic events such as the unemployment rate.

KEY TERMS

Trade-off, p. 3

Scarcity, p. 5

Well-being, p. 6

Economic good, p. 6

Human capital, p. 7

Physical capital, p. 7

Economic environment, p. 9

Ceteris paribus, p. 10

Intelligent mistakes, p. 12

Positive analysis, p. 12

Normative analysis, p. 13

Economic rationality, p. 14

Microeconomics, p. 15

Macroeconomics, p. 15

QUESTIONS AND PROBLEMS

1. Suppose everyone had the same preferences, values, and income. In such a world, could we conclude that all individuals would buy the same economic goods in the same amounts? Explain your answer.

2. Charities depend on people to donate their money or volunteer their time. Predict how a person's mix of money and time donated to a charity changes as he:

   a) gets a raise in his hourly wage.
   b) gets married and has children.
   c) retires from his job.

   Defend each of your predictions.

3. True, false, or uncertain: It is economically rational for a student to cheat to improve her grades, if she knows with certainty that she won't get caught. Explain your answer.

4. Education and exercise are two ways we can increase our human capital. Give two examples of choices we can make that will decrease ("depreciate") our human capital. Explain your answer.

5. Identify a few rational mistakes you have made in your lifetime. Explain why you made them and what you learned from them. Have you ever made an "irrational" mistake—that is, a mistake that you learned nothing from?

6. Suppose an animal is on the brink of extinction. How, as a society, would we determine the amount of resources to commit to preserving the species? Explain your answer.

7. When you use MapQuest.com to get driving directions between point A and point B, MapQuest asks whether you want the shortest route in terms of (a) mileage, or (b) time. What is the opportunity cost to you of choosing to (a) minimize your mileage? Of choosing to (b) minimize your time? Explain your answers.

8. The United States is characterized as a "mixed economy" in that it is neither purely capitalistic nor purely socialistic. Identify three goods whose production and distribution are controlled by the U.S. government, and name three goods whose production and distribution are dictated by market trade between individuals who privately own capital.

9. Think about the last time you made a decision that, in hindsight, you thought was a "bad" or "stupid" decision. What kind of information, if provided in advance, would have kept you from making this decision? Would this information have been costly to get? Explain your answer.

10. Do you think that it makes sense that parents are given the right to make all of their children's decisions before the age of "emancipation"—which is 18 years old in the United States? Do you think that this is the "right" age to hand over all decision making to children? Explain your answer.

11. The Great Recession of 2007–2009 apparently redefined those goods and services that Americans consider "necessities." The Pew Research Center reported the percentage point change between 2006 and 2009 in opinions about the necessity of the following goods.[5]

−21%	Microwaves
−17%	Clothes dryer
−16%	Home air conditioning
−14%	Dishwasher
−12%	TV set
−10%	Cable or satellite TV
3%	Flat screen TV
2%	High-speed Internet
1%	iPod
0%	Cell phone

Given these responses, how do you think that most people define "need" or "necessity?" Are the survey results consistent with the viewpoint that "needs" are often defined relative to the availability of different goods and services? Explain your answer.

12. Economist Paul Krugman, a Nobel Laureate in Economics, writes a column for the *New York Times* that is widely reprinted by other newspapers in the country. Randomly select three of Professor Krugman's recent columns and critique them in terms of whether his writings included any normative statements. For each normative statement you find, discuss whether you believe that Professor Krugman has substantiated his opinion in a systematic fashion.

13. How do people pursue their self-interest in the political arena? How does your answer contrast with the ways in which people pursue their self-interest in the marketplace? Explain your answer.

• • • • • • •

[5]Sharon Jayson, "Recession Redefines 'Necessities.'" *USA Today*, April 24–26, 2009, p.1.

Appendix 1A Basic Graphing and Math Skills Used in Economics

GRAPHING

The purpose of a graph is to illustrate the relationship between two variables. For example, you could examine how much a family spends each year (one variable) relative to its annual income (the other variable). As **Table 1A.1** shows, this information can be arranged in a table with expenditures as the *y* (**dependent**) variable and income as the *x* (**independent**) variable.

Table 1A.1 A Table Illustrating the Relationship between Two Variables	
y Expenditures ($/yr)	*x* Income ($/yr)
20,000	10,000
25,000	20,000
30,000	30,000
35,000	40,000
40,000	50,000
45,000	60,000
50,000	70,000

The data in the table can now be plotted on a grid, like **Figure 1A.1**. The resulting graph allows us to visualize the relationship between income and expenditures.

The line running from left to right across the bottom is referred to as the horizontal axis or the *x*-axis. The line running up and down the left side of the graph

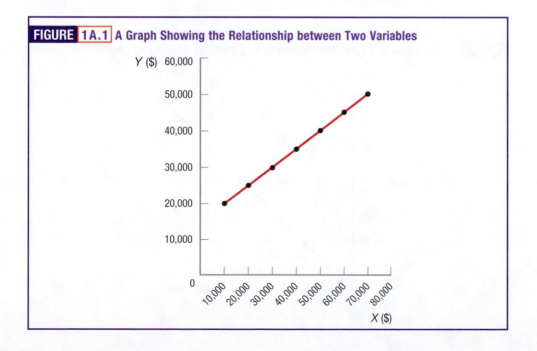

FIGURE 1A.1 A Graph Showing the Relationship between Two Variables

is called the vertical axis or the *y*-axis. The intersection of the horizontal axis and vertical axis is called the *origin*. The origin corresponds to a value of zero for both the *x* variable and *y* variable.

On the graph, each combination of *x* and *y* values is represented by a point on the graph. For example, the first point shows when income is $10,000 per year (measured on the *x*-axis), and expenditures are at $20,000 per year (measured on the *y*-axis). This combination can be written (10000, 20000). In the same manner, the seventh point on the graph can be written (70000, 50000). More generally, points can be expressed as (*x*, *y*).

Calculating the Slope of a Line

The **slope** of a straight line equals the change in the *y* variable associated with a change in the *x* variable, as we move from one point on the line to another. The slope is often described as the line's "rise over run." Its mathematical formula is $\Delta y/\Delta x$, where Δ means "change in." **Figure 1A.2** shows the slope of a line.

Using Figure 1A.2 as an example, we can find the slope of the line between different points on the line. To find the slope of the line between the *x* values of 4 and 6, we use the formula $\Delta y/\Delta x$.

Δy = the change in *y* = the value of *y* when *x* = 6 minus the value of *y* when *x* = 4
$\quad$ = 30 − 20 = 10
Δx = the change in *x* = 6 − 4 = 2

Therefore, the slope of the line between *x* = 4 and 6 = $\Delta y/\Delta x$ = 10/2 = 5.

The line depicted in Figure 1A.2 has a **positive** slope, which means that the relationship between the two variables is positive. Any *increase* in *x* is associated with an *increase* in *y*. Graphs in economics do not always have positive slopes. Consider **Figure 1A.3** and **Figure 1A.4**.

Figure 1A.3 has a **negative** slope: as *x* increases, the value of *y* decreases. Conversely, as *x* decreases, the value of *y* increases. It can also be said that the two values are **inversely** related. Figure 1A.4 has a slope of zero: as *x* increases or decreases, the

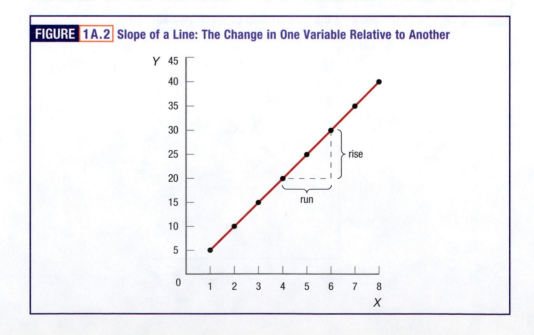

FIGURE 1A.2 Slope of a Line: The Change in One Variable Relative to Another

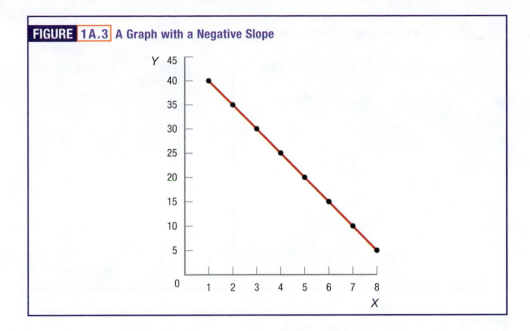

FIGURE 1A.3 A Graph with a Negative Slope

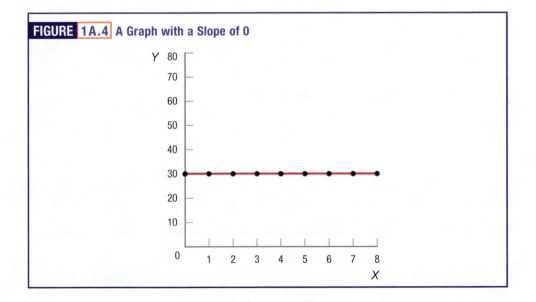

FIGURE 1A.4 A Graph with a Slope of 0

value of y remains constant at $y = 30$. **Figure 1A.5** shows a slope that is undefined: the x value does not change at all as the value of y increases or decreases. (Δx equals zero between all points on the line.)

Finding the y-Intercept of a Line

Looking at **Figure 1A.6**, note that the line crosses the y-axis at the point $x = 0$, $y = 15$. We say that 15 is the **y-intercept** of the line. Technically speaking, the y-intercept of the line is the point at which the line intersects the y-axis. This is the value of y when the value of x is zero.

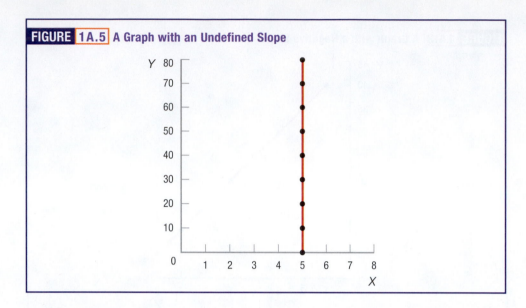

FIGURE 1A.5 A Graph with an Undefined Slope

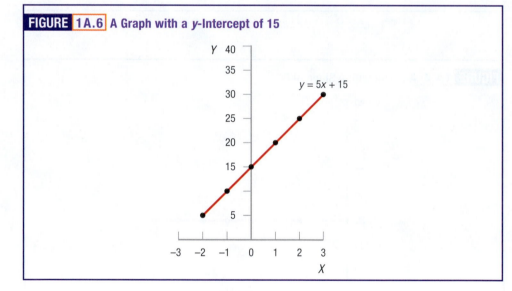

FIGURE 1A.6 A Graph with a *y*-Intercept of 15

$y = 5x + 15$

One way to find the *y*-intercept is to use the formula for a line $y = mx + b$, where

y = the value of y at a given point
x = the value of x at a given point
m = the slope of the line
b = the *y*-intercept

To find the *y*-intercept, we need the slope of the line—which is 5—as well as a value for x and y on the line, such as point (1, 20).

$m = 5$
$y = 20$
$x = 1$

After plugging our numbers into the equation

$$y = mx + b$$
$$20 = 5(1) + b$$

we solve for b:

$$20 = 5 + b$$
$$20 - 5 = b$$
$$15 = b$$

After finding the slope and the y-intercept, we can write the general equation of the line:

$$y = 5x + 15$$

Note: If you are given just the equation of a line, you can simply plug in $x = 0$ to calculate the y-intercept.

Practice Problems

1. Graph the data in the following table.

y	x
10	1800
15	1600
20	1400
25	1200
30	1000
35	800

2. Are x and y positively related or negatively (inversely) related?
3. Using the line you created for problem 1, what is the slope? What is the y-intercept? Write out the equation of the line in the form $y = mx + b$.
4. Suppose you have a second line represented by the data in this table:

y	x
5	0
10	300
15	600
20	900
25	1200
30	1500

Graph this line on the same graph that you created for problem 1. What is the formula for this line in the form $y = mx + b$?
5. By examining the graph you created for problems 1 and 4, find the intersection of the two lines. Write this intersection as the ordered pair (x, y).

Percentage Change

In many cases, you will be asked to find the **percentage change** or **growth rate** in different variables. For example, if the price of a good rises from \$2.00 (P_1) to \$2.50 (P_2) the $\Delta P = (P_2 - P_1) = \$2.50 - \$2.00 = \$0.50$, where Δ means "change in." To calculate the %ΔP, where %$\Delta P = \Delta P/P_1$, we have \$0.50/\$2.00 = 0.25. To convert this number to a percent, multiply by 100. $0.25 \times 100 = 25\%$. More generally, the formula for %ΔP is

$$\%\Delta P = \left(\frac{\Delta P}{P_1}\right) \times 100$$

Note: Although ΔP carries the units of the original variable (P in \$'s, in this example), %ΔP will be a **pure number** with no units because the numerator and denominator units cancel out (as shown in this example).

Practice Problems

1. Find the %ΔP when $P_1 = \$30$ and $P_2 = \$33$.
2. Find the %ΔQ when $Q_1 = 45$ and $Q_2 = 30$.
3. Compute the %ΔQ / %ΔP for the preceding numbers.

Nonlinear Curves

When finding the slope, we assumed that a graph was **linear**, that is, a straight line. Lines are the easiest graphs to work with because they are completely described by their slope and y-intercept. However, many of the relationships you will encounter in economics are not linear. Examining **Figure 1A.7**, we observe that between $x = 0$ and $x = 5$, x and y are positively related. However, for larger values of x, the slope is

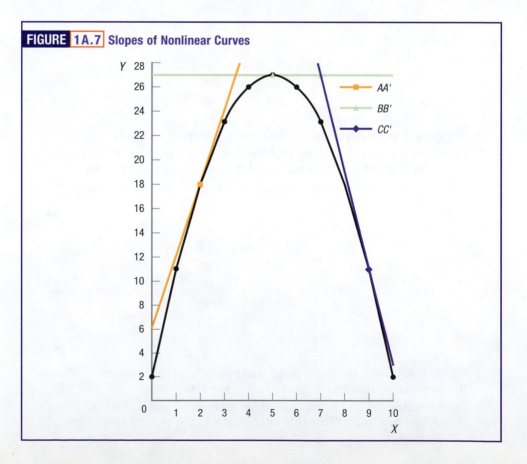

FIGURE 1A.7 Slopes of Nonlinear Curves

negative. That is, *x* and *y* are inversely related. It is clear from the graph that the slope of a **nonlinear curve** is not constant.

The slope of a nonlinear curve at any point is defined as the slope of the tangent to the curve at that point. (This is the best approximation of the slope of a curve at a point without using more advanced math.) Let's look at Figure 1A.7 again, this time focusing on the tangent *AA'*, which just touches the curve at point (2, 18). *AA'* is tangent to the curve where *x* = 2. Along the line *AA'*, if *x* = 1, *y* = 12. We know that at *x* = 2, *y* = 18. Using the formula for the slope discussed in Part 2, we get

$$\Delta y / \Delta x = (18 - 12)/(2 - 1) = 6$$

Therefore, 6 is the slope of the curve at the point *x* = 2.

Practice Problems

1. Find the slope of the curve at *x* = 5 using the tangent *BB'* (use the line and pick another point along that line).
2. Find the slope of the curve at *x* = 9 using the tangent *CC'* (use the line and pick another point along that line).

Computing the Area of a Rectangle and Triangle

The formula for the area of a rectangle like the one shown in **Figure 1A.8** is

Area = (Length) × (Width)

In special situations such as in **Figure 1A.9**, the area of a rectangle on a graph will represent revenue received by sellers or, equivalently, expenditures made by consumers. The following equation shows how the area is computed:

Area = Revenue = (Price) × (Quantity)

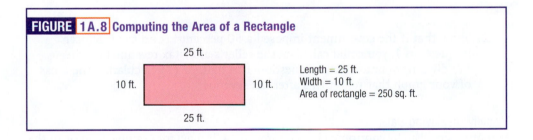

FIGURE 1A.8 Computing the Area of a Rectangle

25 ft.

10 ft.   10 ft.   Length = 25 ft.
                                Width = 10 ft.
                                Area of rectangle = 250 sq. ft.

25 ft.

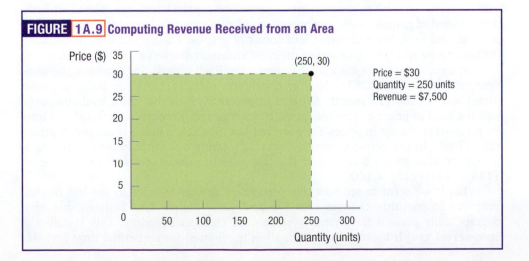

FIGURE 1A.9 Computing Revenue Received from an Area

Price ($)

(250, 30)

Price = $30
Quantity = 250 units
Revenue = $7,500

Quantity (units)

As shown in **Figure 1A.10**, the formula for the area of a triangle is

$$\text{Area} = \tfrac{1}{2}\,(\text{Base}) \times (\text{Height})$$

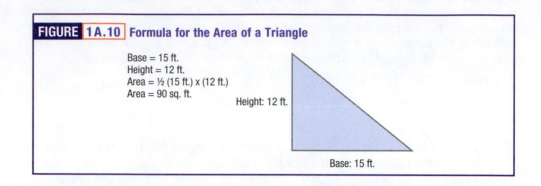

FIGURE 1A.10 **Formula for the Area of a Triangle**

Base = 15 ft.
Height = 12 ft.
Area = ½ (15 ft.) x (12 ft.)
Area = 90 sq. ft.

Height: 12 ft.

Base: 15 ft.

Practice Problems

1. Using a graph with P (Price) on the vertical axis and Q (Quantity) on the horizontal axis, shade in the area that corresponds to total revenue for each of the following sales conditions (use a different color pen to shade in each of these rectangles):

P	Q
$10	200
$12	180
$14	140

2. Show that if the government imposed a 50 percent tax on the producer in question 1, you could calculate the seller's after-tax revenue by either (1) dividing your answers in question 1 in half, or (2) calculating the areas of your graph that reflect this after-tax revenue.

Visually Displaying Data

You often are visually confronted by economic data. It may, for example, appear in the form of a chart of stock prices, a table of figures showing the latest unemployment data, or some kind of graphic displaying how much of a household's budget is spent on food, gasoline, and rent. We will use various forms of graphical display of data throughout this text, so we will introduce you to the most common displays and how to use them.

Some economic data are available over time. Each month, for example, the government announces what the level of consumer prices (actually, an index of those prices) was for the past month. What is important is how that price level compares with the level of prices in previous months, so price levels are typically translated into the percentage change in prices. Suppose that last month the index of consumer prices was 133 and in the previous month it was 125. Using our formula for calculating a percentage change, we find that in the last month, prices increased 6.4 percent = $[(133 - 125)/125] \times 100$.

What if we want to see how this percentage change in price in the last month compares to monthly changes over the past year? **Figure 1A.11** shows one way to graphically present the monthly percentage changes in prices. This is called a **time-series graph** because the information is reported for sequential time periods.

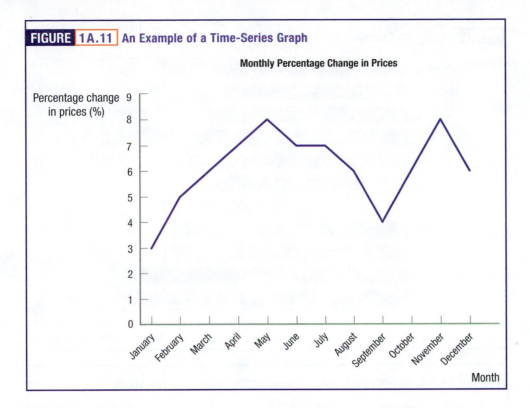

FIGURE 1A.11 **An Example of a Time-Series Graph**

Monthly Percentage Change in Prices

Percentage change in prices (%)

Month

As you can see, the vertical axis reports the percentage change in prices, and the horizontal axis shows the passage of time. From January through May, the percentage change in prices was increasing: prices were rising at a faster rate. This changed in May when these price increases subsided.

Such time-series graphs are useful when we want to see how an economic measure, whether prices or the unemployment rate or the average wage paid to nurses, is changing over time. Once we can visualize this time-series pattern, we can investigate whether some change in the economic environment led to observed shifts in the pattern, such as occurred in May for the price data.

What if instead you wanted to display the value that one economic measure takes on for a number of firms at one point in time? For example, suppose you want to report the prices that different suppliers charge for a good, say gasoline, in the month of May. You could do this by using a chart like the one in **Figure 1A.12**, which is called a **bar chart**. (Bar charts can be shown either horizontally, as in this figure, or vertically.)

A bar chart allows you to quickly see the different prices charged by the different companies at a certain point in time (May). Each supplier's price can be easily compared to that of the competition. In the chart, gasoline sold from Mobil is clearly more expensive than the gasoline sold by Quiktrip.

Bar charts are sometimes used to illustrate data over time as well. **Figure 1A.13** shows the changes in the level of prices from the previous time-series graph, plotted in a bar chart format.

What if you want to apportion the total of some variable—say, annual spending or the 24 hours in a day—into subcategories? Suppose, for example, that there is information about the way in which college students spend their money. You sometimes see survey results reported as "The results of a recent survey of college students revealed that 60 percent of their monthly income was spent on rent, 20 percent on food and gasoline, 15 percent on entertainment, and 5 percent on school-related items."

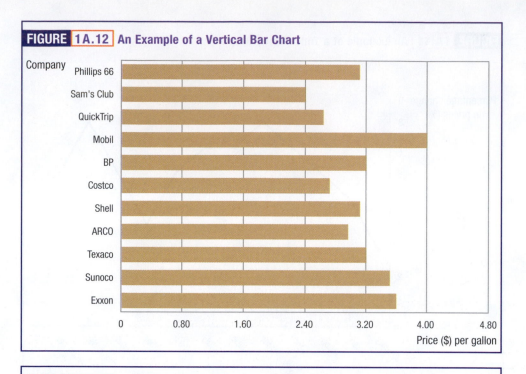

FIGURE 1A.12 An Example of a Vertical Bar Chart

Company

Phillips 66
Sam's Club
QuickTrip
Mobil
BP
Costco
Shell
ARCO
Texaco
Sunoco
Exxon

0   0.80   1.60   2.40   3.20   4.00   4.80

Price ($) per gallon

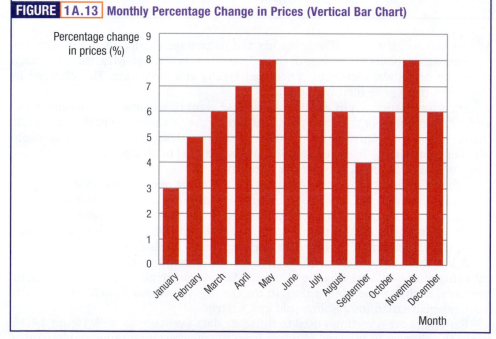

FIGURE 1A.13 Monthly Percentage Change in Prices (Vertical Bar Chart)

Percentage change
in prices (%)

January February March April May June July August September October November December

Month

As shown in **Figure 1A.14**, there is a much easier way to summarize these findings: a **pie chart**. Pie charts are often used to show percentages of a total. Because of this, the "pieces" of the pie must add up to 100 percent.

The pie chart shown reports the distribution of student expenditures across the various categories. You can see very quickly that the lion's share of expenditures goes to rent rather than school-related items.

Finally, to show the relationship between two different variables, a **scatter plot** is sometimes used. A scatter plot can be used to "eyeball" whether two variables appear

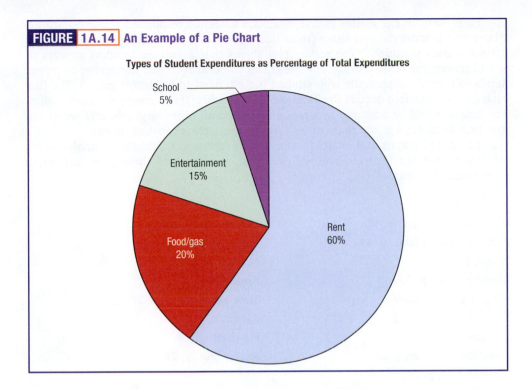

FIGURE 1A.14 An Example of a Pie Chart

Types of Student Expenditures as Percentage of Total Expenditures

School
5%

Entertainment
15%

Food/gas
20%

Rent
60%

to be related, either positively or negatively. For example, suppose you want to see whether an increase in study time (*x*) is related to test performance (*y*). To do so, you would collect data from your classmates about how many hours they studied for a midterm test and what their test grades (in percentages) were. The data you collect show that some students studied very little, and some studied a lot. Some got good grades, and some did not. But are *x* and *y* related in any meaningful way? Plotting the data as a scatter graph, as in **Figure 1A.15,** will help to visualize whether a systematic relationship exists between the two variables.

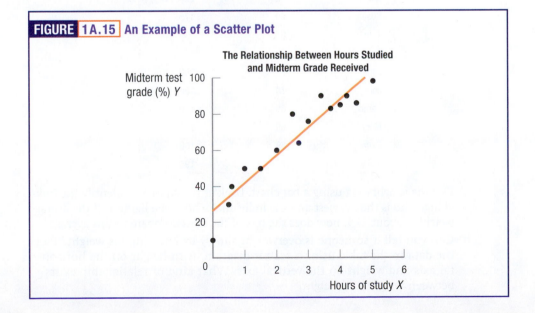

FIGURE 1A.15 An Example of a Scatter Plot

**The Relationship Between Hours Studied
and Midterm Grade Received**

Midterm test
grade (%) *Y*

Hours of study *X*

Each point in the scatter plot represents a student's response to your questions, "How many hours did you study (the student's *x*-value), and what grade did you get (the student's *y*-value)?" The scatter plot shows that a positive relation appears to exist between the hours studied and the grades students received. The scatter of points tends to rise: those students who studied more tended to get better grades. The line that we have inserted depicts the "average" relationship. If there were no relationship, the points would be scattered in a random fashion all over the graph, and we would not be able to draw a line that comes close to connecting most of them.

The use of graphs and charts is common in economics because we analyze a lot of data to test our theories. You will see most, if not all, of these graphical forms throughout the text.

KEY TERMS

Dependent variable, p. 19

Independent variable, p. 19

Slope, p. 20

Positive slope, p. 20

Negative slope, p. 20

Inversely related, p. 20

y-intercept, p. 21

Percentage change, p. 24

Growth rate, p. 24

Pure number, p. 24

Linear, p. 24

Nonlinear, p. 25

Area, p. 25

Time-series graph, p. 26

Bar chart, p. 27

Pie chart, p. 28

Scatter plot, p. 28

PRACTICE PROBLEMS

1. The income and expenditure data shown at the beginning of this Appendix were plotted using what kind of graph? From the plot used there, would you say that income and expenditures are positively or negatively related?

2. Suppose you take a survey in your class asking students for their height and weight. The data you collect are shown in the following table:

Name	Height (inches)	Weight (pounds)
Bill	72	220
Susan	69	175
Tom	65	130
Anne	60	115
Janet	77	200
John	70	180
Sarah	63	180
Mary	68	190
Gary	69	160
Molly	74	195

a) Plot the weight data using a bar chart. Look at the chart and identify the individual who is the heaviest and the individual who is the lightest. If the average weight is about 175, how does the rest of the class compare to this average?

b) Can you tell if someone is overweight simply by knowing his weight? Plot the data in the table using a scatter diagram, with height on the horizontal axis and weight on the vertical axis. What kind of relationship exists between weight and height?

c) You hear on the news that the average weight of individuals has increased over the past 50 years and that this trend must be reversed. Based on your observations in your scatter plot, how might you react to the news story? What questions might you ask?

3. The following pie charts show two companies' expenditures by category. The size of the each pie segment reflects the amount of money spent, as a percent of total expenditures.

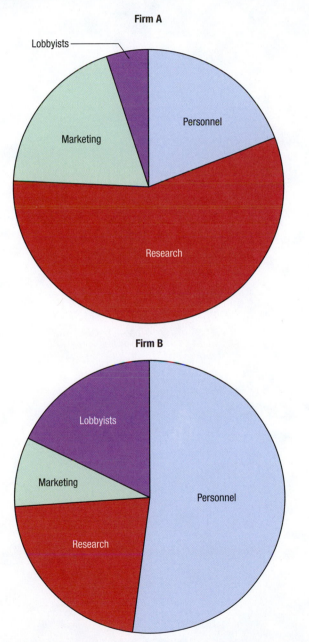

Firm A

Lobbyists

Personnel

Marketing

Research

Firm B

Lobbyists

Marketing

Personnel

Research

a) Given the definitions, which firm is more heavily engaged in research? Which one is spending relatively more money on lobbyists? If "personnel" reflects the salaries paid, which firm might you be more interested in working for?

Making Choices in the Face of Scarcity: Harnessing Life's Possibilities

"A conversation is a dialogue, not a monologue. That's why there are so few good conversations: due to scarcity, two intelligent talkers seldom meet."

Truman Capote, author

Scarcity is apparent everywhere. Your labor is scarce, cars are scarce, clean air is scarce, even the time you spend reading this chapter is scarce. As long as scarcity exists, we simply cannot satisfy every "want" we have. And because we can't always get everything we want, we must make choices. The problem we face in a world of scarcity is how to prioritize our desires so that the scarce resources we do have are used in a way that gives us the greatest possible happiness, or satisfaction, in life. We have already introduced the idea of rational economic decision making. In this chapter, we present an economic model of rational choice that provides a framework for predicting how each of us copes with the scarcity we face.

2.1 Making Choices to Achieve the Greatest Satisfaction Possible

How do you allocate the 24 hours that make up each day? Your choice may be to spend 16 hours sleeping, 4 hours at school, and the remaining 4 hours text messaging friends. Or, perhaps you choose to sleep 6 hours, spend 2 hours at the gym, 8 hours at work, 4 hours at school, and the rest of your day eating out with friends. However a person chooses to devote her scarce time is a personal choice that reflects her individual **preferences**.

PREFERENCES Tastes; basis upon which alternative opportunities are ranked.

EXAMPLE Most Americans prefer to eat dinner early, while Europeans prefer to eat after 8 P.M.

EXAMPLE Most residential college students prefer late morning classes, while commuter students prefer early morning or evening classes.

EXAMPLE Vegetarians prefer tofu burgers at the local barbeque, while carnivores prefer ribs and hamburgers.

Our preferences reflect our individual tastes—our likes and dislikes—that are defined by our experiences, genetics, beliefs, education, and value system. As economists, we do not judge a person's preferences and the resulting choices the person makes. We simply assume that the person acts in an economically rational way and makes decisions she thinks will enhance *her* sense of well-being. In effect, she makes choices that yield the greatest **economic benefit**.

ECONOMIC BENEFIT The satisfaction, happiness, or sense of well-being created when a person allocates a scarce resource to a particular use.

EXAMPLE People spend some of their limited time and income on leisure activities such as vacations and going to baseball games because they get an economic benefit—a sense of well-being—from these activities.

EXAMPLE Parents reap economic benefits from their children's shows of affection, as well as from their performance of such household tasks as setting the table, emptying the trash, walking the dogs, and washing the dishes.

EXAMPLE Couples bestow upon one another an economic benefit through the time commitment each makes to the other.

Economists often give the term "economic benefit" another name: **utility**.

UTILITY Economic benefit or well-being.

EXAMPLE Purchasers of iPhones receive utility from the iPhone's Web-surfing capabilities, GPS directional maps, and other useful apps.

EXAMPLE Music fans get utility from seeing their favorite groups live, in concert.

Why do we say that a person makes choices that she *thinks* will increase her economic benefit, or utility? Because, in reality, it is rare that a person will have complete information about all of the alternatives she faces—it is simply too costly and time-consuming to evaluate all of the possible options.

When we allocate time to attend class, sleep, or work, we are making decisions about how to maximize the well-being we can get from the limited amount of time we have at our disposal. Each choice requires the sacrifice of other potential opportunities: simply stated, we cannot be in two places at once. For example, if you decide to stay home to take care of your children or play video games, you cannot be at work at the same time earning a salary. This means that there is an **opportunity cost** associated with your choice to spend your time at home instead of at work. In this instance, your opportunity cost equals the economic benefit that you *would have* received from the goods and services you *could have* purchased had you earned income instead of staying home. Had you gone to work instead of staying home, there would have been an opportunity cost to that decision as well—the economic benefit you would have enjoyed from staying home with your children or playing video games.

OPPORTUNITY COST The economic benefit given up when one option is chosen over another. The economic benefit you miss out on from your next-best opportunity because of the choice you have made.

EXAMPLE The opportunity cost of spending your vacation fixing up your house is the economic benefit you would have derived from your next-best option, which was sitting on the beach sipping cold lemonade.

EXAMPLE The opportunity cost of taking an early morning class is the economic benefit you would have received from sleeping in until noon.

ECONOMIC FALLACY   Business owners who own their own buildings and don't pay rent can sell their products at a lower price than business owners who lease space and must pay rent.

False. Even if a business owner owns his building and doesn't pay rent, he has spent money to purchase the building. This money has an opportunity cost associated with it. After all, the money could have been invested or spent on things that create well-being. Also, the owner does not have to use the building for his own business; he could rent it out to another company. This forgone rent is an opportunity cost that must be considered when the business figures out the total cost of selling its products.

Going forward, when we speak about the **economic cost** of the choice you make, we are speaking about its opportunity cost—the benefits forgone from the next-best alternative that could have been chosen.

ECONOMIC COST Opportunity cost.

EXAMPLE The economic cost of getting married is the benefit that could have been had by continuing to "play the field."

EXAMPLE The economic cost of purchasing a Starbuck's coffee mocha is the benefit that could have been had by ordering a cafe latte instead.

ECONOMIC FALLACY   If the price of something is zero, then its economic cost is zero.

False. Let's say that you receive a full scholarship to go to college. There is still an opportunity cost of going to college, such as the wages that you forgo by attending classes rather than working. To get the "free" autograph of a sports or film star, you usually must wait somewhere for some time. This waiting imposes an economic cost. People who live in countries where the government provides "free" health care usually wait all day to be seen (in Australia, patients often bring their lunches to their doctor's office!) and months or years more before their surgeries are performed. These are some of the economic costs associated with free health care.

Our examples highlight the fact that economic benefits and opportunity costs encompass much more than monetary considerations: there is a nonmonetary benefit, for example, that comes from catching a few extra hours of sleep, spending time with your child, or hanging out with your friends. If you think about it, money itself provides little, if any, direct economic benefit. If you were stranded on a deserted island, and a bottle washed ashore stuffed with $100 bills, would this money make you any happier? You can't eat or wear money; what money does do is allow you to purchase goods that you want, now or in the future. Having more money makes us happier because we get economic benefits from the things we can purchase with it. Having money in our wallets or bank accounts also reduces our anxiety about our future economic situation. By lessening our uncertainty about the future, we have increased our happiness today.[1]

It turns out that a person will make the best use of his scarce resources by making choices that generate the greatest **net benefit**—that is, by making choices that maximize the *difference* between the economic benefit received and the opportunity cost incurred.

NET BENEFIT The difference between the economic benefit and the opportunity cost of an alternative.

EXAMPLE A working mother can stay at work and earn overtime, in which case, she will have to arrange for child care, which costs $7.50 per hour. The mother will make an economically rational decision to stay at work only if she earns more than $7.50 an hour, in which case, her net benefit is positive.

EXAMPLE A student enrolled in a four-year college is considering taking a summer-school course at his local community college because he can save $750 in tuition. If the additional costs of this option—including parking and transportation costs, as well as the opportunity cost of the time spent on registering for class, getting the credit hours transferred, driving farther, and so on—are less than $750, then the net benefit of taking the course will be positive.

SOLVED PROBLEM

Q You are offered a free ride to go to Florida for your spring vacation. Alternatively, you can spend $299 to fly round-trip to Mexico. You would have been willing to spend up to $399 to fly to Mexico. What is the opportunity cost of going to Florida?

A The net benefit of flying to Mexico is equal to $399 − $299 = $100. If you go to Florida, the net benefit you pass up from flying to Mexico is $100. Therefore, the opportunity cost of accepting the ride to Florida is $100. This assumes that there are no additional costs or benefits of either trip that must be considered (and that everything else—hotel, food, and so on—is the same in both locations).

In the real world, people sometimes deviate from this decision "rule" and ultimately find out that they have made a bad choice. This is because decisions must sometimes be made in the face of limited or erroneous information. For example, if you knew *in advance* that skipping work to study for a final exam would get you fired, you would probably make a different decision than if you think that your boss will

· · · · · · ·

[1]Daniel Gilbert, "What You Don't Know Makes You Nervous." *New York Times*, May 21, 2009.

overlook your absence. Choices must often be made based on our expectations about what will follow, that is, based on our best guess about the amount of net benefit we will get from our decision.

If a person ends up making a "bad" decision, does this mean that he has acted in an "irrational" way, economically speaking? Not at all. In the real world, information itself is a scarce resource. Therefore, we must also consider the economic costs we would incur—spending more time searching for information on the Internet or buying the most recent copy of *Consumer Reports*, for example—to gather more information in advance of making a choice, say, to buy a big-screen television. Most likely, investing enough time to be 100 percent sure about each alternative you can choose from will not be your best strategy. This means that people knowingly make choices to maximize their well-being in the face of what economists call **imperfect information**.

> **IMPERFECT INFORMATION** Limited or erroneous knowledge about the economic cost or benefit of an alternative.

> **EXAMPLE** Investors chose Bernie Madoff to handle their financial affairs based on friends' recommendations and the impressive returns these friends had received. As it turned out, Madoff was a swindler who falsified documents and paid off earlier investors with newer investors' funds. Many people lost their life savings.

> **EXAMPLE** Some colleges publish and distribute instructor evaluation booklets, which report student evaluation scores and comments from the previous academic year. Students at these schools have more complete information on which to base their course selections than students who go to schools that do not publish these results.

2.2 Marginal Analysis and Rational Choice

Every day, people face competing opportunities when it comes to using their scarce resources. Even decisions about leisure activities require some thought. Perhaps you have asked yourself: "Should I rent a DVD or go to the movies? Should I go out to eat or fix dinner at home? If I go out, should I take the kids or find a babysitter?" Each of these options has corresponding economic benefits and opportunity costs. How, exactly, do people make these decisions to achieve the maximum amount of satisfaction they can?

Economists characterize the decision process that ensues as "thinking at the margin." Basically this means asking yourself: "If I spend one more unit of my scarce resource (my time or money) on option 1, on option 2, or on option 3, which will give me the greatest net benefit?" In effect, we describe your thought process as *incremental* in nature, in which you evaluate how to spend the next minute of your time or dollar of your income. This approach is called **marginal analysis**.

> **MARGINAL ANALYSIS** A thought process that compares the net benefit of allocating each additional unit of a scarce resource to one alternative versus another.

EXAMPLE Should you spend another hour studying for your economics midterm exam or use it instead to finish your Spanish assignment?

EXAMPLE Should you spend another dollar to super-size your fast-food lunch, or should you use it instead to buy dessert?

Marginal analysis requires us to compare the **marginal benefit** to the **marginal cost** of spending an additional unit of a scarce resource in a particular way.

MARGINAL BENEFIT (*MB*) The increase in economic benefit that results when an additional unit of a scarce resource is spent on a particular activity.

MARGINAL COST (*MC*) The increase in economic cost that results when an additional unit of a scarce resource is spent on a particular activity.

EXAMPLE What is the net benefit of spending one more hour studying for an economics exam? The answer depends on what you expect this hour to yield in terms of additional exam points (this is your perceived marginal benefit). You would compare this to what you would expect the extra hour to yield if you spent it instead in the next-best way, for example, by studying for a chemistry test (this is your perceived marginal cost). If the difference between the marginal benefit and marginal cost—that is, the net benefit—is positive, you will spend the extra hour studying economics.

EXAMPLE What is the net benefit of spending more money to upgrade to a faster 4G cell phone? This net benefit depends on the marginal benefit you get from saving time uploading to or downloading from the Internet compared to the benefit you *could* have received from spending this money in the next-best way—for example, using it to buy more downloaded music or movies. This forgone benefit is the marginal cost of spending more money to upgrade your cell phone. If the net benefit of the upgrade is positive, then spending the money on a 4G cell phone will maximize your well-being.

Do economists really expect that people consciously engage in this type of incremental comparison before every decision they make? Absolutely not. The best way to think about marginal analysis is that it is as an approximation—a model—that is predictive of people's behavior. The model need not apply perfectly to any or every situation. We only care about whether it is a reasonably good predictor of how people tend to act. Marginal decision making recognizes that we are not typically limited to all-or-none choices when we allocate our scarce resources; that is, we are likely to spend our money or time in a number of ways, at differing levels of intensity.

Marginal analysis is a particularly powerful framework for not only analyzing how we spend each additional hour or dollar at our disposal but also for predicting how these choices change when the world around us changes. For example, marginal analysis predicts that the amount of time a family spends on meal preparation decreases when time-saving technologies such as freshly frozen foods and the microwave become low-cost and widely accessible: the marginal benefit of spending additional time to bake and cook "the old-fashioned way" declines. Likewise, our model would predict that the huge expansion in television programming that has occurred over the past decade has resulted in people spending more time, on average, watching

Table 2.1 Number of Hours per Week Spent on Household Tasks (1965–2003)					
Time Use Category	1965	1975	1985	1993	2003
Food Preparation and Household Chores	14.42	11.55	10.55	8.23	8.01
Men only	1.97	1.98	3.83	2.85	3.46
Women only	24.65	20.23	15.96	12.81	12.43
Shopping	6.09	5.26	5.97	5.35	5.27
Men only	4.73	4.32	4.64	3.90	4.39
Women only	7.20	6.12	7.05	6.58	6.12

Source: Mark Aguiar and Erik Hurst. "The Allocation of Time Over Five Decades." Working Paper 06-2. *Federal Reserve Bank of Boston*, January 2006, Table 2.

TV (assuming program quality hasn't declined). In other words, the marginal benefit of each additional hour spent watching TV has increased.

How accurate is marginal analysis in predicting how people use their time? The U.S. Bureau of Labor Statistics (BLS) collects information about how Americans spend their time on a whole host of work and leisure activities.[2] **Table 2.1** presents a subset of this information, as reported by economists Mark Aguiar and Erik Hurst.[3] These findings are remarkably consistent with what our model predicted about how our allocation of time to household tasks would change over the past five decades, especially for women. We see that women now spend significantly less time performing household tasks such as food preparation, which has left them with more time for work outside the home and leisure activities. Men have picked up only a small fraction of this decline in women's household work time, spending about 1.5 hours more a week than almost 40 years ago.

In observing human behavior, we find that time and time again, people *act in a manner consistent* with marginal analysis. In most circumstances, our choices can be predicted quite accurately by using a "marginalist" model of behavior. We do not know whether some sort of evolutionary process has created neural "hardwiring" so that people act as if they are making marginal calculations, or whether people learn to behave in this way by first making mistakes or observing their parents or peers. In any case, people's choices exhibit a remarkable consistency with marginal decision making from a predictive standpoint. Economists who have studied animals in a lab setting have likewise found that "when put to the test, rats and pigeons [also] conform to the elementary principles of economics," specifically, they act as if they engage in marginal cost–marginal benefit calculations.[4]

Even though it's been shown that almost everyone acts like they think at the margin, there is no reason for us to assume that different people using the *same* decision process will make the *same* choices, even when they are put in the same situation. In other words, even when individuals face the same alternatives and have the same

· · · · · · ·

[2]U.S. Bureau of Labor Statistics, *American Time Use Survey*.

[3]Mark Aguiar and Erik Hurst. "The Allocation of Time Over Five Decades." Working Paper 06-2. *Federal Reserve Bank of Boston*, January 2006, Table 2.

[4]John Kagel, Raymond C. Battalio, and Leonard Green, *Economic Theory: An Experimental Analysis of Animal Behavior* (New York: Cambridge University Press, 1995), p. 3.

amount of resources available, they often make different decisions. This happens because they subjectively value these alternatives differently according to their personal preferences. How often have you dined out with a friend, spent approximately the same amount of money, but ordered entirely different meals? While you are taking this economics course, how many other students are taking philosophy or accounting during the very same class time? The beauty of our economic model of decision making is that it provides a framework for predicting individual choices without imposing uniformity on the actual choices that people make.

Marginal Analysis in Action

Consider a couple discussing the number of children they would like to have (we call this the "fertility" decision). They know that there is a monetary cost to having a child: money spent on medical care, food, a bigger house, child care, and education is money that cannot be spent on sports cars, vacations, upscale restaurants, and other goods and services. In fact, it is estimated that the average cost of raising a child born in 2005 through age 17 is upwards of $250,000 for middle-class families.[5] We also know that nonmonetary costs are associated with raising a child, including the sacrifice of leisure activities or work opportunities, not to mention sleep. These nonmonetary costs differ from person to person, depending on both individual preferences and the alternatives people face. For example, a female college graduate faces a higher opportunity cost of having a child than a high-school dropout. Why? Because the college graduate would have to forgo higher wages if her pregnancy or child-rearing activities led to a decline in hours worked.

How do couples weigh these costs and benefits to determine the number of children that would maximize their well-being? In the real world, couples almost certainly have imperfect information about the full range of costs and benefits arising from parenthood. Extrapolating from others' experiences is, at best, an imperfect gauge, as is drawing conclusions from TV shows. Often, it is only *after* someone has had a child that he more fully appreciates the costs and benefits of being a parent. So, it is possible that a person's initial views on family size will change after he has had a child.

This point deserves emphasis: economic decisions are made at a point in time based on information available at that time. Later decisions may be informed by the experiences arising from earlier decisions, which lead to a change in the perceived benefits and costs of certain alternatives. For example, we often try a variety of brands of cereal, peanut butter, and yogurt before we have adequate information to settle on the brands we prefer.

We can use marginal analysis to model the decision to have a first child. Based on imperfect information, a couple will assess the net benefit of having a first child. If the benefit outweighs the cost—yielding a positive net benefit—they will choose to have the child. If the net benefit is negative, they will defer having a child until such time (if ever) that their circumstances change and the net benefit of doing so becomes positive. For example, if a woman loses her job, the opportunity cost of having a child may fall, and the net benefit of having a child may turn positive at that point in time. If this same woman immediately lands another job at a higher salary, the opportunity cost will increase and likely lead to a negative net benefit. Similarly,

• • • • • • •

[5]"Expenditures on Children by Families, 2005." U.S. Department of Agriculture Publication #1528-2005.

many couples wait until they have finished college to have their first child because the opportunity cost is too high to tend to kids and go to school at the same time. In other words, the net benefit of starting a family is not positive.

What about the decision to have a second or third or tenth child? Parents will again act as if they have engaged in marginal analysis, weighing the benefits and costs of having the additional child. They may even factor in the benefits and costs that they believe will accrue to their existing child(ren): Will the firstborn be a spoiled brat if he is an "only child"? On the other hand, will the existing child(ren) suffer once there is an additional child vying for the family's limited resources, including parental attention?[6] We know, for example, that children from large families tend to earn less as adults than children who come from smaller families because they generally have less education.[7] This suggests that additional children in a family can have a lifelong, negative economic impact on older siblings.

As long as the net benefit of having additional children is positive, a couple will continue to expand its family. This will continue until the couple reaches a point where the benefits of having another child are just outweighed by the costs; that is, where the marginal benefit equals the marginal cost of having the additional child. At this point, the net benefit of having another child is zero. We say that the couple is "at the margin" when it comes to having this last child. That is, they are **indifferent** to having this last child.

INDIFFERENCE A situation in which the net benefit of a particular decision is zero and, as a result, a decision maker doesn't care about the choice that is made.

EXAMPLE Your instructor doesn't care whether you read the textbook before or after class, as long as you read it. She is indifferent to your study routine.

EXAMPLE Most people in the United States don't care whether their child is a boy or girl, as long as it is healthy. They are indifferent to their child's gender.

EXAMPLE Lots of drivers are indifferent to which brand of gasoline they put in their cars.

Reaching this point of indifference, a couple would stop adding to its family. Having more children would result in a negative net benefit. This doesn't mean that an additional child wouldn't add to its parents' sense of well-being or that it wouldn't be loved and cared for. What it means is that the perceived net benefit of having one more child is negative: the benefit is outweighed by the cost. Of course, if the couple wins the lottery, they may reconsider this decision: the opportunity cost of an additional child may decline if a nanny can now be hired, for example. The point is that marginal analysis would likely predict different choices when the world around us changes.

You might be thinking that the application of marginal analysis to such a personal decision as having children is cold and impersonal. In reality, demographers and policy makers use this type of behavioral model to explain why some groups of people or nations tend to have more children than others. Many policy decisions are based on the fundamental assumption that people act as if they are making the kind

• • • • • • •

[6]Jeff Opdyke, "How Many Children?" *St. Louis Post-Dispatch*, October 20, 2002.
[7]Judith Blake, "Family Size and the Quality of Children," *Demography*, 18, no. 2 (November, 1981).

of marginal calculations just described. Countries with low reproduction rates may reduce the marginal cost of having a large family by subsidizing child care or requiring employers to offer paid parental leaves. Countries suffering from overpopulation may offer free birth-control methods or impose large fines on families with more than a certain number of children.

What we are saying is that whether we are talking about having children or eating hot dogs at a baseball game, a person will maximize her satisfaction, or sense of well-being, by engaging in each activity up to the point where the net benefit of additional consumption equals zero. Put another way, an economically rational decision maker will stop consuming a particular good at the point where the marginal benefit derived from the last unit just equals its marginal cost.

The Limits of Marginal Analysis

As it turns out, marginal analysis can be problematic when we are dealing with addictive behaviors because for most addicts, their decision about how to use their scarce resources is an all-or-none decision. They get economic benefit from only one substance or activity—the one to which they are addicted. The initial decision to smoke, drink, or gamble may actually be rational to the extent that people assess their perceived net benefit of engaging in a particular behavior. However, after a person becomes addicted to the activity, he will likely spend a large part of his scarce resources on this addiction; marginal benefits and costs are irrelevant. This is why it is easier to dissuade teenagers from starting to smoke by imposing huge taxes that raise the price per pack. Addicted smokers are far less responsive to increases in cigarette prices. Marginal analysis may not be well suited for predicting how an addict's behavior will change when his economic environment changes, for example, when the penalty for drunk driving increases to include mandatory jail time.

This is not to say that marginal analysis is totally irrelevant when it comes to some choices made by an addict. For example, smokers who are paid to quit smoking are more successful in breaking the habit than those who are not, and the amount they are paid matters.[8] Also, drug addicts seem to systematically engage in the "optimal" type of crime to pay for their habits, based on the particular characteristics of their addiction. Users of methamphetamines favor identity theft because their drug addiction gives them long attention spans during which they can focus on the details that identity theft entails. In contrast, crack cocaine users are more likely to rely on muggings, carjackings, and robberies because crack cocaine gives them a sense of overwhelming strength and power, but only a short attention span.[9] These choices are consistent with marginal analysis. Addicts act as if they recognize that the marginal benefit and marginal cost of using their time to commit different types of crime depend on the specific drug they are using.

2.3 Diminishing Marginal Benefit

Several interesting questions arise from the fertility decision we just discussed: (1) Is the economic benefit that parents receive from the second child the same as it is for the first child, and is the economic benefit of the third child the same as for the

· · · · · · ·

[8]Associated Press, "Money Helps Smokers Quit, Study Says." *St. Louis Post-Dispatch*, February 12, 2009.

[9]John Leland, "Meth Users, Attuned to Detail, Add Another Habit: ID Theft." *New York Times*, July 11, 2006.

second child, and so on? And, (2) is the opportunity cost of the second child the same as it is for the first child, and is the opportunity cost of the third child the same as for the second child, and so on?

If the answers to (1) and (2) are both *yes*, then the marginal cost and marginal benefit are the *same* for each additional child, which means that the net benefit of having a tenth child is the same as the net benefit of having the first child. If this were the case, a couple that chooses to have one child that is perceived to yield a positive net benefit would choose to have as many children as possible, each of which would yield the same net benefit.

In reality, the "average" family in the United States has about two children, far fewer than only a century ago. Also, the average family size in most parts of the world is far less than what the limits of reproductive biology would dictate. This gives us additional insight into the economic costs and benefits of having children: specifically, the net benefit of having additional children must at some point decline.

One reason that the net benefit of additional children or other goods may eventually fall is that the marginal benefit begins to diminish. You and your friends do not eat an infinite amount at all-you-can-eat buffet restaurants. Even though the sense of well-being derived from the first and second helpings of macaroni and cheese is positive, the third, fourth, and fifth helpings just don't deliver the same satisfaction as the first two. Because the marginal benefit of an additional helping decreases at some point, the net benefit (marginal benefit minus marginal cost) of this extra helping must also decline.

This idea has general applicability. Whether it is extra helpings at the local buffet or more children, at some point, the marginal benefits begin to decline. We refer to this phenomenon as **diminishing marginal benefit**.

DIMINISHING MARGINAL BENEFIT A situation in which the economic benefit generated from an additional unit of a good or activity is less than the benefit derived from the preceding unit.

EXAMPLE The first cold lemonade on a hot summer's day will likely create a good deal more well-being than the second.

EXAMPLE Some television commercials are quite funny the first time they are seen. By the 50th viewing, most of the enjoyment is gone.

Another reason economists believe that diminishing marginal benefit sets in at some point is that people enjoy variety in the goods they consume. The more of one good that is consumed—in lieu of another good—the less variety we get. Imagine having the same dinner menu every day; even your most favorite dish will begin to lose its appeal at some point.

Because people differ in their preferences, they are also likely to differ in terms of when diminishing marginal benefits set in. An insomniac will likely get a great deal of satisfaction from watching reruns of *Star Trek* well into the middle of the night; in contrast, this satisfaction will have already diminished considerably by 10 P.M. for those who are used to going to bed by then.

In our example of the all-you-can-eat buffet, the marginal benefit from additional helpings will not just diminish at some point, but it can even turn negative if someone gets sick from overeating. That is, our *overall* happiness or satisfaction starts to decline because we have overindulged in some activity. In effect, what was an **economic "good"**—yielding us additional well-being—has turned into an **economic "bad."**

ECONOMIC "GOOD" An activity, product, or service whose consumption increases well-being.

ECONOMIC "BAD" A product, activity, or service whose consumption reduces well-being.

EXAMPLES Sunshine, intellectual challenges, gourmet meals, and social drinking are typically economic "goods," whereas sunburns, stress, overeating, and binge drinking are economic "bads."

Consuming economic bads lowers our overall sense of well-being. In contrast to an economic good, *less* of an economic bad is always preferred to more.

What may be an economic good for one person could be an economic bad for another. A person may become sick to his stomach and dizzy if he drinks more than two beers; his third beer is an economic bad. In contrast, his date may not suffer any ill effects until her sixth beer, at which point beer becomes an economic bad. Similarly, many children enjoy peanut butter sandwiches every day, whereas others with peanut allergies would go into anaphylactic shock after only one bite.

The principle of diminishing marginal benefit helps us more accurately predict certain behaviors. For example, if people pay a flat fee to connect to the Internet, then their marginal cost of access is zero. As a result, people will use the service until the marginal benefit has diminished to zero, at which point, the net benefit is also zero. Contrast this with what you predict would happen if people were charged instead by the minute or hour of connection time. Given your prediction, how do you think customers have responded to AT&T and other telephone service providers that have dropped their unlimited data plans and have replaced them with prices based on usage?

Returning to the decision about family size, we find that throughout history, the benefits of having more children have clearly diminished depending on the economic environment. Traditionally, firstborn sons were highly prized because they could inherit family lands and thereby perpetuate the family's name (which was attached to the land) and wealth. Because daughters were usually prohibited from owning property, the benefits from having additional children would begin to diminish only after a male heir was produced.[10] The preeminent position of the firstborn son continues today in certain societies. In rural India, a son is still favored over a daughter because he is responsible for working family lands and supporting elderly parents; also, his family does not pay a dowry when he weds.[11] The strong preference for sons in China, along with the government's strict "one child per family" policy (one child in urban areas; two in rural areas), has resulted in a striking gender imbalance in that country: 129 boys for every 100 girls for firstborns, and 147 boys to 100 girls for secondborns.[12]

· · · · · · ·

[10]Gordon Bjork, *Life, Liberty and Property* (Landham, MD: Lexington Books, 1980).

[11]John Donnelly, "Females Routinely Aborted in India, Study Finds." *The Boston Globe*, January 10, 2006.

[12]Howard W. French, "As Girls 'Vanish,' Chinese City Battles Tide of Abortions." *New York Times*, February 17, 2005.

In many countries, including the United States, the trend has been toward smaller and smaller families. One explanation is that as we have evolved from an agrarian economy to an industrial economy to an information services economy, the economic benefit of having additional children has declined. On the family farm of old, children worked the fields and helped with chores. Today's modern farm is technologically advanced and depends on a great deal of labor-saving equipment, thereby reducing the benefits that additional children generate. Also, the introduction of government programs such as Social Security has reduced the perceived benefit of having more children simply to ensure a "cushion" in one's old age. Such changes may explain why the marginal benefit of an additional child now begins to diminish at a lower number than in the past.

Water is another good that clearly exhibits diminishing marginal benefits in consumption. The first gallons of water in our possession generate the greatest benefit; they keep us alive. Additional gallons generate a positive, but smaller, benefit in that we can use them to take a shower and enjoy better personal hygiene. Yet additional gallons generate positive, but even smaller, benefits in that we can use them to water our lawn. We get positive, but diminishing, benefits from each gallon of water we consume beyond the minimal amount required to keep us alive.

2.4 The Principle of Increasing Cost

When we talk about the cost of an alternative, we actually mean its economic, or opportunity, cost. With that in mind, can we say anything about what happens to the marginal cost of using more and more of a good? In the case of water, is there some point at which the opportunity cost of consuming additional amounts of water begins to increase?

When it comes to water production, the lowest cost source of drinking water for a community is rainwater, which is collected by local reservoirs. This water is then filtered and purified before it gets to your house. As more and more water is used, however, the community must tap subterranean water reserves that have to be pumped up to surface water-treatment plants using energy and equipment. This suggests that as more water is consumed, the cost of acquiring the water increases. This additional cost means that some other town activity—say, repairing Main street—will go undone. In other words, the opportunity cost of water rises with increasing levels of consumption. This result is consistent with the **principle of increasing marginal cost**.

PRINCIPLE OF INCREASING MARGINAL COST As more of a good is consumed, the opportunity cost of additional units of consumption begins to rise. That is, the marginal cost of an additional unit starts to increase at some point.

EXAMPLE The cost of heating water in one's home using solar power is low in sunny climates such as the Middle East. However, the cost of shifting more and more of the home's energy needs to solar through the use of solar cells begins to rise dramatically because of the limited capacity of these cells.

EXAMPLE The cost of making budget cuts—whether at the family level or the federal government level—starts to increase as more and more core expenditures are cut, such as those that fund basic food consumption.

The point at which increasing costs set in differs depending on economic conditions. When it comes to water, some regions of the world get a large amount of low-cost rainwater each year, while other areas must turn to more costly alternatives at relatively low levels of water use. In the case of Kuwait, the scarcity of rainwater is counterbalanced by its ample supply of seawater and oil supplies to support its desalinization plants.

When it comes to having more children, the principle of increasing cost says that, at some point, the marginal cost of having another child is greater than the marginal cost of the preceding child. Is this true? Think about the cost of housing as a family grows in size. Adding more children may mean that at some point, the family must relocate to a community that offers larger homes at a lower price. This could mean relocating to the suburbs, resulting in a longer commute to work. Or, consider the possibility that having additional children increases the probability that one is sick on any given day and that a parent must miss work. There are many reasons to believe that the marginal cost of having additional children will rise at some point. Whether it is after the first, second, or third child, the principle of increasing marginal cost has validity even when it comes to the fertility decision.

2.5 The Diminishing Net Benefit of Consumption

The principles of diminishing marginal benefit and increasing marginal cost provide a powerful tool that helps us predict the choices people make. As we consume more and more units of a good or engage in more and more of an activity, the marginal benefit we receive will eventually diminish. At the same time, the marginal cost will eventually rise. This means that at some point, the *net* benefit generated by an additional unit of a good or activity must fall.

Also, at some level of consumption, the marginal benefit of the last unit consumed will just equal its marginal cost. This last unit will generate zero net benefit because the difference between marginal benefit and marginal cost is zero. Because the net benefit is zero, we would not expend any more of our scarce resources to acquire any more units. We can depict the relationship between diminishing marginal benefit and increasing marginal cost using **marginal benefit (*MB*)** and **marginal cost (*MC*) curves**.

> **MARGINAL BENEFIT (*MB*) CURVE** A graphic representation of the incremental benefit received from consuming an additional unit of a good.

> **MARGINAL COST (*MC*) CURVE** A graphic representation of the incremental cost incurred to consume an additional unit of a good.

Figure 2.1 puts both of these curves in the same graph. Notice that the *MB* curve at first increases and then begins to decline as we move out the horizontal (quantity) axis. In contrast, the *MC* curve begins to rise at some quantity level.

Let's use this graph to further analyze a person's decision about how much water to consume each week. The vertical distance between the *MB* and *MC* curves represents the *net* benefit that you receive from consuming each gallon of water. The net benefit of the 10th gallon consumed each week is indicated by the line AB; the net benefit of the 16th gallon is represented by the line CD. As you can see, the net benefit of each additional gallon is decreasing the more we are consuming. At the 20th gallon, the net benefit is exactly equal to zero: at point E, the *MC* curve and the *MB* curve intersect, which means that the marginal cost of the 20th gallon is just equal to the marginal benefit it generates. Beyond this level of water consumption, the net

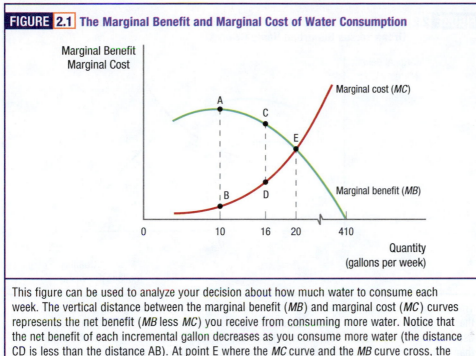

FIGURE 2.1 **The Marginal Benefit and Marginal Cost of Water Consumption**

This figure can be used to analyze your decision about how much water to consume each week. The vertical distance between the marginal benefit (*MB*) and marginal cost (*MC*) curves represents the net benefit (*MB* less *MC*) you receive from consuming more water. Notice that the net benefit of each incremental gallon decreases as you consume more water (the distance CD is less than the distance AB). At point E where the *MC* curve and the *MB* curve cross, the net benefit of consuming one more gallon of water is exactly equal to zero.

benefit from using more gallons is negative: the marginal cost of additional gallons swamps out any additional benefit that may be had. Note that beyond the 20th gallon, the marginal benefit from consuming additional gallons of water is still positive—water is still an economic "good" generating positive marginal benefit. However, at the same time, the marginal cost of consuming additional gallons beyond the 20th gallon outweighs this marginal benefit, thereby resulting in a *negative* net benefit. Our *overall* sense of well-being from consuming water will fall if we consume more than 20 gallons per week.

Irrespective of the marginal cost of water, after we go beyond 410 gallons a week, the *MB* curve crosses into negative territory. We are likely at "flood stage" at this point, such that consuming additional gallons of water diminishes our overall sense of well-being even if they are free. The 411th gallon of water is an economic bad, as are all gallons beyond this quantity.

Keep in mind that whether we are talking about water, education, children, or music downloads, the point at which marginal cost and marginal benefit are equal will probably not be the same for everyone. People's *MB* or *MC* curves may differ. For example, the *MB* curve for water is likely to be very different for a suburban home owner than for an urban condominium home owner without a yard. **Figure 2.2** shows two *MB* curves—one for each type of home owner—along with a common *MC* curve, which assumes that the cost of water delivery is the same for each of the home owners. What you can see is that the level of water use—where the net benefit is equal to zero—differs for the two home owners. The suburban dweller will consume more water even though the marginal cost of the last gallon purchased is higher than the marginal cost of the last gallon purchased by the urban home owner. This makes sense because the suburbanite's *MB* curve is higher and therefore justifies spending more to get additional gallons.

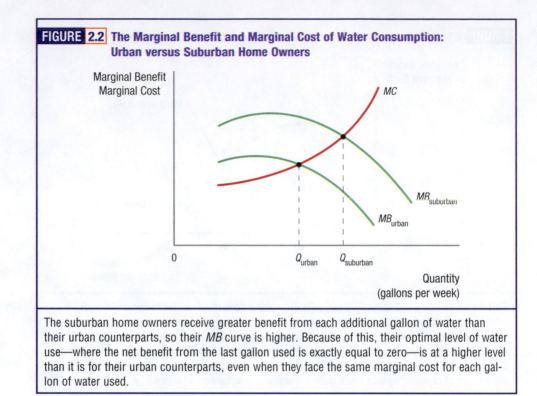

FIGURE 2.2 The Marginal Benefit and Marginal Cost of Water Consumption: Urban versus Suburban Home Owners

The suburban home owners receive greater benefit from each additional gallon of water than their urban counterparts, so their *MB* curve is higher. Because of this, their optimal level of water use—where the net benefit from the last gallon used is exactly equal to zero—is at a higher level than it is for their urban counterparts, even when they face the same marginal cost for each gallon of water used.

If the water company in a drought-stricken community wanted to reduce overall water consumption, our analysis would tell it to raise the water rates paid by suburban home owners. This would cause the *MC* curve for water to shift up, so that the net benefit of using an additional gallon of water would equal zero at a lower level of water use.

What if the *MB* curves of two people are the same, but the *MC* curves they face are different? Consider, for example, a couple that lives in a high-rent city such as New York City versus a couple living in a sprawling suburban housing development in the Midwest. Suppose that there is no other difference between the couples—they earn the same income, have the same preferences, and so on. **Figure 2.3** shows that the NYC residents incur a much higher *MC* curve for additional children due to the cost of expanding their housing space; as a result, we would predict that they will tend to have smaller families than their suburban counterparts. This prediction has been borne out by the facts.[13] For a similar reason—the cost of space—NYC residents also tend to have fewer cars.

We have already acknowledged that we make economic decisions with the imperfect information we currently have on hand but that it can become more perfect with time, experience, and investment in additional information-gathering activities. When better information changes our assessment of the marginal benefit or marginal cost of consuming more of a particular good, the corresponding curves will adjust and lead to a new level of consumption.

• • • • • •

[13]Jeff Opdyke, "Having Children: It's (Partly) About Money." *St. Louis Post-Dispatch*, September 29, 2002.

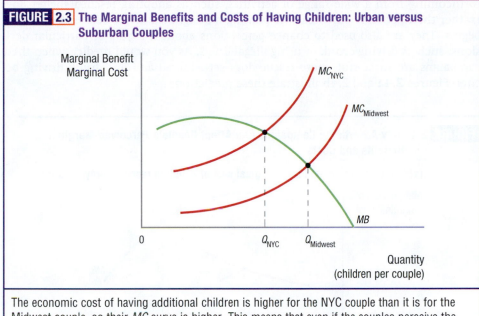

FIGURE 2.3 The Marginal Benefits and Costs of Having Children: Urban versus Suburban Couples

The economic cost of having additional children is higher for the NYC couple than it is for the Midwest couple, so their *MC* curve is higher. This means that even if the couples perceive the same economic benefit from having a first, second, and third child, the NYC family will choose to have fewer children than the Midwest couple.

Marketing gurus understand that it is costly for people to evaluate the benefits they would get from new products and services. For this reason, they often provide free samples or cost-saving coupons to encourage consumers to try their goods. Samples of new cereals are often bundled with the Sunday newspaper. Online news services are advertised offering free trial subscriptions, and infomercials advertise money-back guarantees. Possibly one of the most interesting examples of free giveaways is the Monty Python channel on YouTube, which shows a selection of the comedy group's film clips with links to buy their DVDs online. Their marketing philosophy? As they put it,

> "We're letting you see absolutely everything for free. So there! But we want something in return. None of your driveling, mindless comments. Instead, we want you to click on the links, buy our movies & TV shows and soften our pain and disgust at being ripped off all these years."

The goal, then, is to change people's perceptions about the economic benefits they will receive from a particular good. In the case of Monty Python, online DVD sales increased by 23,000 percent after the free DVD samples were put on YouTube.[14]

Advertising campaigns are geared toward changing people's perceptions about the benefits that would be gained from consuming a particular good. The goal of such campaigns—waged by a wide variety of industries ranging from cosmetic surgery to soft drinks to perfume—is to move the consumer's *MB* curve up, resulting in a higher level of consumption than before. Likewise, "public-service" campaigns conducted by charities or government agencies are aimed at changing perceptions about the *benefits*

. . . .

[14]Stan Schroeder, "Can Free Content Boost Your Sales?" *Mashable: The Social Media Guide*, January 22, 2009. http://mashable.com/2009/01/22/youtube-boost-sales/.

forthcoming from a wide-range of activities, such as adopting rescued shelter dogs (rather than pet store purebreds) or naming a designated driver before the partying begins. They are also used to change perceptions about the *costs* of particular decisions, such as driving drunk or using illegal drugs. As you would predict, when these campaigns are successful, more rescue dogs get adopted and less drunk driving occurs. **Figures 2.4a** and **2.4b** illustrate these predictions.

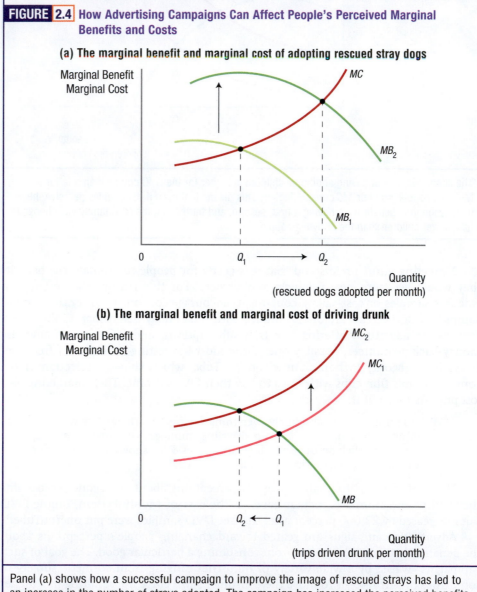

FIGURE 2.4 How Advertising Campaigns Can Affect People's Perceived Marginal Benefits and Costs

(a) The marginal benefit and marginal cost of adopting rescued stray dogs

(b) The marginal benefit and marginal cost of driving drunk

Panel (a) shows how a successful campaign to improve the image of rescued strays has led to an increase in the number of strays adopted. The campaign has increased the perceived benefits people get from adopting stray animals, thereby shifting the marginal benefit curve from MB_1 to MB_2 and the optimal number of stray adoptions from Q_1 to Q_2. Panel (b) shows that a successful campaign against drunk driving results in people taking fewer trips while under the influence by increasing the perceived cost of doing so. It shifts the MC curve up from MC_1 to MC_2 and reduces the number of DUI trips from Q_1 to Q_2.

SOLVED PROBLEM

Q Child labor laws in wealthier countries severely limit the amount of time a child under a certain age can spend as a paid laborer. Leaders of these countries are insisting that poorer countries adopt similar laws to protect their children from exploitation. Show, using *MB* and *MC* curves, the impact of these new laws, if passed, on the optimal number of children that a typical family in a poorer country will have.

A

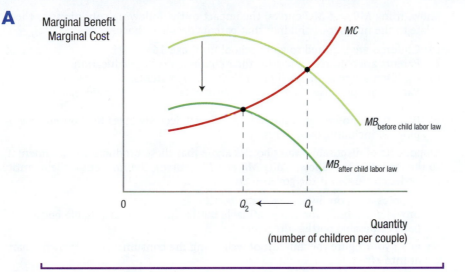

WHAT YOU SHOULD HAVE LEARNED FROM CHAPTER 2

- For each choice a person makes, there is an opportunity cost in terms of the next best alternative forgone.

- Economic costs and benefits include nonmonetary considerations.

- To maximize well-being in the face of scarcity, people must allocate their resources in a manner consistent with marginal analysis. As far as economists are concerned, however, they need only act as if they have examined the marginal trade-offs they face.

- Even when faced with the same alternatives and scarce resources, people often make different choices that reflect their own set of personal preferences.

- Each additional unit of consumption yields a positive but declining amount of well-being (diminishing marginal benefit) and comes at an increasing opportunity cost (increasing marginal cost). This means that the net benefit of consuming an additional unit of a good or engaging in an additional amount of an activity must eventually fall to zero.

- Because information is itself scarce, people usually make decisions based on imperfect information. They may make mistakes (choices that don't maximize their sense of well-being) and adjust their choices as they gain more information.

KEY TERMS

Preferences, p. 33

Economic benefit, p. 34

Utility, p. 34

Opportunity cost, p. 35

Economic cost, p. 35

Net benefit, p. 36

Imperfect information, p. 37

Marginal analysis, p. 37

Marginal benefit, p. 38

Marginal cost, p. 38

QUESTIONS AND PROBLEMS

1. Show, using *MB* and *MC* curves, the impact of the following conditions as they relate to the number of children that parents decide to have.

    a) Children are required to go to school until age 16.
    b) Parents are required to pay for their children's college education.
    c) Children are required to support their elderly parents.
    d) Parents are promised "job security" if they take off for unpaid maternity leave.
    e) Parents are no longer required to pay Social Security taxes for household employees, including babysitters.

2. Opponents of disposable water bottles argue that these products are detrimental to the environment. Show, using *MB* and *MC* curves, the impact on the quantity of bottles consumed if the government:

    a) imposes a tax on disposable water bottles.
    b) provides a subsidy for using refillable bottles instead of disposable bottles.
    c) bans disposable bottles altogether.

    Show on your figure the amount of well-being the consumer loses if such a ban is put into effect.

3. Blockbuster has a sales promotion where for $16.99 per month, you can have two DVDs in your possession at all times and can exchange them for other DVDs at any time during the month. Alternatively, you can rent each video for $3.99 for a two-day rental. Does the marginal cost of a DVD rental vary depending on the rental plan? What is this marginal cost? Will people watch DVDs constantly if they opt for the monthly rental plan? Why or why not?

4. Cell phone companies often give away telephones to their subscribers. Does this mean that the economic cost of these telephones is zero? Why or why not?

5. Show, using *MB* and *MC* curves, that you can reduce population growth in poorer countries by either (1) educating women and giving them greater employment opportunities; or (2) prohibiting the employment of children under a certain age. Do you think that parents would prefer one of these policies to the other? Explain your answer.

6. It is often said that higher education does better—in terms of enrollments—during bad economic times and worse during good economic times. Can you substantiate this prediction using *MB* and *MC* curves? [Hint: Think about the opportunity cost of attending college.]

7. Water companies have a variety of ways to reduce water use during droughts. One way is to increase the price of water. Another way is to prohibit consumers from watering their lawns. Which approach do you think is preferable? Why? Explain your answer.

8. Show, using separate *MB* and *MC* curves for each group, why people tend to go out to more movies in their teens and twenties than in their thirties and forties. Which group do you think better reflects the behavior of retirees? Why? Explain your answer.

9. Some retailers offer a discount when people buy more of a particular product—for example, buy one medium pizza for $7.95 and three medium pizzas for $5 each.
   a) How would you reconcile this pricing practice with the principle of increasing cost?
   b) Why would anyone just buy one pizza? Explain your answer.

10. Predict, using *MB* and *MC* curves, how the number of TripTiks travel itineraries prepared by the Automobile Association of America (AAA) for its members changes as Internet mapping technologies such as MapQuest become increasingly accessible at low cost. What do you think happens to membership in AAA?

    Explain your answer.

11. Using *MB* and *MC* curves, predict how the increasing use of robots in a manufacturing plant changes the optimal number of employees hired by the owner of the plant.

12. Given the rise in Internet shopping, what would you predict about the amount of time spent shopping in 2011? Do you think the time saved is used to earn more income or to pursue additional leisure activities? Explain your answer.

13. In the late 1800s and first part of the 1900s, many people living in rural areas ordered their clothes, tools, and even ready-to-assemble homes from mail-order catalogs such as the Sears, Roebuck and Company catalog. A century later, people began to shop from mail-order online retailers such as L.L. Bean and Amazon. Do you think that the same economic factors contributed to both "cycles" in mail-order buying? Explain your answer.

14. Using *MB* and *MC* curves to depict the food consumption decision of a typical low-income family, show why agri-business companies lobby politicians so hard for the continuation of the food-stamp program. Explain how your analysis could be extended to construction-worker unions that lobby for government home-mortgage subsidies.

15. The total benefit that Professor Allison gets from consuming the first beer at a Red Sox game is (in money terms) $25; it goes up to $40 for two beers, $50 for three beers, $58 for four beers, and $64 for five beers. Suppose the price of each beer is $8.
    a) What number of beers will Professor Allison consume?
    b) What is the total benefit he derives from drinking this amount of beer?
    c) What is the total net benefit he receives?
    d) What is the marginal benefit he receives from the second beer?
    e) What is the net marginal benefit he receives from the second beer?

16. Using marginal benefit (*MB*) and marginal cost (*MC*) curves, show what happened to people's consumption of liquor when Prohibition—the federal government's ban on liquor consumption—was repealed.

17. Using *MB* and *MC* curves, show how a teenager's decision to have one or more children is affected when (1) she is paid $100 each month to remain in school and not become pregnant; (2) she is paid $100 a month in food stamps for each child she has.

The Nature of Economic Costs

"Idealism is fine, but as it approaches reality, the costs become prohibitive."

William F. Buckley, Jr.,
columnist

It bears repeating: we live in a world of scarcity. And, as you learned in the previous chapter, this means that there is an opportunity cost to each and every choice we make. By opportunity cost, we mean *economic cost*—the sacrifice we make in terms of the forgone well-being to be had from our next-best alternative.

Even when something is offered "free of charge," it can come at a substantial economic cost. A "free" dog in need of a loving home requires food, veterinary care, and human playtime. Spending time at the free neighborhood park with family and friends means less time at work, a smaller paycheck, and, consequently, fewer purchases that could have generated well-being. Receiving a full scholarship to attend college does not mean that the economic cost of attending is zero—there are forgone earnings and consumables to consider. And, as the old adage goes, even a "free" lunch isn't usually free.

In this chapter, we explore in more depth the meaning of economic cost. As you will discover, the monetary cost of a choice is often a relatively small portion of a decision's total economic cost. This makes the choice between alternatives more complicated than just knowing how each will impact your wallet.

3.1 Definition and Determinants of Economic Costs

Studies of high-school dropouts reveal that pregnant teenagers are at increased risk of leaving school without a diploma. Teen mothers have an approximately 60 percent chance of graduating from high school by age 25, compared to 90 percent for those who postpone having children until after graduation.[1]

· · · · · · ·

[1] N. L. Leland et al., "Childbearing Patterns: Among Selected Racial/Ethnic Minority Groups—United States, 1990." *MMWR* (1993).

This tells us that the economic cost of teenage pregnancy is greater than simply the medical bills and the cost of baby formula. It also must include the loss in future wages resulting from dropping out and not having a high-school diploma. In contrast, women who defer having children until they have a high-school or college diploma in hand do not bear this economic cost. However, they may incur another type of economic cost—an increased risk of infertility. As women and men age, the probability of successfully having children the "old-fashioned way" declines.[2] This means that the decision to delay having children can result in higher medical bills for infertility treatment and a smaller family than otherwise preferred. This is an important economic cost to consider when it comes to choosing the best time to have children.

Our economic model of choice tells us that even when two people enjoy the same economic benefits from the same alternatives, they will make different choices if they are faced with different opportunity costs. A college-bound suburban teenager faces a substantially higher opportunity cost of having a child in high school than a high-school student who believes that her most promising employment opportunity is bagging groceries. It is critically important to understand that whether we are making predictions about the timing of having a child or whether to adopt a dog, our behavioral model predicts that people will make different choices simply because they face different opportunity costs. We needn't assume that people have different preferences, that is, different morals or values. Ultimately, our decisions depend on what we expect to forgo.

A good example is the increase in property crimes that occurs during economic recessions. The opportunity cost of engaging in criminal behavior is much lower for an unemployed person with few promising job leads than for a person who is successfully climbing the corporate ladder. A similar prediction holds for urban youth who face an unemployment rate that is 20 percent higher than their suburban counterparts: the opportunity cost of engaging in underground, illegal activities is substantially less.

3.2 Explicit versus Implicit Costs

One component of opportunity cost—the most obvious one—is the monetary cost of an opportunity. Economists refer to this type of cost as the **explicit cost** of a choice.

EXPLICIT COST The monetary cost of a choice.

EXAMPLE The explicit cost of going on a date includes the cost of movie tickets, dinner, and transportation (and a babysitter, if necessary).

EXAMPLE The explicit cost of attending college includes tuition and the cost of books and transportation.

EXAMPLE The explicit cost of using a toll bridge is the toll that is paid.

When you spend money on a movie, you forgo the well-being that could have been had from the next-best use of this money. We have already noted that money in itself provides no economic benefit. However, it can be used as a "common denominator" to compare the benefits forthcoming from alternative purchases. Suppose, for

· · · · · · ·

[2]Thurston Hatcher, "Careers and Babies: Fertility Decline Underscores Dilemma." *CNN*, May 2, 2002; Salynn Boyles, "Men, Your Fertility Clock Is Ticking." *WebMD Medical News*, February 5, 2003.

example, that you decide to spend $8 on a movie ticket. Underlying this choice is consideration of the benefit that you will forgo from spending the $8 on your next-best opportunity—buying a large pizza with two toppings from your favorite pizza place.

In addition to the explicit costs of making a choice, we incur **implicit costs** when we make a decision.

IMPLICIT COST The nonmonetary cost of a choice.

EXAMPLE A significant implicit cost of attending college full-time is the time that cannot be spent working to earn money to purchase economic goods or engaging in leisure activities.

EXAMPLE An implicit cost of using a toll-free road is the time spent fighting congestion during rush hour traffic.

Because implicit costs are, by their very definition, nonmonetary, they are not always easy to quantify. Economists often use wage rates to approximate the value of time spent doing "outside-of-work" activities such as attending college or participating in volunteer programs. For example, the dollar value of volunteer time donated to charitable organizations in the United States was estimated at $21.36 an hour in 2010, based on the average hourly wage of nonmanagement, nonagricultural workers.[3] The rationale for this approach is that the implicit cost of devoting time to such activities is roughly equal to the wages that a volunteer could have earned had he spent the time in the workplace instead. In a similar fashion, economists use a person's lifetime earnings potential to estimate the implicit cost of a person choosing to engage in activities that increase the risk of an early death, such as driving without a seat belt or smoking.[4]

When regulatory agencies consider new rules, they often take into account the implicit costs that businesses impose in terms of increasing the risk of disability or death.[5] What is the implicit cost—in terms of increased mortality—of a neighborhood factory that pollutes the local well water? What is the implicit cost that is borne by employees when an employer poorly ventilates a factory? Depending on how these implicit costs are estimated, certain government regulations may or may not be "cost-justified." We know, for example, that reducing factory pollution is not cheap. Will the subsequent reduction in mortality justify the cost of retooling?

Although implicit costs may be difficult to quantify, we know from observing people's behavior that these costs factor crucially into the decision-making process. Notice how people often buy items such as smoke detectors, side air bags, and sunscreen—goods that have no other benefit than to reduce the implicit cost of potential injury or death—despite the difficulty of actually "costing out" these risks. For those who buy smoke detectors, the opportunity cost of *not* buying them is just too high.

We observe that college students carefully consider the implicit cost of alternative class schedules, even when the explicit cost of each class (tuition) is the same. For example, two sections of introductory economics may not be equally attractive

· · · · · · ·

[3]Independent Sector, "Value of Volunteer Time: 2010." (2011). http://independentsector.org/volunteer_time.

[4]Kip Viscusi, "The Value of Life in Legal Contexts: Survey and Critique." *American Law and Economics Review,* 2, no. 1 (2000): 195–210.

[5]Binyamin Appelbaum, "As U.S. Agencies Put More Value on Life, Businesses Fret." *New York Times,* February 16, 2011.

to students, even when the same instructor is teaching both sections. Why is this? Because the implicit cost of each section's scheduled time slot will differ, depending on the student. Each student must consider which other courses are offered in the same time slot and the benefit that could be had from taking one of these alternative courses instead. A freshman who must fit a freshman writing class into her schedule would incur a lower implicit cost if she chooses the economics section that does not conflict with this required course. A business major would incur a lower implicit cost if she chooses an economics section that does not conflict with her managerial accounting class.

The implicit cost of classes scheduled midday is likely lower for nonworking, residential college students than for students who work off-campus to pay for their education or to support their families. Based on this supposition, our economic model would predict that colleges catering predominantly to full-time students schedule the bulk of their classes between 9:30 A.M. and 3 P.M. In contrast, colleges servicing working students offer many more classes at 8 A.M., 6:30 P.M., and even on weekends.

In the previous chapter, we defined the concept of economic cost as the opportunity cost of choosing a particular alternative. This opportunity cost is the sum of both the *explicit* and *implicit* costs of a choice. This is why economists disagree with the commonly held notion that the total cost of attending college is tuition, room, and board. We are confident that the full economic cost—not just the explicit costs—is considered when a person makes a decision about college and, more generally, how to use his scarce resources. How else can you explain the fact that "technogeeks" Steve Jobs and Bill Gates dropped out of college in the 1970s to seek their fortunes in hardware and software development? These students perceived that the *implicit* cost of staying in college for a couple more years was too high relative to the benefits they would get from the degree. They dropped out even though the *explicit* cost of staying in college had not changed. This result is worthy of emphasis: even when the explicit cost of a choice remains unchanged, an increase in its implicit cost can lead to a change in behavior.

3.3 Economic Costs versus Accounting Costs

Now that you better understand the nature of economic cost, it can be compared to other kinds of cost measures. In business, **accounting costs** refer to the ways in which accountants track costs when they prepare a company's ledgers and tax returns. In the accounting world, *accounting costs* are usually limited to money outlays (what we've called explicit costs) and may be defined by a country's tax code.

ACCOUNTING COSTS Explicit costs, or monetary outlays, incurred in the course of doing business.

EXAMPLE A student entrepreneur opens up a day-care center down the street from campus to provide students and faculty with preschool care. She invests $5,000 to fix up the space she has rented and incurs such business expenses as utilities, insurance, renovation costs, and the wages she pays herself. These are the venture's accounting costs.

EXAMPLE The accounting costs for an independent traveling salesman who works out of his car include the money spent on his product inventory, his gasoline purchases, depreciation on his car, and his monthly cell-phone bill.

In the preceding examples, the accounting costs ignore the implicit costs associated with opening the day-care center or selling out of one's car. The student running the day-care center could have invested her $5,000 in another way. The $5,000 could have earned interest in the bank or generated dividends from the purchase of a stock. The salesman does not pay himself a salary for his time but takes whatever profit he makes in lieu of pay.

From an economist's perspective, passing up an investment return or an opportunity to earn a salary is as much of a cost to a business as its rent or gasoline payments. These implicit costs are part of the opportunity cost of pursuing a particular venture and must be considered when the real profitability of a venture is assessed. If a business owner cannot generate sufficient revenue to cover all of his explicit and implicit costs, then he would be better off closing the business. Of course, if the owner gets satisfaction from the business in ways that are independent of profitability, then he might continue to keep a business open even when its economic costs exceed the money taken in.

Consider the case of a physician who leaves her group practice because she wants to see fewer patients each hour in order to give each of them more attention. She walks away from an annual salary of $340,000 a year and starts her own solo practice where she pays herself $150,000 a year and just breaks even in terms of her patient revenues and total explicit practice costs (including her salary). At the end of the first year, she remains delighted with her decision. From an accounting cost perspective, the doctor's expenses just equal her revenues. From an economics perspective, the doctor's total economic costs exceed her revenues by $190,000—the amount of salary that she lost when she left her previous employment. *If* the only consideration is whether the new practice is truly profitable, the physician would close it down and go back to her old group. However, it is clear that she gets a sense of well-being that more than outweighs the money she has passed up and the well-being that would have resulted from the goods and services she could have bought with this money. In effect, this physician is willing to pay for the right to practice medicine the way she wants to by sacrificing the purchases that the $190,000 could have made. So from this economic perspective, keeping the practice open makes sense.

Accounting costs and economic costs are often different when it comes to assigning a cost figure to business assets: manufacturing equipment, computers, buildings, and so forth. Typically, accountants look at the historical cost (original purchase price) of an asset rather than its economic cost. The U.S. Internal Revenue Service (IRS) provides guidelines for using an asset's historical cost to calculate a company's tax liability. This means, for example, that the accounting cost of owning an old office building—situated in a prime location—will be very low when compared to its economic cost. Its economic cost will include the opportunities forgone if the owner continues to operate the building in its present use. The next-best opportunity may be to sell the building and the land on which it sits so that the property can be converted to a higher-valued use such as loft housing.

You probably know someone who has totaled his car and is reimbursed the *Kelly Blue Book* value of the car. This reimbursement is based on the age of the car, its mileage, and the estimated market value of similar cars. We can think of this as the *accounting cost* of the vehicle. For most people, however, the economic cost of wrecking their car is much higher than this. Quite likely, they cannot purchase an exact replacement with the insurance check they receive. This means that the opportunity cost of losing the use of the car is greater than the cost assigned by the insurance company.

Because accounting costs ignore implicit costs, they are typically less than economic costs. Periodically, accounting rules have changed to bring accounting costs more in line with economic cost. Consider, for example, the change in corporate-accounting rules in 1992 that require publicly held companies (those that sell ownership shares to the public) to "book" as a liability the cost of future commitments to retirees to provide them with medical-insurance coverage. Before this change, these costs were excluded from company balance sheets until they were actually paid out. The new accounting rules caused an immediate, one-time decline ("write-down") in company profits, especially for those companies with large future health-care commitments such as the big three U.S. automobile manufacturers. Although the profits reported in each company's balance sheet declined, profitability from an economic standpoint remained unchanged. From an economic perspective, excluding these costs in the first place underestimated the true economic cost of the labor used to build cars. The commitment to retiree medical-insurance coverage was part of the active employees' compensation package. Without it, workers would likely have demanded higher wages.

Because accounting costs and economic costs are not usually the same, we are likely to draw different conclusions about the profitability of a business depending on which cost measure we use. This makes sense because profits are simply the difference between a company's sales revenue and the cost it incurs to produce and market its goods. We can compute a company's **accounting profit** by subtracting its accounting costs from its revenue. In contrast, when economic costs are deducted from revenue, we arrive at the business' **economic profit**.

ACCOUNTING PROFIT Total revenue less total accounting cost.

EXAMPLE Morissa and Max collected $200 from selling cold cans of soda at a local art show. They spent six hours selling the soda, which cost them $128 at Sam's Club. They also paid $20 for a vendor's license to sell at the show. Because they agreed to take no salary, their accounting profit was $52($200 − $128 − $20), which they split between themselves.

ECONOMIC PROFIT Total revenue less total economic cost.

EXAMPLE Suppose that Morissa gave up six hours of work time to help Max with his soda venture. Because she is an experienced ultrasound technician, the earnings she passed up were $28 per hour, or $168 in total. This means that the economic profit of the soda venture is at a minimum $168 lower than its accounting profit which did not take into account the value of her time, or −$116($200 − $128 − $20 − $168).

If economic costs are so difficult to quantify, do entrepreneurs and investors rely solely on a company's accounting information to make decisions? For example, did investor perceptions about company profitability change in 1992, when companies began to "book" their future retirees' health-insurance liabilities? We know there were whopping write-downs as a result of this accounting change; General Motors, for example, took a $20.8 billion write-down. Yet, on the very day that this write-down was announced, GM's share price closed up by over 2.5 percent.[6] As Rick Wagoner, who was GM's CEO at the time noted, the financial community was already anticipating

[6]Doron Levin, "Company Reports; GM Lost $23.5 Billion Last Year." *New York Times*, February 12, 1993.

the write-down. Investors had already considered previously unbooked liabilities when estimating the value of the company. This behavior is consistent with the notion that investors understand the difference between accounting and economic costs—and that they have their eyes on economic profits, not accounting profits.

ECONOMIC FALLACY   The fact that pharmaceutical companies earn profit margins in excess of 15 percent—as compared to 5 percent in the food and retailing sectors—is conclusive evidence that they are gouging consumers by charging too much for their drugs.

False. Profit margins that are reported in annual reports and by the media are accounting profits. These profits do not reflect the implicit costs of production, which in the case of drug companies include the risk that the billions of dollars invested in the research and development of a new drug could be futile. Just as venture capitalists require a higher return on their investment in risky new ventures, investors in drug companies require a higher return to compensate for the risk that a new drug in the pipeline could be shown to be ineffective or for some other reason be denied approval by the U.S. Food and Drug Administration (FDA).

3.4 Sunk Costs

Ever heard the expression, "Let bygones be bygones?" This means that we should let the past stay in the past and not spend more energy or other resources revisiting something that happened in the past. Circumstances inevitably arise where it makes economic sense for a person to walk away from a prior decision and let this past decision stay in the past. Even if this means having already incurred costs that cannot be recouped, it may be best to simply bring an activity to a halt. This may occur because new, previously unavailable, alternatives now exist. Or, it may be that additional information has been gained that now causes you to reconsider your initial decision. In any event, we often bear **sunk costs** when we choose to pursue another option and walk away from our initial choice.

SUNK COSTS Costs that cannot be recouped if you walk away from a prior decision.

EXAMPLE In anticipation of the move to laser discs, Sarah paid $2,500 for a player that she expected would be compatible with new industry standards. As it turns out, laser discs did not catch on, and movie distributors quickly discontinued selling them. Sarah's purchase of the laser-disc player is a sunk cost. She has already borne the cost of this purchase. Sarah can decide to keep the laser-disc player to play her very limited laser-disc collection (which is also a sunk cost), or she can choose to replace it with a Blu-ray player. Whatever she decides, the sunk cost of the player and laser-disc collection will not factor into the decision process.

EXAMPLE A working mother enrolls her baby in a prestigious day-care center. The tuition is a nonrefundable, upfront payment of $9,500 a year. After a few months of this arrangement, the mother decides that she would rather stay home and take care of her child full-time. The economic trade-off the mother faces consists of the net benefit she would derive from goods that she can purchase if she continues to work versus the satisfaction she gets from taking care of her child full-time. The nonrefundable tuition is a sunk cost—it was paid and is nonrefundable—irrespective of whether the mother now decides to work or stay at home. Therefore, it will not factor into her current decision about whether to continue working or not.

As these examples suggest, sunk costs are just that: scarce resources that we have "sunk" into an activity as a result of a previous decision. At first glance, it may not make sense to ignore these costs in our decision process as we move forward. Upon further consideration, however, we see that we are stuck with these costs whether we stand by our original decision or switch to another opportunity. After all, do we really want to continue to "throw good money after bad?" So, if your parents complain about all the money that was wasted when you tell them that you really want to fix cars instead of pursuing a career in accounting, just remind them that the cost of your college education is a sunk cost.

SOLVED PROBLEM

Q Suppose you are hired for a position that requires you to purchase a new wardrobe that you would not normally wear. Six months later, you are offered another job that doesn't require you to dress this way. In making your decision about the new job, will you compare (1) the new salary offer to the salary you are currently getting paid; (2) the new salary offer to the salary you are currently getting paid *minus* the cost of the wardrobe; or (3) the new salary offer *plus* the cost of the wardrobe to the salary you are currently getting paid?

Would your answer change if the new position had its own dress code and required you to buy yet another wardrobe?

A You would compare the new salary offer to your current salary. Your wardrobe purchase for the current position is a sunk cost—you have already paid for it whether you stay in your current job or take the new one. However, if the new job required you to purchase a new wardrobe, then you would compare the new salary offer *minus* the cost of this wardrobe to your current salary. Whereas the money you spent on the wardrobe for your present job is a sunk cost, the cost of the wardrobe for the new position has not yet been incurred. Therefore, it must be considered when you decide whether to stay in your present job or move to the new one.

3.5 Reducing the Cost of Making Choices: The Role That Habits Play

Most of us do not use MapQuest or our Apple GPS app every morning to find the shortest route to school or work. Typically, we take the same route every day unless there is an unexpected change that causes us to rethink our usual choice, either temporarily (there's an accident on the road ahead) or permanently (a new highway or subway line opens). Similarly, after making an initial assessment about the net benefit we will get from different brands of peanut butter or orange juice, we get into the *habit* of purchasing the same brands over and over. We follow **habits** in lieu of active decision-making in situations that are routine and repetitive.

HABITS Routine choices that are made in lieu of actively weighing the costs and benefits of each alternative.

EXAMPLE When Arell goes out to lunch, she always heads for the closest Panera Bread restaurant and ignores other restaurants in the area.

EXAMPLE When Sam surfs the Internet, he always clicks on his Google Chrome desktop icon and ignores other browser options.

Why do we rely on habits, even when they lead to choices that may not always maximize our sense of well-being? A key element in making good choices is more and better information; however, this information can be costly to acquire. Because gathering and evaluating information each and every time we are faced with the same choice (such as choosing a route to school) requires us to use up scarce resources, we often adopt habits as an information-economizing behavior.

Have you ever wondered why nationally branded items such as Clorox or Coca-Cola often sell for a higher price than their generic-brand or supermarket-brand counterparts? Companies understand the role that a brand name plays in fostering habit-based choices. If you have a particular brand of peanut butter that you like, or a hamburger chain that you prefer, it is information-economizing to habitually consume these brands as long as the product is the same each time you purchase it. For example, some of us rely on the McDonald's name when choosing a lunch spot rather than gathering a lot of information about other fast-food restaurants. We know that whether we are in New York City or Tallahassee, McDonald's offers a predictable menu of predictable-tasting food (this may, however, not be the case in certain foreign locales). This reduces the time we have to invest in making a decision about where to have lunch and what to eat.

For its customers to habitually choose McDonald's, however, the company must ensure that its menu, cooking ingredients, and the overall quality of its service are uniform across locations. For this reason, McDonald's requires its franchisees to purchase key ingredients from a corporate-approved supplier, offer a menu approved by the parent company, and train employees a specific way. These franchise restrictions help the corporation protect its brand name so that it can be projected as a reliable information-economizing "signal" to consumers. It is crucial that the company protect its brand name because consumer "signals" (tastiest, freshest, softest, and so on) are costly to create. Even accountants realize that a company's reputation has economic value and includes an asset category called "goodwill" on company balance sheets.

Switching Costs

When do we change a habit? Some people never do. Others will rethink a habit when there is a substantial change in circumstances, whether it is a change in road conditions, the availability of new alternatives, or the price or taste of a good. For example, when Coca-Cola bottlers in the United States began substituting corn syrup for cane sugar in 1985, they lost a large number of Coke drinkers that did not like the new taste. These people switched to other brands that were still using cane sugar. U.S. bottlers also lost market share to Mexican bottlers, who continued to use only cane sugar for sweetness and began to ship Mexican Coke over the border.[7]

When we "break" an old habit voluntarily, we are revealing that we believe there is a net benefit to be had by reevaluating our options. That is, the economic benefit from making a new choice outweighs the **switching costs** we will incur.

SWITCHING COSTS The monetary costs, as well as psychological and time costs, incurred when a person changes brands, providers, or products.

EXAMPLE You are considering changing your e-mail service from AOL to Comcast to save money on the monthly access fees. The question is how long it will take to recoup the switching costs you will incur. These may include the cost of reprinting your business cards, any termination or set-up fees, and the time cost of notifying people of your e-mail address change.

. . . .

[7]Louise Chu, "Is Mexican Coke the Real Thing?" *The San Diego Union Tribune*, November 9, 2004.

EXAMPLE A laundry-soap manufacturer switches to a new, concentrated formula and incurs switching costs arising from the redesign of its packaging and a marketing campaign to convince consumers that the new product is better than the original one that was sold in a bigger box.

Companies recognize that, in some instances, substantial switching costs keep people locked into old decisions. In these situations, companies often provide services to reduce these switching costs. For example, most e-mail service providers now offer a free, automatic forwarding link from a person's old e-mail address, along with an automatic message sent to entries in a new subscriber's old address book.

The federal government also intercedes periodically to reduce consumers' switching costs. In November 2003, the Federal Communications Commissions (FCC) enacted a "local number portability" rule that required cell-phone carriers to let a subscriber take her telephone number when she switched wireless carriers. The industry estimated that more than 30 million subscribers would jump to a new wireless company after the switching cost of having to give up one's telephone number was eliminated.

Sometimes, we are forced to break habits when we would prefer not to do so. Consider the case where your employer changes its employee health-insurance plan, and your family practitioner—whom you have gone to all your life—is no longer in the network of "preferred" providers. You will now have to pay significantly more to continue to see your family doctor. You feel bad about having to switch to a new doctor, and you also must spend a good deal of time gathering information about the doctors that are in the new plan before you make a choice. You incur both psychological and time costs in making the switch to a new doctor. Your decision about whether to switch to a new physician will depend upon whether these switching costs outweigh the additional costs you expect to bear if you remain with your existing doctor.

ECONOMIC FALLACY   More choices always *improve* a person's well-being.

False. Because it can be costly to evaluate the costs and benefits of a new alternative, a person might simply continue to make the same choices as before and maintain his original level of well-being. Depending on the incremental benefit that can be derived from reconsidering a decision, sticking with an old choice might not be a "lazy" response. It may, indeed, lead to the greatest level of well-being possible. In fact, psychologists have documented that an increase in the number of choices people face can sometimes reduce their well-being, leading to indecision and "paralysis." In one study, researchers found that as the number of job possibilities available to college graduates increased, applicants' satisfaction with the job-search process declined.

When Choices Are Not Repetitive

It turns out that habits are not of much use when we are making decisions that are neither repetitive nor routine. For example, the selection of a college is a once-in-a-lifetime decision for many of us. We also think that it is an important decision in terms of future post-collegiate opportunities. As a result, many high-school students and their families make a substantial investment in gathering information about their options. We spend time on the Internet, making trips to various campuses, and discussing alternatives with teachers, family members, and friends. Because the choice is not a repetitive one like choosing a route to work, a habit cannot lessen these information costs. Of course, if students always went to their parent's alma mater without ever considering other opportunities, then we would consider this a habitual choice.

The greater the opportunity cost of making a poor decision, the more we are willing to invest to make a better, more-informed decision. It makes sense for families to spend more of their scarce resources on their children's college-selection process than they do on where they will go out to eat. Similarly, we expect that people will make a greater investment in information before choosing a cardiac surgeon than they do before picking a hairstylist. Even in the case of medical care, however, people become extremely loyal to their surgeons after they have made the initial choice and had a positive experience. Their subsequent choice of surgeon may then become a habit.

3.6 Prices: Signals of Opportunity Cost in the Market

Economists pay a lot of attention to prices. As you will see later on, prices are one way of allocating scarce resources in a society. Higher prices mean that fewer people are going to buy the good. And when prices rise, this may signal that the amount of a good that is available for sale is substantially less than the amount people want to purchase. Scalped tickets to the annual all-star baseball game sell at four times their face value; a similar phenomenon can be observed when the Rolling Stones come to town.

Before we discuss how prices are determined or why they go up or down, there is a much more basic principle to establish: the prices we face serve as signals of the opportunity cost of making trades. The money you spend on a rare comic book is money that is not available to purchase five new video games, your next-best opportunity. The price of the rare comic book and the fact that you are willing to pay it even though your income is limited says that the net benefit you get from it is greater than the net benefit you would get from the five video games. The price of a good—and your willingness to pay it—tells us something about the satisfaction you expect to get from making one purchase in lieu of another.

For example, suppose the tuition at the local state university is $415 for a three-credit-hour course. At the prestigious private university located nearby, the three-credit-hour course costs $1,660. If a student chooses the private university and her parents are willing to pay the bill, they sacrifice an additional $1,245 per course in other consumables than if the student went to the public university.

In effect, a family that chooses the private university option will forgo four times more of other consumables—and the satisfaction that would result—than if the family opts instead for a state-university education. Apparently, if the family elects the private education, the higher price is worth this opportunity cost. In this example, the **relative price** of private versus state higher education is $1,660/$415 = 4.

RELATIVE PRICE The ratio of the price of one good to the price of another good.

EXAMPLE If the price of taking a seven-day vacation to Disney World in Orlando is $1,500, and the price of taking a seven-day vacation to Disneyland in Los Angeles is $1,200, then the relative price of one option versus the other is $1,500/$1,200 = 1.25.

EXAMPLE If the price of buying a pre-owned video game is $12, and the price of buying it new is $39, then the relative price of one option versus the other is $39/$12 = 3.25.

Generally speaking, relative price conveys the opportunity cost of making one purchase versus another; that is, how much of one good you will have to give up to acquire another one instead.

Note that if the prices of two goods both doubled—for example, the tuition at both the private and state universities doubled—their relative price would remain the same. The private school would still be four times more costly than the state school in terms of forgone consumption of other goods ($3,320/$830 = 4). If both tuitions were halved as a result of a new government program that offered a 50 percent tuition tax credit, then their relative price once again remains the same ($830/$207.50 = 4). In contrast, if a new state program provided a $100 tax refund for each public and private-university course that is taken, then the relative price of private versus state education *would* change: ($1,560/$315 = 4.95). Private universities would become relatively more "expensive" than state universities in terms of forgone consumption. According to our model of economic decision-making, this increase in opportunity cost leads us to predict that some students would switch from private to state universities in response to the new state program.

Prices also convey something about a seller's opportunity costs. Think about a garage sale. When you put a price tag of $90 on an old ping-pong table, you are signaling to prospective buyers that at this price, you are willing to give up the use of the table for what the $90 will buy you instead. When someone offers you $70 and you refuse the offer, what you are "saying" is that your best opportunity for spending the $70 will not generate enough benefit to outweigh the opportunity cost of giving up the ping-pong table.

In summary then, the price at which a good is bought and sold reflects its opportunity cost. For the buyer, it is the forgone consumption of other goods that could have been purchased with the money. For the seller, it is the forgone use of the good. There may, of course, be additional costs related to buying or selling a good. People may incur both implicit and explicit costs, such as the time and transportation costs required to make a trade.

SOLVED PROBLEM

Q In March 2006, *Money* magazine featured a story about a pilot who couldn't afford to buy the antique planes he wanted to fly, so he built two of them from scratch. Fred Murrin, an engineer who earns approximately $72,800 per year, estimated that the cost of building both planes was around $39,000 and that they are now worth 10 times this cost. He also estimated that he spent approximately 12,500 hours on the project over the course of 18 years. Murrin emphasized that the value of the planes really wasn't what was most important to him, but that his passion was flying World War I planes. How much cost did Murrin incur to satisfy this passion?

A If we assume that Murrin works a 40-hour week, then the cost of his time is equal to $72,800/2080 where 2080 is (52 weeks × 40 hours/week). This comes out to $35 per hour, Murrin's hourly wage (ignoring taxes). Therefore, 12,500 hours would have an economic cost of $35 × 12,500 = $437,500. If we add the $39,000 in explicit costs, we arrive at a total cost of $437,500 + $39,000 = $476,500. Murrin estimates that the two planes are now worth $39,000 × 10 = $390,000 if he were to sell them. Subtracting the total economic cost of building the planes from this revenue, we get $390,000 − $476,500 = −$86,500. In other words, the costs exceed the monetary benefits by $86,500. If Murrin gets at least this amount of nonmonetary benefit from flying the planes, then he made an optimal decision to engage in his building project.

3.7 Transaction Costs

To better understand the additional costs that may be incurred when buying or selling a good, consider the following situation. Suppose that you are in the market for a used car. You spend days searching for information on the reliability, fuel efficiency, safety record, and average repair costs for the dozen or so models you are considering. You also will likely check out sources such as the *Kelly Blue Book* to get some idea of how much each model will cost if you buy it from a private party or from a certified car dealer. Based on all of this information, you are able to compare the costs and benefits of each option and identify the model that you believe will yield you the greatest net benefit.

The next step in the process is to find someone with the car you want who is willing to sell it to you at a price that is within the range you have in mind. The cost of identifying potential sellers has gone down considerably in the Internet age, now that there are a number of Web sites you can use to locate specific cars for sale. After you have located potential sellers of the car you want, you must assess their willingness to sell to you, which will depend on the price you offer. Bargaining often ensues. While it is in your interest to pay the least amount possible for the car, it is in the seller's interest for you to pay the highest possible price. This can lead to intense, time-consuming negotiations. Will the seller give you the accessories that he bought for the car at the price you offer? Are you willing to accept a cracked headlight at the seller's asking price? Bargaining tends to flush out the net benefit that each party gets from the car.

Even if you and the seller are able to settle on a price for the car (with or without accessories), you have to agree on a form of payment. If the seller will not take a personal check and requires a money order, bank check, or cash, you will have to incur additional time costs and possibly bank fees. In turn, you may want the seller to show you the car's maintenance records or a CARFAX report to ensure that the car has not previously been in an accident. Finally, you and the seller must agree on who will pay for the temporary license plates required until the title is officially transferred, and so on.

When all is said and done, both you and the seller have incurred a whole host of costs to make the trade happen. To summarize, these include search and information costs, time costs, negotiating costs, and costs to enforce the terms of the deal, that is, to make sure that each party holds up his end of the deal. Economists refer to these types of costs as **transaction costs**.

> **TRANSACTION COSTS** Costs incurred in trading goods and services, including search and information costs, bargaining costs, payment costs, and enforcement costs.

> **EXAMPLE** The transaction costs you would bear to buy an airline ticket have been reduced substantially with the introduction of Orbitz and other airfare Web sites that not only provide you with an instant comparison of the fares of different airlines but also accept credit cards and send you electronic boarding passes.

> **EXAMPLE** The transaction costs you bear when you buy a can of Star-Kist tuna fish are the transportation and time costs required to make a shopping trip. There are no bargaining costs because the price is nonnegotiable.

The price of a good might be mutually acceptable to both the seller and buyer and, yet, the trade isn't consummated because of significant transaction costs. For example, most car-rental companies require that their customers pay with a credit card. This gives the companies an easy way to collect if there is damage to the vehicle, if it is returned late, and so on. This means that potential renters who are willing to pay the daily rate to rent a car but haven't got a credit card are turned away.

As we will see later on, scarce resources may be traded within organizations—rather than through markets—to reduce transaction costs. For example, "trades" that take place inside a household can reduce many of the transaction costs we just discussed. Parents let their teenage kids use the car in return for running errands; one adult partner does most of the cooking while the other tends to the lawn and garden. These kinds of long-term understandings make it unnecessary to engage in potentially costly repeat transactions in the market.

WHAT YOU SHOULD HAVE LEARNED FROM CHAPTER 3

- ■ That the opportunity cost of a decision is the well-being forgone from the next highest-valued alternative.

- ■ That costs are more than just money outlays. They include things such as time given up, forgone leisure activities, and lost wages.

- ■ That economic cost differs from accounting cost and, as a result, accounting profits will likely diverge from economic profits.

- ■ That people, facing limited information, will sometimes make choices that they may try to "adjust" later, after they gain more information.

- ■ That sunk costs are irrelevant to current decisions.

- ■ That habits can be an information-economizing approach to making repetitive decisions.

- ■ That brand names can facilitate low-cost, habit-based decision-making.

- ■ That the cost of switching brands, products, or providers can be high enough to discourage breaking a habit.

- ■ That the price of a good reflects its opportunity cost in terms of the benefit that would have been derived by spending the money on the next-best opportunity available.

- ■ That relative prices indicate the opportunity cost of one good versus another in terms of benefits forgone by not spending the money on the next-best opportunity available.

- ■ That trades may not take place because the transaction costs are greater than the net benefit received from the exchange.

KEY TERMS

Explicit costs, p. 56

Implicit costs, p. 57

Accounting costs, p. 58

Accounting profit, p. 60

Economic profit, p. 60

Sunk costs, p. 61

Habits, p. 62

Switching costs, p. 63

Relative prices, p. 65

Transaction costs, p. 67

QUESTIONS AND PROBLEMS

1. True, false, uncertain. Explain your answers.
   a) Accounting profits will always be less than economic profits.
   b) Accounting costs will always be less than economic costs.

c) Sunk costs are included in the explicit cost of a choice.

d) Sunk costs are included in the implicit cost of a choice.

2. The owner of a record store paid $62,000 for tenant improvements to the space he is renting. Last year, he earned $190,000 in (economic) profits in this space. A friend suggests that he move to a more heavily trafficked location, where it is estimated that he will pay $46,000 for tenant improvements and earn $240,000 per year in (economic) profits. Should the store owner make the move? Why or why not. Explain your answer.

3. Currently, it is illegal for people to sell their kidneys to people who require a transplant. An argument in favor of legalizing trade in kidneys is that it would increase the supply and substantially reduce the amount of time someone has to wait for a transplant. Is there an *economic* (not moral) argument against making trade in kidneys legal? Explain your answer.

4. Suppose that people volunteer to staff a town's local fire department. Should the value of their time be included in calculating the economic cost of providing fire protection to the town? Explain your answer.

5. What is the opportunity cost of investing $5,000 to open a new cupcake shop? Explain your answer.

6. Identify three habits in your daily life that you think are information-economizing habits. Is there any other reason that habits form and persist over time? Explain your answer.

7. Suppose that you are shopping for a new digital camera and can buy it online or in an electronics store such as Best Buy. Explain carefully the economic benefits and costs that would contribute to your decision of where to buy the camera (assume that the price of the camera itself is the same for the online and brick-and-mortar store vendors).

8. Mrs. Teeples recently received a letter notifying her that her credit card company was changing from a fixed interest rate for unpaid balances to a variable interest rate. She calculates that she will pay an additional $580 per year under the new terms.

a) What types of switching costs might she incur should she switch to another credit card provider?

b) How much would Mrs. Teeples be willing to spend in switching costs to find a credit card provider that offers the original terms she had?

c) How do credit card companies reduce switching costs to attract new cardholders and their unpaid balances?

9. Your sister Tania, currently a junior in college, has completed all but a few requirements to earn a degree in accounting. Suppose that she calls you and tells you that she is taking her first economics course and is surprised to discover a passion and a talent for the subject. As a result, she is considering switching her major to economics.

a) What costs would factor into her decision about whether to make the change or not?

b) How would you advise her to respond when your parents say to her "look at all the time and money you've already spent on your accounting courses"?

10. McDonald's restaurants in Japan, India, and Israel offer a menu that is substantially different from the one offered in the United States. Coca-Cola uses a different formulation in different countries.

a) What does this tell you about the customers that these companies are targeting for sales in these countries? Specifically, are they local residents or U.S. tourists?

b) Suppose that more American tourists visit Tokyo Disneyland than any other site in Japan. Do you think the Coke sold in the park would taste more like the Coke sold in the United States than Coke sold in Tokyo? Why or why not? Explain your answer.

11. What is the opportunity cost that an employer bears when he discriminates against women or African Americans in the hiring process? In answering this question, first assume that such discrimination is legal. How would your answer change if it becomes illegal?

12. Suppose the government bans the use of a pesticide and is able to catch anyone who violates the law. If this is the case, what is the opportunity cost that a farmer bears if he continues to use this pesticide? Would your answer change if the government is unable to catch all lawbreakers? Explain your answers.

4

Property Rights: The Foundation of Economic Costs and Benefits

"Protecting the rights of even the least individual among us is basically the only excuse the government has for existing."

Ronald Reagan, actor, governor, and 40th president of the United States

How we ultimately allocate our scarce resources depends on the economic costs and benefits of the alternatives we face. This is true whether we are talking about our time, the property we own, or our ideas and inventions. Many factors, including our personal preferences, can affect these costs and benefits. The rights we have over the control and use of our resources—usually dictated by the legal system—have a significant impact on our choices. If you are not permitted to attend school because of your religion, race, or gender, the opportunity cost of going to work instead changes dramatically. If you are not allowed to drive because you are a woman, the economic benefit of owning a car diminishes considerably.

A few years ago, a U.S. district court ruled that it was illegal to download music without the prior consent of the performer or music publisher. As a result, the economic *cost* of using unlicensed Web sites (e.g., Napster) increased, and, at the same time, the economic *benefit* of using a licensed site (e.g., iTunes) increased.[1] It makes sense that sites such as iTunes, which negotiate licenses that permit legal downloads, began to flourish only after the courts ruled against "pirated" downloads and imposed millions of dollars in fines. This example demonstrates that the definition of ownership rights can substantially affect the economic costs and benefits of the opportunities we choose between.

As you will see next, these rights—which we refer to more generally as "property rights"—also play a central role when it comes to voluntary exchange in a market. The bottom line is that what we really buy and sell are property rights, which dictate the ways in which we can use the goods and services we trade.

[1]John Schwartz, "Tilting at Internet Barrier, a Stalwart Is Upended." *New York Times*, August 10, 2009.

4.1 The Nature of Property Rights

How people can use their scarce resources is determined by a society's legal system and its societal and religious norms. These institutions give us permission to enjoy the resources under our control in specific ways and, at the same time, place restrictions on their use. We refer to these rights—and the restrictions they impose—as **property rights**.

> **PROPERTY RIGHT** Legal or social permission to control and use a scarce resource in a particular way.

> **EXAMPLE** International law gives combatants permission to take prisoners of war. It does not give them the right to torture these prisoners for information.
>
> **EXAMPLE** Societal norms permit football spectators to stand up to watch important plays on the field. They do not give spectators permission to demand that the people sitting in front of them remain seated.
>
> **EXAMPLE** As legal guardians, parents are authorized to manage the income their children earn. However, parents do not have permission to gamble with this money.

These examples demonstrate that a property right is not just limited to real property, that is, land or some other asset such as a person's home. In economic terms, property rights apply to all of the scarce resources at our disposal, which encompass virtually all of the choices we make. In the United States, most adults over the age of 18 are entitled to vote. Prior to 1920, women were excluded from this entitlement, or property right. They could not use their time to vote. In other words, property rights often apply to people's *actions* and not just their ownership of tangible property.

Positive property rights give us permission to use our resources in certain ways. *Negative* property rights constrain our choices. We can, for example, drive our cars at 30 miles per hour through downtown Los Angeles—a positive property right—but we cannot drive through a pedestrian walkway if there is a person standing in it—a negative property right. Property rights can be thought of as the "rules of the game." You can't cut a neighbor's tree down without permission, even if it does block the sunlight into your home. The neighbor has the right to benefit from the tree's shade and the value it contributes to his home site. Property rights define the ways in which we can and cannot use the scarce resources at our disposal.

Property rights are created and enforced primarily by the government, through its legislative and judicial systems. However, nongovernmental groups can also establish property rights. For example, a condominium association board may prohibit pets in the building and include this rule (called a covenant) in the contract that every buyer signs. What if you bought a condo in this building and then arrived with your Labrador retriever? The association board can use the courts to enforce the terms under which you purchased the condo. As long as the contract you signed—with the no pet clause—is legal, you will likely be evicted unless your dog is sent elsewhere to live.

In some situations, the courts have ruled that specific clauses contained in some contracts are against the "public interest" and are, therefore, unenforceable. In the United States, for example, a person cannot legally contract with someone else to perform a mercy killing, even if the person who initiates the contract suffers from a painful, terminal illness. You cannot legally contract to sell your kidney to someone else. Generally speaking, property rights that are created through legislative or court action tend to be more enforceable than those created through private, voluntary contracts.

Rights that are legally defined take precedence over private agreements. For example, in many states, the parents of an adult son who is gay have the legal right to make medical decisions in the event that their son is incapacitated, even if the son has a long-standing understanding in place with his partner. This is one reason that same-sex marriage has become such an important issue: a key objective is to change the legal rights that gay partners have relative to one another.

Religious norms can also establish positive and negative property rights. In most religions, adultery is a sin because it violates the property rights conveyed by a marriage contract. "Thou shall not steal" gives people the sole right to access and enjoy their private possessions. Some religions strongly encourage "tithing," which means that congregants must give 10 percent of their income back to the church. In effect, tithing rules give people the right to keep only 90 percent of the fruits of their labor; the remaining 10 percent belongs to the church to do with as it sees fit.

Community and social norms also bestow property rights that affect our everyday decisions. Moviegoers expect that other people in the theater will not talk on cell phones during the movie.[2] Students expect that classmates will not make so much noise that they drown out the instructor. Neighbors expect that others on the block will mow their lawns periodically to maintain property values on the street. In each of these situations, there is an expectation that a person's choices will conform to certain societal norms. These norms—which protect other people's rights to a quiet theater, a useful lecture, or a tidy neighborhood—are enforced by subtle but powerful social mechanisms. These include verbal and nonverbal expressions of disapproval, as well as a call to expel or otherwise punish violators.

However, social expectations about the behavior of others aren't usually *legally* enforceable. A good example of this relates to the socially acceptable use of hallways in New York City apartment buildings. With the exception of clutter and combustible materials that violate the fire code, apartment residents must often contend with each other's use of hallways to store personal effects (baby strollers, shoes, etc.) and even to host children's parties.[3] When space is tight and expensive, social norms regarding the appropriate use of hallways apparently evaporate into thin air.

Property rights may be **private** or **common**.

PRIVATE PROPERTY RIGHT A right that bestows exclusive control over a scarce resource to one person or entity.

EXAMPLE A car owner, subject to state laws, has the sole right to decide who will drive his car and where it will be driven.

EXAMPLE College students age 18 years or older have the sole right to decide who receives a copy of their grade transcripts.

· · · · · · ·

[2]John Kelly, "Radical Civility Works." *Washington Post,* June 29, 2009.
[3]Penelope Green, "Getting Territorial Out of the Hall." *New York Times,* April 26, 2007.

COMMON PROPERTY RIGHT A right that bestows shared control over a scarce resource to a group of people or entities.

EXAMPLE A national park is common property that can be used by anyone who pays the entrance fee.

EXAMPLE The Internet is common property that can be enjoyed by anyone who has the technology to access it.

The National Park Service, an agency of the U.S. government, oversees the public's access to national parks. The Internet is overseen by a nonprofit organization—ICANN (Internet Corporation for Assigned Names and Numbers)—which assigns Web site addresses, domain names, and IP (Internet protocol) numbers. Although the Internet itself is a common property resource, a user can only connect to it through some sort of network service that *is* private property and *can* deny access. Your university server, for example, restricts connectivity to enrolled students, faculty, staff, and, possibly, alumni. AOL requires subscribers to pay a monthly fee to link to the Internet via its network.

The key difference between private and common property rights is whether an owner has exclusive control over the property in question. Can an owner access, consume, share, deny access, or sell the property without the approval of others? In the past, beachfront home owners in Southern California relied on the local police to block nonresidents from accessing "their" shoreline. Similar restrictions were in place along the shoreline of Lake Michigan, where coastal towns required city-issued passes to access local beaches. In both cases, restricting access to the shoreline protected the privacy of beachfront home owners and enhanced the value of their homes. In 2002, the U.S. Supreme Court ruled that these home owners had illegally blocked public access to the beach, which was determined to be common, not private, property. Today, there are public pathways (but not necessarily nearby parking) to the shoreline.[4]

In some countries, scarce resources are predominantly held in common. In Cuba, for example, large tracts of agricultural land, factories, medical clinics, and housing are owned "by the people," which translates into common property under government control. In China, home owners are given the right to develop publicly owned land through 70-year land leases.[5] Yet even in these countries, private property rights exist. For example, people in China can buy food and clothing, which they are not required to share with others.

Even nations with a sophisticated system of private property rights hold some resources in common. In addition to the park and Internet examples we've already discussed, perhaps the most valuable common property we share in the United States is our set of laws, including the Constitution and Bill of Rights, and our legislative and judicial systems. We share access to these legal institutions, which dictate and enforce our private property rights.

As it turns out, countries fall along a spectrum in terms of their mix of private and commonly held property. In the United States, for example, home owners usually gain private property rights to the ground under their homes, including mineral and

· · · · · · ·

[4]Barbara Whitaker, "Ruling Clears Way to Ease Beach Access in California." *New York Times,* October 23, 2002.

[5]Joseph Kahn, "China Approves Property Law, Strengthens Middle Class." *New York Times,* March 16, 2007.

water rights, when they purchase a house. As we mentioned before, this land belongs to the people—represented by the government—in countries like China. In the United States, people routinely get their medical care from private hospitals and physician practices. (Active military and military retirees, who receive their care at government facilities staffed with government-paid medical personnel, are an exception.) In contrast, most of the hospitals and clinics in England are part of the British public-health service; in other words, they are common property resources that provide shared access and are controlled by the government rather than by private entities.

Why is there common property in a country like the United States, which has long trumpeted private property rights? One explanation is that the right to control access to some scarce resources—in order to block unauthorized use—is prohibitively costly. Consider, for example, a scenario where an owner is given private property rights to a city's main streets: it would be costly to control access at each and every possible entry point. Contrast this with a private road in a rural area that is owned and maintained by the landowner who lives at the end of the road and who receives the bulk of the road's benefits.

Another situation in which common property rights arise is when many people can share the use of a particular resource without compromising another's enjoyment. For example, people may share a common property right to a privately run golf course or to a privately run museum. Note that these types of common property are not owned by the government but by community groups that can exclude people if they do not meet membership criteria, such as paying dues. Still, the government does own a lot of common property, including historic sites such as Ellis Island and Fort McHenry, which can be enjoyed by many people at the same time.

Converting Common Property into Private Property

In some instances, property held in common can be converted into private property by people who have the shared right to access the property. Probably the most famous example of this involves the most productive fishing banks in the world—the Grand Banks of Newfoundland. These banks are common property because there is no owner who controls access to them. As a result, questions arise as to how the fish living in these banks will be managed and harvested over time. Who has the right to catch fish? How much catch can be taken from the banks each year? Who will enforce these restrictions?

Although the fishing banks themselves closely fit our definition of common property, the fish—once caught—become private property. A fisherman has the exclusive right to eat or sell the fish she catches, as long as she does not violate local fishing regulations. Fishermen reap economic benefits from the fishing banks only if they can "privatize" the fish that inhabit the commonly-held fishing banks. Meanwhile, the cost of depleting the fishing banks is borne by all of the fishermen, today and in the future.

This creates an economic incentive whose outcome is easy to predict: there will be "overfishing" of the great fishing banks in terms of the number of fish caught now versus in the future. Fishermen will race each other to claim the economic benefits from privatizing the stock of fish that exists in the banks. Ecologist Garrett Hardin coined the term "tragedy of the commons" to refer to such a situation.[6]

· · · · · · ·

[6]Garrett Hardin, "The Tragedy of the Commons." *Science,* 162 (December 13, 1968).

Hardin recognized that people have an incentive to overuse property held in common. As evidence, he cited the problem of overgrazing of common property by cattle and sheep owners in the United States during the nineteenth and twentieth centuries.

What if the fishing banks or common grazing lands had been privately owned in the first place and access to them could be controlled at low cost? The incentive to overfish or overgraze would be eliminated because there would not have been multiple owners racing to capture the private benefit from property held in common. As it turns out, private fish farms follow "best-practice" methods to maximize the value of their fish stock through careful harvesting timetables.

National governments have stepped in with legislation to address the overfishing problem. In 1992, Canada banned all cod fishing in the Grand Banks of Newfoundland after the collapse of its cod fisheries. Iceland has set an annual limit on total fish catches (based on estimates of the stock of fish) and allots fishing quotas, by type and size of fish, to licensed fishermen. These quotas are called "individual transferable quotas" because they are rights that can be bought, sold, or leased through established market exchanges that act just like a stock exchange.

Private Management of Common Property

Based on field studies conducted over several decades, Elinor Ostrom (a political scientist who won the 2009 Nobel Prize in Economics) has suggested that small, local groups can effectively manage resources held in common so that the "tragedy of the commons" can be averted without government intervention. Her research has unearthed a variety of group arrangements that have been successfully used to manage common property resources for hundreds of years. These resources include alpine pastures and forests held in common by residents of Swiss villages, meadows and forests owned by Japanese villages, and irrigation reservoirs and ditches owned in common by farmers in Spain.

Drawing from her observations, Ostrom has identified those design features that are most important to the success of voluntary common property access arrangements. To be successful, members of the user group must agree to a set of community rules that regulate access to the common resource, impose penalties on those who violate these regulations, establish a monitoring system, and block nonmembers from accessing the common property resource. The group's members must also be provided with low-cost mechanisms for conflict resolution and be included in the decision-making process that develops the allocation rules for the resource held in common.[7]

If you think about it, this is exactly the type of system that has been adopted by private voluntary associations in the United States and elsewhere to manage commonly held property such as housing cooperatives, golf courses, and campgrounds. Members of the nonprofit Nature Conservancy have even purchased private property in the Santa Monica, California mountain range and converted it into a commonly held resource whose terms of use are dictated by the organization.

Among the unresolved questions is whether voluntary arrangements can be effective in managing a common resource when the user group is very large, for example, people who breathe and pollute the air. Also, certain common resources, by their very

· · · · · · ·

[7]Elinor Ostrom, "Collective Action and the Evolution of Social Norms." *Journal of Economic Perspectives*, 14, no. 3 (Summer 2000): 137–158.

nature, may be difficult for private groups to monitor and limit access to, such as the oceans or vast underground deposits of natural gas. Finally, to what extent can private groups enforce their voluntary agreements without the backing of government-enforcement mechanisms?

ECONOMIC FALLACY   If owners hold property in common, then no one can be excluded from its use.

False. Owners of a common property resource have the same ability to exclude users who are not owners as owners of private property. Country clubs can exclude nonmembers, as can churches. Publicly held companies can keep those who do not own shares out of stockholder meetings. The only question is whether exclusion is possible at low cost; that is, whether the right to access (or prohibit access to) a common property resource is ultimately enforceable. In the case of breathable air, for example, one group cannot, at low cost, prevent another from accessing the resource. We call this a *public* good because not only is the good held in common, but excluding nonowners is virtually impossible. We address the nature and production of public goods in greater detail in Chapter 16.

4.2 Property Rights and Trade

For trade to flourish, a clearly defined set of property rights must exist. When we buy and sell goods, we *voluntarily* exchange the right to control the use of a good *in a specific way*. Think about the "trade" you made to get a college education. The tuition you paid for this course gives you the right to attend class, have your assignments graded, receive a final grade, and demand time during office hours. It does not, however, give you the right to visit the professor at home, uninvited. Similarly, when you bought your laptop, the seller transferred to you exclusive, private use of the computer. This use does not give you the right to hack into other computers or create and spread a computer virus. In effect, when you voluntarily exchanged your dollars for credit hours or a laptop, you received a set of property rights that specified how you could use your purchase.

What if property rights are not well-defined? How much would a home buyer be willing to pay for a house if she cannot be sure that she will have the right to resell the house in the future and enjoy any gains from the sale? Why would a buyer pay anything for a car if the seller cannot ensure that the transfer of ownership is legally enforceable, that is, that the car comes with a clean title? In situations like these, how can a buyer and seller come to terms about the price of some good if the property rights being transferred are uncertain? This is why well-defined property rights are crucial for a system of voluntary trade to work.

Voluntary exchanges can still take place when property rights are in doubt, but the exchange process becomes much more costly. In such instances, trades often require additional, sophisticated "support systems"—such as insurance, guarantees, warranties, title searches, and so on—which increase the cost of the trade. And, when trading becomes more costly, fewer exchanges take place and economic activity diminishes. It is perhaps no coincidence that nations with more loosely defined property-rights systems and weaker enforcement mechanisms tend to be poorer than countries with rights that are more precisely defined and enforced. At the 2011 World Economic Forum, President Dmitri A. Medvedev of Russia admitted that his country's corrupt legislative and judicial systems undermine economic development, saying that "Russia indeed faces many difficulties in creating the rule of law and building a modern economy."[8]

Involuntary Relinquishment of Private Property: Eminent Domain

In a market, the exchange of property rights is usually voluntary. However, when one of the parties to the exchange is the government, the exchange may be coerced. For example, the law of eminent domain permits government entities—usually cities and states—to buy your home and commercial real estate *even if you are unwilling to sell it.*

EMINENT DOMAIN The right of the government to take private property for public use.

EXAMPLE During the 1950s, the federal government exercised eminent domain to purchase more than 42,000 miles of private property to construct the U.S. Interstate Highway System.

EXAMPLE An Ohio municipality invoked eminent domain to acquire a piece of property to build a continuous bike path through town.

Eminent domain exists so that the government can pursue activities that promote the "public interest." In most instances, eminent domain is used when a government agency wants to acquire properties to construct a public project and faces potential "holdouts"—property owners who do not wish to give up their properties in return for the government's offer of compensation and those who are "holding out" for a better deal. The application of eminent domain has been hotly contested in some instances. For example, is it in the public interest to use eminent domain to acquire land for the private development of shopping centers? Or is this solely in the economic interest of developers and the government (which gains new sources of tax revenue)? Whatever the motive, the U.S. Supreme Court has recently ruled that economic development can justify the legal "taking" of private property through eminent domain.[9]

Even if your family has owned its home for 20 years, or your mother, who is a physician, has owned her clinic building for her entire career, private ownership rights do not protect your family from eminent domain. In other words, when your home or your mother's building was initially purchased, the rights that were conveyed did not include an exemption from future eminent-domain actions. However, your property rights do protect you from having your property seized without "fair" compensation—usually dictated by market value. The last clause of the Fifth Amendment, called the Taking Clause, requires that "just" compensation be paid for property taken under eminent domain. Many countries, including Russia, Venezuela, and China, offer no such protection and often seize private assets for the "public good" without paying any compensation. You can probably imagine the long-term negative impact these activities have on private business investments in these countries.

· · · · · · ·

[8]Eric Pfanner, "At Forum, Medvedev Seeks to Reassure Foreign Investors." *New York Times,* January 26, 2011.

[9]Linda Greenhouse, "Justices Uphold Taking Property for Development." *New York Times,* June 24, 2005.

What if you place a greater value on your home or your mother's practice locale than the market does? Perhaps your home has been in your family for generations, or your mother has no place to relocate her practice that is as convenient for her patients. These types of opportunity costs are not considered when the amount of compensation is determined. This is yet another example of the divergence that can arise between accounting and opportunity costs and its impact on private and public decision making.

Trading Resources Held in Common

If the rights to a resource are held in common, the resource cannot be traded unless each and every owner agrees to the exchange. Alternatively, the owners may agree in advance to a less costly decision process, such as majority rule voting or delegation of authority to a subset of owners, an elected board of directors, or a designated governmental body. For example, local residents typically delegate their decision-making powers to their elected local officials when land-use planning and zoning matters arise in the community.

In some situations, the cost of reaching a decision about the use of a commonly held resource can outweigh the benefits. Think about the amount of time and money Congress spends to reach agreement about the use of publicly owned lands. One piece of legislation proposed to sell more than 240,000 acres of national forest land, the proceeds from which would be applied to fund rural schools and new highways. This proposal has been debated for years, with politicians taking one side or another depending on whether the proceeds from the sale would only go to the regions adjoining the land or would be shared with other regions of the country.[10] As this example illustrates, there can be huge transaction costs when it comes to managing and trading common property resources. These costs will usually be far greater than the transaction costs that arise when private property is exchanged.

4.3 Enforcing Property Rights

If property rights are to have any impact on individual decision making, they must be enforced. Let's say that you have a piece of paper—a deed—which states that you own your home and have exclusive rights to the economic benefits arising from this property. This means that you have the right to exclude anyone else from entering and using your home unless you have explicitly given them permission. This may sound a bit selfish, but having the ability to exclude others from the benefits of the goods that you own is what property rights enforcement is all about.

Think about the purchases you make every day. If there is no one to keep you from simply taking as much gasoline from the pump as you want, why would you ever offer to pay the seller? The owner of the gas station must be able to prevent you from taking gas if he is going to be able to extract payment from you. If he cannot do this, he will have no incentive to purchase gasoline in the first place for resale.

Consider the early days of radio and television, when it was cost-prohibitive to exclude radio and TV owners from tapping into programming signals that were broadcast through airwaves. Because they could not be excluded, radio listeners and TV viewers did not have to pay for access to programs. This forced radio and television companies and their local affiliates to find other ways to cover their programming

· · · · · · · ·

[10]Jacob Luecke, "Controversial Forest Sale Revived." *Columbia Tribune,* February 6, 2007.

costs. It turned out that their transmission signals were valuable to another group that *could* be excluded: corporate advertisers, who wanted to "piggyback" on programming signals to increase sales of their goods. If these advertisers did not pay for air time, they could be blocked from transmitting their commercials to viewers.

A more recent situation has arisen in the world of wireless Internet access. Some wireless users regularly tap into their neighbor's Wi-Fi connection without permission. Economists call these people "free riders" because they freely share in the benefits arising from someone else's property. This can happen when a person's private right to the exclusive use of some good or service cannot be enforced. To protect against the "theft" of Wi-Fi connections, a number of technological fixes have arisen. These include firewalls and password protections.

Similarly, technology has largely resolved the TV broadcasting "problem." Only subscribers can access programming delivered by cable- and satellite-transmission systems; also, these companies have found low-cost ways to identify pirate users. Radio broadcasting has been slower to incorporate such technologies. In fact, commercial-free, subscriber satellite radio networks Sirius and XM (now merged as Sirius XM Radio) have fared poorly in the marketplace since they were introduced in the late 1990s.

Many technological advances have arisen that reduce the cost of enforcing private property rights. Microchips with GPS capability, for example, deter the theft of cars, laptops, pets, and livestock. DNA testing reduces the cost of establishing paternity and enforcing laws that give children the right to financial support from both parents. Retinal and iris scans can now be used to limit access to locations containing valuable private property. Sometimes these new technologies replace or reinforce enforcement mechanisms that have grown less effective due to changing circumstances. For example, sophisticated home-security systems are increasingly used to complement traditional law enforcement, in part because suburban sprawl has increased the emergency response times of local police departments.

As it turns out, some technologies have actually *raised* the cost of enforcing private property rights. There are numerous examples:

- The Internet has reduced the cost of "pirating" music and films.
- Copy machines and scanners have made copyright laws virtually unenforceable. Improvements in copy machine technology have even increased the cost of enforcing the government's exclusive right to print money by reducing the cost of counterfeiting high-quality currency.
- Electronic spyware makes it more difficult to protect our right to privacy.
- High-quality camera cell phones have made it harder to discourage copycats and counterfeiters in the fashion and manufacturing industries.[11] At the same time, camera cell phones can be quite helpful in providing real-time evidence of thefts, carjackings and so forth, thereby helping to enforce private property rights.[12]

Whenever our ability to enforce private property rights is compromised, people are likely to encroach on these rights. The end result is that the value of these rights

••••••

[11]David S. Bennahum, "Hope You Like Jamming Too." *Slate.* December 5, 2003. http://www.slate.com/id/2092059/

[12]David Pepose, "Smile for the Camera, Criminals." *Washington Times,* August 25, 2006.

will decline, as will people's willingness to pay for them. After all, why pay for something that you can have for free? In other words, property rights will have value only if they can be enforced.

4.4 Protecting Intellectual Property Rights: Special Considerations

So far, our discussion has centered around property rights related to goods, such as land and cars; and actions, such as access to a traffic intersection. But as you already know, the definition of an economic good is more expansive than this. We must also consider property rights to "products" that result from our creative activities. *Intellectual property* is a term used to refer to creative outputs such as scientific ideas, inventions, musical compositions, visual art, poetry, and other writings. **Intellectual property rights** are the rights we have to control the use of this type of property.

INTELLECTUAL PROPERTY RIGHTS Control over the use of ideas and products arising from a person's creativity.

EXAMPLE The Moscow Ballet and the band Green Day control access to their digitally recorded performances.

EXAMPLE An artist controls the use of visual reproductions of her works.

EXAMPLE The authors and publisher of this textbook control its duplication and distribution.

Intellectual property rights have value only if the owners of these rights can prevent the unauthorized use of their creative outputs. A songwriter may sell the right to record a song. This is a legal exchange of property rights. At the same time, the songwriter may refuse permission to have his song used as a commercial jingle. A scientist may license production rights to a newly discovered drug but limit its distribution to North America. An author may sell the movie rights to her novel but retain the rights to her characters.

Sometimes, the cost of detecting and prosecuting infringements on established intellectual property rights is so high that these rights end up having virtually no value. For example, how many times have you downloaded an article off the Web and ignored the copyright notice? The fundamental problem is that once creative outputs become public, they can be disseminated at virtually zero cost from one user to another. Musical compositions can be shared, sung, or recorded at virtually no cost after they have been played the first time. Theoretical discoveries quickly spread by word of mouth (or by tweet) after a scientist reports her findings at a professional meeting. People can easily appropriate our words and ideas after they have been expressed. And YouTube users can easily post unauthorized clips from popular TV shows and movies that can then be viewed by others at no cost.[13]

The economic dilemma is that information creation, scientific discovery, and artistic endeavors are not costless; they take time, effort, talent, and materials, which

·······

[13]Laura Holson. "Hollywood Asks YouTube: Friend or Foe?" *New York Times,* January 15, 2007.

are all scarce resources. How can authors, scientists, and songwriters earn a return from their investment if others can appropriate and thereby benefit from their work without permission? Will there be too little investment in these creative activities if intellectual property rights can't be enforced?

Economists face a delicate balancing act in this situation. As we have already noted, the opportunity cost of sharing intellectual property *after* it is created is, in most instances, zero or close to it. For example, it costs practically nothing to download a song or movie after it has been produced or to replicate a fashion design after it has been created. For this reason, most economists favor the dissemination of creative outputs at low or no charge. Also, economists recognize that the faster intellectual property can be shared, the more quickly new intellectual property will materialize. We see this occur frequently in the biomedical realm; breakthroughs in recombinant DNA technology, for instance, have translated directly into the development of "designer" drugs to combat arthritis, diabetes, and other debilitating diseases. Had there not been low-cost access to the new recombinant technologies, these drugs would not have been developed as quickly as they were.

But economists also recognize that less intellectual property will be created when the *private* returns from investing in creative activities are negligible. Even though these activities are likely to continue at some level—by people motivated by fame (a celebrity spot on *The David Letterman Show*?) or by the satisfaction of engaging in creative activities—we know that *more* investment will occur if the creators can control access to their works and the benefits that flow from them.

Balancing the benefits of rapid dissemination against the need for sufficient incentives to encourage creative activity, a number of legal protections for intellectual property have evolved. These include patents and copyrights, which give creators the exclusive, legally enforceable right to control access to their intellectual property for a limited time in return for making the work public.[14] Currently, the length of a patent is 20 years from the date it is applied for, whereas copyright protection extends throughout an author's lifetime plus 70 years.

Patents and copyright protections serve both public and private interests. From the government's perspective, they encourage both discovery and the speedy dissemination of creative works. From an innovator's point of view, they increase the chances that he will enjoy the fruits of his labor. Of course, this assumes that patent and copyright protections can be enforced. In reality, it is extremely difficult to weed out pirated designs, software, movies, and mechanical devices when they are produced in foreign countries whose governments are unwilling to enforce the patent or copyright laws of another nation.[15]

Patent protection is often crucial to the regulatory process, especially in the case of pharmaceuticals. The Federal Drug Administration (FDA) requires that detailed information about a new drug, including its molecular composition, be divulged during the regulatory review process. Because of this, drug manufacturers are among the most likely companies to seek patent protection for a new product as early as possible. When these patents lapse, generic versions of drugs—produced by generic drug manufacturers such as Teva—quickly appear, thereby severely lessening the original drug company's profit stream.

• • • • • • •

[14]United States Patent and Trademark Office, 2005.

[15]Editorial, "China and Intellectual Property." *New York Times*, December 24, 2010, p. A22

ECONOMIC FALLACY   Drug patents reduce competition in the pharmaceutical industry and result in exorbitant drug prices.

Uncertain. Patents increase competition to the extent that the science underlying new discoveries is quickly made available for competitors to "invent around." Patents also reduce the amount of resources wasted on "reinventing the wheel." It is true that drugs under patent protection cost more than if there were no such protection and competitors could copy the drug at virtually no cost. The real question is whether the economic return to drugmakers for *discovery and production* is greater than the opportunity cost of investing in such activities. One anecdotal piece of information in this regard is that generic drug manufacturers—those who produce drugs after patent protection ends—do not engage in virtually any research or development to create new drugs.

Because of the threat posed by copycat producers, some owners of intellectual property have chosen not to seek patent protection. Instead, they rely on private-enforcement mechanisms. In the case of Coca-Cola, the original formula and its updated versions are classified as "trade secrets." To protect these secrets from getting into the hands of competitors, Coca-Cola does not entrust the entire formula to any one employee. The company has chosen to privately enforce its proprietary rights to its formula to limit copycats for a much longer period than the span of patent protection. The same is true for classic perfumes, such as Chanel No. 5, and the "secret recipe of 17 herbs and spices" developed by Colonel Harlan Sanders, the founder of Kentucky Fried Chicken.

The courts have generated a large body of case law that prohibits activities such as industrial espionage and the recruitment of competitors' employees to gain access to trade secrets. Also, the U.S. Department of Justice actively prosecutes insiders who leak military design secrets to foreign nations. The real threat to trade-secret protection is when technologies arise that can "break" the trade secret, for example, the recipe for a specific perfume. Unless there is proprietary ownership of one or more ingredients used to create the product, it will remain unique only in terms of characteristics that are still protected by copyright or trademark laws, for example, the product's brand name, bottle shape, or marketing slogan.

Intellectual property owners sometimes seek government protection while, at the same time, developing private-enforcement mechanisms. For example, the music industry has developed "digital management system" software to block unauthorized music downloads and file-sharing. Software producers have created "locks" to ensure that their computer programs cannot be copied from one user to another. And college textbook publishers have introduced software that terminates students' access to books on DVDs at the end of each semester. When successful, these types of private-enforcement mechanisms encourage more creative activity, leading to more innovation and a larger body of knowledge. In fact, an entire body of research suggests that advances in intellectual property—new knowledge and technology—result in higher rates of national economic growth.

4.5 How Changes in Property Rights Affect Our Economic Decisions

We have just seen that property rights directly affect the costs and benefits of our choices. Using the marginal benefit and marginal cost framework of analysis we developed previously, we can examine the consequences of *changes* in property rights on individual decision making.

Smoking Bans

It has become very popular for local governments to ban smoking in restaurants and bars. These bans affect the property rights of smokers and nonsmokers in very different ways. The benefits that smokers receive from eating at smoke-free restaurants fall: they must now forgo the pleasure they get from smoking while they eat their meals or drink their cups of coffee. In contrast, nonsmokers enjoy a greater benefit from eating out at smoke-free city restaurants: they are no longer subjected to the stench and health risks of secondhand smoke. Smoking bans also impact people's choices about eating at restaurants in adjacent cities that don't have smoking bans. The opportunity cost falls for smokers eating at a suburban cafe where there is no ban, instead of at the best restaurant in the city where the ban is in place. They forgo less well-being when they choose to eat outside the city limits because they can no longer smoke while eating in the city.

Panels (a) and (b) in **Figure 4.1** illustrate the impact that a smoking ban has on a typical smoker's choice of dining venues inside and outside the city's limits. Panel (a) shows that the smoking ban results in a downward shift in the marginal benefit (*MB*) curve for meals eaten in the city with the ban. So, the number of meals that a smoker eats in this city each month declines from 12 to 9. Panel (b) shows that, for the reasons stated earlier, the smoking ban in the city shifts the marginal cost (*MC*) curve down for meals eaten in neighboring cities where smoking is still permitted. The end result is that the smoker increases the number of meals he eats—from 10 to 14—in neighboring cities each month.

This analysis helps explain why city governments are reluctant to impose restaurant smoking bans unless neighboring cities do so as well. Local restaurant owners and bar owners exert tremendous political pressure against localized smoking bans, arguing that the loss of sales revenue they would suffer would translate into substantial declines in local tax collections. However, this opposition diminishes considerably when adjacent cities join together to support a regional smoking ban.

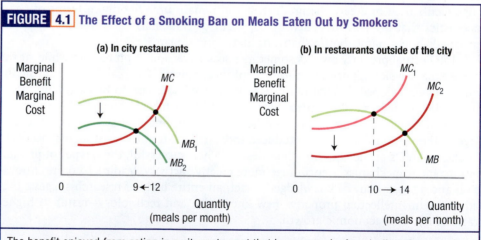

FIGURE **4.1**   **The Effect of a Smoking Ban on Meals Eaten Out by Smokers**

(a) In city restaurants

(b) In restaurants outside of the city

The benefit enjoyed from eating in a city restaurant that is now smoke-free declines for a smoker. This is represented by the downward shift in his *MB* curve in panel (a) as he cuts back the number of meals he eats in city restaurants from 12 to 9 meals a month. As panel (b) shows, the marginal (opportunity) cost of eating a meal outside the city falls because the benefit a smoker gives up by not dining at a city restaurant has declined due to the smoking ban there. This translates into a downward shift in the smoker's *MC* curve. Consequently, the number of meals he eats outside the city increases from 10 to 14 meals a month.

We could have instead applied our marginal benefit–marginal cost analysis to predict how the smoking ban affects the choices of nonsmokers. The net benefit of dining in the city would rise for nonsmokers, leading them to eat more meals in the city with the smoking ban. At the same time, the opportunity cost of eating outside the city rises because nonsmokers are passing up the chance to enjoy a smoke-free meal in the city (not to mention that smokers are now eating *and smoking* more in restaurants outside the city). As a result, there will be a decline in the number of meals that nonsmokers eat in restaurants located outside the city, where smoking is still permitted.

Do our model's predictions fit with actual experience? In April 2004, Talbot County, Maryland imposed a no-smoking ban on restaurants, bars and other public places. In the first six months of the ban, restaurant receipts fell by 11 percent in Talbot County, while sales in the neighboring counties without smoking bans—Caroline and Dorchester Counties—increased by 36 percent and 14 percent, respectively. By the end of 2004, the number of bars and restaurants in Talbot County had fallen from 39 to 29.

SOLVED PROBLEM

Q A public initiative called The Puppy Mill Cruelty Prevention Act was passed in Missouri in 2010. Among other things, it requires puppy breeders to allot a certain amount of kennel space for each dog, have each dog examined annually by a licensed veterinarian, and provide unfettered access to exercise areas and clean water. (1) Using MB and MC curves, show the impact of this new law on how many puppies a breeder will produce each year. (2) What do you think will happen to the price of the puppies sold to local pet stores by puppy-mill operators? (3) What, if any, impact do you think the Puppy Mill law will have on stray rescue adoptions?

A As the following figure shows, the MC curve for breeding puppies will rise, resulting in a reduction in the optimal number of puppies produced.

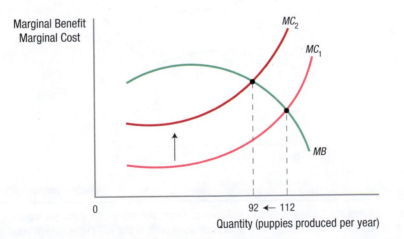

Because the cost of complying with the new regulations has increased the cost of producing puppies, we would expect both the wholesale and retail prices of these dogs to increase as well. As prices rise, we would predict that stray rescue puppies and dogs—which can usually be adopted for a small fee—would become more attractive to people looking for a new pet.

Outlawing Child Slavery

Another example of how changing property rights affects people's decisions relates to the global trade in children and young women. Although not a pretty thought, there are still regions of the world where families sell their sons or daughters to make ends meet for the rest of the family.[16] In Ghana's Volta Lake area, for example, children as young as age four have been sold into forced labor for as little as $100.[17] In these situations, the economic benefit to a parent of having a child increases by the amount that she can be "sold" for. The buyer will value the child based on her economic worth over her productive life, whether as a factory worker, domestic servant, or armed soldier. In some sense, this situation is not all that different from what occurred in the United States during the eighteenth and early nineteenth centuries. Although children were not sold outright, they were highly valued by their parents for their labor productivity on the family farm and in factories.

We depict this situation in **Figure 4.2**. As shown in the figure, when the opportunity to sell children exists, the number of children born to the typical family is seven. However, there has been a concerted effort around the world to eradicate trade in children and young women through the introduction of protective laws.[18] If these laws make the cost of trafficking in children prohibitive, what do you think would happen to the number of children born to the typical family? Eliminating the option of selling one's children results in a decline in the expected marginal benefit from having children, thereby shifting the MB curve down. If the marginal cost of having children has not changed, the optimal number of children born to the typical family will decrease from seven to five.

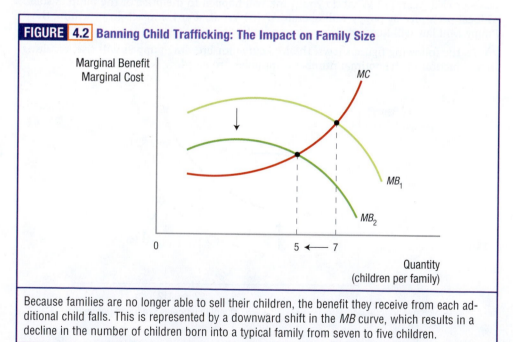

FIGURE 4.2 Banning Child Trafficking: The Impact on Family Size

Because families are no longer able to sell their children, the benefit they receive from each additional child falls. This is represented by a downward shift in the MB curve, which results in a decline in the number of children born into a typical family from seven to five children.

· · · · · · ·

[16]Nicholas Kristoff, "The Good Daughter, in a Brothel." *New York Times,* December 17, 2006.

[17]World Briefing. "Ghana: 116 Child Laborers Rescued." *New York Times,* May 28, 2011.

[18]Amelia Gentleman, "Stricter Law Fails to Diminish the Demand for Child Laborers in India." *New York Times,* March 4, 2007.

SOLVED PROBLEM

Q Suppose that a state enacts a law that increases the drinking age for "hard liquor" to 25, while the drinking age for beer and wine remains at 21. Using *MB* and *MC* curves, show the impact of this law on (1) the consumption of hard liquor; (2) the consumption of wine and beer.

A As the following figures indicate, the opportunity cost of drinking hard liquor will rise, thereby reducing the amount consumed. At the same time, the opportunity cost of drinking beer and wine will decrease, increasing the amount consumed. Of course, these results require that the new law is strictly enforced.

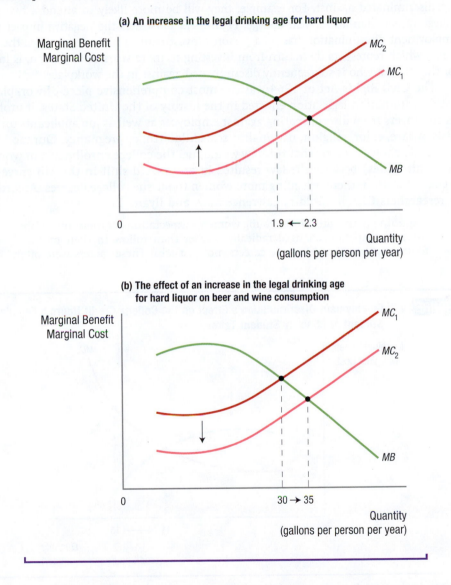

(a) An increase in the legal drinking age for hard liquor

(b) The effect of an increase in the legal drinking age for hard liquor on beer and wine consumption

Antidiscrimination Laws in the Workplace

The benefit that students perceive they will get from a college degree depends, at least in part, on the difference between their expected future earnings and what they would earn with only a high-school diploma. This benefit must be weighed against the cost of obtaining a college degree, including the costs of tuition and books and the income students forgo if they don't work full-time while going to school. Now suppose that discrimination in hiring practices prevents some college grads—due to their gender or race—from landing high-earning positions after college. If these graduates are denied some of the rewards of obtaining a college degree, then the market value of their educational achievement diminishes. That is, the economic benefit from pursuing higher education is reduced. Our economic model predicts that people who are discriminated against in this way—when it comes to finding a job after college—will be less likely to attend college. If they do attend, they are apt to take fewer total credit hours than those who are not discriminated against. For example, they will be more likely to attend a two-year college rather than a four-year college. **Figure 4.3** illustrates the negative impact that employment discrimination has on a person's investment in higher education: the *MB* curve, which represents the return from investing in more years of education, is lower for the student who is subsequently discriminated against in the workplace.

The Civil Rights Act of 1964 was the most comprehensive piece of workplace-antidiscrimination legislation enacted in the history of the United States. It prohibits employers from discriminating against employees as well as job applicants on the basis of race, color, religion, nationality, sex, childbirth, or pregnancy. Our model of economic choice predicts that this law would fuel the college enrollments of women (and minorities) because the law resulted in an upward shift in the *MB* curve for higher education, thereby leading more women to pursue college degrees. According to researchers Claudia Goldin, Lawrence Katz, and Ilyana Kuziemko:

> Beginning in the late 1960s, young women's expectations of their future labor force participation changed radically. Rather than follow in their mothers' footsteps, they aimed to have careers, not just jobs. These careers were often

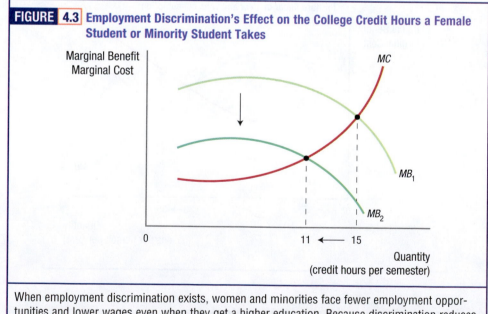

FIGURE 4.3 **Employment Discrimination's Effect on the College Credit Hours a Female Student or Minority Student Takes**

When employment discrimination exists, women and minorities face fewer employment opportunities and lower wages even when they get a higher education. Because discrimination reduces the return from getting a 4-year college education for people who are discriminated against, there is a downward shift in the *MB* curve associated with accumulating college credit hours. As a result, the number of college credits they earn declines from 15 to 11 each semester.

outside of the traditionally female occupations for women. [This explains much of] the increase in the female-to-male ratios of college graduates from the 1970s to the 1990s.[19]

Almost 50 years later, the percent of the U.S. undergraduate college population that is female has risen from 39 percent to 58 percent.[20]

Even in the absence of government laws prohibiting workplace discrimination, employers have often responded to changes in economic conditions by expanding the employment rights of previously underrepresented groups. Take, for example, the changing position of women in the U.S. workforce during World War II. The war thrust many women into the workplace for the first time. Their labor was needed to support the war effort and replace men who were fighting overseas. This eventually led to more liberal societal norms about women working side-by-side with men in U.S. manufacturing plants. In effect, the property rights of working women expanded due to the pressures created by the war economy, and, even after the war was over, these rights remained largely intact.

4.6 When Illegal Markets Become Legal (and Vice Versa)

The Eighteenth Amendment to the U.S. Constitution, which went into effect in 1920, made the sale of alcoholic beverages illegal in the United States. The passage of this amendment ushered in the period known as Prohibition. During Prohibition, anyone who bought "bootleg" (illegally produced and distributed) liquor or consumed home-brewed alcohol broke the law. In fact, the famous gangster Al Capone got his start by selling bootleg liquor during Prohibition. His gang earned over $60 million a year (more than $1 billion in today's dollars) before Capone was arrested in 1934.[21] Clearly, enforcement of the law must have been imperfect because Capone had a ready market for his liquor, customers who were willing to risk arrest to continue buying and drinking alcoholic beverages.

Because supplying liquor during Prohibition was illegal, the costs of production and distribution increased relative to the costs before Prohibition began. It has been estimated that as a result of Prohibition, beer prices increased by more than 700 percent, and the price of distilled corn whiskey increased by approximately 270 percent.[22] Production costs rose partly because smaller brewing facilities that were easier to conceal had to be built and used; these smaller plants couldn't achieve the production efficiencies that larger breweries enjoyed. In addition, suppliers had to pay hefty bribes to local law-enforcement officials and politicians to keep their private drinking clubs ("speakeasies") open.

When the Twenty-First Amendment ending Prohibition took effect in 1933, the right to purchase alcoholic beverages in liquor stores and bars was reinstituted. This reduced the opportunity cost of buying and selling liquor because the legal risks were now gone. The repeal of Prohibition also reduced the economic benefit of buying moonshine, hooch, and other substances of questionable quality. What does our

· · · · · · ·

[19]Claudia Goldin, Lawrence Katz, and Ilyana Kuziemko, "The Homecoming of American College Women: The Reversal of the College Gender Gap." (NBER Working Paper No. 12139), April, 2006.

[20]Tamar Lewin, "At Colleges, Women are Leaving Men in the Dust." *New York Times,* July 9, 2006.

[21]"Prohibition." *Encyclopaedia Britannica.* 2007.

[22]Mark Thornton, "Alcohol Prohibition Was a Failure." *Cato Policy Analysis No. 157,* July, 1991.

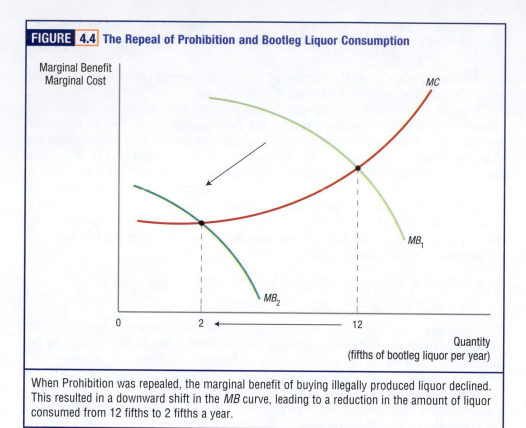

FIGURE 4.4 The Repeal of Prohibition and Bootleg Liquor Consumption

When Prohibition was repealed, the marginal benefit of buying illegally produced liquor declined. This resulted in a downward shift in the *MB* curve, leading to a reduction in the amount of liquor consumed from 12 fifths to 2 fifths a year.

model of economic choice predict about the consumption of liquor once Prohibition ended?

Figure 4.4 illustrates the *MB* and *MC* curves for consuming bootleg liquor during Prohibition: according to this figure, the amount of bootleg liquor consumed by a typical drinker was 12 fifths per year. After Prohibition ended, the marginal benefit of drinking bootleg liquor declined because of the availability of legal substitutes. We show this by shifting the *MB* curve down. This reduced the amount of bootleg a typical drinker purchased from 12 fifths per year to only 2 fifths a year. You might wonder why sales of bootleg liquor did not go to zero. It turns out that the production of moonshine and other illegal liquors continued for a variety of reasons, including their distinctive taste and high alcohol content. Still, the end of Prohibition led to a collapse in the revenue stream for Capone and other gangs, leading them to branch out into other "lines of business" such as gambling and bank robbery.

Many people consider Prohibition to be a historic anomaly, a misguided attempt to legislate private morality. Still, there are a number of countries—such as Saudi Arabia and Kuwait—that prohibit the production and purchase of alcoholic drinks. Our experience with Prohibition yields important insights into the potential impact of taking markets that are currently illegal—such as markets for illicit drugs and human organs— and making them legal. When a product is legalized, its price generally falls.

The Repeal of Blue Laws

From the seventeenth century through the latter half of the twentieth century, virtually every state in the United States enforced Sunday "blue laws," which prohibited retail sales on Sundays. Despite a U.S. Supreme Court ruling that such laws were

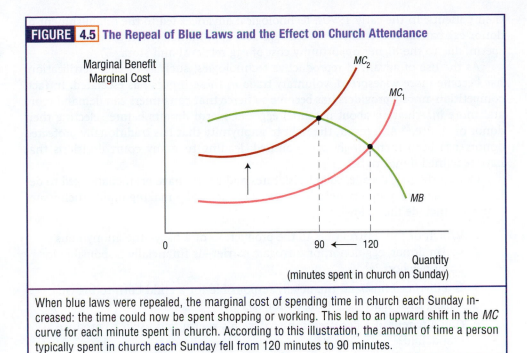

FIGURE 4.5 The Repeal of Blue Laws and the Effect on Church Attendance

When blue laws were repealed, the marginal cost of spending time in church each Sunday increased: the time could now be spent shopping or working. This led to an upward shift in the *MC* curve for each minute spent in church. According to this illustration, the amount of time a person typically spent in church each Sunday fell from 120 minutes to 90 minutes.

unconstitutional, they did not begin to disappear until the 1950s, first for supermarkets, then for other retail stores, and, finally, for sales of alcoholic beverages (only in some states). In Europe, these restrictions are called "Sunday laws," which remain in place in many countries. In 2009, France modified its Sunday closure laws to permit retail sales in tourist areas and its major cities.

According to our model of economic choice, how would rescinding blue laws impact a person's church attendance? **Figure 4.5** shows that the *MC* curve for going to church on Sunday shifts up in the face of newly available shopping and work opportunities.

This leads us to predict that the amount of time people spend in church on Sunday would fall if blue laws were repealed, as Figure 4.5 shows. For some people, the amount of time spent in church might even drop to zero. How accurate is our prediction? A recent study found that the percent of the population that attended Sunday services *at all* dropped measurably—from 37 percent to 32 percent—when blue laws were repealed.[23]

Legalizing the Baby Trade

In most countries, it is illegal to buy or sell a baby. In other words, an entrepreneur cannot broker a deal between a baby buyer and a baby seller (the biological parents of the baby). This is one important way in which the property-rights system has restricted parental rights. Nevertheless, in some parts of the United States, people do have the legal right to buy and sell all of the *inputs* required to create a baby. Sperm, eggs, and, in some states, even wombs (in the form of surrogate carriers) can all be legally purchased. Donor sperm banks, which have existed since the 1950s, compensate anonymous donors and resell the sperm to infertility doctors for use by

· · · · · · ·

[23]Jonathan Gruber and Daniel Hungerman, "The Church vs the Mall: What Happens When Religion Faces Increased Secular Competition?" (NBER Working Paper No. W12410), August, 2006.

their patients. In the early 1990s, technological advances led to the establishment of donor egg banks. (Currently, donated eggs cost approximately ten times the price of sperm, due to the higher opportunity cost of egg retrieval and storage.)

As the use of advanced reproductive technologies, such as in vitro fertilization, has become more widespread, voluntary trade in these inputs has escalated. In fact, competition among providers has become so fierce that consumers can demand more and more information about potential egg and sperm donors before selecting their donor of choice.[24] As a result, the right to anonymity that has traditionally protected donors has been increasingly compromised, leading to many court decisions that have redefined donor rights.

During the past decade, state legislatures and courts have been challenged to define and assign the property rights connected to each baby-making input. Such issues that arise include the following:

- Which of the contributors to the production of a baby—the anonymous sperm donor, egg donor, or surrogate carrier—is financially responsible for an ill newborn?[25]

- Is a divorced husband financially responsible for a child born to his wife, during their marriage, using donor sperm?[26]

- Can a parent of a deceased son retrieve his sperm and use it to produce a grandchild?[27]

To resolve these thorny property rights questions, courts have extrapolated from previous rulings related to adoption and parental responsibilities and rights, as well as from existing contract law.

4.7 Shopping for Favorable Property Rights

Property-rights systems vary from country to country, and even state to state. Because property rights affect the benefits and costs of our decisions, there may be an incentive to "shop" for more favorable property rights by moving from one legal (or religious) jurisdiction to another, either temporarily or permanently. For example, well-known celebrities and racecar drivers[28] shop for citizenship rights in low-tax countries such as Switzerland and the Netherlands to keep more of their wealth; grandparents move to Florida rather than California for more generous estate tax laws; gay couples shop for residency in states that have legalized same-sex marriage; and fugitive financiers shop for international destinations that do not have an extradition treaty with the United States. Whether a person is willing to "vote with her feet" for a more favorable property-rights environment depends ultimately on whether the benefits of this move outweigh the costs.

Suppose that your state decides to increase its corporate tax rate to 10 percent from its current rate of 6 percent. At the same time, a neighboring state decides to maintain its corporate tax rate at 6 percent. In effect, your state has reduced the

· · · · · · ·

[24]Gina Kolata, "Psst! Ask for Donor 1913." *New York Times,* February 17, 2007.

[25]Jaycee v. Superior Court, 42 App. 4th 718 (Calif. 1996).

[26]Mark Fass, "Judge: Paternal Duties Apply to Child Born of Artificial Insemination." *New York Law Journal,* January 24, 2007.

[27]Joel Greenberg, "In Life of Soldier, in Death a Father?" *Chicago Tribune,* January 29, 2007.

[28]Richard S. Chang, "Auto Racing and Taxes." *New York Times,* March 12, 2009.

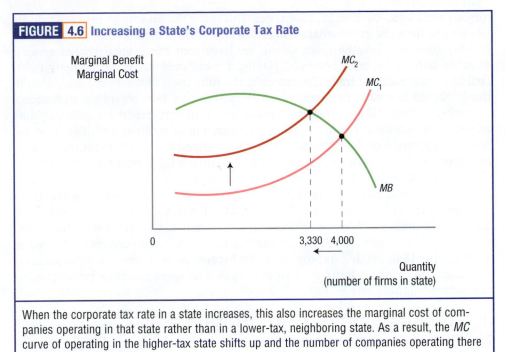

FIGURE 4.6 Increasing a State's Corporate Tax Rate

When the corporate tax rate in a state increases, this also increases the marginal cost of companies operating in that state rather than in a lower-tax, neighboring state. As a result, the *MC* curve of operating in the higher-tax state shifts up and the number of companies operating there falls from 4,000 to 3,750 firms.

share of earned income that corporations have a right to retain. What does our model predict will happen to the number of firms operating in your state versus the neighboring state?

Figure 4.6 shows the effect of an increase in your state's corporate tax on the number of businesses operating in your state, all else the same. When the corporate tax rate increases, so do the opportunity costs of companies located in your state. As Figure 4.6 illustrates, the *MC* curve of these companies shifts up, and the number of companies operating in your state falls from 4,000 to 3,750 firms. Where do the 250 companies go? They relocate to the adjacent state, whose corporate tax rate hasn't changed. You might wonder why all of the companies located in your state do not move across the state line to take advantage of the lower tax rate. The answer is that relocation costs may be quite steep for some firms, especially those with elaborate, customized physical plants or highly localized distribution systems. In other words, "voting with your feet" to a more favorable tax jurisdiction can be prohibitively expensive.

How good is our prediction about the impact of the increase in corporate tax rates on where businesses (re)locate? There are, in fact, a number of studies that demonstrate that the corporate tax structure has a significant impact on the location decisions of firms. And, all else the same, states with higher corporate tax rates tend to experience lower growth in terms of new business starts relative to states with lower corporate tax rates.

Shopping for a more favorable property-rights system has its risks. In the case of same-sex marriages, for example, it is unclear whether states or countries that prohibit these marriages will recognize and enforce them. If they do not, then gay couples who want to enjoy the benefits conveyed by marriage—spousal employment benefits, inheritance rights, parenting and adoption rights, and so on—would have to permanently relocate to states that recognize same-sex marriages. Among the costs of doing so are forgone work opportunities in other states. This is the reason why so many people are lobbying to have the gay-marriage issue addressed at the federal level.

As economies become more global, we have seen the property-rights systems of many nations begin to converge. Having a more uniform set of property rights facilitates international trade. For example, the formation of the European Union in the 1990s led to greater uniformity in member nations' laws regarding professional licensure, agricultural and livestock standards, and import–export tax policies. More recently, international efforts to deter the financing of terrorist activities have put enormous pressure on "tax havens" such as Switzerland to report the sources of asset transfers and bank holdings. This has severely curtailed a person's right to secretly stash wealth in confidential, offshore bank accounts.

Our economic model predicts that in response to this change in property rights, the flow of funds to tax havens will decline, as will the number of financial institutions specializing in offshore banking. This prediction is consistent with the recent report that the number of banks in one tax haven—Antigua—dropped from 90 in 1998 to only 15 in 2003.[29] As property rights become more uniform across countries, states, and other jurisdictions, the cost of shopping for more favorable property rights can become prohibitively high.

4.8 Incomplete Property Rights and Rent-Seeking

Property rights are always changing. In particular, we have seen that technological advances often create situations in which property rights don't exist or are hard to enforce. When this occurs, the property-rights system is said to be "incomplete," and our courts and lawmakers try to fill in the gaps. A U.S. district court ruling addressed the incomplete property rights created by technologies that allow people to download digital music files without paying for them. A similar dispute is still ongoing as to whether people can create freely accessible Web site libraries of downloadable musical scores. The European Union has ruled that this activity infringes on music publishers' copyrights. However, the offending Web site's servers are located in Canada, where copyright laws are much less stringent.[30]

Can actors demand to be paid for movies they made that people share over the Web? Can scientists restrict access to stem cell lines they have genetically modified?[31] What rights does a person have who contributed the original cellular matter that has been altered to create new drug therapies?[32] Uncertainty about property rights in these and similar situations means that voluntary trades that would make people better off may not take place. And, as we discussed earlier, uncertainty over property rights can lead to a suboptimal investment in the production of goods such as medical research or musical compositions.

Property rights can also be incomplete if, in the past, these rights had little value and weren't worth addressing and enforcing. When there were only three major television networks—ABC, CBS, and NBC—scant attention was given to the syndication

· · · · · · ·

[29]Aline Sullivan, "Tax Havens: Going, Going, Gone?" *International Herald Tribune,* March 15, 2003.

[30]Daniel Wakin, "Free Trove of Music Scores on Web Hits Sensitive Copyright Note." *New York Times,* February 22, 2011, p. A1.

[31]Andrew Pollack, "Patents on Stem Cells Are Evoked in Initial Review." *New York Times,* April 7, 2007.

[32]Laura Tangley, "Who Owns Human Tissues and Cells?" *Bioscience* (June, 1987).

rights to television shows after they were canceled. Given the limited amount of on-air time, the three networks rarely ran old episodes of cancelled shows. However, after the number of networks exploded with the introduction of cable and satellite TV delivery systems, the value of syndication rights rose substantially because new stations such as TNT and Nickelodeon needed inexpensive programming to fill their airtime. This, in turn, has created a new fan base for vintage programs, including *I Love Lucy*, *The Addams Family*, and *The Twilight Zone*, resulting in lucrative DVD sales[33] and iPod downloads of old episodes,[34] along with new merchandising deals.

As you might expect, the increased value of these reruns has led to several high-profile court cases dealing with the rights of producers and actors to receive compensation when their old programs are televised and copies are sold. It is not surprising that decades-old Hollywood contracts failed to address the current situation—who would have foreseen the day when 200+ TV channels would exist and when video content could be downloadable inexpensively? Today, with this in mind, it is common for all parties involved in the production and distribution of a new television series to have their rights to future "residual" earnings clearly defined before the first day of filming.

Rent-Seeking

The process of defining, assigning, or redefining property rights is often influenced by intense pressures brought to bear by competing interest groups. The Recording Industry Association of America (RIAA), for example, has initiated more than 200 lawsuits around the country against individuals engaged in the downloading and sharing of music files. As the trade association for major U.S. recording labels, RIAA seeks to extend the copyright protections held by its members to cover downloaded music. The fact that RIAA is willing to spend a great deal of money to force the judicial system to address this "gray area" is clear evidence that the property rights in question have substantial value.

Interest groups also engage in activities to try to influence legislative decisions that create or redefine property rights. The pursuit of favorable property rights through the judicial system or the legislative process is called **rent-seeking**.

RENT-SEEKING Activities that seek to create, redefine, or limit property rights.

EXAMPLE The National Corn Growers Association has lobbied for legislation that stipulates that only corn ethanol can be used as a gasoline substitute in the United States.

EXAMPLE Public-school administrators and teachers' unions have lobbied state and federal legislators to block the introduction of voucher systems that would allow students to use public funds to attend private schools.

EXAMPLE The U.S. steel, automobile, and tire manufacturing industries have lobbied Congress to impose heavy taxes on the imports of foreign competitors.

· · · · · · ·

[33]Greg Hernandez, "TV Shows Old and New Send DVD Sales Soaring." *Los Angeles Daily News*, September 1, 2003.

[34]Ronald Grover, "Dibs on the Download Dough." *Businessweek*, March 20, 2006.

To better understand rent-seeking behavior, ask yourself why lobbyists exist. The role of a lobbyist—whether it is the dairy farmers' lobbyist or your state university's lobbyist—is to protect and even expand the property rights held by the lobbyist's employer. In the case of your state university, this might translate into lobbying against the opening of a competing state-funded college. A new state-funded college could siphon away state resources previously committed to your university or create more competition for students and tuition dollars. The resources that your school is attempting to protect are sometimes referred to as "rents." Rent-seeking activities try to protect and even increase these payoffs.

Rent-seeking takes place in many situations, with different "sides" working to protect or enhance the value of their property rights. Consider labor-intensive businesses—for example, the agricultural, construction, and food-services industries. These industries often lobby for the right to issue more work visas to foreign workers because they want to lower their costs of labor. Similarly, business and educational interest groups have recently begun to lobby for an increase in the number of work visas granted to skilled foreigners,[35] including computer programmers, scientists, and accountants. In contrast, labor unions and some professional organizations often lobby against issuing more visas in order to safeguard the wages of their members.

Factory owners and manufacturing industries often lobby politicians for the right to discharge more pollutants into the atmosphere to keep their production costs low. The opposing position is taken by environmental and public-health groups, which campaign for more stringent regulations to protect the public's "right" to clean air. These are exactly the interest groups that are most vocal during debates over "cap-and-trade" legislation in the United States, which is aimed at limiting producers' rights to pollute the air.

Should it come as any surprise, then, that businesses, unions, and other interest groups invest scarce resources to nudge the legislative process toward their preferred property-rights outcomes? These "wins" are not free, however. They come at the expense of other people and interest groups that are not awarded the right to control the use of the resources in question. In 1981, U.S. automobile manufacturers successfully lobbied Congress to negotiate a "voluntary export agreement" with the Japanese government that limited the right of Japanese car manufacturers to export cars to the United States. Among the winners were U.S. autoworkers and shareholders in U.S. auto and auto-supply companies. The biggest losers were U.S. car buyers who faced higher sticker prices and less selection, as well as the owners and employees of Japanese car dealerships located in the United States.[36]

Why didn't U.S. car buyers lobby against the export agreement? It turns out that the benefits of the agreement were concentrated among only a few interests—primarily the U.S. automakers, their labor union members, and suppliers. In contrast, the costs were spread across a large number of potential consumers. All of the "losers" from the agreement had such a small stake in the matter that it would not have made economic sense for them to invest the scarce resources required to organize themselves to lobby Congress. This is the same reason that consumers have been largely voiceless in the debate over cap-and-trade legislation: the Congressional Budget Office has projected that the cost to a family of four would be only $175 per year. In general, then, lobbying efforts are most successful when the benefits to be

• • • • • • •

[35]Miguel Helft, "A New Push to Raise Cap on H1-B Visa." *New York Times,* November 15, 2006.
[36]Clyde Farnsworth, "Antitrust Problem in Car-Import Curbs." *New York Times,* March 19, 1981.

had are concentrated among only a few individuals or organizations, and the costs are spread over a large number of people or entities.

Those individuals or interest groups that can make their positions heard by political or judicial decision makers at a low cost tend to be more successful in bringing about more favorable property-rights outcomes. This explains why some retired government and elected officials—who can capitalize on their connections—often command hefty lobbyist fees. It may also help explain why the substantial expansion in educational and workplace rights for women and black people didn't occur until members of both groups were able to freely exercise their voting rights to support or oppose political candidates.

WHAT YOU SHOULD HAVE LEARNED FROM CHAPTER 4

- That property rights convey legal rights to use the economic resources we possess or acquire, in specific ways.

- That property rights directly impact the choices that individuals make because they affect the economic benefits and costs of alternatives.

- That private property rights are essential to a well-functioning market system of exchange.

- That common property rights often result in high transaction costs that impede beneficial exchange.

- That there will be a suboptimal amount of creative output—intellectual property—produced when there are no mechanisms to enforce private property rights to such innovations.

- That technology can have a positive or negative effect on the ability to enforce property rights.

- That changes in property rights will have an impact on how we allocate our scarce resources.

- That technological changes can often lead to situations in which property rights aren't well-defined or easily enforceable.

- That people will "shop" for more favorable property-rights systems when the benefits outweigh the costs.

- That interest groups have an economic incentive to engage in rent-seeking behavior to obtain beneficial property rights.

KEY TERMS

Property rights, p. 72

Private property rights, p. 73

Common property rights, p. 74

Eminent domain, p. 78

Intellectual property rights, p. 81

Rent-seeking, p. 95

QUESTIONS AND PROBLEMS

1. Suppose that you have been hired as a consultant to advise a country on how to make the transition from communism (property held in common) to a system of private property. Propose at least two ways that this country could create and distribute private-ownership rights to property that was previously held in common.

2. If it's true that ownership in stars or land on the Moon is not enforceable, then why do people actually pay for these rights? What property right is actually being acquired here?

3. What if the U.S. Supreme Court ruled that a birth father had the same rights as a birth mother to reclaim his child within 180 days of adoption. Using *MB* and *MC* curves, show the impact of this ruling on (1) the number of babies adopted in the United States; (2) the number of babies adopted by U.S. families from countries outside the United States.

4. Several years ago, the federal government enacted the Family and Medical Leave Act (FMLA), which allows employees to take an unpaid leave of absence to tend to family crises without any risk of losing their job. If women are the primary caregivers when it comes to elderly parents and young children, (1) using *MB* and *MC* curves, show the impact of FMLA on the hiring of women; (2) suggest a way in which the government could counteract the result that you predicted in (1).

5. In the late 1960s, the Catholic Church eliminated the requirement that observant Catholics eat fish on Fridays. Using *MB* and *MC* curves, show the effect of this change on the (1) consumption of fish, and (2) consumption of beef by traditional Catholics.

6. AMC theaters recently established a new rule that prohibits babies under the age of two from attending movies shown after 8 p.m. Using *MB* and *MC* curves, show the impact of this rule on (1) evening movie attendance by individuals who do not have children; (2) evening movie attendance by parents with children under two; (3) DVD rentals by parents with young children.

7. One approach to the "tragedy of the commons" is to allocate quotas to individual users of the common property. (1) How would you integrate such a quota into your marginal benefit–marginal cost illustration of economic decision making? (2) What would happen if the *MB* curve for the good that is subject to the quota—for example, fish—shifts up due to new scientific findings about the health benefit of consuming the good? Does the optimal amount of fish caught change? Will it actually change? Do you think that the actual outcome is "optimal" from an economic standpoint?

8. Suppose that you authored a book or wrote a song. If you knew that it would be prohibitively costly to enforce your ownership rights to the material after it was published, would this affect the price at which you sold the first copy? How? Explain your answer.

9. By 2009, the Federal Communications Commission (FCC) had mandated that all analog television broadcast signals were to be converted to digital signals. Using *MB* and *MC* curves, show the impact of this regulation in 2007 on (1) purchases of television sets that receive only analog signals; and (2) purchases of digitally equipped television sets. How easy do you think it was to find an analog television set to buy in 2007? Explain your answer.

10. Consider two neighboring states: Missouri and Illinois. Missouri has one of the lowest tax rates in the country and, as a result, one of the lowest funding levels for higher education. By contrast, Illinois has one of the highest tax rates in the country and is generous in its funding of public colleges and universities. Discuss what would happen if Illinois and Missouri adopted a "reciprocity" agreement to extend in-state tuition to each other's state residents. Specifically, do you think that Missouri would increase, decrease, or leave unchanged its level of funding for higher education?

11. Some countries, such as Spain and Austria, have adopted property-rights systems stating that when a person dies, his organs are available for transplant *unless he opts out* of donating his organs prior to death. This is called the "opt-out" system of organ procurement. Other countries, such as the United States, have an "opt-in" system, which requires potential donors to provide consent to having their organs used for transplants before they die. Using *MB* and *MC* curves for *each* procurement system, predict which approach will generate more organ transplants.

12. Suppose that a restaurant smoking ban is enacted in your town. Using *MB* and *MC* curves, show the impact on the volume of take-out food orders (1) for smokers; (2) for nonsmokers.

13. If people can free-ride on television and radio signals, why do you think that some contribute voluntarily to the support of stations such as Public Broadcasting (PBS) and National Public Radio (NPR)? Explain your answer.

14. Some of the most important discoveries that have improved the well-being of mankind have arisen without any enforceable private intellectual property rights. Two examples are the wheel and fire. Can you think of similar discoveries that have been made in the past century that have not benefited from patent protection or government funding? Are there situations where you think the promise of patent protection or research funding is especially critical to innovation? Explain your answer.

15. The Swiss are considering new banking rules that will make it harder for residents of neighboring countries to "hide" money in Swiss banks to avoid taxes. Using *MB* and *MC* curves, show how this legislation would impact the amount of money that a German citizen will deposit into Swiss bank accounts. Do you think that Swiss banks favor this change? What about German banks? Explain your answer.

Externalities: The Social Benefits and Costs of Our Choices

"Do you mind if I sit back a little? Because your breath is very bad."

Donald Trump, *billionaire real estate developer*

So far we have assumed that when you make a choice, you reap all of the economic benefits and incur all of the economic costs of your decision. Sometimes this is not a good assumption to make. There are times when one person's actions create benefits for others. What about those students in a class who are brave enough to ask all of the questions that everybody else is too intimidated to ask? Or think about the neighbor who renovates her house and thereby enhances the property values for everyone on her street. And the person who volunteers to be the designated driver and must refrain from drinking while allowing his friends to party hard. In all of these cases, one person's decision results in an increase in the well-being of others.

Sometimes a person's choices impose costs on others. Think, for example, about a student with the flu who insists on coming to class. Wouldn't we all have preferred him to stay home in bed and not risk infecting us? Or, consider the infant taken by his parents to a Saturday evening movie who begins to cry just as the plot thickens. Most of the other moviegoers would have preferred that the infant be left home. And, what about a drinker who insists on driving home from the bar and causes a fatal accident? In each instance, one person's decision imposes costs on others.

The question we raise in this chapter is whether people (or companies or governments) do, or *should*, account for these "spillover" benefits and costs when they make a decision. Because we are using the normative term *should*, we must establish some criteria for assessing the goodness of the choices that are made. We do so by looking at what is optimal from an economic point of view.

5.1 Private versus Social Costs and Benefits

To better understand the consequences of spillover costs and benefits, let's first distinguish **private costs** and **private benefits** from **social costs** and **social benefits**.

PRIVATE COST The economic cost that a person bears due to a choice he has made.

EXAMPLE Your private cost of going on your Christmas vacation equals the sum of the explicit and implicit costs that you incur, such as the money spent on vacation and the well-being you forgo from the holiday office party you miss.

PRIVATE BENEFIT The economic benefit that a person enjoys from a choice she has made.

EXAMPLE Your private benefit of going on your Christmas vacation equals the happiness and sense of well-being you gain from spending time with your distant family and friends or visiting new places.

SOCIAL COST The total economic cost borne by everyone as a result of an individual's choice.

EXAMPLE The social cost of your Christmas vacation equals the sum of your private cost plus the implicit cost borne by the children of your fellow employees who must do without a Santa Claus at the office party because you are the only one with a physique appropriate for the role.

SOCIAL BENEFIT The total economic benefit enjoyed by everyone as a result of an individual's choice.

EXAMPLE The social benefit of your two-week holiday vacation equals your private benefit plus the increase in well-being that your teenagers get from being left home unsupervised for two weeks.

In most situations, people are likely to consider only the private benefits and costs of their choices when they decide how to use their scarce resources. Think about when you enroll in a class that already is close to its maximum attendance cap. Do you think about the student who needs the class to graduate at the end of the semester but may be shut out because you chose to take one of the few remaining slots? What about when you pull into a scarce parking spot close to the classroom's building in the dead of winter? Do you consider how your decision to take this spot might affect a middle-aged faculty member who will have to trudge up the hill from a distant parking lot? Or do you think about disabled drivers, if the spot is not reserved for their exclusive use?

As it turns out, many of our actions result in social costs that go beyond our private costs. These social costs equal the sum of the private costs we incur plus any spillover costs that we impose on others. The same holds true for social versus private benefits. In most cases, we do not consider spillover benefits when we make our decisions. One major exception worth mentioning relates to decisions that we know will have an impact on family members or friends. We will often weigh this impact in making our choices because our own well-being often depends, at least in part, on the well-being of people who are central to our lives.

Previously, we examined a couple's choice about how many children to have. Applying our economic framework of decision making, we showed that the couple makes this decision by comparing the private marginal costs and private marginal benefits they receive from each additional child. But shouldn't prospective parents also consider the possible spillover costs or benefits of their decision?

Having children can generate enormous social costs and benefits that are so significant that they have attracted serious attention by government policy makers worldwide. China imposed a one-child-per-family policy for urban families to prevent its population from growing too rapidly. In contrast, Japan, Germany, and many other industrialized countries have introduced programs to counteract their low birthrates, which have fallen below the 2.1 children per couple required to just keep the size of their populations constant.[1] With birthrates well below this "replacement" rate, there has been a dramatic aging of the population in these countries, especially in Japan where more than 20 percent of the population are 65 or older.[2]

This low birthrate phenomenon is also spreading to rapidly developing countries such as South Korea. Why are the governments in these countries adopting policies that provide incentives for people to have more children? They know that an aging population will result in a future labor force that is inadequate to support social programs for the elderly, sustain economic growth, and preserve cultural uniqueness.

How can public policies affect people's decisions about having children? The U.S. income-tax system subsidizes larger families through generous tax breaks, including a child-care tax deduction, an adoption tax deduction, and an "earned income-tax credit" that benefits low-income parents. In several European countries, both mothers and fathers are given paid leaves of absence for 6 to 12 months after each child is born.[3] Some countries, such as France, are actually paying their citizens to have more children. As you can see, there are many ways a society can subsidize the choice to have more children.

These subsidies result in a downward shift in the *private* marginal cost curve ($MC_{private}$) of having additional children: the private opportunity cost of each child is reduced, even though the total social cost remains unchanged. Some of the costs have simply been shifted to society or, to be more specific, to taxpayers.

Figure 5.1 shows how public policies such as these affect a couple's decision about how many children to have. According to the figure, the optimal number of children in a family is three before the introduction of any subsidies. However, after a subsidy is enacted and the private marginal cost of having children falls, the optimal number of children in a family increases to four, assuming that nothing else changes.

Whenever a portion of the private cost of having children is shifted to others (e.g., to taxpayers who pay for public schools and subsidize school-lunch programs and school-based child care while parents work), we predict that the optimal number of children in a family will increase. In fact, we expect that anytime a good or service is subsidized, people are likely to consume more of it because its private marginal cost has fallen. For example, a greater amount of housing will be purchased if residential housing costs are subsidized by the government.

In the United States, the federal government subsidizes housing in a number of ways. The personal income-tax system allows home owners to deduct from their earnings the mortgage interest and property taxes they pay. In addition, via government subsidies, certain home buyers, such as veterans, get lower interest rates on

• • • • • • •

[1] Donald McNeil, Jr., "Subtract Billions; Demographic 'Bomb' May Only Go 'Pop!'" *New York Times*, August 29, 2004.

[2] "World Briefing: Japan Most Elderly Nation." *New York Times*, July 1, 2006.

[3] Sharon Lerner, "The Motherhood Experiment." *New York Times*, March 4, 2007.

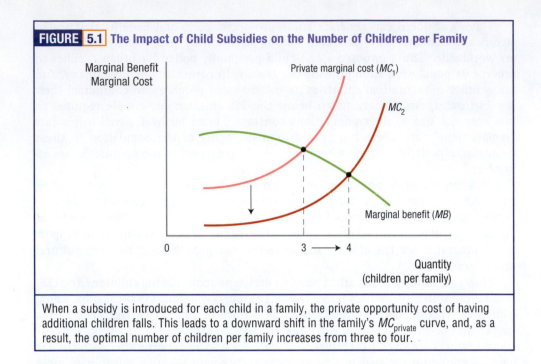

FIGURE 5.1 The Impact of Child Subsidies on the Number of Children per Family

When a subsidy is introduced for each child in a family, the private opportunity cost of having additional children falls. This leads to a downward shift in the family's $MC_{private}$ curve, and, as a result, the optimal number of children per family increases from three to four.

their mortgages. All of these subsidy programs reduce the *private* opportunity cost of owning a home. As a result, buying a home can be less expensive than leasing a home or renting an apartment.

Why does the government subsidize—and thereby encourage—the purchase of homes? Politicians, mortgage lenders, and home builders believe that the spillover benefits to society from widespread home ownership are substantial.[4] Voluntary non-profit organizations, such as Habitat for Humanity, agree. They claim that home ownership creates an incentive for individuals to invest in the upkeep of their houses, which "spills over" to the neighborhood and the community. Home owners also are more likely to support local schools and become involved in local government. From a political perspective, the stability that results from home ownership allows politicians to build long-term relationships with their constituents. And, just as child subsidies lead to bigger families, the subsidies for home ownership increase the number and size of homes that are purchased, which increases local property-tax collections.

If someone knew that others would benefit from the number of children she had or from her housing decision, would this affect her choice? To answer this, consider the following scenario. Suppose a mother decides to offer her teenage daughter's friends a supervised, alcohol-free "hangout" at her home. What would happen if the parents of these teens were brought together and told that the hangout's hours of operation could be extended if all of the families pitched in for junk food and soft drinks? Do you think they would contribute to cover these added expenses? If so, would they contribute an equal amount?

Assuming that the friends' parents enjoy spillover benefits from extending the hangout's hours of operation—after all, their kids are in a safe place and are not at home requiring supervision or being annoying—our economic model predicts that

[4]Jacqueline King, "Homeownership Initiative Targets Minnesota's Emerging Markets." *Community Dividend,* Federal Reserve Bank of Minneapolis, 2, (2005).

these parents would be willing to contribute something toward its cost. Some parents will pay more, some less, depending on how much well-being they get from having the hangout open more hours each day. These payments reduce the *private* cost borne by the mother who is hosting the hangout; as a result, it will be kept open longer. In effect, a voluntary trade has taken place between the friends' parents and the mother: the mother is being paid to expand her services. This tells us that the mother that originated the plan will keep the hangout open *too few hours* if other families pay nothing for the spillover benefits they enjoy.

The problem is that the people who enjoy the spillover benefits are often too numerous or too dispersed to ever come together to compensate the source of these benefits. So instead, social institutions—government, religious-based, and community-based organizations—assume responsibility for encouraging the consumption and production of goods that generate positive spillover benefits. These initiatives focus on "internalizing" spillover benefits so that they enter into a person's decision process, much like the contributions that the parents made to the mother "internalized" the spillover benefits these parents received. When spillover benefits are successfully internalized, people will consider the social benefits of their decisions rather than just the private benefits they get.

As we have already seen, one way to do this is to reduce the private cost of consuming a good or engaging in an activity. Another way is to increase the private benefit that a person gets from making choices that generate spillover benefits. For example, let's revisit the question of why governments issue and enforce patent rights. The idea behind patent rights is to increase the private benefit of coming up with new innovations so as to increase the amount of time and money invested in the discovery process.

In **Figure 5.2**, we see that an enforceable patent system shifts the private marginal benefit ($MB_{private}$) curve upward for innovation activities. Assuming that the private marginal cost ($MC_{private}$) of these activities hasn't changed, the number of

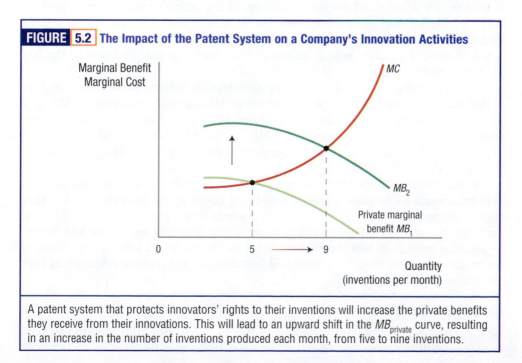

FIGURE 5.2 The Impact of the Patent System on a Company's Innovation Activities

Marginal Benefit
Marginal Cost

MC

MB_2

Private marginal benefit MB_1

0   5 → 9

Quantity
(inventions per month)

A patent system that protects innovators' rights to their inventions will increase the private benefits they receive from their innovations. This will lead to an upward shift in the $MB_{private}$ curve, resulting in an increase in the number of inventions produced each month, from five to nine inventions.

inventions produced increases. That is, the amount of innovation corresponding to where the new $MB_{private}$ curve equals the original $MC_{private}$ curve is greater than in the absence of a patent system.

5.2 Positive versus Negative Externalities

We have just seen that patent protection leads to more innovation than otherwise would occur. Why is the government involved in promoting innovation? Is it simply to enrich people like Bill Gates? No. The spillover benefits to society in terms of economic growth and greater individual well-being sometimes justify government involvement. When the social benefit arising from a person's decision is greater than the private benefit she receives, we say that a **positive externality** exists.

POSITIVE EXTERNALITY A situation in which a decision maker's choices generate economic benefits for others.

EXAMPLE Thomas Edison spent a great deal of his time inventing a long-lasting lightbulb. He became very wealthy, and society enjoyed a positive externality from his efforts—safer, more reliable lighting.

EXAMPLE Jonas Salk and Albert Sabin perfected vaccines against polio. They became famous, and people worldwide enjoyed a positive externality from the virtual eradication of polio.

EXAMPLE Your parents are coming to visit you at college; your roommate's parents are not coming. Your decision to clean the entire dorm room generates a positive externality for your roommate.

Children, home ownership, innovations, and many other economic activities can generate positive externalities for others. The problem, from society's point of view, is that people often don't engage in enough of the activities that produce positive externalities. In other words, the *social* benefit arising from the last unit of a good that a person consumes is greater than its marginal cost. But from an individual's point of view, the private benefit he enjoys just equals the marginal cost of the last unit he consumes.

We can readily use our discussion about scientific innovation to show why this is the case. In **Figure 5.3**, we superimpose the social marginal benefit curve (MB_{social}) onto the private marginal benefit–marginal cost diagram we have been using to represent the individual decision process. The MB_{social} curve includes the spillover benefits arising from a person's choice and, therefore, is higher than the $MB_{private}$ curve, as the figure shows.

What becomes immediately evident is that the number of innovations per year that maximizes an inventor's private well-being (two) is less than the number that maximizes social well-being (four). In other words, more innovations would be optimal from society's standpoint: the problem is that investing more time and money to produce more than two innovations is *not* in the inventor's self-interest. There is no reason to believe that this person will "internalize" the positive externalities that he creates for others.

Negative Externalities

Not all choices generate positive spillover benefits. When the consumption of a particular good or the pursuit of an activity imposes spillover costs on other members of

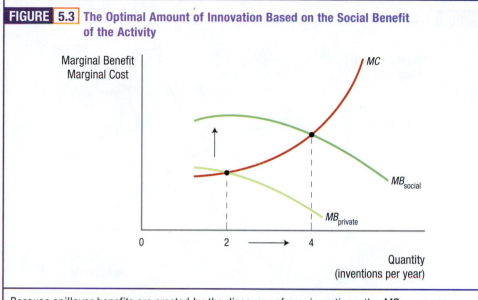

FIGURE 5.3 The Optimal Amount of Innovation Based on the Social Benefit of the Activity

Because spillover benefits are created by the discovery of new inventions, the MB_{social} curve associated with inventions is higher than the $MB_{private}$ curve. The inventor will invest enough time and money to produce four inventions a year only if the social marginal benefits are somehow internalized into his decision process.

society, then the social cost of this choice will exceed the private cost. We say that a **negative externality** exists.

NEGATIVE EXTERNALITY A situation in which a decision maker's choices impose economic costs on others.

EXAMPLE A college student who leaves the door to her dorm building propped open for friends creates a safety risk for all of the other dorm residents.

EXAMPLE People with communicable diseases such as swine flu who go out in public can impose costs on those with whom they come into contact.

EXAMPLE Young families that decide to move to rural areas can inflict substantial costs on longtime residents by overburdening local schools, water and sewage plants, and existing roads and highways.

Suppose families that wanted to move to a rural area were first required to get permission from each of the neighbors who would suffer spillover costs from the move. To get this permission, the families would likely have to compensate these neighbors to offset these costs. The neighbors, in turn, would require enough compensation to make them at least as well off, in terms of economic well-being, as before the families moved into the area.

If we added together all of the compensation required for the families to get permission to move in, we would have a good approximation of the spillover costs imposed on the neighborhood. Of course, these costs must then be added to the private cost borne by the families that are moving to accurately assess the total social cost of the relocation. If the families are not required to pay this compensation—that

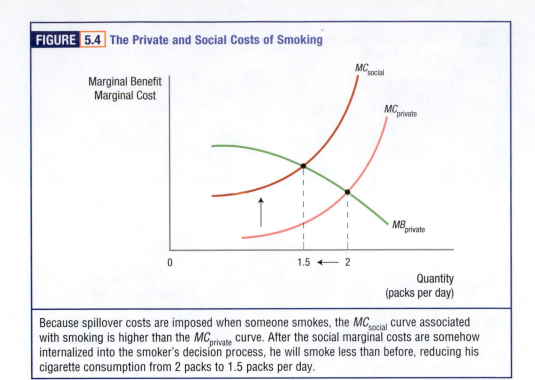

FIGURE 5.4 | The Private and Social Costs of Smoking

Because spillover costs are imposed when someone smokes, the MC_{social} curve associated with smoking is higher than the $MC_{private}$ curve. After the social marginal costs are somehow internalized into the smoker's decision process, he will smoke less than before, reducing his cigarette consumption from 2 packs to 1.5 packs per day.

is, if the families only consider their private costs of making the move—then "too many" families will move into this rural community. When negative externalities exist, people engage in *too much* of an economic activity from society's point of view. People's decisions are based on the private net benefit they get without regard for the spillover costs these choices impose on others.

In the previous chapter, we looked at the effect of smoking bans in public areas such as restaurants. Smokers create a negative externality for nonsmokers. **Figure 5.4** shows a typical smoker's $MC_{private}$ and $MB_{private}$ curves. Also included in the figure is the social marginal cost curve (MC_{social}) of the person's smoking. Notice that the MC_{social} curve is higher than the $MC_{private}$ curve because the MC_{social} curve includes not only the private cost of smoking but also the costs borne by others. The divergence between social and private costs tells us that a negative externality exists.

As we can readily see, the amount of smoking in public that maximizes a smoker's own well-being is determined by the intersection of the $MB_{private}$ and $MC_{private}$ curves. This occurs at 2 packs of cigarettes per day. But the MC_{social} is greater than the marginal cost $MC_{private}$ at that level of smoking. The optimal number of cigarettes that maximizes *society's* net benefit is not 2 packs per day but 1.5 packs per day. This is where the MC_{social} curve just equals the private marginal benefit that the smoker receives. Figure 5.4 tells us that from society's point of view, people "should" smoke less in public places.

Every day, we make choices that generate potentially large positive or negative externalities. Consider your decision about how much money to spend on maintaining your car. You would likely make this decision based on a variety of factors, such as its eventual resale value, its reliability in getting you to and from work or school (and the opportunity cost if you are late!), and its fuel efficiency. But these are all private benefits and costs. Your decision process will not include the costs imposed on others if your car breaks down and backs up traffic for hours during rush hour, or how much air pollution a poorly running engine might create. A socially optimal choice about how much to spend on car maintenance would take these negative externalities into account.

SOLVED PROBLEM

Q Suppose the $MC_{private}$ and $MB_{private}$ curves of a typical smoker are represented by the following graph. Suppose further that there are a million smokers in the United States. Using the graph, indicate how costly the negative externality must be each year to justify a ban on smoking in the United States.

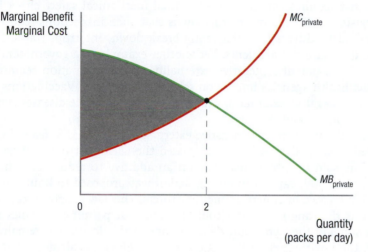

A The shaded area between the $MB_{private}$ and $MC_{private}$ curves indicates the private net benefit that a smoker gets from smoking each year. If we multiply this by 1,000,000, we would get the net benefit that all smokers get each year from smoking. If the well-being of smokers is considered to be as important as the well-being of nonsmokers, then smoking would have to generate spillover costs in excess of this total net benefit each year to justify a total ban on smoking in the United States.

5.3 Internalizing Externalities: Government Solutions

Public policy makers have relied on a variety of mechanisms to get people (and businesses) to internalize the externalities they create. We've already mentioned how government subsidies can prod people to make socially optimal choices regarding the number of children to have and the amount of housing to purchase. The government can also internalize externalities through regulations, taxes, and changes to property rights. When successful, these actions result in *less* of an activity that generates negative externalities and *more* of an activity that generates positive externalities. Let's consider the pros and cons of each type of government intervention.

Government Regulation

Government regulations are "command-and-control" rules that are applied to a variety of externality situations. The federal government, for example, introduced a law in 1996 to require the addition of folic acid to breads and other enriched grain products. The goal was to increase the number of women of childbearing age taking this additive, which has been shown to prevent catastrophic birth defects such as spina bifida.[5] Individuals born with spina bifida or other severe (but not fatal) birth defects can impose large negative externalities on society because private and public medical-insurance programs usually provide lifelong medical support. The law reduced the private marginal cost of taking folic acid by making it more readily available and convenient, which—according to our economic model—would lead to a greater consumption of the nutrient. The end result was a well-documented reduction in the incidence of spina bifida in the United States.

Another example of a government policy aimed at addressing externalities is a state law that requires cars to pass an annual mechanical safety check before they can be registered. The reason for this law is that such inspections reduce the social costs imposed by drivers who frequently break down, interrupt traffic flow, create road hazards, and cause accidents. Yet another example of a government regulation that addresses a potential negative externality is the vaccination requirement that state public health agencies impose on school-age children. Vaccinations reduce the occurrence of negative externalities caused by communicable diseases such as polio, meningitis, and whooping cough.

Perhaps the most massive negative externality that the U.S. federal government has tackled is air pollution. Congress passed the Clean Air Act in 1990, requiring that gasoline sold in urban areas contain an additive to reduce carbon dioxide air emissions.[6] In 2009, cap-and-trade legislation was proposed to limit the amount of air pollution created by American manufacturers. This law sought to cap the amount of emissions that any given firm could produce but permit companies to buy and sell all or some of their emission rights. Although this legislation remains stalled in Congress, the Environmental Protection Agency (EPA) has already instituted a cap-and-trade system to reduce industrial emissions of sulfur dioxide and nitrogen oxides, which are the primary causes of acid rain.

These types of laws encourage individual decision makers to make choices that are closer to the social optimum by changing the trade-offs they face. Often, these regulations come at a cost. In the case of folic acid, bread prices may be higher due to the additional cost of vitamin additives. Mandated automobile inspections raise the private cost of owning a car. And, as anyone who lives in a major metropolitan area can attest to, gasoline additives to reduce harmful emissions increase the price of gasoline. In each case, as long as the benefits to society exceed the additional costs arising from the government policy, then the policy contributes positively to the *net* economic well-being of society as a whole.

"As a whole" is an important caveat: there will always be winners and losers from regulation in terms of who enjoys the resulting benefits and who bears the cost of compliance. If, for example, you own and maintain your home, you will enjoy the benefit when your municipality enforces local ordinances that require your messy neighbor to get rid of all the junk cars on his lawn, an action that imposes private costs on him.

· · · · · · ·

[5]"Adding Folic Acid to Grain Reduces Birth Defects, Study Finds." *New York Times*, September 6, 2005.

[6]Matthew Wald, "Industry Blames Chemical Additives for High Gas Prices." *New York Times*, June 26, 2000.

When the government considers enacting a regulation, just how accurate is it in assessing the law's impact on the well-being of each person in society? After all, we just said that for a regulation to be socially optimal, its net benefit to society as a whole must be positive. For example, when highway speed limits were lowered to reduce gasoline consumption and traffic fatalities, did legislators factor in the loss in economic well-being borne by truckers and owners of trucking companies? When the federal government passed the law that required folic acid additives in bread products, did regulators take into account the loss in well-being borne by people who are allergic to folic acid? As it turns out, we sometimes discover *after* the fact that a regulation has been put into place to promote a "social good" before there was a thorough assessment to assure that its *net* social benefit is positive. In other words, insufficient attention may be paid to the additional costs of the regulation relative to the additional benefits that it will generate.

Even when information about social costs and benefits is readily available (a heroic assumption at best), these costs and benefits likely will change over time. For many years, the Federal Communications Commission (FCC) had regulations in place pertaining to the ownership of local broadcasting stations in order to promote the social good through competition, local control, and diversity in programming. In 2003, the FCC recognized that these rules had become outdated as television, radio, cable, telephone, and Internet providers began to enter each other's markets and compete head-on. In response, the FCC deregulated many of the markets that it had previously regulated.[7] Unless regulations are reviewed periodically—as they were at the FCC—at some point, they might actually reduce social well-being relative to what would have occurred without the regulations.

ECONOMIC FALLACY   A great deal of attention has been paid to the negative effect that a new Walmart Superstore can have on neighboring "mom-and-pop" retailers and grocery stores. The concern is that these smaller stores will go out of business because they cannot compete with Walmart's prices, hours of operation, and its large variety of products. This negative spillover effect gives local governments a legitimate reason to regulate—even prohibit—Super Walmart in their jurisdictions.

False. The entry of Walmart into a market permits consumers to rethink their spending decisions and decide whether to now buy items at Walmart. That is, the success of Walmart depends on voluntary trade that will occur only if it makes the buyer better off. Competition among suppliers for demanders' dollars is the foundation for competitive markets, and it ultimately leads to opportunities that maximize well-being for any given amount of scarce resources a person has under her control. This would not be considered a negative externality.

Economists refer to spillover effects that result solely from price changes as *pecuniary externalities*. In effect, when prices change, there is a redistribution of money and wealth; some people win and some lose. When, for example, the price of the PC fell low enough for the "average Joe" to buy one, many people turned to online news sources. This eventually led newspapers to lay off large numbers of employees. The reduction in PC prices generated a pecuniary externality.

. . . .

[7]"Deregulating the Media; Excerpts from Statements Issued by Commission Members after the Vote." *New York Times,* June 3, 2003.

It is important to distinguish pecuniary externalities from what are called *technological externalities*, that is, the types of spillover effects we have discussed in this chapter. Pecuniary externalities do not result in an inefficient allocation of scarce resources and do not, therefore, require government intervention. Technological externalities result in underuse or overuse of resources and do create a potential justification for government intervention.

Government Subsidies and Taxes

Government subsidies and taxes are sometimes used to internalize externalities. Unlike regulations that force people to change their consumption of a good—as in the case of folic acid—subsidies and taxes nudge people to "voluntarily" change their behavior. When it comes to positive externalities, subsidy programs such as the student-loan program and the tax deductibility of charitable donations and mortgage interest payments are all aimed at reducing the private costs that individuals face when making specific choices. The goal is to increase education, charitable giving, and home ownership, respectively. An alternative way to provide a subsidy is for the government to directly produce goods that are then given away or sold at a subsidized price, such as low-cost vaccinations and public higher education.

When negative externalities exist, taxes are often used to discourage activities that give rise to these externalities. So-called "sin taxes" have been levied on cigarettes, liquor, and other goods to increase the private cost of consuming these products. Recently, there have even been proposals to tax sugary sodas to reduce the negative externalities created by obesity. Whereas the amount of a good that a person consumes usually *increases* when there is a *subsidy*, the amount consumed usually *decreases* when a *tax* is introduced.

Consider how the regulatory approach to a negative externality differs from the tax approach. Think about the difference between instituting a ban on smoking in public places and placing high taxes on each pack of cigarettes purchased. Would you expect these two policies to yield the same outcome in terms of the amount of smoking that takes place in public? Do you think that smokers incur the same increase in private cost under both scenarios?

Using subsidies and taxes to address externality problems can be plagued with practical difficulties. To determine the optimal amount of a subsidy or tax requires extensive information about how members of society value the externality in terms of spillover benefits or costs. To complicate matters, the optimal tax or subsidy is likely to change over time. The government may decide, for example, that timber companies are overharvesting redwood forests from society's point of view. After all, it takes a long time to grow a mature redwood tree, and this species provides a source of recreational pleasure. To reduce the number of trees cut down, Congress might impose a tax on all redwood lumber products sold. However, wouldn't we want to rethink this tax if scientists reported that cut redwood trees are the only source of Taxol, a chemical that prevents the reoccurrence of breast cancer? In other words, what happens if the social costs or benefits from harvesting redwood trees change?

To illustrate this tricky balancing act, **Figure 5.5** compares the private and social costs of harvesting redwood trees. As you can see, before government intervention, the private marginal cost of harvesting trees is lower than its corresponding social cost. This results in overharvesting. Now suppose the government imposes a tax on each tree harvested. If the tax rate is optimal, it will shift the $MC_{private}$ curve upward so that it coincides with the MC_{social} curve. This leads to a decline in the number of

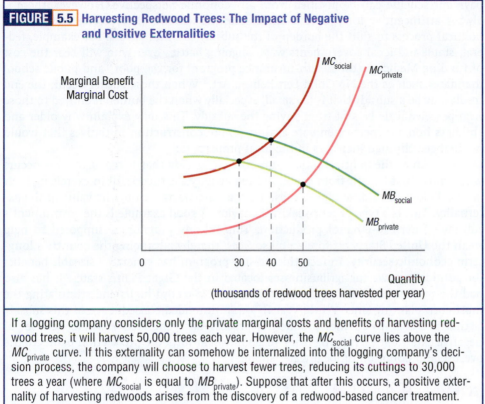

FIGURE 5.5 | Harvesting Redwood Trees: The Impact of Negative and Positive Externalities

If a logging company considers only the private marginal costs and benefits of harvesting red-wood trees, it will harvest 50,000 trees each year. However, the MC_{social} curve lies above the $MC_{private}$ curve. If this externality can somehow be internalized into the logging company's deci-sion process, the company will choose to harvest fewer trees, reducing its cuttings to 30,000 trees a year (where MC_{social} is equal to $MB_{private}$). Suppose that after this occurs, a positive exter-nality of harvesting redwoods arises from the discovery of a redwood-based cancer treatment. Then the social marginal benefit of harvesting trees will be greater than the private marginal ben-efit, and the MB_{social} curve will lie above the $MB_{private}$ curve. If this externality can be internalized into the logging company's decision process, then the number of trees harvested will increase from 30,000 to 40,000 trees a year (where the MB_{social} equals the MC_{social}).

trees that a company will cut down from 50,000 to 30,000 per year, which is the socially optimal level of harvesting.

Now let's consider what happens with the discovery of Taxol, which can only be derived from cut redwood trees. This discovery shifts the benefit curve upward to reflect the new social benefit (MB_{social}) of harvesting redwoods. The optimal number of trees harvested will now equal 40,000, which is more than the previously optimal number (30,000). To get to this new level of redwood consumption, part of the tax must be rescinded. In fact, depending on the value placed on the positive externality created by Taxol, the government may even be required to introduce a *subsidy* large enough to encourage even *more* redwood harvesting than had initially occurred prior to any government intervention in the redwood market.

This example shows that tax and subsidy programs may eventually lead to an allocation of scarce resources that *reduces* social well-being relative to a world without such intervention. The cost of dynamically adjusting taxes or subsidies when there is a change in the economic environment is simply too great to avoid this possibility.

When the government subsidizes an activity, these subsidies must be paid by someone, usually a subset of taxpayers or consumers. If the group that pays the subsidy is, by and large, the same group that receives the spillover benefits, then this payment scheme can be justified from an economic perspective. However, there is always an incentive for people to understate the benefits they receive and use the political process to shift the burden of the subsidy to other payers. For example, federal, state, and local governments wage ongoing battles over who will bear the cost of funding Medicaid (the health-insurance program for the poor) and public school mandates such as the No Child Left Behind Act.[8] When these battles occur, the end result may be a subsidy that is *too small,* especially when the burden is shifted to those who perceive little benefit from paying the subsidy. This may explain why older and childless home owners often vote against school construction initiatives that would be financed through increases in the local property tax.

Sometimes the political process produces a subsidy that is *too large.* This occurs when those that benefit from the subsidized activity are successful in exercising their political clout to achieve higher subsidies than are warranted by the value of the externality. This is a type of rent-seeking behavior. A good example is the government's subsidy of corn-to-ethanol production. This subsidy program is supposed to help wean the United States off foreign oil sources, thereby advancing the country's long-term economic security. In fact, this subsidy program has generated sizeable benefits for politically powerful agribusinesses located in the Great Plains states. It has also had the predictable effect of driving corn prices to record highs and stimulating the most corn planting since World War II.[9] An unintended consequence of this subsidy is that the corn-to-ethanol production process has generated a whole new set of negative externalities, ranging from air pollution around the production plants to the overuse and pollution of local water supplies.

SOLVED PROBLEM

Q In many states, there is a 5-cent deposit paid by people who buy milk, soft drinks, juice, beer, and other drinks packaged in plastic, aluminum, or glass containers. The purpose of this deposit is to encourage people to return their empty containers so that they can be recycled, thereby reducing the amount of litter in the streets and garbage dumped in landfills. (1) Using *MB* and *MC* curves, show the impact of this policy on the number of containers that a person will throw away. (2) Using *MB* and *MC* curves, show the impact of this policy on the number of containers that a person will return to collect her deposit. (3) Suppose that some consumers are simply too busy to return their containers and instead throw them away. If other people specialize in going through trash to reclaim these containers and return them for the deposit money, do these "trash divers" help or hinder the process of achieving the "right" amount of recycling? Explain your answer.

A Panel (a) of the following figures shows that the private marginal cost of throwing away a container increases due to the presence of a deposit that will be lost. This is shown by an upward shift in the $MC_{private}$ curve so that it approaches the MC_{social} curve in the figure. The result is a reduction in the number of containers thrown away, from ten to six each week.

At the same time, panel (b) shows that the $MB_{private}$ of returning a container for recycling increases because of the deposit it will yield. This leads to an upward shift in the $MB_{private}$ curve toward the MB_{social} curve, resulting in an increase in the number of containers returned to the store, from five to seven each week. The end result is that more containers will be recycled and fewer simply thrown away.

· · · · · · ·

[8]Sam Dillon, "Connecticut to Sue U.S. Over Cost of School Testing Law." *New York Times,* April 6, 2005.

[9]Andrew Martin, "Farmers Head to Fields to Plant Corn, Lots of It." *New York Times,* March 31, 2007.

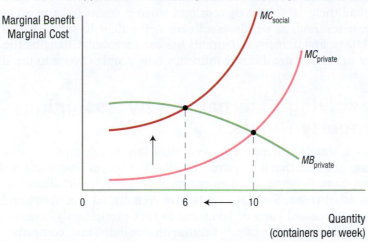

(a) Containers thrown away when a container deposit is introduced

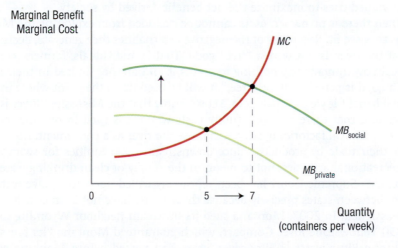

(b) Containers returned when a container deposit is introduced

"Trash divers" who dig through garbage to reclaim containers for the deposit money actually improve the process of internalizing the externality at hand. Their transaction costs are lower than those of the people who actually bought the containers because the value of the trash diver's time is lower. Therefore, they can specialize in delivering containers back to the store and ensuring that the "right" amount of recycling takes place.

Modifying Property Rights

Modifying property rights through legislative or judicial action can help internalize externalities. In the early 1900s, the property rights that parents held to their children were modified to prohibit most forms of child labor in the United States. These child-labor laws internalized a positive externality, namely the societal benefits created by sending children to school rather than to work on farms or in the factories.

Property rights have been modified to deal with a whole host of externalities. In some states, drivers under the age of 18 and over the age of 65 have had their driving rights limited to reduce traffic fatalities.[10,11] In the post-9/11 world, air travelers have had their rights severely restricted when it comes to carry-on baggage and security searches. And, as we discussed earlier, the right to smoke on airplanes, in public buildings, and in many restaurants has been revoked. Changing the allocation of property rights can significantly influence how people choose to use their scarce resources.

5.4 Resolving Externalities by Assigning Property Rights

In some cases, simply assigning a property right can remedy an externality situation. Take the case of a state that lies upstream on the Mississippi River that decides to construct a new dam. Building this dam can create negative externalities for states and water users downstream. Some geologists have even argued that upstream Mississippi River dams have caused parts of Louisiana to sink precipitously because they block the flow of sediment downstream.[12] Because no one individual, company, or political jurisdiction owns the entire Mississippi River, there is no one owner that can control the way this water resource is used. This means that the river may not be put to its highest valued uses to maximize the net benefit derived by society.

When there is no owner, users cannot be excluded from exploiting the Mississippi River as they see fit. Regardless of the negative externalities they generate, decision makers treat the river as if it were a "free" good. That is, individuals, farmers, companies, and local governments pay nothing to access it and are not limited in their use of it. When a good is perceived to be "free," it will be used up to the point where the private marginal benefit it yields equals zero. Yet we know that the Mississippi River is a scarce resource and that there are opportunity costs when it is used in one manner versus another. Chemical factories upstream that use the river as a convenient, no-cost dump site for their toxic by-products reduce downstream opportunities for swimming and other recreational activities, not to mention the supply of clean drinking water.

The U.S. Supreme Court has been repeatedly called upon to resolve water-rights disputes between states precisely because these rights have not been clearly and completely assigned. In 2007, Montana sued its upstream neighbor Wyoming to enforce the 1950 Yellowstone River Compact, which guaranteed Montana "its fair share" of Yellowstone River water.[13] Fifty-seven years had passed before Montana sought to have the Compact enforced. Why? The right to this downstream water became valuable only after Montana experienced exponential growth in commercial and residential development in the late 1990s.

If the Court rules that an upstream state has the legal right to do as it pleases with the river, then downstream states have two options. One is to pay the upstream states enough to assure adequate river water for drinking, irrigation, and other purposes. The other option is to simply do without some or all of this water. Conversely, if

· · · · · · ·

[10]Thomas Dee, et al., "Graduated Driver Licensing and Teen Traffic Fatalities." *Journal of Health Economics,* 24 (2005).

[11]Kathleen Murphy, "Elderly Drivers Pose Growing Challenge for States and Auto Insurers." *Insurance Journal* (May 17, 2004).

[12]"Is Louisiana Sinking? Dams on the Mississippi River Are Causing Parts of Louisiana to Sink as Much as Nine Inches a Year." *USA Today (Society for Advancement of Education),* August, 1997.

[13]"Montana Sues Wyoming in U.S. Supreme Court." Department of Justice, State of Montana, February 1, 2007.

the Court rules that downstream states have the right to enough water flow to meet agricultural and residential water needs, then upstream states would be required to compensate their downstream neighbors in some way if any of this water is diverted by their dams.

The problem is that negotiations between states over how the river water will actually be used will not take place until rights to the river are established. After these property rights are assigned, negotiations can begin to resolve how the river is ultimately used.

To see this, assume that the downstream states are awarded rights to the river and that the value they place on the water outweighs the value to upstream states from damming the river. In this case, any offer made by upstream states to obtain permission to dam the river will be rejected. If, instead, upstream states are awarded rights to the river, the offer made by downstream states should more than compensate them for not engaging in damming activities. Under either property-rights scenario, we expect the same outcome: dams will not be built upstream. The negotiation process reveals the value of the river water to downstream states versus the value placed on damming by upstream states.

These types of negotiations force the parties involved to consider offers to "buy" some or all of their water rights when they make decisions about how to ultimately use the river water. Refusing to accept an offer increases the opportunity cost of using the river exclusively for local purposes because the payment is an opportunity that is forgone when it is refused.

We can use our marginal benefit and marginal cost framework to illustrate the outcome of such negotiations. Panel (a) of **Figure 5.6** shows the optimal number of dams built by upstream states in a ten-year period when these states legally control the river. In this situation, an offer by downstream states to pay for a reduction in damming activities will cause the *MC* curve of damming activities to shift upward because refusing the offer adds to the opportunity cost of building dams. The end result is that upstream states will choose to build fewer dams and, instead, accept some of the money offered by the downstream states.

Now suppose that the Court gives the downstream states legal control over the river. These states have an interest in keeping the water flowing and substantially restricting upstate dam projects. If upstream states want to build dams, they must negotiate with the downstream states to do so. Payments offered by upstream states in exchange for permission to build dams will increase the downstream states' opportunity cost of saying "no" and maintaining unimpeded water flow. As panel (b) of Figure 5.6 shows, this will shift the downstream states' *MC* curve for water upward because the payments offered by the upstream states add to the opportunity cost of protecting the downstream water flow. The end result is that the level of water flowing unimpeded to downstream states will fall, and the downstream states will accept some of the money offered by their upstream neighbors.

Under either ownership scenario, the river will be put to its highest-valued use. The negative externalities that the states impose on each other will be internalized by all of the decision makers when such negotiations take place.

The Coase Theorem

Our Mississippi River example shows that a negotiated solution to an externality can be attained after property rights to the resource in question have been assigned. In theory, *when negotiations are costless,* this solution is socially optimal. That is, the scarce resource will be put to its highest-valued use to maximize the net social

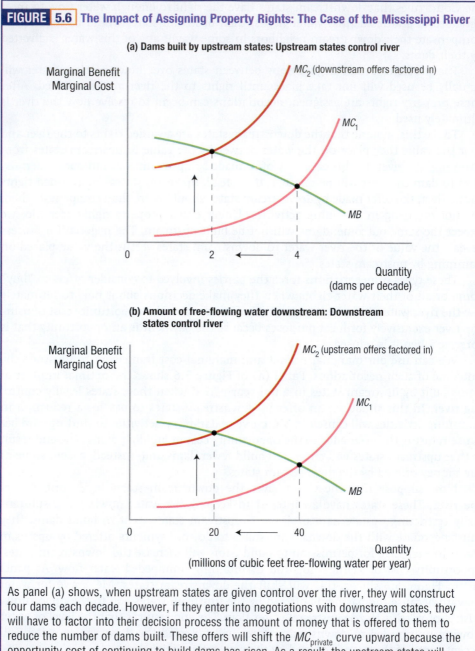

FIGURE 5.6 **The Impact of Assigning Property Rights: The Case of the Mississippi River**

(a) Dams built by upstream states: Upstream states control river

Marginal Benefit
Marginal Cost

MC_2 (downstream offers factored in)

MC_1

MB

0   2   ←   4

Quantity
(dams per decade)

(b) Amount of free-flowing water downstream: Downstream states control river

Marginal Benefit
Marginal Cost

MC_2 (upstream offers factored in)

MC_1

MB

0   20   ←   40

Quantity
(millions of cubic feet free-flowing water per year)

As panel (a) shows, when upstream states are given control over the river, they will construct four dams each decade. However, if they enter into negotiations with downstream states, they will have to factor into their decision process the amount of money that is offered to them to reduce the number of dams built. These offers will shift the $MC_{private}$ curve upward because the opportunity cost of continuing to build dams has risen. As a result, the upstream states will reduce the number of dams built from four to two each decade and accept payment from the downstream states for exercising this restraint. Panel (b) shows that when downstream states are given control over the river, the payments offered by the upstream states add to the opportunity cost of protecting the downstream water flow: this shifts the downstream states' $MC_{private}$ curve for water upward. The level of water flowing unimpeded to downstream states will fall as they accept some compensation from their upstream neighbors.

benefit to members of society. This was exactly the outcome we reached in our earlier example about the mother who converted her home into a safe haven for teenagers. Because there was no dispute over the right of the home owner to control the use of her home, parents were required to compensate her in some fashion to increase the hangout's hours of operation.

This type of negotiation and outcome was envisioned by Nobel Laureate Ronald Coase in his now famous article on the nature of social cost.[14] A key ingredient in the **Coase Theorem** is that property rights must be clearly spelled out for an externality to be internalized through subsequent negotiation. The Coase Theorem also says that it doesn't matter which party is given the right to control the resource that is generating the externality—the same socially optimal use will result as long as all parties to the externality can subsequently engage in negotiations.

> **COASE THEOREM** Regardless of which party is given the property rights to a scarce resource that is creating an externality, the same socially optimal use of that resource will result as long as all parties to the externality can negotiate with each other at low cost.

In our Mississippi River example, the Coase Theorem says that the number of dams and the amount of water flowing downstream will be the same regardless of whether the upstream or downstream states are granted control over the river, *as long as negotiations between the parties can take place.*

The essence of the Coase Theorem underlies recent efforts to address the greenhouse effects and potential climate change resulting from industrial pollution. As we have already discussed, the success of cap-and-trade proposals introduced in the United States in 2009 requires an initial assignment of pollution rights—in terms of type and amount of each particulate—to each company and a subsequent market in which these rights can be bought and sold. The goal is for those producers who "value" pollution rights the highest—perhaps because alternative, nonpolluting production technologies are nonexistent or extremely costly—to purchase and accumulate these rights. At the same time, those businesses that can switch to less-polluting technologies at relatively low cost will receive sufficient compensation from selling their pollution rights to cover this transition.

One of Coase's most important contributions is to make clear that *it takes two (or more) parties to create an externality*: there is no "right and wrong" party to an externality. This means that smokers are no more "guilty" of creating an externality than nonsmokers. Indeed, there would be no externality at all if a smoker landed on a deserted island or lived in a country where everybody smoked. It is only after property rights are assigned that encroachment on them without permission leads to legal penalties.

If Coase's Theorem holds up, then why does it matter who gets control over the Mississippi River or other scarce resources in the first place? After all, we will get the same number of dams and water flowing downstream. The answer is that the initial assignment of property rights creates *wealth effects*. Specifically, the assignment of rights dictates which party to the externality must pay the other in the negotiation process to achieve its objectives. Do upstream users have to compensate downstream users to continue building dams? Or must downstream users compensate upstream states to assure an adequate flow of water downstream?

· · · · · · ·

[14]Ronald Coase, "The Problem of Social Cost." *Journal of Law and Economics,* 1 (1960).

As long as property rights remain unassigned, we have situations that are ripe for unresolved externalities. A 1992 court case illustrates this point. The Tennessee Supreme Court was asked to rule on an unusual property dispute arising in an otherwise typical divorce proceeding. Earlier in their marriage, a couple had voluntarily pursued infertility treatment, which led to the creation of fertilized eggs that were frozen for future use. The judges were asked to decide which of the divorcing partners "owned" these eggs. Was it the ex-wife, who argued that this might be her last viable option for having children? Or was it the ex-husband, who argued that using these eggs would impose a cost on him by forcing him to become a father?

Ultimately, the court ruled that the ex-wife could not use the eggs *without* her ex-husband's permission and that these eggs should be kept frozen "pending the couple's possible future meeting of the minds."[15] Legal rights to the eggs were now clearly defined and assigned, at least in the state of Tennessee. Since this decision, the Supreme Courts of Massachusetts and New Jersey have followed Tennessee's lead and ruled that a person cannot force an ex-spouse to become a parent against his will.

The Tennessee ruling clearly envisioned the possibility that the couple would continue to negotiate over how the eggs would actually be used. Assuming that such negotiations were costless, an outcome consistent with the Coase Theorem might be one in which the ex-wife agrees to put sufficient funds into an escrow account to cover future child-support claims, omit the ex-husband's name from the birth certificate, or waive all or part of her divorce settlement to offset the negative externality resulting from her use of the eggs. The ex-husband would then have the right to approve her use of the eggs under these terms or refuse the offer. Whether he accepts or rejects the offer, the very existence of the offer causes the ex-husband to take into account the value that the ex-wife places on using the eggs to have children. The offer does so by increasing his opportunity cost of keeping the eggs from his ex-wife.

The important point here is that until the legal right to the eggs was decided, these negotiations would not have taken place. As long as the ex-wife considered the eggs to be hers, there was no reason for her to offer her ex-husband any deal, unless it was simply to avoid the possibility of incurring high legal bills. Similarly, there was no reason for the ex-husband to negotiate with his ex-wife over use of the eggs as long as he believed that he had the legal right to them. By clearly assigning the rights to the eggs, the court broke this logjam and opened the way for negotiations to take place.

There are some instances, however, in which assigning property rights will not successfully internalize an externality. Suppose it is so costly to bring all of the parties to the negotiation "table" that these costs outweigh any benefit that would be realized from internalizing the externality. When this is the case, the initial allocation of property rights is likely to dictate the way in which the scarce resource is used. In our previous example, the frozen fertilized eggs would not be used, despite the real possibility that the resulting well-being enjoyed by the ex-wife is greater than the cost borne by the ex-husband.

5.5 How Good Is the Government at Solving Externality Problems?

Government policies aimed at resolving externalities are meant to improve on the decisions that individuals make about the allocation of their scarce resources. The success of such policies depends on their ability to get people to take into account

·······

[15]*David v. David*, 842 S.W. 2d 588 (Tenn. 1992).

the spillover costs and benefits they generate. This will more often be the case if the following conditions are met:

- Low-cost information is available to accurately approximate the spillover costs or benefits generated by each person's choices. Without this information, it is unlikely that a tax or subsidy would be set at an appropriate level to accurately internalize the externality. Consider the fact that many state-highway patrols issue speeding tickets with fines that vary depending on how far over the speeding limit a person is driving. Do these fines accurately reflect the increase in spillover costs resulting from higher and higher speeds? If they do, then they will encourage drivers to slow down to a socially optimal speed level; if not, then traffic may end up traveling at a suboptimal rate of speed.

- The source of an externality can be identified and targeted at low cost so that the externality is fully internalized and socially optimal choices are made. In 1990, the northern spotted owl was added to the threatened species list by the U.S. Fish and Wildlife Service, which led to a virtual ban on logging in older federal forests in the Pacific Northwest. In economic terms, the logging ban meant that the social marginal cost of logging even one tree in the federal forests—in terms of the risk to the spotted owl—was greater than the private marginal benefit of harvesting that tree. Loggers lost jobs, sawmills closed, and towns built up around the logging industry experienced massive economic declines. Twenty years later, this ban is still in effect, and still the northern spotted owl population is declining at a rate of about 3 percent per year in the region and as much as 9 percent per year in the state of Washington. It turns out that a competing species—the barred owl—and the spotted owls' highly restrictive diet of wood rats and flying squirrels, are the primary culprits leading to its extinction.[16]

- Interest groups are unable (at low cost) to "capture" a policy that is aimed at resolving an externality and exploit it to improve their own economic well-being instead. A good example is the licensing of taxicabs in most cities. Local authorities license taxicabs presumably to ensure that cab vehicles and drivers are safe. However, taxicab owners have successfully lobbied to limit the number of licenses granted, ostensibly to promote public safety. Many would argue that the end result has been too few licensed cabs and higher taxicab fares.

- Interest groups are unable (at low cost) to capitalize on the existence of relatively small externalities to justify policies that primarily increase their own economic well-being. For example, U.S. pharmacies and drug companies have lobbied to block Americans from buying drugs from Canada and Europe. The companies argue that the safety of these drugs cannot be assured, thereby creating a negative externality in terms of compromising public safety. Does the magnitude of this potential spillover cost justify prohibiting drug imports, or is this just a way to increase the returns to U.S. drug companies and pharmacies?

- The judicial or legislative process can assign and enforce property rights at low cost. You have already learned that assigning a property right can help resolve an externality problem. However, enforcing this right might be so costly that the externality remains unresolved. For example, consider the

---

[16]William Yardley, "20 Years Later, a Plan to Save Spotted Owls." *New York Times,* July 1, 2011, p.1.

cost of ensuring a home owner's right to peace and quiet when there are multiple bars and restaurants just around the corner whose patrons create a noise externality. Or consider the cost of strictly enforcing a hands-free cell-phone law for drivers to increase road safety and reduce road deaths. Sometimes the cost of enforcing people's rights ends up outweighing the spillover costs or benefits of an externality.

Economists can help formulate policies that try to address externalities. A key contribution of economists is that they identify situations in which private and social costs differ or private and social benefits diverge. After an externality is identified, economists are often called on to put a monetary value on the spillover benefits or costs. Economists may also be asked to analyze how successful a proposed government policy is likely to be and what its impact will be on people affected by the externality. For example, what is the cost to the steel industry and its employees of a cap-and-trade carbon-emissions system? What is the cost to car buyers of more stringent pollution-emissions standards or breathalizers to reduce drunk driving? What is the benefit to be had by nonsmokers if smoking is banned in public buildings?

WHAT YOU SHOULD HAVE LEARNED FROM CHAPTER 5

- That there are often more than just private costs and benefits resulting from our decisions.
- That when others receive benefits from a person's choices, positive externalities arise, and when others are adversely affected by a person's choices, negative externalities are created.
- That society may attempt to "internalize" externalities through regulations, tax and subsidy programs, and the reallocation of property rights.
- That in certain circumstances, defining property rights internalizes externalities by providing the foundation for negotiations and trade between involved parties.
- That the existence of high transaction costs can hinder negotiations to internalize externalities, even when property rights are clearly defined.
- That it may be difficult to identify the source of an externality so that spillover effects can be internalized to the appropriate decision maker.
- That government policies aimed at addressing externality problems may also become vehicles for vested interests to engage in rent-seeking activities to increase their own well-being at a cost to others.

KEY TERMS

Private cost, p. 102

Private benefit, p. 102

Social cost, p. 102

Social benefit, p. 102

Positive externality, p. 106

Negative externality, p. 107

Coase Theorem, p. 119

QUESTIONS AND PROBLEMS

1. Which of the following choices creates a negative or positive externality? Explain your answer.

   a) Driving without your seat belt fastened
   b) Opening a kiosk in the mall to sell jewelry, right outside a jewelry store
   c) Disconnecting the fire alarm in your frat house

    d) Taking the last piece of cake

    e) Wiping off the table after you have finished eating

    f) Taking your coworker's lunch from the refrigerator and eating it

2. Opponents of convenience "wipes" argue that these disposables are detrimental to the environment. Using *MB* and *MC* curves, show the impact on an individual's quantity of wipes consumed each year if the government:

    a) imposes a tax on wipes.

    b) imposes a quota on wipes.

    c) provides a subsidy for using biodegradable cleaning solutions instead.

3. Suppose that environmentalists are successful in their effort to ban fishing off the eastern shores of the United States. Using *MB* and *MC* curves, show the resulting impact on an individual's quantity consumed of:

    a) U.S. harvested fish.

    b) imported fish.

    c) chicken.

4. A classic example of a positive externality relates to the neighborhood beekeeper, whose bees pollinate the nearby apple orchard for free as they fly around looking for nectar to make honey. The story goes that there will be too few bees from an economic standpoint because the beekeeper enjoys only the benefits from the honey produced by his bees, not the benefits reaped from pollination. Explain how a "market" in pollination might work and how property rights could be enforced in such a situation.

5. Several years ago, in an effort to reduce acid rain, the EPA allocated "pollution allowances" to manufacturers emitting sulfur dioxide and nitrogen oxide. These pollution permits capped each company's maximum annual level of emissions. The EPA allowed those companies that did not meet their maximum level of emissions to sell the balance of their allowance to other producers in the form of "pollution credits." Do you think that the pollution-credit market improved or reduced the effectiveness of the pollution-permit program in achieving an optimal level of acid rain? Explain your answer.

6. In most Western countries, there is a law in place requiring that children be vaccinated against such communicable diseases as polio and smallpox. If, in fact, each person benefits from getting vaccinated, and there are only small risks of doing so, why is it necessary to *require* people to get vaccinated (assume that the vaccines are offered free of charge by local public-health agencies)? Explain your answer.

7. The federal government's Pell Grant program reduces the private cost of attending college for many students.

    a) What spillover benefits do you think are created by having more college-educated people in our society?

    b) Do you believe that this is the reason that college subsidies exist?

    c) Given your answers in (a) and (b), how would you explain the fact that government subsidies for college education have declined considerably over the past decade? Explain your answer.

8. When do you think it makes sense to totally ban an economic good or activity? Illustrate your answer using $MB_{private}$ and MB_{social} curves and $MC_{private}$ and MC_{social} curves.

9. Suppose a group of home owners files a lawsuit against a neighborhood pig farm, claiming that the smells are overwhelming and are reducing the value of their homes. If you were the judge in this case, to whom would you award the contested property right? Would it matter to you "who was there first?" Explain your answer. What factors might you take into account in making your ruling?

10. An interesting type of property right is an "air right," which permits real-estate owners to buy control over the use of airspace above or next to their structures.

Discuss how a market in these air rights compares, from an economic point of view, to more traditional government-regulatory approaches (such as zoning) in internalizing the negative externality that can arise when new buildings are erected that block the views of existing neighborhood structures.

11. You are quietly sitting under a tree at a local park, enjoying the newest novel by your favorite mystery writer. All of a sudden, a large family with noisy kids spreads its picnic blanket a stone's throw away. How does this situation illustrate Coase's argument that "it takes two to make an externality?" How would you resolve this externality? What does this resolution imply about the allocation of property rights to this spot in the park?

12. Many negative externalities—such as secondhand smoke or air pollution—jeopardize people's health and increase their risk of dying at an early age. Discuss how you would put a dollar value on these spillover costs so that a policy maker could impose the socially optimal tax on choices that generate these externalities.

13. During the Great Recession of 2007, consumers cut back on their purchases of environmentally friendly "green" products, such as recycled-paper products and biodegradable cleaning supplies. What, if anything, does this behavior tell you about the social benefit of preserving the environment? More specifically, does it vary over time depending on economic circumstances? Explain your answer.

14. In 2011, California Governor Jerry Brown signed into law the Renewable Energy Act, which requires that at least one-third of the state's electricity come from renewable sources, such as wind and the sun, by 2020. Although these sources of energy are renewable at virtually zero cost, it turns out that it takes a lot of land, steel, and other resources to convert them into readily accessible electricity. How, if at all, should these costs have factored into Governor Brown's decision to sign the Renewable Energy Act?

PART 2

From Individual Choices to Market Outcomes

Whether we are consumers or producers of a good or service, we can usually improve on our own well-being by engaging in some form of economic exchange. There are "gains from trade" to be had when buyers and sellers meet face-to-face, online, or through representatives to exchange goods and services. These trades take place in markets. Markets can have a physical location—such as weekly farmers' markets and the New York Stock Exchange—or they can be "virtual"—such as NASDAQ, eBay, and Amazon.

In Part 2, we show how people's individual economic choices provide the foundation upon which markets operate. We develop a supply-and-demand framework to predict the price at which a good is exchanged as well as the total amount of the good that is traded in the market. Based on this approach, we can predict how changes in the economic environment are likely to affect these prices and quantities; how gains from trade are shared between buyers and sellers; and how some government policies—such as price controls—can lead to unintentional and sometimes adverse market outcomes that ultimately reduce people's well-being.

Willingness to Pay and the Demand for Goods and Services

"People are always making a fuss over my $15-20 million salaries. Believe me, the amount is meaningless once my wife finds out about it. She's already spent half of my salary from Terminator 7!"

Arnold Schwarzenegger, actor and former governor of California

So far, we have looked at how to apply our marginal benefit and marginal cost framework of analysis to the everyday economic decisions we all face. We have come quite far in our ability to make predictions about people's choices using this relatively simple approach. These predictions focused on whether a person's consumption of a good would be likely to increase or decrease when there is a specific change in the economic environment.

However, we have sidestepped the question of how we would actually value the benefit that a person receives from each unit of a specific good or service. This measurement question is not easy to resolve. After all, how do we measure happiness, security, satisfaction, pleasure, comfort, or convenience? Yet each of these feelings can be an important component of the well-being we get from allocating our scarce resources in a particular way.

People somehow manage to intuitively value the economic benefit they would derive from each alternative they consider. We see this when it comes to the purchasing decisions that people make. Have you ever chosen to pay more for Reese's peanut butter than the Safeway brand? Somehow, you've decided that the extra money is "worth" spending on Reese's rather than spending it on something else. If we are to spend our money in a way that maximizes our sense of well-being, we must be able to value the options at hand.

When people decide how much they are willing to pay for each unit of a particular good, they have, in effect, "monetized" the benefit they will receive from each unit. This gives them a basis upon which to decide how much, if any, of the good to purchase. Even when people barter one good for another—shoes for dental work, math tutoring for a meal, and so forth—each party to the trade must somehow value the benefits he expects to receive to compare them to the opportunity cost of what he will be giving up in the exchange.

6.1 Willingness to Pay and Reservation Price

People often enjoy different amounts of well-being from the same good because of differences in preferences and in the availability of alternatives. There is no reason to believe, for example, that you and your parents get the same economic benefit from attending the symphony or the latest Black Eyed Peas concert. This means that even when two people have the same income, different tastes will likely lead to differences in their **willingness to pay** for a particular good.

> **WILLINGNESS TO PAY** The maximum amount of money that a person is willing and able to pay for each unit of a good.

> **EXAMPLE** A person who lives on a 300-acre farm is likely to be willing to pay more for a John Deere riding lawn mower than a person who lives in an apartment in New York City.
>
> **EXAMPLE** Meat eaters are willing to pay substantially more for a McDonald's Quarter Pounder than vegetarians.

Economists sometimes refer to your willingness to pay as your **reservation price**.

> **RESERVATION PRICE** Willingness to pay; the maximum amount that a person is willing and able to pay for each unit of a good.

Suppose that the only cost of making a purchase is the price of the good: that is, transportation, information, and other transaction costs are negligible. When this is the case, a person's reservation price equals the monetary value she places on the economic benefits she derives from the good. This means that when the good's price exactly equals this reservation price, the *net* benefit the consumer receives (value of benefits − price) equals zero. She would be *indifferent* to buying the good or not. If the good's price is greater than her reservation price, then the net benefit resulting from buying the good is negative. A rational decision maker would walk away without making a purchase in this case.

There have been numerous studies of people's willingness to pay for a variety of goods and services. Recently, researchers estimated the amount that parents would pay to protect their children and grandchildren from the effects of global warming. People were asked how much more money they would be willing to pay for their electricity service each month to cover the costs of significantly reducing greenhouse gases, which have been linked to climate change. Although the answers varied a great deal, the majority of respondents were indifferent to addressing the problem of global warming when the cost they would bear exceeded $18.75 per month.[1]

ECONOMIC FALLACY   People's willingness to pay to extend their lives an additional day is infinite.

False. We know from observing people's behavior that they often make choices that increase their risk of dying. They drive at high speeds, step out into streets, ride roller-coasters, smoke, and actively engage in other risky activities. This means

• • • • • • •

[1]"The Indifference Point on Global Warming." *St. Louis Post-Dispatch,* June 30, 2009.

that the value they place on living an additional day is not infinite—they are willing to incur some probability of dying in return for the net benefit that risky activities generate. Although it is true that a large percentage of total medical outlays take place in the final six months of a person's life, we cannot take this as a sign that the willingness to pay to continue living is infinite. After all, these end-of-life costs are typically paid by insurance companies or the government, not the patient or his family.

Willingness to Pay Implies Ability to Pay

When economists talk about *willingness to pay,* they are actually talking only about instances in which this willingness can be translated into an actual payment. That is, a person must not only be willing but also able to pay for the good or service desired. Although you might place a high dollar value on the benefits of owning a Porsche Boxster, your *willingness to pay* from an economic standpoint equals the amount you can actually hand over for the car. The fact that our ability to pay for some desired purchases often falls short explains why sellers frequently offer attractive financing plans to help buyers purchase such big-ticket items as homes and cars.

Diminishing Marginal Benefit and Willingness to Pay

An interesting question to ask is whether someone's willingness to pay for the first unit of a good differs from his willingness to pay for the second unit of the same good. What about his willingness to pay for the third unit of the good?

Consistent with the principle of diminishing marginal benefit—which says that the benefit a person gets from the first unit of a good is greater than from the second unit, which is greater than the benefit enjoyed from the third unit—it would make sense that a person's willingness to pay declines as he acquires more and more of a good. Another way to put this is that the **marginal willingness to pay** for each additional unit consumed declines.

> **MARGINAL WILLINGNESS TO PAY** The maximum willingness to pay for each additional unit of a good.

> **EXAMPLE** You may be willing to pay $11 to see a long-awaited movie at your local theater but only $6 to see it again with friends.

> **EXAMPLE** On a hot summer day, you may be willing to pay $4.25 for a 32-ounce soft drink at the ball game but only $1 for a refill.

In **Figure 6.1**, we graphically show someone's willingness to pay for each hot dog purchased from a street vendor during a weekend visit to New York City. The vertical axis represents the visitor's willingness to pay—her reservation price—for *each and every* hot dog.

We adopt the convention here of using a small letter q to represent the quantity demanded by one consumer. Later in this chapter, we use a capital Q to represent the total quantity demanded by all consumers in a market.

We see in Figure 6.1 that there is an inverse relationship between each hot dog's reservation price and the total number of hot dogs consumed. That is, the reservation price for an additional hot dog is less than for the one before. This is why the graph shown in Figure 6.1 is downward sloping. The principle of diminishing marginal benefit "guarantees" this result.

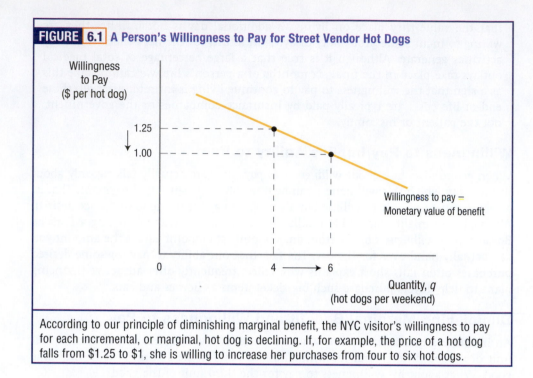

FIGURE 6.1 A Person's Willingness to Pay for Street Vendor Hot Dogs

According to our principle of diminishing marginal benefit, the NYC visitor's willingness to pay for each incremental, or marginal, hot dog is declining. If, for example, the price of a hot dog falls from $1.25 to $1, she is willing to increase her purchases from four to six hot dogs.

Let's say that our tourist can buy as many hot dogs as she wants at $1.25, the going price charged by NYC street vendors. At this price, we see that she will buy a total of four hot dogs during her weekend stay. We know this because her reservation price for each of the first three hot dogs is greater than $1.25, the price that she must actually pay for each hot dog. But when it comes to the fourth hot dog, her reservation price of $1.25 is just equal to the price she must pay, which means that the fourth hot dog yields zero *net* benefit. Therefore, the buyer is *indifferent* to consuming the fourth hot dog. We know with certainty that she will not buy any more hot dogs beyond the fourth hot dog because her reservation price for these additional hot dogs is less than $1.25, resulting in a negative net benefit.

You have seen this type of economic decision making before. If the only cost of purchasing a good is its price, then this is the marginal cost (*MC*) of consuming each unit. And, if the willingness to pay for each unit is the "monetized" value of the benefit received, then this will represent the marginal benefit (*MB*) derived from each unit. Applying our previously developed model of economic choice, we expect that a person will maximize the net benefits she receives by consuming a particular good up to the point where the price of that good is just equal to the willingness to pay—the reservation price—for the last unit purchased.

What would happen if the price of hot dogs dropped from $1.25 to $1? We see that our buyer will buy two additional hot dogs over the weekend—for a total of six during her NYC visit—because her reservation price for the fifth hot dog is greater than $1 and just equal to $1 for the sixth hot dog. Now she is indifferent about the sixth hot dog. As this result suggests, there is an *inverse* relationship between a good's price and the quantity that a person will buy: when price falls, the quantity purchased will typically increase, as long as nothing else changes.

How Convenience Affects a Consumer's Reservation Price

In reality, we know that a good's price often represents only a portion of the total cost that a buyer will incur in making a purchase. There are likely to be other costs—both explicit and implicit—that must be factored in when a buyer sets his reservation price. A Boxster buyer, for example, is likely to incur costs beyond the car's $50,000 price tag. These include the opportunity cost of the time invested in researching alternative sports cars and dealer inventories, as well as the time spent negotiating a deal. And then there are the sales taxes and higher insurance premium the buyer will pay when he switches from his old car to the Boxster.

When such transaction costs exist, we expect that a buyer will reduce his reservation price by the amount of these additional costs. Why? Suppose the maximum you are willing to pay to attend an upcoming concert is $100. Let's say the city in which the concert is being held decides to charge each ticket holder a $5 gate entry fee to pay for the extra security provided for the event. How much would you now be willing to pay for the ticket itself? $95. In other words, your reservation price for a ticket drops by the amount of other costs incurred in making the purchase. The same thing happens when you have to pay shipping on an Amazon.com purchase: you are willing to pay less for the item itself than if there was free shipping.

This tells us that there is an inherent trade-off between your reservation price and other costs incurred in making a purchase. In fact, you can see this trade-off reflected in people's everyday decisions. Think of how many people you know who purchase bottles of soda or water from on-campus machines at a far higher price than if these were purchased at the supermarket. The fact that these on-campus purchases are made tells us that the willingness to pay for these drinks is at least equal to the higher price that is being charged. Does this behavior make economic sense?

On-campus machines are convenient and readily accessible between classes; they eliminate the costs of running to a convenience store off campus. Therefore, students who drink bottled soda or water are willing to pay more for the on-campus drinks. In other words, they will pay more to avoid other transaction costs, in this case, the time required to drive off campus, park the car, stand in the checkout line, find a new parking spot on campus, and so on. This is the same reason that many people—especially those who place a high value on their time—are willing to pay additional "handling fees" to buy concert tickets online rather than standing in line at the box office window or redialing Ticketmaster for hours on end. What we are saying is what you already know—convenience comes at a price.

Suppose, for example, that buyers had to wait in long lines for upwards of 30 minutes to purchase hot dogs from a NYC hot dog street vendor. Our hot dog consumer's willingness to pay for each hot dog purchased will fall, reflecting the additional time costs incurred to purchase each hot dog. She will now purchase fewer hot dogs at the going price of $1.25 because her reservation price for each hot dog has dropped.

What if, instead, street vendors agreed to deliver the hot dogs to your hotel? We would expect our buyer's reservation price for each hot dog to increase—especially in the most bitter winter months—as shown in **Figure 6.2**. At $1.25, more hot dogs are now purchased.

On a much larger scale, we have seen the willingness to pay for convenience soar as the value of people's time has increased. This has been most noticeable with the trend toward greater workforce participation by women during the latter half of the twentieth century. People's willingness to pay for a range of goods and services—dry cleaning, child care, frozen and microwaveable foods, and so on—has increased. Families are now willing to pay more to lessen the amount of time they must devote

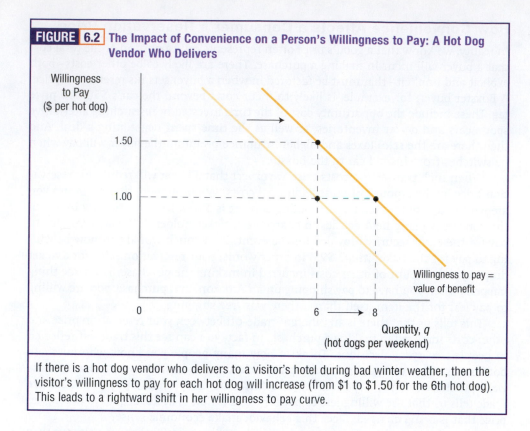

FIGURE 6.2 The Impact of Convenience on a Person's Willingness to Pay: A Hot Dog Vendor Who Delivers

If there is a hot dog vendor who delivers to a visitor's hotel during bad winter weather, then the visitor's willingness to pay for each hot dog will increase (from $1 to $1.50 for the 6th hot dog). This leads to a rightward shift in her willingness to pay curve.

to maintaining their households. Many of the most successful product innovations in recent decades have capitalized on our growing willingness to pay to save time; these include electric toothbrushes and dishwashers; fast-food and pharmacy drive-throughs; iPhones; individually packaged cookies and chips; and Jiffy Lube no-wait car maintenance. Taking advantage of this trend, some doctors have even introduced "concierge" medicine where, for a few thousand dollars a year, patients are seen immediately without having to wait or schedule an appointment months in advance.

In conclusion, then, a person's willingness to pay for a good will increase when the transaction costs of making the purchase fall. This means that more of the good will be purchased at any given price.

6.2 Deriving a Person's Demand Curve

Our analysis of willingness to pay tells us that a person will decide whether to buy a good and, if so, how much to buy based on a comparison between his reservation price and the good's price. This doesn't mean that everyone gets out their calculator or fires up a special "app" on their iPhones before buying lunch or chewing gum, but the idea is that we do, using some internal calculator, act *as if* we are comparing our willingness to pay to the prices we face. This comparison establishes a relationship between a person's reservation price and a good's price, as well as the **quantity** of the good that is **demanded**.

QUANTITY DEMANDED The number of units of a good that a person is willing and able to buy at a specific price.

EXAMPLE When the round-trip airfare from Los Angeles to Washington, D.C. is $350, you are willing to buy three round-trip tickets a year.

EXAMPLE When the price of gasoline is $3 a gallon, you are willing to fill up your tank (16 gallons) once a week.

Notice that quantity demanded is measured in *physical units*—that is, number of trips, gallons, and so on. The units that we use to measure quantity—for example, whether we count up one-way trips or round-trips demanded—will have an obvious impact on the number of units you demand. In the first example, you demanded three round-trip tickets a year, which is the equivalent of six one-way tickets when the round-trip airfare is $350.

We must also specify the time over which the quantity is demanded. Say that you purchase 4 pizzas a month when they cost $9 each. You are likely to purchase somewhere around 48 pizzas a *year* at the same price. This tells us that the quantity demanded of a good or service typically increases the longer the period in question.

Suppose we can collect information on the quantity of some good—say, gasoline—that you would demand at different prices. We assume that nothing else changes except for the good's price, so we can attribute any changes in your quantity demanded to price alone. We call this your **demand** for the good.

DEMAND Quantity demanded at *each and every* price, assuming that all else remains unchanged.

EXAMPLE When the round-trip airfare from Los Angeles to Washington, D.C. is $350, you are willing to buy three round-trip tickets a year. When the fare drops to $250, you are willing to buy five round-trip tickets. And when the fare is $450, you are willing to buy two round-trip tickets.

EXAMPLE When the price of gasoline is $3 a gallon, you use up one tank (16 gallons) of gas a week. When the price drops to $2 a gallon, you use up two tanks of gas a week. And when it rises to $5 a gallon, you use up only one tank of gas a month.

We can represent the demand for a good by creating a **demand schedule** that shows the quantity demanded at each and every price.

DEMAND SCHEDULE A table that shows the quantity demanded at each and every price.

Table 6.1 shows the number of courses that Janet, a college student, is willing to "buy" each semester. We see that as the price of a course drops, she will enroll in more classes each semester. Why does this make sense? Notice that Janet's willingness to pay for each additional course is falling; a direct result of our principle of diminishing marginal benefit. Therefore, the price of a course must also drop to entice Janet to take another class. If, instead, the price per course were to rise, say from $600 to $900, Janet will reduce the number of courses she takes each semester from four to three because her willingness to pay for the fourth course is less than $900.

Table 6.1	Janet's Demand Schedule for College Courses
Price per Course	Number of Courses Demanded per Semester
$1,500	1
1,200	2
900	3
600	4

We can graph Janet's demand schedule to arrive at her **demand curve**.

DEMAND CURVE A graphical representation of a demand schedule. The demand curve plots various price–quantity combinations that a buyer is willing to accept.

Figure 6.3 is a graphical depiction of the data in Table 6.1. By convention, the price per unit of the good is on the vertical axis, and the number of units, or quantity demanded (q) by a single consumer, is on the horizontal axis.

Even though this graph is called a demand "curve," it is often depicted as a straight line. The actual shape of a person's demand curve depends on how he responds to price changes in terms of changes in quantity demanded. Irrespective of its actual shape, a demand curve must always slope downward because, as we've already shown, a person's willingness to pay for each additional unit declines. So when the price of a good goes down, you are willing to buy more of it, and when its price goes up, you are willing to buy less of it, as long as nothing else changes.

LAW OF DEMAND The price of a good and the quantity demanded are inversely related. When price rises, the quantity demanded falls, and when price falls, the quantity demanded rises, assuming that nothing else has changed.

FIGURE 6.3 Demand Curve for College Courses

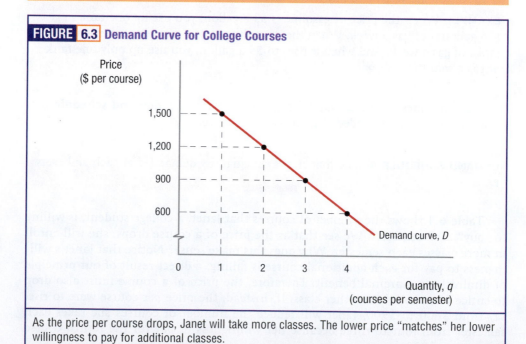

As the price per course drops, Janet will take more classes. The lower price "matches" her lower willingness to pay for additional classes.

The points shown in Figure 6.3 are the four price and quantity demanded pairs taken from Table 6.1. But, instead of just showing the demand relationship as these distinct points, we can connect the "dots." That is, we can introduce additional price and quantity demanded combinations so that the graph becomes increasingly smooth.

The demand curve reveals two very important pieces of information. If we pick a value for the quantity demanded, the *height* of the demand curve at this point represents Janet's willingness to pay for the very last, or marginal, unit demanded. For example, if we read *up* to the demand curve at three courses a semester, we see that Janet's willingness to pay for a third course is $900. We know this must be the case because she is willing to enroll in this third course at a price of $900.

If, instead, we read *over* to the demand curve from the vertical price axis at $900, we can read off the *total* quantity (three courses) that Janet demands at this price. In other words, Janet will enroll in courses up to the point where the price per class is just equal to her willingness to pay.

Movements along the Demand Curve

We have demonstrated that when the price of a course increases, Janet will enroll in fewer courses each semester. When the price goes down, she will enroll in a greater number of classes. Once again, this is because of the diminishing marginal benefit that Janet receives from each additional course. Janet's response to a change in price, assuming nothing else has changed, is to move up or down her demand curve. This is referred to as a **movement along her demand curve**.

> **MOVEMENT ALONG THE DEMAND CURVE** Increase or decrease in quantity demanded when only the price of the good changes.
>
> **EXAMPLE** While you typically download five songs a day to your MP3 player when the price per song is $2, you increase your number of downloads to eight a day when the price per download drops to $1. You have moved *down* your demand curve for downloaded music in response to the price change (assuming nothing else has changed).
>
> **EXAMPLE** When the price of pedicures is $13, your sister gets one every week. When the price increases to $18, she cuts back to one every other week. She has moved *up* her demand curve for pedicures in response to the price change (assuming nothing else has changed).

6.3 Movements along a Demand Curve versus Shifts in the Curve

We have already noted that even when people have the same income, they are unlikely to have the same willingness to pay for a particular good. This means that the demand curve for a specific good will likely differ across individuals. For example, when it comes to new cars, people who do not have a driver's license—perhaps due to a medical condition or age—have a reservation price of zero and will not purchase even one car no matter what the price. Another person with 17-year-old triplets in her household is likely to be willing to pay a substantial amount for one or more cars. Still others, such as people living in New York City, enjoy low-cost, convenient mass transit and will have a relatively low reservation price for a car. As these situations demonstrate, the willingness to pay for cars depends on many factors.

Suppose we compare the demand curves for weekly child care for a household where both adults work versus one in which only one adult works, assuming that the total household income is the same for both families. Arguably, a family's willingness to pay for each hour of child care is greater when both adults work. We can illustrate this in **Figure 6.4**. In panel (a), we show each family's willingness to pay each week for child care. Panel (b) translates these results into each family's demand curve for

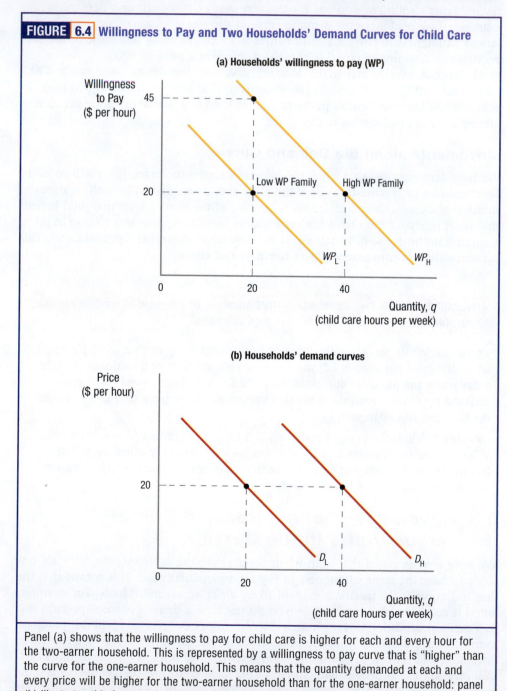

FIGURE **6.4** Willingness to Pay and Two Households' Demand Curves for Child Care

(a) Households' willingness to pay (WP)

Willingness to Pay ($ per hour)

Low WP Family   High WP Family

WP_L WP_H

Quantity, q
(child care hours per week)

(b) Households' demand curves

Price ($ per hour)

D_L D_H

Quantity, q
(child care hours per week)

Panel (a) shows that the willingness to pay for child care is higher for each and every hour for the two-earner household. This is represented by a willingness to pay curve that is "higher" than the curve for the one-earner household. This means that the quantity demanded at each and every price will be higher for the two-earner household than for the one-earner household: panel (b) illustrates this for a market price of $20 per hour.

weekly child care. A household with a greater willingness to pay for child care will have a demand curve that sits to the right of the demand curve of a household that has a lower willingness to pay. To verify this, recall that the vertical distance up to the demand curve at any given quantity level reflects the willingness to pay for the last unit consumed. In this case, if we look at 20 hours of child care a week, we see that the willingness to pay for the 20th hour is, in fact, higher for the demand curve to the right. And, because this is so, the demand curve on the right indicates that more child care will be purchased at each and every market price. For instance, if the price of child care is $20 per hour, Figure 6.4 shows that the household with the greater willingness to pay will demand 40 hours of child care per week, compared with 20 hours per week demanded by the household with the lower willingness to pay.

As you can see, these families differ in their willingness to pay even though their incomes are the same. The reason for this is that the opportunity cost of taking care of one's own children is higher for one family versus the other because in one case both adults work outside the home.

We can generalize this result: a demand curve that is to the right of another reflects a greater willingness to pay for each unit of the good in question. This means that if a person's willingness to pay for a good increases for some reason, her demand curve will shift to the right. At each and every price, a greater quantity is demanded. Conversely, if her willingness to pay for each unit declines, her demand curve will shift to the left. At every price, a smaller quantity is demanded.

A person's willingness to pay for a good can change for many reasons. For example, we have already discussed how increases in the opportunity cost of our time have increased our willingness to pay for convenience goods. This, then, leads to a rightward shift in the demand curve for these goods: *at each and every price*, a higher quantity is now demanded. We call this a **shift in the demand curve**.

> **SHIFT IN DEMAND CURVE** A movement of the demand curve to the left or right. This movement reflects the change in quantity demanded at each and every price due to a change in something other than the good's price.

> **EXAMPLE** When a city builds a conveniently accessible subway system, each commuter's demand curve for gasoline shifts to the left.

> **EXAMPLE** After a heavy snow, people's demand curves for shovels and road salt shift to the right.

In our earlier example about Janet's demand for college courses each semester, we saw that a change in the price of a course led her to increase or decrease the number of courses she demanded. Why don't these price changes cause a shift in Janet's demand curve? No shift occurs because her willingness to pay for each course has not changed; *only the price has changed.* For a demand curve to shift, something *other than* the good's price must change; something that alters a buyer's willingness to pay for each unit of the good.

6.4 Why a Change in Income Shifts the Demand Curve

When income rises, it is likely to increase a person's willingness to pay for units of a particular good, such as vacations and dinners out. This then translates into rightward shift in the individual's demand curve for these goods. Why? First of all, we know that your income ultimately determines your ability to pay, which is a necessary prerequisite for willingness to pay (recall that wishful thinking itself doesn't translate into willingness to pay). Second, as your income increases, you may be able to splurge on goods that you would otherwise be unable to afford. Conversely, if your income falls, you are likely to do without some goods as you "tighten your belt."

How exactly does a change in income affect your willingness to pay and corresponding demand curve? It depends on the kind of good we are talking about.

Normal versus Inferior Goods

Let's say that your income increases substantially. Instead of earning $16,000 a year working for a fast-food restaurant, you land a manager's job that pays $23,000 a year. If this happens, do you think you would continue to buy the very same things you did before? Would you continue to buy all of your clothes at a secondhand shop? Would you continue to wait until a movie comes out on DVD before you see it? Or would you start to shop at retail clothing stores and take in a few movies when they first open at the local movie theater? Economists have noticed that when people's incomes change—whether up or down—their buying habits also change. How these purchasing patterns change depends on each individual's preferences for specific goods. Some people may consider secondhand clothes to be the ultimate in chic, while others wouldn't be caught dead in recycled-clothing stores if they had the money to shop elsewhere.

As a general rule, when an increase in income leads to an increase in a person's willingness to pay for each unit of a good, we say that this is a **normal good**.

NORMAL GOOD A good that a person is willing to pay more for as her income increases and less for when her income declines.

EXAMPLE Most people treat eating out at a restaurant as a normal good.

EXAMPLE Most couples treat children as a normal good.

EXAMPLE Most readers treat books as a normal good.

When we look at how a person's buying habits change in response to a change in income, we assume that nothing else has changed except for income. This means that there has not been a coinciding change in the individual's preferences, the alternatives that he faces, or the price of the good. This is important because it means that we can attribute any change in purchases that we observe *solely* to the person's change in income.

When it comes to normal goods, people are willing to pay more for each unit when their incomes rise and less when their incomes fall. We can show graphically the impact of a change in income on the demand curve for a normal good. A normal good's demand curve *shifts to the right* when a person's income increases. It *shifts to the left* when his income decreases. We can illustrate this effect in **Figure 6.5**, which shows Dan's demand for tickets to Boston Red Sox baseball games. At his initial level of income, say $10,000 a year, his demand curve for Red Sox tickets is D_1. At a price of $20, Dan is willing and able to buy a ticket to 8 games. If Dan's income were to increase to $15,000 a year, his demand curve for Red Sox tickets shifts right to D_2 assuming that Dan treats these tickets as a normal good. At a price of $20, Dan is now willing and able to buy a ticket to 15 games. Notice that

FIGURE 6.5 **The Demand for a Normal Good Following an Increase in Income**

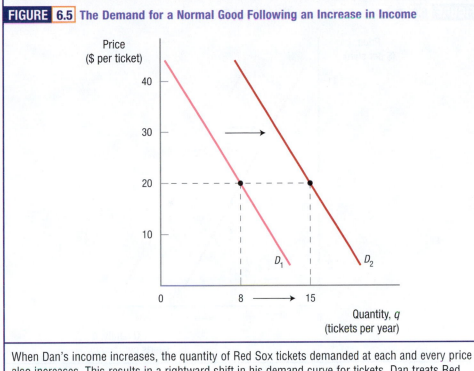

When Dan's income increases, the quantity of Red Sox tickets demanded at each and every price also increases. This results in a rightward shift in his demand curve for tickets. Dan treats Red Sox tickets as a normal good.

Dan's willingness to pay for each and every ticket is now greater than it was before his income increased.

Not all goods are normal goods. In some cases, when income rises, a person's willingness to pay for each unit of a particular good falls. And conversely, when income drops, a person's willingness to pay for each unit rises. Whether this happens or not *depends solely on a person's preferences* about the good in question. When this does happen, we call this an **inferior good**.

INFERIOR GOOD A good that a person is willing to pay less for as her income increases, and more for when her income declines.

EXAMPLE Secondhand clothing and used cars are usually inferior goods.

EXAMPLE Day-old bakery bread is typically an inferior good.

EXAMPLE "Staycations" (vacations spent at home) are usually inferior goods.

When someone treats a good as inferior, she purchases *less* of it at every price when her income rises and *more* of it when her income falls.

In **Figure 6.6**, we show the relationship between income and the demand curve for an inferior good, in this case, Pam's demand for secondhand clothing. At her initial level of income, Pam's demand curve for secondhand clothes is represented by the curve D_1. If the price of a secondhand shirt is $5, Pam buys five shirts each month. Now suppose that Pam's income increases, and her demand curve for secondhand

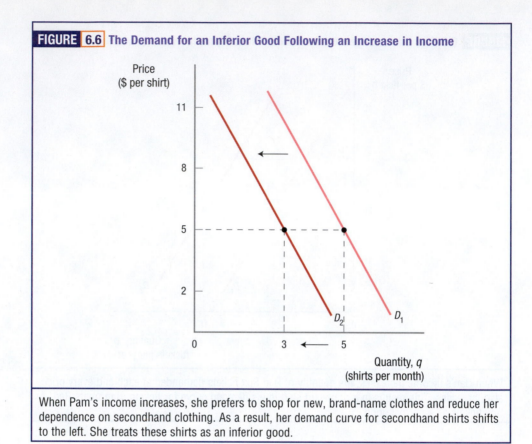

FIGURE 6.6 **The Demand for an Inferior Good Following an Increase in Income**

When Pam's income increases, she prefers to shop for new, brand-name clothes and reduce her dependence on secondhand clothing. As a result, her demand curve for secondhand shirts shifts to the left. She treats these shirts as an inferior good.

shirts shifts leftward to D_2, which is a sign that she treats these shirts as an inferior good. We see that at the $5 price, the number of secondhand shirts that she is willing and able to buy drops to three. In fact, *at each and every price*, the quantity of secondhand shirts that Pam demands is lower than before her income increased. In other words, Pam's willingness to pay for each secondhand shirt is less than it was before her income increased.

As a rule, an inferior good's demand curve shifts to the *left* when a person's income increases. It shifts *right* when the person's income falls.

It is very important to understand that inferior goods are still economic "goods"—that is, they contribute positively to a person's sense of well-being. Also, the term "inferior" has nothing to do with the inherent quality or chemical composition of the good. It is simply an economic term used to describe a person's preferences about a good and indicate how changes in income will affect his demand for it. We often observe distinct differences around the world in what people perceive to be normal or inferior goods. For example, in some countries, processed baby formula is considered a normal good while breast milk is considered an inferior good. In the United States, the reverse is true for many mothers. Many people in the United States consider used cars to be inferior goods. In Mexico, used cars that are exported from the United States are considered normal goods.

People's perceptions about whether a good is inferior or not can change over time. For many years, most people considered purebred puppies to be normal goods. In contrast, older and mixed-breed dogs were considered to be inferior goods. As family incomes grew, people sought out breeders of pricey purebred puppies rather than adopting dogs from the local pound. Over the past few decades, however, these perceptions have changed radically. In wealthy communities such as Aspen, Colorado, it has become an "in" thing to adopt animals rescued from the streets and local puppy mills. The ASPCA, local media outlets, and Animal Planet programs have all brought about this change in preferences by shining a spotlight on the benefits to be had from adopting rescued dogs. As a result, these dogs are now viewed by many as normal rather than inferior goods: families adopt more rescued dogs and puppies when their incomes increase.

In the retail sector, Walmart has embarked on an ambitious campaign to change people's perceptions that it carries "inferior" clothing and home decor. Concerned with the flight of higher-income shoppers to its primary competitor (Target), Walmart has revamped its product lines, store displays, and advertising to distance itself from its image as "cheap and low priced." The goal is for people to remain Walmart shoppers even when their incomes rise and they can shop elsewhere.

ECONOMIC FALLACY   Although the price of gasoline declined after an unprecedented run-up to over $4 per gallon, this has not led to a resurgence in purchases of big SUVs. This means that consumers' preferences have changed, and smaller cars are now considered preferable to larger, gas-guzzlers.

False. Consumers have long memories. They recall what it was like to be "stuck" in a previous, costly decision to drive a large gas-guzzler when gasoline prices soared over $3 a gallon. The fact that there has been no movement back to these large cars with the fall in gasoline prices most probably indicates that people believe that gas prices will increase again in the near future. When gas prices spiked higher in the 1970s, people did not return to large cars until over a decade after gas prices once again subsided. After they did, however, they did so in a *big* way: this was the period when SUVs and minivans were first introduced into the market.

In the United States, many consumers treat name-brand detergents such as Tide and Cheer as normal goods. In contrast, "private-label" or store-brand detergents are viewed as inferior goods. The same is true for name-brand versus store-brand soda, chips, toilet paper, and ibuprofen. Generally speaking, when people's incomes rise, their purchases of name-brand products increase while their purchases of store brands decline. We see ample evidence of this buying pattern. Companies that produce name-brand consumer products—such as Procter and Gamble, Kellogg's, and Pepsi—experience higher sales volume when people's incomes are growing. In contrast, store-brand manufacturers do better when people's incomes are shrinking or stagnant. This is why the stock prices of many name-brand producers fall during economic recessions—when personal income is lagging—and rise during economic expansions.

Transitory versus Permanent Changes in Income

When a person views a change in income as **transitory** in nature, his demand curve for a good may respond differently than if the income change is expected to be permanent.

TRANSITORY INCOME Short-term or one-time increases or decreases in income.

EXAMPLE Wage bonuses, temporary job layoffs, one-time tax assessments or tax refunds, and lottery winnings are all transitory changes in income.

Often, transitory declines in income are offset by using savings or borrowing money, whereas transitory increases in income may be banked or used for one-time "splurges" such as a vacation. In such instances, the demand curve for a normal good might not shift at all despite the change in current income.

6.5 Why Changes in Property Rights Can Shift a Demand Curve

Just as changes in income affect a person's willingness to pay and his demand curve, changes in property rights can have a similar impact. Consider the following situation. When the Supreme Court ruled in 2005 that downloading music without permission violated publishers' copyright protections, there was an increase in many music listeners' willingness to pay for legal downloads. This meant that the demand curve for iTunes downloads, for example, shifted to the right—more downloads were demanded at each and every price because the free alternatives were now illegal.

In general, changes in property rights affect a person's willingness to pay for units of a good because they change the value of the benefits derived from the good. The value of legal iTunes downloads increased when the free alternative became illegal. In contrast, when the U.S. Supreme Court refused to hear an appeal of a lower court's ruling granting public access to California beaches,[2] the willingness to pay of home buyers for California beachfront homes declined. Beachfront home owners suffered a loss of privacy and exclusive use of the beach. As a result, the demand curve for California beachfront properties shifted to the left. Whenever property rights are redefined in a way that reduces the perceived value of the benefits derived from a good, the demand curve will shift to the left. Conversely, when a change in property rights increases a good's perceived benefits, the demand curve will shift to the right.

Often, a change in property rights will affect the demand curve for more than one good. For example, to reduce automobile emissions and encourage people to purchase fuel-efficient cars, the state of Virginia passed a law in 2000 that allowed single-occupant hybrid (gasoline-powered and electric-powered) vehicles to use the less-congested carpool (high-occupancy vehicle, HOV) highway lanes. California followed with similar legislation in 2004. As a result, the property rights associated with owning a hybrid became more valuable. Drivers gained an added benefit from driving a hybrid—the amount of time they now saved commuting on congested highways. This increased their willingness to pay for these types of cars. At the same time, the opportunity cost of driving traditional 100 percent gasoline-powered cars rose, thereby reducing people's willingness to pay for these types of cars.

We can illustrate how the change in property rights related to access to HOV lanes affected the demand for hybrids and 100 percent gasoline-powered cars. In panel (a) of **Figure 6.7**, we depict a California family's demand for hybrids before they could individually use HOV lanes. At some price, say $26,000, we show that the family is willing to buy two hybrid cars every four years. Panel (b) shows the demand for gasoline-powered cars during the same period. At the same ($26,000) price, the family is willing to also buy two gas-powered cars every four years.

Once individual drivers of hybrids are allowed in the HOV lanes, the willingness to pay for hybrids increases while, at the same time, the willingness to pay for gasoline-powered cars declines. This leads to a rightward shift in the demand curve

· · · · · · · ·

[2]Barbara Whitaker, "Ruling Clears Way to Ease Beach Access in California." *New York Times*, October 23, 2002.

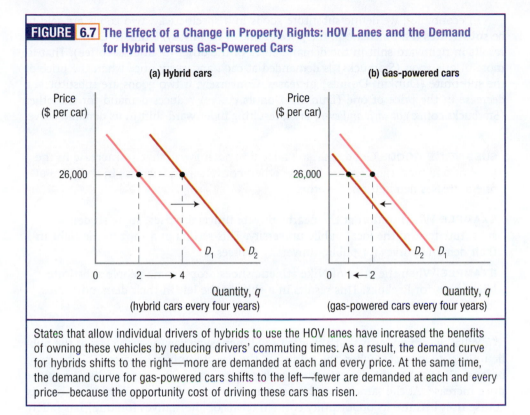

FIGURE 6.7 The Effect of a Change in Property Rights: HOV Lanes and the Demand for Hybrid versus Gas-Powered Cars

States that allow individual drivers of hybrids to use the HOV lanes have increased the benefits of owning these vehicles by reducing drivers' commuting times. As a result, the demand curve for hybrids shifts to the right—more are demanded at each and every price. At the same time, the demand curve for gas-powered cars shifts to the left—fewer are demanded at each and every price—because the opportunity cost of driving these cars has risen.

for hybrids and a shift to the left in the demand curve for gasoline-powered cars. Now, the number of hybrids the family is willing to purchase at the $26,000 price increases to four, while the number of gasoline-powered cars purchased at the same price drops to one. In other words, the family's willingness to pay for each and every gasoline-powered car falls while, at the same time, its willingness to pay for hybrids rises. This example illustrates that changes in property rights can change people's perceptions about the value, or net benefit, of purchasing a good.

Ironically, Virginia's program to stimulate hybrid-car purchases by giving individual drivers access to HOV lanes has resulted in traffic congestion in HOV lanes that is now just as great as in the non-HOV lanes. The same is beginning to prove true in California. As a result, both states are now grappling with ways to ration HOV permits for hybrid vehicles. To the extent that this benefit is curtailed, so too will be the demand for hybrids.

6.6 Why the Price of a Substitute Good Can Shift a Demand Curve

Two goods are said to be substitutes if a buyer perceives that they approximate each other in terms of use and economic benefit. For example, you may treat coffee from Dunkin' Donuts as a good substitute for Starbucks coffee. Close substitutes are viewed as stand-ins for each other when it comes to the choices people make. When two goods are close substitutes, small changes in the price of one can have a substantial impact on demand for the other. Whether a good is a close substitute for another depends solely on an individual's preferences. Some people would never drink Pepsi instead of Coke, whereas others are relatively indifferent between the two cola drinks.

In economics, we define substitute goods in a specific way: two goods are said to be **substitutes** if an increase in the price of one of them (say, Dunkin' Donuts coffee) results in rightward shift in the demand curve of the other (Starbucks coffee). That is, more of one good (Starbucks) is demanded at each and every price when the price of the substitute (Dunkin' Donuts) increases. Conversely, if two goods are substitutes, a decrease in the price of one (Dunkin' Donuts coffee) reduces demand for the other (Starbucks coffee) *at each and every price*, resulting in leftward shift in its demand curve.

SUBSTITUTE GOODS Goods that are related in such a way that an increase in the price of one increases demand for the other; conversely, a decrease in the price of one decreases demand for the other.

EXAMPLE When tuition at the nearby private university rises, some students substitute toward the local public university. This results in a shift to the right in their demand curves for public-university courses.

EXAMPLE When the price of Nike athletic shoes drops, some people substitute Nike shoes for Reeboks. This results in a shift to the left in their demand curves for Reeboks.

What we are saying is that a student's willingness to pay for each class at the public university increases when the tuition at the private university rises. This happens because the *net* benefit she gets from each private-university course falls due to the price increase. At the same time, the net benefit she gets from each public-university course rises because its opportunity cost (in terms of alternatives forgone) has fallen. This is the case even though the public university's tuition rates *have not changed*.

One way we can assess the degree of substitutability between two goods is by observing the amount by which one good's price must increase before people begin to switch from that good to another. For example, it may take a very dramatic increase in the price of gasoline for people to switch from driving their own cars to using mass transit. This would lead us to predict that gasoline and mass transit are "weaker" substitutes for one another than, for instance, fuel-efficient cars versus gas-guzzling SUVs.[3]

To see the impact that the price of a substitute can have on another good's demand curve, consider the following situation. The price of adopting babies born in Russia and Romania fell with the demise of the Soviet Union in 1991. As the price of adopting foreign babies fell, U.S. couples moved *down* their demand curve for these children, as illustrated in panel (a) of **Figure 6.8**. That is, the decline in price led to an increase in the quantity of babies demanded from Russia and Romania. Meanwhile, the cost of adopting children born in the United States remained unchanged. This meant that the price of adopting a child from the United States rose *relative to the price* of adopting from Russia or Romania. For those adoptive parents who viewed U.S.-born and Russian-born children as close substitutes, the fall in price for foreign-born babies resulted in a leftward shift in the demand curve for U.S.-born babies, as shown in panel (b). The quantity of U.S.-born babies demanded at each and every price declined because a close substitute had become relatively less expensive.

· · · · · · ·

[3]"One-Third of Consumers Looking at More Fuel-Efficient Cars." www.consumeraffairs.com. May 24, 2006; John Machacek, "Demand for Fuel-Efficient Cars Puts Pressure on Congress." *USA Today,* July 9, 2006.

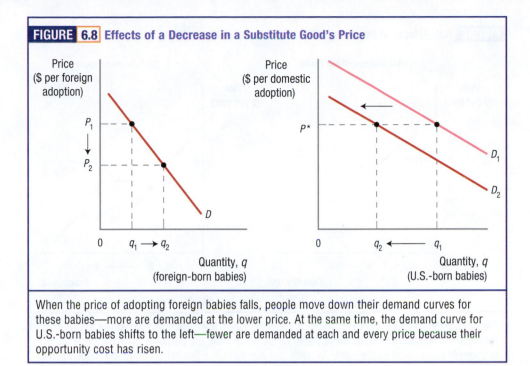

FIGURE 6.8 Effects of a Decrease in a Substitute Good's Price

When the price of adopting foreign babies falls, people move down their demand curves for these babies—more are demanded at the lower price. At the same time, the demand curve for U.S.-born babies shifts to the left—fewer are demanded at each and every price because their opportunity cost has risen.

We often hear about the impact that a change in one good's price has on the demand for a substitute when government trade policies are discussed. You might hear arguments that "cheap" imported goods threaten jobs in U.S. industries. Political pressure inevitably arises to enact protectionist trade policies that will increase the price of imports in the United States. This will reduce the quantity of imports demanded by U.S. consumers and result in a rightward shift in demand for U.S.-made products.

Suppose, for example, that at a price of $28, you are willing and able to buy two pairs of jeans each year that are made in the United States. This is depicted in panel (b) of **Figure 6.9**, which shows your demand curve for U.S.-manufactured jeans. You are also willing and able to purchase four pairs of jeans made in China, which are selling for $22, as illustrated in panel (a).

If U.S.-made and foreign-made jeans are reasonably close substitutes, then a change in the price of foreign-made jeans will affect your demand for jeans manufactured in the United States, and vice versa. What if the U.S. government wants to stimulate purchases of U.S.-made clothing? One way to do this is to enact trade policies that cause the price of foreign-made jeans to rise to $40. This price change decreases the quantity of foreign-made jeans you demand, so you will move *up* your demand curve for foreign-made jeans, as indicated in panel (a). But because U.S.-made jeans are a close substitute, this price increase will cause the demand curve for U.S.-made jeans to shift to the right. Your willingness to pay for each pair of U.S.-made jeans increases because the opportunity to purchase foreign-made jeans has become more expensive. With the price of U.S.-made jeans unchanged at $28, the quantity demanded at this price will increase.

A common way for the federal government to increase the price of foreign-made jeans or other imported goods is to impose a tax (called a *tariff*) on these imports. At one time or another, tariffs have been imposed on steel and automobile imports, as well as on toys and imported clothing. American manufacturers and their workers benefit

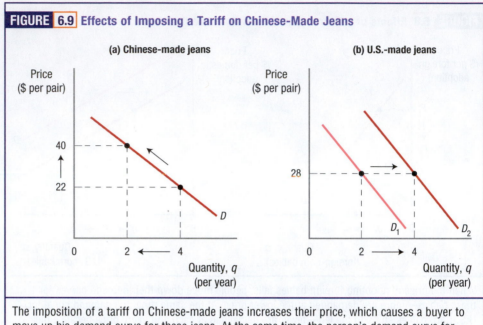

FIGURE 6.9 Effects of Imposing a Tariff on Chinese-Made Jeans

The imposition of a tariff on Chinese-made jeans increases their price, which causes a buyer to move up his demand curve for these jeans. At the same time, the person's demand curve for U.S.-made jeans shifts to the right—at each and every price, a greater quantity will be demanded. This occurs because the opportunity cost of purchasing U.S.-made jeans has fallen, and these are considered to be close substitutes for the Chinese-made jeans.

at the expense of foreign producers and workers. At the same time, American consumers "lose" because a lower-priced alternative has disappeared. They will now have to spend more of their income on jeans, cars, toys, and so on than before the tariffs were imposed. In effect, tariffs reduce the purchasing power of American consumers.

Producers may also substitute one input for another when an input price changes. Consider the local grocery store that pays a full-time checker $20 an hour, including any payroll taxes for which the employer is responsible. How will the store owner respond if there is an increase in the price of labor due, perhaps, to a new federal law that requires employers to pay an additional 9 percent of wages to fund a public health-insurance program? The store owner's new price of labor will be $21.80, including this new tax. How will she respond in terms of the number of work hours she demands from her employees? The increase in the price of labor causes the store owner to move up her demand curve for labor, leading to a reduction in the quantity of labor demanded. This would translate into shorter workdays or layoffs. At the same time, what if there is a substitute available for the grocery checkers?

During the past few decades, self-checkout scanning technology has become readily available to grocery stores and other retail outlets. Reacting to the increasing price of labor, many grocery store owners have increased their purchases of self-checkout scanners. That is, each store owner's demand curve for self-checkout scanners has shifted to the right. In fact, according to the Food Marketing Institute, nearly half of U.S. supermarkets offered a self-checkout option in 2005, compared with only 6 percent in 1999.[4] In other words, grocery-store owners have substituted away from

· · · · · · ·

[4]Doug Desjardins, "Shoppers Tapping into High Tech." *DSN Retailing Today*, January 10, 2005.

checkout workers and toward scanners in response to upward pressures on the price of labor.

A similar response to wage pressures occurred in the fast-food industry during the 1990s, when a booming economy put upward pressure on the wages of unskilled workers. Many fast-food chains turned to self-serve soda machines and automatic fryers to reduce the quantity of labor demanded. In other words, they moved up their demand curve for labor while their demand curve for new types of labor-saving equipment shifted to the right.

6.7 Why the Price of a Complementary Good Can Shift a Demand Curve

Some goods are not treated as substitutes for each other but, rather, as **complements**. By this we mean that the goods tend to "go together" when they are consumed. Obvious examples include hot dog buns and hot dogs, or shoe laces and shoes.

COMPLEMENTARY GOODS Goods that are usually consumed with one another.

EXAMPLE Cell phones and call minute plans are complementary goods.

EXAMPLE iPods and iTunes are complementary goods.

EXAMPLE Chips and dip are complementary goods.

What happens to a good's demand curve if the price of a complementary good changes? For example, how would a family's demand curve for calling minutes change if the price of cell phones dropped?

Figures 6.10 shows a family's demand curve for cell phones and its demand curve for calling minutes. At an initial price of $120 per phone, the quantity of phones demanded is two per year as depicted in panel (a). When the price of phones drops, say to $85, the quantity of cell phones demanded increases, from two to four per year. In other words, the family moves *down* its demand curve for cell phones. But notice what happens to the demand curve for calling minutes. Because cell phones and calling minutes are complements, the decline in the price of cell phones causes the family's demand curve for calling minutes to shift to the right, as shown in panel (b). At a price of ten cents per minute, the family is now willing to purchase 1,000 minutes per month instead of 500 minutes.

The fact that cell phones have become cheaper means that the family is now willing to give additional members of the family a cell phone, which leads them to increase their call minutes plan. This complementarity between phones and minutes goes a long way toward explaining why wireless services such as AT&T and Sprint benefit when they align themselves with low-cost cell-phone manufacturers. In fact, we often find wireless providers heavily subsidizing the purchase of cell phones to encourage people to switch to their calling plans. For example, Verizon recently offered free Blackberry Storms—retailing at $499.99—to new calling-plan subscribers.

This finding also explains why cell-phone makers are actively involved in political initiatives to reduce or eliminate taxes and other government fees that have been imposed on wireless-service providers. As a seller, it can sometimes be more "politically correct" to lobby for favorable tax and regulatory treatment of a complementary good than for your own good.

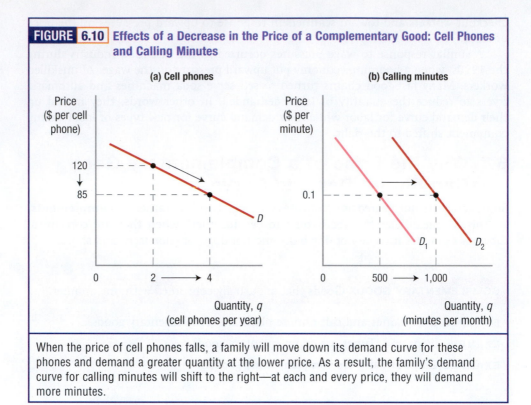

FIGURE 6.10 Effects of a Decrease in the Price of a Complementary Good: Cell Phones and Calling Minutes

(a) Cell phones

Price ($ per cell phone)

120
↓
85

D

0   2 → 4

Quantity, *q*
(cell phones per year)

(b) Calling minutes

Price ($ per minute)

0.1

*D*₁   *D*₂

0   500 → 1,000

Quantity, *q*
(minutes per month)

When the price of cell phones falls, a family will move down its demand curve for these phones and demand a greater quantity at the lower price. As a result, the family's demand curve for calling minutes will shift to the right—at each and every price, they will demand more minutes.

Our example of cell phones and cell minutes suggests that goods that are strongly complementary may be sold together. We call this "bundling." There are many examples of bundling, such as motherboards and disk drives (but not always monitors), cell phones and charger cords, and picture frames and glass. Because both goods are usually required if either is to be used, bundling them together serves as a convenience to buyers. For many years, Microsoft bundled its spreadsheet and word-processing software with its Windows operating system and distributed the bundle to computer manufacturers to install before selling the computers. This practice ended when the federal government sued Microsoft, arguing that this bundling had only one objective—to monopolize the market for computer software. Today, most PC buyers get a computer with the Windows operating system already installed, but must elect—often at an additional cost—to have the suite of Microsoft software also installed.

An intriguing economic question is why some complementary goods are bundled together all the time, others bundled some of the time, and still others never bundled together. Men's suits, which bundle a jacket and pants, are popular retail offerings. In contrast, "separates" tend to dominate women's clothing lines. Men's pants rarely come with belts, while women's pants often do.

One possible explanation for the observed increase in demand for bundled goods is that the opportunity cost of our time has increased. As a result, the cost of the time required to purchase complementary goods separately has also risen, leading to a higher willingness to pay for bundled goods. Today's grocery shelves are full of these goods, including packaged crackers and cheese, premade sandwiches and salads,

Table **6.2** A Review: Factors That Can Shift a Person's Demand Curve
▶ **A person's demand curve shifts to the right when:**
1. His preferences change, thereby increasing the net benefit derived from the good.
2. The price of a complementary good decreases.
3. The price of a substitute good increases.
4. For normal goods, his income increases.
5. For inferior goods, his income decreases.
6. Property rights change and increase the net benefit of the good.
◀ **A person's demand curve shifts to the left when:**
1. His preferences change, thereby reducing the net benefit derived from the good.
2. The price of a complementary good increases.
3. The price of a substitute good decreases.
4. For normal goods, his income decreases.
5. For inferior goods, his income increases
6. Property rights change and reduce the net benefit of the good.

and new versions of the original bundled meal—frozen TV dinners. At the same time, other bundled goods such as laundry detergent with fabric softener, and peanut butter and jelly blended in one jar have not fared as well. For bundled goods to succeed in the marketplace, consumers must derive a net benefit from the bundling. This in turn depends on whether the value of the benefit gained from the bundling outweighs the higher price that is usually paid for the bundled good relative to the sum of the prices of the unbundled goods.

We've discussed many factors that can shift a person's demand curve. **Table 6.2** summarizes them.

6.8 From Individual to Market Demand Curves

So far, we have talked exclusively about a single consumer's demand curve for various goods. But most economic discussions focus on the total demand that groups of buyers have for a particular good and how this demand responds to some change in the economic environment. It is not uncommon to hear analysts asking such questions as:

- How have unit sales of SUVs fared in Minneapolis since gasoline prices started to rise in 2008?
- How many units of single-family houses have been purchased in Phoenix, Arizona, since the beginning of the 2007 Great Recession?
- What has happened to unit sales of laptops since the introduction of the iPad tablet?

It is quite straightforward—both conceptually and computationally—to "add together" individual demand schedules to arrive at a group demand schedule that shows the total quantity demanded at each and every price. In a similar way, we can add together individual demand curves to get a total demand curve for the group.

Table 6.3 The Demand Schedule for College Credit Hours							
Price per Credit Hour	$100	$200	$300	$400	$500	$600	$700
Number of credits demanded per year by Gail (q_1)	10	8	6	4	2	0	0
Number of credits demanded per year by Jay (q_2)	7	6	5	4	3	2	1
Total credits (Q) demanded per year by both Gail and Jay	17	14	11	8	5	2	1

We illustrate this approach with a simple example: consider a world in which there are only two college students, Gail and Jay. Now suppose each has the demand schedule for college credits reported in **Table 6.3**.

To calculate the total quantity demanded for college credits at each price, we *add* together the quantity demanded by each student at that price. Graphically, this translates into a *horizontal* summation of the two demand curves, as illustrated in **Figure 6.11**. Notice that because we are now talking about the quantity demanded by more than one person, we use the capital letter Q to represent quantity demanded, where Q equals the sum of q_1 and q_2 at each price.

One of the things we know right away about this total demand curve is that it must be downward sloping because each of the individual demand curves that we "summed over" is downward sloping.

FIGURE 6.11 Deriving the Market Demand Curve for Credit Hours

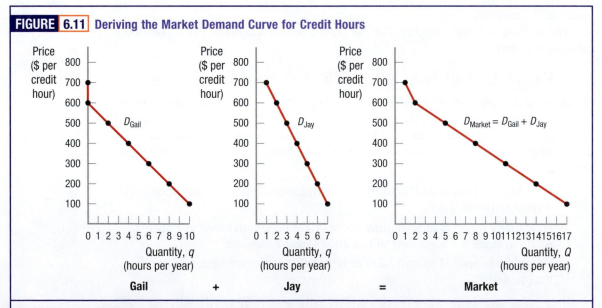

To find the market demand for credit hours, we add together the quantity demanded by Gail and Jay at each price. For example, at $600 per credit hour, the total number of credit hours demanded equals 0 + 2 = 2 credit hours. We repeat this calculation for each and every price per credit hour to get the market demand curve. This process is sometimes referred to as a *horizontal* summation of the two demand curves.

Obviously there are more students who demand college credits in the real world than just Gail and Jay. To find the total demand for college credits when there are more than two students, we follow the same approach. By adding up the quantity demanded by each student at each price, we end up with a demand schedule and demand curve for the total credit hours demanded by all of these students at each and every price.

Market Demand

Suppose we want to shed some light on the question of how the total demand for single-family houses in Phoenix has changed since the beginning of the 2007 Great Recession. To address this question, we have to know something about the total demand for single-family houses in Phoenix before and after the recession began. Based on our previous discussion, we could simply add up the demand of all potential buyers of Phoenix single-family houses, both before and after the recession began. Notice that we have not added in the demand for single-family houses in Tucson or Boston. Neither have we added in the demand for condominiums or horse ranches in Phoenix. We have not done so because we are solely interested in how total demand *for single-family houses in Phoenix* has changed over time.

Generally speaking, economists are interested in looking at the total demand of consumers who are purchasing the same good in the same market. By **market**, we mean a physical or virtual place such as eBay where buyers and sellers meet to voluntarily exchange goods and services.

> **MARKET** A place or circumstance in which buyers and sellers meet, either directly or through representatives, to voluntarily exchange goods and services.

> **EXAMPLE** The New York Stock Exchange (NYSE) is located in New York City. It is filled with traders who "match" buyers and sellers of shares of stock in companies listed on the exchange.

> **EXAMPLE** Amazon.com is an international virtual Web site that brings together buyers and sellers of a diverse array of goods, including books, music, shoes, and movies.

> **EXAMPLE** Most cities have weekly farmers' markets, where local farmers sell their produce to local residents.

For any given good and any given market—such as single-family houses in Phoenix—we can derive the total quantity demanded at each and every price by adding together the individual demand schedules of buyers in the market. From this market schedule, we can derive a **market demand curve**.

> **MARKET DEMAND CURVE** A graphical representation of the relationship between a good's price and the total quantity demanded in the market, at each and every price.

EXAMPLE At a price of $4 per gallon, 1 million gallons of gasoline are demanded each week in the greater Los Angeles area.

EXAMPLE Two million cans of Coke are demanded nationwide each month when the price is $1 per can.

In many instances, calculating market demand is much harder than it sounds. It isn't always easy to know which individual demand schedules should be added together to create the market demand schedule and corresponding demand curve. Can one person's demand for chunky peanut butter be added to another's demand for reduced-fat peanut butter? Is there, in fact, a single market demand curve for peanut butter, or are there separate demand curves for different types of peanut butter?

Some of us who buy hot, delivered pizzas are sensitive to a change in the price of frozen, premium pizzas—we tend to buy a lot fewer delivered pizzas when the price of the premium frozen pizzas drops. Does this mean there is only one pizza market, or are there several distinct pizza markets—frozen, delivered, handmade, and so on—each with its own market demand schedule? You may think that this distinction is simply academic. If so, you might be surprised to learn that the question of how to define the pizza market was *the* central issue in a Wisconsin court case. The judge was asked to rule on whether a proposed merger between a boxed-pizza manufacturer and a frozen-pizza producer would reduce competition in "the" pizza market.

Our pizza example highlights that the *degree of substitutability* between goods can be an important factor in determining which goods actually "belong" in the same market. We can ask the same question about brand-name sneakers. Do consumers consider Nike and Reebok shoes to be pretty much the same good—brand-name athletic shoes—such that each individual's demand for Nike *and* Reebok shoes can be added together to obtain the market demand for brand-name athletic shoes?

Another complication that can arise in estimating the market demand for a good is that the market may be geographically defined. We know, for example, that people who work in New York City are much more likely to demand housing in New York, New Jersey, and Connecticut than in Phoenix (except perhaps for the snowbirds). People living in Missouri will demand gasoline that can be purchased in Missouri (and possibly Illinois and Kansas) but not in California. In other words, *where* a good is purchased can be an important factor when it comes to deriving the market demand for a good. This is particularly true when the good is costly to transport. This goes a long way toward explaining why international Internet retailers such as eBay predominantly trade goods with low shipping costs—DVDs, jewelry, and SIM cards—while more localized trading sites such as Craigslist specialize in heavier items—furniture, large fish tanks, and cars—that are costly to transport long distances. While eBay faces an international market demand curve encompassing individual demand schedules from around the world, the market demand curve for Craigslist tends to primarily reflect the demand schedules of local residents.

With all of these issues in mind, we must assume that we can accurately define a market and identify those individual demand schedules that contribute to this market's total demand schedule. One thing we do know is that the "adding up" process used to compute market demand ensures that the quantity demanded at each price will increase when we add more individual demand schedules. So, the corresponding market demand curve must shift to the right when additional buyers "enter" the market. More units of the good are now demanded at each price. Conversely, when the number of buyers in the market declines, the market demand curve will shift to the left.

Consider what happened when the federal government introduced college grant and loan programs. Because of these programs, more people were able to attend college. Adding the demand schedules of these new students to the preexisting market demand led to an increase in the total quantity of courses demanded at every price. Graphically speaking, there were new individual demand curves to add to the preexisting market demand curve. The end result was that the market demand curve for college credits shifted to the right.

Another example of how adding new buyers shifts the market demand curve to the right relates to recent regulatory changes in Mexico that now allow older U.S. cars to be imported into Mexico. Adding in the individual demand schedules of Mexican buyers shifts the market demand curve for older U.S. cars to the right. More generally, whenever international markets are "opened" by free-trade agreements that eliminate barriers to trade, the market demand curve for exported goods shifts to the right. American farmers experienced a substantial increase in market demand for their products when NAFTA (the North American Free Trade Agreement) was introduced in 1992. At the same time, however, the market demand curve for industrial parts manufactured in the United States shifted to the left, with buyers instead taking advantage of lower-priced industrial parts made in Mexico.[5]

Factors That Shift the Market Demand Curve

As you can probably guess, market demand curves shift *in the same direction* as their underlying individual demand curves. In other words, market demand curves are affected by the same factors that shift individual demand curves. Recall that these include changes in income, in the price of a substitute or complementary good, in preferences, and in property rights. To understand why this is the case, remember that the market demand curve is simply the sum of the underlying individual demand curves. So if individual demand curves shift to the right, for whatever reason, then the market demand curve must also shift to the right (a greater quantity of the good will be demanded at each and every price). Even if only one person's demand curve shifts due to a change in the economic environment, the market demand curve must also shift in the same direction. However, this shift is likely to be imperceptible because each individual is only one of numerous buyers who contribute to market demand.

Short-Run versus Long-Run Changes in Individual and Market Demand Curves

It is important to realize that it may take some time for people to alter their purchasing habits in response to changes in the economic environment. Therefore, individual and market movements along the demand curve, as well as shifts in individual

5Elizabeth Becker, et al., "Free Trade at Age 10: The Growing Pains Are Clear." *New York Times*, December 27, 2003.

and market demand curves, may not be instantaneous. Consider what happens when the price of gasoline rises. In the short run, a person might not be able to reduce his gas consumption and move up his demand curve for gasoline because he is limited by where he lives and works, and the type of car he owns. In the long run, however, he can relocate, change jobs, or trade in his car, thereby moving up his demand curve for gas and buying less of it at the higher price. In a similar fashion, if one of the workers in a two-income household loses his job, it may take time for the household to actually reduce its demand for child care. If the family has entered into a 12-month contract with its child-care provider, then the family's demand curve cannot actually shift during the period of the contract. Only in the long run, when the contract expires, is the household able to act upon its new circumstances and purchase less child care at each and every price, which results in a leftward shift in its demand curve for child care.

This means that individuals and, consequently, the market, may be adjusting to a change in the economic environment over an extended period of time. For example, government policies that lower mortgage rates may not translate into a higher demand for new homes and an increase in building permits for months or even years into the future. Compare this to government food subsidies for low-income pregnant women, which tend to stimulate an immediate increase in the quantity of food demanded at each and every price.

SOLVED PROBLEM

Q Using market demand curves, show the impact of e-mail and instant messaging on (1) the high-speed cable services market, and (2) the postage-stamp market.

A E-mail and instant messaging are substitutes for mailed letters. Therefore, the introduction of electronic communications has resulted in a shift to the left in the market demand curve for "snail mail" (and, hence, postage stamps), as illustrated in panel (a) below. In contrast, e-mail and instant messaging have led to a rightward shift in the market demand for complementary goods, in this case, high-speed cable access to the Internet, as illustrated in panel (b). At each and every price, more cable services will be demanded.

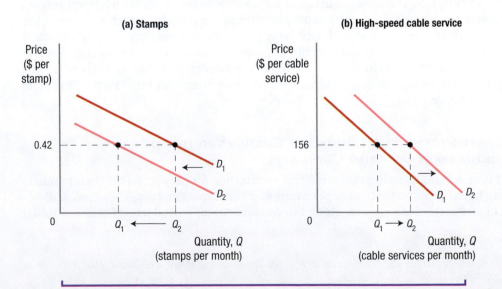

6.9 Summarizing the Factors That Shift Demand

We have identified several factors that lead to shifts in the individual and market demand curves for a good. To reiterate, one of these factors is *not* a change in the price of the good itself: a change in the price of a good moves you along (up or down) the good's demand curve, changing the quantity demanded. What causes the demand curve to shift? **Table 6.4** summarizes the factors that lead to a shift in an individual's demand curve and the corresponding market demand curve.

ECONOMIC FALLACY   The price of housing rose rapidly until recently and with it, the number of housing units purchased. This shows that demand curves can slope upward.

False. In the past decade, falling interest rates gave more people the ability to pay for housing through low-interest mortgages. Also, the number of people willing and able to pay for more expensive housing increased due to the baby boomers coming into their peak earning years, as well as an influx of wealthier immigrants. Both of these factors caused the market demand curve for housing to *shift* to the right—not slope upward.

Table 6.4   Factors That Lead to a Shift in the Market Demand Curve

Income changes
- ▶ to the right if the good is normal, and incomes increase;
- ◀ to the left if the good is normal, and incomes decrease;
- ▶ to the right if the good is inferior, and incomes decrease;
- ◀ to the left if the good is inferior, and incomes increase.

Preferences change
- ▶ to the right if the good becomes more valued;
- ◀ to the left if the good becomes less valued.

Price of a complementary good changes
- ▶ to the right if a complementary good's price decreases;
- ◀ to the left if a complementary good's price increases.

Price of a substitute good changes
- ▶ to the right if a substitute good's price increases;
- ◀ to the left if a substitute good's price decreases.

Change in Property rights
- ▶ to the right if the change increases the value of the good;
- ◀ to the left if the change decreases the value of the good.

Number of buyers changes
- ▶ to the right when the number of buyers increases;
- ◀ to the left when the number of buyers decreases.

SOLVED PROBLEM

Q Suppose that due to a parts shortage, there is a run-up in the price of eReaders (electronic-book readers). Using a separate market demand curve for each good, show the impact of this price increase on (1) the demand for eReaders, (2) the demand for electronic books (e-books), and (3) the demand for paperback books.

A As the following figure shows, buyers will move up their demand curves for eReaders: the quantity demanded at the higher price will be less than before the price increase. And, because e-books are complements to eReaders, the market demand for these e-books will shift to the left—fewer e-books will be demanded *at each and every price*. Finally, because paperback books are substitutes for e-books and eReaders, the market demand for them will shift to the right—more paperback books will be demanded *at each and every price*.

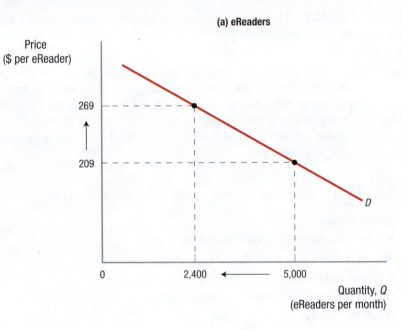

(a) eReaders

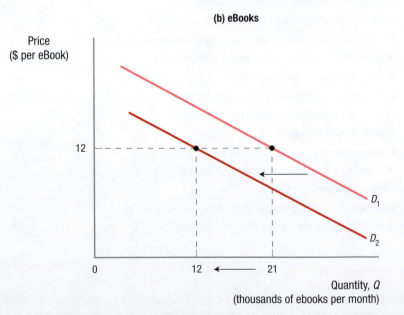

(b) eBooks

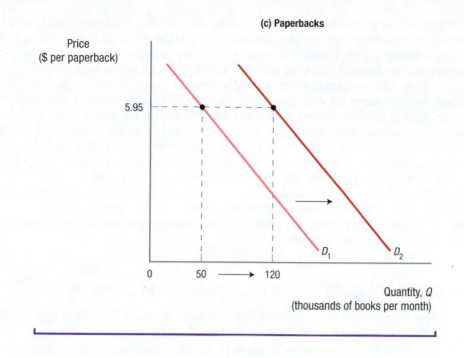

(c) Paperbacks

6.10 Derived Demand

Suppliers usually use inputs in their production process. For instance, carpenters require nail guns and saws, and car producers require steel. Even workers require food and sleep if they are to supply labor services. These production requirements create a demand for *inputs into production*.

The quantity of an input demanded at each and every price depends critically on the demand for the end product. In other words, a producer's willingness to pay for various inputs depends on the willingness of consumers to pay for his output. This is why the demand for inputs is referred to as a **derived demand**.

DERIVED DEMAND The demand for an input, which is dependent upon the demand for the good(s) that it is used to produce.

EXAMPLE When the demand for cars dropped in the previous recession, the derived demand for autoworkers declined, and some autoworkers lost their jobs.

EXAMPLE When the demand for laptops increased, the derived demand for lithium batteries also increased.

To illustrate the concept of derived demand, consider the impact that the aging population in Japan has on Japan's future demand for grade-school teachers. It is well-known that the population in Japan is getting older and that there are fewer children being born there. This means that the demand for grade-school education will decline in the future, resulting in a leftward shift in the demand curve for grade-school education. Because there will be fewer students, this reduction in demand for education will also reduce the derived demand for teachers. One way that teachers' unions can counteract this trend is to successfully lobby for regulations that reduce student–teacher ratios, thereby preserving the same number of classes as before. Absent this, the demand curve for teachers will shift to the left as well.

Generally speaking, when a good's demand curve shifts to the right, the derived demand curve for each input into its production also shifts in the same direction. This interdependence between the demand for inputs and outputs explains why workers—who supply labor services—and other input suppliers are often strong advocates for policies that increase the demand for the goods they help to produce. It should come as no surprise that U.S. steelworkers often lobby alongside U.S. steel companies to impose tariffs on imported steel products. And why the United Automobile Workers (UAW) and auto-part manufacturers strongly supported the 2009 "Cash for Clunkers" subsidy program to stimulate the purchase of new cars. After all, these workers' own economic survival was closely linked to the market demand for the goods they produced.

WHAT YOU SHOULD HAVE LEARNED FROM CHAPTER 6

- That the principle of diminishing marginal benefits means that the marginal willingness to pay for additional units of a good declines.

- That because the marginal willingness to pay falls, consumers will buy more of an item when its price falls and less when its price rises.

- That a demand schedule reflects the number of units of a good that a person will purchase at each and every price, assuming that nothing else has changed.

- That the height of the demand curve represents a person's willingness to pay for different units of a good.

- That the demand curve also indicates the number of units of a good that an individual will purchase at each price.

- That when there is a change in the price of a good, a buyer will move up or down his demand curve, thereby adjusting the quantity of the good he demands.

- That a demand curve will shift to the left or right if something other than the good's price changes.

- That the demand curve for normal and inferior goods will respond differently to changes in a person's income.

- That a substitute good is a close replacement for another, based solely on individual perceptions; changes in the price of a substitute will shift the demand curve for the other good.

- That a complementary good is typically consumed with another good (hot dogs and hot dog buns; cars and gasoline), and changes in the price of one complement will shift the demand curve for the other good.

- That a market is a place where buyers and sellers get together directly or indirectly to voluntarily exchange goods and services.

- That a market demand curve will move in the same direction as its underlying individual demand curves in response to a change in the economic environment.

- That a market demand curve will shift right if more individual demanders are added to the market, and it will shift to the left if individual demanders leave the market.

- That the demand for inputs into production is dictated by the demand for goods produced using these inputs.

KEY TERMS

Willingness to pay, p. 128

Reservation price, p. 128

Marginal willingness to pay, p. 129

Quantity demanded, p. 132

Demand, p. 133

Demand schedule, p. 133

Demand curve, p. 134

Law of demand, p. 134

Movement along the demand curve, p. 135

Shift in the demand curve, p. 137

Normal good, p. 138

Inferior good, p. 139

Transitory income, p. 141

Substitute goods, p. 144

Complementary goods, p. 147

Market, p. 151

Market demand curve, p. 151

Derived demand, p. 157

QUESTIONS AND PROBLEMS

1. The use of dry cleaners has declined in the United States during the past few decades, even though people's incomes have increased. Is this sufficient information to conclude that dry-cleaning services are an inferior good? Why or why not? Explain.

2. True, False, or Uncertain. During economic expansions (when income is high), demand for higher education declines. Therefore, higher education is an inferior good. Explain your answer.

3. For the following markets, indicate whether there is a movement along the demand curve or a rightward or leftward shift in the demand curve, in response to an increase in gasoline prices:

   a) SUV market
   b) Mass-transit market
   c) Gasoline market
   d) Automobile tire market
   e) Telecommuting software

4. Over the past decade, the "green" movement has campaigned against the purchase of bottled water because the plastic is not biodegradable. Using two individual demand curves, show the impact of this campaign on:

   a) The demand for bottled water
   b) The demand for refillable bottles

   In your opinion, has the campaign been successful in changing individual preferences about bottled water?

5. Show the impact that the adoption of Chinese babies by U.S. families has on the market demand curve for Chinese au pairs (young people who travel to the United States to take care of children).

6. Indicate how the following events affect the market demand curve for hard-copy college textbooks:

   a) The federal government cuts its funding of college Pell grants and loans.
   b) The price of hard-copy college textbooks falls.
   c) The price of electronic textbooks falls.
   d) The courts rule that students may not resell their hard-copy textbooks.

7. Identify two U.S. industries (other than those already discussed) that were "helped" by NAFTA. Identify two U.S. industries that were "hurt." Why do you think this was the case? Explain your answer.

8. Suppose that a person must have a medication—such as insulin or nitroglycerin—to survive. What would his demand curve for this medication look like? Explain.

9. The Taxpayer Relief Act of 1997 exempted from taxation the first $500,000 of profits received when an owner-occupied home is sold. Show the impact that this policy change had on the market demand curve for owner-occupied housing.

10. Using one individual demand curve for gasoline and a second for recreational vehicle rentals, show the impact of an increase in the price of gasoline on the:
    a) quantity of gasoline demanded.
    b) quantity of RV rentals demanded.

11. With the weakening of the American dollar versus most foreign currencies, foreigners have enjoyed an increase in their purchasing power for American goods. The exact opposite has happened for Americans purchasing foreign goods. Using a separate market demand curve for each of these goods, show how this has affected the market demand curve for:
    a) vacations in the United States by foreign tourists.
    b) vacations in Europe by U.S. tourists.

12. When an individual demand curve shifts because of a change in income, will the new demand curve always be parallel to the old one? Why or why not? Would your answer change if we were talking about a shift in the demand curve resulting from a change in the price of a substitute or a complement? Explain your answer.

13. Transplant surgeons have become ardent proponents for laws that would make organs more widely available. Why do you think this is the case? Explain your answer.

14. Log on to Amazon.com and compare the prices of a specific book (1) when shipping is free, and (2) when there is a shipping and/or handling charge. Is the price of the book with free shipping higher, lower, or the same as the one that has a shipping charge? Explain your findings.

15. Retailers often cluster together in indoor malls or strip malls—even when they are direct competitors, such as Eddie Bauer and American Eagle. And, car sellers often locate on the same street even though they are competing for the same buyers. Explain why this makes good business sense.

16. In such European cities as Barcelona, local shop owners close their stores between 1 P.M. and 4 P.M. for a lengthy lunch break. They then reopen and close at 9 P.M. International chains such as Gap and Walmart that are located in the same cities remain open during these lunch breaks. If all else were the same, which type of store would you predict to have higher prices? Suppose you conduct a study to test your prediction and you find out that the local merchants have higher prices. Is this consistent with your prediction? If not, why do you think you were wrong? Explain your answer.

Appendix 6A An Indifference Curve Analysis of Consumer Choice

Chapter 6 showed how you can derive a person's downward sloping demand curve from our basic economic-choice model. As you already know, people engage in an activity up to the point where the marginal benefit they obtain from the last unit they consume is equal to its marginal cost. If the only cost of acquiring a good or service is its price, and willingness to pay reflects the benefits enjoyed from each unit of the good, then we can say that people will consume up to the point where their willingness to pay from the last unit consumed is equal to the good's price. Economists use *indifference curves* and *budget lines* to model this decision-making process in a more formal way in order to draw additional conclusions about how consumers respond to changes in the trade-offs they face. This appendix provides an overview of this analysis and the types of conclusions that can be drawn from it.

REPRESENTING A CONSUMER'S INCOME CONSTRAINT

People's purchasing decisions are constrained by the income they have at their disposal. We have seen that when an individual's income changes, so does her demand curve. We can formalize a person's income constraint as follows: suppose a buyer has to decide how to divide her monthly income between two goods: food (X) and rental housing (Y). In reality, we know that there are lots of other goods she will buy each month, but for simplicity, we will assume here that there are only two goods. One of the implications of this assumption is that our buyer spends all of her income on food and rent each month because we do not allow for saving, which would be a third "good."

Table 6A.1 shows two sets of combinations of food and rent she can buy if her initial monthly income is $1,000 and then if her income grows to $4,000 a month. The actual amount of each good she can buy is dictated not only by her income but also by the good's price. Let's assume that the price of a unit (some standardized bundle) of food is $5. Let's also assume that price of rental housing is $2 per square foot per month.

Table 6A.1	Combinations of Food and Housing that Exhaust a Person's Income
Income = $1,000 per month	
Food Units	**Rental Housing (sq. ft.)**
200	0
150	125
100	250
40	400
0	500
Income = $4,000 per month	
Food Units	**Rental Housing (sq. ft.)**
800	0
600	500
400	1,000
160	1,600
0	2,000

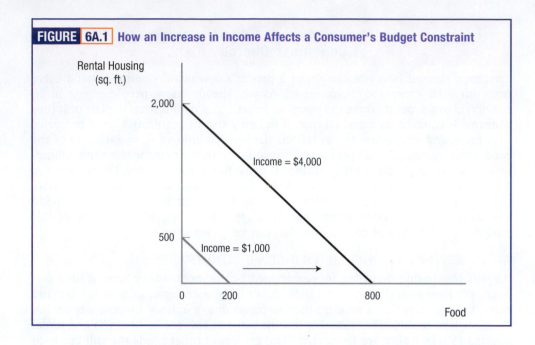

FIGURE 6A.1 How an Increase in Income Affects a Consumer's Budget Constraint

Rental Housing
(sq. ft.)

2,000

Income = $4,000

500

Income = $1,000

0   200   800

Food

In **Figure 6A.1**, we graph these two sets of food and rental housing combinations. The lower line shows how much of each good the consumer can buy with a monthly income of $1,000. The upper line shows the combinations if her income increases to $4,000. We call these lines **budget lines** or **budget constraints**.

> **BUDGET CONSTRAINT** A line comprised of all bundles of goods that a person can afford at a given set of prices and income.

We call these budget *constraints* because, at the given prices, the buyer cannot buy more than the combinations shown. If her income is $4,000, for example, she cannot buy more than 800 units of food. If she spends all of her income on rental housing, she could buy no more than 2,000 square feet of housing.

However, if the consumer is willing to trade off some housing for food, then she will find herself somewhere *along* the budget constraint. And, because we are assuming she spends all of her income, she will not choose some combination inside this budget constraint. Finally, because the budget line indicates the maximum combinations of food and housing that the consumer can buy, she cannot choose some bundle outside of her budget line. So where along the budget line will the consumer end up?

Before we answer this question, a few questions about the budget constraint must be addressed. First, why is its slope negative? Recall that the slope of a line is measured as "the change in rise (Y) given a one unit change in run (X)." In the current context, this translates into the trade-off between food and housing—that is, how much additional housing (ΔY, where Δ means "change in") could be purchased if the consumer cut back on 1 unit of food (ΔX). The prices of the goods dictate this trade-off; it is completely independent of the consumer's preferences or income. We know that giving up 1 unit of food will "free up" $5 that can be used to rent 2.5 square feet more of housing. So less food yields more housing, which is consistent with the negative slope.

Second, why are the budget constraints parallel to one another? The lines are parallel because the market's trade-off between the two goods doesn't change with income. The trade-off, dictated by the relative prices of the two goods, remains constant: giving up 1 unit of food will free up 2.5 square feet of housing. The slope of both budget constraints ($\Delta Y/\Delta X$) equals -2.5. Because the slopes of the two budget constraints—one corresponding to $1,000 a month and the second to $4,000 a month—are the same, they must be parallel to one another.

What *does* happen when the consumer's income increases is that her budget line shifts to the right: at the higher income, more of one or both goods can be purchased. The Y-intercept in our example, which represents the maximum amount of rental housing that can be purchased if no income is spent on food, increases from 500 square feet ($1,000/$2 per sq. ft.) to 2,000 square feet ($4,000/$2 per sq. ft.). Similarly, the X-intercept increases from 200 to 800 units.

What if instead of an increase in income, there was an increase in the price of food, say from $5 to $7.50 per unit? If this consumer is spending all of her income on housing, then this price change wouldn't matter to her. That is, she can still purchase as much housing as she did before the increase in the price of food. Graphically, the Y-intercept of the budget line remains the same as before. However, if the consumer purchases any food at all, she will now be unable to purchase her original bundle of food and housing due to the price increase. She will have to cut back on food, housing, or both because her income has not changed.

Figure 6A.2 shows how the budget constraint associated with $1,000 per month "pivots" or rotates inward as a result of an increase in the price of food, *holding the price of housing and income unchanged*. The X-intercept, which was originally $1,000/$5, or 200 units of food, falls to $1,000/$7.50, or 133.3 units of food. Fewer units of food can now be purchased when all of the consumer's income is spent on food. We also can see that the budget line becomes steeper. This reflects the fact that the trade-off between food and housing has changed: for every unit of food given up, $7.50 is now freed up to be spent on housing, yielding an additional 3.75 square feet. Now the new trade-off between food and housing is 1:3.75, or

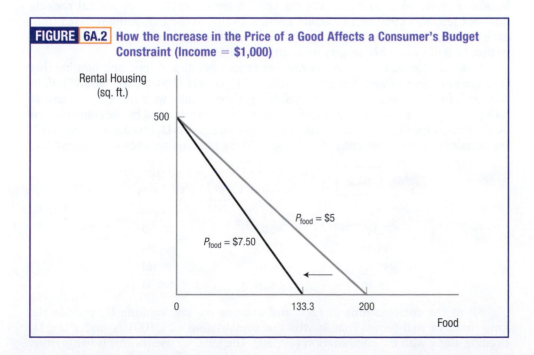

FIGURE 6A.2 **How the Increase in the Price of a Good Affects a Consumer's Budget Constraint (Income = $1,000)**

Rental Housing (sq. ft.)

500

$P_{food} = \$5$

$P_{food} = \$7.50$

0   133.3   200

Food

1 unit of food for 3.75 square feet of additional housing: the slope of the budget line has therefore increased from -2.5 to -3.75.

We can easily use the same approach to figure out what the new budget constraint would look like for different price changes in one or both goods.

Characteristics of Budget Constraints

We can summarize our findings about the budget constraint as follows:

- The budget constraint shifts parallel to the right when a person's income increases.

- The budget constraint shifts parallel to the left when a person's income decreases.

- The budget constraint "pivots" inward when the price of X increases (the Y-intercept remains unchanged) and outward when the price of X falls.

- The budget constraint "rotates" inward when the price of Y increases (the X-intercept remains unchanged) and rotates outward when the price of Y falls.

- The budget constraint will be the same for consumers who face the same prices and have the same incomes.

A GRAPHIC REPRESENTATION OF CONSUMERS' PREFERENCES

We know that consumers make choices based on both the price of various goods and their willingness to pay for each. Willingness to pay depends on personal *preferences*: vegetarians are not made better off when a juicy steak is placed before them. Similarly, most teenagers get little satisfaction from watching black-and-white silent movies.

This means that even when people have the same budget constraint, they are likely to make different purchasing decisions when it comes to such goods as food and rental housing. Suppose that a person can rank different combinations of food and rental housing according to the well-being he gets from them. Without worrying about putting an actual number on this level of well-being, he simply assigns a ranking: this bundle is preferred to that one. We call this an *ordinal ranking*. An ordinal ranking does not require a consumer to actually assign a value to the well-being received from each bundle, nor does he have to figure out how much more or less well-being (twice as much? half as much?) he gets from one bundle versus another.

Now suppose we want to group together various bundles of food and housing that yield the same level of well-being, say U_0, U_1, and U_2 (where U stands for "utility"). If, in fact, both food and housing generate well-being, then bundles with the least amount of *both* goods will generate the lowest level of utility. This is represented by the combinations yielding utility level U_0. By contrast, the highest level of utility is U_2 because its corresponding bundles offer the most units of both goods. These rankings are shown in **Table 6A.2**.

Table	6A.2	Combinations of Food and Housing that Yield the Same Level of Well-being		
U_0		U_1		U_2
25, 100		50, 200		75, 300
30, 80		60, 160		90, 240
40, 60		80, 120		120, 180
60, 30		120, 60		180, 90

All of the combinations of food and housing in, say, ranking U_0 provide the same level of well-being. That is why the combination (25, 100) is under the U_0 heading along with the combination (60, 30). The term we use for this is *indifference*.

The idea is that the consumer is indifferent—the amount of well-being he derives is the same—whether he consumes the (25, 100) bundle of food and housing or the (60, 30) bundle.

We have all experienced indifference like this many times in our lives. Suppose you have a tuna sandwich for lunch, and your office mate has an egg-salad sandwich. When asked if you would trade half of your sandwich for half of your office mate's sandwich, you weigh the costs and benefits of making such a trade. If you view the new sandwich combination as making you no better or worse off, then you would rank this new lunch "bundle" the same as your original sandwich, and you would be *indifferent* to making the trade.

Returning to Table 6A.2, we would expect that our consumer of food and housing prefers all of the combinations in U_1 to those in U_0 because there is more food and/or housing in the bundles associated with U_1 than U_0. Of course, this assumes that more food or housing, or both, is better in terms of improving his well-being.

We can graphically illustrate these preferences. In **Figure 6A.3**, we plot each of the food/housing bundles for each of the "Us" from Table 6A.2. The curves that result are called **indifference curves**.

INDIFFERENCE CURVE A curve that shows all bundles of goods that yield the same level of well-being.

Each indifference curve shows all of the bundles of food and housing that generate the same level of well-being for the consumer. As you can see, there are separate indifference curves for each of the levels of well-being labeled U_0, U_1, and U_2. Because greater amounts of one or both goods increase well-being, these curves must move up and to the right.

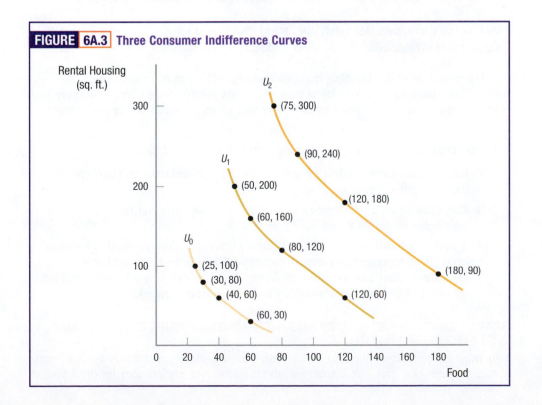

FIGURE 6A.3 **Three Consumer Indifference Curves**

The first thing to notice is that the indifference curves slope downward. Why is this the case? If a person is given more of one good, say food, then he must give up some housing to remain indifferent. The second thing to notice is that the indifference curves are "convex to the origin." That is, they bow in toward the origin of the graph. This means that the slope of the indifference curve isn't constant. Why? Recall that the principle of diminishing marginal benefit states that the incremental well-being from additional units of a good declines as more of the good is consumed. What this means is that when a person has a large amount of housing and not much food, he will be willing to give up a lot more housing to obtain a little more food. A similar phenomenon occurs if he has a lot of food but no housing. He will be willing to give up a lot more food to obtain a little bit of housing. If the amount he is willing to trade didn't vary with how much of each good he had, the slope of the indifference curve would be constant and the indifference curve would be a straight line. As you can see, it's not.

Table 6A.2 indicates that the *trade-off* between food and housing that keeps the person at the same level of well-being changes as the amounts of food and housing in the bundles change.

We actually know something more about this trade-off and the slope of the indifference curve. For every 1 unit reduction in food, the loss in well-being equals the marginal benefit generated by that unit (MB_{food}), which is also referred to as marginal utility (MU_{food}). How many square feet of housing are required to compensate the consumer for this loss in well-being? It depends on the marginal benefit that additional square feet of housing will yield. Therefore, the trade-off between food and housing that leaves the individual indifferent is equal to the ratio of the marginal benefit of the two goods, $MB_{food}/MB_{housing}$.

If, for example, the unit of food the consumer gives up reduces his well-being by 50 and an additional square foot of housing increases his well-being by 100, then .5 square feet of housing will compensate him for 1 less unit of food: $MB_{food}/MB_{housing}$ equals 50/100 or 1/2. We call this ratio the **marginal rate of substitution (MRS)**.

> **MARGINAL RATE OF SUBSTITUTION (MRS)** The rate at which a consumer is willing to trade off one good for another and remain indifferent.

The principle of diminishing marginal benefit tells us that a consumer's MRS will decline (in absolute value) as he moves down his indifference curve: for every one unit increase in food, the amount of square feet given up gets smaller and smaller.

Characteristics of Indifference Curves

We can generalize our findings about indifference curves as follows:

- Indifference curves reflect people's individual preferences and are, therefore, likely to differ across people.
- The slope of an indifference curve represents the marginal rate of substitution between goods *X* and *Y*.
- A person's indifference curves will never intersect. (We know this because each curve represents a unique level of well-being, and no combination can yield more than one level of well-being. So there can be no bundle that lies on two indifference curves, which an intersection requires.)

HOW BUDGET CONSTRAINTS AND INDIFFERENCE CURVES, TOGETHER, DICTATE CONSUMER CHOICE

You may have noticed that our discussion about budget constraints ignored consumer preferences, and our discussion about consumer preferences ignored budget constraints. Budget constraints reflect the trade-off between food and housing that the market dictates through the prices it sets, irrespective of consumer preferences. Indifference curves reflect the trade-off between food and housing that is derived from a consumer's preferences, irrespective of market prices. To see this, look at the bundles that deliver the same U_0 level of well-being in Table 6A.2: they do not cost the same. Bundle (25, 100) costs \$325, bundle (30, 80) costs \$310, and bundle (60, 30) costs \$360.

So how do budget lines and indifference curves come together to tell us something about a consumer's decision process? We know that people consider both their preferences and the prices they face when choosing the mix of goods that will maximize their well-being for any given level of scarce resources (in this case, income). If you were the consumer, what bundle of food and housing would you choose, given your income? Your decision can be illustrated by combining your budget constraint and indifference curves, as **Figure 6A.4** shows.

This figure shows a budget constraint corresponding to an income of \$4000 and two indifference curves. The budget constraint reflects the maximum bundles of food and housing that can be purchased given their prices (\$5 and \$2, respectively) and your income. The two indifference curves, labeled U_0 and U_1, show bundles of food and housing associated with two levels of well-being. Of course, you would rather have the bundles lying along indifference curve U_1 than those lying along U_0 because you would prefer to have more of one or both of the goods rather than less of either or both.

Consider the bundle of food and housing (150, 1,200). This bundle puts you on indifference curve U_0. As you can see in Figure 6A.4, choosing this bundle puts you inside the budget constraint, which means that at the given prices, you could afford to buy more of one or both goods and doing so would increase your well-being. But how much more of each should you buy? Our model of consumer choice predicts that you will end up with the bundle marked by point B (400 units of food and 1,000 sq. ft. of housing) because this bundle satisfies two basic economic requirements. First, this

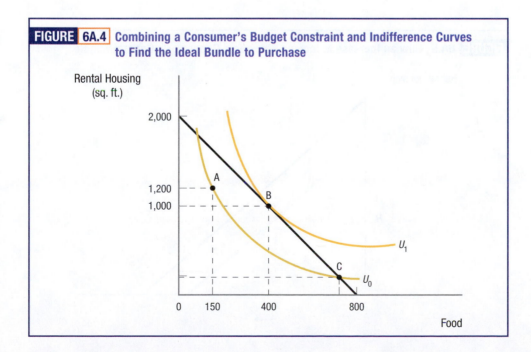

FIGURE 6A.4 **Combining a Consumer's Budget Constraint and Indifference Curves to Find the Ideal Bundle to Purchase**

bundle exhausts your income. You cannot buy more of either good given your budget constraint, nor would you want to buy less. In contrast, the bundles represented by points A and C are not "optimal" in terms of achieving your goal, which is to maximize your well-being. Second, the bundle at point B—and every other one on the indifference curve U_1—is preferable to any bundle on indifference curve U_0. However, the bundle at B *is the only bundle* on U_1 that you can purchase, given your income. Given your income and your personal preferences, this is the best you can do. Notice that this bundle is located at the point where your budget constraint is just *tangent* to your indifference curve U_1. Economists sometimes refer to this as a *tangency solution*.

Changes in an Individual's Income

What happens to a consumer's choice of bundle when there is a change in income? Look at **Figure 6A.5**. There we've replicated Figure 6A.4, leaving out the numbers. Figure 6A.5 shows an increase in your income, while holding prices and your preferences constant. At a higher level of income, your budget constraint shifts to the right. Now which bundle will you choose?

   The bundle of food and housing at point B no longer maximizes your well-being. Because your income is higher, you can buy more of one or both goods until you've once again exhausted your income, landing you somewhere along your new, higher budget constraint *and* on a higher indifference curve. The bundle at which this occurs is located at point D. This bundle will maximize your well-being. How does this translate into your demand for food and housing? Your income increased and, given the original prices of food and housing, you bought more of each good to maximize your well-being. Therefore, both goods must be *normal goods*: your demand for each good will shift to the right when your income increases.

Changes in the Price of a Good

Suppose there is no change in your income or the price of housing, but the price of food increases. We already showed that this will cause the budget constraint to

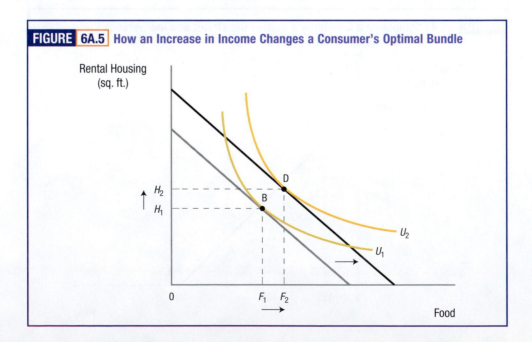

FIGURE 6A.5 How an Increase in Income Changes a Consumer's Optimal Bundle

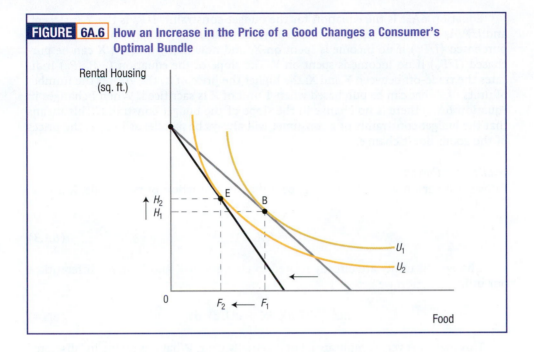

FIGURE 6A.6 How an Increase in the Price of a Good Changes a Consumer's Optimal Bundle

rotate inward; there will be no change in the Y-intercept, but the X-intercept will get smaller. **Figure 6A.6**, which shows this change in the budget constraint, reveals that your original bundle B is no longer attainable—it sits outside your new budget constraint. The highest indifference curve that you can now reach is lower than before the price increase.

This is an important but logical finding: a price increase reduces a consumer's well-being. We see that the best you can now do is to choose the bundle at point E, which is the point where your new budget constraint is just tangent to indifference curve U_2. The bundle at E contains less food. In other words, when the price of food increased, you bought less of it. This is exactly what the law of demand predicts. As it turns out, bundle E also contains more housing—whose price did not change—than before. In fact, your purchases of housing could have gone up or down, depending on how much more of your income you decided to spend on food to cover the price increase.

A MATHEMATICAL REPRESENTATION OF CONSUMER CHOICE

We can restate our analysis in mathematical terms.

Budget Constraints

Given the prices P_X and P_Y, all of the combinations of X and Y that would just exhaust the consumer's monthly income (I) can be represented by the following income constraint:

$$P_X X + P_Y Y = I \tag{6A.1}$$

We can graph this relationship—with X and Y on the horizontal and vertical axes, respectively—using the following equation derived directly from equation 6A.1:

$$Y = I/P_Y - P_X X/P_Y \tag{6A.2}$$

Equation 6A.2 is the equation for the budget constraint. I/P_Y is the Y-intercept, and I/P_X is the X-intercept. The intercept values tell us how many units of Y can be purchased (I/P_Y) if no income is spent on X, and how many units of X can be purchased (I/P_X) if no income is spent on Y. The slope of the equation ($-P_X/P_Y$) indicates the trade-off between Y and X: the higher the price of X, the greater the number of units of Y that can be purchased when 1 unit of X is sacrificed. When I changes in equation 6A.2, there is no change in the slope of the budget constraint. This means that the budget constraints of a consumer will always be parallel as long as the prices of the goods don't change.

Indifference Curves

Consider a person whose well-being, or utility, is a function of two goods, X and Y. That is,

$$U = f(X, Y) \tag{6A.3}$$

Changes in utility are directly related to changes in X and Y. If we differentiate our utility function we get

$$dU = dU/dX \, dX + dU/dY \, dY \tag{6A.4}$$

This may look very complicated, but it actually isn't. What it is saying in "discrete" terms is that

$$\Delta U = MU_X \, (\Delta X) + MU_Y \, (\Delta Y) \tag{6A.5}$$

That is, a change in well-being (ΔU) occurs when there is a change in the amount of good X (ΔX) or good Y (ΔY) you have, weighted by their respective marginal utility (MU_X, MU_Y) or benefit you gain.

Along an indifference curve, ΔU is equal to zero. As a result, along an indifference curve, the following must hold:

$$0 = MU_X \, (\Delta X) + MU_Y \, (\Delta Y) \tag{6A.6}$$

Rearranging, we get

$$MU_X/MU_Y = -\Delta Y/\Delta X = -\text{slope of indifference curve} \tag{6A.7}$$

Utility Maximization

Given the income level I_0, what is the bundle of X and Y that will maximize a person's level of well-being? Mathematically speaking, we are looking for the values of X and Y to

$$\text{Maximize } U = f(X, Y)$$

such that

$$I_0 = P_X X + P_Y Y$$

We have already shown that the X, Y combination that yields the highest level of well-being is where the budget constraint is just tangent to the indifference curve. At this point, the slope of the indifference curve is just equal to the slope of the budget constraint. That is,

$$P_X/P_Y = \text{MRS}_{X,Y} = MU_X/MU_Y \qquad (6A.8)$$

This result is a necessary condition for *consumer equilibrium*. By equilibrium, we mean that a consumer will stop trading with the market and adjusting his bundle of goods when this equality is met.

Rearranging equation 6A.8, we get

$$MU_X/P_X = MU_Y/P_Y \qquad (6A.9)$$

This tells us that a consumer has maximized her well-being only when the last dollar she spends on good X yields that same increase in well-being as the last dollar she spends on good Y. This result explains why, when the price of a good increases, a person will tend to buy fewer units of that good and more of other goods whose prices have not changed: the marginal benefit gained per dollar spent on these other goods is now greater than what is gained from spending these dollars on good X. In other words, your dollar doesn't "go as far" anymore when you buy X.

KEY TERMS

Budget constraint, p. 162

Indifference curve, p. 165

Marginal rate of substitution, p. 166

PRACTICE PROBLEMS

1. What would a consumer's indifference curve look like if she were choosing between a "good" and a "bad"—say, going to movies and sitting in traffic? Explain.

2. What would a person's indifference curve look like if she were choosing between two "perfect" complements that had to be used together in a specific combination—say, athletic shoes and shoelaces? Explain.

3. What does a straight-line indifference curve tell you about a person's preferences in terms of the two goods, X and Y? Explain. If the indifference curve was a straight line, what would this mean in terms of consumer equilibrium? Explain.

4. Could a budget constraint ever be curved? Explain.

5. What would the indifference curves look like for a drug addict who is choosing between cocaine and food? Explain.

Translating Demand into Reality: The Supply of Goods and Services

*"I am like any other man.
All I do is supply a demand."*

*Al Capone,
bootlegger and bookie*

So far we have focused on the impact that factors such as preferences, property rights, income, and the price of alternatives have on a person's willingness to pay for a good. This willingness to pay is represented by an individual's demand curve. When we add all of these individual demand curves together, we get the market demand curve.

Unfortunately for consumers, the fact that there is an economic demand for a good does not guarantee that this demand will be filled, that is, that a trade will ensue. Just because people are "willing and able" to pay for certain quantities of goods doesn't necessarily mean that these goods are available for purchase. Think about the times you were willing to pay for a certain style of shoes or jacket, but these styles were nowhere to be found when you wanted them.

For trade to occur, a supplier must be willing and able to sell the good for a price equal to or less than a buyer's willingness to pay. Put another way, a consumer's reservation price must be sufficiently high to persuade a supplier to part with a good he has produced from his own scarce resources. For example, most people's willingness to pay for space travel is not enough to cover the resources used up in routine space trips. Still, a handful of private citizens have already flown on space-docking missions with the Russian Federal Space Agency for the mere sum of $20 million.[1] It remains to be seen whether suborbital space trips, which will be offered by Virgin Galactic in the next few years, can generate a sufficient amount of demand at the estimated price tag of $200,000.[2]

When a person's reservation price is not enough to cover the cost of supplying a good, the potential buyer will walk away empty-handed or with a quantity that

· · · · · · ·

[1]"Space Tourist Hails 'Trip to Paradise.'" *BBC News*, May 6, 2001.
[2]John Schwartz, "Space Tourists: A New Niche?" *New York Times*, October 24, 2004.

falls short of the preferred amount. The bottom line is that suppliers behave just like anyone else. They try to maximize the net benefit they get from the scarce resources under their control. In this chapter, we explore the choices and constraints that producers face in deciding how to allocate these scarce resources.

7.1 The Behavior of Individual Suppliers

All of us are suppliers of some sort. Most of us supply our time to the labor market in the form of work, and many of us supply money to banks and other lenders through our savings. Therefore, from an economic perspective, all of us are "suppliers." This means you shouldn't think of suppliers as only retailers or corporations that produce "things" for sale in the market. The economic model of supplier behavior that we will develop applies to all types of supply activity, including your own.

Every potential supplier in every market must decide whether it makes sense to use scarce resources to produce a particular good or service. A farmer has to decide whether to grow corn, soybeans, or nothing at all. A worker has to decide whether to work in his mother's local business, take a job in another city, or go back to school. Sometimes suppliers take a risk in choosing what to produce—it may turn out after the fact that there are no buyers for the product. Even successful companies such as McDonald's can occasionally get it wrong when it comes to consumer demand for new products. Its hula burger—a cheeseburger with a slice of pineapple in place of the burger—was a resounding flop when McDonald's founder Ray Croc introduced it in the early 1960s. In later years, McDonald's McSpaghetti, McLobster, and McPizza were rolled out with great fanfare, only to be withdrawn within months of their debut.

Suppliers not only create new products but also enter existing markets when they expect there is a net benefit to be had from augmenting the scarce resources already committed to these markets. In other words, they anticipate that the economic benefit of supplying additional units of an existing good or service outweighs the opportunity cost. Recall that opportunity cost reflects the forgone net benefit that would have been enjoyed from putting resources to their next-best use. This means that suppliers must consider the net benefit they would receive from a wide variety of supply activities before choosing which market to participate in. A salesperson, for example, must choose which line of products to sell, that is, which product markets to participate in as a supplier. A restaurant owner must decide whether he wants to be a supplier of take-out food, focus on the dine-in crowd, or serve both markets. And an education major must decide whether she wants to teach at the preschool, elementary, middle-school, or high-school level.

The Opportunity Cost of Production: Increasing Marginal Cost

We have already introduced the principle of increasing marginal cost, which tells us that the cost of producing additional units of a good rises at some point. This phenomenon can occur from the very first unit onward or kick in at some higher level of production. **Figure 7.1** illustrates this principle. You can see that as additional units of the good are produced, the marginal cost of each of these units is higher than for the unit before.

Why does the assumption of increasing marginal cost make sense? Recall that in the case of water, the first gallons of water can be supplied at low cost simply by catching rainwater in a bucket or reservoir. To increase the supply further, groundwater sources could be tapped and pumped up from under the earth's surface, a more

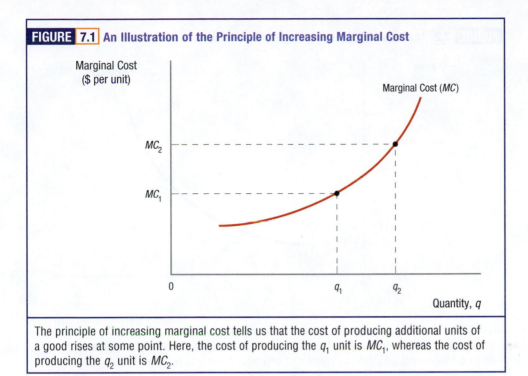

FIGURE 7.1 **An Illustration of the Principle of Increasing Marginal Cost**

The principle of increasing marginal cost tells us that the cost of producing additional units of a good rises at some point. Here, the cost of producing the q_1 unit is MC_1, whereas the cost of producing the q_2 unit is MC_2.

expensive process than simply collecting rainwater. As more water is supplied, the cost of supplying additional gallons rises.

The concept of increasing marginal cost applies to virtually everything that is produced. Think about starting a home-based business that provides catering services for your friends. Your existing kitchen setup—your oven, refrigerator, pots and pans—is perfectly adequate to meet your friends' demands for catering their special events. However, as word of mouth spreads and your client list expands, you will likely outgrow this low-cost production setting and have to move to a larger facility. Quite likely, you will have to hire more staff and lease or purchase more cooking equipment. As a result, the cost of servicing additional clients and events is likely to rise. Each additional catered event (assuming the same menu and number of guests) costs more to produce than the one before.

Closer to home, we observe that the "production" of household services—cleaning, cooking, mowing the lawn, and so forth—also exhibits increasing marginal cost. This happens because we tend to get tired and bored the more chores we do, thereby increasing the cost of performing additional services around the house.

You have already learned that a person will maximize the net benefit obtained from an activity if she engages in it to the point where its marginal benefit equals its marginal cost. There is no reason to believe that this would be any different for suppliers. After all, each supplier is trying to maximize the return she gets from the scarce resources that she owns. In the case of price-taking suppliers, the "benefit" they get when they sell each unit of a good is equal to the price (P) they receive for the unit. This means that the quantity supplied that will maximize a producer's net benefit is where the good's price just covers the marginal cost of the very last unit produced.

Figure 7.2 shows a typical marginal cost (MC) curve, which exhibits increasing marginal cost, for the production of bottled water. As we can see, if the price of

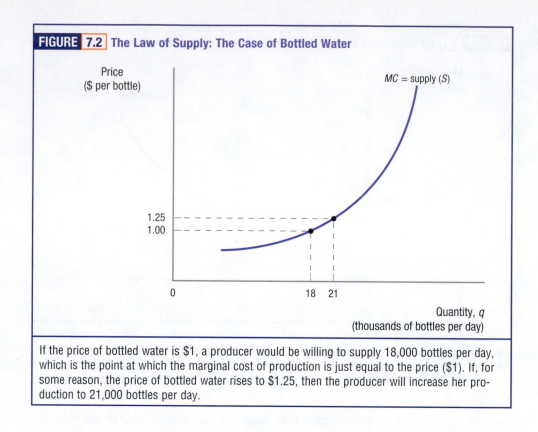

FIGURE 7.2 The Law of Supply: The Case of Bottled Water

If the price of bottled water is $1, a producer would be willing to supply 18,000 bottles per day, which is the point at which the marginal cost of production is just equal to the price ($1). If, for some reason, the price of bottled water rises to $1.25, then the producer will increase her production to 21,000 bottles per day.

bottled water is $1 per bottle, the producer would be willing to supply 18,000 bottles per day, which is the point at which the marginal cost of producing the very last bottle is just equal to the price ($1) she receives for it.

Why is 18,000 bottles per day the "best" output level to choose? Suppose that the bottler chose instead to produce more than 18,000 bottles a day. At this higher output level, the marginal cost of each of the additional bottles is greater than $1, the price she receives for each bottle. This means that she is losing money on all of the bottles produced beyond 18,000 bottles a day; that is, the net benefit received from these additional bottles is *negative.* Rational economic decision makers will never engage in an activity that generates negative net benefits. They will stop at the point where the marginal benefit is just equal to the marginal cost.

Suppose instead that the supplier decides to produce only 12,000 bottles of water a day. The marginal cost of producing the 12,001th bottle of water is less than $1, meaning that if she expanded her output, she could capture additional net benefit. This will be the case up to the 18,000th bottle of water. As you have already learned, she won't receive any additional net benefit from the 18,000th bottle supplied because the price she receives for it ($1) is just equal to the marginal cost of producing it ($1). Unless her marginal cost of production goes down, or the price goes up, she won't be inclined to supply any more units.

The Law of Supply

Suppose that the price that the bottler receives rises to $1.25. How will she respond to this change in her economic environment? She will choose a new output level, where the marginal cost of producing the last unit is now just equal to $1.25. Figure 7.2

shows that the supplier is willing to increase her output level to 21,000 bottles per day when the price is $1.25 because the higher price will cover the higher marginal cost of producing additional bottles. As the price rises, the producer is "enticed" to move up her marginal cost curve and increase the quantity of bottled water supplied.

The fact is that higher prices tend to persuade suppliers to supply more output. A higher wage will entice you to work overtime. A higher interest rate will entice you to save more. When a price increases, the marginal benefit of supplying additional units rises. This encourages producers to supply more, even though they incur higher marginal costs of production. This result leads directly to the **law of supply**.

LAW OF SUPPLY When a good's price increases, suppliers are willing to offer more units for sale, all other things held constant. Conversely, when the price falls, suppliers cut back on the number of units they are willing to sell.

EXAMPLE You work an eight-hour shift as a waiter at a local restaurant, after which you are dead on your feet. Your boss offers you double time—twice your regular wage—to cover the next shift for a sick employee. You agree, but only because you will receive twice the money for the second shift.

EXAMPLE When interest rates rise from 1.5 percent to 12 percent, people tend to save more money because the opportunity cost of spending it now has risen.

A Producer's Supply Curve

In the previous chapter, we discussed the relationship between the price of hot dogs in New York City and the number of hot dogs that a tourist will buy during her weekend visit there. Let's now look at how many hot dogs a typical street vendor in New York City is willing and able to supply at different prices. **Table 7.1** shows the hot dog vendor's **supply schedule**.

SUPPLY SCHEDULE A table that shows various prices of a good and the number of units a producer is willing to sell at each price during a specific time period.

As you can see, this supply schedule is consistent with the notion that as the price of hot dogs increases, so does the street vendor's willingness to sell more hot dogs. At a lower price of $1 per hot dog, the vendor is only willing to supply five dozen each day. As the price rises to $1.25, however, he is willing to increase production and

Table 7.1 Supply Schedule of Hot Dogs	
p	*q*
Price per hot dog ($)	No. of hot dogs supplied each day (in dozens)
1	5
1.25	10
1.50	15
1.75	20

supply an additional five dozen hot dogs, for a total of ten dozen each day. The price has to rise to elicit this additional supply because the vendor will incur higher marginal costs of production, say from working later hours in the cold or having to buy a lot more ice to keep a greater number of hot dogs cold all day.

As we did with the demand schedule, we can use the information in the supply schedule to construct a **supply curve**.

> **SUPPLY CURVE** A graphic representation of a supplier's supply schedule. The supply curve plots various price–quantity combinations that an individual producer is willing to accept.

A supply curve, like the one shown in **Figure 7.3** for hot dogs, plots the various price–quantity combinations that the supplier is willing to accept. By convention, the price (P) of the good is on the vertical axis, and the number of units, or quantity (q), of the good that an individual supplier is *willing to supply* is on the horizontal axis. We adopt the convention of using a lowercase "q" to represent the quantity that an individual supplier is willing to supply.

In Figure 7.3, the height of the supply curve at any given output level reflects the opportunity cost of supplying the last, or marginal, unit. For example, the marginal cost of supplying the tenth dozen of hot dogs equals $1.25 per hot dog. Therefore, the supplier must be paid at least $1.25 per hot dog to provide this much output. At $1.25, the vendor is indifferent to whether he supplies the last (tenth) dozen of

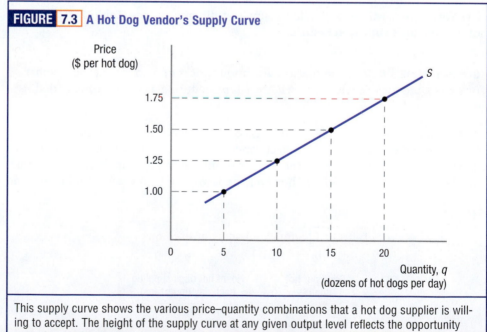

FIGURE 7.3 **A Hot Dog Vendor's Supply Curve**

Price ($ per hot dog)

This supply curve shows the various price–quantity combinations that a hot dog supplier is willing to accept. The height of the supply curve at any given output level reflects the opportunity cost of supplying the last, or marginal, hot dog. At a price of $1 per hot dog, the vendor is willing to supply five dozen hot dogs a day. When the price rises to $1.25, he is willing to supply ten dozen hot dogs, and so on.

hot dogs or not because the marginal benefit (price) received is just equal to marginal cost, resulting in zero net benefit.

It is important to recognize that the supply curve reveals the amount of a good that a producer is willing to sell at different prices. But just because he may be willing to sell different amounts at these different prices doesn't mean that there will be buyers for his output at all of these prices. Our street vendor might be willing to supply 80 dozen hot dogs per day if the price was $25 a hot dog, but at that price, the amount actually sold will likely be little or none. Similarly, you might be willing to supply 90 hours of work each week for $500 an hour. The trouble is you are likely to have a hard time finding an employer who will hire you at that wage. So if the prices that suppliers are willing to sell at are higher than even one buyer's willingness to pay, no voluntary exchanges will take place at all in this market.

The Supply of Labor

To better understand the concept of a supply curve, we turn to an example that is likely to be of particular interest to you—your supply of labor. Because we "own" our time in free societies, we must be paid to supply labor services (unless we are willing to volunteer our time). How much we must be paid depends on the opportunity cost of our time. That is, what is the net benefit we pass up from our next-best activity if, instead, we go to work?

We may be paid by the hour, day, or year. Regardless of how we are paid, there is a price at which we are willing to supply some labor services. When it comes to labor services, we call this price a **wage**.

WAGE The price at which labor services are supplied.

EXAMPLE The going wage for economic tutoring is $9.50 per hour. Ben is willing to work six hours a week at that wage.

EXAMPLE A telecommunications company offered a consultant $100 per hour to testify as an expert witness in a trial. She turned it down, saying that her going consulting rate was $175 an hour.

To maximize your economic well-being, you will weigh the benefits of working against the opportunity cost of working. This decision process will dictate how much time you spend at work and how much you spend on your next-best alternative. As you dedicate more and more of your time to work, there is less and less time left over for other activities that also give you pleasure. The more you work, the less time you have to sleep, go to school, play sports, or pursue other leisure activities.

Sure, the additional wages you earn will increase the amount of goods you can buy in the marketplace. Even so, these goods generate declining contributions to your personal satisfaction if the principle of diminishing marginal benefit holds. And, as the remaining time that is available for other activities declines, it becomes all the more valuable when put to these uses. Working more than 50 hours a week can even jeopardize your health by increasing the risk of high blood pressure and related health problems.[3] Therefore, if you are to be enticed into working extra hours, the wage you get for these additional hours must increase. Conversely, if the wage rate drops, it

[3]"Overtime: Good for Your Wallet but Bad for Your Health." *St. Louis Post Dispatch*, October 1, 2006.

will no longer cover the opportunity cost of working these extra, higher-cost hours. People will move down their labor supply curves, devoting more time to leisure activities and less to work.

This work–leisure trade-off is consistent with the observed behavior of employers and employees. For example, employers have a long history of paying more for "overtime" hours to persuade workers to put in more than a 40-hour workweek. In 1938, during the Great Depression, labor groups successfully lobbied Congress for "time-and-a-half" wages to be paid to hourly employees who worked more than 40 hours a week. Their rationale was that employees should be compensated for sacrificing additional leisure opportunities when they worked overtime. Congress supported the "time-and-a-half" initiative for quite a different reason. It wanted to penalize employers for extending the workweek for existing workers instead of hiring more employees. Whatever the underlying rationale, we know that according to the law of supply, an increase in the wage for overtime hours encourages workers to work more hours per week, all other things remaining the same.

ECONOMIC FALLACY   When salaries go up, some people work less, not more. This means that the law of supply must not apply to labor markets.

False. Recall that the law of supply states that when the price of a good or service—in this case, the wage—goes up, more of it will be supplied—in this case, hours worked. You will also recall that this prediction holds *ceteris paribus*, that is, when everything else remains unchanged. In fact, the *ceteris paribus* condition is violated when we talk about a person's responsiveness to wage changes. The reason for this is that when wages change, so does the income of the worker. If we believe that leisure activities are normal goods, then more income would lead to greater consumption of leisure. However, this means that more time will be spent on leisure activities, leaving less time for work. We call this the *income effect* of a change in the wage rate.

It still remains true, however, that an increase in the wage rate increases the opportunity cost of pursuing more leisure activities because more goods can now be purchased for every hour worked. This is referred to as the *substitution effect* between leisure and consumables. In most cases, the substitution effect outweighs the income effect, so that a greater quantity of labor services is supplied when the wage rate rises and a lesser quantity is supplied when the wage rate declines. The income effect usually doesn't outweigh the substitution effect except at very high wage rates, where an individual's labor supply curve actually becomes *backward-bending*.

And even though there may be backward-bending supply curves when it comes to an individual's labor supply, after we aggregate all these curves to obtain the market supply curve, we expect that it will still conform to the law of supply and be upward sloping.

7.2 Supply in the Short Run versus the Long Run

Even though supply curves are upward sloping, this does not tell us exactly how much *more* quantity is supplied when the price of a product increases or what the magnitude of the reduction will be if its price drops. We can get a better handle on a supplier's responsiveness to price by looking at the slope of her supply curve. Usually, suppliers are less responsive to price changes in the short run than in the long run. Given more time to adjust, suppliers have greater freedom (meaning that they face fewer costly constraints) to respond fully to price changes. For example, a manufacturer may be able to expand her production in the long run at low cost because over time, she can train additional employees and avoid paying overtime to existing workers. Or, she can build additional production facilities to accommodate more workers rather than pay employees a premium to work night shifts. Therefore, we expect a supplier's *long-run* supply curve to be flatter than the *short-run* supply curve.

In the very short run, called the **market period**, a supplier is unable to respond at all to a change in the price offered for his product. The quantity he supplies to the market cannot contract if the price falls or expand if the price rises.

MARKET PERIOD The length of time during which a supplier cannot make any adjustment to the quantity he supplies to the market.

EXAMPLE After a farmer has planted his crops for the season, he cannot change the volume or mix of agricultural products he supplies to the market.

EXAMPLE In the fall, clothing retailers submit their orders for spring fashions. These retailers are then locked into the styles and volume of clothing they have on hand to sell in the spring.

Consider the situation where your boss offered you $200 an hour to work 4 more hours after you have already worked an 18-hour shift. You probably wouldn't be inclined to accept his offer because you need some sleep. Similarly, if we look at the supply of residential housing, we know that in the market period, the supply of new houses is unresponsive to changes in price. It takes time to find land, get building permits, and construct a new house. Given more time, builders may be able to convert warehouses into lofts or apartments into condos at a relatively low cost in response to increases in housing prices. We refer to the period in which this type of partial response occurs as the **short run**.

SHORT RUN The length of time during which a supplier is able to only partially adjust the quantity she supplies to the market in response to a change in the good's price.

EXAMPLE A manufacturer of a hit toy can expand her output somewhat in response to an increase in the toy's price by adding a third shift to her firm's current production schedule.

EXAMPLE When the price of plywood rose as a result of Hurricane Katrina, Gulf Coast suppliers of building materials could only modestly increase the quantities they had to sell by buying from suppliers in nearby states.

In the **long run**, a supplier can fully respond to a change in price by expanding or contracting all inputs into production at low cost.

LONG RUN The length of time required for a supplier to be able to fully adjust the quantity she supplies to the market in response to a change in the good's price.

EXAMPLE When tofu and other soybean products became a mainstay of the American diet and led to higher soybean prices, it took farmers several years to fully transition from wheat to soybean production.

EXAMPLE When the world price of oil increases, it can take oil producers years to bring new offshore oil rigs on line.

When it comes to the housing industry, it will take much longer for builders to increase the supply of homes built from the ground up than to retrofit apartment buildings or warehouses in response to higher housing prices.

Figures 7.4 shows how the housing supply curve changes from the market period to the short run, and, finally, to the long run. In the market period, the supply curve (S_{mp}) of a typical builder in Atlanta is vertical at the current quantity of new, vacant houses he has available for sale—say 12 units. In this case, notice that even if housing prices increase from $220,000 to $270,000, there is no increase in the quantity supplied. The other two supply curves represent the short run (S_{sr}) and the long run (S_{lr}). As you can see, over time, the builder is able to respond more fully to price increases. In the short run, a price increase from $220,000 to $270,000 results in an increase in available housing from 12 to 18 units per year. Over a longer period of time, the same price increase elicits even more supply, increasing the available quantity from 18 to 24 units per year.

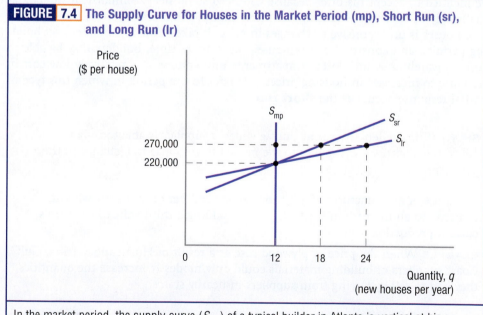

FIGURE 7.4 **The Supply Curve for Houses in the Market Period (mp), Short Run (sr), and Long Run (lr)**

In the market period, the supply curve (S_{mp}) of a typical builder in Atlanta is vertical at his current quantity of new, vacant houses—12 units. Even if housing prices increase from $220,000 to $270,000, the quantity supplied remains at 12 units during the market period. The other two supply curves represent the short run (S_{sr}) and the long run (S_{lr}). In the short run, a price increase from $220,000 to $270,000 results in an increase in available housing from 12 to 18 units per year. In the long run, this same price increase elicits an increase in quantity from 18 to 24 units per year.

A frequently asked question is how long—in terms of actual time—it takes for a supplier to "get to" the long run. The answer depends on the good in question and the constraints that the supplier faces. Suppliers with a lot of unused capacity, such as fiber-optic network suppliers, can readily expand their services in a very short period of time. In contrast, an airline running at nearly 100 percent seating capacity requires significantly more time to expand its services, especially if the expansion requires new planes, new airport gates, and the hiring and training of new pilots and crews.

It can also take time for a supplier to downsize operations and reduce the quantity he produces. In 1989, the U.S. government enacted regulations that have since required employers to give employees 60 day advance notice of a plant closure. These new laws have slowed the ability of U.S. producers to respond to dramatic reductions in price. Similarly, car manufacturers that have negotiated multiyear contracts with unionized workers can't quickly scale back production when car prices drop. This is one reason that major U.S. car manufacturers sought bankruptcy protection during the 2007 Great Recession. Under bankruptcy protection, they were able to renegotiate the terms of their labor union contracts before these agreements had expired.

Because different industries respond to price changes on different timetables, it can be difficult to precisely pinpoint the impact that government policies have on various sectors of the economy. For example, when the Federal Reserve reduces interest rates, it's likely that the automobile industry will improve—in terms of sales and employment levels—before the housing industry because the production cycle for housing is 12 to 15 months long compared to just 30 days for cars.

7.3 Movements along a Supply Curve versus Shifts in the Supply Curve

When a good's price changes, a supplier responds by changing the quantity of the good she is willing to produce (as long as we are not in the market period). As you saw in Figure 7.3, an increase in the price of hot dogs leads to an increase in the quantity of hot dogs that a typical street vendor is willing to sell, if he is able. If the price of hot dogs falls, the vendor will reduce the number of hot dogs supplied. Unlike the demand curve, the supply curve exhibits a positive relationship between price and quantity supplied. That is, the quantity supplied moves in the *same* direction as the change in price. A price increase, therefore, moves a supplier up along his supply curve.

What leads to a shift in the supply curve? If you recall, a shift in the demand curve means that there is a change in the quantity demanded *at each and every price*. It turns out that we have an analogous situation for the supply curve. In **Figure 7.5**, we have drawn a supply curve for cell phones that has the now-familiar upward slope. At $100, we see that the quantity of cell phones supplied by Qualcomm, a producer of cell phones, is 1,000,000 units per year.

What if the price of cell phones increases to $130? At this higher price, you can see that Qualcomm is willing to *move up* its supply curve and provide 1,250,000 phones for sale each year. A decrease in the price would have had the opposite effect.

For Qualcomm's supply curve to shift, there must be a change in its economic environment that results in a change in its willingness to supply *at each and every price*. Consider the shift in Qualcomm's supply curve from S_1 to S_2. At S_2, Qualcomm is now willing to supply 1,500,000 phones at $100; that is, the quantity supplied has increased even though the price of the cell phone hasn't. This tells us that something

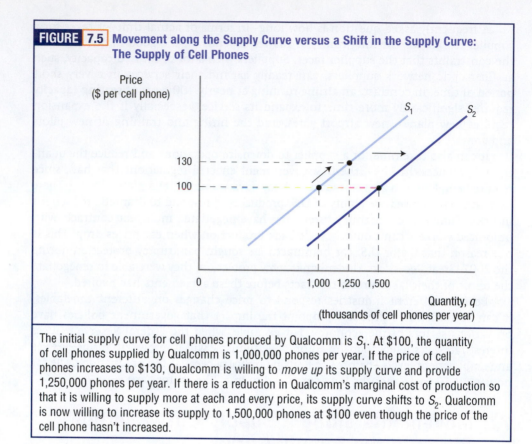

FIGURE 7.5 Movement along the Supply Curve versus a Shift in the Supply Curve: The Supply of Cell Phones

The initial supply curve for cell phones produced by Qualcomm is S_1. At $100, the quantity of cell phones supplied by Qualcomm is 1,000,000 phones per year. If the price of cell phones increases to $130, Qualcomm is willing to *move up* its supply curve and provide 1,250,000 phones per year. If there is a reduction in Qualcomm's marginal cost of production so that it is willing to supply more at each and every price, its supply curve shifts to S_2. Qualcomm is now willing to increase its supply to 1,500,000 phones at $100 even though the price of the cell phone hasn't increased.

in the economic environment has changed that affected Qualcomm's decision process, and it wasn't the price of the cell phone.

A rightward shift in the supply curve means that there is an increase in the quantity supplied at each and every price. A leftward shift in the supply curve means that there is a decrease in the quantity supplied at each and every price. What can cause the supply curve to shift? We address this question next.

7.4 Factors that Shift a Supply Curve

When we discussed factors that shift an individual's demand curve, we considered changes in income, property rights, the price of alternatives, and preferences. These changes shift the demand curve so that the quantity demanded is now higher or lower at each and every price. When it comes to the supply curve, a change in the opportunity cost of production leads to a shift in the curve. That is, anything that affects the marginal cost of producing an additional unit of output will result in a shift in the supply curve so that the quantity supplied *at each and every price* changes.

Although a number of things can change a supplier's marginal cost of production, perhaps the most obvious is a change in the price of an input used in the production process. We look at this next.

Changes in Input Prices

If the marginal cost of production changes, it changes the net benefit that a supplier receives for each unit produced. Why? The net benefit per unit is simply the difference between its marginal benefit and marginal cost or, in this case, the difference between the price received for the unit and its marginal cost of production. When there is an increase in the cost of hiring workers, for example, the marginal cost curve will shift upward and, given that there is no change in price, the supplier will cut back on the number of units he is willing to produce.

Whether we are talking about labor, machinery, or other resources used up in the production process, each has a price. Workers are paid wages, and equipment owners are paid a lease payment. We call these **input prices**. An input price tells us the price of a "unit" of an input—the wage per hour, the price per barrel of oil, the monthly lease rate for a scanning machine, and so forth.

INPUT PRICE The price of one unit of an input used in production.

EXAMPLE Animators are employed to produce Disney films such as *The Lion King*. The wage they receive per hour, day, or week is an input price.

EXAMPLE Oil is used to produce rubber, steel, plastics, and other basic manufacturing materials. The price of oil per barrel is an input price.

Let's take a closer look at how a change in the price of an input affects the supply of a good. Consider the impact that an increase in animators' wages has on Disney's supply of animated movies each year. **Figure 7.6** depicts the supply curve, labeled S_1, of animated movies that Disney is willing to supply each year based on its current costs of production.

FIGURE 7.6 **How an Input Price Shifts the Supply Curve: A Wage Increase for Movie Animators**

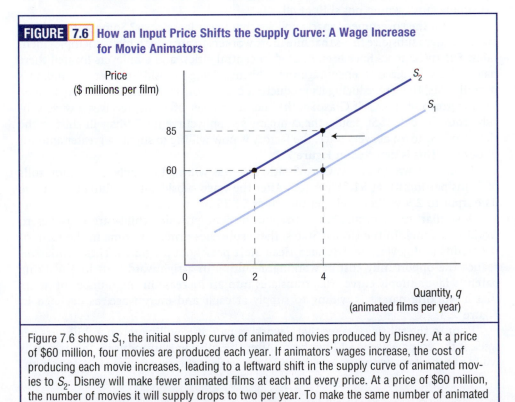

Figure 7.6 shows S_1, the initial supply curve of animated movies produced by Disney. At a price of $60 million, four movies are produced each year. If animators' wages increase, the cost of producing each movie increases, leading to a leftward shift in the supply curve of animated movies to S_2. Disney will make fewer animated films at each and every price. At a price of $60 million, the number of movies it will supply drops to two per year. To make the same number of animated films (four) per year as before the wage increase, Disney must now receive $85 million per movie.

If film distributors are willing to pay $60 million per movie, then Disney will supply four films per year. Now what if animators' wages increase by one-third, perhaps because the opening of a new animation studio (Pixar) increases their opportunities? The cost of producing each movie increases as a result. As the marginal cost of each movie increases, the net benefit from producing each movie declines. Consequently, the supply curve of animated movies shifts to the left, to the supply curve labeled S_2. Disney will make fewer animated films at each and every price. If Disney expects to sell each movie at the same price as before ($60 million), the number of movies it will supply will drop to two per year. To acquire the same number of animated films (four) as before the wage increase, the film distributors must now offer $85 million per movie. This is because the marginal cost of producing the third and fourth movie is now higher than the original price tag of $60 million per movie.

Virtually all goods use labor in either their production or distribution stages. This means that an increase in wage rates will translate directly into an increase in the cost of supplying most goods. As we have just shown, this will result in a leftward shift in the supply curve for these goods. At any given price, a lesser quantity of the good is now supplied. Suppose, for example, that the government required all employers to provide workers with health-insurance coverage or a new paid holiday (e.g., Super Bowl Monday). The employer's cost of labor services would increase, and the supply curve for its product would shift to the left. One way of seeing this is to recognize that after the leftward shift in the supply curve, the *vertical height* of the new supply curve, which reflects the marginal cost of producing each unit, is greater at all levels of output. Of course, if there is a supplier who is not subject to the new law—perhaps because he has a small number of employees or is located outside the country—then his supply curve would not shift at all.

What if the government enacts policies that lower labor costs? Some state and federal initiatives subsidize firms that hire more workers in areas with high-unemployment rates. *Enterprise zones* have been created in central cities, and employers located there have been subsidized to encourage more hiring.[4] Wage subsidies lower a company's payroll costs, thereby reducing its production costs. Consider the Tums factory located in downtown St. Louis. If GlaxoSmithKline, the maker of Tums, receives a wage subsidy from the city of St. Louis, the company's supply curve for Tums will shift to the right from S_1 to S_2: at every price, the factory is now willing to supply a greater amount of output. This is depicted in **Figure 7.7**.

Before the wage subsidy, GlaxoSmithKline was willing to supply 1.5 million rolls of Tums per month at $1.25 per roll. After the wage subsidy, it is willing to increase its output to 2.9 million rolls per month at $1.25 per roll.

A similar result occurs when the government provides child-care subsidies to working parents. In the United States, these subsidies primarily come in the form of tax credits and government-funded Head Start preschool programs. These initiatives reduce the opportunity cost of working, resulting in a rightward shift in a working parent's labor supply curve. This translates into an increase in the number of hours that a working parent is willing to supply at each and every wage, as depicted in **Figure 7.8**.

Prior to the subsidy, we see that a working parent is willing to work 35 hours per week if the going wage is $12 per hour. After the subsidy is introduced, this parent is willing to increase her hours worked to 39 per week at the going wage of $12 per hour.

⋯⋯⋯

[4]Robert Pear, "Congress Revives Bill on Investment in Poor Areas." *New York Times*, December 14, 2000.

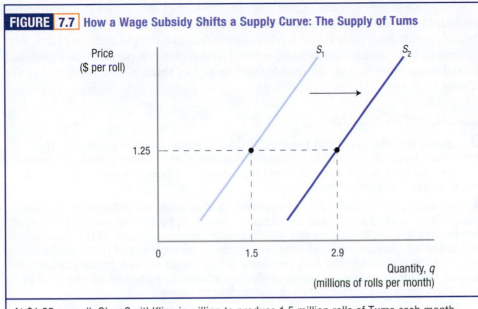

FIGURE 7.7 **How a Wage Subsidy Shifts a Supply Curve: The Supply of Tums**

At $1.25 per roll, GlaxoSmithKline is willing to produce 1.5 million rolls of Tums each month. Wage subsidies reduce the marginal cost of producing each roll of Tums. As a result, the supply curve shifts to the right, from S_1 to S_2, leading the company to increase its supply to 2.9 million rolls per month.

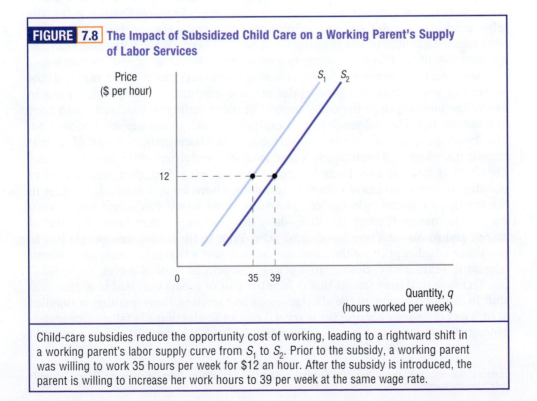

FIGURE 7.8 **The Impact of Subsidized Child Care on a Working Parent's Supply of Labor Services**

Child-care subsidies reduce the opportunity cost of working, leading to a rightward shift in a working parent's labor supply curve from S_1 to S_2. Prior to the subsidy, a working parent was willing to work 35 hours per week for $12 an hour. After the subsidy is introduced, the parent is willing to increase her work hours to 39 per week at the same wage rate.

This response is precisely the reason why, in 1996, then-President Clinton incorporated child-care subsidies into the U.S. government's new welfare-to-work program. The idea was to encourage single mothers on welfare to return to the labor force. And it seems to have worked: on average, women who received these child-care subsidies worked more months and had double the earnings of those who did not receive the subsidy.[5]

SOLVED PROBLEM

Q Suppose that the U.S. dollar becomes "weaker" relative to other currencies. This means that each dollar is able to purchase less in the world market, including foreign-produced oil. How would this affect the supply curve of a producer such as U.S. Steel, which is heavily dependent on oil imports.

A The dollar price of each barrel of imported oil rises when the dollar weakens, even though there is no change in the actual resources—labor, equipment, and so forth—that foreign suppliers use to produce this oil. As a result, the supply curve of U.S. Steel will shift to the left: its marginal cost of producing each and every ton of rolled steel rises. Generally speaking, when the dollar weakens, it leads to an increase in the production costs of any domestic supplier whose production process is dependent on imported inputs. This results in a leftward shift in the producer's supply curve.

Technology (Knowledge) and Production Costs

Technological breakthroughs often lead to new, cost-saving production processes. As we noted in Chapter 6, grocery stores introduced labor-saving price-scanning registers to reduce their costs; fast-food restaurants turned to automatic and self-serve drink-filling machines; and banks began to offer a wide range of services through automatic teller machines (ATMs) and online banking. These cost-reducing technologies have increased the quantity of services supplied at each and every price. Banks, for example, are now able to offer 24-hour access to your money without additional service fees.

An important example of how cost-saving technology can increase supply in the absence of any change in a good's price was the invention of the printing press in 1440. The press replaced the costly process of using scribes to handwrite each copy of a manuscript. The end result was an explosive growth in the supply of books and, as a by-product, an increase in knowledge and its dissemination. Think of it: that knowledge, which had been largely locked away in the cloisters of the monks, infused the world at large at a relatively low cost. You are living through a similar kind of transformation: advances in computer technology have led to a dramatic increase in the supply of low-cost information. More and more people can access a wide variety of information through the Web—daily stock prices, weather forecasts, musical scores, and so on—at a very low or zero price. Prior to these advances, people had to pay a much higher price for the same access: there was a charge to access the 24-hour telephone weather line, closing stock prices, and printed musical scores.

Technological innovations that reduce the cost of production lead to a rightward shift in the supply curve of the affected goods and services. More quantity is supplied *at each and every price* because the marginal cost of production has fallen. Computer-generated animation technologies, for example, have substantially reduced the cost

·······

[5]Sandra Danziger, et al., "Childcare Subsidies and the Transition from Welfare to Work." *Family Relations,* November 2003.

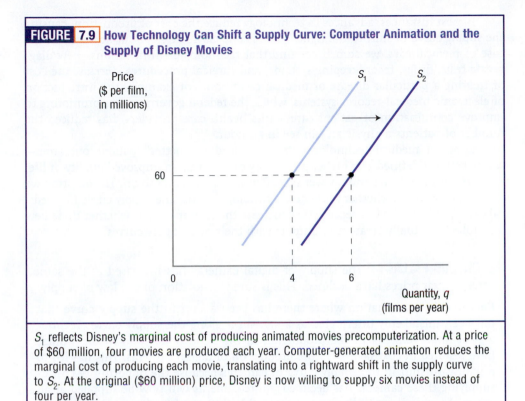

FIGURE 7.9 **How Technology Can Shift a Supply Curve: Computer Animation and the Supply of Disney Movies**

S_1 reflects Disney's marginal cost of producing animated movies precomputerization. At a price of $60 million, four movies are produced each year. Computer-generated animation reduces the marginal cost of producing each movie, translating into a rightward shift in the supply curve to S_2. At the original ($60 million) price, Disney is now willing to supply six movies instead of four per year.

of producing animated features because animators are no longer needed to draw each individual film cel by hand. In fact, Disney produced its first fully computer-animated movie, *Chicken Little,* in 2005.

To see how technological change might impact the supply of animated movies, **Figure 7.9** shows the supply curve, labeled S_1, of animated movies precomputerization. At a price of $60 million, four movies are produced each year. Computer-generated animation reduces the marginal cost of producing each movie, translating into a rightward shift in the supply curve to the new supply curve labeled S_2. At the original ($60 million) price, Disney is now willing to supply six movies instead of four per year. Now, the marginal cost of producing the fourth and fifth movies is less than $60 million, and the marginal cost of producing the sixth movie is just equal to $60 million. The vertical distance of the supply curve at each and every unit of output is lower than before because the marginal cost of producing each film has fallen.

There are many other examples of how advances in technology have lowered the cost of production and increased supply without any increase in the price of the good. E-mail and the Internet have both reduced the cost of working because they permit people to work at home rather than commuting to an office. Many work costs—a professional wardrobe, transportation, and even child care—can be substantially reduced when telecommuting is introduced into the workplace. Your professor, for example, can now hold "virtual" office hours from her home via e-mail, after the kids have been put to bed. When this happens, there is a rightward shift in her supply of office hours; she is willing to offer more virtual hours without an increase in her pay.

In most instances, advances in technology reduce the cost of production, causing the supply curve to shift to the right. There is one glaring exception, however. In the case of medical care, we sometimes find that technological innovations—new diagnostic tests, drugs, recordkeeping systems, and surgical procedures—*increase* the cost of treating a particular disease or medical condition. For example, the introduction of electronic medical-records systems, which the federal government is promoting to improve coordination of patient care across health-care providers, has reduced the number of patients a physician can see in an hour.

Advanced medical technologies typically lead to "better" patient outcomes—where better is defined as a higher probability of survival, an improved quality of life, a shorter recuperation period, fewer side effects, less pain, and so on. The question we leave unanswered is whether these new technologies cause the supply curve for medical care to shift to the left because they increase the cost of care, or whether these new technologies actually create new outputs with their own supply curves.

ECONOMIC FALLACY   The supply of digital cameras has increased at the same time as their prices have declined. This is surely a violation of the law of supply.

False. This is a situation where there has been a *shift* in the supply curve that has been mistakenly interpreted as a *movement* along the supply curve. Technological improvements in the production of high-end optics and media storage have resulted in cost savings in the production of digital cameras. This has led to a rightward shift in the supply curve of cameras because the opportunity cost of supplying these cameras has declined. More cameras will now be supplied at all prices. As we will see in the next chapter, this shift right in the supply curve will cause the market price for cameras to decline.

As this example shows, when the *ceteris paribus* assumption is violated (i.e., something other than a good's own price changes), the supply curve will shift, and the law of supply will mistakenly appear to be contradicted.

Property Rights and Production Costs

Changes in property rights can have a substantial impact on the decisions that suppliers make. Some of these changes reduce the marginal cost of production, while others increase the cost.

Consider, for example, the impact of court rulings which have established that victims of drunk drivers have the right to sue bars that serve the drivers. This new property right increases the cost of operating a bar and selling drinks because bar owners now have to pay higher insurance premiums to cover their additional liability. As a result, there is a leftward shift in the supply curve for bar drinks.

In contrast, some state legislatures have limited the liability of physicians by placing caps on the size of medical malpractice awards. We would expect this change to reduce the malpractice insurance premiums doctors pay. **Figure 7.10** shows the supply curve for a doctor who provides obstetrical services (the care of pregnant women and delivery of their babies). We define output in this case as the number of babies delivered each month.

At the price of $1,200 per delivery, we can see that this doctor is willing to "supply" 17 deliveries per month. Her cost of doing business includes her malpractice insurance premium, which increases with the number of deliveries she does each month. That is, it is part of her marginal cost curve. The cap that is now placed on medical malpractice

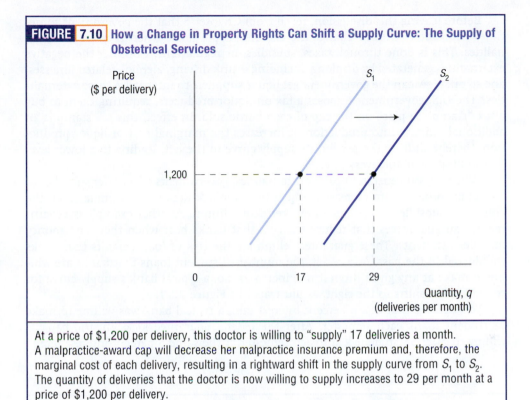

FIGURE 7.10 How a Change in Property Rights Can Shift a Supply Curve: The Supply of Obstetrical Services

At a price of $1,200 per delivery, this doctor is willing to "supply" 17 deliveries a month. A malpractice-award cap will decrease her malpractice insurance premium and, therefore, the marginal cost of each delivery, resulting in a rightward shift in the supply curve from S_1 to S_2. The quantity of deliveries that the doctor is now willing to supply increases to 29 per month at a price of $1,200 per delivery.

awards will decrease malpractice insurance premiums and, therefore, the marginal cost of each delivery. This leads to a rightward shift in the supply curve to the new supply curve labeled S_2. The doctor is now willing to supply 29 deliveries each month. The 18th through 28th deliveries now have a marginal cost that is less than $1,200, and the marginal cost of providing the 29th delivery is exactly equal to $1,200. As it turns out, after passage of these malpractice caps, the supply curves for obstetrics, neurosurgery, and other medical services that result in frequent malpractice lawsuits did, in fact, shift to the right.[6] However, not all states have passed laws to cap malpractice awards, so this rightward shift in supply has not occurred everywhere.

There are many examples of government regulations that affect the cost of supplying a good. Examples include workplace standards, reporting requirements, restrictions on how certain inputs can be handled or used in the production process, and waste-disposal rules. Regulations have the same impact on supply curves as government taxation. For example, whether the government requires all employers to offer health insurance to their workers or taxes them to fund a public health-care plan for all employees, the result will be qualitatively the same: labor costs will rise, leading to an increase in the marginal cost of production and a leftward shift in the employer's supply curve. Of course, the actual monetary impact of the two policies on an employer's payroll costs may be different if the tax does not equal the cost of directly providing employees with insurance.

· · · · · · ·

[6]William E. Encinosa and Fred J. Hellinger, "Have State Caps on Malpractice Awards Increased the Supply of Physicians?" *Health Affairs*, May 2005.

Before leaving this discussion, recall from Chapter 5 that the government sometimes deliberately tries to change the choices people make when they create externalities. This is done through taxes, subsidies, or regulations. Consider the negative externalities generated by drinking, including drunk driving, alcohol-related illnesses, and so on. How can the government get liquor suppliers to internalize these externalities? The U.S. government imposes a tax on liquor producers, requiring them to buy a tax "stamp" to place on the cap of each bottle sold. In effect, this tax stamp is an additional "input" into production. It increases the marginal cost of liquor production, thereby shifting the producer's supply curve to the left, leading to a lower level of output at each and every price.

When a good generates positive externalities, governments often offer subsidies to encourage producers to increase the quantity supplied. Recall our example about the child-care subsidies implemented by President Clinton. Another example is government loan guarantees that reduce the cost that banks bear when they lend money to college students. These guarantees eliminate the risk of loan defaults that banks shouldered in the past. As a result, the number of student loans that banks are willing to make at any given interest rate increases. So, a typical bank's supply curve for student loans shifts to the right, as illustrated in **Figure 7.11**.

You can see that at a 6 percent interest rate, a typical bank was willing to make 18 student loans each semester. After the federal guarantee kicks in, the bank is willing to offer 38 student loans each semester at the same 6 percent interest rate.

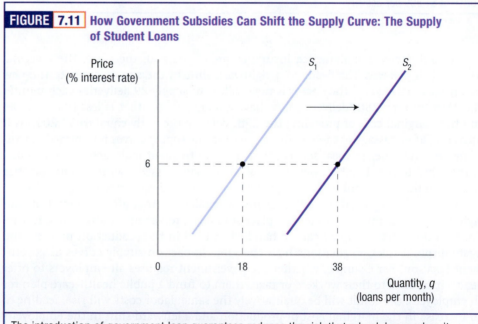

FIGURE **7.11** **How Government Subsidies Can Shift the Supply Curve: The Supply of Student Loans**

The introduction of government loan guarantees reduces the risk that a bank bears when it lends money to college students. Because there is no longer a risk of loan default, the bank's supply curve for student loans will shift to the right: at each and every interest rate, it is willing to supply a greater number of loans. At a 6 percent interest rate, the bank was willing to make 18 student loans each semester in the absence of government guarantees. After the federal guarantee kicks in, the bank is willing to offer 38 student loans each semester at the same 6 percent interest rate.

7.5 From Individual to Market Supply Curves

Recall that the market demand curve was derived by summing up the quantity demanded by each person at each and every price. In a parallel fashion, we can derive the **market supply curve** by adding up the quantity supplied by each producer at each and every price.

> **MARKET SUPPLY CURVE** A graphical representation of the total number of units of a good supplied at each and every price by all producers in a market during a specific period of time.

Note that while we represent an individual producer's quantity supplied by a lowercase q, we denote the total amount of output supplied in the market at each and every price by Q.

Our ability to derive a market supply curve is subject to the same challenges that arose in the derivation of a market demand curve. Defining the market and identifying suppliers who trade in the same market may, in reality, be quite difficult. Assuming that we can resolve these issues, how do we derive a market supply curve?

Let's revisit our earlier example of the hot dog vendor. In the first panel of **Figure 7.12** we show his supply curve. At a price of $1 per hot dog, this vendor is willing to sell 5 dozen hot dogs a day. The second panel shows the supply curve of the vendor on the next street corner. Notice that the two vendors' supply curves are not identical, which tells us that there are differences in the vendors' costs of production. Perhaps the second vendor has a lower cost of production because he

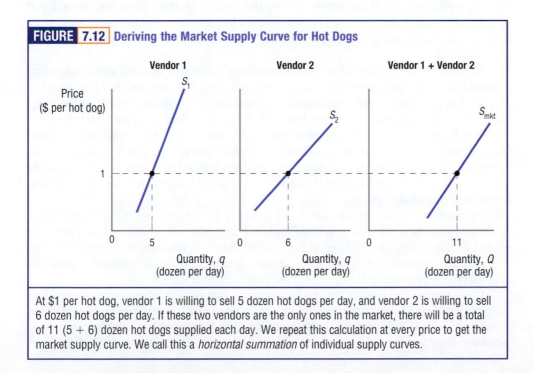

FIGURE 7.12 **Deriving the Market Supply Curve for Hot Dogs**

At $1 per hot dog, vendor 1 is willing to sell 5 dozen hot dogs per day, and vendor 2 is willing to sell 6 dozen hot dogs per day. If these two vendors are the only ones in the market, there will be a total of 11 (5 + 6) dozen hot dogs supplied each day. We repeat this calculation at every price to get the market supply curve. We call this a *horizontal summation* of individual supply curves.

doesn't have to pay for napkins—the theater down the street has given them to him to hand out to promote a new play. Because his marginal cost of production is lower, the second vendor is willing to supply 6 dozen hot dogs a day if the price is $1. If these are the only vendors in the market, then the market supply curve, as shown in the third panel of Figure 7.12, reveals the total market supply at each and every price. As indicated, at a price of $1, the combined quantity supplied is equal to 11 dozen hot dogs per day. We call this a *horizontal summation* of the individual supply curves. It directly parallels what we did with individual demand curves to obtain a market demand curve.

To derive a market supply curve when there are more than two suppliers, we follow the same approach, only adding in many more suppliers. By adding up the quantities (*q*) supplied at each and every price, we arrive at a market supply curve.

Because the height of the individual supply curves reflects the cost of producing each incremental unit, the height of the market supply curve will likewise represent the cost of supplying the marginal unit to the market. It is the lowest marginal cost possible given the cost considerations that each supplier faces. If one supplier enjoys lower costs than another, perhaps because he is exempt from paying a tax, this lower-cost supplier will be the only supplier in the market until the point where his cost of supplying one more unit just equals the marginal cost of the first unit supplied by the next-lowest cost supplier.

All of the factors that shift individual supply curves will likewise shift the market supply curve because the market supply curve is simply the summation of these individual curves. An increase in an input price that causes each producer's supply curve to shift left also causes the market supply curve to shift left. If only a few suppliers are affected by this increase, however, and there are many suppliers in the market, then the market supply curve may not shift very much at all. Imagine if a small city imposed a per drink tax on all of the bars located within its city limits. If this happened, the supply curves for drinks offered by local bars would shift to the left, but the supply curves of all the other bars in the greater metropolitan area would not change. As a result, the market supply curve for bar drinks in the entire metropolitan area would hardly budge as long as there are a large number of bars that lie outside the taxing city.

Whenever the number of suppliers increases, there will be additional individual supply curves to "add into" the market supply curve. This means that the quantity supplied at each and every price increases, resulting in a rightward shift in the market supply curve. Conversely, if the number of suppliers decreases, the market supply curve will shift to the left. For example, those states that have enacted medical-malpractice caps have seen an influx of "high-risk" specialists, which has resulted in a rightward shift in the market supply curves for these medical services. At the same time, the supply curves in states that have not enacted malpractice caps have shifted to the left due to this exodus.

As markets become more global, the number of suppliers in many markets has increased dramatically. For example, low-cost access to the Internet has promoted global e-commerce, thereby expanding the number of retailers who are willing to supply U.S. consumers with DVDs, art, books, and electronics at low cost. This shifts the market supply curve for each of these products to the right.

Or, consider the impact that technology has had on the labor supply curves facing U.S. employers. The Internet and secure, high-speed telecommunication services have enabled skilled workers living in India and elsewhere to supply accounting, software-development, and customer-support services to U.S. employers. "Offshoring"

FIGURE 7.13 **The Impact of Foreign Suppliers: The Supply of Accounting Services in the United States**

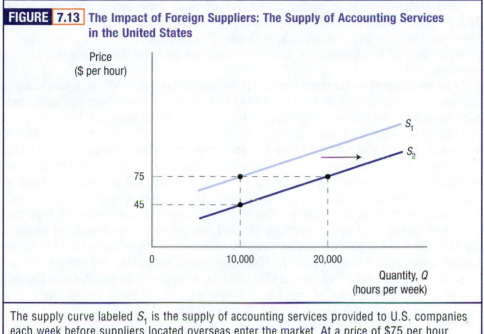

The supply curve labeled S_1 is the supply of accounting services provided to U.S. companies each week before suppliers located overseas enter the market. At a price of $75 per hour, accountants in the United States are willing to offer a total of 10,000 hours in services per week. After accountants located in India enter the market from their remote location, the amount of accounting services supplied to U.S. companies at each and every wage rate increases. There is a rightward shift in the supply curve to S_2. At $75 an hour, the total number of hours of accounting services supplied increases sharply, to 20,000 per week. The original number of accounting hours supplied at $75 an hour (10,000 hours) will now be supplied at $45 an hour.

these kinds of jobs to workers located outside the United States shifts the supply curve of labor services available to U.S. employers to the right. Foreign workers augment the number of workers actually living in the United States who are willing to work at each and every wage. We show this effect in **Figure 7.13**.

The supply curve labeled S_1 is the supply of accounting services provided to U.S. companies pre-Internet. At a price of $75 per hour, accountants in the United States are willing to offer a total of 10,000 hours of services per week.

Now let accountants living in India "enter" the market, providing accounting services to U.S. clients from their foreign locale. The supply curve of accounting services available to U.S. employers shifts right to S_2, reflecting the greater number of suppliers of accounting services. Also, because these foreign accountants often incur lower opportunity costs of working, they tend to supply more services at each and every wage. This means that the market supply curve for accounting services shifts to the right not only because there are more suppliers of these services but also because the marginal cost of these new suppliers is lower. At the initial price of $75, the total number of hours of accounting services supplied increases sharply, to 20,000 per week. The original number of accounting hours supplied at $75 (10,000 hours) will now be supplied at a price of $45 an hour. These hours will be supplied by the lowest-cost suppliers in the market—primarily by the foreign accountants.

The vertical distance between the old (S_1 and new supply curves (S_2) at 10,000 hours tells us that the marginal cost of supplying the 10,000th hour is now lower than before—$45 instead of $75. Employers—who are consumers of accounting services—benefit from using the lower-cost services provided by accountants living overseas.

Not everyone views this trend toward globalization favorably. What if, for example, the American Accounting Association (AAA) believes that its members will suffer economically from the increased reliance on foreign accounting services? After all, as we just saw, this is likely to reduce the wages of accountants working in the United States. We would expect the AAA to lobby the government to intervene to "protect" U.S. accountants from any loss of income. In many markets, the entry of foreign suppliers and the resulting growth in the quantity of imported goods and services purchased by U.S. consumers has led to an angry "push back" in the form of new tariffs and trade sanctions, along with subsidies for American producers. In one example, high tariffs on imported steel once effectively blocked foreign steel suppliers from entering the U.S. market. When they were repealed in 2003, the supply curve for steel in the United States shifted to the right.[7] In 2002, the United States imposed steep tariffs on Canadian lumber imports to protect U.S. jobs in the lumber industry. Because Canada had been a major supplier of wood to U.S. markets, these tariffs caused the supply curve of lumber available in the United States to shift to the left.[8]

The United States is not the only country that imposes these types of trade barriers on imports and exports. Following a drought in 2006, India banned the export of lentils for fear there would be domestic shortages of the product.[9] Because of this export ban, the quantity of lentils available at each and every price to U.S. consumers, including Indian restaurants, declined dramatically. The absence of Indian lentil suppliers translated into a leftward shift in the supply curve of lentils in the United States.

SOLVED PROBLEM

Q Suppose the state of Oregon passes a law that nurse-midwives can deliver babies in lieu of obstetricians. (1) What is the impact on the supply curve for delivery services? (2) Why do you think the state would pass this law? (3) Do you think that obstetricians would support enactment of this law or not?

A (1) The supply curve for delivery services will shift to the right from S_1 to S_2: there are now a greater number of suppliers of the service. These additional suppliers are likely to also face lower costs for each delivery, which also causes the supply curve to shift right. This means that at any price, more services will be provided. At $1,200 per delivery, for example, the total number of deliveries that will be supplied by obstetricians in Oregon before the new law was 480 a month. After the law passes, obstetricians and midwives are willing to perform 720 deliveries a month. (2) By allowing midwives to deliver babies, the state is supplementing the local supply of doctors available to deliver babies. (3) It is likely that obstetricians would oppose the law, arguing that it could compromise the health of the mother and baby. As we will see in the next chapter, the law is also likely to reduce the price that doctors receive for each delivery.

• • • • • • •

[7]Dan Ackman, "Bush Cuts Steel Tariffs, Declares Victory." *Forbes Magazine*, December 5, 2003.

[8]Major Garrett, "Bush Imposes Canadian Lumber Tariffs." *Money.cnn.com*, March 22, 2002.

[9]Corey Kilgannon, "Little India Hoards Lentils as Prices Rise." *New York Times*, September 29, 2006.

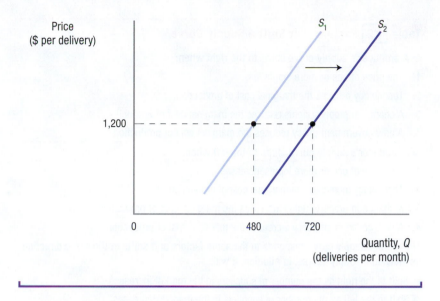

7.6 Summarizing the Factors that Shift Supply

Now that we have identified all of the factors that affect the supply of goods and ser-vices, we can summarize our findings. First, a change in the sales price of a product leads to a change in quantity supplied: each producer moves up or down his supply curve. The individual supply curves—and, consequently, the market supply curve—*will not shift* when the price of the good changes, assuming all else remains unchanged.

Second, a supplier will increase the quantity he is willing to supply at each and every price when his marginal cost of production falls. This will happen if (1) the price of one or more inputs falls; (2) cost-saving technology becomes available; (3) a change in property rights reduces the cost of supply; or (4) a government policy is enacted that provides a subsidy for each unit of the good produced or in some other way reduces a supplier's marginal cost of production. In each of these cases, the sup-ply curve shifts to the right: more is supplied *at each and every price*. And, the vertical height of the supply curve at any level of output, which reflects the cost of producing the marginal unit, is lower than before.

Conversely, a supplier will reduce the quantity he supplies at each and every price when his costs of production increase. This will happen if (1) the price of one or more inputs increases; (2) cost-increasing technology is introduced; (3) a change in property rights increases the cost of supply; or (4) a government policy is enacted that increases the marginal cost of producing each unit. In each of these cases, the supply curve shifts to the left: less is supplied *at each and every price*. The vertical height of the supply curve at any level of output is now higher than before.

Table 7.2 provides a summary of the impact that each of these factors has on individual supply curves and the market supply curve. It also reminds us that when the number of suppliers grows, the total quantity supplied in the market at each and every price also increases, and the market supply curve shifts to the right. On the other hand, if the number of suppliers falls, the total quantity supplied to the market at each and every price also falls, and the market supply curve shifts to the left.

To summarize, demanders are willing to pay a certain amount for each unit of a specific good. Likewise, suppliers are willing to supply units of a specific good if their costs of production are covered. If we assume that a free market economy exists—in

Table 7.2 Factors that Shift a Supply Curve

▶ A producer's supply curve shifts to the right when:

1. The price of one or more inputs falls.
2. Technology reduces the marginal cost of production.
3. A change in property rights reduces the marginal cost of production.
4. A new government policy reduces the marginal cost of production.

◀ A producer's supply curve shifts to the left when:

1. The price of one or more inputs increases.
2. Technology increases the marginal cost of production.
3. A change in property rights increases the marginal cost of production.
4. A new government policy increases the marginal cost of production.

The market supply curve responds to the same factors and shifts in the same direction as individual supply curves. In addition, it will:

▶ Shift to the right as the number of suppliers in the market increases.

◀ Shift to the left as the number of suppliers in the market decreases.

which voluntary trade can occur without interference—under what conditions will demanders and suppliers actually buy and sell goods? To explore this key question, we put the two "sides" of the market together in the next chapter.

WHAT YOU SHOULD HAVE LEARNED FROM CHAPTER 7

- That a supplier is just like every other economic decision maker—he is seeking to maximize the net benefit derived from his scarce resources.

- That the net benefit a supplier gets from selling a good or service in a market is equal to the price she receives for each unit minus the marginal cost of producing that unit.

- That the law of supply states that when a good's price increases, a supplier is willing to increase the quantity supplied of that good, all else remaining the same. Conversely, when a good's price falls, a supplier is willing to supply less of the good.

- That a supplier's supply schedule shows the amount of output that he is willing to provide at each and every market price.

- That the supply curve is a graphical representation of the supply schedule; its height at any level of output reflects the marginal cost of supplying the last unit.

- That long-run supply curves are usually flatter than short-run supply curves; that is, suppliers are more responsive to price changes in the long run.

- That input prices, technology, and property rights all have an impact on the amount a supplier is willing to supply at each and every price; therefore, changes in any of these factors usually lead to a shift in the individual supply curve.

- That the market supply curve is the horizontal summation of individual supply curves.

- That the same factors that shift individual supply curves will also shift the market supply curve in the same direction.

- That the market supply curve will shift to the right when the number of suppliers increases and shift to the left when the number of suppliers declines.

KEY TERMS

Law of supply, p. 177

Supply schedule, p. 177

Supply curve, p. 178

Wage, p. 179

Market period, p. 181

Short run (supply), p. 181

Long run (supply), p. 181

Input price, p. 185

Market supply curve, p. 193

QUESTIONS AND PROBLEMS

1. Maura goes to school full-time and moonlights as a security guard nights and weekends. When her hourly wage increased from $10 per hour to $12 per hour, she requested a cut in her scheduled hours. How would you explain the observed negative slope of her supply curve for labor? Does this tell you anything about whether nonwork activities are inferior or normal goods for Maura?

2. a) Draw the supply curves for two individual suppliers of lettuce, one who produces lettuce in California and the other who produces lettuce in Mexico. Assume that the suppliers are identical; that is, they both face the same opportunity cost of production.
   b) Select a price P, and show that both suppliers will supply the same quantity to the marketplace at this price.
   c) Using these same supply curves, now show what happens to the quantity supplied by each producer when the U.S. government requires that suppliers located in the United States pay a tax on every head of lettuce harvested. Assume that the price remains at P.
   d) If the U.S. government and the Mexican government permit free trade between their countries, who do you think will supply lettuce to U.S. consumers? Explain your answer.

3. Suppose the government imposes a quota on each fisherman to prevent overharvesting of fish. Show what the fisherman's supply curve looks like after the quota is imposed. What does the market supply curve look like?

4. Opponents to free-trade agreements such as NAFTA argue that they don't lower the true costs of supply because many countries—including the United States—heavily subsidize many of their domestic industries. Explain how subsidies "undermine" the ability of free-trade agreements to promote suppliers with the lowest economic costs of production.

5. Suppose that accounting firms can now either send accounting work to accountants in India via data-transmission technologies or import accountants from India to do the work. Explain carefully what factors might impact their decision. More specifically, under what conditions would it make more sense to send the work overseas?

6. Medical technology has advanced to the point where organs such as the liver can be split, with pieces transplanted into two patients rather than one. Show the impact of this technological change on the market supply curve for transplantable livers.

7. A California court ruled that a dentist was liable for a car accident involving a patient who was given "laughing gas" (nitrous oxide) earlier in the day. Show how the market supply curve for dental treatments using gas as a pain reliever/relaxant changed as a result of this change in property rights.

8. Several states are considering legislation that would give children with sperm donor "daddies" the right to contact these fathers when they reach the age of 21. If these new laws pass, what, if anything, do you think will happen to the market supply curve of sperm for infertility procedures?

9. The federal government has passed a number of regulations in recent years that impact the way in which medical practices operate. Among these regulations are

requirements that (1) medical records are now kept in special cabinets in locked rooms to protect patient privacy; and (2) electronic medical-records systems are introduced into the practice. Show how the market supply curve for LASIK surgeries is affected by these new regulations. Suppose the amount that each LASIK surgeon receives for each procedure remains unchanged. Can you predict what will happen to the number of procedures each surgeon will perform each month after these regulations are put into place?

10. In the long run, how do owners of commercial property reduce the market supply of properties in response to a decline in lease rates? Explain your answer.

11. Environmental-protection groups are delighted that plastic-bag manufacturers have become more attuned to environmental concerns and are now producing bags containing 40 percent recycled materials. Can you think of another reason that these producers have moved in this direction, independent of any environmental concerns? (Hint: plastics contain relatively large amounts of oil.)

12. At what wage rate would you consider working *fewer* hours each week? What types of considerations would factor into your answer? Explain.

13. When the United States eliminates tariffs on steel and chemical imports, more of the steel and chemicals that U.S. customers use are produced overseas. This means that the amount of pollution generated by these industries in the United States is lessened. How, if at all, do you think that pollution should factor into decisions about imposing or eliminating tariffs? Explain your answer.

The Makings of a Trade

"Teach a parrot the terms 'supply and demand' and you've got an economist."

Thomas Carlyle, essayist and historian who first called economics "the dismal science"

Now that we understand the fundamentals of both individual and market demand and supply, we turn to the crucial question: When will a trade actually take place? Is it enough that both demanders and suppliers simply co-exist in the same market, or must a buyer and a seller meet specific conditions for an exchange to occur? Will the price in the market be high enough to entice suppliers of a good and, at the same time, low enough to attract customers?

Both buyers and sellers have a "say" in whether a trade takes place. It takes both parties to a trade—demanders and suppliers—to determine the terms of this trade including the price, quantity, and specific property rights that will be exchanged. As the noted economist Alfred Marshall, once said:

> We might as well reasonably dispute whether it is the upper or under blade of a pair of scissors that cuts a piece of paper, as whether value [price] is governed by utility [demand] or cost of production [supply].[1]

Either party can always walk away from a deal if he is not satisfied with the terms. This means that a buyer cannot reap benefits at the expense of a seller's well-being, nor can a seller improve his own well-being at the expense of a buyer. *Voluntary* trade must be mutually beneficial to take place. The voluntary nature of trade is an integral component of free markets. This is in distinct contrast to situations in which a ruler or government requires people to consume a particular good or service (such as the requirement to buy health insurance) or coerces suppliers to provide a certain good or service (such as a military draft to meet a country's demand for soldiers).

The supply-and-demand framework that we will develop is relied upon for virtually every predictive model that economists develop, whether the subject matter is international trade, monetary policy, tax initiatives, population growth, or

- - - - - - -

[1]Alfred Marshall, *Principles of Economics*, 8th ed. (London: Macmillan, 1964), p. 348.

health-care reform. In this chapter, we explore how supply-and-demand analysis can be used to predict price changes in response to a change in the economic environment. We will also see why obstacles that impede the interactions between supply and demand in a market can lead to undesirable outcomes from an economic standpoint.

8.1 Market Supply and Demand, Together

When we introduced the concept of individual demand, we discussed the notion of willingness to pay for a good, which depends on the marginal benefit received. Likewise, we talked about a supplier's willingness to provide a good, which is dictated by the marginal cost of production. To identify under what conditions an actual trade will take place, we must first understand the way in which both market demand and supply *together* determine the market price. Will this price be equal to or lower than a demander's willingness to pay? Will it be equal to or higher than a supplier's marginal cost? When both of these conditions are met, trade will normally occur. We say "normally" because in some instances high transactions costs can derail otherwise viable trades.

As you will recall, a market demand curve has a negative slope—it tilts downward—and a market supply curve has a positive slope—it tilts upward. Suppose, for example, that the market demand and supply schedules for a specific type of memory chip are as reported in **Table 8.1**. (We continue the convention of using a capital Q for quantity to indicate that we are talking about *market* quantities, not *individual* supplier or demander quantities.) We can readily see that as price increases, the quantity demanded declines while the quantity producers are willing to supply increases.

We can graph the demand and supply schedules on the same diagram, as shown in **Figure 8.1**. A word of caution: if the price were really zero, wouldn't the quantity demanded be limitless rather than 300? We report values at a zero price simply for purposes of this example. In reality, as the price gets closer and closer to zero, we'd expect the quantity demanded to become astronomically big.

You can see that the demand and supply curves intersect at a unique price and quantity combination, in this case, at a price of $6 and quantity of 150,000 per month. What makes this combination unique is that at $6—and only at $6—the quantity demanded (150,000) exactly equals the quantity supplied (150,000). We say that $6 is the **market-clearing price**.

Table 8.1	The Market Demand and Supply Schedules for Memory Chips	
	(Thousands per Month)	
P	Q_d	Q_s
$0	300	0
$2	250	50
$4	200	100
$6	150	150
$8	100	200
$10	50	250
$12	0	300

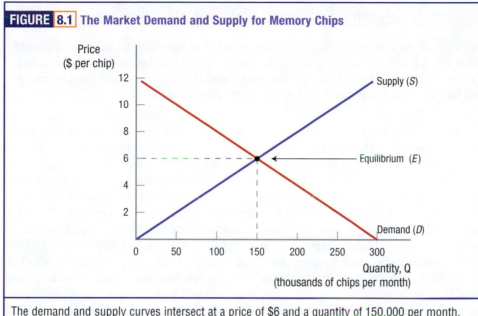

FIGURE 8.1 The Market Demand and Supply for Memory Chips

The demand and supply curves intersect at a price of $6 and a quantity of 150,000 per month. At $6, the quantity demanded exactly equals the quantity supplied, which makes it the market-clearing or equilibrium price.

MARKET-CLEARING PRICE The price at which the quantity demanded just equals the quantity supplied.

EXAMPLE At a price of $2.95 a gallon, dairy farmers are willing to bring 49,000 gallons to market each day, and consumers are willing to purchase 49,000 gallons of milk each day. In this instance, $2.95 is the market-clearing price for milk.

EXAMPLE At a price of $7.50 an hour, local babysitters are willing to supply 780 hours of babysitting each week. At that same price, parents are willing to purchase 780 hours of babysitting each week. In this case, $7.50 per hour is the market-clearing price for babysitting services.

We call this market-clearing price the **equilibrium price** in the market. The quantity demanded and supplied at this price (which are equal) is called the **equilibrium quantity**.

EQUILIBRIUM PRICE The price at which the quantity demanded is exactly equal to the quantity supplied; the market-clearing price.

EXAMPLE At a price of $96 a barrel, the world's daily demand for barrels of oil just equals the world's daily supply of barrels of oil. In other words, $96 is the equilibrium price of a barrel of oil.

EQUILIBRIUM QUANTITY The quantity bought and sold at the equilibrium price.

EXAMPLE At a price of $96 a barrel, the number of barrels of oil sold on the world market—85 million barrels a day—is just equal to the number of barrels purchased a day. In other words, 85 million barrels per day (bpd) is the equilibrium quantity of barrels of oil bought and sold in the world market each day.

Equilibrium price and quantity have very important economic meanings. Recall that the height of the demand curve represents consumers' willingness to pay for each additional unit of a good. The height of the supply curve reflects the marginal cost of supplying this unit. If we look at our memory-chip example (refer to Figure 8.1), the height of the demand curve is just equal to the height of the supply curve at the equilibrium price of $6. This means that the willingness to pay for the 150,000th chip purchased just equals the marginal cost of supplying the 150,000th chip. Both exactly equal $6, the equilibrium price. At a quantity greater than 150,000, demanders are not willing to pay enough to cover the marginal cost of supplying even one more chip. They will walk away from buying more chips rather than pay a price that is greater than their willingness to pay. Similarly, suppliers will walk away rather than expand output beyond 150,000 chips because consumers' willingness to pay does not cover the marginal cost of producing these additional chips.

It should come as no surprise that equilibrium occurs at the price and quantity where willingness to pay just equals marginal cost. We have already seen that when people make choices about how to allocate their scarce resources, their net benefit is maximized when the marginal benefit just equals the marginal cost for the last unit consumed of a good. And, as we showed in Chapter 6, willingness to pay is simply the monetary value that demanders assign to marginal benefit. So going to the point where willingness to pay equals marginal cost is consistent with our basic model of economic decision making.

Another way to think about equilibrium price and quantity is to realize that no other price–quantity pair makes sense. For example, if the price were higher than $6, say $10, as depicted in **Figure 8.2**, the quantity demanded (50,000) is less than the quantity supplied (250,000).

From your own personal experience, what usually happens when there is a lot more of some good for sale than there is demand for it? You're right if you predicted that the price must be reduced to "clear" the market. That is exactly what the dynamics of Figure 8.2 suggest will happen: at $10, the quantity supplied is greater than the quantity demanded, so there will be downward pressure on price. This downward pressure will be totally alleviated at the equilibrium price of $6 because the quantity demanded and supplied are exactly the same at that price.

What if, instead, the price of a chip was lower than $6, say $4? Here, the quantity supplied (100,000) will be less than the quantity demanded (200,000). If you've ever faced this situation—where there is too little of a good sold to satisfy the demand for it—you know that there will be upward pressure on price to "ration" the good among potential buyers. This often occurs with "hot" sporting events or concerts: tickets sell at a price substantially higher than their face value.

How can we be sure that a market will eventually "find" its equilibrium price and quantity? As individual suppliers and demanders independently adjust their quantities in response to the price they face, there will be a *convergence* toward equilibrium price and quantity. Over time, suppliers will expand their production

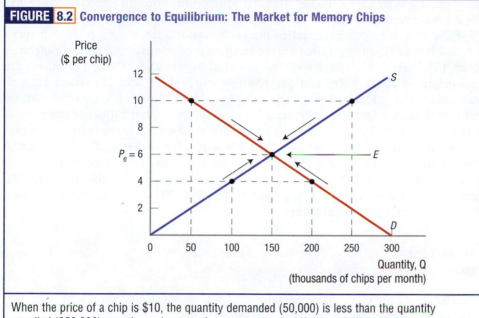

FIGURE 8.2 Convergence to Equilibrium: The Market for Memory Chips

When the price of a chip is $10, the quantity demanded (50,000) is less than the quantity supplied (250,000), creating a downward pressure on price. If, instead, the price of a chip is $4, the quantity supplied (100,000) is less than the quantity demanded (200,000). There will be upward pressure on price to "ration" the chips among potential buyers. It is only at $6, the equilibrium price (P_e), that there is no pressure on price to change.

if willingness to pay is higher than they had expected. At the same time, consumers will increase or decrease the quantity they demand when the price is lower or higher than their willingness to pay. We do not know how long it will take for these responses to fully work through the system, that is, until equilibrium price and quantity are finally attained.

We do know that after this equilibrium is reached, suppliers and demanders will not be inclined to further adjust the quantity they supply or purchase. The market-clearing, equilibrium price will remain in effect until there is a change in the economic environment that causes the market supply or demand curve to shift. We will examine the effects of supply and demand shifts later in this chapter.

8.2 Price Takers in a One-Price Market

We have just seen that after a market's equilibrium price is achieved, it will not change unless the market supply or market demand curve shifts. This suggests that the equilibrium price cannot be influenced by individual buyers or sellers. Each buyer and each seller must take the market price as a "given" and adjust the quantity purchased or sold accordingly. In the context of our previous example, each memory-chip demander and supplier decides how many—if any—chips to buy or sell at $6 per chip.

In other words, each and every buyer and seller *quantity-adjusts* in response to the equilibrium price. A consumer will walk away without buying anything at all if she doesn't "like" the price she faces: that is, if the price is higher than her willingness to pay for even one unit of the good. She cannot coerce a seller to trade at a price below equilibrium. Similarly, a supplier will walk away from even one sale if the price is less than his marginal cost of supplying the good. He cannot force a buyer to purchase his good at a price that is higher than the equilibrium price. In effect, everyone has the ultimate recourse, which is to "vote with their feet" and walk away from a deal.

How well does this portrayal of market behavior approximate reality? It turns out that it is sufficiently precise to make accurate predictions about market outcomes when (1) there are many *actual* and *potential* buyers and sellers; (2) buyers are well informed about prices and purchasing opportunities; and (3) sellers are well informed about prices and sales opportunities. When these conditions are met, an individual market "player"—whether a buyer or seller—cannot influence the price at which a good is traded. A single buyer cannot insist on a price lower than equilibrium if there are many other buyers willing to pay sellers the higher equilibrium price. A single seller cannot insist on being paid a price higher than equilibrium if there are many other sellers willing to supply consumers at the lower equilibrium price. To summarize, in a world in which no party to a trade has any influence over price, everyone behaves as a **price taker**.

> **PRICE TAKER** A potential buyer or seller who takes price as "given" and can only quantity-adjust in response to this price.

> **EXAMPLE** You can enroll for as many classes at your college as you wish, but you cannot negotiate a lower per credit hour tuition.

> **EXAMPLE** When Uncle Orville takes his cattle to market, he must accept the current day's price; he cannot negotiate a higher price.

A One-Price Market

When a market is comprised of price takers, there will be only one price in the market—typically the equilibrium price—at which trades take place. We refer to this outcome as a **one-price market**.

> **ONE-PRICE MARKET** A market in which each and every unit of the good trades at the same price.

> **EXAMPLE** At any given point in time, each ounce of gold trades at the same price.

> **EXAMPLE** At McDonald's, a small order of French fries is bought and sold for $1—it is on the restaurant's Dollar Menu.

One-price markets are common for commodities, which are products that are not perceived to be materially different from one another. Gold, oil, and wheat are examples of commodities. Some consumers even consider air travel to be a commodity, choosing their flights solely based on price. We can illustrate the idea of a one-price market by considering the online market for new CDs and DVDs. After you factor in the shipping and handling costs, and vendor reliability (measured by customer-satisfaction ratings), you'll find that a specific DVD sells for pretty much the same price on every Web site. Lots of one-price markets arise in cyberspace, largely because it is so easy to compare prices and trading opportunities. Sites such as bizrate.com, Nextag.com, and Amazon.com have cropped up to make it even easier to compare prices across large numbers of product vendors.

Widespread use of the Internet has also led to greater price convergence across geographically distant markets. For example, now that you can go online to price a 1972 Volkswagen ragtop in St. Louis, Chicago, and Miami, that price knowledge gives you better information about buying opportunities. It also means that sellers are better informed about their competitors' prices. As a result, the prices of VWs of similar quality and with similar features will be much closer to one another than they otherwise would be.

ECONOMIC FALLACY   All of us have seen gas stations across the street from one another selling gas at different prices. Similarly, when we use price-comparison Web sites, we see vendors selling the same product at different prices. This must mean that buyers and sellers are not price takers because these are not one-price markets.

False. Before we can conclude that a market is not a one-price market when the "same" good is apparently selling at different prices, we must be sure that the goods really are the same. In the gas station example, one station might include a discounted car wash whereas the other doesn't. One might take credit cards, whereas the other requires cash. One might be located on a site that is easier to enter and exit. Finally, one gas station may sell a name-brand gasoline that someone believes is higher quality and is willing to pay more for. We must be sure that we are truly comparing "apples to apples" before we can conclude that a market violates the one-price result.

Similarly, price-comparison Web sites often exclude shipping costs from the prices that are quoted. Also, some of the vendors sell refurbished products, whereas others sell only brand-new goods. Some accept credit card payments, whereas others require use of an Internet payment system, such as PayPal. Suppliers may or may not offer warranties and generous return policies. Finally, one vendor might have a higher ranking than another in terms of reliability and consumer satisfaction. Once again, we must be sure that we are comparing the prices of the same good before we can conclude that the one-price outcome has been violated.

8.3 Consumer and Producer Surplus

As we previously mentioned, voluntary trade will take place only when it is mutually beneficial for both the buyer and the seller. The question that arises is how much of the gains—or net benefits—generated by a trade is captured by the buyer versus the seller.

We have already seen that in a one-price market, consumers will not actually pay their full willingness to pay for each unit they purchase. In our memory-chip example, demanders' willingness to pay for the first 50,000 memory chips is at least $10 a chip. Nevertheless, these chips will actually be purchased at the equilibrium price of $6 each. Because competition among price takers leads to a one-price market, consumers enjoy **consumer surplus** on all but the last unit purchased.

CONSUMER SURPLUS The difference between a person's willingness to pay for a unit of a good and the amount that is actually paid.

EXAMPLE You are willing to pay up to $15 for the newest book in the Harry Potter series. The book turns out to sell for $10.47, including tax. The difference between what you were willing to pay and what you actually paid—$4.53—is your consumer surplus.

EXAMPLE You are willing to pay up to $2 for the first bottle of Coke Zero you drink each day at school, $1.60 for the second bottle, and $1 for the third bottle. Each bottle sells for $1 at the campus vending machine. Your consumer surplus is $1.60 a day ($1 from the first bottle, 60 cents from the second, and no surplus from the third).

In **Figure 8.3**, which refers to our memory-chip example, the red-shaded area represents the total amount of money that consumers actually pay for the 150,000 chips sold each month: $6 (height of rectangle) × 150,000 (length of rectangle) or $900,000. The consumer surplus that chip buyers enjoy is represented by the blue-shaded area. Notice that the amount of surplus contributed by each additional unit purchased declines because the willingness to pay for each unit falls according to our principle of diminishing marginal benefit. Therefore, the gap between willingness to pay and the actual price paid ($6) decreases as we move toward the last (150,000th) unit purchased. This last unit generates no consumer surplus.

To understand consumer surplus, think about what a demand curve represents: at various prices, the demand curve shows the quantity of a good that

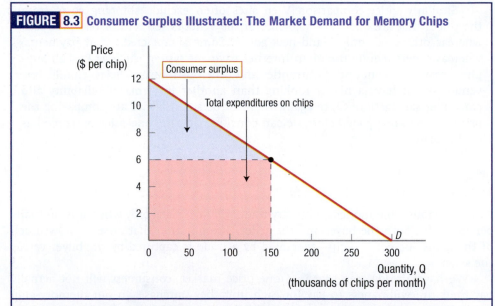

FIGURE 8.3 Consumer Surplus Illustrated: The Market Demand for Memory Chips

The red-shaded area represents the total amount of money that consumers actually pay for the 150,000 chips sold each month: $6 (height of rectangle) × 150,000 (length of rectangle) or $900,000. The consumer surplus that chip buyers enjoy is represented by the blue-shaded area. Notice that the amount of surplus contributed by each additional chip purchased declines because the willingness to pay for each of these chips falls according to the principle of diminishing marginal benefit. Therefore, the gap between willingness to pay and the actual price paid ($6) decreases as we move toward the last (150,000th) chip purchased. This last chip generates no consumer surplus.

consumers are willing and able to buy. At $6, buyers are willing and able to buy 150,000 memory chips, which is more than the amount they are willing to buy at higher prices. At $10, for example, consumers are still willing to buy 50,000 memory chips. So, even though buyers are willing to pay more for the first 50,000 chips when the price is $6, they don't have to. They get to keep some of what they were willing to pay—this is their consumer surplus. Because of this consumer surplus, buyers are not indifferent to making a trade. Consumer surplus represents *the gains from trade* precisely because consumers pay less than their willingness to pay for all but the last unit they purchase. Buyers attempt to maximize these gains when they trade in a market.

Can we actually put a dollar amount on the consumer surplus that buyers receive? The answer is yes. When the demand curve is linear, as it is in Figure 8.3, we simply calculate the area of the shaded triangle, which represents consumer surplus. At a price of $6, this consumer surplus is equal to

$$\text{Consumer surplus} = \tfrac{1}{2} [150,000 \times (\$12 - \$6)] = \$450,000$$

For demand curves that are actually curved, we would need to estimate the area under the demand curve up to the equilibrium price and quantity, and then subtract from this the actual expenditures on the good.

Measuring consumer surplus is especially important when cost–benefit evaluations are made of proposed government-funded projects. Suppose, for example, that the government is contemplating a new bridge in the San Francisco Bay area. The value that drivers place on this new bridge equals the consumer surplus they would receive from it—which would be the entire area under the market demand curve if the bridge is toll-free. This amount would have to be estimated so that policy makers can gauge the net benefit of erecting the bridge, that is, the benefits that the bridge bestows minus the cost of building it.

Producer Surplus

Referring back to Figure 8.3, we see that if the price of memory chips rises for some reason, the amount of consumer surplus falls. As a result, the gains from trade that buyers enjoy also fall. This makes sense—we always prefer buying things at a lower versus higher price.

Where does this loss in consumer surplus go? To answer this question, we must first look at how suppliers fare in a one-price market. The first thing to recognize is that because sellers receive the same price for all the units they sell, this price is higher than the marginal cost of production for all but the very last unit sold. **Figure 8.4** shows the supply curve for the memory-chip industry. The height of the supply curve at any output level tells us the marginal cost of the last unit produced. For example, the marginal cost of producing the 150,000th unit equals $6, while the marginal cost of the 100,000th unit equals $4. At the equilibrium price ($6), the marginal cost of the very last chip sold just equals the price that the supplier receives. For all of the other units sold, the price received is greater than the marginal cost of production. The difference between the equilibrium price and each unit's marginal cost is represented by the blue-shaded area in Figure 8.4.

We call this shaded area **producer surplus**.

PRODUCER SURPLUS The difference between a supplier's marginal cost of producing each unit of output and the price received for that unit.

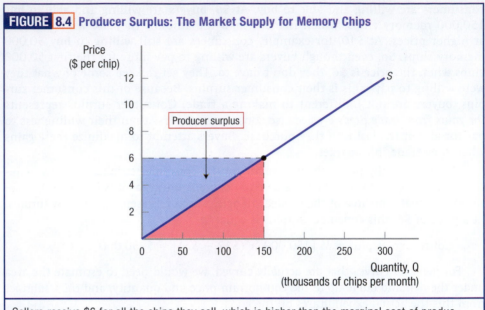

FIGURE 8.4 **Producer Surplus: The Market Supply for Memory Chips**

Sellers receive $6 for all the chips they sell, which is higher than the marginal cost of production for all but the very last chip sold. We know this because the height of the supply curve at any output level represents the marginal cost of the last chip produced. For example, the marginal cost of producing the 150,000th chip equals $6, while the marginal cost of the 100,000th chip equals $4. Producer surplus is the difference between equilibrium price and each chip's marginal cost, as represented by the blue-shaded area.

EXAMPLE Your opportunity cost of providing babysitting services to a neighbor on Saturday evenings is $7 an hour. However, you are paid the "going rate" of $9 an hour. You enjoy $2 an hour of producer surplus every time you babysit.

EXAMPLE It costs your local water utility $1 a gallon to distribute its first million gallons to the community and $1.50 a gallon for the next million gallons. If the utility is paid $1.50 for each gallon distributed, it will earn $500,000 ($0.50 × 1 million) in producer surplus.

To understand producer surplus, think about what a supply curve represents: at various prices, the supply curve shows the quantity of a good that suppliers are willing and able to supply to the market. At $6, producers are willing and able to sell 150,000 memory chips, more than the amount they are willing to supply at $4. But even at $4, producers are willing to supply 100,000 memory chips. So even though sellers are willing to take $2 less ($6 − $4) for the first 100,000 chips, they don't have to. They earn producer surplus on these 100,000 memory chips because all of the 150,000 chips are sold at one price ($6).

The existence of producer surplus means that sellers are not indifferent to making a trade. In fact, they enjoy a net benefit because they are paid more than their marginal cost of production for all but the very last unit sold. In terms of rational economic decision making, the marginal benefit they receive from devoting their scarce resources to producing a particular good—its price—is greater than marginal cost for all but the last unit. Producer surplus represents the *gains from trade* that suppliers capture.

We can measure the actual value of producer surplus the same way we do consumer surplus. At a price of $6, the triangle representing producer surplus in Figure 8.4 has an area equal to the following:

Producer surplus = ½ [150,000 × ($6 − 0)] = $450,000

It turns out that in this particular example, consumer and producer surplus are equal at the equilibrium price of $6. But most often this will not be the case. What if the price rose for some reason to $10? Consumer surplus would fall to only ½ [50,000 × ($12 − $10)] or $50,000. This is consistent with what we already showed graphically: when there is an increase in price, consumer surplus declines. Producer surplus rises to ½ [250,000 × ($10 − 0)] or $1,250,000.

We can now go back to our original question of what happens to the "lost" consumer surplus when there is an increase in price. We all know that consumers prefer lower prices, whereas suppliers prefer higher prices. Now we know why: the price dictates how much of the gains from trade will translate into consumer surplus versus producer surplus. Price changes tend to redistribute these gains from trade from consumers to producers and vice versa.

Determinants of Consumer and Producer Surplus: The Slopes of the Supply and Demand Curves

Panels (a) and (b) in **Figure 8.5** show two sets of the market supply and demand curves for some good, let's say coffee. Suppose that in both instances, the market-clearing price is $10 a pound, and 400 pounds of coffee are traded in the market each

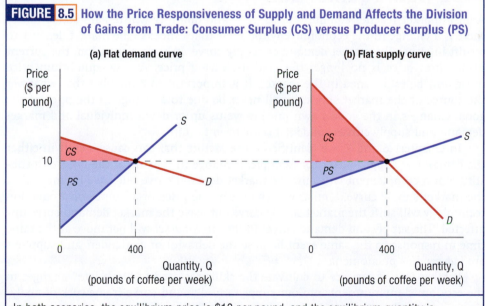

FIGURE 8.5 **How the Price Responsiveness of Supply and Demand Affects the Division of Gains from Trade: Consumer Surplus (CS) versus Producer Surplus (PS)**

In both scenarios, the equilibrium price is $10 per pound, and the equilibrium quantity is 400 pounds of coffee per week. Consumer surplus is the red area highlighted above this price and below the demand curve. Producer surplus is shown by the blue-shaded area under this price and above the supply curve. The market with a flatter demand curve and steeper supply curve (panel a) generates less consumer surplus and more producer surplus than the market with a flatter supply curve and steeper demand curve (panel b), which generates more consumer surplus and less producer surplus.

week at that price. Based on our previous discussion, consumer surplus is the red area highlighted above the equilibrium price and below the demand curve. Producer surplus is shown by the blue-shaded area under the equilibrium price and above the supply curve.

The two versions reveal that the amount of surplus each group enjoys depends on the slopes of the supply and demand curves. Even when the equilibrium price ($10) and quantity (400) are the same, a flatter demand curve and steeper supply curve, as shown in panel (a), generates less consumer surplus and more producer surplus. Why is this so? A flatter demand curve means that consumers' willingness to pay for the first and last unit purchased are not very different. In contrast, the steeper supply curve indicates that the marginal cost of production is increasing rapidly.

A steeper demand curve and a flatter supply curve, shown in panel (b) generates more consumer surplus and less producer surplus. The steeper demand curve means that consumers' willingness to pay falls substantially between the first and last units purchased. And the flatness of the supply curve indicates that the marginal cost of producing the first unit is not very different from the last unit produced.

In the next chapter, we will talk in great detail about those factors that affect the sensitivity of demand and supply to price. These factors influence the slopes of the demand and supply curves and, as shown, the division of the gains from trade between consumers and producers.

8.4 Market Disturbances: Reaching a New Equilibrium

After a market reaches equilibrium, its price and quantity will remain stable unless there is a change in the economic environment that "shocks" the market, leading to a shift in either the market demand or supply curve. In such a situation, the current equilibrium price is no longer the market-clearing price. A new equilibrium price must now be established in the market. It is important to remember that whatever the source of the market shock, it will never be due to a change in the price of the good. Changes in the good's own price move us up or down individual and market demand and supply curves *but do not cause them to shift.*

In Chapters 6 and 7, we identified those factors that can cause a shift in either the demand or supply curve. For example, a change in income or the price of a substitute or a complement will shift the market demand curve but have no impact on the market supply curve. Similarly, a change in the price of an input or production technology will shift the market supply curve but leave the market demand curve unaffected. The supply and demand curves *in the same market* will *not* move at the same time in response to the same event because the behavior of demanders and suppliers are *independent* phenomena.

It takes lots of practice to cultivate the skills required to "translate" changes in the economic environment into our supply-and-demand curve framework of analysis. Sometimes it will be difficult to determine whether a change leads to a shift in the demand or supply curve, or no movement at all. You might find yourself referring back to Chapters 6 and 7 frequently to confirm which factors shift the demand curve and which shift the supply curve. Nevertheless, by honing these skills, you will develop a powerful tool that will enable you to systematically predict how equilibrium prices and quantities respond to changes in the economic environment. Some examples follow.

Example: The Price of Gasoline Rises

We can use our supply-and-demand framework to analyze an event that you have likely experienced: a significant increase in the price of gasoline. Such an increase will affect many markets, from the market for suburban homes to hybrid vehicles, to public transportation and overnight-delivery services such as FedEx. In the case of suburban homes, an increase in gas prices increases the cost of commuting to work from the suburbs. Because the cost of commuting increases, the quantity of suburban homes demanded falls at each and every price. This translates into a *leftward* shift in the market demand for suburban homes.

The quantity of gas-saving hybrids demanded at each and every price will increase following an increase in the price of gasoline, causing a *rightward* shift in the market demand curve for such cars. People will substitute away from large, gas-guzzling sport-utility vehicles (SUVs), which now cost more to drive, resulting in a *leftward* shift in the demand curve for SUVs. When public transit is available, people will substitute toward this alternative and away from driving, causing the market demand curve for public transportation to also shift *to the right*. Finally, because gasoline is an input into the provision of overnight-delivery services—jets must also fuel up—the supply curve for overnight-delivery services will shift *to the left*. The opportunity cost of delivering the current quantity of mail and packages rises.

Given these varied responses to an increase in gas prices, let's illustrate each, using supply and demand, to predict how each market's equilibrium will be affected. Because we want to know how the equilibrium price and quantity are impacted by the gasoline price increase, we need to compare the equilibrium in each market before and after this increase. In **Figure 8.6**, we show each separate market and the shift in the demand or supply curve based on the previous discussion. In each market, we have assigned initial equilibrium prices and quantities.

Look first at the market for suburban homes. As noted previously, the increase in gas prices leads to a leftward shift in the demand curve. This shift—along with the unchanged supply curve—yields a lower market-clearing price and a smaller equilibrium quantity. In the market for hybrid cars, the rightward shift in the demand curve means that the equilibrium price will increase as will equilibrium quantity. A similar outcome occurs in the market for public transportation: the shift in the demand curve results in a higher price (fare) and a larger number of riders. Finally, the shift left in the supply curve of overnight-delivery services leads to a higher market-clearing price and a lower equilibrium level of delivery services.

These results are striking in a number of ways: First, isn't it astonishing to realize that so many markets can be affected by just one price change? While we have analyzed the impact of a change in gasoline prices on four markets, literally hundreds of other markets are also affected. In just the labor market alone, an increase in the price of gasoline will impact the employment and wages of autoworkers, transit employees, airline pilots, suburban construction workers, and car-leasing agents, among others. Second, our predictions about how equilibrium price and quantity change vary depending on the market in question: sometimes the price and quantity both increase (hybrid cars), other times price and quantity decline (suburban homes), and in still other instances, price increases and quantity declines (overnight-delivery services). This example shows why it is so difficult to make accurate predictions when a supply-and-demand framework is not used to analyze the impact of market shocks.

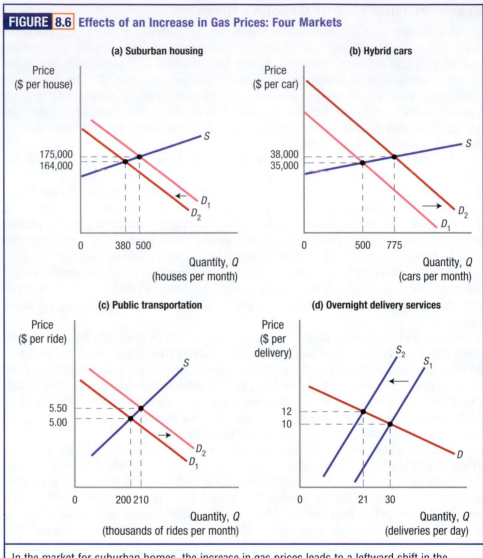

FIGURE 8.6 **Effects of an Increase in Gas Prices: Four Markets**

In the market for suburban homes, the increase in gas prices leads to a leftward shift in the demand curve. This shift in the demand curve—along with the original supply curve—leads to a lower market-clearing price and a lower equilibrium quantity. In the market for hybrid cars, the rightward shift in the demand curve means that the equilibrium price will increase as will equilibrium quantity. A similar outcome occurs in the market for public transportation: the shift in the demand curve results in a higher price (fare) and a greater number of tickets sold. Finally, the leftward shift in the supply curve of overnight-delivery services leads to a higher market-clearing price and a lower equilibrium level of delivery services.

Moving from One Equilibrium to Another

You have just seen that a disturbance in the economic environment can lead to a shift in either the supply or demand curve and that this shift leads to a new equilibrium price and quantity. Exactly how does a market reach its new equilibrium price and quantity?

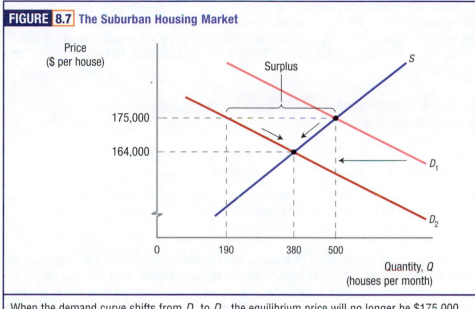

FIGURE 8.7 **The Suburban Housing Market**

When the demand curve shifts from D_1 to D_2, the equilibrium price will no longer be $175,000. Although builders are still willing to supply 500 houses for sale per month, the quantity demanded from the buyers' side of the market at a price of $175,000 has dropped from 500 houses per month to only 190. Because the quantity supplied is greater than the quantity demanded, there will be downward pressure on price. As the price drops, the quantity supplied decreases, and the quantity demanded increases. Only after this adjustment process has taken place do we end up at the new market-clearing price ($164,000) and a new equilibrium quantity of houses traded (380 homes per month).

Figure 8.7 replicates the suburban house market graph from panel (a) in Figure 8.6. We use it to dig deeper into what moves the market from the initial equilibrium to the one resulting from the shift in the demand curve.

Given the leftward shift in the demand curve, the first thing to ask is "why wouldn't the equilibrium price stay at $175,000?" At this price, builders are still willing to supply 500 houses for sale per month. But at $175,000, the quantity demanded from the buyers' side of the market has dropped from 500 houses per month to only 190. Another way of saying this is that after the increase in gas prices, the market for suburban houses no longer "clears" at $175,000. It is now in **disequilibrium**.

DISEQUILIBRIUM A situation in which quantity demanded does not equal quantity supplied.

EXAMPLE At their face value of $95, there were ten times more people demanding tickets to Bruce Springsteen's last concert at the old Giants Stadium than the number of tickets available. The market for these tickets was in disequilibrium at the $95 ticket price.

EXAMPLE When American Airlines introduced the first nonstop flights from Los Angeles to New Zealand, it set the economy airfare at $1895 round-trip. At that price, the flights were 35 percent empty. The market for these nonstop flights was in disequilibrium.

Because the housing market is in disequilibrium, the going price must change to once again become a market-clearing, or equilibrium, price. In Figure 8.7, the specific problem is that at $175,000, suppliers are willing to supply more houses than buyers are willing to purchase. A **surplus** of houses is now available. In other words, there is **excess supply**.

SURPLUS/EXCESS SUPPLY A situation in which quantity supplied exceeds quantity demanded.

EXAMPLE At its cover price of $34.95, there were vast numbers of unsold, surplus copies of *A Dummy's Guide to Changing Lightbulbs*.

EXAMPLE At $18 million per passenger, there are unfilled, surplus seats on a private rocket to the International Space Station.

Because there is a surplus of houses, their price begins to drop as suppliers attempt to sell their inventory of homes. You may have experienced this yourself: parents who get transferred and must sell one home to buy another in a different town often start with one price but then "settle" for one much lower, especially if they are moving in the middle of a recession. As the price drops, two things happen: First, the quantity demanded rises as consumers *move down* their *new* market demand curve in response to the lower price. Second, the quantity supplied decreases as suppliers *move down* their original market supply curve in response to the lower price. Only after this adjustment process has taken place do we end up at the new market-clearing price ($164,000) and a new equilibrium quantity of houses traded (380 homes per month).

What if the price of gasoline eventually falls, and the demand curve shifts back to its original position? In this situation, the initial equilibrium price would be $164,000, and the quantity supplied would be 380 homes per month. But after the rightward shift in the demand curve, the 380 homes supplied will be less than the quantity demanded at this price, which can be seen by extending a line from $164,000 over to the new demand curve. Once again, the market is in disequilibrium, only this time, the market suffers from a **shortage** of homes at the going price. This shortage in supply leads to **excess demand**.

SHORTAGE/EXCESS DEMAND A situation in which the quantity demanded exceeds the quantity supplied.

EXAMPLE For its 50th anniversary celebration, McDonald's ran out of the hamburgers it was selling for 29 cents each. There was a shortage of hamburgers at that price.

EXAMPLE There was a shortage of World Series tickets priced at face value.

You know what happens when something is in short supply: its price increases. In the presence of excess demand, buyers scramble to purchase the existing supply of the good, and suppliers attempt to ration this short supply by increasing its price. As price rises, two things happen: First, the quantity demanded declines as individuals *move up* their new demand curve in response to the higher price. Second, the quantity supplied increases as suppliers *move up* their original supply curve in response to the higher price. Eventually these movements will lead to a market-clearing price where quantity demanded is just equal to quantity supplied.

How long does this adjustment process take? In most cases, prices and quantities do not instantly move to their new equilibrium values. It may take some time, for example, for home builders to ramp up production, that is, move up the market supply curve. In some markets, however, adjusting to a shift in the demand or supply curve can happen quite quickly. In financial markets, for example, a change in demand or supply conditions leads to almost instantaneous changes in the prices of financial assets, such as stocks and bonds. Consider the impact of government regulatory decisions concerning the approval or withdrawal of a certain prescription drug, or a breaking-news bulletin that people have died from consuming a tainted product. The stock price of the producer in question—along with substitute and complementary goods producers—responds almost instantaneously, reflecting expectations about how consumer demand will change.

Through this type of adjustment process, markets can eventually reach a new equilibrium. This assumes that there are no further shocks to the market that arise during the adjustment period. Whether new, independent shocks arise during or after the adjustment period, they will once again create a disequilibrium situation and redirect the market toward another equilibrium price and quantity. The fact that some prices vary a great deal over time suggests that the underlying demand conditions and supply conditions may be highly unstable.

SOLVED PROBLEM

Q Using a market supply curve and market demand curve, show what happens in the residential mortgage-loan market if the value of housing declines and thereby increases the risk of making these loans. How does consumer and producer surplus change as a result of this change in the lending market?

A The increase in risk increases the opportunity cost of making residential loans, which results in a shift left in the supply curve of available money. The equilibrium interest rate increases, and the equilibrium number of loans made declines. As depicted below, there is a reduction in both consumer and producer surplus.

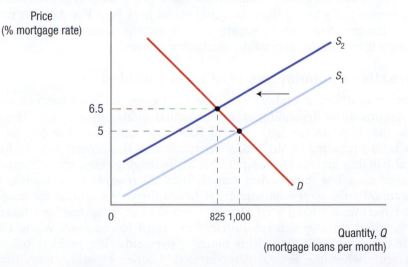

8.5 Market Bubbles

If markets adjust in such a predictable way, you might be asking why they seem to sometimes go haywire and create **market bubbles** that burst and often wreak havoc on the economy.

> **MARKET BUBBLE** A run-up in the price of an asset that is eventually followed by a crash in its price.
>
> **EXAMPLE** In the mid-1990s there was a rapid run up in the prices of shares of technology and Internet companies. In March, 2000, the bubble burst, and the technology-laden NASDAQ stock exchange suffered close to a 10 percent drop within only 6 days.
>
> **EXAMPLE** Between 1998 and 2006, inflation-adjusted housing prices grew at an average rate of almost 7 percent per year, peaking in the first half of 2006. The housing bubble then burst and the value of U.S. housing fell by $9.8 trillion by December 2010.

While most economists and financial experts are quick to recognize a market bubble *after* it has burst, it can be very difficult to identify one in advance. After all, there are many reasons that prices may have a rapid run-up, including a reduction in the supply of a product due to unavoidable production glitches or an increase in demand due to changes in consumer preferences. The price of an ounce of gold, for example, rose from $840 at the end of 2007 to $1,850 in the third quarter of 2011. This translates into an almost 30 percent increase in price per year. Is this a market bubble that is going to burst in the near future (as has been the case in the past for gold), or does it reflect a move towards a new equilibrium price based on buyers' expectations that the American dollar, the Euro and other currencies will be weakened by the worldwide debt crisis? (People often purchase gold as a "safe" investment when the purchasing power of currencies falls.)

The key feature of a bubble is that the price of an asset rises to a level that cannot be justified by the asset's "fundamental value." For example, dot.com share prices rose astronomically higher than what they would have been based on the most optimistic estimates of each tech company's future income stream. Why did these prices seemingly diverge from their stable, equilibrium values?

Alternative Explanations of Market Bubbles

A number of different explanations have been given for price bubbles. Often the explanations differ depending on the particular bubble in question. The housing bubble that burst in the latter half of 2006 has been blamed largely on low interest rates promoted by the U.S. government and the Federal Reserve Bank, the central banking organization responsible for managing those rates. Not only were mortgage rates low, but lenders reaped financial rewards from lending to risky applicants, homebuyers who would not have otherwise qualified for home loans. These buyers were offered what are now referred to as "subprime" mortgages, often at low, teaser rates, which subsequently increased to the point where borrowers couldn't keep up with their rising monthly payments. The problem became even more acute when the Federal Reserve made a series of adjustments that raised market interest rates from their low of 1 percent in 2002 up to 5.25 percent in 2006. When low-interest loans were plentiful, there was an on-going rightward shift in the demand curve for housing. When interest rates rose and subprime mortgages began to sour, the demand curve for housing shifted back to the left. This would help explain the run-up in housing prices followed by the fall in prices—in other words, a price bubble that burst.

However, most analysts argue that the run-up in housing prices far exceeded the price rise justified by lower interest rates. They argue that home prices escalated because buyers engaged in speculative activities, intent on "flipping" homes for a quick profit. A *speculative bubble* is fueled by expectations that future prices will continue to rise. Some economists have argued that speculators are uninformed investors who suffer from an irrational *herd mentality*. They make investment choices based solely on the choices that others make: when they see that other people are investing in a particular asset and are doing well, then they, too, want to share in these gains. Even relatively uninformed speculators are likely to know that they have overpaid for an asset. Nevertheless, they are willing to pay this amount because they think that there is a "greater fool" that will pay even more for the asset in the near future. A central feature of herd mentality is that the investor realizes that an asset is overvalued and is still willing to purchase it.

Speculation will feed a market bubble as long as these expectations are met; however, any downturn in price will severely dampen the enthusiasm of speculators and can lead to a substantial decline in demand, thereby accelerating the fall in the price. Moreover, there can be multiple run ups and falls before prices stabilize. Whatever the reason that demand skyrockets and then rapidly recedes, whether its rational or not, the market works to accommodate these shifts in demand and achieve a new equilibrium price and output level.

8.6 Government Policies That Prevent Markets from Reaching Equilibrium

We have seen that markets tend to "self-correct" when shortages or surpluses exist. In both cases, suppliers and demanders adjust their behavior, and these adjustments lead to a new equilibrium price where, once again, quantity demanded equals quantity supplied. It is indeed remarkable that the independent price-taking behavior of individual consumers and suppliers can achieve such a result. Adam Smith likened this phenomenon to an "invisible hand" that guides a market to equilibrium.

There are instances in which the government—prompted by such concerns as fairness or protection of particular interests—creates an artificial impediment that keeps certain markets from attaining equilibrium. In every instance, the goal of the policy is to keep some price from rising too high or falling too low. Some of the most famous examples have had to do with the price of rental housing in big cities (e.g., Los Angeles and New York City) and the price of energy resources (e.g., natural gas). Recently, there has been a great deal of political debate over the fees (interest rates) charged for payday loans and the pricing of adjustable-rate mortgages (ARMs). In these instances and others, governments have introduced price "guidelines" that attempt to set market prices at a level other than their equilibrium level. These guidelines are called **price controls**, and they take various forms.

PRICE CONTROLS Prices set by a government authority rather than by the market.

EXAMPLE State usury laws place a cap on the interest rate that lenders can charge borrowers.

EXAMPLE State regulators set the rates that electric and gas utilities can charge their customers.

EXAMPLE The federal government and some state governments set the minimum wage that employers can pay employees.

Price controls take the form of *price ceilings* or *price floors*. We will deal with each separately.

Price Ceilings

A price ceiling exists when a market's price is artificially set *below* the equilibrium price that would be established by supply and demand. Just as a balloon cannot fly above a room's ceiling, the price of a good cannot go above the government's price ceiling.

PRICE CEILING The maximum price that can legally be charged for a good.

EXAMPLE The New York State Division of Housing and Community Renewal sets the maximum rent that can be charged for 50,000 rent-controlled apartments in New York City.

EXAMPLE The federal government sets the maximum prices that doctors can charge patients enrolled in its Medicare health-insurance program for seniors.

When a price ceiling is in effect, shortages often exist because the quantity demanded exceeds the quantity supplied, and excess demand goes unfilled.

Price ceilings can lead to some very interesting and important outcomes. Consider the market for kidney transplants in the United States. Did you know that there are price controls in this market? Live kidney donors can legally be paid for supplying their kidneys, but they can only be paid an amount equal to the cost of their medical expenses. The families of deceased donors receive nothing. However, the opportunity cost of donating a kidney in either circumstance could very well be greater than the payment allowed by law. A live donor could suffer from lost wages, not to mention pain and potential long-term health problems. The families of deceased donors might suffer mental anguish at the thought of having their loved ones cut open for organ retrieval. The reimbursement "cap" imposed on donors is, in effect, a price ceiling. **Figure 8.8** depicts this situation.

Figure 8.8 presents a hypothetical market demand and supply curve for transplantable human kidneys. If a free market for kidneys existed, the market-clearing price would be $50,000, and 100 kidneys per month would be made available at that price to recipients by living donors and the families of the deceased. However, the "price" of kidneys is capped by a price ceiling, which just covers the reasonable medical expenses for live donors and is otherwise zero for deceased donors. Suppose the ceiling for live donors is $25,000. At this price, suppliers are only willing to provide 50 kidneys a month, but demanders would like to "buy" 200. At the price ceiling, there is a shortage of kidneys (in this case, 150 kidneys) available for transplant. Notice that the opportunity cost of supplying the 51st kidney is less than the willingness to pay for it, but it is greater than the maximum price of $25,000.

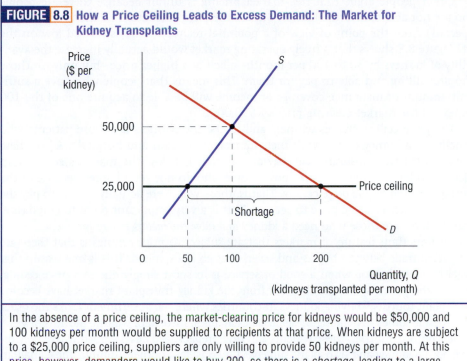

FIGURE 8.8 How a Price Ceiling Leads to Excess Demand: The Market for Kidney Transplants

In the absence of a price ceiling, the market-clearing price for kidneys would be $50,000 and 100 kidneys per month would be supplied to recipients at that price. When kidneys are subject to a $25,000 price ceiling, suppliers are only willing to provide 50 kidneys per month. At this price, however, demanders would like to buy 200, so there is a *shortage*, leading to a large waiting list of transplant candidates. At the price ceiling, the opportunity cost of the 51st kidney is less than the willingness to pay for it, but it is greater than the legal maximum of $25,000.

Because of this artificially low price, a large waiting list of potential recipients exists. As of 2010, more than 93,000 patients were registered on the official kidney waiting list of the United Network for Organ Sharing (UNOS) in the United States alone.

So who will get the kidneys that are in short supply? This question has continued to vex economists, philosophers, transplant surgeons, and ethicists. Society's unwillingness to depend on unfettered markets to allocate kidneys means that the market's willingness to pay is ruled out as a basis for distributing kidneys. So the allocation process must take place based on an alternative system of distribution. Should the sickest among the potential recipients go to the head of the list (in which case, the number of lives actually saved through kidney transplants would likely go down)? Should a patient's age matter? Should alcoholics or diabetics be excluded from the recipient pool? What about illegal immigrants or high-school dropouts?

The "correct" answer depends on the goals of those who design the allocation rules. Even transplant surgeons are at odds over how kidneys "should" be allocated. Some surgeons argue that organs should be used within the same geographic area in which they are collected. In other words, kidneys harvested in the Midwest would be transplanted into patients in the Midwest. Others have vied for a national system of distribution. Because kidneys are essential to their livelihoods, transplant surgeons are particularly concerned about the allocation rule that is ultimately adopted. This may also explain their keen interest in new technologies that reduce their dependence on donor kidneys or increase the success of partial-kidney transplants.

Other people argue that free-market pricing is unfair because there are people who are not able to afford a kidney. But are the other allocation methods any *fairer*—especially from the point of view of a potential recipient who is ranked low on the list? Figure 8.8 shows that a freely operating market would actually increase the availability of kidneys by 50 to 100 per month—albeit at a higher price—but only for those who are willing and able to pay for them. This means that people who have a sufficient amount of insurance coverage or income will be able to acquire one of the 100 kidneys at the market-clearing price of $50,000.

The price ceiling creates winners and losers: the winners are those patients who actually get a kidney (along with their transplant surgeon and hospital). All of these recipients (or their insurers) will pay a price that is below the market's equilibrium price. Who loses in this system? Those people who do not get a kidney because of the shortage created by the price ceiling. That is, those who were actually willing to pay the $50,000 market-clearing price to get one. This is a very important point to emphasize: these "losers" are those who need a kidney *and have the means to pay for one.*

An important feature of markets that are subject to price ceilings is that there are gains from trade between buyers and sellers that go unexploited. This is one reason that illegal markets develop when a good or service is in short supply due to a price ceiling. Some of the patients who are shut out from the kidney-transplant market have become "transplant tourists," buying kidneys in countries where the government looks the other way when it comes to policing these illegal exchanges. Instead of waiting months or years in their home countries, these patients can find prepackaged deals abroad where they receive both a kidney and transplant surgery.[2] Or consider another example: the Canadian health system reimburses Canadian surgeons at a below-equilibrium rate, which leads to long waits for surgical procedures such as hip replacements or hernia repairs. So, although it isn't illegal to do so, some Canadians venture into the northern United States, where they pay the full tab to receive timelier surgeries. In both the Canadian and kidney examples, we see that some of the excess demand created by a price ceiling "leaks" into other markets in which there is either no price ceiling or one that is not tightly enforced.

We see a similar result in the credit markets. Many states have usury laws that set a maximum interest rate that can be charged to a borrower. As a result, regulated lenders will not lend to individuals or businesses at high risk of default because they cannot charge enough to make it worthwhile to assume such risks. People with poor credit are forced into the illegal loan-shark market or the unregulated payday-loan market if they are in need of money. The interest rates in these markets have been documented to be as high as 2400 percent (borrow $1, pay back $24), far less than the 6 to 24 percent usury limits set by most states.

Price ceilings can even affect the market at which currencies trade around the globe. Some countries put a ceiling on the "price" at which their currencies trade with other international currencies. The price of the Chinese yuan, for example, has been artificially "pegged" at a price below equilibrium so that Chinese products remain cheap when they are bought with foreign currency on the world market. By keeping the value of the yuan below equilibrium, the Chinese government can stimulate exports and accumulate foreign currency. The price ceiling also lessens the amount of imports in China purchased with yuan because so many more yuan are required to buy these foreign products.[3]

· · · · · · ·

[2]Larry Rohter, "The Organ Trade: A Global Black Market; Tracking the Sale of a Kidney on a Path of Poverty and Hope." *New York Times*, May 23, 2004.

[3]Lloyd Norris, "Weak Dollar? Not So Much in China." *New York Times*, October 15, 2009.

SOLVED PROBLEM

Q Suppose the government is concerned that the rise in mortgage lenders' interest rates due to the increased risk of making mortgage loans (see the previous Solved Problem) will adversely affect the ARMs of thousands of home owners and lead to numerous fore-closures. Show how the imposition of a price ceiling on interest rates will impact the results in the first Solved Problem. Who wins and who loses when this price freeze is introduced?

A The price ceiling, say at the original equilibrium mortgage rate of 5 percent, leads to excess demand for loans: the quantity of loans demanded equals 1,000, but the quantity supplied is only 750. The winners are those who already have adjustable loans whose rates are frozen. The losers are those who are willing to pay a higher interest rate for a home loan but are unable to get one because of the interest rate freeze (see the following figure).

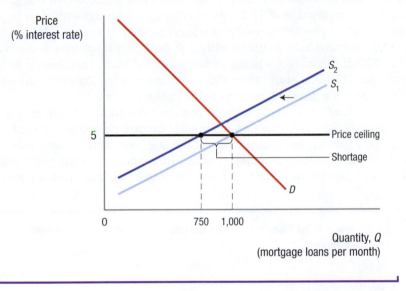

Price Floors

Sometimes, the pursuit of "fairness" leads to government policies that attempt to keep a market's price *above* its market-clearing level. That is, they create a **price floor** in the market.

PRICE FLOOR The minimum price that can legally be charged for a good.

EXAMPLE Employers cannot hire employees at a wage below the minimum wage set by the federal government. The minimum wage is a price floor.

EXAMPLE The Civil Aviation Administration of China has set a price floor for seats on each of the routes flown by its domestic airlines.[4]

Just as a ball cannot fall below the floor of a room, the price at which trades take place cannot fall below a price floor. The most well-known price floor in the United States is the minimum wage, which requires employers to pay workers no less than

- - - - - - -

[4]Xin Dingding, "Price Floor to Be Set for Air Tickets." *China Daily*, January 14, 2009.

a specified amount per hour—currently set at $7.25 by federal law. Some states have enacted a higher minimum wage.

The federally set minimum wage is most likely to come into play in unskilled-labor markets because highly skilled employees already receive wages above this legal minimum. On occasion, however, state governments single out certain skilled labor markets—for example, public school teachers—for their own special minimum wage, which is often above the equilibrium wage.

Figure 8.9 illustrates the effects of imposing a price floor on the hourly wage earned by dishwashers in the fast-food industry. Typically, these jobs are held by young and inexperienced workers. Let's suppose that the market-clearing wage for these workers is $5.50 an hour. At this price, Figure 8.9 shows that there would be 670,000 jobs available and filled nationwide. Now suppose that the government imposes a minimum wage of $7.25. As you can see, this wage—which is higher than the equilibrium wage—creates a surplus (excess supply) of workers. At the minimum wage, 800,000 individuals would be willing to work, but employers demand and hire only 520,000. If the market was left to determine the wage, there would be more job opportunities (150,000 more) than with a minimum wage. As with a price ceiling, a price floor creates a disequilibrium situation in the market.

When a price floor is in place, there are gains from trade between buyers and sellers that go unexploited. In our minimum-wage example, employees want to work up to the point where the opportunity cost of the last hour worked just equals the wage received. At the same time, employers would hire labor up to the point where their willingness to pay for an additional hour just equals the wage rate. In other words,

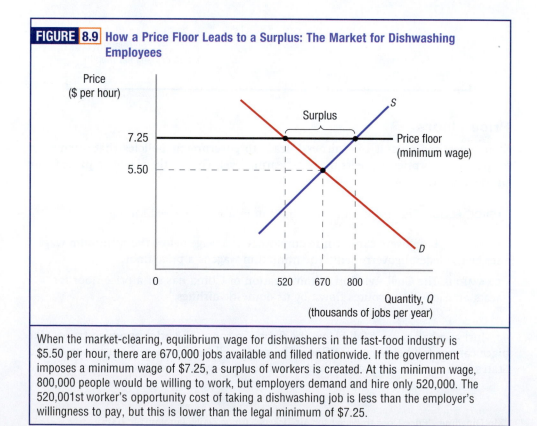

FIGURE 8.9   How a Price Floor Leads to a Surplus: The Market for Dishwashing Employees

When the market-clearing, equilibrium wage for dishwashers in the fast-food industry is $5.50 per hour, there are 670,000 jobs available and filled nationwide. If the government imposes a minimum wage of $7.25, a surplus of workers is created. At this minimum wage, 800,000 people would be willing to work, but employers demand and hire only 520,000. The 520,001st worker's opportunity cost of taking a dishwashing job is less than the employer's willingness to pay, but this is lower than the legal minimum of $7.25.

employers and employees, left alone to trade, will go to where the height of the supply curve just equals the height of the demand curve—that is, to the equilibrium of $5.50 an hour and 670,000 jobs. However, employers are unable to hire employees at this wage rate because it falls below minimum wage. The shortfall in employment that results is sometimes referred to as the "underemployment" effect of minimum wage.

Because price floors create a disequilibrium condition in the market, a number of questions arise: Who will be hired when there is an excess supply of labor? That is, how will jobs be "rationed"? How does the outcome from this rationing process compare to the outcome when employment opportunities are allocated by the market? Who wins and who loses as a result of minimum-wage laws? And how are related markets affected by the introduction of this price floor?

When there is a surplus of workers at minimum wage, employers can decide who to hire based on factors other than the wage they will pay the worker. These factors may include the applicant's work history, education, hair length, number of facial piercings, or general attractiveness. Employers are no longer able to hire unskilled, high-risk applicants at a wage that is justified by their productivity because this wage tends to be below the minimum wage. It is not surprising that many empirical studies have found that minimum-wage laws have the greatest negative impact on the employment rates of unskilled minority males, especially teenagers and young adults.[5]

While there is an underemployment effect created by the minimum wage—the quantity hired is less than the quantity willing to work—not everyone loses when the minimum wage takes effect. As you can see in Figure 8.9, those who are employed enjoy a higher wage than they would if there were no minimum wage. The losers are people who would have been employed if the market-clearing wage of $5.50 prevailed. Notice that the number of losers does not equal the surplus of workers at the minimum wage. Many of these people would not be willing to work at the lower equilibrium wage. What we know is that there are gains from trade that 150,000 unemployed workers—the amount of unemployment resulting from moving above the equilibrium wage to the minimum wage—and potential employers want to exploit but cannot do so because it is illegal. This is the reason why some minimum-wage workers are willing to (illegally) work extra hours after they clock out, which reduces their actual wage per hour below the minimum wage. Other employees are willing to (illegally) accept cash wages that are below minimum wage. While unions and federal agencies argue that these illegal activities are a form of worker exploitation, in many cases, these deals arise from voluntary agreements struck between employees and their employers to circumvent minimum-wage laws.

Minimum-wage laws can also have a significant impact on markets in which labor is a major input into production. Recall that an increase in input costs leads to a leftward shift in the market supply curve. An increase in the minimum wage can result in a significant leftward shift in the supply curve in markets where there is heavy dependence on unskilled labor. Such markets include agriculture, food services, and textile manufacturing. A leftward shift in the supply curve—with the demand curve unchanged—leads to a higher equilibrium price and a lower equilibrium quantity of the good. This creates a very interesting dilemma for policy makers: raising the minimum wage improves the living standards for those minimum-wage workers who have jobs but may result in an increase in the price of the goods and services that these very workers consume.

· · · · · · · ·

[5]David Neumark, "Minimum Age Effects in the Post-Welfare Reform Era." *Employment Policies Institute*, January, 2007.

The increase in labor costs associated with the introduction of a minimum wage or an increase in the minimum wage creates incentives for employers to pursue production processes that reduce their dependence on labor. In the food-services industry, for example, the increase in minimum wage over time has encouraged adoption of self-serve soda machines at fast-food outlets. The U.S. textile industry has responded by relocating its mills and manufacturing facilities overseas to take advantage of lower-cost workers who are not subject to U.S. minimum-wage laws.

ECONOMIC FALLACY   When teachers' unions negotiate higher than equilibrium salaries for their members, the total amount spent on teachers rises.

False. Those teachers who continue to have jobs at this higher wage will earn more in total as long as there are rules that block any reduction in their hours. However, there will be teachers who will not be hired at the higher wage. The total amount spent on teachers may or may not increase, depending on each school district's ability to substitute other personnel for teachers or increase the student–teacher ratio. In any event, the union's most senior members will tend to be winners to the extent that seniority becomes the rule by which scarce teaching positions are allocated.

8.7 Are Government Price Controls Really That Bad?

Most often, government price controls are imposed to create more fairness in the market. For example, many developing nations impose price ceilings on basic foodstuffs so that people of lower economic means can buy bread—even though there may be less bread supplied overall. Sometimes, governments impose price ceilings to reduce their own outlays on particular goods and services. The best example of this in the United States is the price ceiling placed on medical providers by Medicare, the federal government's medical-insurance program for the elderly. The question that must be asked is what the economic cost is of using price controls to accomplish these goals.

Virtually every economist and policy maker will agree that price ceilings create shortages, and price floors lead to surpluses. The crucial question is just how *much* distortion is really introduced into the market? For example, how many more kidneys would really be available if they could be bought and sold? How many more people really lose their jobs when a minimum wage is introduced or increased? These questions focus on the actual number of winners and losers created by price controls, along with how the winners' gains compare to the losers' losses.

It turns out that the actual magnitude of the shortage or surplus resulting from a price control depends crucially on how a market's demand and supply respond to price changes. That is, how much do buyers cut back when prices rise and how much do suppliers cut back when prices fall?

To illustrate this point, let's again consider the impact the minimum wage has on the supply of dishwashers. Let's first assume that the supply of labor is not very responsive to increases in the wage. This could occur if there are regulations that limit the number of hours that employees can work or the size of the labor pool were constrained due to geographic isolation (e.g., a Steak 'n Shake in rural North Dakota). This is depicted in **Figure 8.10**.

When supply is totally unresponsive, as shown by the supply curve S_2, the labor supply curve will be vertical. The quantity of labor supplied does not change at all when

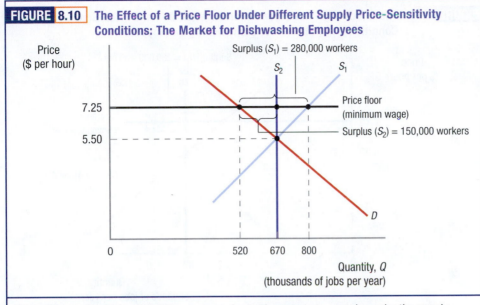

FIGURE 8.10   **The Effect of a Price Floor Under Different Supply Price-Sensitivity Conditions: The Market for Dishwashing Employees**

When the supply of labor is totally unresponsive to the wage rate—as shown by the supply curve S_2—the labor supply curve will be *vertical*. The market-clearing wage in this case is $5.50 per hour. Now impose a minimum wage equal to $7.25 an hour. In this example, the amount of surplus labor equals 150,000 workers (670,000 minus 520,000). Compare this to the surplus that would arise if the labor supply curve is S_1. If the supply curve is S_1, the number of surplus workers would be 280,000 (800,000 minus 520,000). The surplus—that is, the amount of unemployment—resulting from the minimum wage is greater the more sensitive labor supply is to a change in the wage rate.

the wage goes up or down. The market-clearing wage in this case is $5.50 per hour. Now suppose the government imposes a price floor (minimum wage) of $7.25 an hour. In this example, the amount of surplus labor equals 150,000 workers. Compare this to the surplus that would arise if the labor supply curve were S_1. If the supply curve is S_1, the number of surplus jobs created by the minimum wage is 280,000. As you can readily see, the surplus—that is, the amount of unemployment—resulting from the minimum wage is greater the more sensitive labor supply is to a change in the wage rate.

On the other side of the market, when employers (who hire dishwashers) are totally unresponsive to an increase in the wage rate, the demand curve for labor will be vertical, as shown in **Figure 8.11**. This could occur because there are government regulations that set the number of workers that employers must have on the premises, or there are union requirements that stipulate the number of workers per shift, or a production process does not permit employers to easily substitute away from labor. Now what happens when a minimum wage is imposed?

Figure 8.11 shows that setting the wage higher than the market-clearing wage creates a surplus of labor. Compare the magnitude of the surplus if demand for labor is D_1 versus D_2. As you can see, the surplus of workers is much greater when the demand curve is flatter. In other words, the introduction of a minimum wage leads to greater unemployment when demand for labor is more sensitive to changes in the wage rate, as depicted by D_1.

The impact of price controls is likely to vary over time. One reason is that the economic environment changes, too. Suppose, for example, that the minimum wage results in substantial underemployment in the unskilled-labor market in New Jersey. Now suppose that the demand for unskilled labor increases at each and every wage rate—that is,

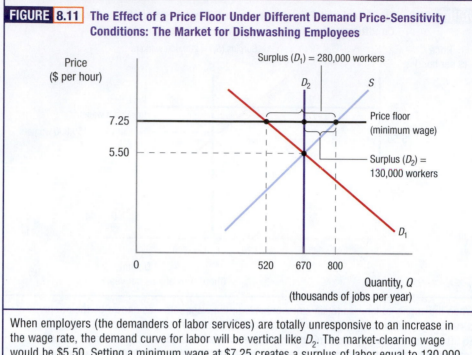

FIGURE 8.11   The Effect of a Price Floor Under Different Demand Price-Sensitivity Conditions: The Market for Dishwashing Employees

When employers (the demanders of labor services) are totally unresponsive to an increase in the wage rate, the demand curve for labor will be vertical like D_2. The market-clearing wage would be $5.50. Setting a minimum wage at $7.25 creates a surplus of labor equal to 130,000 workers (800,000 minus 670,000). Compare the surplus if the demand for labor is D_1 instead. Now the surplus is 280,000 workers (800,000 minus 520,000). Here, employers cut back on hiring when the wage rate increases, which means that the number of surplus workers grows more under D_1 than D_2. We can generalize this result: the flatter the demand curve, the greater the surplus will be in the presence of a price floor.

the demand curve shifts to the right—because the overall economy is expanding and, in particular, the New Jersey casino industry is growing rapidly. What happens?

Figure 8.12 represents the market for unskilled labor in New Jersey. At the minimum wage P_{min}, there is a surplus of labor. Now let consumer demand for casino services increase. This leads to an increase in the demand for casino employees, resulting in a rightward shift in the demand curve for unskilled New Jersey workers from D_1 to D_2. As Figure 8.12 illustrates, this shift in demand substantially reduces the unemployment effect of the minimum wage. In fact, if the shift in demand is substantial, the new equilibrium wage can even be *above* the minimum wage. When this occurs, the minimum wage is no longer a factor: the labor market will achieve an equilibrium price. This may explain why studies of the increase in minimum wage in New Jersey during the economic expansion of the mid-1990s revealed the state had no surplus of unskilled labor. Rather, the authors found that employment in the state was actually *higher* after the minimum wage increased.[6] The question that remains, of course, is whether minimum-wage laws magnified the unemployment effect when there was a leftward shift in the demand curve for labor during the Great Recession of 2007.

• • • • • • •

[6]David Card and Alan B. Krueger, "Minimum Wages and Employment: A Case Study of the Fast-Food Industry in New Jersey and Pennsylvania." *American Economic Review*, 84, no. 4 (September 1994): 774–775.

FIGURE 8.12   **Minimum Wage and a Shift in Demand for Workers: The New Jersey Labor Market**

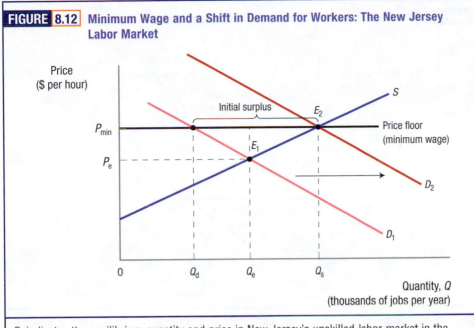

E_1 indicates the equilibrium quantity and price in New Jersey's unskilled-labor market in the absence of a minimum wage. After a minimum wage (P_{min}) is imposed, there is a surplus of labor. If there is an increase in the demand for unskilled labor—say due to growth in the casino industry—then there will be a rightward shift in the demand curve for labor from D_1 to D_2. A rightward shift in demand can substantially reduce the unemployment effect of the minimum wage. In fact, if the shift in demand is substantial, the minimum wage may no longer have any impact: in this example, the demand for workers shifts sufficiently to the right so that the minimum wage is now the equilibrium wage in the market. This new equilibrium is labeled E_2.

8.8 Using Market Mechanisms to Enforce Price Controls

Our actual experiences with price controls in both the United States and the world has demonstrated the difficulty that even governments face in maintaining the disequilibrium that occurs when price ceilings and price floors are imposed. The "invisible hand" of the market constantly pushes us towards equilibrium price and quantity. This push occurs because people—both as buyers and sellers—naturally look for trades that increase their own well-being. As long as a supplier's cost of producing more of a good is less than a consumer's willingness to pay for it, both the seller and buyer have an incentive to maneuver around any obstacles to make the trade.

Therefore, government price controls must be enforced vigilantly. But short of arresting violators and imposing high penalties, are there ways that price controls can be enforced by taking advantage of the "natural" market mechanism?

Suppose that the Indian government sets a price ceiling of P_c in the lentil market to make this food staple more affordable for its population. **Figure 8.13** shows the market for lentils in India. P_c is the price ceiling, which is lower than the market price P_e. To sustain this price ceiling, the Indian government must either police each and every trade that takes place or create a situation where this price effectively becomes the new equilibrium price. Figure 8.13 shows that this can be done by enacting a

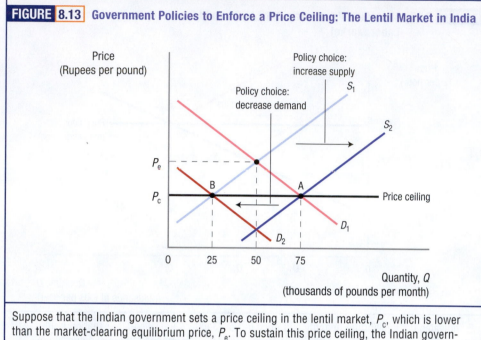

FIGURE 8.13   **Government Policies to Enforce a Price Ceiling: The Lentil Market in India**

Suppose that the Indian government sets a price ceiling in the lentil market, P_c, which is lower than the market-clearing equilibrium price, P_e. To sustain this price ceiling, the Indian government can enact a policy, such as subsidizing lentil production, which shifts the supply curve for lentils to the right. Or, it could enact a policy such as subsidizing lentil *substitutes*, that shifts the demand curve for lentils to the left. These policy options lead to equilibrium points A and B, respectively.

policy that shifts the supply curve for lentils to the right. Or, it could enact a policy that shifts the demand curve for lentils to the left. These alternatives lead to equilibrium A and B, respectively, in Figure 8.13. (The government could also use some combination of the two policies.)

What kinds of policies would have this effect? The supply curve would shift rightward if the government imported a vast quantity of lentils to supply to the domestic market or banned the export of lentils produced in the country.[7] The demand curve for lentils would shift left if, for example, the government subsidized the price of lentil *substitutes*. If the Indian government can get these policies "just right," there would no longer be a shortage of lentils, and the market-clearing price would now be at the price ceiling. Notice that the new equilibrium quantity would differ depending on which policy is pursued: when the demand curve shifts left, the equilibrium quantity of lentils declines, while a shift right in the supply curve would lead to a greater equilibrium quantity of lentils.

Now consider the enforcement of a price floor P_f on dairy products, in this case, cheese. As **Figure 8.14** shows, the price floor is above the equilibrium price, thereby creating a surplus. At the price floor, too much cheese is being produced.

Once again, the government could use the market's own internal tendencies to support this price. It could enact policies that bring about a rightward shift in the demand for cheese, or it could pursue strategies that shift the supply curve to the left. If it achieves either goal in exactly the right measure, the price floor (P_f) becomes the

· · · · · · ·

[7]Corey Kilgannon, "Trouble in Queens as Lentil Prices Rise." *New York Times*, September 29, 2006.

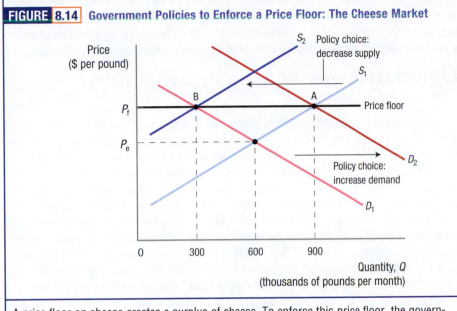

FIGURE 8.14   **Government Policies to Enforce a Price Floor: The Cheese Market**

A price floor on cheese creates a surplus of cheese. To enforce this price floor, the government could enact policies, such as buying up cheese with taxpayer dollars, which bring about a rightward shift in the demand for cheese, or it could pursue strategies that shift the supply curve to the left, such as paying dairy farmers to reduce their herds. If it achieves either goal in exactly the right measure, the price floor (P_f) becomes the new market-clearing, equilibrium price at points A and B, respectively.

new market-clearing, equilibrium price at equilibrium A or B, respectively. (Again, the government could use some combination of the two policies.)

The U.S. government has, in fact, used both approaches to enforce a price floor in the cheese market. In 2009, the Obama administration purchased surplus cheese from dairy farmers, thereby shifting the demand curve for cheese to the right and creating support for a price higher than the market's equilibrium price.[8] This surplus cheese was then distributed to food pantries in the United States and overseas. The government has also paid farmers to reduce their dairy herds, which shifted the supply curve for dairy products to the left. Once again, if the government can get it "just right," it can maintain its price floor by capitalizing on the market's own tendencies. This is much harder than you may think. One failed policy—which actually led to spot shortages of milk—offered cash payments to dairy farmers who were willing to turn some of their dairy cows into hamburger.[9]

Of course, depending on the strategy adopted, the quantity of cheese produced will be less or more than the equilibrium quantity produced at the market's "natural" equilibrium price. In either case, however, the American consumer ends up paying more at the grocery store for cheese products. And both approaches can be costly to taxpayers. From a policy standpoint, you might ask whether paying dairy farmers to

· · · · · · ·

[8]Associated Press, "President Signs Emergency Aid for Dairy Farmers." *New York Times*, October 21, 2009.

[9]"Why Milk Consumers?" *New York Times*, April 4, 1989.

reduce their herd sizes or buying up surplus cheese is a good use of taxpayer dollars. But at the same time, ending these policies may lead to severe hardship for dairy farmers and those whose incomes depend on the dairy business. As you can imagine, these policies involve a complicated mix of economics, lobbying, and politics.

8.9 What Happens When a Price Control Is Abolished?

For a variety of reasons, price ceilings and price floors are often abolished at some point in time. Perhaps they were imposed during war time and the war has ended. Or perhaps there has been a change in the composition and philosophy of regulatory agencies or Congress. When a price control is removed, the outcome is straight-forward: the market moves to the market-clearing price and equilibrium quantity dictated by the original demand and supply curves. Neither of these curves shifts. We say "original" to reference the demand and supply curves that existed before the government intervened to support its regulated price through policies—such as purchasing surplus output—that may have shifted the market's demand or supply curve.

It is important to recognize that other markets will be affected when price controls are lifted. Removing a price control might cause the demand or supply curve in a *related* market to shift, pushing that market into disequilibrium and, eventually, to a new equilibrium. This possibility is discussed next. As you'll see, this will lead to some predictions that are initially counter-intuitive but can be readily explained upon further consideration.

Lifting a Price Ceiling

The classic case of a price ceiling is rent control in New York City. Many apartments in New York City are subject to some form of rent ceiling or rent-stabilization guide-lines. This creates a shortage of apartments in the city. There are more people who are willing to pay to live in the city than there are units to lease. Where do the renters go who cannot get an apartment in the city? Many move to nearby New Jersey, which does not have rent control and is readily accessible via bridges, ferries, and public transit. In other words, the demand for apartments in New Jersey is greater than it would be if New York City did not have rent control.

What would happen if rent control in the city ended? Panels (a) and (b) in **Figure 8.15** illustrate the effect that lifting rent controls in New York City has on rentals in both New York City and its close substitute, New Jersey. As you can see, the rental rate for city apartments would rise to the market-clearing price, and the num-ber of available units would increase to the equilibrium quantity. Where do many of the new tenants come from? From New Jersey, of course! Despite the fact that rental rates in the city *rise*, people who were willing to pay the higher equilibrium price but were previously shut out by rent control will now able to find apartments and move to the city. As a result, the demand for New Jersey apartments declines, represented by the leftward shift in the demand curve for New Jersey apartments. The end result is a lower equilibrium rental rate in New Jersey and fewer units rented.

You may be uncomfortable with this result. After all, rents *rise* in the city, and yet the number of apartments rented also rises. Doesn't this violate the Law of Demand? The answer is a resounding *no*. Rent control forces out of the market people who are willing to pay the equilibrium price. After the artificially low rental rates are elimi-nated, renters can maximize their well-being by moving *along* their demand curves to the point where their willingness to pay is just equal to the market-clearing

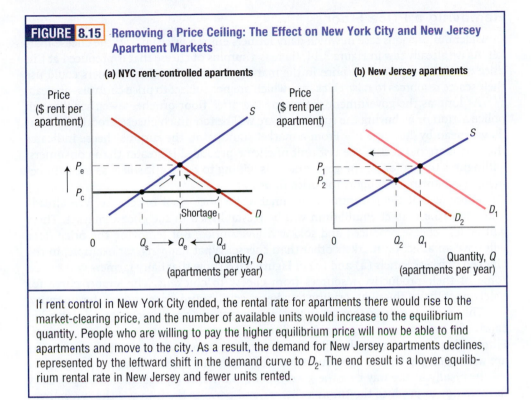

FIGURE 8.15 **Removing a Price Ceiling: The Effect on New York City and New Jersey Apartment Markets**

If rent control in New York City ended, the rental rate for apartments there would rise to the market-clearing price, and the number of available units would increase to the equilibrium quantity. People who are willing to pay the higher equilibrium price will now be able to find apartments and move to the city. As a result, the demand for New Jersey apartments declines, represented by the leftward shift in the demand curve to D_2. The end result is a lower equilibrium rental rate in New Jersey and fewer units rented.

price. This also explains why our general rule—which says that people substitute away from a good when its price increases—doesn't hold in this special situation. The city-apartment market is not in equilibrium as long as rent controls are affecting it. The price and quantity that results from rent control is *not* a price–quantity combination that lies on the market demand curve. This means that some people are unable to pursue the housing choice that would maximize their level of well-being—that is, living in New York City rather than New Jersey.

The same scenario arose when the price of natural gas was deregulated and allowed to rise to its equilibrium level.[10] During the period in which a price ceiling on natural gas was in effect, there were shortages in the United States. Providers were unwilling to build gas pipelines and distribution networks to supply customers in higher cost, inaccessible areas of the country. As a result, residential and commercial developments in low-density locations were often deprived of natural gas as an option to meet their heating, cooking, and other energy needs. To alleviate the upward pressure on oil prices created by the price ceiling on natural gas, the Reagan administration began the process of deregulating the natural gas market. The end result was that in spite of the increase in the price of natural gas as it converged to its equilibrium level, the number of natural gas customers increased. Correspondingly, the demand curve for electricity and heating oil shifted to the left, leading to less electricity and heating oil use. In the longer run, the higher unregulated price of natural gas stimulated not only an expansion in gas distribution systems but also greater investment in gas exploration, which has actually led to a decline in natural gas prices.

• • • • • • •

[10]Robert D. Hershey, Jr., "Issue and Debate; Deregulation of Natural Gas." *New York Times*, May 16, 1981.

Removing a Price Floor

Consider our previous case in which dairy farmers enjoy a price floor in the cheese market. As we already saw in Figure 8.14, there is a surplus of cheese that is produced at this price relative to equilibrium price in the market. Suppose that these farmers could use their scarce resources to raise chickens—which are not subject to price controls—instead.

As long as the government maintains the price floor on cheese—either through police action or by buying the surplus—there will be too much cheese produced. What do we mean by "too much"? From a market standpoint, the surplus cheese indicates that the marginal cost of the last unit of cheese produced is greater than consumers' willingness to pay for it. The government is willing to pay for it solely as an enforcement mechanism to support the price floor.

Suppose that the government eliminates the price floor on cheese. We already know that the market equilibrium will be reestablished in the cheese market. There will be less cheese produced and sold at a lower price. But removing the price floor will have an affect on markets other than cheese. What happens, for example, in the chicken market? Panels (a) and (b) of **Figure 8.16** show that dairy farmers will switch some of their productive resources from cheese to chickens. The supply curve for chickens shifts to the right, leading to a lower equilibrium price and greater quantity.

This analysis tells us that when too many resources are attracted to a market because of a price floor, a higher price will result in complementary producer markets. Eliminating a price floor will redirect scarce resources to markets in which consumers are willing to pay for the opportunity cost of additional units of output.

Ironically, if the way that the government maintains a price floor is to pay dairy farmers not to produce the surplus cheese—and permits them to use these resources instead in other productive activities—there will actually be too much supply in the chicken market. In this case, "too much" refers to the fact that some of the resources diverted to the chicken market should, from an economic perspective, have been used in cheese production instead. To see this, notice that in order for there to be no excess

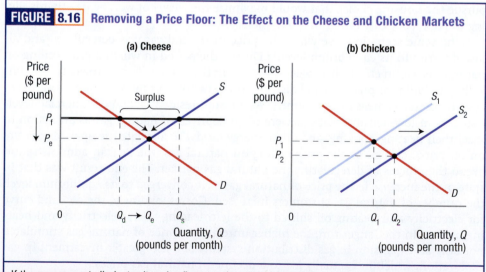

FIGURE 8.16   **Removing a Price Floor: The Effect on the Cheese and Chicken Markets**

If the government eliminates its price floor on cheese, market equilibrium will be reestablished in the cheese market. There will be less cheese produced, and it will be sold at a lower price. Dairy farmers will switch some of their productive resources from cheese to chickens. The supply curve for chickens will shift to the right, leading to a lower equilibrium price and greater equilibrium quantity.

supply, the quantity supplied would have to be Q_d. But the price-quantity combination (P_f, Q_d)—is not even a point on the dairy farmers' market supply curve. And, at Q_d, consumers' willingness to pay for additional cheese exceeds the opportunity cost of expanding production.

Rescinding the price floor and the payment program aimed at reducing production levels would lead to a lower market-clearing price for cheese and, at the same time, greater supply as dairy farmers move down their market supply curve to equilibrium. This apparent anomaly in supply behavior—where the quantity traded increases as the price goes down—can be explained by the previous observation that suppliers were not even operating along their supply curve when the price floor was in effect and, therefore, that the cheese market was in disequilibrium.

WHAT YOU SHOULD HAVE LEARNED FROM CHAPTER 8

- That the intersection of a market's demand and supply curves establishes equilibrium price and quantity.

- That equilibrium price is also called the market-clearing price because quantity demanded equals quantity supplied at this price.

- That at equilibrium, the price of a good is equal to the marginal cost of producing the last unit sold and is also equal to the willingness to pay for the last unit purchased.

- That individual suppliers and demanders respond to price—they are price takers. They have no power to influence price, but they can walk away from a trade.

- That in the presence of price-taking behavior and information about prices, a one-price market will result.

- That a one-price market creates consumer and producer surplus, the amount of which depends on the slopes of the market demand and supply curves.

- That when there is a surplus in a market, price begins to fall as suppliers attempt to sell off excess supply. As this happens, consumers move down the market demand curve, and suppliers move down the market supply curve, until equilibrium is once again restored.

- That when there is a shortage in a market, price begins to rise as demanders bid up the price to obtain the scarce good. As this happens, consumers move up the market demand curve and suppliers move up the market supply curve, until equilibrium is once again restored.

  - That a market bubble arises when rapidly increasing demand for an asset pushes its price above the asset's fundamental underlying value.

  - That speculators often fuel the rapid run-up in prices associated with a market bubble and that this may be driven by herd mentality.

  - That a market bubble bursts when there is a drastic reduction in demand for the asset whose price has been rapidly run-up.

- That a price ceiling is the maximum price at which a good can be legally traded.

- That a price floor is the minimum price at which a good can be legally traded.

- That government must actively pursue policies to enforce price controls because there is a natural tendency to move back to equilibrium as individuals pursue their self-interest.

- That eliminating a price control will not lead to a shift in the demand or supply curve in the price-regulated market.

- That eliminating a price control can cause the demand or supply curve in related markets to shift.

KEY TERMS

QUESTIONS AND PROBLEMS

1. Using supply-and-demand analysis, show what happens if the going price in a market is below the equilibrium price. Explain how pressures on price will lead the market to its equilibrium price and quantity.

2. A price floor only works when the market-clearing, equilibrium price is *lower* than the regulated price. Why?

3. A price ceiling only works when the market-clearing, equilibrium price is *higher* than the regulated price. Why?

4. U.S. residents have increasingly turned to Canada as a cheap source of prescription drugs. They are traveling across the border and using mail order Web sites to buy these drugs. Using supply and demand curves, show the impact of these activities on the equilibrium quantity and price of:

   a) prescription drugs in U.S. drugstores located near the Canadian–U.S. border.
   b) Canadian drugstores located near the U.S. border.
   c) bus tickets from major northern U.S. cities to Canadian cities.

   Indicate, using your answer to (b), how much U.S. senior citizens would be willing to pay in fines (for breaking the law) to continue to purchase Canadian prescription drugs.

5. Using supply and demand curves, show the impact on the equilibrium quantity and the price of menu items when restaurants:

   a) introduce free delivery to homes and businesses.
   b) introduce the acceptance of credit cards in lieu of cash-only.
   c) provide self-serve soda machines.
   d) eliminate reservations (i.e., seat people "first come, first served").

6. Using supply and demand diagrams, show how cost-saving improvements in the production technology for plasma screens impact equilibrium price and quantity in:

   a) the plasma TV market.
   b) the high-definition cable-services market.
   c) the movie theater market.
   d) the LCD TV market.

7. Using supply and demand diagrams, show the impact of an economic contraction on equilibrium price and quantity in the:

   a) jewelry market.
   b) used car market.
   c) new car market.
   d) store-brand toilet paper market.

8. Using supply and demand diagrams, show the impact of reductions in international supplies of crude oil on equilibrium price and quantity in:
   a) the U.S. gasoline market.
   b) the SUV market.
   c) the car tire market.
   d) the hybrid car market.
   e) the mass-transit market.

9. Using consumer demand curves, explain why it makes economic sense for a cell-phone company to virtually give away its phones to cell-phone users.

   True, false, uncertain. Explain: The price of cellular phones increases when:
   a) cell-phone numbers are transferable between cell-phone companies at no cost.
   b) the cost of early termination of a cell-phone contract declines.

10. Suppose that U.S. lumber companies are successful in ending current limits on the amount of trees that can be harvested in our national forests. Using supply and demand diagrams, show the impact on equilibrium price and quantity in:
    a) the lumber market.
    b) the new housing market.
    c) the carpet market.
    d) the wood stain/varnish market.
    e) the lumberjack labor market.

11. As a result of the Iraq War and rebuilding effort, the worldwide demand for U.S. raw materials such as lumber and steel has skyrocketed. Using supply and demand diagrams, show the impact of the war on equilibrium price and quantity in:
    a) the U.S. automobile market.
    b) the U.S. carpet market.
    c) the U.S. construction industry.
    d) the U.S. autoworker labor market.

12. In response to recent corporate financial scandals, the Federal government has enacted laws that make accountants personally liable for inaccuracies reported in audited financial statements, irrespective of the source of the error. Accountants must not only sign their name to any and all audited reports, but they are liable for criminal and civil penalties as well. Using supply-and-demand analysis, show the impact of this change in rules on equilibrium wage and quantity in:
    a) the accountant market.
    b) the corporate-audits market.
    c) the umbrella liability insurance-policy market (provides malpractice insurance for accountants).

13. To generate voting support from dairy producers, Congressional representatives from dairy-producing states have supported the use of price supports (floors) on milk and cheese. Using supply and demand diagrams, show the impact of such policies on price and quantity in:
    a) the milk market.
    b) the pizza market.
    c) the juice market.
    d) the cereal market.

    Identify one policy that the government can use to ensure that the price floor is not eroded over time.

14. Using supply and demand diagrams, show the impact of removing the price ceiling on natural gas on quantity and price in:
    a) the natural gas market.
    b) the electric-furnace market.
    c) the natural gas oven market.
    d) the heating-oil market.

15. In response to the rapid rise in the price of gasoline, some politicians have argued for a temporary or permanent suspension of the federal tax on gasoline (18.4 cents per gallon). Using supply and demand diagrams, show the impact of removing this tax on equilibrium quantity and price:

   a) for the gasoline market.
   b) for the car tire market.
   c) for FedEx and other delivery companies.

16. Political leaders in Los Angeles are leading a campaign to raise the minimum wage in the city (for all employment in the city) to a higher, "living" wage. Using supply-and-demand analysis, show the impact on:

   a) the skilled labor market in the city.
   b) the unskilled, teenage-worker market in the city.
   c) the fast-food industry in the city.

   Who "wins" and who "loses" if the minimum wage is raised?

17. Assume that the demand for cocaine is totally unresponsive to price, and assume further that users get the funds to pay for cocaine by stealing. Suppose the government is successful in intercepting shipments of the drug and, therefore, is able to reduce supply.

   a) Using supply-and-demand analysis, show the impact of the government's activity on the equilibrium price of cocaine.
   b) What will happen to the amount of crime committed by cocaine users?
   c) Does the government's activity have any effect on the amount of consumer and producer surplus enjoyed by buyers and sellers in the illegal drug market? Explain your answer.

18. Describe at least one mechanism that can be used to allocate economic goods when price is below equilibrium and there is excess demand. Explain the rationale for the government keeping prices below equilibrium (e.g., rent control); and private suppliers keeping prices below equilibrium (e.g., concert tickets).

19. Suppose the federal government imposes a tax on suppliers of soft drinks that contain sugar or corn syrup—soda, sports drinks, and so on—to discourage consumption and reduce obesity.

   a) Using supply-and-demand analysis, show the impact of this tax on equilibrium price and quantity in the regular soda market.
   b) Does consumer or producer surplus change as a result of this new tax? Explain your answer.

Price Elasticity: Measuring the Sensitivity of Buyers and Sellers to Changes in Price

"Let every nation know . . . that we shall pay any price . . . to assure the survival and success of liberty."

John F. Kennedy, 35th president of the United States

You have already learned that demand curves slope down and supply curves slope up. The steepness, or *slope*, of the demand and supply curves gives us a sense of how responsive buyers and sellers are to changes in price. The steeper the demand curve for a good is, the less responsive the quantity demanded is to a change in price. Similarly, the steeper the supply curve is, the less responsive quantity supplied is to price changes.

The slopes of the demand and supply curves tell us, all else held constant, the change in the number of units of a good demanded or supplied when its price changes by 1 cent, 1 dollar, or 1 kroner (if that is how price is measured). Let's suppose that your demand curve for weekly purchases of Blu-ray movie discs has a slope of -4. This means that you are likely to buy one more disc each week if the price drops by $4. And, for every $4 increase in the price of the discs, you would reduce your weekly purchases by one movie. We can interpret the slope of a supply curve in the same way. A producer of Blu-ray movie discs whose supply curve has a slope of $+2$ will supply 100,000 more discs to the market when the price increases by $2 (assuming that quantity supplied is measured in 100,000s of units).

Unfortunately, these slopes are not very good measures of price sensitivity. To see this, suppose that instead of looking at your weekly demand for Blu-ray discs, we looked at the number of discs you demand annually. If you purchase 1 more movie each week in response to a $4 decline in price, then you will purchase an additional 52 movies a year when price declines by $4. This means that the slope of your *annual* movie demand curve is $-4/52$ instead of $-4/1$, even though your responsiveness to the $4 price cut hasn't changed at all. This example demonstrates that the actual magnitude of a slope is sensitive to the "units" in which price and quantity are measured, where "units" refers to the measures used for price (dollars, pesos, euros, millions of dollars), quantity (pints, quarts, gallons, millions of units), and time period (day, week, year).

In the early twentieth century, a famous economist named Alfred Marshall introduced an alternative measure of price responsiveness that is not sensitive to this "units" problem. He called his measure *price elasticity*. One of Marshall's goals in devising this measure was to be able to compare price sensitivity across goods, consumers, and time. Are the French, for example, less responsive to changes in the price of wine than Americans? Does the annual supply of milk respond more to changes in milk prices than the weekly supply? As we will see next, Marshall's price elasticity measure conveys a wealth of valuable information to decision makers, whether they are individuals, corporations, or government agencies.

9.1 Price Elasticity of Demand: An Overview

Whereas the slope of a demand curve tells us the change in the number of units of a good demanded when there is a change in price, the **price elasticity of demand** tells us the *percentage* change in the number of units of a good demanded in response to a *percentage* change in its price.

> **PRICE ELASTICITY OF DEMAND** The percentage change in the quantity of a good demanded in response to a percentage change in its price.

> **EXAMPLE** When the price of gasoline increased from $3 to $4 a gallon (a 33 percent increase), purchases of gasoline dropped by 9 percent. This means that the price elasticity of demand for gasoline equals −9% / 33%, or −0.27.

> **EXAMPLE** When the price of housing dropped by 19 percent in Phoenix, the number of homes purchased increased from 1,200 to 1,500 a month (a 25 percent increase). The price elasticity of demand for housing in Phoenix equals 25% / −19%, or −1.32.

We can express price elasticity of demand as

$$\text{Price elasticity of demand } (\varepsilon_d) = \frac{\text{percentage change in quantity demanded}}{\text{percentage change in price}}$$

where the Greek letter epsilon (ε) is our shorthand symbol for elasticity.

Using percentage changes instead of the actual changes in the *number* of units demanded or the *dollar* change in price eliminates the units problem that plagues the slope calculation. Let's show this using our movie-download example. If the price of a download falls by $4—say, from $5 to $1—then the percentage change in price is equal to

$$\text{percentage change in price} = \frac{\text{new price} - \text{old price}}{\text{old price}}$$
$$= \frac{\$1 - \$5}{\$5}$$
$$= -\$4 \ / \ \$5$$
$$= -0.8 \text{ or } -80\%$$

−0.8 is called a "pure number." It is unit-free because the units ($) in the numerator are cancelled out by the units ($) in the denominator of the calculation. The same must therefore hold for −80 percent.

Calculating the percentage change in quantity also leads to a pure number, which eliminates the units problem when we switch between different measures of quantity or time. If you buy one more Blu-ray movie disc each week (e.g., 8 instead of 7) and 52 more per year (e.g., 416 instead of 364) when there is a $4 price cut, then the *percentage* change in quantity demanded is equal to

percentage change in quantity demanded

$$= \frac{\text{new quantity demanded} - \text{old quantity demanded}}{\text{old quantity demanded}}$$

$= (8 - 7) / 7 = 0.14 \text{ or } 14\%$ Weekly

$= (416 - 364) / 364 = 0.14 \text{ or } 14\%$ Annually

Because the numerator and the denominator of each calculation share the same time period, these cancel each other out, and we get the same percentage change in quantity whether we are measuring quantity demanded in weeks or years.

Using the definition of price elasticity of demand given earlier, your price elasticity of demand for Blu-ray movie discs can be calculated as

$$\text{Price elasticity of demand} = \frac{14\%}{-80\%} = -0.175$$

Because this price elasticity measure is unit-free, its value can be used to compare price sensitivity across different buyers, products, and markets. Notice also that the price elasticity of demand is negative. In fact, because of the Law of Demand, it can never be positive. When a product's price increases, more of it will never be purchased (holding everything else unchanged). And when a product's price falls, less of it will never be bought. As a result, many economists report price elasticities without their negative signs as if they were positive numbers. We will do this, too, from now on.

How exactly do we compare price elasticities of demand? Does a price elasticity of 0.175 mean there is greater or less responsiveness to price changes than if the price elasticity equals 2.00? We turn to this next.

Comparing Price Elasticities of Demand

How does the hypothetical price elasticity we just calculated for Blu-ray discs (0.175) compare to the price elasticity of demand for airline tickets, for example? Let's suppose that the price of a round-trip airline ticket from New York to Los Angeles decreases from $450 to $350, which amounts to a 22 percent decrease in price:

Percentage change in price $= (350 - 450) / 450 = -0.22 = -22\%$

Suppose that in response to this price decline, the total number of round-trip tickets you will purchase during the next 12 months increases from 2 to 3. This equals a 50 percent increase in tickets demanded, which means that your price elasticity of demand for airline travel between NYC and LA equals 50% / −22% = −2.27. After we get rid of the negative sign, we are left with a price elasticity of demand for Blu-ray discs of 0.175 versus a price elasticity of demand for airline tickets of 2.27, which is nearly 13 times greater.

These two numbers tell us that a 1 percent decline in the price of Blu-ray discs leads to a very small (just a 0.175 percent) increase in the number of Blu-ray discs purchased. In contrast, a 1 percent decline in the price of an airline ticket results in a 2.27 percent increase in the number of tickets purchased. Your demand for airline tickets is much more price sensitive than your demand for Blu-ray movie discs. How does this translate to everyday life? When airline companies advertise cheap tickets to select cities, they know that a relatively small drop in price will bring about a relatively large increase in ticket purchases by leisure travelers, even to snowbound cities such as Minneapolis in the dead of winter. As we will see later on, the size of the price elasticity of demand for a good actually tells us a lot more than simply whether one person or market is more or less responsive to price than another.

9.2 Price Elasticity and Consumer Expenditures on a Good

Robert Crandall, the former head of American Airlines, believed that every airline executive should have a working understanding of price elasticity of demand. He was quoted in the *New York Times* as saying:[1]

> "Much—indeed most—of our [industry] problems can be attributed to managements who seem to believe their mission in life is to put every living human being on an airplane at any price and who have failed to do their economic homework on subjects such as price elasticity."

Crandall was referring to the incessant fare wars in the air-travel market, which were filling seats on planes but reducing the airline industry's profitability. He rightly understood that the price elasticity of demand is arguably one of the most important economic concepts in the business world.

Why is this so? As we will see in a moment, price elasticity of demand tells us something about how a buyer's *total expenditures* on a good change when the good's price changes. So far, we have been looking at the actual *number* of units of a good that someone buys over a specified period of time. The total amount of money that is spent on this good equals the number of units purchased multiplied by the price that is paid for each unit. Every dollar that a consumer spends on a good translates into a dollar of *revenue* that the supplier receives (assuming away taxes and other price add-ons). For this very reason, suppliers such as American Airlines want to know how a consumer's total expenditures on airline tickets will change in response to changes in airfares. They know that the company's *revenue* stream is what ultimately matters, not the *number* of tickets sold.

Pricing strategists at Apple, for example, have examined the impact of a reduction in the price per download from $2 to 99 cents on the total amount of money buyers would spend on iTunes. They already know that more songs would be downloaded, but that is not the question at hand. The question is how total expenditures on iTunes would change. Similarly, eye surgeons who offer laser vision-correction surgery have lowered the price of surgery from $2,600 to $1,000 per eye to see what would happen to their revenue stream (it went down).

Policy makers also rely on information conveyed by a good's price elasticity of demand. For example, they may be concerned about the extent to which eliminating the tax deduction for mortgage-interest payments—which would increase the price of housing actually borne by the home owner—would affect the housing market. How would expenditures on housing change if the deduction is eliminated? What effect

---

[1]Agis Salpukas, "American Airlines Reins in Growth." *New York Times*, September 12, 1991.

would this eventually have on state and local property tax receipts? While we know from the Law of Demand that the number of units of housing demanded would decrease if the mortgage deduction is eliminated, we do not know how total expenditures on housing would change.

Think about a situation in which the price of a credit hour at your school increases from $100 to $160, which is a 60 percent increase in price. We know that the *number* of credit hours demanded will decline, but will this decline offset the increase in price that the university receives for each credit hour still taken? Suppose that in response to this credit-hour price increase, you reduce your credit-hour load from 20 hours each semester to 16, which is a 20 percent reduction. Your total tuition bill will go from $2,000 ($100 × 20 credit hours) to $2,560 ($160 × 16 credit hours) each semester. Your total expenditures will increase, even though you are getting fewer credit hours for your money. Notice that because you have reduced your credit hours when the price goes up, you are behaving exactly in line with the Law of Demand. But you have not cut back *enough* credit hours to totally offset the price increase. You would have to reduce your credit hours to 12.5 per semester ($160 × 12.5 credit hours = $2,000) to keep your total tuition payments the same as before the price increase. The end result is that while you take fewer credit hours, your university still collects more tuition dollars from you.

This example illustrates an important point: total expenditures on a good (such as college credit hours) can move in a *different* direction from the quantity demanded. That is, when price increases and quantity demanded decreases, total expenditures might increase or decrease, depending on the degree to which consumers cut back their purchases. Likewise, when the price of a good falls and quantity demanded increases, the total amount that consumers spend might increase or decrease, depending on the degree to which consumers increase their purchases. And all the while, the Law of Demand still holds.

Vertical Demand Curves

Consider what happens when there is an increase in the price of some good that buyers simply must have and for which there are few, if any, substitutes. Certain medications such as insulin that are essential to maintaining people's health are a good example. The result is a very steep, perhaps even vertical, demand curve for these drugs. When the demand curve is vertical, buyers are not sensitive to price at all: they will buy the same quantity of the good regardless of the price. Of course, the demand curve for even an "essential" good can be vertical only over a certain range of prices because, at some point, a buyer will have exhausted his entire income or so much of it that what remains for food and other necessities is severely compromised. In the case of insulin, we observe diabetics cutting back on their insulin use when it becomes too pricey for them (e.g., after they lose insurance coverage for prescriptions), sometimes substituting exercise or dietary changes in an effort to control their diabetes. Many times, they will apply for public or drug-company subsidies to reduce their out-of-pocket prescription drug costs.

Figure 9.1 shows the market demand curve for insulin. Starting from an initial price of $6 per unit and a quantity of 2 million units per day, what happens if the price increases to $9? The total amount of money that diabetics spend on insulin must increase because there is no change in the quantity demanded. The increase in total expenditures is ($9 − $6) × 2 million, or $6 million per day, represented by the pink-shaded area. This equals the increase in total revenue that insulin suppliers receive.

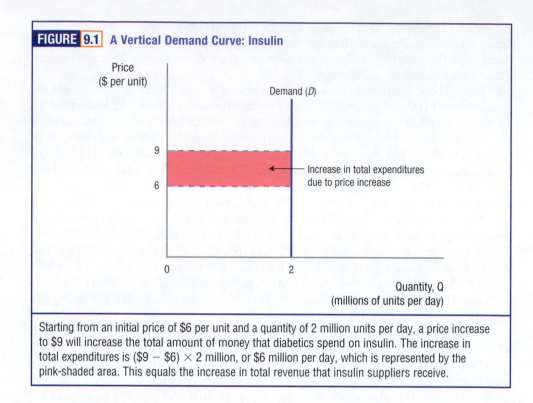

FIGURE 9.1   A Vertical Demand Curve: Insulin

Starting from an initial price of $6 per unit and a quantity of 2 million units per day, a price increase to $9 will increase the total amount of money that diabetics spend on insulin. The increase in total expenditures is ($9 − $6) × 2 million, or $6 million per day, which is represented by the pink-shaded area. This equals the increase in total revenue that insulin suppliers receive.

Conversely, if the price of insulin falls from $6 to $4 per unit, total expenditures on insulin will drop by ($4 − $6) × 2 million, or −$4 million a day. Clearly, suppliers would prefer the higher price to the lower one because they are producing and selling the same amount of insulin in either case. This means that they are incurring the same production costs whether the price is $4, $6, or $9. Thus, the profitability of insulin producers—which is the difference between their total revenue and total costs—*always* increases when the price of insulin increases. You should not jump to the conclusion, however, that insulin producers will raise their prices as high as possible—after all, they are still price takers in the competitive market for insulin.

Downward Sloping Demand Curves

Compare the insulin result to what happens when the price of iTunes digital-music downloads falls. Because Apple controls a large segment of the digital-music download business, it must evaluate alternative pricing strategies. It knows that a price cut leads to an increase in the quantity of downloads demanded. However, Apple doesn't know whether buyers' total *expenditures* on digital music will increase, decrease, or stay the same after the price change. **Figure 9.2** illustrates this situation by showing that a price decline from $3 to $1 leads to an increase in the quantity of downloads demanded (from 12 million per week to 18 million per week). How does the total amount spent on iTunes change in response to this price change? The price falls by $2 per download, but the quantity demanded increases by 6 million per day. The question about how total expenditures change boils down to how much of the price cut is offset by additional download purchases.

Selling digital-music downloads at the lower price of $1 means that Apple receives less revenue from the original 12 million units sold; this loss in revenue is

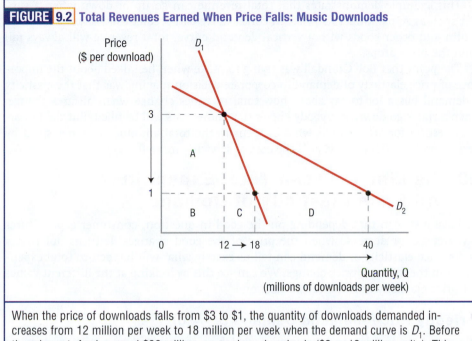

FIGURE 9.2 Total Revenues Earned When Price Falls: Music Downloads

When the price of downloads falls from $3 to $1, the quantity of downloads demanded increases from 12 million per week to 18 million per week when the demand curve is D_1. Before the price cut, Apple earned $36 million per week on downloads ($3 × 12 million units). This is represented by area A plus area B. But after the price cut, even though it sold an additional 6 million units per week, its total revenue declined to $18 million ($1 × 18 million units). This is represented by area B plus area C. Notice that area A plus area B is greater than area B plus area C. However, we would arrive at a different result if the demand curve was D_2: the drop in price would increase the total number of downloads to 40 million per week. This would generate $40 million per week ($1 × 40 million units), which is represented by areas B, C, and D. Area B plus area C plus area D is greater than area A plus area B.

($1 − $3) × 12 million, or −$24 million per week. To predict whether Apple's revenues increase, decrease, or remain unchanged after the price cut, we must compare the gain in total expenditures resulting from the increase in quantity demanded to the loss in total revenue associated with the price reduction. Before the price cut, Apple earned $36 million per week on downloads ($3 ×12 million units). This is represented by areas A and B. But after the price cut, even though it sold an additional 6 million units per week, Apple only earned $18 million ($1 × 18 million units), which is represented by areas B and C. Notice that area A plus area B is greater than area B plus area C. In this case, we see that the price cut *reduces* the total revenue Apple earns on music downloads by $6 million. Even though the *number* of downloads increases dramatically, the increase is not enough to offset the reduction in price. If you were the CEO of Apple, would you drop the price of a download from $3 to $1?

What if instead of an increase from 12 million to 18 million downloads per week, the price cut resulted in a total of 40 million downloads per week, which is an increase of 28 million downloads? This would generate $40 million per week ($1 × 40 million units), which is represented by areas B, C, and D. Area B plus area C plus area D is greater than area A plus area B, so Apple will earn more revenue if it drops the price to $1.

This example demonstrates that total revenue can go up or down when a supplier such as Apple lowers its price. In contrast, we can predict that when it comes to insulin and other goods with a vertical demand curve, total revenue will always fall when the price drops.

The point that Bob Crandall was trying to make when he talked about the importance of price elasticity of demand in corporate decision making was that the elasticity of demand has a lot to say about how total revenues change when airfares change. When airfares go down, everybody knows that more seats will be filled. But the important question for an airline is what happens to the total amount of money spent by fliers when fares fall (and what is the cost of servicing more fliers)?

9.3 The Link between Total Expenditures and Price Elasticity of Demand

We have just seen that depending on the good in question, consumer expenditures may increase or decrease when the price of the good changes. It turns out that a good's price elasticity of demand can tell us exactly what will happen to total expenditures in the face of a price change. We can see this by looking at the different values that price elasticity of demand can take on.

Perfectly Price Inelastic Demand ($\varepsilon_d = 0$)

Let's return to the demand for insulin, which is represented by a vertical demand curve over some range of prices. What is the price elasticity of demand for insulin? Because there is no change at all in the quantity demanded when price changes, the numerator of the price elasticity calculation is zero, no matter what the value is of the denominator. This means that the price elasticity of demand for insulin equals zero. Demand is said to be **perfectly price inelastic**.

> **PERFECTLY PRICE INELASTIC DEMAND** A situation in which the quantity of a good demanded is totally unresponsive to a change in its price. A good whose demand curve is vertical.

> **EXAMPLE** The demand for emergency medical care is perfectly price inelastic.
>
> **EXAMPLE** The demand for oxygen tanks is perfectly price inelastic after a deep-sea diver is underwater.

As you saw earlier in Figure 9.1, when the quantity demanded of a good such as insulin is independent of price, the total amount of money spent on it must rise when price goes up. This has to be the case because the increase in price is not met with any decrease in quantity demanded. In fact, total expenditures on a good such as insulin must increase by the *same percentage* as the price increases: if the price of insulin goes up by 20 percent, so will total expenditures. Conversely, a drop in price results in the same percentage fall in total expenditures: if price falls by 15 percent, so will total expenditures on perfectly price inelastic goods such as insulin.

Price Inelastic Demand ($\varepsilon_d < 1$)

What if you would cut back on a good—but not by very much—if its price rose? Gasoline, diapers, and toilet paper may be good examples. Unless the price of gas increases dramatically, the quantity purchased tends not to change very much, at least in the short run. So, even though the demand for gas is not *perfectly* price inelastic, it is still somewhat price inelastic.

What does this mean? An increase in the price of gasoline results in only small cutbacks in the number of gallons purchased because only discretionary driving is affected. In other words, most of us must drive to work or to school because there are few viable alternatives. Therefore, only a fraction of the price increase can be offset by reducing the number of gallons purchased. Conversely, when the price of gas falls, we increase the quantity of gas we purchase, but this increase is usually fairly small and does not fully offset the price decline.

Suppose that at a price of $2 per gallon, 6 million gallons of gasoline are sold per day in the state of California. Now let the price increase to $3 per gallon, as illustrated in **Figure 9.3**. According to this figure, the quantity demanded falls to 5 million gallons per day. After the price increase, total expenditures on gasoline increase from $2 × 6 million, or $12 million per day, to $3 × 5 million, or $15 million per day. In other words, area A in the figure far outweighs area B, which represents the savings from cutting back on the number of gallons purchased.

How does this match up with the real world? Researchers have estimated that the price elasticity of demand for gasoline is approximately 0.2. That is, a 10 percent increase in the price of gasoline will, all else held constant, lead to only a 2 percent decline in the number of gallons purchased. For example, if the price of gasoline rose from $2 to $2.20 (a 10 percent increase), the number of gallons per year that you are likely to purchase would fall by 2 percent, say from 1,000 gallons to 980 gallons. In other words, your total expenditures on gasoline would increase from $2 × 1,000 gallons, or $2,000 a year, to $2.20 × 980 gallons, or $2,156 a year.

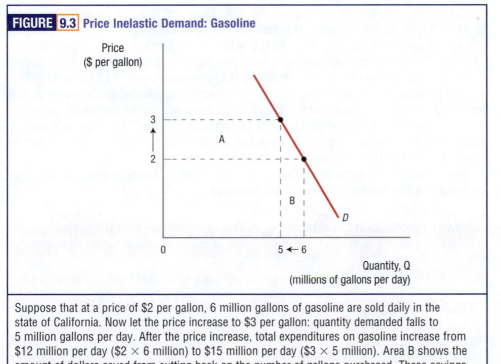

FIGURE 9.3 **Price Inelastic Demand: Gasoline**

Suppose that at a price of $2 per gallon, 6 million gallons of gasoline are sold daily in the state of California. Now let the price increase to $3 per gallon: quantity demanded falls to 5 million gallons per day. After the price increase, total expenditures on gasoline increase from $12 million per day ($2 × 6 million) to $15 million per day ($3 × 5 million). Area B shows the amount of dollars saved from cutting back on the number of gallons purchased. These savings, however, do not outweigh the price increase on the gallons still purchased (area A).

We can generalize this result to show that when a good exhibits a price elasticity of demand equal to 0.2, total expenditures (not quantity) will increase by approximately 0.8 percent when the price of the good increases by 1 percent.

Although 0.8 percent may not seem like a large increase in total expenditures, consider the fact that U.S. consumers spent more than $2.47 trillion[2] on gasoline in 2004. At that level, every 1 percent increase in the price of gasoline translates into almost $2 *billion* more spent on gasoline that is no longer available for other purchases.

Anytime a good has a price elasticity of less than 1, price increases lead to an increase in total expenditures on the good, and decreases in price result in lower total expenditures. This occurs because the percentage change in quantity demanded is always smaller than the percentage change in the price. We say that the demand for such goods is **price inelastic**.

PRICE INELASTIC DEMAND ($\varepsilon_d < 1$) A situation in which the percentage change in the quantity demanded is less than the percentage change in price.

EXAMPLE The demand for coffee, diapers, toilet paper, and salt is price inelastic.

Unitary Price Elasticity of Demand ($\varepsilon_d = 1$)

What if, instead, we consider a good that people budget for, each and every month? For example, suppose you set aside $40 a month to spend on take-out food. Based on this budgeting rule, your total monthly expenditures on take-out food will never vary—they will always be $40 regardless of whether the price of take-out food goes up or down. This means that when the price of the food changes, the quantity you purchase must change to exactly "offset" the price change.

Let's say that the price of your favorite Taco Bell burrito goes down—from $1.99 to $1.69. This price cut will permit you to buy more burritos each month and still spend only $40. In fact, because the price of the burrito fell by approximately 15 percent, you can increase your fast-food purchases each month by approximately the same percentage—15 percent (assuming that you only spend the $40 on Taco Bell burritos). Because the percentage change in quantity demanded is the same as the percentage change in price (except that it is positive instead of negative), the price elasticity of demand must equal 1. So, if the price of Taco Bell burritos increases by 20 percent, you would have to cut back the *number* you purchase by 20 percent to keep your total fast-food expenditures at $40 a month.

When people budget a fixed amount of dollars to a particular good, we say that the good exhibits **unitary price elastic demand**.

UNITARY PRICE ELASTIC DEMAND ($\varepsilon_d = 1$) A situation in which the percentage change in quantity demanded is exactly equal to the percentage change in its price.

EXAMPLE Suppose you have been given a gift card to a local clothing store. You can buy four shirts that are 50 percent off or two shirts that are not on sale (all of them originally sold for the same price). Your demand for the store's merchandise is unitary price elastic in that your total expenditures will always equal the value of the gift card.

[2]*Statistical Abstract, 2008.* Table 896.

A popular stock market investing strategy is called *dollar-cost averaging*. This investment strategy recommends investing the same total dollars each month in your mutual fund or stock portfolio. This means that the actual *number* of shares you purchase will depend on the price per share at the time you make each monthly investment. If an investor buys $240 worth of Walmart shares each month, she will receive six shares when the stock is $40 per share and four shares when the price per share is $60. The rationale for this approach is to "average out" short-term fluctuations in stock prices as well as to avoid the temptation to "time" the market—which is usually a losing proposition. Investing the same amount of money each month to buy shares means that your demand for these shares is unitary price elastic.

Of course, many goods exhibit unitary price elasticity regardless of how individual consumers budget for them. Tires are one example. When the price of tires goes up by a certain percentage, purchases (in terms of the total number of tires bought) fall by roughly the same percentage.

Price Elastic Demand ($\varepsilon_d > 1$)

Our New York to Los Angeles airline travel example showed that your demand for airline tickets is highly sensitive to changes in ticket prices: the price elasticity of demand in that example was 2.77. What does this tell us about how your total expenditures change as the airfares rise or fall? Given a price elasticity of demand equal to 2.77, a 10 percent change in ticket prices will result in a 27.7 percent change in the *number* of tickets you purchase.

Consider **Figure 9.4**. Suppose the round-trip airfare between New York and Los Angeles is $300. At this price, you buy an average of 8 round-trip tickets per year.

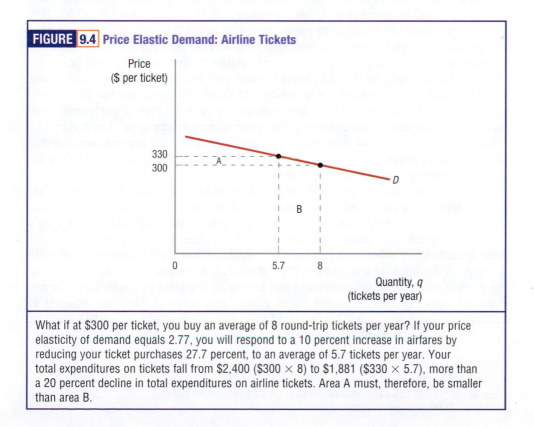

FIGURE 9.4 **Price Elastic Demand: Airline Tickets**

What if at $300 per ticket, you buy an average of 8 round-trip tickets per year? If your price elasticity of demand equals 2.77, you will respond to a 10 percent increase in airfares by reducing your ticket purchases 27.7 percent, to an average of 5.7 tickets per year. Your total expenditures on tickets fall from $2,400 ($300 × 8) to $1,881 ($330 × 5.7), more than a 20 percent decline in total expenditures on airline tickets. Area A must, therefore, be smaller than area B.

Now let the airfare increase by 10 percent, from $300 to $330. According to your price elasticity of demand, you would respond by reducing your ticket purchases by 27.7 percent, to an average of 5.7 tickets a year. Your total expenditures on tickets fall from $2,400 ($300 × 8) to $1,881 ($330 × 5.7). So a 10 percent increase in airfares leads to more than a 20 percent decline in total expenditures on airline tickets. In other words, you have cut back the number of trips by more than the 10 percent required to just offset the price increase. In fact, you have cut back so much that the total amount you spend on tickets has fallen off sharply—by more than 20 percent.

Now suppose the price of travel declines by 10 percent. The resulting increase in the number of tickets you purchase more than offsets this price cut. Your total expenditures will increase by more than 20 percent. When it comes to airline tickets and other goods that exhibit a price elasticity of demand greater than one, you always adjust your quantity demanded by a greater percentage than the percentage change in price. This holds whether price is going up or down. Such behavior reflects a great deal of sensitivity to price. We call this **price elastic demand**.

PRICE ELASTIC DEMAND ($\varepsilon_d > 1$) A situation in which the percentage change in quantity demanded is greater than the percentage change in price.

EXAMPLE Vacations, plastic surgery, and jewelry are all goods for which demand is price elastic.

Area B in Figure 9.4 represents the reduction in total expenditures resulting from the decrease in the number of tickets purchased at the higher price of $330. This more than offsets the increase in expenditures on the 5.7 tickets that are still purchased after the price increase, which is represented by area A. Generally speaking, the more price elastic a good's demand is, the *flatter* its demand curve will be.

How can a company that has some control over pricing use information about the price elasticity of demand for its product to make pricing decisions? Music producers, who get a share of iTunes revenues in the form of royalty payments, have argued that listeners are insensitive to the price of new releases, or "hot tracks." In effect, they are saying that demand is price inelastic and total expenditures on this music would increase substantially if these tracks were priced higher than Apple's flat rate of 99 cents per song. Are these producers right?

It turns out that the demand for a just-released downloadable hot track becomes highly price elastic within a matter of only weeks of its release.[3] Even though listeners might be initially willing to pay higher prices around the time of a song's release, this price insensitivity dissipates quickly as other new releases compete for their attention. In effect, the presence of substitute hot tracks increases the price elasticity of demand for any one specific hot track. This means that if Apple followed the pricing advice of music producers and increased the price of a new song for any extended period of time, it would suffer a decline in revenue. The total amount of money that listeners are willing to spend on a new song would fall only a week or two after the song's release date.

·······

[3]Sean Ryan, "Music Label Unhappiness with iTunes—A Price Elasticity Debate." August 28, 2005. www.sharkjumping.com.

The price elasticity of demand for digital music has already been estimated for a 50 percent cut in Apple's flat-rate price—from 99 cents to 49 cents. The estimates reveal that this price cut would increase total expenditures on downloads of digital music anywhere from 300 percent to as much as 1,000 percent.[4] Working backward from these estimates, we calculate that the price elasticity of demand for digital music may be as high as 40. This means that if the price of downloads increased instead of decreased—even for hot tracks—there would be a huge decline in Apple's total revenue and the royalties passed on to music producers.

By contrast, the price elasticity of demand for downloaded movies is estimated to be far lower than for hot tracks. This is likely due to the relatively longer time period between new movie releases as compared to new music releases, which means that fewer new movie substitutes are available. In 2006, 23 percent of broadband users said they would download a movie if its price were $10, whereas only 14 percent would do so if the price were $15. This translates into a price inelastic demand of 0.18.[5]

Perfectly Price Elastic Demand ($\varepsilon_d = \infty$)

We have previously described the behavior of price-taking suppliers, who can only respond to the market's price by adjusting the quantity they supply. They cannot increase their price above their competitors, or they will lose all of their customers. And there is no reason to drop their price below the competition because each supplier is so small relative to the size of the market that she can sell as much as she wants at the going market price.

Price-taking behavior is the norm in agricultural markets, for example, because consumers tend to be unconcerned about who actually supplies their celery or peaches. Likewise, cereal producers are indifferent to which wheat or corn growers provide them grain, unless there are discernible differences in the type or quality of grain supplied (e.g., whether it has been genetically altered or not). More generally, we see price-taking behavior by suppliers in a market when consumers perceive that they are all providing the same good.

Figure 9.5 shows a horizontal demand curve—horizontal from the point on the price axis that corresponds to the market's equilibrium price—which economists use to represent the demand curve facing a price-taking supplier. It is important to recognize that the horizontal nature of the demand curve is a *representation* of how price-taking suppliers perceive the demand they face. Its slope is equal to zero, so there is no change in price even when there is a change in the quantity that a price-taking producer supplies. Once again, this is because the producer is small—and virtually inconsequential—when it comes to determining the market price. Each producer perceives that consumers will purchase any and all of the quantity he supplies at the market price of $6.

A horizontal demand curve translates into a price elasticity of demand of infinity. A supplier who reduces his price an infinitesimal amount below the going market price will experience a huge percentage increase in quantity demanded

....

[4]Victoria Shannon, "Music Business Finds Little to Sing About." *International Herald Tribune,* January 23, 2006.

[5]Brad Cook, "Research Firm: Only 14% Would Pay $15 for an iTunes Movie." September 6, 2006. www.ipodserver.com.

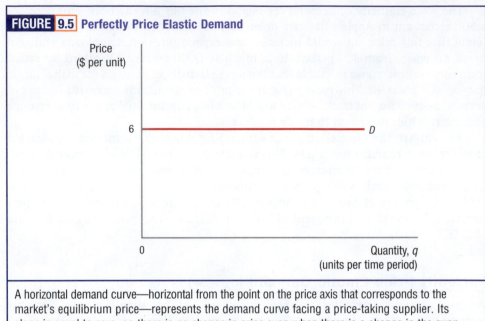

FIGURE 9.5 Perfectly Price Elastic Demand

A horizontal demand curve—horizontal from the point on the price axis that corresponds to the market's equilibrium price—represents the demand curve facing a price-taking supplier. Its slope is equal to zero, so there is no change in price even when there is a change in the quantity that a price-taking producer supplies. This is because the amount supplied by one producer is small—and virtually inconsequential—when it comes to determining the market price. From an individual supplier's point of view, consumers will demand any and all quantities supplied at the market price of $6.

(from an infinitesimal piece of the market's total demand to the entire market demand). And, when a supplier increases his price an infinitesimal amount above the going market price, he will experience a huge percentage decline in quantity demanded (from an infinitesimal piece of the market's total demand to zero). We call this **perfectly price elastic demand**.

PERFECTLY PRICE ELASTIC DEMAND A situation in which the quantity demanded is so sensitive that it goes to zero when the price increases by only an infinitesimal amount.

EXAMPLE If a dairy farmer tries to sell a gallon of milk at a price higher than the equilibrium price, he will lose all of his customers to farmers who sell their milk at this lower equilibrium price.

EXAMPLE If a seller of gold tries to raise his price per ounce above the market price, he will lose all of his customers to other gold sellers.

Table 9.1 recaps the relationship between the magnitude of the price elasticity of demand measure and the way that total expenditures (TE) change with changes in price. We've also included some examples of goods that fit into each category.

Table   9.1   A Summary of the Price Elasticity of Demand

Perfectly Price Inelastic Demand

Examples: insulin, emergency medical care

$\varepsilon_d = 0$ When P goes up, Q doesn't change, and TE goes up.

When P goes down, Q doesn't change, and TE goes down.

Price Inelastic Demand

Examples: toilet paper, salt, coffee, gasoline

$\varepsilon_d < 1$ When P goes up, Q goes down, and TE goes up.

When P goes down, Q goes up, and TE goes down.

Unitary Price Elastic Demand

Examples: stocks (dollar-cost averaging), movies

$\varepsilon_d = 1$ When P goes up, Q goes down, and TE doesn't change.

When P goes down, Q goes up, and TE doesn't change.

Price Elastic Demand

Examples: jewelry, restaurant meals, manicures

$\varepsilon_d > 1$ When P goes up, Q goes down, and TE goes down.

When P goes down, Q goes up, and TE goes up.

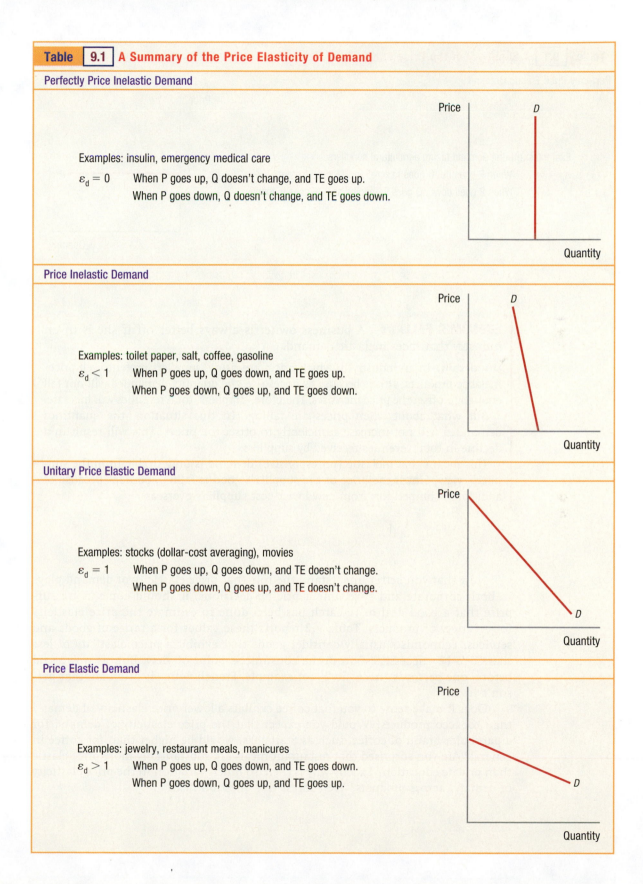

| Table | 9.1 | A Summary of the Price Elasticity of Demand (*continued*) |

Perfectly Price Elastic Demand

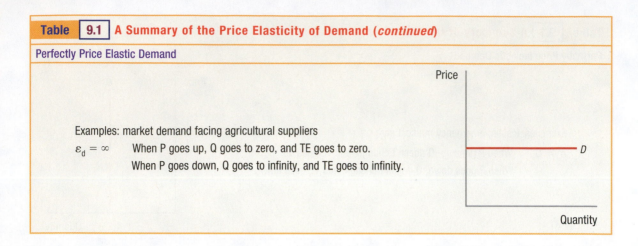

Examples: market demand facing agricultural suppliers

$\varepsilon_d = \infty$ When P goes up, Q goes to zero, and TE goes to zero.
When P goes down, Q goes to infinity, and TE goes to infinity.

ECONOMIC FALLACY   A business owner is always better off if she is in an industry that faces inelastic demand.

Uncertain. In an industry in which prices are rising, suppliers prefer to sell price-inelastic products. This is because as prices rise, the quantity demanded will not fall enough to offset the price increases. Therefore, suppliers' total revenues will increase.

But what about when prices are falling? In this situation, the quantities demanded will not increase sufficiently to offset the prices. This will result in a decline in total revenues received by suppliers.

This means that inelastic (unresponsive) demand is undesirable from the supplier's viewpoint if the price of the supplier's good is falling, perhaps because of additional competition from new lower-cost suppliers overseas.

Now that you better understand the role that price elasticity of demand plays in both corporate and government pricing decisions, it should come as no surprise that a good deal of research has been done to estimate the price elasticity for a variety of products. **Table 9.2** reports these values for a range of goods and services. Economists usually consider goods that exhibit a price elasticity of less than 1 to be "necessities" from the consumer's point of view. But, as we've said before, one person's "necessity"—for example, French wine—is often another person's luxury.

Does it make sense to you that coffee exhibits a lower price elasticity of demand than tobacco products? Would you expect that the price elasticity of demand for a particular brand of coffee, such as Starbucks, would be higher than for coffee in general? Are you surprised that restaurant meals are substantially more price elastic than private education? Exactly why is there so much variation in the price elasticity of demand across products? We address this question next.

Table 9.2	Estimated Price Elasticities of Demand for Various Goods and Services
Goods by Elasticity	**Estimated Elasticity of Demand**
Inelastic	
Salt	0.1
Matches	0.1
Toothpicks	0.1
Airline travel, short run	0.1
Gasoline, short run	0.2
Gasoline, long run	0.7
Residential natural gas, short run	0.1
Residential natural gas, long run	0.5
Coffee	0.25
Fish (cod) consumed at home	0.5
Tobacco products, long run	0.45
Legal services, short run	0.4
Physician services	0.6
Taxi, short run	0.6
Wine, short run	0.7
Approximately Unitary Elastic	
Movies	0.9
Housing, owner occupied, long run	1.2
Shellfish, consumed at home	0.9
Oysters, consumed at home	1.1
Private education	1.1
Tires, short run	0.9
Tires, long run	1.2
Wine, long run	1.2
Beer, short run	1.2
Radio and television receivers	1.2
Elastic	
Restaurant meals	2.3
Foreign travel, long run	4.1
Airline travel, long run	2.4
Fresh green peas	2.8
Automobiles, short run	1.9
Automobiles, long run	2.2
Chevrolet automobiles	4.0
Fresh tomatoes	4.6

Sources: Patrick L. Anderson, et al., "Price Elasticity of Demand." Mackinac Center for Public Policy, November 13, 1997. www.mackinac.org/1247; Irvin B. Tucker, *Survey of Economics* (Mason, OH: South-Western Cengage Learning, 2009), p. 102; William A. McEachern, *Economics: A Contemporary Introduction* (Mason, OH: South-Western Cengage Learning, 2009), p. 107; Robert Frank and Ben Bernanke, *Principles of Microeconomics* (Homewood, IL: Richard D. Irwin, 2004), p. 95.

9.4 Why Goods Exhibit Different Price Elasticities of Demand

How sensitive a good's demand is to price changes depends on a whole host of factors. These include the availability of substitute goods, the proportion of a person's income that the item accounts for, whether the good is viewed to be "essential" or a luxury, the time horizon over which we are measuring price elasticity, and whether the price changes are perceived to be permanent or transitory. We explore each of these factors in the following subsections.

Availability of Substitutes

Do consumers *perceive* that substitutes are available for a good whose price has increased? If the answer is no, then the good's price elasticity of demand will be very low: consumers will not reduce their purchases very much when there is an increase in price. Importantly, they very likely will not cut back enough to reduce their expenditures on the good. In effect, they are stuck. In the most extreme case—when demand is perfectly price inelastic—the same amount of the good will be purchased regardless of its price.

In our earlier discussion of individual demand curves, we noted that the existence of a substitute depends largely on a consumer's preferences, which reflect his *perceptions* about the substitutability of two goods. Are cloth diapers a "good" substitute for disposables? What about Pepsi versus Coke? Or, for that matter, what about courses offered by a state university versus a community college? When it comes to substitutes, it is truly the case that "perception is reality."

Because it is ultimately consumers' perceptions that determine whether a substitute good exists or not, it is in a supplier's self-interest to distinguish her product—in the minds of consumers—from potential substitutes. One method of doing this is to provide consumers with comparative product and service information through advertising and product reviews. Every supplier strives to create a market "niche" that insulates her from the full force of competition and thereby reduces the price elasticity of demand for her product. In the case of agricultural markets, country-of-origin labels and organic labels have reduced the substitutability of "apples for apples" for at least some consumers. Building a brand name is another common strategy to differentiate one's own product from potential substitutes. For example, Lipitor—the blockbuster, brand-name, cholesterol-reducing prescription drug—emphasizes in its ads that there are no generic drugs available that can substitute for it. Starbucks emphasizes the quality of the coffee beans it uses and the fact that these beans are "fair traded" (i.e., they are purchased at a price that does not exploit native workers). The more successful this strategy of product differentiation is, the greater the pricing power a supplier will have: she will be able to command a higher price for her product than others in the market and still retain buyers. In effect, she has reduced the price elasticity of demand that she faces, so her demand curve will no longer be horizontal.

SOLVED PROBLEM

Q Suppose two groups of consumers are in the market for new automobiles. For the first group, which is comprised of young people, new cars exhibit a price elasticity of demand equal to 14. For the second group, which is comprised of older workers and business owners, new cars exhibit a price elasticity of 2. If there are exactly the same number of consumers in each of the two groups, and if young people buy 20 percent of the new cars sold each year (the rest are purchased by the second group), what is the price elasticity of demand for the market as a whole?

A In this example, new cars are far more elastic for young people. Perhaps used cars are reasonable substitutes when it comes to meeting the transportation needs of the individuals in this group. In contrast, older employees and business owners are relatively more "stuck" on new cars, perhaps because these individuals have different preferences or larger incomes. You might be tempted to say that because the two groups have the same number of consumers, the market's price elasticity of demand must equal the average of the two groups' elasticities, or 8 (14 + 2 / 2). But that wouldn't be accurate. To calculate the price elasticity of demand for the entire market, we need to *weight* each group's price elasticity of demand by the percentage of the quantity demanded that they each account for

Market price elasticity = (14 × 0.2) + (2 × 0.8) = 4.4

In other words, the price elasticity of demand for the entire market is 4.4—not 8.

Generalizing this result, we see that a market's price elasticity of demand is most sensitive to the elasticity of demand of consumers who are the biggest buyers in the market.

The Proportion of Income Allocated to the Good

In the course of your daily routine on campus, you may get into the habit of buying a can of Coke from the vending machine outside your second class of the day. You don't think much about this because it's "only" $1, which represents a very small fraction of the money that you have to spend. In this type of situation, you are likely to be less sensitive to price changes—that is, your price elasticity of demand for cans of Coke will be very low. In fact, over some range of price increases, perhaps up to $1.25 a can, you may actually exhibit perfectly price inelastic demand when it comes to your daily soda purchase. In this case, it would take a price increase of over 25 percent to begin to affect your soda-purchasing patterns.

Contrast this situation to changes in the price of a college credit hour. It is quite likely that a hefty share of your income (or your parents' income) is devoted to making tuition payments. If the price of a credit hour increases by even a small amount, say 4 percent, this will have a substantial impact on the amount of money remaining to spend on other goods, such as car payments, food, and gasoline. In effect, the opportunity cost of a 4 percent price increase in tuition is substantially higher than the 25 percent increase in the price of soda. This is why economists predict that consumers will be far more price sensitive—that is, have a higher price elasticity of demand—when it comes to goods that account for a large share of their income.

ECONOMIC FALLACY   If the demand for gasoline is perfectly inelastic, when its price rises, the consumption of gasoline and other goods will be unchanged.

False. If the price elasticity of demand for gasoline equals zero, then the quantity purchased when its price rises stays the same. This means that people's expenditures on gasoline go up. To the extent that gasoline is a key component in people's budgets, an increase in its price can substantially depress the quantity of goods demanded in many other markets, even those that are not directly related to gasoline and transportation. This is because people have limited incomes, so their purchases of one or more other goods must fall—even though the prices of these goods haven't changed! When the price of a major component of our consumption bundle rises, there is an *income effect* that affects our consumption of other unrelated goods. This would not be the case for people who use mass transit, for example, as long as the price of this type of transportation doesn't change.

Whether the Good Is Perceived to Be "Essential" or a Luxury

We have already seen that in the case of insulin and other life-sustaining medications, the price elasticity of demand is zero or close to it. Diabetics treat insulin as an essential good when it comes to their well-being. They grit their teeth when the price rises, but buy it anyway.

You have probably felt the same way when the price of gasoline rises, and you must still fill your gas tank so that you can go to work, school, the bank, and so on. Higher prices reduce your sense of well-being because you have less money left over to buy the "frills" that you enjoy so much. Yet, you probably cut back on gasoline purchases very little, at least in the short run. In contrast, if the price of one of these frills—say, designer athletic shoes or handbags—rises, you are more likely to reduce your purchases, choosing instead a less-expensive substitute or hoping that the price will come down again. What your choices tell us is that the more essential you feel a good is to your daily life, the less elastic your demand for it will be. And the more of a luxury a good is to you, the higher its price elasticity of demand will be.

The Short Run versus the Long Run

Another factor that affects a product's price elasticity of demand is the amount of time people have to respond to any given price change. Over time, people can rid themselves of costly commitments and respond more freely to changes in market conditions. For example, until his car lease expires, a person leasing a gas-guzzling SUV cannot fully adjust the amount of gas he purchases when the price of gasoline rises. **Table 9.2** reports both the short-run and long-run price elasticities of demand for a number of goods, including natural gas, tires, and air travel. We can see that the price elasticity of demand is consistently greater in the long run than in the short run. Put another way, demand curves for these goods tend to become *flatter* over time as consumers move away from goods whose prices have risen and toward substitutes whose prices have remained unchanged. Or, people may be able to defer their purchases of durable goods—such as tires—into the future in response to a price increase.

The amount of time it takes to fully respond to a price change varies according to the good in question. It may take years for people to adjust to higher gas prices, especially if the adjustment involves moving closer to work or saving up to buy a new fuel-efficient automobile. In contrast, consumers standing in the produce section of their local grocery store may quickly adjust to a price increase in oranges by switching to apples or pears.

Over time, new substitutes also are likely to appear in the market. This is exactly what happens in the pharmaceutical market after the patent on a brand-name drug expires. Generic drugmakers can then legally enter and compete against the original producer of the drug, typically at a far lower price (as much as 80 percent lower). Both public and private medical-insurance plans contend that these generic drugs are "therapeutically equivalent" to their branded counterparts. Given this presumption, it makes sense that insurers almost always require that prescriptions be filled with generics, when available, rather than brand-name medications. Nonetheless, branded drug companies have not gone quietly away in the face of these cheaper generic substitutes, arguing with some success that the inert compounds in some generic drugs can severely compromise their clinical efficacy.[6]

· · · · · · ·

[6]Leslie Alderman, "Not All Drugs Are the Same After All." *New York Times*, December 18, 2009.

Technological innovations often create new substitutes in the longer run, thereby increasing a good's price elasticity of demand. Think about downloadable television programs versus satellite TV, cable TV systems, and over-the-air broadcast stations; cell phones and broadband versus wired landlines; and scanners and e-mail versus the U.S. postal system. In each case, the price elasticity of demand for the older product becomes greater after higher quality and often lower cost products are introduced. Sometimes the demand for the older product will disappear completely: VCRs have been competed out of existence by DVDs and Blu-ray disc players, and tube TVs have been replaced by LCD and plasma flat-screen TVs. And 80 percent of individual post offices were losing money in 2011, which will inevitably lead to widespread closures and a reduction in services.

Temporary versus Permanent Price Changes

Think about how you react when there is a sale on your favorite jeans. You are likely to be extremely responsive to this temporary price cut and may stock up for the next several months. Conversely, when you see that the price of the jeans has risen, you are apt to defer your jeans purchases as much as possible, hoping that the price goes back down. In other words, you respond in a highly sensitive fashion to these temporary price changes by shifting the *timing* of your purchases. This means that your price elasticity of demand may be greater in response to temporary price changes than to more permanent changes in price.

9.5 Relating Price Elasticity of Demand Back to the Demand Curve

Prior to introducing the concept of price elasticity of demand, we relied on the slope of the demand curve to indicate price sensitivity. We also said that using the slope in this way was problematic. Even so, is there a connection between these two measures of price sensitivity?

Let's investigate this question more closely by looking at a straight-line demand curve. It's only natural to presume that if a demand curve is a straight line—which means that its slope is constant—then the price elasticity of demand must also be constant. Is this presumption correct?

Remember that the slope of a demand curve tells us how the *number* of units purchased of a good changes when its price changes. For example, if college tuition goes up $50 per credit hour at your school, you might enroll in one less three-credit-hour class. If your babysitter reduces her hourly rate by 50 cents, you might hire her to babysit an additional four hours per week. In contrast, price elasticity of demand tells us how your total *expenditures* on credit hours or babysitting change when price changes. It turns out that the slope of the demand curve is only one component that factors into the price elasticity of demand computation.

Consider **Figure 9.6**, which shows three points on a parent's weekly child-care demand curve. These points represent quantity and price pairs. The points are A (48, $4); B (32, $5); C (16, $6).

Notice that whenever the hourly wage increases by $1, the total hours of babysitting demanded each week declines by the same amount—16 hours. This behavior is represented by a straight-line demand curve with a constant slope of $-1/16$. Now let's calculate the price elasticity of demand along this demand curve.

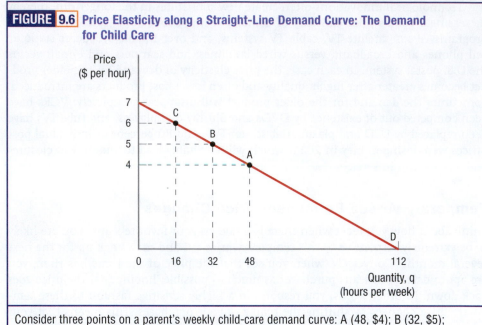

FIGURE 9.6 Price Elasticity along a Straight-Line Demand Curve: The Demand for Child Care

Consider three points on a parent's weekly child-care demand curve: A (48, $4); B (32, $5); C (16, $6). For every $1 increase in the hourly wage, the total hours of child care demanded each week declines by 16 hours. This means that the slope of this demand curve equals −1/16. However, the percentage change in quantity demanded as we move from A to B is different from the percentage change in the quantity demanded as we move from B to C. The same holds for the percentage change in price. This means that the price elasticity of demand when price increases from $4 to $5 is different from the price elasticity when price increases from $5 to $6.

Moving from point A (48 hours at $4 per hour) to point B (32 hours at $5 per hour), we calculate the price elasticity as

$$\text{price elasticity of demand} = \underbrace{[(32 - 48) / 48]}_{\%\ \text{change in } Q_D} / \underbrace{[(\$5 - 4) / 4]}_{\%\ \text{change in } P} = 1.33$$

We can also compute the price elasticity of demand corresponding to a move from point B (32 hours at $5 per hour) to point C (16 hours at $6 per hour). We get

$$\text{price elasticity of demand} = \underbrace{[(16 - 32) / 32]}_{\%\ \text{change in } Q_D} / \underbrace{[(\$6 - 5) / 5]}_{\%\ \text{change in } P} = 2.50$$

The price elasticity of demand for babysitting has changed: it has increased (ignoring the negative sign) as the parent *moves up* his demand curve. How is this possible given that the *number* of babysitting hours the parent demands falls by the same amount in response to each $1 increase in the price of babysitting? There is a 16-hour cut in hours demanded when the parent moves from A to B, and another 16-hour cut when he moves from B to C. So how can we make sense of our price-elasticity result?

Because the parent is purchasing fewer and fewer hours of child care as its price rises, cutbacks of an equal number of hours (16) translate into greater and greater *percentage* changes in the quantity of babysitting demanded, causing the *numerator* of the elasticity measure to progressively increase. At the same time, as the price keeps rising, each dollar increase translates into a smaller and smaller *percentage* increase in the babysitter's price. This means that the term in the *denominator* of the elasticity computation progressively decreases. When the numerator of a fraction increases, and the denominator decreases, they work in the same direction to increase the value of the fraction. So the elasticity number must increase as we move up the demand curve, even though the slope of the demand curve is unchanged. In other words, the price elasticity of demand moves from elastic to inelastic as we move down a straight-line demand curve.

At the midpoint of a straight-line demand curve—that is, at the point that corresponds to the midpoint values of price and quantity—the product's price elasticity of demand is *unitary elastic.* In Figure 9.6, this midpoint corresponds to the point (56, $3.50).

The Midpoint Method of Calculating Price Elasticity

Perhaps you have already detected an anomaly when we compute the price elasticity of demand along our straight-line demand curve: we get different answers when we move *down* the curve (e.g., from B to C) versus up the curve (from C to B). When we compute the price elasticity of demand moving from point C back to B, we get

$$\text{price elasticity of demand} = [(32 - 16) / 16] / [(\$5 - 6) / 6] = 6$$

$$\underbrace{}_{\text{\% change in } Q_D} \quad \underbrace{}_{\text{\% change in } P}$$

Clearly there is a problem because we already calculated that the elasticity value for the move from point B to C is 2.50. Shouldn't this simply be the "mirror image" of the price elasticity when we move from C to B? What if the price of child care increases from $8 per hour to $12 per hour—because it's a holiday, perhaps? Shouldn't the responsiveness in quantity of hours demanded by a parent be the same—only in the opposite direction—as when the price goes back down from $12 per hour to $8? If this were not the case, then every time the price went up and then fell back to its original level, a parent would not end up on the same demand curve as before!

This anomaly arises due to a simple, computational issue. Specifically, when we move from B to C, we are computing the percentage changes using the initial position B (32, $5) as our base; when we move from C back to B, we use C (16, $6) as our base. Whenever you calculate percentage changes and there is a substantial difference in the before and after values—whether it is calculating the percentage change in your GPA between semesters or the percentage change in the number of registered voters between presidential elections—your result will be sensitive to whether you use the starting point or ending point as the base for calculating the percentage.

When it comes to measuring price elasticity, this problem can be remedied by using an alternative computational approach called the **midpoint method**.

MIDPOINT METHOD A method that calculates percentage changes using the midpoint of the starting and ending values as the base.

This approach uses the midpoint between the initial and subsequent price values as the base on which the percentage change in price is calculated, and the midpoint between the initial and subsequent quantity values as the base on which the percentage change in quantity is calculated. Applying the midpoint method to our example, the price elasticity of demand moving from point B to C is

price elasticity of demand
= [(16 − 32) / (32 + 16) / 2] / [($6 − $5) / (5 + 6) / 2] = 3.67

We can show that this result is exactly what we would get if we used the midpoint method to compute the price elasticity of demand moving from point C to point B:

price elasticity of demand
= [(32 − 16) / (16 + 32) / 2] / [($5 − $6) / (6 + 5) / 2] = 3.67

The price elasticity of demand that is computed using the midpoint method is sometimes referred to as the **arc elasticity of demand**.

ARC ELASTICITY OF DEMAND The price elasticity of demand calculated using the midpoint method.

In every other way, arc elasticity is identical to the price-elasticity measure that we have been using until now. (This latter measure is sometimes referred to as the "point" elasticity of demand to distinguish it from the arc elasticity of demand.) Using the midpoint method isn't necessary when price and quantity changes are small; in such instances, you can simply use the point elasticity calculation that we first presented, the one developed by Alfred Marshall more than 100 years ago. When the change in a good's price or quantity demanded is large, however, it is especially important to use the midpoint method so that your results are not sensitive to whether price is increasing or decreasing. The midpoint method can also be used to compute other elasticity measures—presented in the following sections and in the next chapter—when there is a large difference in the starting and ending values of the numerator or denominator.

In reality, most estimates of price elasticity of demand are now derived using computer software. So the most important thing to know is the meaning of price elasticity of demand and what kinds of information it conveys to help you succeed as a marketer, policy maker, or price setter.

SOLVED PROBLEM

Q Suppose the U.S. dairy industry is successful in its campaign to shift the demand curve for milk products right by using celebrities to advertise the positive benefits of drinking milk. Show how this campaign affects the price elasticity of demand at each and every price.

A Let's assume for the moment that the campaign causes the market demand curve to shift right so that it's parallel with the original market demand curve. This means that the slope of the demand curve hasn't changed. What about ε_d? Suppose that price drops from P_1 to P_2. The percentage change in price is the same for both the old and new demand curves. And, the change in the *number* of units purchased is exactly the same for both the old and new demand curves (because they share the same slope). This means that $Q_{12} − Q_{11} = Q_{22} − Q_{21}$. However, the *percentage* change in the quantity demanded will be *higher* before the shift in the demand curve, because the base on which the percentage is calculated (Q_{11}) is smaller than after the shift (Q_{21}). Therefore, when there is a rightward, parallel shift in the demand curve, the price elasticity of demand goes down (in absolute value) at each and every price.

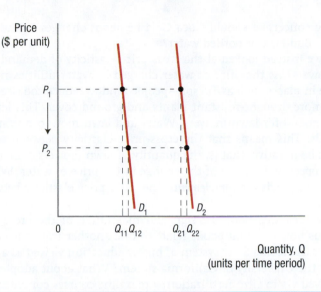

9.6 Cross-Price Elasticity of Demand

You learned in Chapter 8 that when a price changes in one market, it is likely to have an impact on other, related markets. Markets tend to be related when their goods are substitutes for, or complements to, each other. We can extend our analysis of price elasticity to capture the magnitude of these cross-market effects by measuring the extent to which the quantity demanded of one good—say, oranges (X)—changes in response to a price change in another good—apples (Y). This measure is called the **cross-price elasticity of demand**.

> **CROSS-PRICE ELASTICITY OF DEMAND (ε_{xy})** The percentage change in the quantity of a good demanded in response to a percentage change in the price of another good.

The cross-price elasticity of demand is measured in a similar way to price elasticity. That is,

$$\varepsilon_{xy} = \frac{\text{percentage change in the quantity demanded of good } X}{\text{percentage change in the price of good } Y}$$

Suppose the price of a credit hour at all of the University of California campuses increased from \$200 to \$320 per hour for in-state residents. This corresponds to a 60 percent increase in price. If, in response, the market demand for credit hours at schools in the California State University system increases by 30 percent, then the cross-price elasticity between the two school systems equals 30% / 60% = 0.50.

In this example, the cross-price elasticity is positive. In other words, a tuition increase in the University of California system leads to an increase in the demand for credit hours in the California State University system. Whenever the cross-price elasticity of demand is *positive* between two goods, we know that at least some demanders perceive them to be *substitutes*. And, the greater the cross-price elasticity, the stronger this substitutability is from the perspective of consumers. From a supplier's perspective, the cross-price elasticity of demand reveals who his competitors really are. For example, how concerned should Coca-Cola be about changes in the price of Pepsi, Safeway Cola, Bud Lite, or bottled water?

What if we instead looked at the cross-price elasticity of demand between water and lawn mowers? As the price of water charged by water utilities rises—which has been the case in places such as Tucson—people tend to reduce the size of their lawns, substituting more drought-resistant plants and ground cover. This leads to a reduction in the demand for lawn mowers. Water and lawn mowers are, in fact, complementary goods. This means that the cross-price elasticity between water and lawn mowers must be negative; that is, the quantity of lawn mowers demanded in Tucson moves in the *opposite* direction of the change in the price of water. Whenever people perceive that two goods are *complements*, the cross-price elasticity between the goods will be *negative*.

Generally speaking, both the sign and magnitude of the cross-price elasticity measure tell us how different goods relate to one another from the consumers' perspective. Is the California State system of higher education viewed as a strong or weak substitute for the University of California system? What about adopted babies versus babies conceived via in vitro fertilization? Are online courses complements or substitutes for campus-based learning? What about gasoline and hotel stays? Cross-price elasticity permits us to measure the strength of relationships such as these.

Producers are very interested in estimating cross-price elasticities of demand. Having this information helps them forecast how demand for their product might change—and their need for additional capacity or employees—when the price of another good increases or decreases. Examples of this are car-rental companies and hotel chains, both of which keep a keen eye on airfare changes because air travel is a strong complement to the services they offer. Likewise, the administrators of public-transportation systems (buses, light rail, etc.) closely monitor the price of gasoline, because it affects their riders' decision to drive a car, which is a strong substitute for public transportation.

A few years ago, college textbook publishers anxiously began to track the success of Amazon.com's new online site where students could buy or sell used textbooks. They were concerned that Amazon would make it much easier (lower cost) for people to buy used copies of a textbook at a significant discount from the price publishers charged for a new copy. Publishers assumed that the cross-price elasticity between used and new copies was quite high. If true, a reduction in the price of used copies or an increase in the price of new books would severely impact new copy demand. What's the evidence?

It turns out that despite the emergence of Amazon as the largest reseller of textbooks, the cross-price elasticity between new and used copies has remained quite low. The evidence? A 10 percent increase in the price of a new textbook translates into less than a 1 percent increase in used book sales. This means that the cross-price elasticity is 0.10, which is quite small (1% / 10%).[7] Why is this so? Aren't used and new books close substitutes for one another?

Apparently, new books—without any markings or ripped pages—are preferred by at least some students. Probably more important is the fact that students often receive financial aid to purchase new textbooks in their school's bookstore but are unlikely to receive the same type of aid when they purchase their books on the Web. At the same time, most students prefer to resell their used books on Amazon at the end of

· · · · · · ·

[7]Hal Varian, "Reading between the Lines of Used Book Sales." *New York Times*, July 28, 2005.

the semester because they receive a higher price than their bookstores will pay. This higher resale price reduces the *net* cost (the difference between the price of a new copy and a used copy) of buying a new textbook in the first place, making new book buyers *less* sensitive to new textbook prices.

Cross-price elasticity of demand figures into many public-policy debates. For example, in 2004, the FAA (Federal Aviation Administration) proposed a rule that would require parents to buy a heavily discounted seat for children under the age of two, rather than holding them for free on their laps, as was then permitted. This proposal came in response to a few well-publicized incidents where "lap babies" were seriously injured due to in-air turbulence. However, after analyzing estimates of the cross-price elasticity of demand between air and auto travel, the FAA withdrew the proposal. Why?

The cross-price elasticity between air and auto travel is estimated to be approximately 0.356, which means that a 1 percent increase in the price of airfares leads to a 0.356 percent increase in auto miles driven. That is, people tend to substitute driving for flying when the price of flying increases. Although a cross-price elasticity of 0.356 may seem small, it turns out that the 21 percent increase in airfare resulting from the purchase of a seat for a lap baby would have led to approximately 7.5 percent additional miles in auto travel. And, because the risk of death per mile traveled by auto is almost 30 times greater than for air travel, the FAA concluded that a rule that required all children to have an airline seat would lead to *more* infant deaths than if no such rule were in place.[8]

The following list summarizes our findings about cross-price elasticity of demand:

- When the cross-price elasticity between two goods is positive, these goods are perceived to be substitutes by at least some consumers. The greater the cross-price elasticity, the stronger the substitutability between the two goods.

- When the cross-price elasticity between two goods is negative, these goods are perceived to be complements by at least some consumers. The more negative this cross-price elasticity is, the stronger the complementarity between the two goods.

9.7 Price Elasticity of Supply

Just as we can capture consumer price sensitivity through price elasticity of demand, we can expand on this approach to measure the price responsiveness of suppliers. **Price elasticity of supply** is calculated as the percentage change in the quantity of a good supplied in response to a percentage change in its price.

> **PRICE ELASTICITY OF SUPPLY (ε_s)** The percentage change in the quantity of a good supplied in response to a percentage change in its price. The computational formula looks a lot like price elasticity of demand:
>
> $$\text{price elasticity of supply} = \frac{\text{percentage change in quantity supplied}}{\text{percentage change in price}}$$

· · · · · · ·

[8]Shane Sanders, Dennis L. Weisman, and Dong Li, "Child Safety Seats on Commercial Airliners: A Demonstration of Cross-Price Elasticities." *Journal of Economic Education* (Spring 2008).

EXAMPLE Suppose you are offered an increase in your hourly wage rate from $10 to $15 (a 50 percent increase) if you will work both weekend days rather than only one weekend day. You respond by increasing your total weekend hours worked from 8 hours to 16 hours (a 100 percent increase). This means that your elasticity of labor supply equals 2 (100% / 50%).

EXAMPLE What if the price of new housing falls by 15 percent, and, in response, the number of new housing building permits declines by 25 percent? This corresponds to a price elasticity of supply of 1.66 (−25% / −15%).

As is the case for price elasticity of demand, price elasticity of supply can be calculated for an individual supplier or for an entire market of suppliers.

We know that supply curves have a positive slope. When the price of a good goes up, the quantity supplied also increases (or, in the rare case, remains unchanged). Conversely, when price declines, the quantity supplied also falls. From these results, it follows that *price elasticity of supply must always be either positive or zero.*

Suppose we are in the very short run, a period so short that the supply of a product cannot change regardless of any change in its price. We have previously referred to this as the "market period," which is represented by a vertical supply curve. Think about the fresh fish that is brought to market on any given day. **Figure 9.7** depicts this situation; we see that when the price of fish rises from $9 to $14 per pound, the quantity supplied is unchanged. The increase in price serves solely to ration the fixed supply to consumers with the highest willingness to pay. It does not stimulate additional supply.

Because there is no change in the quantity supplied, the numerator of the price elasticity of supply equals zero, which means that the price elasticity is also equal to

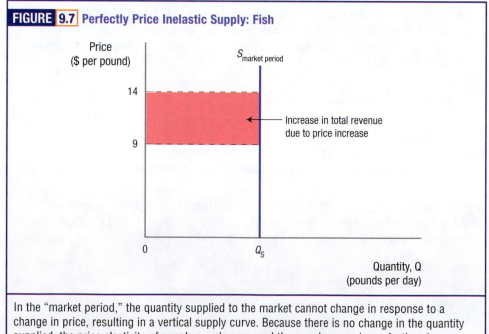

FIGURE 9.7 **Perfectly Price Inelastic Supply: Fish**

In the "market period," the quantity supplied to the market cannot change in response to a change in price, resulting in a vertical supply curve. Because there is no change in the quantity supplied, the price elasticity of supply equals zero, and the supply curve is *perfectly price inelastic.* The total revenue that suppliers receive goes up or down by the *same* percentage as the change in price because there is no change in the quantity supplied.

zero. Economists call this a *perfectly price inelastic* supply curve. As you can see, in this situation, the total revenue that suppliers receive goes up or down by the *same* percentage as the change in price because there is no change in the quantity supplied.

While perfectly price inelastic supply is rare, it is most prevalent in the market period when output cannot be easily adjusted or stored at low cost to be sold when there is an increase in price. Even then, suppliers have been known to destroy perishable goods, such as milk, rather than sell them when the market price falls below their production costs.[9]

The magnitude of the price elasticity of supply is extremely important to market and government decision makers. Take the rapid increase in fossil-fuel prices over the past few years. This run-up has led to a resurgence in interest in building more nuclear power plants in the United States (despite recent events in Japan). The problem is that nuclear power plants require uranium to operate, and it's not clear whether the worldwide supply of uranium can expand sufficiently to meet the increase in the demand for it.

Some researchers have estimated uranium's price elasticity of supply to be as high as 2.3 to 3.3. That is, a 1 percent increase in its price would stimulate up to a 3.3 percent increase in the quantity of uranium supplied to the market.

Others have argued that the supply of uranium is, in fact, price inelastic—that suppliers aren't very responsive to increases in the price of uranium because it is extremely costly to mine currently untapped deposits.[10] If this is true, then the global price of uranium would have to rise substantially to attract additional supply into the market. This rise in uranium costs could more than offset any potential cost savings to be had by adding nuclear-power capacity to meet our energy needs.

Over longer periods of time, we expect that suppliers can adjust more fully to price changes, resulting in a greater price elasticity of supply. In response to a price increase, new suppliers will have time to gear up and enter the market. At the same time, existing suppliers can expand their facilities, develop new production technologies, and train more employees. When prices decline, firms can, over time, lay off employees and shut down plants. The amount of time it takes to fully adjust to price changes depends on a producer's contractual commitments as well as the regulatory environment. For example, the federal government's WARN Act (Worker Adjustment and Retraining Notification Act) requires U.S. employers to give employees a minimum 60-day layoff notice prior to any plant closing. Delaying plant closures simply postpones the inevitable reduction in quantity supplied that must occur when there is a decline in the price of a product.

Regulation's Impact on Price Elasticity of Supply

Even in the long run, there are instances in which a product's supply is insensitive to price changes. We see this most often when government regulations limit the growth in supply of a particular good. For example, virtually every state limits the number of nursing-home beds that each provider can offer, irrespective of people's willingness to pay for them. Similarly, New York City limits the number of taxicab "medallions" (licenses) it issues, thereby restricting the number of cabs that can legally pick up passengers. At one time, the now defunct CAB (Federal Civil Aeronautics Board) regulated whether an airline could enter *or exit* a particular air route, say from Poughkeepsie to Chicago. Government policies such as these—that restrict

• • • • • • •

[9]Stephen Castle, "European Farmers' Anger Spills into the Streets of Brussels," *New York Times*, October 5, 2009.

[10]Ux Consulting Company, "Supply Elasticity of Uranium." *Ux Weekly*, September 27, 2004. www.uxc.com.

Table 9.3	Price Elasticity of Supply Estimates for Housing, by Major Metropolitan Area, 1979–1996*
Dallas	29.9
Tampa	27.4
Atlanta	21.6
Charlotte	17.0
Houston	12.8
Indianapolis	11.0
Tulsa	8.25
St. Louis	6.89
Memphis	5.63
Baltimore	5.52
Detroit	4.74
Salt Lake City	4.69
Minneapolis	4.21
Los Angeles	3.73
Philadelphia	3.09
Chicago	2.48
Boston	1.77
Pittsburgh	1.43
San Jose	0.33
San Francisco	0.14

*Elasticities computed based on lagged housing prices, not current.

Source: Richard K. Green, Stephen Malpezzi, and Stephen K. Mayo. "Metropolitan-Specific Estimates of the Price Elasticity of Supply of Housing and Their Sources." *American Economic Review* (May, 2005).

the entry, expansion, or exiting of suppliers—reduce the long-run price elasticity of supply in a market.

A recent study of the elasticity of supply in housing in 45 major metropolitan areas found that burdensome land-use regulations tended to reduce the responsiveness of new housing starts to price changes.[11] **Table 9.3** reports how the price elasticity of supply varies across a subset of these cities. San Francisco—one of the most regulated areas in terms of land use—exhibited an elasticity of supply equal to 0.14, which means that a 1 percent increase in the price of housing stimulates only a 0.14 percent increase in housing starts. In contrast, the Dallas metropolitan area, which has far fewer land-use restrictions, enjoys a price elasticity of supply equal to 29.9. This means that a 1 percent increase in housing prices stimulates an increase of almost 30 percent in housing starts. As you might expect, the study found that the geographic density of a city, along with its population size and growth, also contributed to each area's price elasticity of housing supply.

· · · · · · ·

[11]Richard K. Green, Stephen Malpezzi, and Stephen K. Mayo. "Metropolitan-Specific Estimates of the Price Elasticity of Supply of Housing, and Their Sources." *American Economic Review* (May, 2005).

WHAT YOU SHOULD HAVE LEARNED FROM CHAPTER 9

■ That economists prefer to use elasticity as a price-sensitivity measure because it is unit-free and comparable across products and time periods.

■ That a product's demand is elastic when the percentage change in the quantity demanded divided by the percentage change in price is greater than one; that it is inelastic when the percentage change in the quantity demanded divided by the percentage change in its price is less than one; and that it is perfectly inelastic when the percentage change in the quantity demanded equals zero when its price changes.

■ That the magnitude of a good's price elasticity of demand can tell us what happens to the total revenues generated by a product when its price rises or falls.

■ That the value of a good's price elasticity of demand depends on a number of factors, including the existence of close substitutes, whether the good is viewed to be "essential" or a luxury, the proportion of a person's income spent on the good, whether we are talking about the short run or long run, and whether the price change is perceived to be temporary or permanent.

■ That when price changes are large, the arc elasticity of demand computational method should be used to calculate elasticity.

■ That the cross-price elasticity of demand is the percentage change in the quantity of one good demanded in response to a percentage change in the price of another good.

■ That if the cross-price elasticity of demand is negative, good X is a complement to good Y. By contrast, if the cross-price elasticity is positive, good X is a substitute to good Y.

■ That the elasticity of supply is a measure of suppliers' responsiveness to changes in the price of products. It will always be positive or zero.

■ That when a product's price elasticity of supply equals zero, there will be no change in the quantity supplied as its price changes; this situation is most typical during the short run or when the market is regulated by government agencies.

KEY TERMS

Price elasticity of demand, p. 240

Perfectly price inelastic demand, p. 246

Price inelastic demand, p. 248

Unitary price elastic demand, p. 248

Price elastic demand, p. 250

Perfectly price elastic demand, p. 252

Midpoint method, p. 261

Arc elasticity of demand, p. 262

Cross-price elasticity of demand, p. 263

Price elasticity of supply, p. 265

QUESTIONS AND PROBLEMS

1. Indicate whether the price elasticity of demand is perfectly inelastic, inelastic, unitary elastic, or elastic in the following situations:

   a) The price of babysitters goes up. Mary responds by hiring babysitters less frequently, but she still has less money to spend on other things.

   b) A new law requires utility companies to have two supervisors on duty every day.

   c) The price of movies goes down. Rik responds by going to the movies more often and still has more money left to spend on other things.

   d) Every year at the annual Dillard's department store half-off sale, Ms. Garcia buys four times as much as she would at regular prices.

   e) The minimum wage rises from $5.50 to $6.05 per hour, and the hiring of minimum-wage employees falls by 20 percent.

2. Suppose that Norm, a college student, spends all of his income on two goods: gasoline and credit hours.

   a) If a $2 increase in the price of gasoline does not change the amount of credit hours the student purchases, what is the price elasticity of demand for gasoline?

   b) If the price increase in gasoline results in an increase in the number of credit hours taken, what do we know about the price elasticity of demand for gasoline?

3. The dean of admissions at UZ State argues that increasing students' tuition will reduce the university's total revenue.

   a) What is she implying about the price elasticity of demand for course credit hours at UZ state?

   b) If, in fact, admissions fall but revenues rise after tuition increases, what does this say about the price elasticity of demand for credit hours at UZ state?

4. Assume that the demand for cocaine is perfectly price inelastic and that users get the funds to pay for cocaine primarily by stealing. Suppose, too, that the U.S. Drug Enforcement Agency successfully intercepts shipments of the drug from foreign sources and, therefore, reduces the availability of cocaine.

   a) Show, using supply and demand curves, the resulting impact on the price of cocaine.

   b) What will happen to the amount of crime committed by cocaine users?

5. Over the past few years, the U.S. government has pushed for the production of more ethanol-based fuels in lieu of fossil fuels. A major component of ethanol is corn. The result has been that the price of corn has increased astronomically. What does this tell you about corn's price elasticity of supply?

6. In the United States, the cross-price elasticity of demand for U.S.-trained engineers versus German-trained engineers is very high, whereas the cross-price elasticity of demand for U.S.-trained doctors versus German-trained doctors is very low. Why do you think this is so?

7. If the demand curve facing a price-taking supplier is horizontal (perfectly price elastic), what is the price elasticity of demand facing a supplier who has no current or potential competitors?

8. True, False, or Uncertain: If the cross-price elasticity of demand between goods X and Y is positive, and the cross-price elasticity of demand between goods Y and Z is negative, then the cross-price elasticity of demand between goods X and Z must also be negative. Explain your answer.

9. Mortgage lenders often advise home buyers that their mortgage, real-estate taxes, and home insurance should be no more than 28 percent of their family income.

   a) If home buyers follow this advice, what can you say about their price elasticity of demand for housing, assuming their income doesn't change?

   b) What if interest rates increase from 5.5 percent to 8.5 percent, and families stick to the 28 percent "rule." Are they violating the Law of Demand by doing so?

10. We have proven that the price elasticity of demand varies along a straight-line demand curve. Can you construct a demand curve along which the price elasticity of demand is constant?

11. Suppose the government increases the "sin" tax on such goods as cigarettes and liquor. Do you think increasing this tax will increase or decrease tax revenues? [Hint: First answer for current smokers and drinkers and then for future smokers and drinkers.]

12. In years where there is a drought or late freeze, the total output of American farmers declines. When weather conditions are optimal, farmers reap substantially larger, bumper crops. If the price elasticity of demand for agricultural products is less than one, predict what happens to the income of American farmers when the weather is good versus bad.

13. As the director of finance for the city's MetroLink subway system, you are asked for your opinion as to whether fares should be raised to cover a large increase in fuel prices that the system faces. You have read that the price elasticity of demand for such commuter services is approximately 0.80. Based on this information, what would your recommendation be? Would your answer change if the price elasticity of demand is 1.4?

14. A new innovation has recently occurred in the college textbook distribution industry: "rent-a-textbook." Do you think that the cross-price elasticity between rented books and new books is high? What about between rented books and books resold on Amazon? Explain. Do you think there will be a lot of demand for rented textbooks? Why or why not.

15. In 2010, American Airlines decided it no longer wanted to sell its tickets through online ticket brokers such as Orbitz and Expedia. It said that it wanted to cultivate its own brand and customer loyalty. How do you think online brokers of airline tickets affect the price elasticity of demand for each airline's tickets? If American Airlines is successful, what will happen to the price elasticity of demand for American Airlines tickets? Explain your answer.

PART 3

Comparative Advantage, Specialization, and Trade

In Parts 1 and 2, you learned that market exchanges generate gains from trade that are usually shared by both buyers and sellers. In Part 3, we look at why gains from trade arise and how scarce resources can be allocated to maximize the total gains and the resulting economic "pie." This does not happen because of government planning but, rather, because individuals strive to maximize the well-being they get from the resources under their control.

We begin by looking at the allocation and coordination of resources within a producing organization. We first examine the most common type of organization in the world, the household, but we could have just as easily chosen General Motors or your local soup kitchen. You will learn how the household maximizes its total well-being given its scarce resources and how exploiting the comparative advantage of each household member can increase its well-being. This will lead to a better understanding of why voluntary exchange takes place not only within the marketplace but also *within* producing organizations. In this regard, we examine how the bargaining process—rather than prices—determines the division of gains from trade within organizations. Finally, we look at the impact that government policies, specifically taxes and subsidies, have on the use of market-based services in lieu of household-based production.

We conclude Part 3 with a discussion about how households—and other producing organizations, for that matter—make decisions about investing some of their current resources to potentially improve their well-being in the future. How much, if anything, should they invest? What should they invest in? What special considerations might be given to investing in one's own human capital and the human capital of others in a household? Lastly, we discuss the returns household members can expect to receive in the labor market by investing in education and whether these returns may help explain the growing income inequality in the United States.

10

Gains From Trade in the Household and in the Market

"Personal relationships are the fertile soil from which all advancement, all success, all achievement in real life grows."

Economist and actor Ben Stein

We have seen how buyers and sellers trade in the market to increase their own well-being. The existence of producer and consumer surplus tells us that gains from trade are realized through these voluntary exchanges. A key feature of market trade is that both consumers and suppliers respond to market price when deciding how much of a good to buy or sell. Prices "coordinate" market transactions by signaling to both buyers and sellers the opportunity cost of different goods. As long as a buyer's willingness to pay is equal to or greater than a supplier's marginal cost of production, trade will take place. The price mechanism inherent in free markets—along with private property rights—assures that the "right" amount of resources is committed to the production of various goods and services in our economy; that is, scarce resources are directed to their highest valued uses.

You might be wondering whether trade can take place in the absence of prices. That is, are there gains from trade that can be exploited without a price signal to govern the exchange? It turns out that gains from trade can also arise in *nonmarket* settings. In fact, the most trades—even in the most advanced economies—take place *inside* organizations, without any price signals at all. One such organization is the household. In every household, members—parents, partners, children, and siblings— trade their own scarce resources to enhance the well-being of themselves and others in the household. Time is often the scarcest resource that a family member has: a child may have to give up play time to set the table for dinner, while a parent may leave work early to coach a daughter's soccer team.

It is within the context of the household that we explore two important issues. First, how and why does trade take place? Second, what does this tell us about the underlying rationale for trade in the marketplace?

10.1 Economic Coordination within Firms

The market is an exceptionally efficient institution for directing scarce resources: buyers and sellers freely respond to the prices they face in terms of the quantities of goods and services they purchase and sell. In turn, these prices direct scarce resources into the production of each good. Given the advantages that market exchange offers, why would we ever observe resources being directed *within* an organization through nonprice signals and mechanisms? This is exactly the question that Nobel Laureate Ronald Coase asked when he explored the nature of the firm.[1] Coase concluded that in certain situations, transaction costs—the costs of executing a trade that we first discussed in Chapter 3—can make the market a very costly venue for voluntary exchange. When this is the case, the possibility arises that resources can be allocated at lower cost *within* an organization without explicit price signals.

To illustrate Coase's point, think about the steps that a buyer must go through to complete a market transaction. He must first locate a supplier of the good he wants to purchase. Next, he must confirm the terms of the trade. This includes the price, terms of payment and delivery, product description and quality specifications, warranties, and so forth. Whether this deal is written or verbal depends on the complexity of the good and the number of contingencies (the "what ifs") that are part of the arrangement. After agreeing to the seller's terms, or negotiating better ones, the buyer must arrange receipt of the good and inspect it to verify that the terms of the trade have been met. Likewise, the seller must take similar steps to protect her own interests. In effect, each and every market-based exchange entails its own separate contract—implicit or explicit—between a buyer and seller.

Sometimes the process just described takes place seemingly instantaneously. When you shop at the grocery store or buy a movie ticket, the cost of this market transaction is extremely low because the terms of trade are relatively simple: if you give the cashier $1.89 (plus tax), you will take ownership of a jar of Jif peanut butter. The market handles these types of trades very efficiently—that is, at a very low transaction cost.

There are, however, other types of trades that the market is not as efficient at handling. When might this be the case?

Coase focused his attention on two situations, the first being when the same buyer and seller make the same trade over and over. Instead of incurring the cost of negotiating each and every time, the parties can come to a long-term understanding about how to coordinate their resources. This is exactly what happens when you take a job in which you supply hours of work in return for a paycheck. You don't renegotiate the terms of your employment every day but, rather, agree to a wage rate and work schedule. Beyond that, your work time is managed by your supervisor, within certain mutually agreeable bounds (e.g., you won't clean toilets).

A second, related situation that Coase considered is when a buyer and a seller find it desirable to enter into a long-term agreement to avoid the transaction costs arising from ongoing, but potentially different, trades. We know that the market performs efficiently when there is a *single* trade that extends over a long period of time. For example, when you get a five-year loan to purchase a car, you receive a payment schedule, and both you and your lender know what to expect from each other (assuming that you both understand the contract you have signed). This situation is very different from long-term contracts that entail ongoing exchanges of goods throughout the contract period.

· · · · · · ·

[1]Ronald Coase, "The Nature of the Firm." *Econometrica* (November, 1937).

Think, for example, about a container manufacturer that sells a variety of cans and bottles to Coca-Cola. Quite likely, it would want to enter into a long-term agreement with Coca-Cola rather than separately negotiate each and every container sale to the soft drink company. In this way, it could reduce its own transaction costs and those borne by Coca-Cola.

However, this long-term agreement is likely to be fraught with uncertainty. Over time, the expectations that each party has of the other can change. Quite likely, Coca-Cola will not be able to stipulate up-front and in great detail the type of container it will want in two years; this will depend on its product line and marketing at the time. Therefore, its long-term contract with the container supplier can specify in only the broadest of terms what is expected in the future. Because of this uncertainty, long-term agreements between buyers and sellers may not be viable, despite the potential savings in transaction costs. This may explain why Coca-Cola's bottlers in North America purchase their plastic bottles from manufacturers that they jointly own and, in Europe, manufacture their bottles and other packaging internally. Similarly, prior to its acquisition by InBev, Anheuser-Busch owned its own container-manufacturing plants, which produced cans, bottles, labels, and packaging for Anheuser-Busch beverage products. By coordinating container manufacturing internally, Coca-Cola and Anheuser-Busch reduce their transaction costs and assure an adequate supply of containers that meet their current specifications.

Consider this scenario: Suppose you want to open a landscaping business and are trying to decide whether to use day laborers or hire regular employees. Most likely, day laborers can be used for specific tasks such as planting trees, laying down sod, raking leaves, and so forth. For these assignments, you can easily convey the requirements of the job to random workers and what you expect of each of them. The short-term contract that is struck between you and the day worker will function quite well; they can be hired by the task at a negotiated rate of pay.

What if you also need workers to handle recurring tasks that are less easily described, or vary from day to day and in the future? You might, for instance, need someone to handle your bookkeeping and customer billing. You certainly wouldn't want to negotiate a new labor contract every time a bill needs to be sent out or a deposit has to be made. Moreover, unforeseen tasks can pop up—dealing with bounced checks, delinquent accounts, income tax inquiries, and so on. This makes it difficult (and therefore costly) to meet your bookkeeping and billing needs by hiring day labor in the market. Hiring from a temporary accounting placement agency is rarely cost-effective when your needs are recurrent, variable, and entail some independent judgment on the part of the worker. This is exactly the type of situation in which Coase predicted that long-term "relationships" will arise: rather than relying on market exchange, people form organizations within which they internally manage and coordinate their resources. Coase called these organizations **firms**.

FIRM An organization that internally manages and coordinates inputs in the production process, rather than relying on prices and market exchange to perform these functions.

EXAMPLE The Ford Motor Company internally manages workers, steel, and other inputs to produce cars and trucks. However, the firm still purchases tires and GPS devices from suppliers in the market rather than producing them in-house.

EXAMPLE Most restaurants cook and bake the menu items that they serve, combining a whole host of inputs and labor services to produce a variety of offerings. However, they still purchase their raw ingredients—eggs, flour, and salt—from the market rather than producing them in-house.

Coordinating some factors of production within a firm can lessen costly interruptions in the production process. After all, if you don't have to stop every morning to negotiate with day laborers or instruct them on the nuances of each job, your firm can complete more landscaping jobs.

Another reason for coordinating resources in-house has to do with quality control. When the quality of an input into production is especially important and is difficult to assess, it might be less costly to assure that quality standards are met by producing it within the firm. For example, the Ford Motor Company ensures that its car doors fit its automobile frames by producing both the doors and frames internally. In a similar vein, Coca-Cola can assure itself an uninterrupted supply of containers whose shapes and labels "fit" its ever-changing marketing campaigns.

10.2 The Household as a Firm

When you think about firms in our economy, you probably think of well-known corporations such as Google and McDonald's. Yet the most common firm in every economy is the household. In the United States, there are more than 112 million households—more than all other types of producers added together.

Households are in the business of producing, sustaining, and growing people's human capital: they provide food and housing, children and child care, companionship, financial management, health, and even love. Within the household, many of the same productive activities occur repeatedly, sometimes even several times a day. Household members empty the dishwasher, walk the dog, take out the trash, pay bills, and drive each other to work and leisure activities. Can you imagine household members negotiating "the terms of a trade" every time one of these jobs needed to be done? If this were the case, then there would be a lot of valuable economic resources—such as time—eaten up by transaction costs.

Just like a "regular" firm, household production takes place over long periods of time and is subject to a great deal of uncertainty. Parents don't know for sure the demands that child care will place on them before their children are born. Every child is different. Some children require special care due to their physical or emotional makeup. Even after a child is born, it is often difficult to identify each and every aspect of child care that must be provided. Complicating this is that these services undoubtedly change over time as the child grows older. This makes it difficult for parents to negotiate contracts for all of their child-care needs. Obviously, child-care options are available in the market that can meet *some* needs of *some* children for *some* part of the day. However, no one would equate these services with the parental responsibilities assumed by a household. Just ask a parent whose child is sent home from day care because she is running a fever or has broken out with measles.

In contrast, households may find it somewhat easier to have their laundry, cleaning, meal preparation, and landscaping needs met by purchasing these services in the market. Still, someone must coordinate these services, monitor their quality, and manage the variable nature of these tasks over time. Who will decide the daily menu for the household? Who will follow through to make sure that the ingredients are at hand and that the meals are actually prepared? Who will sort laundry into piles for the dry cleaner and for the white and colored washes? And who will supervise the landscaper to make sure that the wrong tree isn't cut down?

Sometimes, there is no supplier in the market that can offer an acceptable, affordable alternative to meet a household's specific needs. Or, there may be so much uncertainty about what is actually required that it's simply more efficient for household members to perform the task themselves. A good example of this is when people have to take their pets to the vet or their children to the doctor. Parents and pet owners often have to make important treatment decisions on the spot, based on information that the medical specialist has just provided them at the visit. How easy would it be to hire someone to take on this responsibility, knowing that treatment options may have to be decided on immediately? Not very.

We mentioned that the output of a household usually includes companionship and love, both of which arise from the reliability and trust that people cultivate between themselves over time. Over long periods of time, there is tremendous uncertainty about what each member of a household expects from the others. What happens if your partner gets sick, hurt, or is laid off from work? What tasks will be shifted between members of the household? This uncertainty makes it difficult to find the same quality and continuity of companionship through a series of short-term, market-based trades or "encounters."

Certainly, there are markets that provide escort services, health-care aides, and even visiting companion dogs.[2] Each of these suppliers is paid for a clearly defined service that is rendered over a specific time period. However, most people would agree that these market-based services are poor substitutes for the companionship, affection, and even love produced within a household, by and to its members (including pets).

In summary then, the household is exactly the type of firm that Coase envisioned would benefit from managing and coordinating scarce resources internally, rather than through the market. In other words, personal resources are "traded" between household members without explicit price signals to guide this process. Obviously, gains from trade exist even when there are no prices and the trade does not take place in a market.

The Value of Household Production

Quite likely, we overlook the household as a firm precisely because the scarce inputs it uses in production—such as time—do not come with a price tag. Members of the household who cook do not receive a paycheck, nor do those who balance the checkbook or drive others to school or jobs. And because no one pays wages for these services, they are not subject to sales or payroll taxes. This means that people who work exclusively in unpaid household production are not eligible for Social Security retirement income or Medicare retirement health-insurance coverage, both of which are funded largely through payroll taxes. However, the U.S. Congress has instituted a Social Security retirement benefit for unpaid, *married* partners of wage earners.

Why does it matter whether household production is explicitly valued by the market? Consider a situation in which a household decides to purchase all of its meals, transportation, and accounting services in the market. The prices paid for these services represent their opportunity cost of production. Because these purchases

[2]Vincent Mallozzi, "For a Temporary Best Friend Fix, Rent a Dog (Kibble Included) for a Day." *New York Times*, March 30, 2008.

carry a price tag, they can be valued and included in the calculation of a country's gross domestic product (GDP)—a measure of its total economic output. In contrast, the value of unpriced but comparable in-home production is excluded.

To get a sense of the amount of household production that *isn't* included in the calculation of GDP, consider the following statistic: in 2010, the estimated market value of an "average" stay-at-home mother in the United States was over $118,000.[3] Multiply this amount by the 5 million or so stay-at-home mothers in the United States (U.S. Census, 2010), and we get over $590 billion per year, or almost 4 percent of the country's GDP in 2010. Obviously, this is an understatement of the true value of unpaid household production because it excludes the unpaid work of men and women who are also wage earners. In fact, the Organization for Economic Co-Operation and Development (OECD) recently estimated how much unpaid work is worth as a percentage of GDP for the 25 OECD countries (which excludes the United States). It found that the total amount of unpaid work—primarily in the household—equals about one-third of GDP in OECD countries, ranging from 19 percent in Korea to 53 percent in Portugal.[4] Yet none of this unpaid work or the output that it generates is counted in GDP. Because of this omission, relying on comparisons of GDP over time or across countries to assess relative well-being is often problematic.

10.3 A Household's Production Possibilities Frontier

Within each household, goods and services are produced that improve the well-being of its members. One or more members provide food services by shopping for groceries and doing the cooking; they nurture a family of children and pets by ensuring their safety, taking them to the doctor, and teaching, training, and socializing them. Other types of household production that use up individuals' scarce resources include financial-management activities—such as maintaining the household's budget—party and vacation planning, home maintenance, and so on. Importantly, the household requires that at least one member earn an income so that it can purchase some goods and services in the market. (This assumes away the possibility of government support programs or other unearned sources of income.)

Suppose that there are two adult partners in a household—a husband and wife; mother and adult child; two sisters, and so on. Can we predict how these tasks will be divided up?

To answer this question, we must first identify the economic choices facing these partners. We need not make any assumptions about the personal nature of the partners' relationship except to assume that it is long term in nature. Why make this assumption? Because such a commitment is central to the creation of trust, which reinforces the partners' mutual agreement to use their scarce resources on behalf of others in the household. We initially assume that the partners cooperate to maximize the well-being of the household, rather than pursuing their own individual preferences.[5] Later, we will relax this assumption and see what this implies about resource allocation within the household.

• • • • • • •

[3] http://www.marketwire.com/press-release/Salarycoms-10th-Annual-Mom-Salary-Survey-Reveals-Stay-Home-Moms-Would-Earn-US117856-1160364.htm

[4] http://www.nestfinance.co.uk/family-finances/2011/04/12/true-value-of-unpaid-work-a-signifcant-part-of-gdp

[5] Gary S. Becker, *Treatise on the Family.* (Cambridge: Harvard University Press, 1981; rev., 1991).

For the purpose of the current illustration, suppose that household members produce two types of outputs: household-based outputs (H) and market-based consumption (C). The quantity of H produced is represented as Q_H, and the quantity of C produced as Q_C. To produce a unit of C, a person must first earn income that can then be used to purchase goods and services. Because we are talking about a person's actual purchasing power, we are only interested in the take-home wage she receives.

An obvious constraint on production activity is that each household member has a maximum of 24 hours each day to (1) produce Q_H or Q_C, and (2) sleep or otherwise meet basic biological needs. Thus, the scarce resource here is time. In reality, household members also devote time to a third type of activity—leisure—which includes the time they spend consuming the "fruits of their labor," so to speak. Ignoring leisure will not compromise our basic analysis because the framework we develop can be readily extended to include a whole host of ways in which household members use their time and earnings.

Finally, let's suppose that the average number of hours a person sleeps each night is a given, dictated perhaps by his or her genetic profile. People who require less sleep have a "leg up" in terms of the amount of time available to produce H and C. The genetic makeup of these people gives them more time to be productive. (You have perhaps read stories about wealthy entrepreneurs and CEOs who say they only need a few hours of sleep every night.) This superior "endowment" can be thought of as a valuable form of human capital. It is really no different from inheriting the genes that increase the likelihood that a person will live longer and have more time to accumulate wealth, or those that increase the probability of a person developing into an all-star pitcher in the major leagues.

Given these conditions, consider the following scenario:

- Partner I—Fred—requires 6 hours of sleep per night to be productive the rest of the day. This leaves him with 18 hours per day to produce H or C. His take-home market wage is $10 per hour, and he can produce one (standardized) unit of household outputs in 30 minutes.

- Partner II—Wilma—requires 8 hours of sleep per night to be productive the rest of the day. That leaves her with 16 hours per day to produce H or C. Her take-home market wage is $12 per hour, and she can produce one (standardized) unit of household outputs in 40 minutes.

We can derive a **production possibilities frontier (PPF)** for each of these partners. The PPF shows the maximum combination of market-based consumption (Q_C) and household outputs (Q_H) that each partner can produce in any given 24-hour period.

> **PRODUCTION POSSIBILITIES FRONTIER (PPF)** A graph that shows the maximum combination of outputs that can be produced from a given amount of scarce resources during a specified period of time.

Figure 10.1 shows Fred's PPF. He can spend all of his waking hours in the labor force, in which case, he will earn $180/day ($10 per hour × 18 hours) that can be used to purchase goods in the market. This is represented by point A on the PPF. Or, Fred can spend all of his waking hours in household production, generating 36 units (2 units per hour × 18 hours) of household outputs (point B). Finally, he can spend a portion of time in the labor force and use the balance of his time to produce household outputs. An example of this would be point C. At

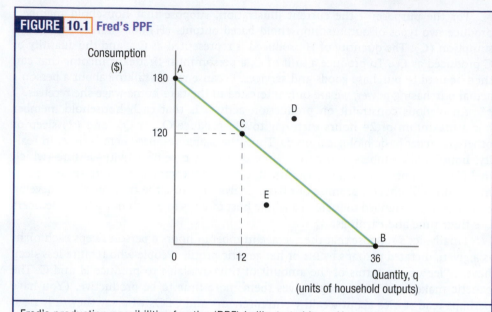

FIGURE 10.1 Fred's PPF

Fred's production possibilities frontier (PPF) is illustrated here. He can spend all of his waking hours in the labor force, in which case, he will generate $180 per day ($10 per hour × 18 hours) that can be used to purchase goods in the market. This is represented by point A on the PPF. Or, Fred can spend all of his waking hours in household production, generating 36 units (2 units per hour × 18 hours) of household outputs (point B). Finally, he can spend a portion of time in the labor force and use the balance of his time to produce household outputs. An example of this would be point C. At point C, Fred spends 6 hours on household production and 12 hours per day in the labor force. Notice that Fred cannot attain the bundle of H and C represented by point D on the graph. He also won't choose bundle E because he can get more H or C, or both, rather than staying at E.

point C, Fred spends 6 hours on household production and 12 hours in the labor force. This generates 12 units of household outputs and $120 in market-based consumption.

Keep in mind that Fred's PPF reflects all of the bundles of H and C that he can achieve. Fred cannot reach combinations of H and C that are outside of his PPF—for example, point D—because he is constrained by his total number of awake hours and his earnings capacity. And, as long as more household services or more goods bought in the market increase his well-being, Fred will never want to choose a combination of H and C—for example, point E—that lies within the PPF. Operating within the PPF means that time is being wasted: it could be used to produce more H or C that would inevitably increase well-being.

We can derive Wilma's PPF in like fashion.

Figure 10.2 indicates that if Wilma spends all of her available hours in the labor market, she will generate $192 per day ($12 × 16 hours) in market purchases (point A'). Alternatively, if she spends all of her time producing household outputs (point B'), she will produce 24 units during her 16 waking hours each day. Like Fred, she can dedicate some of her time to the labor market and the rest to producing household outputs. Point C' is an example of this. At point C', Wilma spends 10 hours on household production and 6 hours in the labor force. This generates 15 units of household outputs and $72 in market-based consumption.

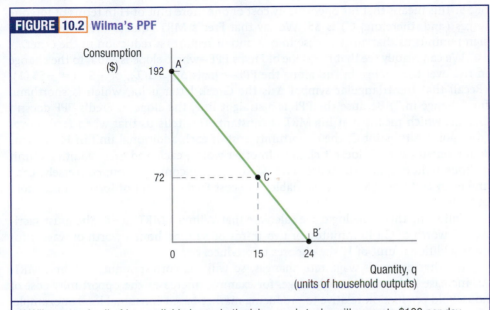

FIGURE 10.2 Wilma's PPF

If Wilma spends all of her available hours in the labor market, she will generate $192 per day ($12 × 16 hours) in market purchases (point A′). Alternatively, if she spends all of her time producing household outputs (point B′), she will produce 24 units of output during her 16 waking hours each day. She can also dedicate some of her time to the labor market and the rest to producing household outputs. Point C′ is an example of this. At point C′, Wilma spends 10 hours on household production and 6 hours in the labor force. This will result in $72 in consumption and 15 units of household outputs produced.

The Shape of the PPF

You might wonder if a PPF must always be downward sloping. In fact, a PPF must always be downward sloping as long as an increase in one good is accompanied by a reduction in the other. That is, if we must take away scarce resources from the production of one good to expand production of the other, then the trade-off between the two goods must be negative. In Fred and Wilma's case, the amount of household outputs (H) produced cannot be expanded without reducing the amount of consumables (C) that can be purchased. Both take time to produce, and time is a scarce resource that can be allocated to only one type of production at a time.

The shape—or slope—of a PPF reflects the actual magnitude of the trade-off between the two types of outputs. We call the slope of the PPF the **marginal rate of transformation (MRT)**. The MRT tells us how much of one output (H) must be sacrificed to produce one more unit of another output (C).

MARGINAL RATE OF TRANSFORMATION (MRT) The rate at which two outputs can be traded off for one another. It is the *opportunity cost* of producing one more unit of one good in terms of forgone units of the other good.

To better understand the MRT, let's take another look at our original example. Fred's MRT is dictated by his wage rate ($10 per hour) as well as his efficiency when it comes to producing household outputs (30 minutes per unit). Thus, gaining one additional unit of household output requires the sacrifice of one-half hour of wages, or \$5. This means that his opportunity cost of one more unit of H in terms of forgone wages (and, therefore, C) is \$5. We say that Fred's MRT equals −\$5. The negative sign reminds us that any increase in one output requires a reduction in the other.

We can readily see that the slope of Fred's PPF—where slope is equal to the change in rise over the change in run along the PPF—equals $\Delta Q_C / \Delta Q_H$, or −\$5 (= −\$5/1). (Recall that the triangular symbol Δ is the Greek letter delta, which is shorthand for "change in.") Because the PPF is a straight line, the slope of Fred's PPF doesn't change, which means that his MRT is constant. This tells us that when Fred moves from point A to point C, the opportunity cost of each additional unit of H in terms of forgone units of C doesn't change. In other words, each and every additional unit of household outputs will "cost" Fred \$5 in forgone consumption; conversely, each and every additional \$5 of consumables will cost Fred one unit of forgone household outputs.

Following this same logic, we calculate that Wilma's MRT is −8. She must sacrifice \$8 worth of C (40 minutes, or two-thirds of \$12, an hour's worth of wages) for every additional unit of H she chooses to produce.

If either partner's wage rate changes, so will the corresponding PPF and MRT. An increase in Wilma's hourly wage, for example, increases the opportunity cost of household production relative to producing market-based consumables. For example, if she earned \$24 an hour, the opportunity cost of the 40 minutes required to produce one more unit of household output would now be \$16 (= \$24 × 2/3 hours). The exact opposite is true for a wage reduction. For example, if Fred suffers a cut in his hourly wage or if there is an increase in payroll (or income) tax rates, his take-home wage falls. Consequently, the opportunity cost of producing one more H in terms of forgone C falls: any additional time used in household production buys less C than before. This leads us to predict that higher tax rates and lower wage rates discourage labor market activity and favor household production. Conversely, lower tax rates and higher wage rates favor labor market activity in lieu of household production.

A PPF with More Than One Slope

Suppose that Fred is offered the opportunity to earn overtime pay—"time and a half"—for all of the hours he works beyond the first eight on any given day. What would his PPF now look like?

As we can see from **Figure 10.3**, the slope of the PPF changes after the first 8 hours of work (point A). This is because the wage rate changes from \$10 per hour to \$15 per hour beyond the first 8 hours of work. The 30 minutes that it takes Fred to produce additional units of H now have an opportunity cost of \$7.50. That is, Fred's MRT with respect to overtime hours equals −\$7.50.

We can generalize from this result that whenever a person's wage rate increases, her PPF becomes steeper. In other words, her opportunity cost of household production increases compared with working outside the home. This result goes a long way toward explaining why the increase in women's wage rates and employment prospects over the past 50 years have led to an increase in women's labor force participation, at the expense of in-home production activities.[6]

This phenomenon has, in turn, created tremendous demand for market substitutes to replace household production—hired child care, take-out food, laundry

----

[6]Mark Aguiar and Erik Hurst, "Measuring Trends in Leisure: The Allocation of Time Over Five Decades." *The Quarterly Journal of Economics*, 122, no. 3 (2007): 969–1006.

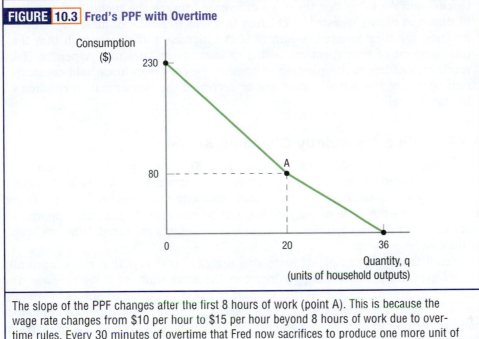

FIGURE 10.3 Fred's PPF with Overtime

The slope of the PPF changes after the first 8 hours of work (point A). This is because the wage rate changes from $10 per hour to $15 per hour beyond 8 hours of work due to overtime rules. Every 30 minutes of overtime that Fred now sacrifices to produce one more unit of household output has a new, higher opportunity cost of $7.50. That is, Fred's MRT as it relates to overtime hours equals −$7.50.

services, and so on—which we will explore at length in the next chapter. In addition, the increasing opportunity cost of household production has been a catalyst for the explosive growth in time-saving household technologies—such as dishwashers, microwave ovens, clothes dryers, permanent press clothing, online banking services, and even automatic sprinkler systems. These innovations reduce the amount of time that it takes to produce a specific household service. For example, Fred or Wilma may now be able to pay all of the household's bills online at a time cost of 15 minutes a week, rather than the 60 minutes it once took to write checks and put them in the mail.

These labor-saving technologies reduce the opportunity cost of producing H in terms of forgone C. In fact, it turns out that whether a woman works outside of the home or not, she now spends less time on household production than she did during the past century. Time spent on household work dropped an average of 15 hours per week from 1965 to 2003 for women who were not in the labor force. For those who were working outside the home, it fell from 18 to 12 hours per week during the same time period.[7]

ECONOMIC FALLACY The average number of children per family in the United States declined from 3.06 in 1900 to 1.86 in 2000. This means that less time is now being spent taking care of children in the household, and more time is being devoted to outside employment and other activities (e.g., leisure).

· · · · · · · ·

[7]Ibid.

Uncertain. We know that there is a difference between the *quality* and *quantity* of time and money invested in children in a family. As the number of children declines, the time invested *in each child* can increase sufficiently such that the total amount of time spent on raising children doesn't change. Appendix 10A specifically addresses the question of whether the change in household composition over time has actually increased or decreased the investment in children's human capital.

A PPF with a Constantly Changing Slope

In our original Fred and Wilma example, the MRT of each person is constant: the trade-off between H and C doesn't change. In contrast, if we are talking about a community's PPF—say, its production possibilities with respect to producing food and drinking water—the slope of the PPF may not be constant. That is, the opportunity cost of one output may increase as more and more of it is produced. Why might this be the case?

Recall that the principle of increasing marginal cost says that the opportunity cost of expanding a good's supply increases the more units of it we produce. The rationale for this assumption is that we have to use more scarce resources to produce each additional unit of the good—in other words, the lowest-cost methods of production are the first to be exploited and exhausted. We first illustrated this principle in Chapter 7 by reflecting upon the ways in which a community supplies water to its residents. The lowest-cost source of drinking water is rainwater, captured by reservoirs. Surface water—which comes from higher-altitude snow melt—is the next lowest-cost source of water. Groundwater is more costly because of the need to locate and pump this water to the surface and filter it before distribution. Finally, seawater is the most expensive source of drinking water because of the high costs of desalinization.

The principle of increasing marginal cost tells us that expanding the supply of drinking water requires more and more resources per gallon produced—such as energy, capital equipment, labor, and "raw" water—that can no longer be used for the production of other outputs such as food. Conversely, the more food we want to produce, the less residual resources there will be to produce drinking water. In fact, we have seen that the opportunity cost of expanding the supply of drinking water to growing populations in the southwest United States isn't constant in terms of food forgone: more and more food output has to be given up for each incremental increase in drinking water supplies. This scenario is currently being played out in California. Colorado River water diverted to farmers in the state's Central Valley is not available to people downstream for drinking water and other personal needs. For crop yields to keep expanding, more and more water is needed to irrigate less fertile, more arid land. Moreover, farmers have begun to expand into more water-intensive crops, planting fruit trees and growing strawberries, for example. This also increases the opportunity cost of marginal increases in the food supply in terms of forgone drinking water.[8] Recognizing this inherent trade-off between food production and drinking water, the Metropolitan Water District of Southern California has begun to pay upstream farmers to leave their ground fallow. Farmers can earn more than $500 an acre, more than the market value of many crops.[9]

· · · · · · ·

[8]Felicity Barringer, "Rising Calls to Regulate California Ground Water." *New York Times*, May 13, 2009.

[9]Felicity Barringer, "Empty Fields Fill Urban Basins and Farmers' Pockets." *New York Times*, October 24, 2011.

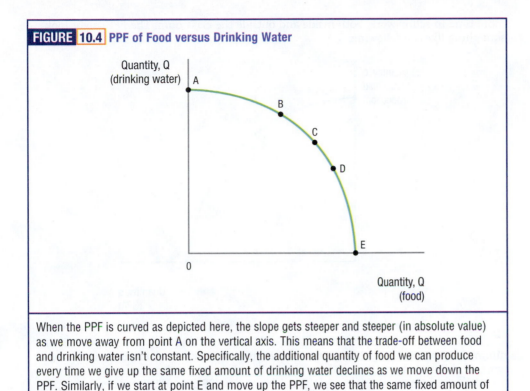

FIGURE 10.4 **PPF of Food versus Drinking Water**

When the PPF is curved as depicted here, the slope gets steeper and steeper (in absolute value) as we move away from point A on the vertical axis. This means that the trade-off between food and drinking water isn't constant. Specifically, the additional quantity of food we can produce every time we give up the same fixed amount of drinking water declines as we move down the PPF. Similarly, if we start at point E and move up the PPF, we see that the same fixed amount of food that is given up yields smaller and smaller increases in water output.

When there are increasing costs of production, the PPF will be "concave to the origin," as depicted in **Figure 10.4**.

Figure 10.4 shows a curved PPF, one with a slope that is getting steeper and steeper (in absolute value) as we move away from the vertical axis. This means that the trade-off between food and drinking water isn't constant. Specifically, the additional quantity of food we can produce every time we reduce our drinking water by the same fixed amount declines as we move from point A to point B to point C. This follows directly from the principle of increasing marginal cost. As we move down the drinking water (vertical) axis, the same reduction in drinking water "buys us" less and less additional food output. In contrast, as we move up from point E where no drinking water is being produced, each unit of food we give up yields less and less additional drinking water. In other words, the last unit of water produced becomes more and more "expensive" in terms of the amount of food that must be forgone.

SOLVED PROBLEM

Q Suppose we extend our household model to include children who are under 16 and cannot legally join the workforce. What would a typical child's PPF look like?

A A lot depends on the child's age and whether the child could produce any units of H. Let's assume we are talking about a 12-year-old boy or girl. Then we could draw a PPF that shows the trade-off between producing units of H (setting the table; emptying the dishwasher; folding the laundry; walking the dog) and producing units of G, where G represents the child's grade point average (GPA). To increase G, a student must invest more time in schoolwork, both inside and outside the classroom. The PPF might look something like the following:

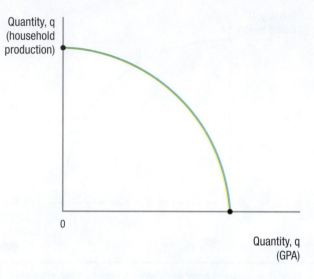

This concave PPF shows that the trade-off between H and G is changing—there are diminishing returns to spending more and more time studying or engaging in housework. A child gets bored, mentally or physically exhausted, and so on.

The interesting question is what the slope of the PPF tells us. It represents the MRT between housework and a child's GPA. It is negative, which means that the more housework a child does, the lower his GPA would tend to be. (Recall that in this simple example, all of the child's time is spent either studying or doing housework.) In effect, the slope is telling us the opportunity cost of doing more housework in terms of the expected reduction in GPA. Instead of earning a wage, the child is "earning" a GPA.

Improving One's PPF

Is there a way that individuals or communities can improve on the trade-offs reflected by their PPFs? We will see in Chapters 13 and 14 that when someone such as Wilma invests in her human capital through education and the development of marketable skills, she is likely to increase her future wages. This will cause her future PPF to "rotate outward." **Figure 10.5** shows that this future PPF will permit Wilma to achieve a higher level of C for her household without having to give up any H. Bundle D′ could not have been attained in the *future* without making the investment *today*.

Similarly, investing in technological innovations today can improve future trade-offs. We have already seen this in the example of time-saving household innovations, which allow people to produce the same level of H and increase their time in the labor market. This also means that the household can increase both H and C. When a community invests in technological innovations—such as desalinization plants, advanced water distribution systems, or water-conserving agricultural processes—it, too, can push its PPF outward and enjoy more of each output.

Is there any way that a household or community could improve upon its PPF *today*? It turns out that by having members *specialize* in production, we can potentially reach a higher level of well-being than individual PPFs would permit.

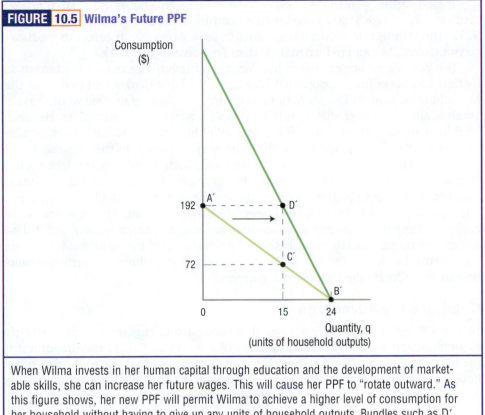

FIGURE 10.5 Wilma's Future PPF

When Wilma invests in her human capital through education and the development of market-able skills, she can increase her future wages. This will cause her PPF to "rotate outward." As this figure shows, her new PPF will permit Wilma to achieve a higher level of consumption for her household without having to give up any units of household outputs. Bundles such as D′ could not be attained in the future had she not made the investment in her education.

10.4 Absolute Advantage, Comparative Advantage, and Specialization

Look again at the PPFs of Fred and Wilma: Figures 10.1 and 10.2 indicate that Fred can produce household outputs at the rate of 30 minutes per unit, compared with the 40 minutes it takes Wilma, and he needs less sleep. As a result, Fred can produce more units of household outputs during his waking hours (36 units) than Wilma (24 units). Fred has what economists call an **absolute advantage** when it comes to household production. He is able to produce more of H than Wilma on any given day.

ABSOLUTE ADVANTAGE The ability to produce more output than other producers using the same amount of resources.

EXAMPLE Angola, Botswana, South Africa, Russia, Canada, and Australia have an absolute advantage in producing more raw diamonds per worker because of their abundance of diamond mines.

EXAMPLE Climate and soil conditions give Ecuador, the Philippines, and Costa Rica an absolute advantage in producing more bananas per worker.

If each partner were to spend every one of their waking hours in the labor market, Fred would generate $180 in market-based consumables, and Wilma would generate $192. This tells us that Wilma has an absolute advantage when it comes to producing consumables: She can produce more C than Fred on any given day.

Is it possible for one partner to have an absolute advantage in *both* production activities? To answer this, suppose that Fred tested the labor market and found out that he could actually make $13 per hour by switching jobs. As a result, Fred would have an absolute advantage in producing *both* household services and consumables. He would be able to produce 36 units of H if he spent all of his time in the household, or $234 (= $13 × 18) of C if he spent all of his time working outside of the household.

If Fred has an absolute advantage in producing both H and C, you might ask why Fred would still keep Wilma around. The fact of the matter is that even if Fred has an absolute advantage in both types of production, he cannot spend all of his time producing household services and, *simultaneously*, earning income. This is where Wilma comes in. Despite the absence of an absolute advantage in either activity, she still has a scarce resource that can contribute to the well-being of the household: her time. This means that it is in the interest of the household as a whole to jointly determine how to best allocate the time of both partners.

Comparative Advantage

To simplify our analysis, let's assume that each partner engages in just one of the two production activities. We also assume that a unit of C is just as important to the household as a unit of H. In such a case, it turns out that the well-being of the household as a whole would be maximized if each partner allocates his or her time solely according to that person's **comparative advantage**.

> **COMPARATIVE ADVANTAGE** The ability to produce a particular good at a lower opportunity cost than other producers.

> **EXAMPLE** India, Vietnam, and China have a comparative advantage in producing labor-intensive goods such as clothing and linens.

> **EXAMPLE** Israel has a comparative advantage when it comes to producing high-tech and scientific innovations.

In our household example, what is Fred's opportunity cost of producing one more unit of household outputs (H)? At a wage rate of $13 per hour, the household will lose $6.50 (30 minutes of wages at $13 per hour) worth of C to gain an additional unit of H. Thus, the opportunity cost of H in terms of forgone C is −$6.50. What is the household's opportunity cost of having Wilma produce one more unit of H? To produce this additional unit, she would have to sacrifice $8 (40 minutes of wages at $12 per hour) worth of C. In other words, her opportunity cost of producing one unit of H is $8. Therefore, Fred has a lower opportunity cost when it comes to household production. While Fred would generate $6.50 more in C if he reduces his production of H by one unit, Wilma will earn the household $8 in consumables—$1.50 more—if she reduces her production of H by one unit.

Because Fred's opportunity cost of household production is lower than Wilma's, we say that he has a *comparative advantage* when it comes to producing household services. Wilma has a comparative advantage when it comes to earning wages that can be used to purchase market-based consumables. What this means is that even though Fred has an absolute advantage in producing C, he benefits the household more by staying home and producing 36 units of H. Wilma benefits the household most by going to work each day and producing $192 worth of C.

ECONOMIC FALLACY   The fact that China has become the primary supplier of steel to the United States reflects its comparative advantage in steel production.

Uncertain. China's large and relatively uneducated population has made the country's opportunity cost of producing labor-intensive outputs such as steel low compared to the United States. However, other factors have also led to the emergence of China as a powerhouse in the global steel marketplace. For example, the Chinese government owns 100 percent of eight of its top-ten steel producers and holds a majority ownership share in many of the remaining Chinese steel producers. In this ownership role, the government has heavily subsidized its steel producers. This distorts the true opportunity cost of China's steel producers—in terms of real resources used up—and the comparative advantage they have relative to U.S. steel producers. Just because China has a *cost advantage* does not mean it has a *comparative advantage* (in terms of real resources) in production.

In 2007, the U.S. Department of Commerce protested China's steel subsidies by filing a complaint with the U.S. International Trade Commission (ITC), an independent federal agency that investigates allegations of unfair trade practices of foreign companies and assesses the harm to specific U.S. industries. In 2008, the ITC imposed stiff penalty tariffs (taxes) on Chinese steel pipe imported into the United States, thereby offsetting China's subsidies and significantly increasing the price of Chinese steel pipe in the U.S. market.

Specialization

If Fred concentrates his time on household production—for which he has the comparative advantage—and Wilma uses her time solely to earn income, this **specialization** in production will maximize the household's overall well-being.

SPECIALIZATION Circumstance in which a person (or country) engages in a limited range of productive activities.

EXAMPLE Household members may specialize in the kinds of household outputs they each produce. One may take care of the garden, while another one takes care of meal preparation, and still another does the laundry.

EXAMPLE Ophthalmologists are surgeons that specialize in treating eye problems, while cardiac surgeons specialize in heart-related problems.

To verify that specialization improves overall well-being, consider what would happen if Fred took a job to buy C, and Wilma specialized in producing household outputs. While the household could now earn $234 and buy more C, it would end up with 24 units of H, which is less than the 36 units enjoyed when each partner's area of specialization is dictated by comparative advantage. Put another way, Fred is *so* much more efficient at household production compared to Wilma that it makes sense for him to work within the household and for Wilma to enter the labor force.

Of course, if Fred and Wilma place relatively little value on household services, Fred might also enter the labor force on a part-time or full-time basis. However, as we have just seen, the opportunity cost in terms of forgone household production would be substantial.

In this example, Fred and Wilma engage in what is referred to as "strong specialization" in that they each do only one thing—produce C or H. In reality, we know that whether because of boredom or some other reason, members of households tend to specialize in one activity but still contribute to others. So, for example, Wilma may be the chief breadwinner for the family, but she also cooks gourmet dinners. Fred may be the primary homemaker but may also have a side job preparing tax returns at home. In the real world, Fred and Wilma have PPFs that are not straight lines but, rather, are concave just like the community PPFs we discussed previously. Their incremental productivity begins to fall because they are dedicating their time to just one activity.

Why Specialization Leads to Prosperity

We can generalize our findings about the household to other producing organizations and to the economy at large. When workers specialize in production activities for which they have a comparative advantage, the amount of output produced by the workers as a group is maximized. Why is this so? According to Adam Smith—probably the most famous economist of all time—specialization in production means that workers no longer have to shift back and forth between unrelated tasks. Moreover, by focusing on just one task, a worker is more likely to discover new ways to improve upon his own productivity. This, in turn, increases each worker's output, thereby pushing out the PPF. In the case of our household, this might translate into Fred finding more efficient (less time-consuming) ways to clean the windows and pay the bills while Wilma discovers ways to purchase more units of C for the same amount of money she earns.

We have arrived at a central principle in economics: specialization enables us to exploit the comparative advantage we each have, leading to an increase in the total amount of output that can be produced for any given amount of scarce resources available. In other words, the total "economic pie" grows larger through specialization because we each do what we do best. In the case of our household, determining each partner's comparative advantage allows the household to maximize the amount of output that can be generated from the combined 34 hours (the scarce resource) per day available to Fred and Wilma.

Limits to Specialization

The degree to which members of a household can specialize depends on how many members there are and the number of productive opportunities that exist. For example, when there is only one adult in a household, she must produce H *and* earn income to buy C (assuming for now that she cannot buy all of the household outputs in the market). She cannot specialize in one activity or the other. (We explore this further in Appendix 10A.) Consider, too, that in a primitive economy that has not yet developed markets within which people can trade consumables—in other words, everything is produced within the household—everyone engages solely in the production of H, although we would expect specialization to arise within the household itself.

Division of Labor

So far, we have discussed specialization as it relates to people choosing different productive activities according to their comparative advantage. Some of us become NBA players, while others of us become economists or pastry chefs. It turns out that we can extend the concept of specialization to the way in which production of a particular good or service is organized. **Division of labor** occurs when workers are responsible for specific subtasks that are part of the production process.

> **DIVISION OF LABOR** Concentration of a worker's full work effort on a subtask that contributes to the production.

> **EXAMPLE** Along an automobile assembly line, some employees are responsible for installing windshields, while others work on installing engine blocks.

> **EXAMPLE** In most restaurants, servers do not "bus" tables; busboys are responsible for cleaning and setting tables.

Assigning workers to specific subtasks permits them to develop task-specific skills that increase their time efficiency. In effect, division of labor can help workers create a comparative advantage in a particular subtask. The goal is to generate a greater amount of output than if each worker were responsible for producing a good from start to finish.

The degree to which an organization engages in division of labor depends crucially on two things: First, can the production process be neatly broken down into subtasks that can be completed by different workers? And second, is there sufficient demand for the good to justify the costs of dividing production into these subtasks?[10] If we look at physicians' offices, for example, we see that some division of labor occurs. Most physician offices have, at the very least, a front desk person in addition to the physician. The doctor does not make appointments, sign in patients, or collect fees. Her time is put to its highest valued use: examining patients and evaluating their medical situation. Sometimes, there is even a medical technician who takes a patient's blood pressure reading and temperature before the doctor arrives for the exam. Rarely, however, do we find that the doctor's exam is broken into further subtasks that are performed by other people. The patient is not put on a production "assembly line" in the office, where one doctor examines the ears and another examines the throat, and so on. This further division of labor simply does not lend itself to increasing patient "throughput" and the practice's total daily production level.

Still, there has been a division of labor of sorts that has occurred in the production of medical care as the demand for diagnoses and procedures has grown (largely due to the explosion in medical knowledge and technology). For example, during the late twentieth century, the specialty of EENT (Ear, Eye, Nose and Throat) split into two subspecialties—eye and ENT. And, more recently, the subspecialty of eye (called ophthalmology) has split into subspecialties, including cornea, retina, glaucoma, and ocular plastics. While patients are not passed along an assembly line in the same way as an automobile under production, they are likely to be referred from one subspecialist to another to address specific eye problems.

Specialization and the Division of Labor Require Cooperation

Suppose that Fred and Wilma specialize in the production of H and C, respectively. As long as both partners value H and C, then their individual well-being will not

....

[10]George Stigler, "The Division of Labor Is Limited by the Extent of the Market." *Journal of Political Economy*, 59 (June, 1951).

be maximized if they consume only the good that they produce. This, then, gives us an economic rationale for voluntary exchange. Trade gives Fred and Wilma the opportunity—through specialization—to make themselves better off both individually and jointly as a household.

Think about what would happen if you were stranded alone on an island. You would have to produce each and every good that you ultimately consumed. By contrast, if you were one of a group of people stranded on the island, you could allocate tasks among yourselves according to each person's comparative advantage. For example, a youngster in the group could be assigned the task of gathering firewood, while a talented knitter makes fishing nets and an athletic person uses the nets to catch fish. According to our earlier discussion, this would result in a greater amount of goods to share among the entire group. As long as members of the group engage in trade—wherein the fisherman trades fish for nets, the firewood collector trades wood for fish, and so on—each person would no longer have to perform each step in the process required to produce a fish dinner. This exchange permits each person to specialize in the activity for which he or she has the lowest opportunity cost.

Gains from Trade

The greater the differences in the comparative advantage of trading partners, the greater the gains from trade will be. Think, for example, about a household member who does not drive and her partner, who cannot vacuum because he has a dust allergy. They would clearly increase each other's well-being by specializing and trading services. The same holds for a partner who is handy at home repairs but burns even the toast and her partner who is a gourmet cook.

Over time, gains from trade can change because there is a change in a person's comparative advantage. For example, if Wilma is laid off from her job, her next best wage offer might lead her and Fred to switch roles. He might leave household production and go into the labor force to earn consumables, while she now takes responsibility for producing household services. A similar result might occur if there is a change in property rights that affects the earnings opportunities of one partner. Or, as we will see in the next chapter, market opportunities arise so that it makes sense for both partners to enter the labor force and purchase some household services instead of directly producing them.

A household's composition can also impact the comparative advantage of its members. For example, the number of children in the typical household has substantially declined during the past 50 years in the United States. With fewer children at home, a mother's comparative advantage in household production has likely diminished relative to her partner. As it turns out, labor-market trends in the United States suggest that there has been a convergence in the comparative advantage of women and men, especially among the most educated partners.[11]

Specialization in a Global Economy

We can extend our analysis of comparative advantage and specialization in the household to the global economy. Suppose, for example, that the United States can produce both lumber and lasers at a lower resource cost than Canada. In other words, the United States has an absolute advantage in producing both goods. Nevertheless, there is an opportunity cost of using scarce labor, machinery, fuel, and so forth to

· · · · · · · ·

[11]Joyce P. Jacobsen, *The Economics of Gender* (Blackwell: Malden, MA, 1998).

harvest trees rather than produce lasers. Even a country as large and well-endowed as the United States faces scarcity, which means that it can't produce everything for which it holds an absolute advantage.

It is likely that the United States holds the comparative advantage in producing lasers while Canada has the comparative advantage in producing lumber (given its expansive forests and fewer number of high-tech production facilities). Therefore, it would make sense for the United States to produce lasers and for Canada to produce lumber. This specialization will maximize the total output of lasers and lumber for the two nations together. As long as the nations agree to subsequently trade lasers for lumber, they will both be made better off by engaging in specialization.

This point is worth emphasizing. Whether we are talking about members of a household or member states in the global community, specialization will not occur unless trading opportunities exist. Wilma will not specialize in producing C if she is not assured that Fred will "trade" at least some of the H he produces in return for some of the consumables that she brings home. Similarly, even though Pacific Rim countries have had a longstanding comparative advantage in the production of clothing because of their abundance of unskilled labor, the U.S. clothing industry would never have withered away had there not been trading opportunities that permitted consumers in both countries to capitalize on each others' comparative advantage.

When there is unimpeded trade in the global economy, we say that a perfectly **open economy** exists. This is what is meant by the term "free trade."

OPEN ECONOMY An economy that has few, if any, costly barriers preventing trade from taking place.

EXAMPLE NAFTA (the North American Free Trade Agreement) eliminated tariffs and trade barriers that impeded trade among Mexico, the United States, and Canada. The rationale for establishing the EU (European Union) was to do the same for European countries.

SOLVED PROBLEM

Q Suppose that the productivities of American and Canadian workers in lumber and steel—as measured by the average daily output of one worker—are as follows:

Country	Tons of Lumber	Tons of Steel
U.S.	0.9	1.0
Canada	0.8	0.8

a. In which product does the United States have an *absolute* advantage? A *comparative* advantage? What about Canada?

b. If each country has 1 million workers and allocates half of its workers to steel production and the other half to lumber, how much steel and lumber would the two countries produce together?

c. Suppose that each country now specializes according to its comparative advantage. How much lumber and steel will now be produced by the two countries together?

d. If the United States and Canada specialize according to (c), and the United States trades 410 tons of steel for 390 tons of Canada's lumber, are both countries made better off as a result of specialization and trade?

A a. The United States has an *absolute* advantage in both lumber and steel—it can produce more of each per labor hour. It has a *comparative* advantage in producing steel because the opportunity cost of a ton of steel is 0.9 tons of lumber, while the opportunity cost of Canada producing a ton of steel is a ton of lumber. So Canada has the comparative advantage in producing lumber.

  b. If each country allocates half their workforce to each productive activity, the total output per day would be

  United States: 500,000 tons steel + 450,000 tons lumber

  Canada: 400,000 tons steel + 400,000 tons lumber

  TOTAL: 900,000 tons steel + 850,000 tons lumber

  c. If Canada uses all of its workforce to produce lumber, and the United States uses 92 percent of its workers to produce steel and the rest to produce lumber, total output would equal 920,000 tons steel (U.S.) plus 72,000 tons of lumber (U.S.) plus 800,000 tons of lumber (Canada), or a total of 920,000 tons of steel plus 872,000 tons of lumber. So by specializing, there are more of both outputs produced by the two countries together (note that while Canada is strictly specializing, the United States is not).

  d. Absolutely. Suppose that the United States trades a total of 410,000 tons of steel for 390,000 tons of lumber. Based on the numbers in (c), the United States would end up with 510,000 tons of steel and 462,000 tons of lumber, more than what it had in (b). Canada would end up with 410,000 tons of lumber and 410,000 tons of steel, also more than in (b).

10.5 Sharing the Gains from Trade

In our original example, we saw that by specializing in those activities in which they held the comparative advantage, Fred and Wilma could generate 36 units of household outputs per day and $192 in market-based consumables. According to our initial assumption, both partners are motivated to maximize the well-being of the household, which means maximizing the total outputs they jointly produce. What if, however, we relaxed this assumption and let each partner pursue his or her own well-being based on personal preferences? In other words, what if partners made choices to maximize their own well-being rather than the household as a whole?

Think of two unrelated roommates—Max and Sam—who live together solely to save on rent but have little, if any, interest in each other's well-being. In such a situation, it makes sense to ask how the roommates will divide up the total output produced by the "household." What are the terms of trade? For example, if Max is a student who dedicates his time to producing household outputs (H) such as meals and clean clothes, will Max pay less rent than Sam, who holds down a full-time job and eats the meals that Max prepares? Or will Max be paid by Sam for providing these household services? If Sam hands over 25 percent of his income to Max, how much H can he expect to receive in return? Will he have a hot meal waiting for him when he walks in the door and his laundry washed and folded? Will Sam be able to rely on Max to take out the trash, load and unload the dishwasher, and walk and feed Sam's dog?

Unwritten, social agreements (sometimes referred to as "social contracts") often dictate the terms of trade in nonmarket settings. These terms tend to be dictated by the same factors that determine the terms of trade in a market. Each person's willingness to "pay" for another's outputs depends on the opportunity cost of producing the outputs oneself, along with the availability and cost of substitutes. The existence of low-cost microwaveable dinners, for example, might lower the amount that Sam is willing to pay Max for preparing meals. This is because the microwave has reduced the opportunity cost of Sam preparing his own meals.

> **ECONOMIC FALLACY**   As women's wage rates have risen relative to men's in the past half century, the amount of time working wives spend with their children relative to the amount of time their husbands do has fallen significantly.
>
> **Uncertain.** Among married women who work outside the home, the amount of time spent in household production has fallen; nevertheless, the amount of time spent in child care has *increased*. By contrast, married men have increased their household production by about 4 hours per week, primarily in the areas of food preparation and indoor tasks.
>
> One study estimated that from 1965 to 1993, working women reduced the amount of time committed to household production *other than* child care by more than 12 hours per week.[12] Some of this decline is due to technological advances that have reduced the time required to perform many household tasks, such as cleaning. Married partners have also increasingly outsourced the production of some household outputs to the market, including, meal preparation.

Bargaining in a Household

While it often occurs without much forethought, bargaining does take place within households—whether it is between members of a family or unrelated household members like Max and Sam. This bargaining determines how the gains from specialization will be distributed among the members. The bargaining power of each partner ultimately depends on the net benefit that each one gets from belonging to the household. More precisely, the household member whose net benefit from being in the household is the greatest—where net benefit equals the total benefit minus the opportunity cost—will have less bargaining power than the member whose net benefit is low. When the opportunity cost of staying in the household is high, a member is more likely to exit if there are not substantial gains from trade to keep her in the household. In the next chapter, we explore this dynamic in greater detail and assess the impact that bargaining power has on the consumption patterns of households.

Finally, just as buyers and sellers can enter or exit markets in response to trading opportunities, members may also enter or leave their household. The ease of entry and exit depends on the property-rights system that governs the formation and dissolution of households. In the United States, for example, the availability of "no fault" divorce has substantially reduced the cost of exiting from a married household. As you might expect, this has significantly influenced the way in which resources are allocated within households because it provides a near costless exit strategy for members when their net benefit of staying in the household becomes negligible. This, in turn, strengthens the bargaining power of the members that receive the lowest net benefit from remaining in the household. The Appendix to this chapter further explores how changes in divorce laws potentially impact the composition and resource-allocation decisions of households.

· · · · · · ·

[12]Mark Aguiar and Erik Hurst, "Measuring Trends in Leisure: The Allocation of Time Over Five Decades," *The Quarterly Journal of Economics*, 122, no. 3 (2007): 969–1006.

WHAT YOU SHOULD HAVE LEARNED FROM CHAPTER 10

■ That trade can occur within producing organizations, which we call "firms."

■ That firms coordinate and direct resources from within, without the aid of price signals.

■ That resource coordination within firms typically occurs because of high transaction costs associated with using the market and its price mechanism.

■ That transaction costs can be high when the same buyer and seller engage in a series of trades over time, or when there is a long-term agreement to exchange resources and there is uncertainty about what trading partners will expect of each other over time.

■ That the most prevalent firm in every economy is the household.

■ That the PPF reflects the maximum combination of outputs that can be produced from a given amount of scarce resources.

■ That the rate at which one output can be traded off for another is called the marginal rate of transformation (MRT); graphically, it equals the slope of the PPF.

■ That the person who has an absolute advantage in producing a certain good might not have a comparative advantage in producing that good.

■ That if a person's opportunity cost of producing an output is lower than the opportunity cost of her trading partners, she is said to have the comparative advantage.

■ That specialization and trade allow each person's comparative advantage to be exploited to maximize the total amount of output that can be generated for a given amount of scarce resources.

■ That the gains from trade will not be exploited through specialization unless there is cooperation between trading parties.

■ That because they impact the distribution of gains from trade, property rights affect the degree to which individuals actually specialize and engage in voluntary exchange.

KEY TERMS

Firm, p. 277

Production possibility frontier (PPF), p. 281

Marginal rate of transformation (MRT), p. 283

Absolute advantage, p. 289

Comparative advantage, p. 290

Specialization, p. 291

Division of labor, p. 293

Open economy, p. 295

QUESTIONS AND PROBLEMS

1. A.J. and J.J. have set up housekeeping with each other, and must decide who will take care of their eight-month-old child and who will go to work to "put bread on the table." Suppose that their PPFs are as follows (assume that their non-sleeping hours are spent either working or taking care of the child):

A.J.:

Net wages per day:	$140	$100	$50	$20	$0
Child care hours per day:	0	4	9	12	14

J.J.:

Net wages per day:	$204	$156	$96	$60	$0
Child care hours per day:	0	4	9	12	17

a) Who has the absolute advantage in terms of producing market-based consumption, Q_C?

b) Who has the absolute advantage in terms of providing child care?

c) Who has the comparative advantage in terms of providing child care?

d) Who will go to work, and who will stay home?

e) What is A.J.'s hourly wage rate? How about J.J.'s hourly wage rate?

f) What is the maximum amount of consumables (in dollars) this family can achieve if the partners specialize, given their PPFs?

g) Would your answers to (d) and (f) change if a babysitter were available at $11 per hour? What about at $8 per hour?

2. Courts often have to estimate the value of nonmarket production. This occurs, for example, when a homemaker is severely disabled or killed by a negligent driver. We call this estimate the "imputed value" of the homemaker's future, forgone services. Indicate whether you think this imputed value would increase, decrease, or remain unchanged depending upon:

a) the number of minor children in the homemaker's home.

b) the age of the homemaker.

c) the educational level of the homemaker.

d) the age of the homemaker's youngest child.

3. Show how the PPF in Figure 10.4 would change if California:

a) invests some of its current resources into plant research and development.

b) implements drip-irrigation hothouse technologies.

c) discovers a low-cost way to extract salt from seawater.

d) increases the number of immigrant workers it permits to work in farming.

e) wins a court case that gives the state a larger entitlement to water from the Rio Grande river.

4. Because the state of Georgia is suffering from an unprecedented drought, it is considering filing suit to challenge the location of its border with Tennessee. Relocating the border would give Georgia control over the water flow of the Tennessee River. If Georgia is successful in its challenge, what will the impact be on its PPF? What about Tennessee's PPF?

5. Using the concept of comparative advantage, explain why the United States is:

a) an exporter of computer technology.

b) an importer of clothing.

c) an exporter of wheat.

d) an importer of oil.

e) an exporter of higher education.

6. Recently the value of the U.S. dollar has been falling. This has made products produced in the United States less costly for foreigners. Is it possible for American suppliers to gain a comparative advantage in the production of certain goods simply because there has been a devaluation of the dollar?

7. Nobel Laureate George Stigler once wrote that the division of labor is limited by the size of a market. Explain the meaning of Stigler's statement.

8. European companies have invested heavily in manufacturing technologies to create or preserve their comparative advantage in the production of such things as turbines.[13] In contrast, U.S. companies have exploited the comparative advantage of producing abroad, locating newer plants overseas and outsourcing jobs to countries with lower labor costs. Discuss the relative merits of the European versus United States approach to global competition in terms of (1) maximizing the country's well-being in the short-run and (2) in the

· · · · · · ·

[13]Nelson Schwartz, "In a Recession, Europe's Focus on Saving Jobs Pays Off." *New York Times*, February 4, 2010, p. B1.

long-run. Which approach do you think puts investment dollars to their highest valued use? Explain your answer.

9. China has enjoyed an ever-growing trade surplus with the rest of the world, including the United States. President Obama has cried "foul" over the Chinese government's policies that keep the Chinese currency (yuan) "undervalued." Explain carefully what the difference is between a country like China having a *cost advantage* versus *comparative advantage* in production of a good or service. Who wins and who loses from the undervaluation of the yuan? Do these policies maximize the output that can be produced on a global scale from the world's limited resources? Why or why not?

10. Suppose that Fred and Wilma live in a country where women are not allowed to work in places that have male employees, nor can they interact with male customers (e.g., in a supermarket). What would Wilma's PPF now look like? What would you predict that she would specialize in—producing C or H? Would you now say that Wilma's comparative advantage had changed? Explain.

11. Suppose that a country adopts a progressive income tax system that calls for:

   ◼ a 10 percent tax on the first $25,000 earned.
   ◼ a 25 percent tax on the next $25,000 earned.
   ◼ a 50 percent tax on the next $50,000 earned.
   ◼ a 90 percent tax on all additional dollars earned.

   If you spend 16 hours a day, five days a week, producing either H or C, and your wage rate in the labor market (before taxes) is $20 per hour, what would your *annual* PPF look like? [HINT: Your PPF is based on after-tax income.]

12. Within the animal kingdom, researchers have observed a division of labor among wolves according to gender: females typically care for their young while males forage for food. In contrast, in an ant colony, the division of labor—breeding, foraging, caring for the queen, and so on—is according to age. Why do you think that the division of labor differs for wolves versus ants? Can you think of other examples of the division of labor within the animal world?

13. There is an old adage about marriage that says that "opposites attract." Can you restate this saying within the context of comparative advantage?

14. Why do you think that countries vary so much in unpaid household production as a percentage of GDP? Explain your answer.

15. At one time or another, many developing countries have pledged to become self-sufficient, thereby reducing their dependence on foreign natural resources such as oil. What would you say to the residents of these countries about the "goodness" of this goal with respect to overall well-being? Explain your answer.

16. Using what you have learned about specialization and trade, explain why an economic boycott of a country that "misbehaves"—such as Cuba or Iran—can have a significant impact on the standard of living of U.S. residents. How likely do you think it is that the United States would boycott China or Saudi Arabia? Explain your answers.

Appendix 10A The Composition of Households and Their Production Decisions

The composition of American households has changed dramatically over the past several decades, in some cases due to changes in the economic environment, and in other cases, due to changes in people's personal preferences and values. Whatever the reason, the end result is that this change in composition has had a significant impact on the internal workings of households and, in particular, the level and mix of household production.

In the first part of this Appendix, we report on the trends in household composition within the United States over the past half century. In Part 2, we identify changes in the economic environment that have contributed to these trends. Finally, in Part 3, we discuss the implications for household production in the future.

PART 1: TRENDS IN HOUSEHOLD COMPOSITION

Households by Marital Status

The days of households such as the one depicted in the TV show *The Simpsons* are fading fast. According to the Pew Research Center, in 1960, the percentage of households headed by a married couple that had children under 18 living with them was 45 percent. By 2010, this had declined to 21 percent. Moreover, the number of people living alone (excluding widows and widowers) grew from 8 to 14 percent of all households during the same period, and the number of people living with children but no spouse grew from 6 percent to 10 percent. When widowed individuals are factored in, the most common household type in the United States is now a person living alone. These one-person households accounted for 27 percent of all U.S. households in 2010, more than double the percentage in 1960.[1]

The trend in marriage rates can be explained in part by the fact that people are delaying marriage: As **Table 10A.1** shows, the median age at time of first marriage rose for men, from 22.8 years in 1960 to 28.2 in 2010, and for women, from 20.3 to 26.1 over the same period. In 1960, 68 percent of all twenty-somethings were married; in 2008, just 26 percent were.

Table	10A.1	Median Age of First Marriage: Various Years	
Year		Males	Females
1960		22.8	20.3
1970		23.2	20.8
1980		24.7	22.0
1990		26.1	23.9
1995		26.9	24.5
2000		26.8	25.1
2005		27.0	25.5
2008		27.6	25.9
2009		28.1	25.9
2010		28.2	26.1

Source: U.S. Census Bureau

....

[1]"Interactive: The Changing American Family." Pew Research Center, *Pew Social and Demographic Trends,* November 18, 2011. http://www.pewsocialtrends.org.

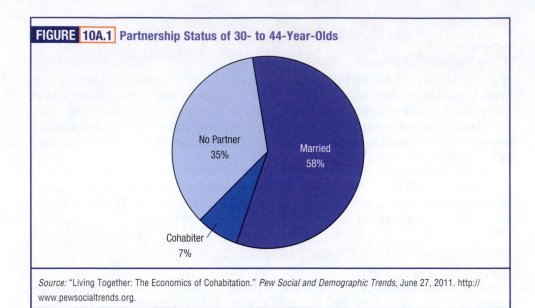

FIGURE 10A.1 Partnership Status of 30- to 44-Year-Olds

No Partner
35%

Married
58%

Cohabiter
7%

Source: "Living Together: The Economics of Cohabitation." *Pew Social and Demographic Trends,* June 27, 2011. http://www.pewsocialtrends.org.

At the same time, there has been a rise in unmarried, opposite-sex partners living together: The percentage of 30- to 44-year-old unmarried, cohabiting adults has nearly doubled since the mid-1990s. **Figure 10A.1** shows that in 2009, 7 percent of people in this age cohort were cohabitating. Although more than half of these cohabiting couples eventually marry, almost 40 percent break up within the span of five years.

In addition to cohabiting partners, the U.S. Census estimates that the number of couples identifying themselves as same-sex and living together grew from 358,390 in 2000 to 646,464 in 2010, an increase of more than 80 percent. In 2010, nearly 20 percent of these same-sex couples reported that they were married.

Households with Children

Given the decline in households with two parents and their children, it is not surprising that the percentage of children living with married parents dropped from 92 percent in 1960 to 66 percent in 2010. The number living with a parent who was never married or divorced rose from 5 percent to 29 percent, with approximately 85 percent of these households headed by single mothers.

Consistent with this finding, births to unmarried mothers rose from 5 percent of all live births in 1960 to 41 percent in 2009. At the same time, nearly 20 percent of American women in 2008 had not borne a child by age 44, compared to only 10 percent in the 1970s.

PART 2: ECONOMIC FACTORS CONTRIBUTING TO THE DECLINE IN MARRIED HOUSEHOLDS

In Chapter 10, we showed how the overall well-being of a household can increase as a result of exploiting the comparative advantage of members in the household. Although we did not speak specifically about these benefits within the context of marriage, it is easy to imagine that many of the trades that take place are more reliable and stable if the partners have made a long-term commitment to each other. For example, it makes more sense for a married couple to invest its joint resources so that one of the partners can move up the corporate ladder than it would for a less stable, cohabiting couple. In the latter situation, there is less incentive for partners to share the returns from their professional success. By contrast, in a married household, there is likely to be a legal obligation to do so, if only when it comes to dividing up the household's assets should the couple divorce.

The Economic Benefits of Marriage

The economic benefits associated with marriage go beyond the gains from trade between household partners. Marriage confers a unique legal status to partners in a variety of ways. Married partners can more easily adopt children, with each adoptive parent granted legal status with respect to the child. A person's Social Security retirement income includes an additional 50 percent in payments for spouses. Most employers offer subsidized health insurance and other benefits to spouses. And, in the event of a life-threatening health crisis, a marital partner has the right to make medical decisions for his or her spouse if the spouse is unable to do so. A surviving partner also does not have to pay estate taxes when his or her spouse dies. And when it comes to immigration, foreign spouses receive preferential treatment. This means that marriage conveys valuable rights, which undoubtedly explains the fight for the right to marry by nontraditional, same-sex couples.

With all of these benefits, why has marriage's popularity waned over the past several decades, to the point that it now accounts for a minority of all U.S. households?

The Impact of Women's Growing Educational and Work Opportunities

Most economists look to the exponential growth in women's educational and earnings opportunities as the primary explanation for the changing composition of households.[2] Women have generally outpaced men in both educational attainment and earnings growth since the 1970s. In decades past when relatively few women worked, they depended on their husbands' earnings to meet the household's market-based consumption needs. During this time, researchers D'Vera Cohn and Richard Fry (2010) contend that "marriage enhanced the economic status of women more than men." However, they argue that "In recent decades, the economic gains associated with marriage have been greater for men than for women." Men can now look forward to a second breadwinner who will increase the household's income and consumption opportunities.

Increasing Life Spans

A second phenomenon that has had a major impact on household living arrangements is the increase in people's life spans over the past 50 years. The life expectancy rate among individuals 65 years and older is steadily rising. While the number of persons in the United States under age 65 has tripled since 1900, the number of persons 65 or over has jumped by a factor of 11. Consequently, the over 65 population, which comprised only 1 in every 25 Americans in 1900, made up 1 in 8 a hundred years later. The fastest growing segment of this population has been among people age 85 and older. This group increased by 38 percent during the 1990s alone. In 1900, there were a mere 100,000 people in this age category. In 2008, there were 5.7 million.

As **Table 10A.2** shows, adults over 65 are the most likely age group to live alone. The percentage (30.1 percent) that lived alone in 2009 was more than double the percentage that lived alone in 1950 (13.7 percent).

· · · · · · ·

[2]D'Vera Cohn and Richard Fry, "Women, Men and the New Economics of Marriage." *Pew Social and Demographic Trends,* Pew Research Center, January 19, 2010.

Table 10A.2 Share of Adults Who Lived Alone in 2009	
Age Group	Percentage
18–29	7.3
30–49	9.5
50–64	15.6
65+	30.1

Source: Pew Research Center tabulations of Annual Social and Economic Supplement to the Current Population Survey, 2009, U.S. Census Bureau

In particular, women over the age of 65 are much more likely than men of the same age to live alone, in large part because wives tend to outlive their husbands. Currently, nearly four in ten older women live by themselves—more than double the proportion of older men who do so (38.8 percent versus 18.7 percent, respectively).

Reforming Divorce Laws

A final factor that has contributed significantly to the change in household living arrangements has been the reform of divorce laws, which began with the introduction of "no-fault" divorce in California in 1970 and slowly spread to the remaining 50 states by late 2010. No-fault divorce laws permit partners to dissolve their marriage without having to provide evidence of one another's wrongdoing or a breach of the marital contract. Currently, more than 80 percent of no-fault divorces are "unilateral," meaning that both partners have not consented to the divorce.

While the debate continues over the magnitude of the effect of unilateral divorce on divorce rates, there is general agreement that it has led to a decline in the duration of marriages. This, in turn, has fueled the growth in single-parent households: in 2009, more than half of all single mothers (53 percent) had been previously married.

PART 3: HOW CHANGES IN HOUSEHOLD COMPOSITION AFFECT HOUSEHOLD PRODUCTION AND INVESTMENTS IN CHILDREN

With the introduction of safe and effective birth control in the early 1960s, women were given the choice to delay their childbearing years and instead pursue educational and workplace opportunities. This, in turn, increased their earning power, which increased the opportunity cost of having children. Perhaps not surprisingly, as **Figure 10A.2** shows, the percentage of women ages 40–44 who have never had children has been climbing fairly steadily over the past two decades. In addition, the rate of childlessness among college graduates is now nearly 25 percent while among high-school graduates, it is only 18 percent. Whereas having children had once been a major motivation for getting married, this impetus has largely disappeared. This goes a long way toward explaining why the average size of U.S. households has been declining for decades—from 3.1 persons in 1960 to 2.6 in 2010—although the 2007 Great Recession has resulted in a 10 percent jump in multifamily households, partially offsetting this trend.[3]

Historically speaking, a major component of household production was childbearing and child-rearing, that is, investing in the human capital of one's children. With the decline in the number of children per household, we would expect a similar decline in the *total* time and money dedicated to child-rearing. However, it is unclear how changes in household composition have affected the amount invested per child.

· · · · · · · ·

[3]Gregory Warner, "Why Rent When You Can Nest?" *New York Times*, September 24, 2011.

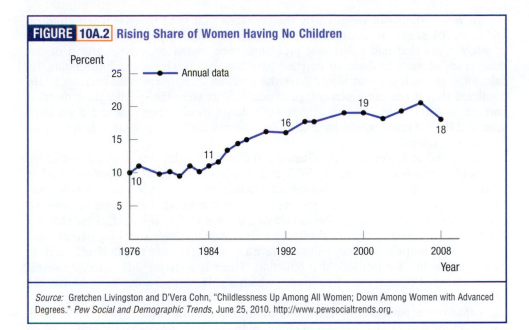

FIGURE 10A.2 **Rising Share of Women Having No Children**

Source: Gretchen Livingston and D'Vera Cohn, "Childlessness Up Among All Women; Down Among Women with Advanced Degrees." *Pew Social and Demographic Trends,* June 25, 2010. http://www.pewsocialtrends.org.

If there are fewer children in a household, for example, do they each receive a greater amount of parental investment? It turns out that this depends on the structure of the household. Ron Haskins, Senior Fellow at the Brookings Institution testified before Congress, stating that[4]

> Children do best when reared by their married parents. From this perspective, the trends in family composition in recent decades have been disastrous for children. Although most of the trends have stabilized in recent years, in previous decades, marriage rates fell, divorce rates rose, and nonmarital birth rates soared.
>
> Nonmarital births occur primarily among poor and minority women. In fact, children born to unmarried mothers are likely to live in poverty and to require support from the welfare system. Mothers who give birth outside marriage are also more likely to be high-school dropouts, to live in poverty, and to be unemployed, all of which are correlated with poor developmental outcomes for children.

One of the reasons suggested for the poor outcomes described by Haskins is that cohabiting and single parents tend to have less time and money to spend on each child. Single, working mothers are often stuck in low-wage jobs and may even pick up second jobs to meet the household's basic food and shelter requirements. They also tend to live in poorer neighborhoods that offer their children low-quality educational opportunities. Likewise, most divorced families experience enormous drops in income because of the financial drain of maintaining two households. Delinquencies in child-support payments exacerbate this problem. Researchers have found that the risk of children of divorced parents dropping out of high school nearly doubles, regardless of their household income prior to the divorce.[5]

· · · · · · · ·

[4]http://www.brookings.edu/views/testimony/haskins/20060503.pdf.

[5]Mary Parke, "Are Married Parents Really Better for Children?" *Center for Law and Social Policy*, 2003. http://www.clasp.org/admin/site/publications_states/files/0086.pdf.

To what extent can we quantify the problems that tend to arise when children are raised by single or divorced parents? Professor Paul Amato examined a group of adolescents that had behavioral problems; then, based on a comparison of the occurrence of each problem in married-parent versus single-parent households, he calculated the number that would have the problem if marriage rates increased.[6] He predicted that if the same percentage of adolescents were living with their married parents in 2002 as in 1980, nearly 300,000 fewer would have repeated a grade in school, 216,000 fewer would have been delinquents, and nearly 29,000 fewer would have attempted suicide.

According to Betsey Stevenson, unilateral divorce laws have created a disincentive for married couples to invest in children and other household production.[7] Rather than specializing in market or household production activities when it is economically appropriate to do so, both parents are more apt to work full-time to preserve their individual economic well-being should a divorce ensue. In effect, these married parents end up making choices similar to those made by single, working parents and single-person households: they will now have a greater tendency to substitute market-based production for household production. There is a major difference, however. Better-educated partners tend to marry, which significantly boosts their household earnings potential, whether separable or jointly. This translates into a greater financial capacity for outsourcing household production to the market, which preserves parental time that can be invested in children. In contrast, single-parent and cohabiting households tend to be poorer and are less likely to have the wherewithal to access high-quality market substitutes for meal preparation and other household tasks.

Researchers have found that working, single parents spend far less time preparing meals at home.[8] This means that government efforts to educate low-income households about the purchase of low-cost, healthy meals and to provide financial assistance to do this through food stamps is likely to be less effective when it comes to working, single-parent households. It is more likely that food stamps will be spent on labor-saving, convenient prepared foods, which often have low nutritional value and may even be unhealthy in terms of fat content, sodium, and so on.

In summary, then, changes in composition have tended to reduce household economic well-being. Households are now less able to exploit the gains from trade between their members, especially when there is only one adult reliably attached to the household. Moreover, because almost half of the children born in the United States are now born into single-parent or cohabiting households, there is a significant disparity in human capital investment in these children versus those raised in married households. At a time when income inequality has become a national concern, the changing composition of American households is likely to further exacerbate this inequality as children of single-parent households reach adulthood.

[6]Paul R. Amato, "The Impact of Family Formation Change on the Cognitive, Social, and Emotional Well-Being of the Next Generation." *The Future of Children*, 15, no. 2 (Fall 2005): 89, Table 2.

[7]Betsey Stevenson, "The Impact of Divorce Laws on Marriage-Specific Capital." *Journal of Labor Economics*, 25 (2007): 75–94.

[8]Lisa Mancino and Constance Newman, "Who Has Time to Cook?" *USDA Economic Research Report*, Number 40, May 2007.

Expenditure Decisions and the Income Elasticity of Demand

"Money frees you from doing things you dislike. Since I dislike doing nearly everything, money is handy."

Comedian Groucho Marx

As you have seen, the individual and household purchases people make are, by and large, limited by the amount of money they earn in the labor market. These earnings might be supplemented by savings, loans, gifts, prize winnings, government payments such as Social Security, and other "unearned" sources of money. The sum of a person's earned and unearned income is the amount he or she has available for market-based consumption at any given point in time.

Like any other good, income is scarce: most of us do not have as much as we would like. The first issue we address in this chapter is how a household makes its purchasing decisions. Are these decisions made jointly by all of its members? Does it matter who actually earns the money or who is responsible for household production? Does the type of relationship that exists between household members matter?

After we have explored the question of how purchasing decisions are made, we continue on to consider how changes in income impact these expenditure patterns. Within this context, we introduce an elasticity concept—*income elasticity of demand*—that looks much like the previous elasticity measures you have studied.

11.1 Making Household Purchasing Decisions

In our initial analysis of household behavior, we assumed that everyone shared the same objective: to maximize the household's overall well-being. You will recall that to accomplish this goal, members will allocate their time according to their comparative advantage and subsequently share their outputs with each other. In this world, it makes no difference which member actually earns income when it comes to predicting purchasing patterns. In effect, this approach treats the household as a single decision maker that makes decisions so as to maximize its well-being. We call this a **unitary model of the household**.

UNITARY MODEL OF THE HOUSEHOLD A predictive model which assumes that household members jointly pursue a commonly held set of objectives.

EXAMPLE The members of a farm family typically share a common goal—producing the largest crop yield possible each year.

EXAMPLE The members of many households share a common goal—owning their own homes.

When household decision making is consistent with this unitary model, we can use our economic model of individual choice to predict its behavior. However, adopting this unitary model for analyzing household decisions creates its own complications. How realistic is it to assume that members have objectives that are perfectly aligned with one another? If their goals are not exactly the same, how are these differences reconciled prior to making household decisions? Do all household members have equal "say" when it comes to market-based consumption, or does the member who earns the income or owns the household's assets have more "say" in how these resources are spent? To what extent do differences in objectives prevent the household from attaining an outcome that maximizes its overall well-being?

Well into the twentieth century, property-rights systems in the United States and elsewhere reinforced the commonly-held view that male heads of households were the primary (and typically only) household earners and should rightly serve as the primary decision makers when it came to household spending. In some countries, it was even illegal for women to own property in their own names. In more recent times, courts, legislatures, and society have come to realize that households are not simply run by the male "heads" of households. In fact, households are comprised of individuals, each with his or her own set of preferences, labor-market opportunities, and unearned income and assets. This realization has led to the development of more realistic economic models about household purchasing decisions.

Why does this matter to anyone outside of sociologists and historians? It turns out that producers of consumer goods are keenly interested in how household purchasing decisions are made—and who makes them—so that they can better target their marketing activities. For example, should a producer of household detergent run its television spots during televised Worldwide Wrestling matches, during evening sit-coms, or during *Ellen* in the afternoon? Will children's hospitals generate more patients and donors if they advertise in news magazines such as *Time* or *Newsweek*, in a glamour magazine such as *Vogue*, or in the local newspaper? Public policy makers are also interested in the household's purchasing-decision process when it comes to implementing policies that stimulate certain consumption activities and discourage others. What is the most effective way, for example, to increase child vaccination rates, reduce smoking, or increase purchases of hybrid cars? The answers to these questions depend crucially on who is actually making the purchasing decisions for the household.

A Divorce-Threat Model of Household Decision Making

It's reasonable to conclude that the adult members of a household have much in common with one another. Whether we are talking about elderly parents and adult children, husbands and wives, or longtime cohabiting partners, a decision process has already occurred that usually results in a more uniform set of values and objectives *within* the household than *outside* of it. Still, it is naive to assume that members' preferences are identical in all respects. For example, a husband might prefer to vacation at a remote resort that offers golf and surfing, whereas his wife might prefer to vacation in a major city with great restaurants, theaters, and shopping.

These differences in preferences may lead you to wonder whether the unitary model does a very good job of predicting household expenditure patterns. How can we incorporate differences in the preferences of household members to create a more powerful predictive model of household decision making?

To answer this, consider the following situation. Suppose we have two people—Sylvia and Morris—who are thinking about moving in together and forming a household. If they remain separate, each can achieve some level of personal or "economic" satisfaction that we have been calling well-being or *utility* (U). Let's define U_S^* as Sylvia's utility if she doesn't move in with Morris and U_M^* as Morris's utility if he doesn't move in with Sylvia.

Economics suggests that Sylvia and Morris will move in together only if they each believe that the utility they will get *after* the move is at least as great as *before* the move. This makes intuitive sense. Both Sylvia's and Morris's pre-move levels of satisfaction represent their opportunity cost of merging their households. If the benefit that Sylvia gets from moving in with Morris outweighs this opportunity cost, then she will opt to move in. Morris's decision process will be exactly the same. If *both* find it advantageous to move in together, then a new household is formed. Within this household, each partner gains well-being not only from the goods that each individually consumes, but from the shared consumption of such goods as companionship, love, a well-maintained home, children, and so on.

Suppose that Sylvia and Morris do decide to move in together. For them to remain together, they must each continue to achieve a level of well-being that is at least as great as if they were living separately (assuming they could return to their independent status at any time, at low cost). Economists call these minimum thresholds of well-being—U_S^* and U_M^*—**threat points**.[1]

THREAT POINT The minimum level of well-being that a person must receive to join and remain in a household.

EXAMPLE Ms. Smiley is a corporate CEO who has a well-paid, prestigious position at a marketing agency in Los Angeles. Her career is extremely important to her. It is unlikely that she would achieve or surpass her current level of well-being (her threat point) if she had to move elsewhere to live together with her partner.

A great deal of research has been done on the behavior of household members living in the "shadow of divorce." These studies assume that each member continually re-evaluates her level of well-being within the household relative to her threat point and, based on the result, decides whether to remain in the household or obtain a divorce. Economists call this behavioral model a **divorce-threat bargaining model** of the household.

DIVORCE-THREAT BARGAINING MODEL A behavioral model in which household resources are allocated so that each member receives at least as much well-being as what could be obtained by leaving the household.

. . . .

[1]Shelley Lundberg and Robert Pollack, "Bargaining and Distribution in Marriage." *Journal of Economic Perspectives*, (Fall, 1996): 139–158.

While the term "divorce" is used in popular parlance to refer to the dissolution of a marriage, the divorce-threat bargaining model can be applied to other household-like situations as well—adult parent and adult child, cohabiting adults, college roommates, and so on. It can even be applied to business partnerships.

The goodness of the divorce-threat model in predicting a household's choices depends crucially on the assumption that divorce is an option for either partner at any time, at relatively low cost. This will be true when there is no legally enforceable or social obligation to remain together. However, when partners are bound by legal or religious requirements that commit them to each other in some way, the cost of exiting the relationship can be significant. The cost of dissolving a marriage depends on prevailing social norms and the legal environment, as well as on the provisions of a prenuptial contract, if one exists. Some countries and religious communities permit only the husband to initiate divorce proceedings. When this is the case, a married woman's divorce threat is not credible, and her bargaining power within the household with respect to the allocation of resources is severely compromised.

In the United States and elsewhere, divorce laws have changed markedly over the past 50 years. A major change has been the introduction of "no-fault" divorces, which do not require parties to document the grounds for divorce—abandonment, adultery, and so forth. In 1970, California enacted no-fault divorce laws, which spread quickly throughout the country. This has dramatically reduced the cost of one partner exiting a marriage unilaterally. In 1960, 16 percent of first marriages in the United States ended in divorce; by 1996, it rose to almost 50 percent. Within five years after no-fault divorce was first introduced, the national divorce rate increased to almost 40 percent.[2]

Along with reducing the cost of getting a divorce, these changes in law slashed the financial obligations of one ex-partner to the other. In most cases, alimony—long-term financial support for an ex-spouse until she remarried—was no longer awarded. This has had a profound impact on each partner's threat point because it has changed the level of well-being each could expect should there be a divorce. The well-being of the partner who would have paid alimony has increased, while the well-being of the ex-spouse who would have received alimony has decreased. Changes in state laws related to the distribution of marital property have also affected the post-divorce well-being of household partners. Perhaps it is not surprising that the introduction of no-fault divorce has been identified as a major contributor to the rise in poverty among women, especially those with children. According to the sociologist Alice Rossi, "millions of women are [now] a divorce away from destitution."[3]

SOLVED PROBLEM

Q According to the divorce-threat bargaining model, children have no bargaining power in a family because the opportunities they face outside the household are fairly bleak-they would become wards of the state (this assumes that they are not physically abused in the household). Yet we know that children have a lot of "say" in the family as to how the household's resources are spent. Does this mean that the model is a poor predictor of actual behavior?

A Children bestow a great deal of happiness upon parents—they are consumption goods of a sort. It's been said that a parent is only as happy as her least happy child.

. . . .

[2]Elizabeth Schoenfeld, "Drumbeat for Divorce Reform." *Policy Review* (May/June, 1996).

[3]Alice Rossi, "Destitution Is Just a Divorce Away." *New York Times,* April 27, 1986.

So parents will go to great lengths to make their children happy even though these kids have no real bargaining power in the household. Children do not make decisions about whether a household will remain intact or dissolve, which is what the divorce-threat bargaining model focuses on. However, they do direct resources to the extent that what makes them happy makes their parents happy. If you had parents who really didn't care about whether you were happy or not, then only your parents would have a say in how the resources of the household are directed, based on their relative bargaining power.

Determinants of Threat Points

A partner's threat point depends on the opportunities she would enjoy outside of the current household. The attractiveness of these alternatives, in terms of generating well-being, depends on the person's earning potential, the possibility of other living arrangements (e.g., whether she can go home to mom), prospects for attracting another partner, her privately owned assets, the availability of government transfer payments, and so forth.

What this means is that the property-rights system within which the household operates is crucially important when it comes to determining each partner's threat point. We have already mentioned the impact of discriminatory divorce laws on women's threat points. If women have only limited labor-market opportunities or cannot own certain types of assets, then their threat points will also be lower than otherwise. The explosive growth in educational and workforce opportunities since the mid-twentieth century has greatly increased the threat points of women in most countries. The introduction of reliable birth-control technologies has had a similar effect in that they permit women to be less dependent on the earnings of their partners.

A Household's Utility Possibilities Frontier

Figure 11.1 indicates the maximum amount of well-being that Morris and Sylvia can each attain from their joint resources if they form a household; this is called their *utility possibilities frontier*. It looks a lot like the production possibilities frontier (PPF) first introduced in Chapter 10. Notice that after Morris and Sylvia are on this frontier, any move from one point to another will make one partner better off at the expense of the other. For example, a move from point B to point A will improve Morris's well-being at the expense of Sylvia's. Conversely, a move to point B to point C will improve Sylvia's well-being at the expense of Morris's. As in the case of a production possibilities frontier, outcomes inside the frontier—point D—are "inefficient." At point D, there are ways to redeploy the resources of the household to achieve higher levels of well-being for both members or for one member without making the other worse off.

Each partner's threat point is also shown. These are designated by points E and F. At no time will *both* partners agree to "bundles" of personal well-being that are located along the frontier beyond these threat points.

Cooperative Bargaining Outcome

How can Morris and Sylvia assure themselves that they are allocating their scarce resources in a way that puts them on their frontier and not inside it? Suppose, for example, that it makes economic sense for Morris to stay home and specialize

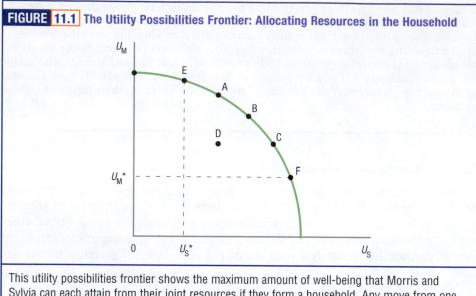

FIGURE 11.1 The Utility Possibilities Frontier: Allocating Resources in the Household

This utility possibilities frontier shows the maximum amount of well-being that Morris and Sylvia can each attain from their joint resources if they form a household. Any move from one point to another along the frontier—say, from A to B—will make one partner better off at the expense of the other. They won't choose point D: it is "inefficient" because there are ways to redeploy the resources of the household to achieve higher levels of well-being for both members or for one member without making the other worse off. Points E and F reflect the individual partners' threat points. At no time will *both* partners agree to "bundles" of well-being along the frontier beyond these points.

in unpaid household production and for Sylvia to go to work to earn income to buy consumables. As you will recall, the potential gains from this type of specialization were explored in the previous chapter. If they both go to work and both engage in household production, they may end up at outcome D, that is, an outcome that is inefficient because each person's comparative advantage has been ignored and, therefore, the *total* well-being of the two partners together is not maximized.

What will it take for both partners to agree to specialize according to their comparative advantage? It turns out that Morris and Sylvia are more likely to behave this way if they have agreed in advance about how they will share the gains that arise from specialization. Will they move from outcome D to outcome A, B, or C on the frontier? Clearly, this will matter because it determines how the gains from "trade" are shared within household. As we will see later, this is where the bargaining power of each partner comes into play.

Morris and Sylvia must not only agree on how they will share in each other's production, but this "understanding" must be enforceable. Consider what would happen if Sylvia is the sole breadwinner in the household and earns her MBA courtesy of her employer. At the same time, Morris stays home and prepares all of Sylvia's meals, takes care of the kids, and keeps Sylvia's clothes clean and pressed. Is there an enforceable agreement that says that Sylvia owes Morris a share of the future earnings arising from her MBA degree, whether they stay together in the future or not? When such understandings exist and are enforceable, a **cooperative outcome** can come about that puts the partnership on its utility possibilities frontier.

> **COOPERATIVE OUTCOME** An allocation of resources that is based on a voluntary, enforceable agreement about how the resulting net benefits will be shared.

It is not unusual for these implicit marital agreements to be "tested" when a household dissolves. When the legendary CEO of GE—Jack Welch—filed for divorce from his wife of 13 years, she asked for half of the property and earnings that he had accumulated during the marriage. She argued that she had specialized in unpaid household production—raising the children and entertaining business associates—which contributed to her ex-husband's financial success. Unfortunately for both partners, there was apparently no enforceable understanding between the two of them about the division of wealth upon divorce. This meant that a judge had to determine an equitable distribution of the couple's wealth. Given the uncertainty that this posed for both partners, the Welches settled just prior to trial.[4]

John Nash, Nobel Laureate and the central character in the movie *A Beautiful Mind,* discovered that if household partners deploy their resources to maximize *the product of the additional well-being* they each receive beyond their threat points, the household will always be on its utility possibility frontier. This is called a **Nash bargaining solution**.

> **NASH BARGAINING SOLUTION** A bargaining outcome such that there is no way to reallocate resources to make someone better off without making someone else worse off; an outcome that is on the utility possibilities frontier.

Of course, no one expects that Morris and Sylvia will negotiate according to Nash's "rule" before they use the resources at their disposal. The important point here is that if they *do* end up on their utility frontier, their allocation of resources will achieve Nash's bargaining solution.

Even if a couple reaches their utility frontier, there are any number of outcomes still possible, represented by the segment of the utility frontier lying between the threat points. Morris would like to be higher up on the curve, while Sylvia would like to be lower on the curve. The bargaining power of each person will ultimately determine where they "land" on the frontier. This in no way implies that household members fight "to the death" or bargain ferociously over every household decision. Still, the bargaining power of each person in a household is likely to contribute to how important family decisions get made—such as whether the household purchases a two-seater convertible or a minivan, relocates in Los Angeles or Minneapolis, or has one or two children.

The Source of Bargaining Power

What determines a person's bargaining power? It turns out that this power is derived from the threat point itself. A partner who can achieve high levels of utility *outside* the household will have more bargaining power *inside* the household. Consider the bargaining power of a Hollywood star that moves in with her hairdresser. Unless the hairdresser is quickly elevated to star status (which actually did occur when Barbra Streisand's hairdresser-partner of ten years, Jon Peters, became a prominent movie

· · · · · · ·

[4]Del Jones, "Welches Reach Divorce Settlement Before Trial Begins." *USA Today,* July 3, 2003.

producer), his bargaining power in the relationship will pale in comparison to his movie-star partner. This means that the star will be able to exert greater control over the resources of the household and purchasing decisions. Notice that this is not because the star actually earns more income; indeed, she may have decided to take a hiatus from acting to enjoy her new relationship. Rather, it is because the star's threat point—which is a function of what she *could* earn—is substantially higher. In other words, she doesn't have to actually earn income to be in control of the household's resources. In fact, it turns out that in many households, money management is the primary responsibility of the person specializing in household production who isn't earning any income at all.

While *actual* earnings do not affect a partner's bargaining power, it's a different story when it comes to actual asset holdings. The greater the wealth that a partner individually holds, the greater his threat point and bargaining power will be. This is the case because a partner's well-being if he left the household is a function of the amount of assets under his sole control. By assets, we mean not only financial assets and land, but the value of the person's human capital as well. Advanced educational degrees, professional credentials, personal reputation, and physical fitness all enhance the value of this human capital and the well-being of a partner should he leave the household.

A number of studies have examined household purchasing patterns in relationship to which partner owns assets or receives government assistance. These researchers have found that children fare better in households in which mothers control more of the household resources.[5] A recent study of households in Ghana found that as the fraction of household assets owned by women grew, so did the percent of income devoted to food. A smaller percent was spent on alcohol, tobacco, and recreation. For every 1 percent increase in the total household assets owned by women, food purchases increased by almost one full day of consumption a month.[6,7]

Household Production and Bargaining Power

Each partner's efficiency in household production may also translate into bargaining power.[8] Suppose, for example, that Sylvia is a gourmet cook and for this reason assumes the primary responsibility for meal preparation. She is much more productive—as measured by the quality and quantity of meals prepared during a given time period—than Morris. This will increase Sylvia's bargaining power; Morris's bargaining power is diminished to the extent that he values these meals and cannot easily replace them if he were to leave the household. Of course, if he could find low-cost substitutes for Sylvia's cooking—at the gourmet bistro down the street or through another partner who is just as productive as Sylvia in the kitchen—his bargaining power would not be diminished much by Sylvia's extraordinary cooking skills.

. . . .

[5]Shelley Lundberg and Robert Pollack, "The American Family and Family Economics." *Journal of Economic Perspectives,* 21, no. 2 (2007).

[6]Cheryl Doss, "Testing Among Models of Intrahousehold Resource Allocation." *World Development,* 24, no. 10 (1996).

[7]Cheryl Doss, "Conceptualizing and Measuring Bargaining Power within the Household." In Karine Moe, *Women, Family and Work: Writings on the Economics of Gender* (Malden, MA: Blackwell. Publishers, 2003).

[8]Robert Pollack, "Bargaining Power in Marriage: Earnings, Wage Rates and Household Production." *NBER Working Paper* 11239, National Bureau of Economic Research, Inc., March, 2005.

Noncooperative Outcomes

What if partners can't come to a voluntary, enforceable agreement about how the gains from trade will be shared? In such a situation, each person is likely to make choices independent of the other to maximize his own well-being. This behavior tends to lead to an inefficient outcome, like D. Still, as long as D delivers a level of well-being greater than each member's threat point, the partnership will remain intact. However, the "wrong" mix of household-based and market-based production will likely occur; each member will work and contribute to household production based on his own sense of well-being. The end result may be too few children, too little investment in education, too little earned income in total, and so on. We call this a **noncooperative outcome**.

> **NONCOOPERATIVE OUTCOME** The allocation of resources that results in the absence of an enforceable agreement about how the gains from trade will be shared.

What a noncooperative outcome means in economic terms is that the parties do not work together to exploit each other's comparative advantage. A noncooperative outcome doesn't necessarily suggest that there will be marital discord within the household. It simply means that each member acts independent of the other when it comes to allocating the scarce resources they each control. This is, in effect, how most college roommates act: they come and go as they like, fix their own meals, empty the trash when they see fit, keep their rooms in whatever state of order they prefer, and so on. This is not to say that roommates don't gain well-being from living together. By splitting the rent, the cost of the big-screen TV and one set of living room furniture, their individual well-being increases over what it would be if they lived alone. However, they are likely not to have an enforceable agreement about who performs specific tasks on behalf of the household, nor will they share their earnings to increase each other's well-being.

11.2 How Changes in Income Affect Household Purchases

Let's assume that the bargaining power of members in the household remains constant. How would we expect changes in total income to affect the household's expenditure patterns? We know, for example, that families operating at a minimum level of subsistence must commit all of their resources to such basic "needs" as water, housing, and food. However, as people's incomes increase, the quality and quantity of goods they purchase change. For example, higher-income households purchase more fresh vegetables and fruits and less canned or frozen substitutes. Likewise, they consume more fresh fish and meat and less pasta and potatoes. In fact, a whole host of additional goods can be purchased when household incomes increase beyond subsistence level. Economists have long been interested in the impact that changes in income have on the purchase of various goods and services in the marketplace.

The Engel's Curve

One of the first researchers to study the relationship between household income and purchases was a German statistician by the name of Ernst Engel. Engel was interested in finding out how a family's food purchases changed when income changed. Based on data that he collected, he graphed family income on the horizontal axis and the amount of food purchased on the vertical axis. A more general version of this graph—which shows how purchases of a specific good change with income—is now commonly called an **Engel's curve**.

> **ENGEL'S CURVE** A graph that shows the relationship between income and the quantity of a good purchased.

Panel (a) of **Figure 11.2** presents two Engel's curves—one positively sloped and the other negatively sloped. The positively sloped curve tells us that the quantity of the good purchased *increases* with income. As you may recall from Chapter 6, this means that the good is a normal good. The negatively sloped curve indicates that the quantity purchased *decreases* with increases in income, which means that the good is an inferior good.

What did Engel's work reveal about family food purchases? Not surprisingly, he found that food is a normal good. However, food purchases do not keep pace with a family's increase in income. Graphically, this translates into an Engel's curve that is upward sloping but with a slope that diminishes as income increases. This is illustrated in panel (b) of Figure 11.2. What this means is that, at some income level, the percentage of the family's income spent on food will actually begin to fall. The family can only eat so much food after all.

Marketing firms focus a great deal of attention on the Engel's curves for products they promote. By understanding how a consumer's purchases change with income, marketers can more precisely target their placement of advertising and their location of new retail outlets. Payday-loan offices and bakery outlet stores, for example, tend

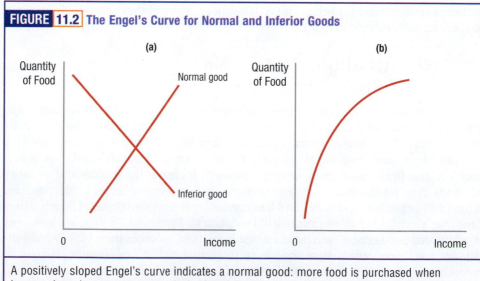

FIGURE 11.2 The Engel's Curve for Normal and Inferior Goods

A positively sloped Engel's curve indicates a normal good: more food is purchased when income rises. In contrast, a negatively sloped Engel's curve represents an inferior good: less is purchased as income rises. Engel found that food is a normal good but that the amount purchased does not keep pace with a family's increase in income. This translates into the Engel's curve in panel (b), which has an upward slope that diminishes as the family's income increases.

to be located in areas populated with lower-income households, while fur centers and LASIK eye surgery centers tend to locate in higher-income neighborhoods. For corporate decision makers, the Engel's curve tells them how sales volume will fare during recessions (periods of slow income growth and high unemployment) versus economic expansions (periods of robust income growth), thereby providing crucial information for plant- and equipment-investment decisions.

NPD Group—a market research firm—recently studied the ways that mothers spend money on their children. Not surprisingly, the researchers found that mothers in poorer households spend a higher percentage of their income on their children. They also reported that 51 percent of mothers with household incomes below $35,000 spent at least 5.5 percent of their income on fast food, books, clothing, movies, and video games for their youngest child. In contrast, only 10 percent of mothers with household incomes of $75,000 or more spent at least 5.5 percent of income on similar purchases for their youngest child.[9]

11.3 Income Elasticity of Demand

In Chapter 6, we introduced and distinguished between inferior and normal goods. This distinction tells us the directionality of the shift in the demand curve when income changes: it shifts to the left for a normal good when income goes down, to the right for an inferior good when income goes down, and so on.

The question that naturally arises is whether there is a more precise way to measure the extent to which purchases of a good change when there is a change in income. For example, how many more university credit hours would you "buy" if your family's income increased by $10,000 a year? How many fewer pizzas would you order per month if your work hours—and resulting income—are cut back by 20 percent? How much more (or less) total consumption will occur in response to a tax rebate of $1,600 for all U.S. families versus a $2,500 tax rebate only for families earning less than $60,000 a year?

To isolate the impact of income changes on purchases, we must be able to track the quantity of a good purchased when a household's income rises and falls—all the while holding prices and people's preferences constant. This is not an easy task. First of all, we know that over the course of their lives, people spend their income differently. As shown in **Figure 11.3**, young adults tend to borrow money, which they invest in education, cars, and so forth. As a result, their savings are negative at this point in their lives. In contrast, people tend to save more money up through their middle-age years. At the same time, they spend more on durable goods, such as furniture and appliances. Once they are empty nesters, household partners spend more on such things as vacations and health care. To assess the impact of income changes on purchases, we must be able to somehow "control for" this life cycle effect on consumption patterns.

Other kinds of problems arise when we try to estimate the impact of income changes on purchases by looking *across* households with different levels of income. The problem with this approach is that we know that different people have different preferences that affect the way they respond to changes in their income: a vegan will not eat filet mignon no matter how great his income grows. Therefore, we cannot accurately assess the impact of changes in income on the demand for specific products unless we are able to control for differences in preferences that exist across households.

· · · · · · ·

[9]Alex Mindlin, "Fast Food's Portion of Parents' Dollars." *New York Times*, June 2, 2008, p. C4.

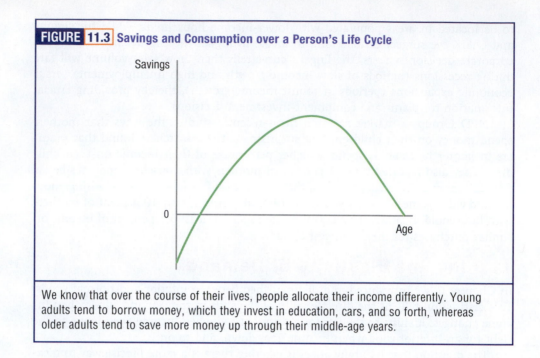

FIGURE 11.3 Savings and Consumption over a Person's Life Cycle

We know that over the course of their lives, people allocate their income differently. Young adults tend to borrow money, which they invest in education, cars, and so forth, whereas older adults tend to save more money up through their middle-age years.

Suppose we can overcome these types of estimation problems. We can then measure the impact that changes in income have on the quantity of a good purchased using a metric that has much in common with a measure we introduced in Chapter 9—price elasticity of demand. We call this new measure **income elasticity of demand**.

INCOME ELASTICITY OF DEMAND (ε_I) The percentage change in the quantity of a good purchased in response to a percentage change in income, holding everything else constant.

EXAMPLE A person gets a raise, and her salary increases from $28,000 to $30,000. She spends some of the raise on a new pair of jogging shoes, increasing her collection from two to three pairs. Her income elasticity of demand with respect to jogging shoes is

$$\text{INCOME ELASTICITY OF DEMAND} = \frac{(3 - 2) / 2}{(\$30,000 - \$28,000) / \$28,000} = 7$$

As this example demonstrates, we compute income elasticity in much the same way we have calculated all of our previous elasticity measures. Using I to represent income, we have

Income Elasticity of Demand =

$$\frac{\% \text{ change in Quantity Demanded}}{\% \text{ change in Income}} = \frac{(Q_2 - Q_1) / Q_1}{(I_2 - I_1) / I_1}$$

For large changes in income, we can apply the midpoint computational method previously introduced for price elasticity, where the "base" for computing the percentage changes in quantity and income is the midpoint of Q and I, respectively. That is,

$$\text{Midpoint } \varepsilon_I = \frac{(Q_2 - Q_1) / (Q_1 + Q_2) / 2}{(I_2 - I_1) / (I_1 + I_2) / 2}$$

Like the price elasticity of demand, income elasticity of demand is an index number, free from any units. This means that we can compare the *relative* sensitivity of demand to income changes for a variety of goods. Is there, for example, greater income sensitivity when it comes to buying eyeglasses, contact lenses, or laser vision-correction surgery?

We already know a lot about the income elasticity of demand from our earlier discussion about normal and inferior goods in Chapter 6. When people's purchases of a good go up as their income increases, this good is a normal good. By contrast, when people's incomes go up, and the quantity demanded goes down, this good is an inferior good. What this means is that the numerator and denominator of the income elasticity calculation must *move in the same direction* if a good is normal, and they must move *in the opposite direction* if a good is inferior. To see this, consider the case where income increases by 20 percent and a person's demand for new books goes up by 10 percent, yielding an income elasticity of ½. Both income and quantity demanded increase, which means that both the numerator and denominator of the income elasticity measure have the same positive sign, resulting in a positive income elasticity measure. Since both income and new book purchases grew, a new book must be a normal good. Compare this to the demand for used books, where the same 20 percent increase in income leads to a 15 percent decline in the quantity of used books purchased. The numerator of the income elasticity measure is negative while the denominator is positive, resulting in a negative income elasticity of $-3/4$. When the income elasticity of demand is negative, the consumer perceives that the good is inferior.

This tells us that the *sign* of the income elasticity of demand is important because it tells us whether a good is inferior or normal. If it is negative, then the good is an inferior good; if it is positive, then the good is a normal good. That is,

If income elasticity of demand ≥ 0, the good is **normal**.

If income elasticity of demand < 0, the good is **inferior**.

Some normal goods exhibit a very high income elasticity of demand, meaning that when people's incomes rise, there is a disproportionate response in terms of increased purchases. If a 10 percent increase in income leads to an 80 percent increase in the quantity of gold jewelry that is purchased, then the income elasticity of demand for gold jewelry is 8. We sometimes refer to these goods as *superior* or *luxury* goods. Researchers have found that when incomes rise, people tend to buy luxury goods that are more "conspicuous" and thereby convey status, such as Rolex watches and Coach handbags.[10]

In contrast, the income elasticity of demand for many goods may be quite low or even zero. These goods are often referred to as *necessities* because the quantity purchased is much less dependent on income. Some of these necessities—such as toilet paper or life-saving medications—also tend to be price inelastic.

· · · · · · ·

[10]Alan Krueger, "Doctoral Thesis Says Rich People Spend More on Conspicuous Things." *New York Times*, January 6, 2005.

SOLVED PROBLEM

Q Suppose that you budget $100 a month to spend on movies, popcorn, and soda at your local theater. When your income goes up by 10 percent, you increase this amount to $120 a month, spending the extra money on a second movie (a double feature) that you see whenever you go to the theater. Your popcorn and soda refills are free. What is your income elasticity of demand for movies? For popcorn and soda?

A The number of movie tickets you buy increases, which tells us that movies are a normal good, with an income elasticity of demand greater than zero. What else does your behavior tell us about your income elasticity of demand for tickets? If your income rises and you don't spend any more on popcorn and soda—because you don't increase your number of theater visits and refills are free—then the income elasticity of demand for these products is *zero* (the numerator of the elasticity computation is zero). This means that more income ($20 more, to be precise) is spent on movie tickets. This must be more than a 20 percent increase because you were initially spending no more than $100 on tickets (and quite likely, less because you like popcorn and soda). So we know that your income elasticity of demand for tickets is greater than 1.

11.4 The Relationship Between Income Elasticity and Expenditures on a Good

The magnitude of a good's income elasticity of demand yields important information about how individuals and households budget for that good. That is, it tells us how the fraction—or share—of income spent on the good changes when income changes. We call this the good's **budget share**.

> **BUDGET SHARE** The fraction of income spent on a particular good or category of goods.

> **EXAMPLE** The religious principle of "tithing" expects that 10 percent of a person's income will be given to the church, irrespective of income level.

> **EXAMPLE** Some families budget a certain percentage—say 5 percent—of their income for eating out each month. Other families may increase this percentage when their incomes increase.

As you recall, Engel found that as a family's income rises, the budget share dedicated to food begins to decline at some point. In other words, while the quantity of food purchased increases as incomes grow, this increase does not keep pace with the growth in income. We can generalize this result: the budget share allocated to goods that are *necessities* tends to fall at some point as income rises. It turns out, as we will see next, these goods exhibit an income elasticity of demand that is less than one.

Unitary Income Elasticity of Demand

If you look back at the equation for income elasticity, you will see that this measure can only equal 1 if the percentage change in quantity demanded of a good (the numerator of the income elasticity measure) exactly equals the percentage change in income (the denominator). So, for example, the demand for movie tickets would be unitary elastic if, when incomes rise by 10 percent, the *number* of tickets demanded also rises by 10 percent. Conversely, when incomes fall by 10 percent, the number of tickets demanded falls by 10 percent.

What does this tell us about the percentage of income that is dedicated to movie tickets when a household's income changes? Because the change in the quantity of tickets demanded always just keeps pace with the change in income, the household's budget share dedicated to movie tickets remains constant. (This assumes that the price of movies and other goods doesn't change.) In this case, we say that the good exhibits **unitary income elasticity**. The same fraction of income is always spent on unitary elastic goods regardless of income level.

UNITARY INCOME ELASTICITY A situation in which the quantity of a good purchased grows or declines at the same rate as any change in income, all else remaining unchanged. Unitary income elastic goods account for a fixed budget share at all levels of income.

EXAMPLE The typical rule of thumb in the mortgage-lending industry is for people to budget 27 percent of their income for housing. If people follow this rule, then housing will exhibit unitary income elasticity of demand. When incomes increase by 10 percent, for example, the quantity of housing demanded will likewise increase by 10 percent, so that 27 percent of the total income is always spent on housing. When incomes fall by 10 percent, the reverse will occur.

If you allocate the same *percentage* of your income each month to each of your budget categories—food, clothing, insurance, education, and so forth—regardless of your total income, then you are acting in a unitary elastic way. The same holds true for a company that always allocates the same percentage of its total budget to various cost categories, such as advertising, employee benefits, and travel, regardless of its total expenditures.

SOLVED PROBLEM

Q Suppose that dining at fast-food restaurants is a unitary elastic good. Show, using supply and demand curves, the impact of (1) an economic expansion on the equilibrium price and quantity in the fast-food restaurant market. (2) What happens if instead there is a recession? (3) Show the impact of an economic expansion and recession on microwaveable dinners, a less-preferred substitute for dining out.

A The demand curve for dining out shifts to the right during an expansion as shown in panel (a) of the following figure. The price and quantity increase such that the new ($P \times Q$) corresponds to the same *share* of income people spent in restaurants before the expansion. Conversely, as panel (b) shows, the demand curve for fast food shifts to the left during a recession. The price and quantity decrease such that the new ($P \times Q$) corresponds to the same *share* of income people spent in restaurants before the recession.

A recession will translate into a rightward shift in the demand curve in the microwaveable-dinner market. The share of income spent on microwaveable dinners must decline during an expansion and increase during a contraction if they are perceived to be inferior goods.

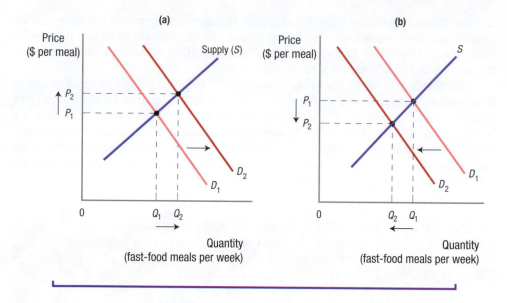

When the Income Elasticity of Demand Is Greater Than One

What if the income elasticity of demand is greater than one? In this case, the percentage change in the quantity demanded of a good (the numerator of our income elasticity measure) is greater than the percentage change in income (the denominator). This means that when incomes rise by 10 percent, the quantity of the good demanded rises by more than 10 percent. Conversely, when incomes fall by 10 percent, the quantity demanded falls by more than 10 percent. As a result, the share of income spent on the good increases when incomes grow and declines when incomes fall. We call these **income elastic goods**.

> **INCOME ELASTIC GOOD** A situation in which the quantity of a good purchased increases more, percentage-wise, than the corresponding percentage increase in income; and, conversely, where the quantity of a good purchased decreases more, percentage-wise, than the corresponding percentage decrease in income.

> **EXAMPLE** Select cuts of beef, brand-name footwear, jewelry, and airline travel tend to be income elastic goods.

The higher the value of the income elasticity of demand, the more sensitive the quantity purchased is to changes in income.

As we have already mentioned, products with high income elasticities of demand are called luxury goods. It is interesting to note that some luxury goods at the turn of the twentieth century have lost this status because of technological changes that have occurred since then. For example, at one time, only the wealthiest households enjoyed fresh fruit and vegetables year-round because it was costly to transport produce from far away growers when it was out-of-season locally. Instead, most people consumed canned, frozen, and preserved fruits and vegetables when fresh alternatives were unavailable from local growers. With the introduction of refrigerated transport—train cars and trucks—as well as the development of a national highway system, more and more families now enjoy fresh produce all year long, irrespective of their incomes or location. What once were luxury goods became normal goods, courtesy of technological innovations.[11]

The share of income that households spend on income elastic goods tends to rise during economic expansions. During recessions, it falls. When a recession sets in, some people expect that their incomes will fall due to the threat of unemployment or wage cuts. In response, they reduce their purchases of income elastic goods by more than their income actually falls. This is why we see that the first whiff of recession is accompanied by a decline in the stock prices of companies that produce luxury goods (Tiffany & Co., Royal Caribbean Cruises, Coach, etc.). This reflects investor sentiment that these companies will experience declines in sales volume and profits when the recession finally takes hold.

When the Income Elasticity of Demand Is Less Than One

Building on our previous results, we can see that when a good's income elasticity is between 0 and 1, we are still talking about a normal good but one where the numerator of the income elasticity measure is less than the denominator. This means that when income grows, the percentage increase in the quantity of the good demanded is less than the percentage increase in income. Conversely, when income falls, the percentage decrease in quantity demanded is less than the percentage decrease in income. This means that if income rises by 10 percent, the quantity demanded will rise by less than 10 percent, and if income falls by 10 percent, the quantity demanded will fall by less than 10 percent. As a result, the budget share of the good declines when income increases and increases when income falls. This is most often the case with consumer staples that people cannot easily do without, such as the basic foodstuffs that Engel studied. We say that these goods exhibit income inelastic demand or are **income inelastic goods**.

> **INCOME INELASTIC GOOD** A situation in which the quantity of a good purchased decreases less, percentage-wise, than the corresponding percentage decrease in income; and, conversely, where the quantity of the good purchased increases less, percentage-wise, than the corresponding percentage increase in income.

> **EXAMPLE** Diapers, toilet paper, and milk tend to be necessities that exhibit income inelastic demand.

Although consumer "staples" such as basic foodstuffs tend to be income inelastic, specific items within this category can actually be quite income elastic. Chicken breasts tend to be income elastic, whereas chicken thighs and legs tend to be income inelastic. Fresh food products are typically income elastic, whereas frozen or canned alternatives are income inelastic or may even exhibit a negative income elasticity of demand (i.e., be inferior goods). And, there may be a disproportionate increase in purchases of income elastic brand-name products such as Charmin toilet paper, Pampers diapers, and so on when incomes rise, whereas their generic substitutes exhibit income inelastic (or negative) income elasticity.

· · · · · · · ·

[11]Carolyn Shaw Bell, *Consumer Choice in the American Economy* (New York: Random House, 1967).

The demand for income inelastic goods will not increase dramatically in an economic expansion, nor contract substantially in an economic downturn. We also expect that there won't be a great deal of variation in consumption patterns for inelastic goods across people in different income classes. As a result, the stock prices of companies that make consumer staples—such as General Mills (cereals), Clorox (bleach), and Anheuser InBev (beer)—rise at the beginning of a recession because stock buyers know that these companies will be the least adversely impacted in terms of declining sales and earnings. This investing behavior is often referred to as a "flight to safety."

When the Income Elasticity of Demand Equals Zero

There are a handful of goods, at most, that exhibit an income elasticity of zero. When this is the case, the numerator of the income elasticity measure must equal zero. This means that there is no change in the quantity demanded of the good when there is a change in income. We call these **perfectly income inelastic goods**.

PERFECTLY INCOME INELASTIC GOOD A situation in which the quantity of a good purchased remains unchanged when there is an increase or decrease in income.

EXAMPLE Prescription drugs such as insulin tend to approximate perfectly income inelastic goods.

EXAMPLE For some people, their morning coffee at Starbucks approximates a perfectly income inelastic good.

What characterizes a perfectly income inelastic good is that the quantity of the good purchased does not change when a household's income changes, which means that the budget share dedicated to the good will go down when a household's income rises, and up when it falls. In reality, it is very difficult to find a good that is perfectly income inelastic. Even in the case of prescription drugs, researchers have found that some consumers delay refilling prescriptions or skip doses when their incomes fall, such as during the 2007 Great Recession.[12]

Table 11.1 reports the estimated income elasticity of demand for a wide range of goods, listed in decreasing order of magnitude. It should come as no surprise that wine is highly income elastic: when household incomes increase by 1 percent, the consumption of wine increases by almost 2.6 percent. In contrast, the consumption of pork increases by only 0.14 percent.

People can differ in terms of their income elasticity of demand for the same good, even when they have the very same incomes, because income elasticity depends on personal preferences. We often observe, for example, that cross-country cultural differences lead to differences in cross-country income elasticities of demand. As **Table 11.2** reveals, chocolate is an income elastic good in Switzerland: for every 1 percent increase in income, chocolate consumption rises by 1.06 percent. In contrast, it is highly inelastic in Japan, where a 1 percent increase in income leads to a mere 0.08 percent increase in chocolate consumption.

· · · · · · ·

[12]Walecia Konrad, "Health Care You Can't Afford to Not Afford." *New York Times,* January 16, 2009.

Table 11.1   The Income Elasticity of Demand for Various Products

Income Elastic Goods	Estimated Income Elasticity
Wine	2.59
Transatlantic air travel	1.91
Audio, video equipment	1.71
Recreation	1.42
Medical care	1.35
Beef	1.06
Income Inelastic Goods	
Clothing/footwear	0.88
Gasoline	0.60
Cigarettes	0.50
Beer	0.46
Chicken	0.28
Pork	0.14
Inferior Goods*	
Bread	−0.08

Sources: Taylor, *Principles of Microeconomics*, p. 98
Mansfield and Yohe, *Microeconomics*, p. 76
Salvatore, *Microeconomics*, p. 138
*As reported by Carolyn Shaw Bell (1967) for high-income nonfarm families in 1955.

Table 11.2   Cross-Cultural Differences and the Income Elasticity of Demand

Country	Estimated Income Elasticity for Chocolate
Switzerland	1.06
United States	0.79
Germany	0.39
Japan	0.08

Source: www.west-dunbarton.gov.uk

ECONOMIC FALLACY   When we look across income groups, we see that the demand for cigarettes is inversely related to income. This tells us that cigarettes must not be addictive, which would require that demand be perfectly income inelastic.

Uncertain. If we look across income groups, we find that the consumption of some goods like cigarettes—that are perfectly income inelastic for *an individual*—exhibit a nonzero income elasticity of demand. This appears to be the case for cigarette purchases: the quantity demanded of cigarettes by smokers is largely independent of their incomes, yet the actual quantity of cigarettes demanded falls as we move to higher income classes. Of the lowest-income Americans, 34 percent smoke, compared with only 13 percent of those earning $90,000 or more per year.[13] And, a study conducted in New Zealand found that while over 4.5 percent of household incomes were spent on tobacco in low-income families, less than 1.5 percent of incomes were spent on tobacco by the top income households.[14]

One explanation for these seemingly contradictory results is that income has an impact on the decision to begin smoking in the first place; that is, smoking as an activity is an inferior good. However, once people begin to smoke, the income elasticity of demand is equal to zero, probably because they become dependent upon smoking a certain amount each day.

Interestingly, we find that in developing countries, smokers view local cigarette brands as inferior goods relative to foreign, branded cigarettes (e.g., Marlboro). As people's incomes increase, the market share held by these foreign brands also increases. However, as the people in these countries continue to grow richer, cigarette smoking as an activity—regardless of brand—becomes an inferior good, and fewer people develop the habit.

11.5 Income Elasticity over Time

As with all elasticity measures, we expect that income elasticity of demand will be higher as we move from the short run to the longer run. The housing market, for example, might not experience much of an increase in demand at the very start of an economic expansion because consumers are locked into their current housing choices. By the time the expansion is several years old, however, buyers are able to freely respond to the change in their incomes. Similarly, when a recession begins, occupancy rates for retail space might not instantaneously fall because retailers are locked into multiyear lease commitments.

The Permanent Income Hypothesis

Income elasticity in the longer run can also vary because people treat income changes that they believe are *permanent* differently from the way they treat income changes they believe are *transitory* or temporary.[15] Workers who receive overtime pay during the holiday season are likely to spend this money in a very different way than if they received a comparable increase in their base pay. Taxpayers who get "one-time" tax rebates as part of a federal stimulus package tend to spend this windfall in a different way than if there was a permanent cut in their tax rate. For example, when people were polled about how they would spend the $300–$1,200 rebate that was part of the U.S. government's 2008 stimulus package, 45 percent said they would use it to pay their bills; 32 percent said they would save it; and only 19 percent said they would spend it.[16] This pattern in income use is quite different from the way that people typically spend their income. As evidence of this, consider the fact that the overall savings rate in the United States was less than 5 percent in 2007—a far cry from the 32 percent of the one-time 2008 stimulus dollars people said they would save.

· · · · · · ·

[13]Lydia Saad, "Cigarette Tax Will Affect Low-Income Americans Most." *Gallup News,* April 1, 2009.

[14]Nick Wilson and George Thomson, "Tobacco Tax as a Health Promoting Policy." *The New Zealand Medical Journal,* April 2005.

[15]Robert E. Hall and Frederic S. Mishkin, "The Sensitivity of Consumption to Transitory Income: Estimates from Panel Data on Households." *Econometrica,* 50, no. 2, (March 1982), pp. 461–481.

[16]Jeannine Aversa, "Tax Rebates Will Wing Their Way to Consumers." *St. Louis Post Dispatch,* February 14, 2008.

Many economists, following the lead of Nobel Laureate Milton Friedman, maintain that people use transitory income to "even out" their lifetime consumption stream. Friedman's famous "permanent income" hypothesis suggests that people's consumption patterns depend on their expectations about the steady stream of income they will earn over their entire lifetime. In other words, what you *expect* to earn over your lifetime has a far greater effect on your purchases today than what you are currently earning. This may explain why recipients of one-time tax rebates use them in a very different way than they do their "regular" income—saving more and spending less to even out their lifetime consumption stream.

The permanent income hypothesis suggests that if you are an economics major, you are likely to spend more during your college years—even if it means going into debt—than your English major counterparts because you expect your lifetime income to be higher. If the permanent income hypothesis is correct—that purchases are determined by permanent income over the life cycle—then the income elasticity of demand measure is more likely to reflect changes in demand due to changes in the lifetime income people expect rather than changes in their current income.

11.6 Income Elasticity and the "Fairness" of a Tax System

Income elasticity of demand can provide important insights into the "fairness" of different types of tax systems and how such systems "should be" designed. Of course, fairness is often in the eye of the beholder: some people think that a "flat" tax—which collects the same percentage of income from everyone regardless of their income—is fair. Others think that people with higher incomes should pay a greater *share* of their income in taxes, and those with lower incomes should pay a lower share. Coming up with a universally accepted standard for fairness is beyond the scope of this discussion. Nevertheless, income elasticity of demand permits us to identify which income classes will bear the tax burden when various types of goods are taxed.

Take, for example, a new 6 percent sales tax on food and clothing purchases proposed by the budget-strapped state of Connecticut. We know that food and clothing are normal goods, which means that households buy more of these goods when their incomes rise. This would result in additional tax payments when household incomes rise. However, we also know that the *fraction* of income devoted to food and clothing begins to fall at some point as incomes grow—that is, the purchases of these goods do not keep pace with the growth in income. **Table 11.3** reports that the income elasticity of demand for clothing is substantially different for the lowest and highest income groups included in a survey of New Zealand households. These goods are income *elastic* for the lowest income group—which means that the budget share devoted

Table **11.3** Sample Income Elasticities for the Lowest- and Highest-Income Groups in New Zealand, 1981–1982		
Good	Lowest Income Group	Highest Income Group
Tobacco and alcohol	2	0.85
Clothing	1.29	0.98
Transportation	1.50	0.90

Source: Jack Hirshleifer and David Hirshleifer, *Price Theory and Applications,* 6th edition, (New Jersey: Prentice Hall), 1992, p.133.

to them rises with income—but are income *inelastic* for the highest income group. In other words, within the highest income group, food and clothing purchases grow at a slower rate than income, so their budget share falls.

If the *share* of income spent on food and clothing falls at some point as income rises, then the *share* of income paid in taxes must likewise fall because tax payments are simply 5 percent of the total expenditures on these goods. Another way to see this is that upper-income households tend to save and invest more, along with buying lots of goods besides clothing and food. These other expenditures are not taxed under the tax proposal. Therefore, while the *total* amount of tax dollars paid by higher-income households will increase with their income, the *share* of their income spent on taxes will fall. This means that the *tax rate*—the percentage or share of a taxpayer's income paid in taxes—also falls.

A tax rate that decreases as individual or household incomes rise is called a **regressive tax**.

REGRESSIVE TAX A tax that accounts for a lower share of income as income rises.

EXAMPLE Taxes on cigarettes are regressive because the percentage of households that smoke declines with income.

EXAMPLE Sales taxes on basic consumer goods such as food tend to be regressive because they account for a higher share of a lower-income household's budget than for a higher-income household's budget.

It is important to emphasize that even when a tax is regressive, higher-income people pay more taxes in total than lower-income people. This is because higher-income households buy a greater quantity of the taxed good. Nevertheless, it is the *share* or *percentage* of income that is paid in taxes—not the actual dollar amount of taxes paid—that determines whether a tax is regressive or not.

According to our income elasticity results, goods that exhibit income elasticity less than 1 (including inferior goods) account for a smaller and smaller share of income as it grows, and a larger and larger share as it falls. Therefore, a tax system that relies predominantly on these categories of goods for its tax base tends to be regressive in nature. For example, a "sin" tax on cigarettes is regressive because the income elasticity of demand for cigarettes is around 0.5 (refer to **Table 11.1**). Nevertheless, sin taxes are popular among voters as a way to encourage people to curb their consumption of goods that the public thinks are "bad."

Taxing these purchases also generates lots of tax revenue because buyers are relatively price insensitive and will not cut back consumption much due to the tax increase.[17] For this reason, the 2007 Great Recession has led revenue-strapped states to propose taxes on soda, video games, gambling, and even topless bars to balance their budgets.[18] In California, a recent ballot initiative was defeated that would have legalized marijuana. The initiative was motivated in part to generate badly needed government revenue.[19]

• • • • • • •

[17]William Safire, "The Syntax of Sin Tax." *New York Times,* April 13, 1998.

[18]Mark Bittman, "Soda: A Sin We Sip instead of Smoke?" *New York Times,* February 12, 2010.

[19]Brad Knickerbocker, "Prop 19 in California: Legalized Marijuana Goes Up in Smoke." *Christian Science Monitor,* November 3, 2010.

What if, instead, a sales tax was placed only on goods that exhibit unitary income elasticity of demand? Because the fraction of income devoted to unitary elastic goods remains constant as incomes rise, the fraction of income that households will pay in taxes—regardless of their income—will stay the same. In other words, when incomes rise, the actual amount of tax dollars the government collects from taxing goods with unitary income elasticity of demand will increase at exactly the same rate as the growth in income. We call this a **proportional tax**.

PROPORTIONAL TAX A tax that collects the same percentage of income from taxpayers, regardless of their income level.

EXAMPLE According to Table 11.1, the income elasticity of demand for beef is approximately 1. If this were the case at all income levels, then a 10 percent tax on beef purchases would translate into a proportional tax.

It is important to understand that taxing a good with unitary income elasticity will not necessarily mean that the same dollar amount of taxes is paid by individuals or households with the same level of income. It is true that households that exhibit a unitary price elasticity of demand for beef will pay the same *share* of their income in taxes as their income grows or declines. However, households of like income can still differ in the amount of taxes they pay because beef may account for a different share of their budgets. Vegans, for example, would escape a tax on beef entirely, irrespective of their income level.

One type of proportional tax system that has gotten a lot of attention lately is a "flat" income tax rate that would apply the same tax rate to the income of each and every household. This means that people in all income groups would pay the same rate, although the actual amount of taxes they pay would still increase with income. By taxing income rather than specific goods, the amount of taxes paid is no longer influenced by taxpayers' consumption patterns.

In contrast, a **progressive tax** is one that extracts an *increasing* share of income from households as their incomes increase.

PROGRESSIVE TAX A tax that accounts for a larger percentage of income as incomes rise.

A progressive tax would tax the purchase of goods that exhibit income elasticities substantially greater than one. We know that the fraction of income spent on these goods increases, all else the same, when a household's income increases and falls when the household's income falls. This means that the amount of tax dollars paid—in total and as a share of a person's income—will rise with income. In 1990, the George H. Bush administration introduced a 10 percent luxury tax on high-priced jewelry, boats, private aircraft, furs, and cars. By 1993, the producers of these goods had successfully lobbied to have the tax repealed. They argued that the tax had severely dampened their sales and level of employment.

The U.S. personal income tax system attempts to be progressive by applying an increasingly higher tax rate to additional dollars of income received. In other words, different ranges of the same person's income are taxed at different rates, in a stair-step fashion. This is accomplished by establishing a set of "tax brackets" that are

Table 11.4	2010 U.S. Income Tax Rate Schedule for a Single Person			
Single				
Taxable income is over	But not over	The tax is	Plus	Of the amount over
$0	8,375	$0.00	10%	$0
8,375	34,000	837.50	15%	8,375
34,000	82,400	4,681.25	25%	34,000
82,400	171,850	16,781.25	28%	82,400
171,850	373,650	41,827.25	33%	171,850
373,650		108,421.25	35%	373,650

defined by ranges of income; income within a bracket is taxed at the same tax rate, while income in higher brackets is taxed at higher rates.

In 2010, the first $8,375 earned by a millionaire was untaxed just like the first $8,375 earned by a farm worker. However, the millionaire's last $8,375 earned was taxed at a far higher rate, 35 percent. **Table 11.4** reports the 2010 tax brackets and corresponding tax rates for a single person.

In reality, the U.S. income tax system is so cluttered with "adjustments" to income—deductions for mortgage interest, charitable contributions, and so on—that the true tax rates are substantially less progressive than this Internal Revenue Service tax rate schedule would imply.

Figure 11.4 shows that tax systems will be regressive, proportional (flat), or progressive depending on how the total amount of taxes paid varies with income. As you

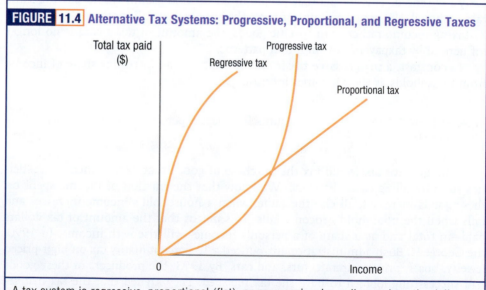

FIGURE 11.4 Alternative Tax Systems: Progressive, Proportional, and Regressive Taxes

A tax system is regressive, proportional (flat), or progressive depending on how the dollar amount of taxes paid varies with income. As you can see, under any of these systems, the dollar amount of taxes paid grows with income. The issue is *how much more* in taxes should be paid when income rises, that is, what is the appropriate rate of growth in tax payments as incomes rise?

can see, under any of these systems, the total dollar amount of taxes paid grows when a person's income increases. The issue at hand is *how much more* in taxes should people pay when their incomes rise.

11.7 Income Elasticity and Global Development

We have focused thus far on how the spending patterns of households change in response to internal bargaining power, control over assets, and changes in income. It turns out that as countries become richer, they, too, experience systematic changes in the goods they demand. The fraction of a country's GDP attributable to various categories of goods changes as its economy grows: for example, a greater share of GDP is spent on automobiles and a smaller share on food and clothing as a country grows richer. We also observe greater public and private investment in higher education and pollution-control technologies.[20] Investments in health care and public sanitation—clean water and sewage treatment—likewise increase. Once a country is no longer struggling to meet the subsistence needs of its population, it can begin to invest in such "luxury" goods as clean air and water. For example, China is slowly weaning itself off from cheaper, polluting sulfur-laden oil as it becomes wealthier and can afford cleaner fuels.[21] Because poorer countries face a high opportunity cost of adopting policies that address such global problems as air pollution, world organizations have argued that wealthier nations should disproportionately reduce their own air pollution relative to the rest of the world.[22]

Income Elasticity and Nutrition

The income elasticity of demand measure has been modified to quantify changes in nutrition and health in developing countries. **Calorie-income elasticity of demand** measures the impact of changes in income on people's nutritional intake.

> **CALORIE-INCOME ELASTICITY OF DEMAND** Percentage change in calories consumed during a specified time period resulting from a percentage change in income, all else remaining the same.

This measure is particularly important when it comes to determining how to most effectively reduce malnutrition in poorer countries. Can nutrition be improved simply by giving people more income? Or must foreign aid continue to provide actual foodstuffs (e.g., rice, grains, and dried milk)? Delivering food to impoverished populations throughout the world is quite costly in terms of transportation, distribution, and storage. It would be much less costly if international aid organizations such as the World Bank could achieve their nutritional goals through cash relief instead. The same issue arises in the United States: Would cash subsidies to the poor accomplish the same objectives as food stamps, but in a more cost-effective way?

· · · · · · ·

[20]Jim Yardley, "China Vows to Clean Up Polluted Lake." *New York Times,* October 27, 2007.

[21]Keith Bradsher, "China Pays the Price for Cheaper Oil: Sulfur-Laden Fuels Contribute to Growing Pollution Problem." *New York Times,* June 26, 2004.

[22]Jim Yardley, "China Says Rich Countries Should Take Lead on Global Warming." *New York Times,* February 7, 2007.

Economists have focused considerable attention on the cost-effectiveness of alleviating hunger around the world through direct food relief versus cash relief.[23] By and large, they have concluded that cash relief delivers a bigger bang for the buck but only when recipients have access to competitive food markets. In a 2001 pilot project initiated by Save the Children, a British organization, families in certain areas of Ethiopia were given cash supplements in lieu of food rations.[24] The choice of beneficiaries did not differ from those who had previously received food aid. The organization found that

> Beneficiaries of cash transfers consumed more diverse foodstuffs than their food-aid receiving counterparts. Cash-receiving households [also] spent more on essential non-food items (coffee, salt, pepper, and kerosene), clothes, and other household needs (such as school materials).

It concluded that cash-relief operations are about one-third more cost-effective than food aid in meeting nutritional goals as long as food was sufficiently available in local markets. However, no attention was paid to whether "kleptocrats"—government officials who siphon off foreign aid—were more successfully deterred under one system of relief versus the other.

ECONOMIC FALLACY   Most studies have found that calorie-income elasticity of demand is close to zero. This means that augmenting people's incomes will not reduce malnutrition.

False. Just because the number of calories consumed per day or week does not change significantly with one's income, this does not mean that increases in income will not reduce malnutrition. Calories come from a number of sources, some of which are healthier than others. We know, for example, that consumption of canned vegetables in the United States declines when people's incomes increase because they are an inferior good when compared to fresh fruits and vegetables. In both developing countries and the United States, high-calorie carbohydrates such as potatoes are inferior goods when compared to lower-calorie but more expensive sources of protein such as meat and nuts.

The point here is that even if a person's daily caloric intake doesn't change with his or her income, the sources of the calories will likely change and will, therefore, have a substantial impact on the person's malnutrition.

WHAT YOU SHOULD HAVE LEARNED FROM CHAPTER 11

- The consumption and saving decisions of households will be affected by the bargaining power of its members, assuming that their preferences are not identical.

- The opportunity cost of being a household member is the well-being he forgoes as a result of giving up his next-best living arrangement. This is called the person's "threat point."

- Bargaining power is not a function of the amount of income earned but of the amount of income that could be earned by a partner.

- A person's bargaining power increases if she controls assets.

⋯⋯⋯

[23]Stephen Coate, "Cash Versus Direct Food Relief." *Journal of Development Economics*, 30, no. 2 (April 1989).

[24]http://www.odi.org.uk/resources/libraries/cash-vouchers/scf_cash_report.pdf.

■ Income elasticity of demand measures the sensitivity of demand to changes in income, holding all else unchanged.

■ Income elasticity of demand for a product is computed as the percentage change in the quantity demanded of the good divided by the percentage change in income.

■ If a good's income elasticity of demand is positive, the good is a normal good. If a good's income elasticity of demand is negative, the good is an inferior good.

■ When a good's income elasticity of demand is greater than one (e.g., Rolex watches), the good is said to be income elastic and is sometimes referred to as a luxury good. The share of income going to this type of good increases as a household's income increases, and decreases when income falls.

■ When a good's income elasticity of demand is between zero and one, the good is said to be income inelastic (e.g., food) and referred to as a necessity. The share of income going to the good goes down when a household's income increases, and vice versa.

■ When a good's income elasticity of demand equals zero, the good is said to be perfectly income inelastic (e.g., prescription drugs). The amount of money spent on this type of good does not vary with income, which means that the share of income spent on it declines when income rises, and vice-versa.

■ When a good's income elasticity of demand is less than zero (e.g., Ramen Noodles), it is an inferior good. The share of income going to this type of good goes down when a household's income goes up, and vice versa.

■ If the permanent income hypothesis is true, then a person's consumption patterns will change only when his expectations change about his lifetime permanent income.

■ The income elasticity of goods that are taxed will dictate whether the tax is regressive, proportional, or progressive.

■ Economies as a whole exhibit an income elasticity of demand for various goods. This is reflected in the change in share of GDP dedicated to different goods or economic activities as national income rises.

■ Calorie-income elasticity of demand is a measure that has been used to evaluate the role that income growth plays in reducing a country's malnutrition rates.

KEY TERMS

Unitary model of the household, p. 307

Threat point, p. 309

Divorce-threat bargaining model, p. 309

Cooperative outcome, p. 312

Nash bargaining solution, p. 313

Noncooperative outcome, p. 315

Engel's curve, p. 316

Income elasticity of demand, p. 318

Budget share, p. 320

Unitary income elasticity, p. 321

Income elastic good, p. 322

Income inelastic good, p. 323

Perfectly income inelastic good, p. 324

Regressive tax, p. 328

Proportional tax, p. 329

Progressive tax, p. 329

Calorie income elasticity of demand, p. 331

QUESTIONS AND PROBLEMS

1. Suppose that Steve prefers golfing vacations, while Emily prefers visiting major metropolitan areas (e.g., New York City). Explain how, if at all, the probability of going on a golfing vacation changes (increases or decreases) if:

   a) Emily has a PhD in economics rather than a PhD in philosophy.

   b) Steve is the son of Bill Gates of Microsoft fame.

c) Emily is thin, tall, and very attractive.

d) Steve is a movie star, but Emily is not.

2. Explain how you would apply the divorce-threat model to a law firm with two partners. What do you think would happen to your outcome as additional partners are added to the firm? Explain your answer.

3. Suppose that two household partners, Ed and Jane, have different income elasticities when it comes to red wine. Ed's income elasticity equals zero—he drinks one glass of wine daily only to achieve the health benefits from red wine. Jane's income elasticity is unitary. If both partners "count" equally in making purchasing decisions, what would be the income elasticity for red wine for the household as a whole? How, if at all, would your answer change if Ed earned and controlled 75 percent of the household's income? Explain your answer.

4. Identify whether the income elasticity of demand is perfectly inelastic, inelastic, unitary elastic, or elastic in the following situations:

a) The number of household workers hired increases by 50 percent when household incomes double.

b) Amy always spends $18 a week eating out.

c) Marni always spends 18 percent of her income eating out.

d) When the income tax rate is increased 5 percent for the wealthiest taxpayers, they reduce their purchases of Corvettes by 15 percent.

5. Suppose that a city introduces an entrance fee for its publicly owned swimming pool and that more lower-income people use the pool than higher-income people (who have their own private pools). Would you consider this entrance fee a regressive tax? Why or why not. Explain your answer.

6. If the United States ever adopts a flat income tax to replace its current tax system, it will likely exempt families with income below a certain level. Will the resulting tax system be proportional, regressive, or progressive? Explain your answer.

7. Suppose that the principle of diminishing benefits applies to money; that is, the last dollar earned and spent generates less additional well-being than the dollar before. Explain how this principle can be used to promote the introduction of a progressive income tax system.

8. The Laffer curve—shown below—makes the argument that increasing income tax rates can lead to a decline in total tax revenues collected by the government. Explain under what conditions this could happen and whether you think that Laffer's prediction makes sense.

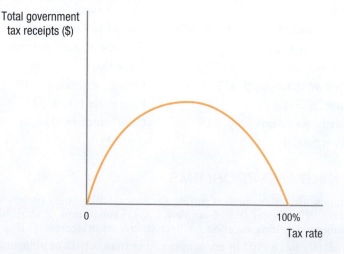

9. Many churches encourage their members to "tithe" 10 percent of their income to the church. If a church member scrupulously follows this rule, what is her income elasticity of demand with respect to church donations?

10. Indicate whether you think the following taxes are regressive, proportional, or progressive. Explain your answers.

    a) A payroll tax
    b) A tax on consumption
    c) A property tax
    d) A gasoline tax
    e) An estate tax (a tax on your wealth when you die)

    Which of these taxes do you think is the "fairest"? Why? Explain your answer.

11. A "lump-sum" tax is a fixed-dollar tax that is collected from every person or household. It is sometimes called a "head tax." Is this tax regressive, proportional, or progressive? What kinds of government services do you think should be funded through a lump-sum tax? Why? Explain your answer.

12. In some countries, polygamy is still legal or, at the very least, condoned (police "look the other way"). Let's say that we are talking about a household with one man and several wives. Explain how, if at all, the bargaining power of each wife varies with the total number of wives. Do you think it matters whether the wife is the first, second, or last wife married? What about whether the wife has had children with the man? Explain your answer.

13. Mr. Huntley and Mr. Brinkley are partners in an accounting firm. How does their bargaining power—when it comes to such things as where to locate the office, employee hiring, and hours of business—compare if:

    a) Mr. Huntley has a CPA and Mr. Brinkley does not.
    b) Mr. Brinkley has grown up in the community while Mr. Huntley has not.
    c) Mr. Brinkley is married to a wealthy woman and Mr. Huntley is not.
    d) Mr. Huntley can speak several foreign languages, while Mr. Brinkley only speaks English.

14. We know that in the overall economy, the income elasticity of demand for farm products is low, while the income elasticity of demand for education, health, and other services is high. What does this tell you about the "importance" of the agricultural sector vis-à-vis the service sector as per capita income in the United States grows? Explain your answer.

15. Some local municipalities have, or are now considering, a *wheel tax* that is levied on each automobile and lightweight pickup registered in the city. The state adds a $10–$20 tax when it collects its annual license plate renewal fee and issues a sticker that goes on the vehicle. Is this a regressive, flat, or progressive tax? Explain your answer.

Purchasing Household Outputs: The Impact of Subsidies and Taxes

"The avoidance of taxes is the only intellectual pursuit that carries any reward."

John Maynard Keynes, British economist

As you have learned, the optimal division of labor in a household is determined by the comparative advantage of each of its members. Whether this division of labor actually takes place depends on the ability of household members to achieve a cooperative outcome about how the gains from specialization will be shared. So far, we have assumed that certain outputs—such as meals, financial management, and child care—are produced within the household and that other goods and services are produced by the market and purchased by performing paid work. In reality, the distinction between household-based and market-based production is a fuzzy one. For example, in some societies, virtually all of the bread that households eat is baked at home. In other societies, households are more likely to purchase their bread in a supermarket.

One question you might ask is under what circumstances will we substitute market production for household production? The answer depends, in part, on whether we consider these market options as reasonable substitutes for in-home production. To what extent do parents think that day-care centers are good substitutes for in-home care? Do you think that take-out food is a good substitute for a homemade meal? Personal preferences dictate whether a person is willing to substitute a good produced in the market for one that is produced within the household. Another consideration is the relative cost of purchasing market alternatives rather than producing the goods ourselves. This, of course, depends on the price of the good compared to the opportunity cost of producing it within the household.

In this chapter, we explore these issues. We pay particular attention to the impact that government subsidies and taxes have on the decision to substitute market-based goods for household production. In effect, our inquiry takes us back full circle to the original question posed by Ronald Coase in Chapter 10: When is it more efficient to trade in the market rather than coordinate resources *within* a firm such as the household?

12.1 Market Substitutes for Household Production

Many times, market substitutes for household production are less than ideal. For example, few parents think that child care provided by strangers is as good as what they themselves can provide. Similarly, restaurants often strive to meet—but fall short of—the caliber of "mom's home cooking." Why, then, do we ever turn to the market to provide these types of services?

Using our basic framework for economic decision making, the answer must be that the opportunity cost of producing these goods ourselves is too high relative to alternative uses of our scarce time. That is, we are willing to purchase imperfect substitutes so that we can put our own time to higher-valued uses such as generating more income and consumables, volunteering for church and civic organizations, spending time with our children, and pursuing leisure activities. Inasmuch as each of us has different opportunities and preferences, we are likely to differ in the amount of market substitutes we use in lieu of household outputs.

Consider again, our simple model of the household that was first described in Chapter 10. We saw there that Wilma's comparative advantage was to enter the paid labor market to earn income to buy market-based consumables. Fred had the comparative advantage in household production. Suppose that Fred's neighbor approaches him with an offer to take care of Fred's kids and, at the same time, perform the rest of Fred's household responsibilities such as laundry and meal preparation. This neighbor asks for $7.50 an hour as compensation. Fred and Wilma both like this neighbor and think that he would be a great substitute for Fred. Does it make economic sense for Fred and Wilma to accept this neighbor's offer, that is, hire him as a market substitute to perform Fred's household work?

In our earlier example, Fred's after-tax wage was $10 an hour. That's $2.50 more than his neighbor's asking wage. Assuming that Fred's only opportunity cost of going to work is his forgone household production, it makes sense to hire the neighbor and redirect Fred's time to earning income. In this way, the household's total market-based consumables can be increased without forgoing any household output. The couple will go from $192 ($12 per hour × 16 hours) earned solely by Wilma to $192 plus $180 ($10 per hour × 18 hours) earned by Fred *minus* $135 ($7.50 per hour × 18 hours) that they pay the neighbor. Fred and Wilma's income will rise by $45 a day ($2.50 per hour × 18 hours) to $237.

Notice that the crucial comparison is between Fred's *after-tax* hourly wage and the neighbor's hourly wage. It doesn't matter whether Fred earns $11.50 or $15 an hour before taxes are taken out of his paycheck. He will compare his after-tax wage, which measures the amount of consumables he can buy, to what he would pay his neighbor. For example, if Fred earned a dollar more per hour ($11 an hour) before tax but had $4.50 an hour taken out for taxes, his after-tax wage would be $6.50, and he would not hire the neighbor at $7.50 an hour. You can see from this example that payroll taxes can play a significant role in Fred's decision about whether to enter the paid labor market or not.

There are many ways in which societies encourage or discourage market-versus home-based production, whether purposely or not. In Norway, there are generous state subsidies for day care, which are designed to encourage both parents to go back to work; in contrast, Italy has resisted efforts to introduce day-care subsidies so as to promote family-based child care.[1] Both subsidies and taxes can have a major effect on people's decisions to enter the labor force. As you will see, subsidies and taxes affect not only the choice between household and market-based production but also the behavior of suppliers of these market substitutes.

12.2 The Impact of Subsidies on Household Production

Consider the Fred and Wilma household again, and imagine what would happen if Fred died or left the household for some other reason. Suppose that there are one or more children living at home that are under the age of 12. If there aren't any affordable child-care options in the marketplace (relative to Wilma's wage rate) and there is no extended family network that can provide child care, Wilma will no longer be able to work to provide food, housing, and other necessities. She will be forced to specialize in household production, unless she chooses to break the law and leave her children alone without adult supervision. Wilma is more likely to stay at home with her kids if she receives unearned income that she can use to purchase food and other goods. Her one-parent household is exactly the type of household that government "safety net" programs—such as welfare, Medicaid, and food stamps—target.

In 1996, at the behest of the Clinton administration, Congress enacted a major piece of legislation dubbed the welfare-to-work program. The goal of the legislation was to substantially reduce the amount of cash assistance that the federal government was giving, on an ongoing basis, to the poor.[2] States were encouraged to adopt innovative approaches to steer single, stay-at-home parents into the labor force. The most frequently implemented policy was to subsidize the use of market-based child care.

By making child care more affordable, states have tried to reduce the private opportunity cost that single parents bear when they enter the labor force. We would predict that this would make it economically advantageous for some parents earning a lower wage to work outside the home. If, for example, a single parent must pay $9 an hour for child care, he will stay home if his take-home wage is less than or equal to $9. With the introduction of a government subsidy that reimburses 33 percent of child-care expenses—lowering the subsidized price of child care to $6 per hour—parents with a take-home wage greater than $6 would enter the labor force (assuming they have no additional work costs, such as transportation). In other words, we would predict that lower-wage positions would now attract single parents. How good are our predictions? So far, about a million children have been enrolled in market-based child-care programs as a result of the welfare-to-work initiative.[3]

More often than not, government subsidies take the form of a **tax credit**, payable to eligible recipients. What this means is that the amount of income tax that a person owes is *lowered* by the amount of the subsidy. Or, if the person does not owe any taxes, she will receive a cash payment from the government in the form of a tax refund.

· · · · · · · ·

[1]Russell Shorto, "No Babies." *New York Times,* June 29, 2008.

[2]Dan Franklin, "Welfare's Changing Face." *Washingtonpost.com,* July 23, 1998.

[3]Tamar Lewin, "Study Finds Welfare Changes Lead a Million into Childcare." *New York Times,* February 4, 2000.

TAX CREDIT An amount of money "credited" against a person's tax liability. When this results in a negative tax liability, a cash payment is made in the form of a tax refund.

EXAMPLE The tax credit for child-care and dependent-care expenses—which equals up to 35 percent of these expenses—is available to working parents with earnings below a certain threshold.

EXAMPLE In 2010, the federal government offered a 30 percent tax credit (up to $1,500) for home owners who installed energy-efficient doors, windows, and insulation.

In some instances, government subsidies are given directly to market providers. For example, federally approved Head Start preschool programs receive government subsidies, as do preschool programs at public schools.

In reality, it turns out that it doesn't matter whether a subsidy is given directly to providers or consumers of child care—both groups will usually benefit from the subsidy. How can this be the case? Before we get to the nuts and bolts of the analysis, consider this: When a good is subsidized, consumers who buy it enjoy a lower, subsidized price. Similarly, the providers of the good enjoy an increase in demand because the subsidy effectively lowers the purchase price to consumers. We will see a bit later in this chapter that this occurs regardless of who actually receives the subsidy check. This is why consumers of child care or any other good purchased in the market are always delighted when the suppliers of these goods receive a government subsidy. In the same way, suppliers often support programs that provide subsidies to the consumers of their goods and services.

Consumer Subsidies

Let's assume that certain consumers of market-based child care receive a $2 tax credit for each hour of care they purchase rather than provide themselves. In the presence of this subsidy, the quantity of child care demanded when the market price is $8 will be higher than in its absence. This comes about because the quantity demanded of a good depends on a consumer's willingness to pay for units of that good. In the presence of a $2 per hour subsidy, consumers are willing to pay $2 more for each hour of child care—that is, pass along to providers the entire subsidy they receive—and be no worse off than if the subsidy didn't exist. This means that at the market price of $8, the quantity demanded *after* the introduction of the subsidy will equal the quantity that was demanded at $6 *before* the subsidy was introduced. The net price to consumers remains $6 per hour after factoring in the subsidy ($8 − $2).

Another way to look at this is that the willingness to pay for each hour of child care increases because there is now another party—the government—that is willing to pay $2 toward each hour of child care. The height of the demand curve—which represents this willingness to pay—must, therefore, increase by $2 at every level of output. A parent is indifferent between paying $8 without the subsidy and $10 with the $2 subsidy, $10 without the subsidy or $12 with the $2 subsidy, and so on. This translates into a parallel, rightward shift in the demand curve for child care, as illustrated in **Figure 12.1**. The vertical distance between the original and new demand curves is exactly equal to $2, the per hour subsidy.

The market price on the vertical axis is the hourly rate that the parent actually pays the child-care provider. This price will be greater than the *net* price that the

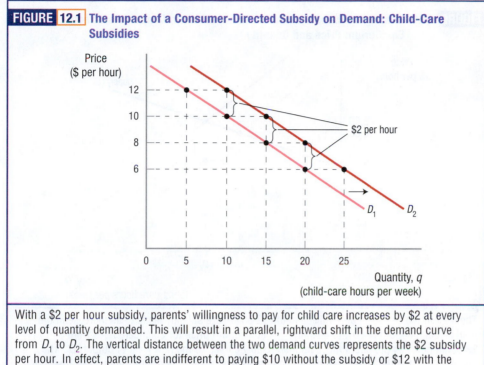

FIGURE 12.1 The Impact of a Consumer-Directed Subsidy on Demand: Child-Care Subsidies

With a $2 per hour subsidy, parents' willingness to pay for child care increases by $2 at every level of quantity demanded. This will result in a parallel, rightward shift in the demand curve from D_1 to D_2. The vertical distance between the two demand curves represents the $2 subsidy per hour. In effect, parents are indifferent to paying $10 without the subsidy or $12 with the subsidy, $8 without the subsidy or $10 with the subsidy, and so on.

parent ultimately pays (i.e., after getting the tax credit back). In effect, the subsidy creates a **price wedge** in the market, where the price that the supplier receives is not the price that the consumer ends up actually paying.

> **PRICE WEDGE** Difference in the price paid to suppliers and the net price actually paid by consumers.

> **EXAMPLE** A home owner pays her mortgage lender a monthly sum that includes interest on the loan, say at 5.5 percent. She gets a portion of this back when she files her federal and state income-tax returns because she can deduct the interest payment from her taxable income. This means that depending on her income-tax bracket, her after-tax interest rate may be closer to 4 percent than the 5.5 percent she paid her lender.

How does the shift in the demand curve resulting from the $2 child-care subsidy affect the market's equilibrium price and quantity? **Figure 12.2** compares the old and new market equilibrium for child care.

Suppose that the equilibrium price before the subsidy is $8 per hour. After the subsidy is introduced, the equilibrium price for child care—that suppliers receive—rises from $8 to $8.60 per hour. This comes about because providers must move up their supply curves in response to the increase in demand, thereby incurring higher opportunity costs as they increase their level of output. Perhaps day-care centers have to expand their staffing disproportionately to comply with staffing regulations for larger facilities, or perhaps they have to move into more expensive facilities.

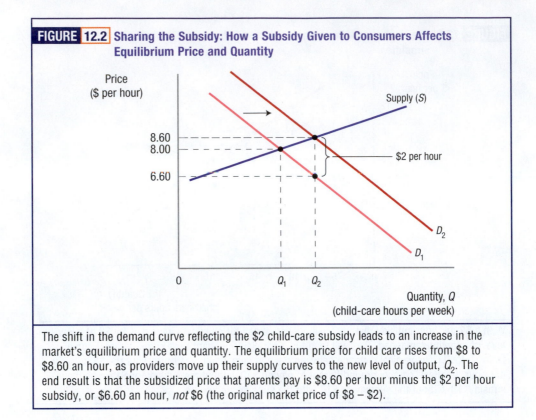

FIGURE 12.2 Sharing the Subsidy: How a Subsidy Given to Consumers Affects Equilibrium Price and Quantity

The shift in the demand curve reflecting the $2 child-care subsidy leads to an increase in the market's equilibrium price and quantity. The equilibrium price for child care rises from $8 to $8.60 an hour, as providers move up their supply curves to the new level of output, Q_2. The end result is that the subsidized price that parents pay is $8.60 per hour minus the $2 per hour subsidy, or $6.60 an hour, *not* $6 (the original market price of $8 − $2).

Whatever the reason for the market's upward-sloping supply curve, some of the subsidy must be passed along to suppliers in the form of a higher market price to entice them to increase their level of services. In our example, this results in an increase in market price from $8 to $8.60. The end result is that the subsidized price that parents pay is $8.60 minus $2, or $6.60 an hour, *not* $6 (the original market price of $8 − $2).

When subsidies lead to an increase in market price, suppliers are said to "enjoy" some of the subsidy, even though the subsidy is paid *directly to consumers*. It is worth emphasizing that this higher market price is necessary to (1) elicit greater supply to meet the increased demand for child care arising from the subsidy, and (2) "ration" the supply of child care among demanders, who now have a higher willingness to pay for these services. The market price does *not* go up because suppliers hear about the subsidy and unilaterally raise their prices "to grab some of it for themselves." Child-care suppliers are *price takers* operating in a competitive market; the market price rises as suppliers move up the market supply curve in response to the increased demand for child care.

SOLVED PROBLEMS

Q Carrier, a manufacturer of residential air conditioning units, offered home owners a $25 rebate check to have their air-conditioning units inspected and serviced by local Carrier dealers. Using supply and demand graphs, show how much of the $25 rebate that home owners actually enjoyed.

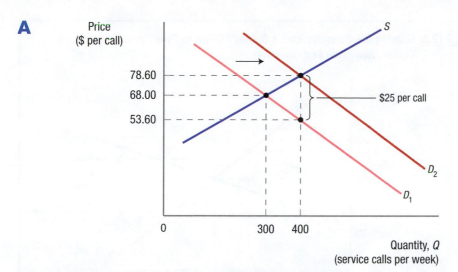

A

As the figure indicates, the subsidized, net service fee that homeowners pay is $53.60, not $43($68 − $25).

Q Why do you think Carrier offered this subsidy to home owners?

A Carrier expected that the service calls would reveal problems with older units that would generate new air-conditioner sales or require the replacement of expensive parts.

Producer Subsidies

The impact of a subsidy on equilibrium price and quantity is the same regardless of whether the supplier or the consumer receives the subsidy check. To prove this, consider the case where, instead of subsidizing parents, child-care suppliers receive the $2 subsidy for each hour of child care they provide. As shown in **Figure 12.3**, this causes a rightward shift in the supply curve: the *private* opportunity cost of providing each hour of care, as represented by the height of the supply curve, is now $2 less per hour. If this per hour subsidy is the same for every hour of child care provided, then the new supply curve will be parallel to the original one, and the vertical distance between them will equal $2.

In effect, the government is now shouldering $2 of the cost of providing each hour of child care. We can derive a new equilibrium price and quantity based on the new supply curve and original demand curve, which has not changed because parents no longer receive the subsidy. The new market price paid by the consumer to the supplier is $6.60. Because this is less than the original price, the consumer still benefits from the subsidy, even though it has been paid directly to the provider. However, the market price has not dropped by the full amount of the subsidy. The net price that suppliers now receive is $6.60 plus $2, or $8.60. This is 60 cents more than the original $8 per hour before the subsidy was introduced.

It is not coincidental that the way the $2 subsidy is divided between consumers and suppliers (consumers receive $1.40, and suppliers receive 60 cents) is the same as when consumers received the subsidy. To prove this to yourself, notice that the vertical distance between the original and new demand curves in the first analysis is equal to the vertical distance between the original and new supply curves in the second analysis. This vertical distance—which represents the $2 subsidy—is "dissected" in the same way in both analyses. As a result, consumers and suppliers enjoy the same share of the subsidy regardless of who actually *receives* the subsidy from the government.

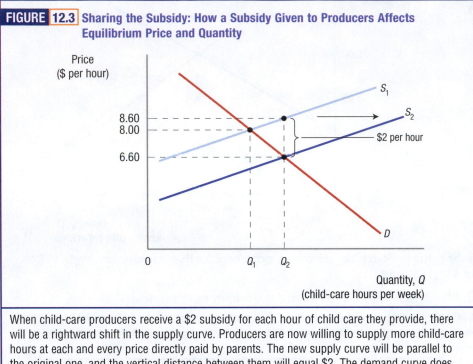

FIGURE 12.3 Sharing the Subsidy: How a Subsidy Given to Producers Affects Equilibrium Price and Quantity

When child-care producers receive a $2 subsidy for each hour of child care they provide, there will be a rightward shift in the supply curve. Producers are now willing to supply more child-care hours at each and every price directly paid by parents. The new supply curve will be parallel to the original one, and the vertical distance between them will equal $2. The demand curve does not change because parents no longer receive the subsidy. The new market price paid by parents is $6.60 per hour. Because this is less than the original price of $8, the consumer benefits from the existence of the subsidy, even though it has been paid directly to the provider. However, the market price has not dropped by the full amount of the subsidy. The *net* price that suppliers now receive is $6.60 plus $2, or $8.60, not $10 (the original market price of $8 + $2).

Do Buyers or Sellers Benefit Most from a Subsidy?

If the division of the subsidy between consumers and suppliers does not depend on who actually receives the money from the government, then what does affect the amount that each group enjoys? To answer this question, let's go back to our analysis of the $2 per hour child-care subsidy that is given directly to parents. Panels (a) through (c) in **Figure 12.4** indicate the new market equilibrium in three scenarios that differ only in terms of the price responsiveness of buyers and sellers. Panel (a) depicts a situation in which supply is relatively responsive to price changes; panel (b) depicts a situation in which demand is relatively unresponsive to price changes; and panel (c) depicts a situation in which both demand and supply are relatively responsive to price changes.

These figures show that when parents are relatively unresponsive to changes in price, the subsidy will stimulate only a small increase in quantity of child care demanded. Because there is less upward pressure on market price, more of the subsidy will remain in parents' pockets. And, the more responsive child-care suppliers are to an increase in the price they receive, the smaller the amount of the subsidy that must be passed along to them to boost the quantity supplied. These results hold whether the subsidy is given directly to parents or providers.

Based on these results, we can say that a government-subsidy program that is meant to reduce the subsidized (net) price consumers pay will be most successful when it targets goods whose supply is *highly responsive to price*: a small increase in

FIGURE 12.4 The Impact of Suppliers' and Demanders' Price Sensitivity on Who Enjoys the Subsidy

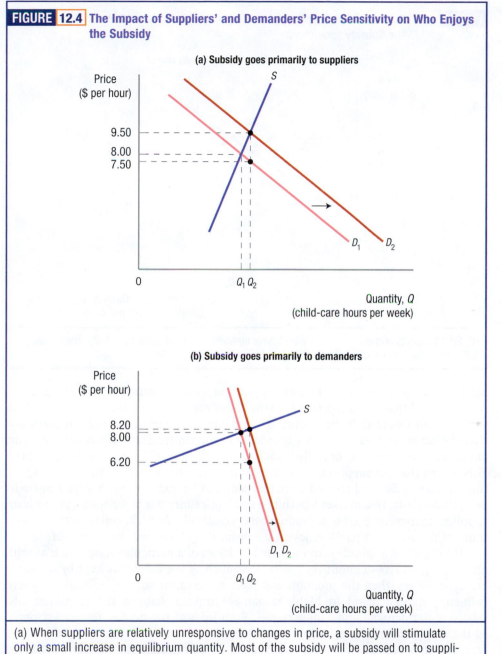

(a) Subsidy goes primarily to suppliers

Price
($ per hour)

9.50
8.00
7.50

S

D_1 D_2

0   Q_1 Q_2

Quantity, Q
(child-care hours per week)

(b) Subsidy goes primarily to demanders

Price
($ per hour)

8.20
8.00

6.20

S

D_1 D_2

0   Q_1 Q_2

Quantity, Q
(child-care hours per week)

(a) When suppliers are relatively unresponsive to changes in price, a subsidy will stimulate only a small increase in equilibrium quantity. Most of the subsidy will be passed on to suppliers in the form of a higher market price.

(b) When parents are relatively unresponsive to changes in the price of child care, a subsidy will stimulate only a small increase in quantity demanded at each and every price. Parents will enjoy most of the subsidy in the form of a lower net price.

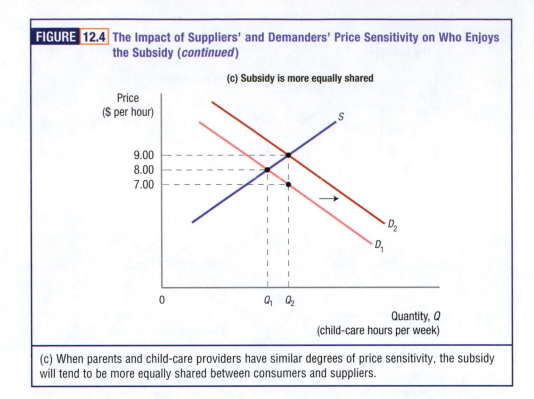

FIGURE 12.4 The Impact of Suppliers' and Demanders' Price Sensitivity on Who Enjoys the Subsidy (*continued*)

(c) Subsidy is more equally shared

(c) When parents and child-care providers have similar degrees of price sensitivity, the subsidy will tend to be more equally shared between consumers and suppliers.

market price will trigger a lot more output. For example, suppose that the government decided that it is important for families to eat more beef and introduces a beef subsidy. This would shift the market demand curve for beef to the right. It turns out that the supply of beef is readily expandable in the United States because there is an abundance of cattle and unskilled workers willing to work at meatpacking plants.[4] This means that the supply curve for beef is relatively flat which, in turn, means that the increase in demand created by the subsidy can be met without a large run-up in production costs. In a market like this, a small price increase is sufficient to motivate suppliers to increase their beef production dramatically. As such, consumers will keep more of the subsidy, thereby enjoying a substantially lower net price for beef.

If the goal of a subsidy is to increase purchases of a particular good—such as milk and dairy products—without regard to how much of the subsidy is kept by consumers or suppliers, then the program will have the greatest success in markets where *both* supply and demand are highly responsive to price changes. This translates into relatively flat demand and supply curves. Both sides of the market respond strongly to the introduction of a subsidy: consumers will demand a lot more of the good in response to a very small decline in net price, and producers will supply a lot more even if market price increases only slightly.

What if, instead, the government's goal is to increase the market price of a good, perhaps to protect suppliers in "core" industries such as agriculture and automobile manufacturing or to reward corporate donors to an elected official's campaign? In this case, the subsidy program would be most successful if it targeted goods whose supply is *highly unresponsive* to price. In markets such as these—with very steep supply

· · · · · · · ·

[4]Kirk Semple, "An Influx of Somalis Unsettles Latin Meatpackers." *New York Times*, October 16, 2008.

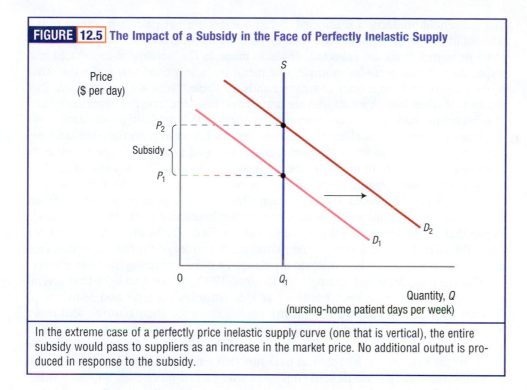

FIGURE 12.5 The Impact of a Subsidy in the Face of Perfectly Inelastic Supply

In the extreme case of a perfectly price inelastic supply curve (one that is vertical), the entire subsidy would pass to suppliers as an increase in the market price. No additional output is produced in response to the subsidy.

curves—the market price must go up substantially for there to be any additional output produced. The oil market is a good example, at least in the short run. In the extreme case of a good with zero price elasticity of supply—where the market supply curve is vertical, as illustrated in **Figure 12.5**—the entire subsidy would pass to suppliers as an increase in the market price, and no additional output would be produced in response to the introduction of the subsidy.

We have already seen that in competitive markets, vertical supply curves are more likely to exist during the market period than in the longer run. Vertical supply curves are also more common when the supply of a good cannot expand because of government regulations. In most states, for example, government regulators limit the supply of highly subsidized nursing-home beds based on an assessment of local "needs." This means that if a government subsidized long-term care insurance program is introduced to reduce the price that patients pay for nursing-home care, there will be virtually no increase in the number of patients served: the subsidy will only drive up market price. The end result is that if state regulators do not permit the nursing-home industry to expand, much of this care will continue to be provided within the household by family caregivers.

In summary then, subsidizing a good or service may or may not lead to additional output and market-based consumption: it all depends on the price sensitivity of suppliers and demanders. This will also dictate the amount of the subsidy that is enjoyed by each "side" of the market.

12.3 The Impact of Taxes on Household Production

You have just seen how government-subsidy programs can encourage households to substitute market goods and services—such as child care—for household production. In reality, government tax policies often end up discouraging this substitution. Recall that household production is untaxed. Because wages are not paid to members of the household for the goods and services they produce for internal consumption, no income or payroll taxes are collected. Products made in the household are shared and traded among members—for example, one member shovels the snow while the other cooks dinner—with no money changing hands, so these trades also go untaxed. This means that when market substitutes are taxed, these taxes increase the opportunity cost of substituting market-based consumption for (untaxed) household production.

Taxes on earnings will affect your decision about whether to enter the labor market—and if so, how much to work—or specialize in household production. The opportunity cost of each hour spent in unpaid home production, in terms of the amount of market-based consumables forgone, drops when a person's earnings are taxed. Going back to Fred and Wilma's household, Fred must earn a take-home wage of more than $7.50 an hour to justify hiring his neighbor to take over the household work. We have already shown that depending on the size of the payroll tax, Fred may be discouraged from entering the labor force. Moreover, if the payroll tax is also levied on the wages that Fred pays his neighbor, then this, too, could discourage Fred from entering the labor market.

Consider the following example. In the mid-1990s, it came to light that several nominees for such high-level positions as U.S. Attorney General and Secretary of Defense had failed to pay Social Security payroll taxes for their nannies and other household workers. The resulting imbroglio was called "Nannygate." In response to the Nannygate scandal, the government enacted the 1994 Social Security Domestic Employment Reform Act. Its goal was to ensure that employers would pay taxes for all part-time and full-time household employees who earned more than $1,750 a year.[5] For many of these employers, the new rules meant that for the very first time, they would actually have to pay a 7.65 percent payroll tax on top of the wages they paid directly to their domestic employees. The Internal Revenue Service estimated that this tax would generate more than $11 billion annually from nannies' wages alone and an equally substantial amount for gardeners, house cleaners, and so on.

How would enforcing the collection of the payroll tax affect the equilibrium wage and the level of domestic employment? We can build upon our analysis of government subsidies to answer this question.

To simplify our analysis, suppose that instead of paying a federal tax of 7.65 percent per dollar of wages, the household pays a tax equal to 76.5 cents for every *hour* that its domestic employees work (this analysis can be readily extended to incorporate a *percent* of payroll tax).

Because the household must pay the government for every hour that it employs these workers, the tax reduces the household's willingness to pay *employees* for domestic services. The household's willingness to pay will therefore decline by exactly 76.5 cents per hour, the amount that is now diverted to the government. In other words, households don't care how much they pay employees *versus* the government; they simply know the maximum they are willing to pay the two parties *together* for each hour of household work provided.

Figure 12.6 illustrates the effect of a 76.5 cents hourly tax on the demand for in-home workers: there is a leftward shift in the demand curve. At any and all market wage rates—the wages paid directly to employees—fewer hours of work are now demanded. In effect, unlike a government subsidy, which shifts the demand curve to the right, a tax shifts the demand curve in the opposite direction—to the left. This makes sense because a tax is simply a negative subsidy; instead of giving consumers a certain

- - - - - - - -

[5]"Opinion: Addressing Nannygate." *New York Times,* March 30, 1994.

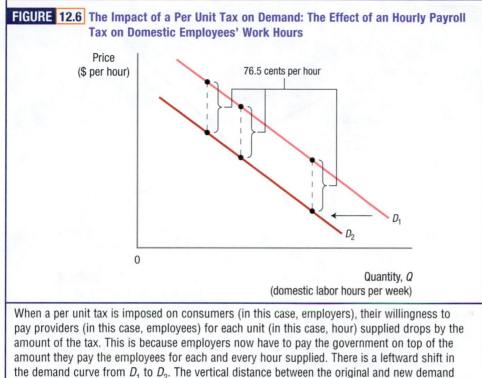

| FIGURE 12.6 | The Impact of a Per Unit Tax on Demand: The Effect of an Hourly Payroll Tax on Domestic Employees' Work Hours |

When a per unit tax is imposed on consumers (in this case, employers), their willingness to pay providers (in this case, employees) for each unit (in this case, hour) supplied drops by the amount of the tax. This is because employers now have to pay the government on top of the amount they pay the employees for each and every hour supplied. There is a leftward shift in the demand curve from D_1 to D_2. The vertical distance between the original and new demand curves equals the per unit tax.

amount of money for each unit of a good purchased, a tax *takes* a certain amount of money for each unit purchased (or, in this case, each hour hired).

As we saw in the case of subsidies, the *vertical* distance between the two demand curves reflects the difference between the willingness to pay employees before and after the tax is imposed. Whereas consumers who receive subsidies end up paying *less* than the market price, consumers who are taxed end up paying *more* than the market price—in this case, the wage rate they pay directly to the worker.

Given the new demand curve, we can determine the new equilibrium wage and quantity of labor hired. The supply curve in **Figure 12.7** shows the willingness of domestic workers to supply hours at different wage rates. Putting this supply curve together with our new demand curve for paid household workers, we see that the equilibrium quantity of labor hired and the market wage both fall. This means that households are likely to engage in more of their own household production and rely on fewer paid hours supplied by domestic employees. Those domestic workers that are still hired will end up with a lower hourly wage than before the tax.

Clearly, employees are hurt by the introduction of the payroll tax because the amount of work hours demanded declines, and the market wage per hour decreases from $10 to $9.50. Workers end up bearing 50 cents of the tax through a reduction in their hourly wage even though it is *the employer* who is actually paying the tax. However, the market wage has not fallen by the full 76.5 cents. This tells us that household employers are also bearing a portion of the tax in terms of the after-tax wage they end up paying. The amount of the tax actually borne by employers is 76.5 cents minus 50 cents, or 26.5 cents per hour. In other words, the household will pay employees $9.50 an hour and pay the government 76.5 cents an hour on top of

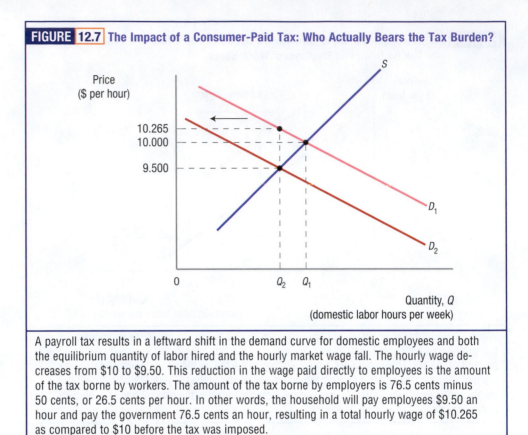

FIGURE 12.7 The Impact of a Consumer-Paid Tax: Who Actually Bears the Tax Burden?

A payroll tax results in a leftward shift in the demand curve for domestic employees and both the equilibrium quantity of labor hired and the hourly market wage fall. The hourly wage decreases from $10 to $9.50. This reduction in the wage paid directly to employees is the amount of the tax borne by workers. The amount of the tax borne by employers is 76.5 cents minus 50 cents, or 26.5 cents per hour. In other words, the household will pay employees $9.50 an hour and pay the government 76.5 cents an hour, resulting in a total hourly wage of $10.265 as compared to $10 before the tax was imposed.

this, resulting in a total wage of $10.265 an hour, which is 26.5 cents more than the $10 wage that existed before the payroll tax was levied.

We have just demonstrated that anytime employers are subject to taxes on the wages they pay, a portion of these taxes is likely to be passed along to employees in the form of a lower wage rate. This is the case whether we are talking about in-home workers, college professors, or hospital technicians. And, we can generalize this result even further: when a consumer must pay a tax on the purchase of a good or service, the supplier is likely to receive a lower price and thereby end up bearing part of the tax. Exactly how the tax is shared between demanders and suppliers—or employers and employees—is called the **tax incidence**.

TAX INCIDENCE The way in which the burden of a tax is shared between consumers and suppliers.

EXAMPLE When Chile reduced its payroll taxes from 30 percent to 5 percent in the early 1980s, researchers discovered that all of these tax savings were passed on to workers in the form of higher wages.[6] In other words, the workers had been bearing all of the payroll tax that employers paid to the government.

Panel (a) of **Figure 12.8** depicts a situation in which the supply of labor is relatively unresponsive to the wage rate. By contrast, panel (b) depicts a situation in which

· · · · · · ·

[6]Jonathan Gruber, "The Incidence of Payroll Taxation: Evidence from Chile." *Journal of Labor Economics*, 15, no. 2 (July 3, 1997): S72–S101.

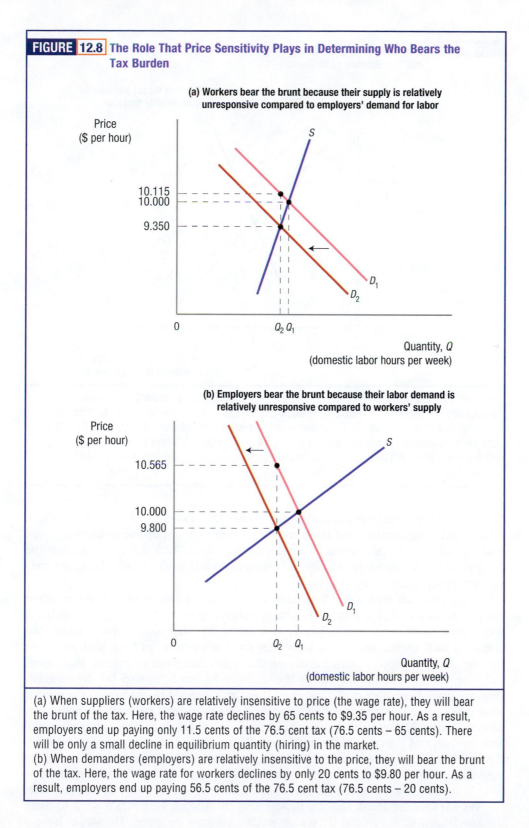

FIGURE 12.8 The Role That Price Sensitivity Plays in Determining Who Bears the Tax Burden

(a) Workers bear the brunt because their supply is relatively unresponsive compared to employers' demand for labor

(b) Employers bear the brunt because their labor demand is relatively unresponsive compared to workers' supply

(a) When suppliers (workers) are relatively insensitive to price (the wage rate), they will bear the brunt of the tax. Here, the wage rate declines by 65 cents to $9.35 per hour. As a result, employers end up paying only 11.5 cents of the 76.5 cent tax (76.5 cents – 65 cents). There will be only a small decline in equilibrium quantity (hiring) in the market.
(b) When demanders (employers) are relatively insensitive to the price, they will bear the brunt of the tax. Here, the wage rate for workers declines by only 20 cents to $9.80 per hour. As a result, employers end up paying 56.5 cents of the 76.5 cent tax (76.5 cents – 20 cents).

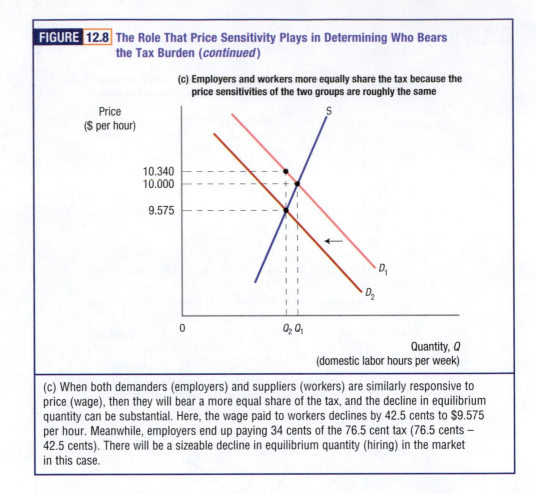

FIGURE 12.8 The Role That Price Sensitivity Plays in Determining Who Bears the Tax Burden (*continued*)

(c) Employers and workers more equally share the tax because the price sensitivities of the two groups are roughly the same

(c) When both demanders (employers) and suppliers (workers) are similarly responsive to price (wage), then they will bear a more equal share of the tax, and the decline in equilibrium quantity can be substantial. Here, the wage paid to workers declines by 42.5 cents to $9.575 per hour. Meanwhile, employers end up paying 34 cents of the 76.5 cent tax (76.5 cents – 42.5 cents). There will be a sizeable decline in equilibrium quantity (hiring) in the market in this case.

the demand is relatively unresponsive to the wage rate. Panel (c) shows a situation in which both labor demand and labor supply are relatively responsive to the wage rate, leading to a more equal sharing of the tax burden. Figure 12.8 demonstrates that the amount of the tax borne by employers (consumers) and workers (suppliers) depends on each group's sensitivity to price.

Employers can pass along a greater amount of the tax to their workers when their demand for labor is relatively more responsive to wage rates compared with the responsiveness of workers who supply that labor. In other words, if employers can easily cut back on the amount of labor they use but workers *can't* cut back much on the amount they supply—perhaps because they can't find work elsewhere—employees will bear the brunt of the tax. This is the situation depicted in panel (a). By contrast, employers will bear more of the tax when they can't respond to changes in the market wage rate as readily as their workers. That is, if employers *can't* cut back on their labor demand easily, but workers can cut back their hours supplied, then, employers will bear the brunt of the tax, not the employees. This is the situation shown in panel (b). If parents, for example, cannot cut back much on the total number of child-care hours they require—perhaps because they have few alternatives or little flexibility in their work schedules—then they will get stuck paying more of the tax on in-home child care.

Why is this so? Think about a person who must work 40 hours a week to meet the conditions of his prison parole or welfare-to-work program. He would have a vertical supply curve at 40 work hours per week. Because he cannot cut back on his hours, a payroll tax can be passed along in full to him in the form of a lower wage rate. Similarly, when employers are "stuck" in terms of their demand for employees, they will bear the entire tax. Think about an ill household member who requires the assistance of in-home medical aides when his partner is working outside the home. Or, what about a situation in which government regulations or union contracts require that a certain number of employees be working on-site at all times because of health or safety concerns (e.g., lifeguards on the beach, teachers in preschools, or inspectors in nuclear power plants). When employers have virtually no flexibility in adjusting the number of labor hours they use when the wage rate changes, they will end up bearing the brunt of the tax, at least in the short run. [We discuss their long-run response in Chapter 16.]

As with subsidies, it does not matter who actually pays the tax bill. When a payroll tax is collected from employers, the wage they pay workers will likely decline. This decline essentially shifts some of the tax burden to employees. A similar result occurs in the real-estate market. A potential home buyer takes into account the annual property taxes she must pay when deciding her willingness to pay a seller for his home—the higher the taxes, the lower the offer price will be. As a result, home sellers will bear at least part of a property tax increase in the form of a lower sales price.

What if the payroll tax is collected directly from workers, that is, deducted from their paychecks? The wage that these employees (suppliers) are willing to accept will likely *rise*, essentially shifting part of the tax burden to their employers (demanders). The same dynamic occurs when a gasoline tax is imposed on gas stations—the market price of gasoline rises, shifting some of the tax burden to consumers.

To prove this is so, remember that at any level of output, the height of the supply curve reflects the marginal cost of producing that last unit of output. If the 76.5 cents per hour payroll tax is withheld from worker paychecks instead of being collected from employers, there will be a leftward shift in the labor supply curve to reflect the additional cost of supplying each hour of work. The *vertical distance* between the original and new supply curves is exactly equal to 76.5 cents at each and every level of quantity supplied. The tax is, in effect, an additional opportunity cost: workers must pay the government 76.5 cents for each hour they work. **Figure 12.9** shows the impact this tax has on the labor market: the equilibrium wage rises to $10.265, and the equilibrium number of hours worked falls.

The *after-tax* wage that employees receive is $10.265 minus 76.5 cents, or $9.50, exactly the same amount they would have received if the tax were collected directly from their employers instead.

To prove this equivalence, notice that the vertical displacement of the supply curve by 76.5 cents is exactly the same as the vertical displacement of the demand curve in Figure 12.6. Using Figure 12.9, you can prove that regardless of which curve actually shifts—that is, which side of the market is taxed—the way in which the tax burden is shared remains the same.

We have now debunked one of the greatest illusions about taxes that people have—that we can escape paying taxes if we are not the ones directly taxed by the government. Taxes get passed "backward" to suppliers and "forward" to demanders all the time, whether we are talking about taxes on wages, gasoline, or cigarettes. Now you understand why, whenever goods or services—including your own labor—are taxed, *both* buyers and sellers can expect to pay part of this tax, at least in the short run. We will come back to this result in Chapter 16, when we discover that there are some exceptions to this conclusion, especially in the long run.

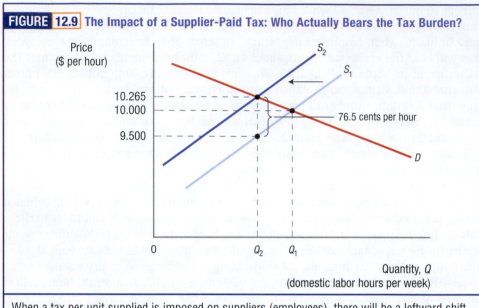

FIGURE 12.9 The Impact of a Supplier-Paid Tax: Who Actually Bears the Tax Burden?

When a tax per unit supplied is imposed on suppliers (employees), there will be a leftward shift in the supply curve: the opportunity cost of supplying each and every unit (hour) increases by the amount of the tax. When the 76.5 cent per hour payroll tax is withheld from workers' pay-checks instead of being paid directly by employers, they must pay the government 76.5 cents for each hour they work. As a result, the market wage rises to $10.265 per hour, and the equilibrium number of hours worked declines. The after-tax wage rate that employees receive is $10.265 *minus* 76.5 cents, or $9.50 per hour, exactly the same amount they would have received if the tax were paid directly by their employers instead.

The Deadweight Loss from Taxes

In addition to having to pay part of the tax, demanders and suppliers are made worse off in another way. In panel (a) of **Figure 12.10**, the consumer surplus that demanders enjoyed pretax is equal to the red-shaded area. Recall that this surplus represents the gains from trade that consumers enjoy because they don't actually hand over their total willingness to pay for each and every unit of the good they purchase. Likewise, pretax, producers enjoyed gains from trade-producer surplus-equal to the blue-shaded area because each unit is not sold at its actual marginal cost of production.

Now let's look at how the consumer and producer surpluses change after a per unit tax is imposed that is collected from suppliers (employees). Consumer (employer) surplus shrinks to the *red*-shaded triangle in panel (b); the *green*-shaded rectangle is lost surplus that represents the taxes that the consumers indirectly bear through the higher market price (wage) they now pay suppliers. Producer surplus shrinks to the *blue*-shaded area; the *orange*-shaded rectangle is lost surplus that equals the taxes that are borne by the suppliers. The problem here is that if we add together the after-tax amounts of consumer and producer surplus plus the total amount of taxes paid, we fall short of the total amount of surplus that consumers and producers enjoyed prior to the imposition of the tax. This shortfall is represented in panel (b) by the *purple*-shaded triangle and the *pink*-shaded triangle, which, respectively, represent losses in consumer and producer well-being that are not accounted for by the tax

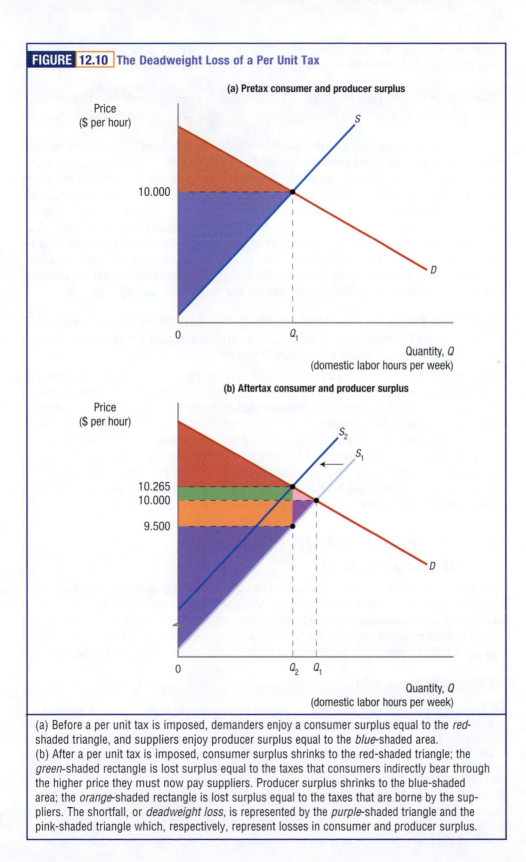

FIGURE 12.10   **The Deadweight Loss of a Per Unit Tax**

(a) Pretax consumer and producer surplus

(b) Aftertax consumer and producer surplus

(a) Before a per unit tax is imposed, demanders enjoy a consumer surplus equal to the *red*-shaded triangle, and suppliers enjoy producer surplus equal to the *blue*-shaded area.
(b) After a per unit tax is imposed, consumer surplus shrinks to the red-shaded triangle; the *green*-shaded rectangle is lost surplus equal to the taxes that consumers indirectly bear through the higher price they must now pay suppliers. Producer surplus shrinks to the blue-shaded area; the *orange*-shaded rectangle is lost surplus equal to the taxes that are borne by the suppliers. The shortfall, or *deadweight loss*, is represented by the *purple*-shaded triangle and the pink-shaded triangle which, respectively, represent losses in consumer and producer surplus.

payments. This means that consumers and producers are harmed by more than the taxes that they are forced to pay. We call this a **deadweight loss**.

> **DEADWEIGHT LOSS** The reduction in consumer and producer well-being—beyond the amount of taxes paid to the government—when a tax is imposed.

Why are we concerned about deadweight losses in a market? The reason is that these losses represent gains from trade that disappear and no longer benefit consumers, producers, or even the government. They arise because there are units of the good that are not produced, even though the willingness of consumers to pay (represented by the height of the demand curve) is greater than the marginal cost of supply (represented by the height of the supply curve). According to our basic economic principles, these units *should be* produced and sold. Why aren't they? Because the tax per unit is greater than the gains from trade that would be reaped, these units will not be traded. Consumers lose, producers lose, and even the government loses additional tax revenue that could be collected if it lowered the tax on the marginal units, $Q_1 - Q_2$.

> **ECONOMIC FALLACY** The 2009 Health Care Affordability Act will require all employers to provide comprehensive, subsidized health insurance to their employees. This will make employees better off.
>
> **Uncertain.** You have learned that when an employer is required to pay a tax over and above the wage she pays her employees, the wage rate tends to fall. This analysis can be extended to a legal requirement that employers must provide subsidized medical insurance to their employees; the employees' wage rate is likely to fall. Because the wage rate of employees paid the minimum wage cannot legally fall, they will face a greater likelihood of losing their jobs after the health-insurance mandate goes into effect. Higher-earning employees will also be made worse off if they prefer higher wages to subsidized health insurance; this is especially likely for young, healthy workers who are not heavy users of medical services.

12.4 The Impact of Differential Taxes and Subsidies

Have you ever been frustrated when you didn't qualify for a government subsidy—say, for a student loan—or were taxed more at a Walmart in one city versus another? Have you ever made a conscious decision to buy a product on the Internet rather than from a local retailer to avoid paying sales taxes? If so, you are aware that government taxes and subsidies can vary from individual to individual, place to place, and good to good.

SOLVED PROBLEM

Q Cash-strapped states are lobbying the federal government to require Internet retailers to collect state sales taxes for all sales made on their Web sites, just like "box" retailers now collect sales tax at the point of sale. Opponents argue that taxpayers are already required to pay taxes on their Internet purchases at the same time that they file their annual state income-tax return. If, as we've argued, there really is no difference whether the buyer or seller pays the tax, then why are the states making such a fuss over this at the federal level?

A We have shown that it doesn't matter whether a (sales) tax is collected from purchasers or sellers—the quantity purchased, amount of taxes paid, and the tax incidence will remain the same. However, in the case of Internet sales, it is far easier for states to collect the taxes owed them by putting the burden on Web retailers to collect these taxes. Why is this so? It is far easier to audit the sales of the Web retailers—and sort them by the buyer's state of residence—than to audit each and every taxpayer's purchases and figure out when sales tax had and hadn't been paid. So the bottom line is that there is a differential cost of compliance that underlies the states' lobbying efforts.

Many times, governments consciously target subsidies or taxes to a subset of people or markets. For example, subsidized college loans and subsidized child care are targeted to households with incomes below a certain level. Sin taxes are often imposed on "undesirable" goods (e.g., whiskey) but not on other goods (e.g., milk). And, even when a tax is uniformly imposed on every supplier or demander in a particular geographic region or country—like the U.S. Social Security payroll tax—it often doesn't extend to other regions or countries. This lack of uniformity can have a significant impact on the well-being of those who are subsidized *and* those who are not and, similarly, of the taxed *and* the untaxed.

Consider the child-care subsidy given to welfare-to-work mothers. As we have shown, this leads to an increase in the market price of child care. The higher price must be paid by subsidized and unsubsidized parents, alike. As a result, the opportunity cost of unsubsidized parents going to work rises. Depending on the magnitude of the price increase, it may discourage some of these unsubsidized parents from remaining in the labor force and encourage them to return to in-home production activities.

The same phenomenon arises when only a select group of suppliers must pay taxes on the goods and services they sell. Eventually, those who are taxed are likely to be pushed out of the market because their costs are higher than their untaxed competitors. Hospitals and other nonprofit organizations that are exempt from paying sales, property, and income taxes can provide their services at a lower price than for-profit competitors who are subject to these taxes. This has the effect of pushing for-profit suppliers out of the market when both types of suppliers compete to sell the same goods and services.

Recently, attention has been called to the differential subsidy that corporations get when they buy tickets to sporting events—they can deduct the expense from their taxes while individual fans cannot. The end result is that ticket prices rise substantially and allegedly keep these fans from attending games. [7]

We see the same scenario play out in international markets. For example, nations often accuse one another of subsidizing their "home" producers to give them a cost advantage in their own domestic markets and in foreign markets relative to other suppliers. China has been accused of "dumping" heavily subsidized steel and chemical products into the world market.[8] The United States has been criticized for its large agricultural subsidies, which amount to over $20 billion a year. These agricultural subsidies have been blamed for the collapse in the world price of cotton and, consequently, the failure of large numbers of subsistence cotton growers in Africa.[9] And fuel subsidies—that governments such as Mexico, India, and China give their citizens—may have quelled street protests and political unrest but have also contributed to the worldwide increase in oil prices.[10]

· · · · · · ·

[7]Richard Schmalbeck and Jay Soled, "Throw Out Skybox Tax Subsidies." *New York Times*, April 10, 2010.

[8]Steven Weisman, "U.S. Says China Agrees to End Some Subsidies." *New York Times*, November 29, 2007.

[9]Gumisai Mutume," Mounting Opposition to Northern Farm Subsidies." *Africa Recovery*, 17, no. 1 (May, 2003): 18.

[10]Keith Bradsher, "Fuel Subsidies Overseas Take a Toll on U.S." *New York Times*, July 28, 2008, p.1.

More recently, President Obama and other world leaders have stepped up the pressure on China to revalue its currency (the renminbi, or Chinese yuan) upward relative to other currencies.[11] The "cheaper" the Chinese currency is, the less expensive Chinese exports are to buy with other currencies. It has been estimated that the Chinese government has artificially suppressed the value of its currency by as much as 25 percent, which is, in effect, a 25 percent across-the-board subsidy to all exporting producers in the Chinese economy. It encourages consumers in other countries to purchase Chinese goods rather than higher-priced products produced in their own countries.

Even when a government doesn't directly subsidize its own producers, it often imposes taxes (called *tariffs*) on imports of foreign-made products. The impact on the home market is the same: the entry of foreign producers is essentially blocked because the tariffs they must pay make them uncompetitive relative to domestic producers.

Consider the differential impact of U.S. Social Security payroll taxes. These are paid by employers on wages earned by employees who work in the United States but not by foreign workers who fill jobs that are offshored. Nor are they collected from employers located in Mexico and elsewhere. As a result, the cost of hiring U.S. employees rises and makes them increasingly noncompetitive relative to foreign, untaxed workers who can readily substitute for them. U.S.-based employees will keep their jobs only if there are no cheaper substitutes elsewhere or if their wages sink low enough to cover the bulk of the payroll taxes collected from their employers.

From an economic standpoint, are differential taxes and subsidies "good" or "bad" in terms of the allocation of scarce resources? To answer this question, consider the case of foreign shrimp suppliers who are the lowest-cost producers in the world but are effectively blocked from the U.S. market because of highly subsidized U.S. producers. Although the market price for shrimp will likely end up being lower in the United States due to the subsidies, the real resource cost of producing the shrimp is higher than if it were produced by the lowest-cost foreign suppliers. Scarce resources have not been put to use in a way that maximizes the global production of shrimp and other goods: more resources are devoted to shrimp production than in the absence of the subsidy. Foreign suppliers who have the comparative advantage in production—that is, those with the lowest opportunity cost—end up producing too little shrimp. Ironically, even though the global resource cost of supplying shrimp rises, U.S. consumers who purchase subsidized shrimp are likely to be made better off at the expense of taxpayers who pay for the subsidies.

Cities are also affected by the presence of differential subsidies or taxes. Think about a city that imposes a steep payroll tax on everyone who works or lives in that city. If there are reasonably close work and living opportunities in untaxed adjacent communities, what do you think will happen to the city in terms of residents and jobs? As long as consumers and producers can escape the tax by "voting with their feet," the city with the payroll tax will become an increasingly undesirable location for employers, employees, and households.

ECONOMIC FALLACY   Regardless of whether a government "protects" its domestic industries by imposing tariffs on foreign suppliers or subsidizing domestic producers, the outcome in the domestic market—in terms of the good's equilibrium price and quantity—will be the same.

. . . .

[11]David Sanger, "Obama Presses China to Let Currency Rise." *New York Times*, September 24, 2010.

Uncertain. As we have shown, producer subsidies usually reduce the price that consumers pay for a good. In contrast, tariffs increase the cost of importing goods, thereby shifting the supply curve of foreign products to the left. The result is an increase in price and a decrease in the quantity of foreign-produced goods that are imported. As these imported goods drop out of the domestic market, the price of the domestically produced alternatives may rise, depending on the amount of competition in the domestic market.

Given this result, you might ask why a government would ever use tariffs instead of subsidies to protect its own industries. The answer is simple: tariffs don't "cost" the government anything (and even enhance the government's tax receipts). By contrast, subsidies must come out of government revenues and taxpayers' pockets.

WHAT YOU SHOULD HAVE LEARNED FROM CHAPTER 12

- A household will weigh the relative cost of purchasing goods and services produced in the market versus the opportunity cost of producing them within the home.

- Subsidies and taxes affect people's opportunity costs and the activities they decide to engage in, including whether to join the labor market or not.

- Because household production is untaxed, imposing taxes on market goods and services will discourage the substitution toward market-based production.

- Regardless of who actually *receives* a subsidy, it will be shared between demanders and suppliers in exactly the same way.

- Regardless of who actually *pays* a tax, it will be borne by demanders and suppliers in exactly the same way.

- The amount of a tax or subsidy attributable to consumers and producers is dictated by their relative responsiveness to price. The share of the tax or subsidy attributable to consumers and producers declines the more sensitive they are to price.

- When a tax is imposed on a good or service, demanders and suppliers lose more than the amount of tax they bear. They also suffer a deadweight loss in terms of the surplus they receive.

- If taxes or subsidies are differential in nature—that is, they are not applied uniformly across all consumers, suppliers, or markets—they will bestow a differential competitive advantage on a subset of economic players.

- When the value of a currency is kept artificially low, the government provides an indirect, across-the-board subsidy to its exporting industries.

KEY TERMS

Tax credit, p. 340

Price wedge, p. 341

Tax incidence, p. 350

Deadweight loss, p. 356

QUESTIONS AND PROBLEMS

1. Environmentalists are pushing the government to impose a tax on disposable diapers because after they are used, they take up space in landfills and are non-biodegradable. Using supply and demand diagrams, show the effect that such a tax would have on the equilibrium price and quantity of

a) disposable diapers;

b) cloth diapers; and

c) Ivory Snow laundry detergent (a product used primarily to wash cloth diapers).

d) Show, in diagram (a), how much of the burden of the tax is borne by consumers and how much by producers.

2. To finance research on the effects of smoking, then-California governor Arnold Schwarzenegger successfully campaigned for a law that increased the state tax on cigarettes to $3 per pack. Using supply and demand graphs,

a) show how much of this tax is borne by California cigarette buyers versus California cigarette sellers.

b) Using supply and demand diagrams, indicate how, if at all, your answer would change if you were looking only at potential smokers rather than existing smokers.

c) What do you think will happen to the number of trips California smokers take annually to Nevada, where cigarettes aren't taxed? Explain your answer.

3. Suppose the government agrees to pay a $5 per hour subsidy per child to parents who use licensed child-care providers. Graph the effect this will have on the equilibrium quantity and price of child care in

a) the licensed child-care market and

b) the unlicensed babysitting market.

c) Show how the subsidy would be shared between licensed child-care providers and parents. What determines who benefits from the subsidy?

4. England is considering funding hospital care for the poor by imposing a 6 percent tax on prescription drugs sold at private pharmacies throughout the country. Using supply and demand graphs, show the impact this tax would have on

a) the equilibrium price and quantity of pharmacy prescription drugs;

b) the equilibrium price and quantity of nonprescription drugs such as over-the-counter pain killers;

c) the equilibrium price and quantity of foreign drug imports that are exempt from the tax; and

d) the number of pharmacists employed in England and their equilibrium wage.

5. When gasoline prices soar, the federal government often considers temporarily suspending the 18.4 cent per gallon federal tax on gasoline. Using supply and demand diagrams, show how removing this tax would affect the equilibrium quantity and price in

a) the gasoline market;

b) the automobile tire market;

c) the taxicab market.

d) Indicate on the graph you drew in (a) who benefits from removal of the tax.

6. In an effort to balance the budget of the U.S. federal government, Congress has discussed dropping its hefty subsidy of U.S. farm products. Using supply and demand graphs, show the impact this change would have on equilibrium price and quantity in

a) the corn market;

b) the market for agricultural land;

c) the market for cornflakes; and

d) the market for ethanol (fuel made from corn).

7. Suppose that the U.S. government decides to subsidize oil exploration and production to eventually reduce gas prices in the United States. Who will actually benefit from this subsidy? Explain your answer.

8. *True, False, or Uncertain:* To stimulate demand for its products during a housing slump, Corning introduced a $500 rebate to be paid directly to purchasers of its fiberglass insulation. As a result, the price after rebate paid by consumers dropped by $500. Explain your answer.

9. If grocery stores install self-checkout registers and lay off their cashiers, they no longer will have to pay federal payroll taxes on cashier wages. What would you predict will happen to other grocery-store employees as payroll taxes continue to rise? Will your prediction hold for all grocery employees, including meat inspectors? Explain your answer.

10. In 1989, the United States' Special Supplemental Nutrition Program for Women, Infants, and Children (WIC) radically changed its subsidy structure, replacing subsidies for infant formula with subsidies for enriched infant cereals, eggs, and other dairy products. Why do you think it made this change?

11. In 2011, Congress debated the merits of continuing its 41 cents a gallon subsidy paid to ethanol gas refiners (ethanol is produced from corn). A major proponent for renewing the subsidy was the corn growers' trade association.

    a) Using a supply and demand diagram, show why corn growers were so vocal about supporting a subsidy that it was not directly receiving.
    b) Using a supply and demand diagram, now show why cereal producers were so supportive of abolishing the subsidy.

12. The U.S. Social Security and Medicare payroll tax is paid by *both* employees and employers: 7.65 percent of wages is paid directly to the government by employers and 7.65 percent is withheld from employee paychecks. Using supply and demand graphs, show

    a) the impact of this "dual" tax on equilibrium wages and the quantity of employees hired and
    b) that the distribution of the burden of the total tax—15.3 percent—between employees and employers would not change if the entire amount was collected from employers.

13. Using supply and demand graphs, show how a tax that is a percentage of sales revenue (rather than a per unit tax) affects a market's equilibrium price and quantity. Is it still the case that the burden of the tax will be shared between consumers and suppliers in the same way, regardless of who actually pays the tax? Explain your answer.

14. In an effort to curb obesity and rein in medical costs, Congress is considering the introduction of a $1 tax on each Big Mac (and similar fast-food sandwiches) purchased. Using the following diagram, calculate the deadweight loss that would result from this tax.

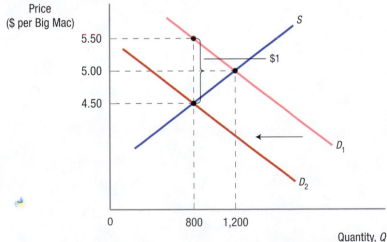

15. For many years, state and local governments borrowed funds to finance capital projects (prisons, parks, roads, etc.) by issuing *tax-free* bonds. These bonds have attracted lenders by offering interest payments that are free from federal and local income taxation. The federal government recently introduced an alternative taxable bond program—"Build America Bonds"—which provides a 35 percent subsidy to states and municipalities for the interest they pay on the bonds they issue but requires bondholders to pay taxes on all of the interest they receive. Using a supply and demand diagram, show how—if at all—this change in policy will affect the amount of money borrowed by municipalities and the after-tax interest rate received by bondholders.

Investing for the Future: Accumulating Human and Other Types of Capital

"If a man empties his purse into his head, no man can take it away from him. An investment in knowledge always pays the best interest."

Benjamin Franklin, signer of the Declaration of Independence and the U.S. Constitution, inventor, printer, and author

As you have learned, households interact with the market economy in two ways. First, they are *demanders* of goods and services and, second, they are *suppliers* of labor for market-based production. In reality, as we will see in this chapter, households provide a whole host of inputs to the market, ranging from financial capital to a wide variety of labor services. This means that the household is actually a more complex organization than previously described, in that it does not always spend all of its income to maximize its immediate level of well-being. As incomes rise and households meet and exceed their subsistence needs, they sometimes look for opportunities that can increase their future well-being, even if it means lower current well-being. In other words, people allocate some of their scarce resources—money and time—to activities that promise a better future for themselves and those they care about. We say that these people are *investing for the future*.

One of the primary roles of households is to build the *human capital* of its members. You will recall from Chapter 1 that human capital refers to the skills, talents, appearance, and other attributes of people that translate into higher returns in the labor market and into greater personal well-being. Household members contribute to each other's human capital by providing safe and warm shelter, clean drinking water, and nutritious meals; seeking medical care when needed; instilling core values, a work ethic, and socialization skills; and by pursuing educational opportunities. Most of these activities have a significant investment component, because they lead to a future pay off in terms of higher wages, longer lives, and a higher quality of life. That you and your family are willing to make these types of investments—forgoing some well-being now for a greater amount of well-being in the future—is reflected by your enrollment in this class.

In this chapter, we discuss the inherent trade-off between consuming and investing, and we explore alternative investment strategies. We also focus on ways in which you can invest in your own human capital to increase the future value of your labor and, consequently, your lifetime flow of consumption (including leisure) and well-being.

13.1 Consumption versus Investment

Households spend the bulk of their income and time producing and using up "consumables" that create immediate well-being. We have already seen that a good deal of time is spent in unpaid household production to produce goods that are immediately consumed, such as meals, clean clothes, and child care. Similarly, a large portion of a person's earned income is spent on the purchase and **consumption** of items such as food, clothing, rock concerts, and cafe lattes.

CONSUMPTION Activities that create immediate well-being and that use up resources in the process.

EXAMPLE When we go to a movie, we use up some of our time and money.

EXAMPLE When we go on vacation, we use up both time and money.

In contrast, **investment** activities provide little, if any, current well-being, but they offer the possibility of increasing future well-being. Investing builds different kinds of wealth holdings—which we call *assets* or *capital*. Investing often takes discipline because it requires that you not only live *within* your means, but that you set aside some of your current resources in the hope that you will gain sufficiently greater future well-being.

INVESTMENT Current resources that are allocated for the purpose of building an accumulation or stock of capital to potentially increase your future well-being.

EXAMPLE Your employer withholds $100 each month from your paycheck to deposit into your 401(k) retirement account. Your goal is to accumulate financial assets that will increase your well-being after you have retired.

EXAMPLE Your parents buy gold coins as a hedge against future inflation to ensure that their future purchasing power results in an adequate level of well-being.

When people talk about their investments, they often refer to their financial wealth, including their bank accounts, stock portfolios, and mutual-fund balances. And, until the 2007 Great Recession that seriously deflated housing prices, people often also spoke about their homes as their greatest investment. Such wealth-accumulation activities often require the investment of both time and money. While households make investments to build their financial and human capital, business owners invest their earnings and borrowed money to acquire land, equipment, software, and so forth to increase their future profitability. Scientists build their intellectual capital by investing money and time to obtain graduate degrees and postdoctoral training. Even nations invest in building their stock of physical and human capital by spending money on roads, clean-water facilities, and education to increase future economic growth rates.

There are many types of capital that investors can accumulate. These tend to differ in terms of their payoff, riskiness, and timeliness of payback. We can classify these assets into three categories:

- Physical capital: for example, land, equipment, and structures
- Financial capital: for example, government and corporate bonds, stocks, bank CDs, and mutual funds
- Human capital: for example, health, beauty, educational attainment, computer skills, personal reputation, and social networks

By accumulating these kinds of capital, we are often able to shift our future production possibilities frontier (PPF) outward, which means we will be able to consume more of one or more goods without having to give up consumption of any other goods. For example, earning a college degree tends to increase a person's wage rate, thereby increasing the amount of market-based goods and services she can purchase per hour worked. As a result, a college graduate will be able to consume more than a high school graduate and still have the same amount of time left over for household production and leisure activities. **Figure 13.1** illustrates this outcome: the PPF rotates out to the right, reflecting the increase in goods that can be purchased for any given amount of household outputs.

Sometimes, we allocate our resources to goods and services that provide immediate well-being but also offer the potential to accumulate wealth. We consume housing services from the homes we own but also benefit from an increase in wealth if our homes, as assets, increase in value in the future. We enjoy reading good books that may, at the same time, improve our vocabulary and thereby augment our human capital and labor market opportunities. A provocative economics class can entertain you and, at the same time, give you a lifelong perspective about the world around you.

More commonly, however, we face a trade-off between consumption and investment and cannot have both at the same time. In other words, a dollar saved is a dollar that cannot be spent now. An hour spent in class is an hour that cannot be used to earn money that can be spent on consumables. How does an individual or household choose between current consumption and investing for the future? How much, if anything, should be invested in each of the many investment opportunities available?

FIGURE 13.1 **How Accumulating Capital Changes a Person's Production Possibilities Frontier**

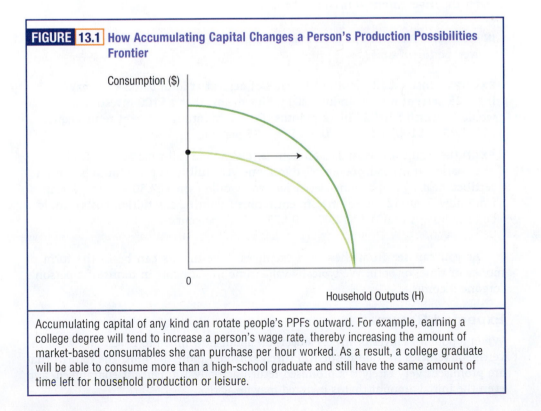

Accumulating capital of any kind can rotate people's PPFs outward. For example, earning a college degree will tend to increase a person's wage rate, thereby increasing the amount of market-based consumables she can purchase per hour worked. As a result, a college graduate will be able to consume more than a high-school graduate and still have the same amount of time left for household production or leisure.

These decisions are made according to our basic economic model of choice—people act as if they have compared the economic (opportunity) cost of each investment alternative to the benefit they would receive in the future. In other words, they assess the *net benefit* of investing in the accumulation of different types of capital, just like they do for alternative consumption opportunities. We already know that your opportunity cost of investing is the well-being you would have enjoyed today from the money and time that you invest instead. Remember that "time is money" in that you could have used the time you invest in building your stock of capital to earn income and purchase consumables—such as a new iPhone—or enjoy leisure activities such as going to the movies.

A Bird in the Hand?

How does an economic decision maker evaluate the benefits of making an investment? Specifically, what would it take for someone to agree to delay gratification until sometime in the future? All else equal, we would all prefer to have a new car or a designer wardrobe today rather than waiting a year for the same car or wardrobe. In other words, current well-being always trumps an equal amount of well-being in the future. After all, who knows what tomorrow will bring? Accumulating capital of any kind and waiting for it to pay off is risky business. Perhaps there will be no payoff in the future or the investor won't be around to enjoy it. Or, inflation could erode the value of the future payoff.

Investors must expect that the gain in their future well-being will more than compensate them for the "pain" (reduction in well-being) inflicted from giving up some of their current consumption. This is why banks must pay interest to attract savers' money—no one would put $100 in a savings account if all they would get in a year is $100. This is also why the longer an investor must wait to be paid back, the greater the **investment return** must be.

INVESTMENT RETURN The percentage change in the value of an investment over a given period of time.

EXAMPLE Insured 12-month certificates of deposit at local banks were paying 1.25 percent interest in July, 2011. This means that a $100 investment would be worth $101.25 in 12 months. The 12-month investment return equals ($101.25 − $100) / $100 = 0.0125 = 1.25 percent.

EXAMPLE You could earn $12 an hour if you worked full-time at your Dad's pizza parlor. If instead, you enrolled in a one-year full-time program to become a certified heating and cooling electrician, you would earn $22.50 an hour a year from now. Your 12-month investment return (ignoring any tuition costs) would be ($22.50 − $12.00) / $12.00 = 0.875 = 87.5 percent.

As you can see from these two examples, investments can be in the form of money or time, or both. We typically value time investments in terms of a person's forgone income.

Expected Return

When a potential investor makes a decision about how much to invest and what investment vehicles to choose, she will surely consider more than just the returns that are promised. Very rarely is a promised return actually 100 percent guaranteed, and even the initial amount that is invested may be at risk.

To assess the net benefit of making an investment, the uncertainty that the future payoff will actually occur must also be considered. This investment risk is factored in by *weighting* the promised return by the probability that it will actually materialize. We call this the **expected investment return**.

EXPECTED INVESTMENT RETURN An investment's return weighted by the probability that it will actually materialize.

EXAMPLE Suppose that you are offered the opportunity to invest in the bonds of a floundering company that is desperately in need of a cash infusion. These bonds will pay 30 percent annual interest. The probability that the company will file for bankruptcy within the year and return your initial investment without any interest is 60 percent. Then the expected return for each $100 you invest equals $[(0.4 \times \$130) + (0.60 \times \$100)] - \$100] / \$100 = .12$ or 12 percent.

In the preceding example, there are two possibilities that an investor must confront: she will get $130 back 40 percent of time, and her original $100 back with no interest 60 percent of the time. This means that the expected investment return can be computed by a simple weighting of the two possible investment returns: $(0.4 \times 30\%$ interest$) + (0.6 \times 0\%$ interest$) = .12$ or 12 percent. (Note that the weights—0.4 and .06—must sum to 1 because one outcome or the other must occur.)

SOLVED PROBLEM

Q Suppose that in the preceding example there is now a 10 percent chance that you will lose your initial investment; a 50 percent chance that you will get your initial investment back without interest; and a 40 percent chance that you will get your investment back with 30 percent interest. What is the expected return of an investment of $1,000?

A The expected return for each $1,000 invested equals $[(0.10 \times \$0) + (0.50 \times \$1,000) + (0.40 \times \$1,300) - \$1,000] / \$1,000 = .02$ or 2%.

Risk Premiums

The greater the perceived risk that all or part of an investment will be lost, the greater its promised return must be. An investor must be paid a **risk premium**, an additional return over and above what it would take simply to compensate him for deferring consumption to a future date.

RISK PREMIUM The additional return that must be given to induce a decision maker to engage in a risky activity such as a risky investment.

EXAMPLE People who invest in risky venture capital funds will require a promise of higher average returns to compensate them for the greater probability that many of these ventures will fail to return a penny (including the initial investment).

EXAMPLE People who engage in risky work activities—such as capping out-of-control oil wells—must be paid very high wages to compensate them for the increased likelihood of serious injury or death.

To gauge the riskiness of an investment activity, we can estimate the risk premium embedded in its expected return by comparing this return to a risk-free investment's rate of return. U.S. Treasury bonds and notes ("Treasuries") are "loans" that investors make to the U.S. government; they are considered among the world's safest investments because they are backed by the "full credit" of the United States. As long as Treasuries are perceived by investors to be risk-free, they will not include any risk premium in their rates of return. They must only compensate investors for deferring consumption and for the risk of inflation—that is, the risk that the future payoff will be in dollars that are worth less in terms of purchasing power.

During the global financial market "meltdown" in 2008, there was a "flight to safety" as investors from around the world moved their money into U.S. Treasuries. Overseas investors bought more than two-thirds of the Treasuries purchased during this period. The sudden upsurge in demand swamped the supply of Treasuries available, pushing the price of Treasuries up and the corresponding rates of return down to almost zero (the yield on three-week notes actually dropped to zero for a short time).[1] Why would anyone defer their consumption in the hopes of receiving a future return close to or equal to zero? Recall that during this period, the solvency of even the largest banks—such as Citibank and Wachovia—and large investment firms such as Goldman Sachs was unclear. Panicked investors looked for a short-term safe haven to "park" their money that would simply assure that they would get their investment dollars back. While small investors can conceivably protect their savings by stuffing it into a mattress, U.S. Treasuries have been the "mattresses" for large institutional investors.

Our "Taste" for Risk

How big will the risk premium be? For any given amount of uncertainty, the corresponding risk premium depends on how risk-averse people are. Economists have observed that people vary in terms of their risk tolerance or "risk preferences", that is, their willingness to take on risk. To test this premise, look around a casino and you will see people playing a variety of games with different chances of winning. We also observe that the willingness to engage in risky ventures changes as people age because the opportunity cost of taking risks changes as well. It's not surprising that most middle-aged parents—people who have accumulated lots of human capital along with lots of financial responsibilities—are more risk-averse when it comes to bungee jumping than their teenage children. Add to this the generally accepted fact that teenagers are biologically predisposed to risky choices because their brains are still maturing.

People fall into three categories when it comes to their risk preferences. Suppose a 5-year U.S. Treasury bond's risk-free return is 3.7 percent. Those who are "risk-averse" would require that a risky investment's expected return be *greater than* 3.7 percent for them to consider the investment. A "risk-neutral" person would require that the expected return be *at least* equal to 3.7 percent. By contrast, a "risk-preferring" person might be willing to make an investment even when its expected return *is less* than 3.7 percent if she believes there's at least a small chance the investment will return far more than that. Risk-preferring people often get a thrill from taking certain risks, that is, they get well-being just from taking the risk. People who play nickel slot machines in Las Vegas get a fun rush now and then, but the expected return is far less than at the nearby poker tables and significantly less than a nickel.

· · · · · · ·

[1]Vikas Bajaj and Michael Grynbaum, "Investors Buy U.S. Debt at Zero Yield." *New York Times,* December 9, 2008.

The Tax Treatment of Investment Returns

Different types of investments are often taxed differently. As a result, investment decisions can be significantly affected by tax policies. Municipal bonds—issued by municipalities such as state governments and cities—are often "double tax free," meaning that their interest payments are not taxable at either the federal or state level. And the interest paid on savings accounts is taxed at a higher income tax rate than the returns received from the sale of stocks that have appreciated in value.

Because it is the after-tax investment return that is important to an investor, he will require a higher pretax return on an investment that is more highly taxed than one that is taxed at a lower rate or is totally tax free. This explains why so many private institutions—such as universities, hospitals, and even football stadium owners—lobby their state governments to permit them to issue tax-free construction bonds. When successful, these groups can substantially reduce the returns they must offer investors, thereby significantly reducing their cost of borrowing money for their projects.

How Much Should You Invest?

After an investor identifies those opportunities that offer the highest expected after-tax returns, he must decide if these returns are high enough to entice him to defer his current consumption.

People differ in their opportunity cost of deferring well-being. For example, older people or those in ill health would be more likely to prefer current well-being rather than an increase in future well-being. In other words, these types of people have relatively short **time horizons**.

TIME HORIZON The time period that people consider when making economic decisions.

EXAMPLE People growing up in countries with shorter life expectancies tend to have a shorter time horizon than those living in countries with longer life expectancies.

EXAMPLE Children raised in urban areas plagued by high murder rates tend to have shorter time horizons than children raised in safer neighborhoods.

EXAMPLE People diagnosed with a terminal disease tend to have a shorter time horizon than those given a clean bill of health.

The shorter a person's time horizon, the greater the expected return must be to entice him to defer consumption into the future. In fact, people with shorter time horizons will often "eat up" their existing capital faster than if they had longer time horizons. Terminally ill patients may gift their savings to friends, relatives, and charities, or they may spend them on dream vacations. Young people with shorter time horizons may run down whatever human capital they have by smoking, using drugs, or engaging in risky gunplay. In effect, just as we can build our capital through investing, we can reduce it by "dissaving."

The bottom line is that a rational economic decision maker will require a higher expected return:

- The greater the riskiness of the investment
- The longer the wait for the payoff
- The greater the tax liability triggered by the investment payoff
- The shorter the investor's time horizon

13.2 Investing in Human Capital

We turn now to one specific class of capital that households tend to heavily invest in: **human capital**.

> **HUMAN CAPITAL** The stock of personal characteristics that contribute to the market value of a person's labor and market-based consumption opportunities. These include health status, intelligence, work ethic, educational attainment, strength, beauty, reputation, and social networks.

> **EXAMPLE** Working out at the gym every morning increases your stock of human capital by improving your health and giving you more energy when it comes to your labor market and leisure activities.

> **EXAMPLE** Beauty pageant contestants often have cosmetic surgery to improve their chances of winning.

We are all born with an "endowment" or stock of human capital. Within bounds, we can grow this initial stock of human capital by investing time and money in a wide variety of activities. However, not all aspects of our initial endowment can be augmented. For example, an adult who is 5 feet, 3 inches tall cannot, with today's available technology, invest resources to achieve a height of 6 feet, 10 inches tall. In contrast, today's eye-surgery options permit people to invest to correct the nearsightedness they were born with or developed in their early years so that they will no longer require glasses or contacts. Clearly, the state of today's technology has a substantial effect on the ways in which we can build our own human capital and that of others.

As is the case for other investments, a household builds its members' human capital to rotate their future PPFs outward. When successful, these investments increase the future return to each member's participation in the labor market. If you learn to speak Chinese today, this will undoubtedly expand your future employment opportunities. Other types of human capital investments, such as preventative health care (e.g., vaccinations), exercise, and healthy eating habits can increase your life span. And, of course, the longer you live, the longer you can receive returns to the investments made in your human capital.

Figure 13.1, shown earlier, depicts the effect that investment in human capital— in this case, gaining a college education—has on a person's PPF. Such investments rotate the PPF outward, reflecting the higher level of market-based consumption that can be gained for any given amount of leisure (or in-home production). The slope of the PPF has increased in absolute value, corresponding to the increase in wage rate that changes the trade-off between consumption and leisure.

As with all investment decisions, people will act as if they have compared the expected return of each human capital investment option with its opportunity cost. It is not necessarily the best economic choice for every person to earn a college degree; some people have a comparative advantage investing in method-acting classes or working as journeymen apprentices in a building trade. Human capital that is built through on-the-job training programs can yield excellent returns depending on the type of training, position, and industry. For example, an employer is apt to invest in a worker's on-the-job training when the know-how that the worker will gain—such as pipefitting and steel-welding skills—is "specific" to the firm or industry. This increases the probability that the employer will earn a return from making this investment in his employees in terms of higher employee productivity. (Interestingly, research has shown that nonwhite male workers enjoy a higher rate of return per hour from on-the-job training than their white counterparts.[2])

Labor-market conditions play an important role in determining the returns to human-capital investment opportunities. In societies where women are still largely excluded from the workforce, for example, parents are understandably less apt to invest a great deal in their daughters' formal educations. Instead, they invest heavily in their sons' higher education opportunities and in their daughters' development of household-production skills.

The Spillover Benefits of Investments in Human Capital

The investments people make in their own human capital and the human capital of other household members often generate spillover benefits in the community. For example, people around the world have invested time and money to obtain vaccinations against such communicable diseases as smallpox. This has led to the virtual eradication of these diseases. We have already discussed situations in which *positive externalities* can arise from a person's choices. We know that there will be a suboptimal amount of investment in activities that generate spillover benefits if people make decisions based solely on their private costs and benefits. This means that the community must either increase these private benefits or reduce the private costs that people face if it is to achieve the socially optimal level of investment in these activities. This is why, for example, vaccination programs in the United States and worldwide are often offered at low cost or even free by public-health agencies or highly subsidized nonprofit organizations.

According to many economists, educating children can generate significant positive externalities,[3] especially when it comes to primary and secondary education.[4] These spillover benefits include the following:

- An informed, literate population that contributes to civil stability and well-functioning democratic institutions
- A more productive labor force that promotes economic growth[5]
- A creative labor force that is technologically innovative
- A population that pursues healthier lifestyles
- A population with a common language and a shared set of values
- A more tolerant population that embraces diversity and an "open" society and economy

Even Nobel Laureate Milton Friedman, the champion of private markets, argued early in his career that primary and secondary education generated large positive externalities, thereby justifying government intervention in the form of public

· · · · · · ·

[2]Emily Blank, "Changes in the Stock of On-the-Job Training: Race and Wage Growth." *Review of Black Political Economy,* 17, no. 4 (March, 1989).

[3]Burton A. Weisbrod, *External Benefits of Education* (Princeton, NJ: Princeton University, Industrial Relations Section, 1964).

[4]James Poterba, "Government Intervention in the Markets for Education and Health Care: How and Why?" in Victor Fuchs (ed.) *Individual and Social Responsibility* (Chicago, IL: University of Chicago Press, 1996).

[5]Robert Barro, "Human Capital and Growth." *American Economic Review,* 91, no. 2 (May, 2001).

education.[6] It took him more than two decades to revise his position on the merits of direct government provision of educational services.[7]

The question that researchers continue to address is not whether spillover benefits from education exist but, rather, their magnitude.[8,9] With respect to higher education, there is general consensus that the only positive externality generated is the creation of new knowledge.[10]

Encouraging Greater Private Investment in Education

If spillover benefits arise from educating a country's children, how can societies ensure that households will invest a sufficient amount to do so? In the United States, both the federal and state governments have focused on policies to promote greater investment in education. These policies generally fall into one of two categories:

- Regulations, for example, compulsory-education laws
- Subsidies, for example, subsidized preschool programs such as Head Start

Regulations, in a sense, impose a tax on people by forcing them to invest in something that they might not have otherwise invested in. Compulsory-education laws—in effect in all states since 1918—are an example of this. They require that children be in class rather than working in the fields or factories to increase family income. The *1948 Universal Declaration of Human Rights* adopted by the General Assembly of the United Nations treated compulsory education through the primary grades as a basic human right. Although compulsory-education laws in the United States were crafted so that children could do agricultural work during the summer, the introduction of the laws still reduced the economic well-being of most households by eliminating a source of income. Not surprisingly, it was politically unattractive to also require that families assume the cost of the educational programs.

Instead, both in the United States and worldwide, taxpayers have traditionally borne most of the explicit costs of compulsory education. In China, for example, the government has "guaranteed" nine years of free compulsory education to all residents, both urban and rural. In reality, however, funding shortfalls in rural provinces have forced families to pay additional educational fees to comply with the law. These fees have been as much as 25 percent of the average farmer's family income. In response, some rural farmers—among the poorest in the country—have given up their land and become migrant workers simply because migrant workers' children are exempt from compulsory-education laws. Other rural farmers have just ignored the compulsory-education law. To remedy this situation, China's central government has begun a campaign to eliminate the fees in the nation's poorest counties.[11]

In the United States, local and state governments have financed compulsory education by building schools and paying for teachers and books. Initially, taxpayers in small,

•••••••

[6]Milton Friedman, *Capitalism and Freedom.* University of Chicago Press, 1962.

[7]Milton Friedman and Rose Friedman, *Tyranny of the Status Quo* (University of California: Harcourt Brace Jovanavich, 1984).

[8]Joshua Hall, "Positive Externalities and Government Involvement in Education." *Journal of Private Enterprise*, 11, no. 2 (Spring, 2006).

[9]Kerry King, "Do Spillover Benefits Create Market Inefficiency in K-12 Public Education?" *The Cato Journal*, 27, (2007).

[10]*Ibid.*

[11]Jim Yardley, "China Plans to Cut School Fees for Its Poorest Rural Students." *New York Times*, March 13, 2005.

rural communities would offer free education by providing a one-room school and a teacher who taught children in all grades, together. The town paid for these services by taxing property owners. Back in the days when children tended to remain in their communities throughout their lives, taxing property owners was a way to force residents to pay for the spillover benefits they enjoyed from having educated town members.

In urban areas, supporters of compulsory education included (1) people who wanted children out of factory sweatshops, and (2) community members who wanted young, nonworking children off the streets while their parents worked. Seemingly strange "bedfellows," child advocates and labor unions joined forces—both in the United States and worldwide—to promote compulsory education and increase the number of years of education required. Beyond any kindly motives they may have had, union members benefited from compulsory education to the extent that it eliminated child labor, a low-cost substitute for higher-paid adult workers.

In countries such as India, where labor organizations are scarce or weak, employers continue to circumvent compulsory-education laws. Children in India are now banned from working in hazardous jobs; still, they provide a ready supply of workers for labor-intensive industries such as rug making and household domestic work. Even though international pressure has been brought to bear, compulsory-education laws continue to be ignored in poorer countries. The introduction of laws that prohibit children under 14 from working as domestic servants or in hotels and restaurants appears to have helped little in this regard.[12] The issue is whether employers and families in poorer countries can afford the opportunity cost of compulsory education in terms of forgone low-cost labor and family income, even when the education itself is free of charge.

13.3 Government-Subsidized versus Government-Provided Education

We have offered a plausible reason for why governments intervene to promote private investment in education. The question that still remains is whether this intervention requires governments to actually *provide* educational services or simply *subsidize* them. Why, for example, did local governments in the United States create public-school systems—including university systems—rather than simply offer subsidies to encourage people to invest more in private educational opportunities?

There is a long history of government involvement in the provision of educational services, ranging from the one-room schools in rural communities to today's complex public-school systems. Despite differences in their size and offerings, these systems tend to have one characteristic in common: schools largely service students living within specific geographic boundaries—city blocks, school districts, states, and so on. Such an approach can be justified when students remain in, or return to, these narrowly defined communities after graduation, in which case they will bestow spillover benefits on local property owners who largely foot the educational bills.

However, assigning students to specific schools according to geographic boundaries also means that public schools do not compete with one another to attract students. While parochial and private secular schools remain options, they are not free. Families that opt for one of these private alternatives are still required to pay taxes to support the free public-school system.

By and large, the only way households can switch from their neighborhood school to another public school is to buy a home or rent an apartment in the neighborhood

••••••••

[12]"India: Ban on Child Labor in Homes and Hotels." *New York Times*, August 3, 2006.

served by their preferred public school—an often costly proposition. However, the desegregation movement of the 1970s did result in an important educational innovation—public "magnet schools"—which offer science, performing arts, visual arts, and other specialty curriculums, and are open to children from different school districts. Magnet schools often have lengthy waiting lists which, in turn, has led to bureaucratic rules that ration these scarce student openings. For example, the Los Angeles school district currently rations magnet school slots according to a point system, where students get points for their minority status and for being previously rejected by a magnet school. As a result, some families "work" the system by applying to highly competitive magnet schools in the hopes of accumulating sufficient rejection points to gain admission to a less-competitive magnet school of their choice. Despite the rationing, over one million children in the United States have "voted with their feet" and attend magnet schools rather than their neighborhood schools.[13]

Ensuring the Quality of Public Education

We have already seen that in private markets, consumers express their willingness to pay by engaging voluntarily in trade. Suppliers of goods and services for which there is little or no demand disappear from the scene, leaving only those producers who can meet consumer demand at a cost that is less than or equal to consumers' willingness to pay. In this way, competition ensures that consumers receive the types of goods and services for which they are willing to pay.

In contrast, we have just seen that households must often incur high costs to "vote with their feet"—that is, to switch to an alternative public or private school in lieu of their public neighborhood school. And those households that send their children to private school must still pay property taxes to support their local schools no matter how unsatisfied they are with them. In such a situation, market-based incentives are lacking to ensure that public schools offer the quality and type of educational programs demanded by the neighborhood's families. What, then, does determine the quality and mix of public education offerings?

Local, state, and federal governments have tried to impose quality standards by enacting regulations, which, among other things, dictate teacher-certification requirements, the length of the school day and school year, and building codes to ensure that school structures are safe. Standardized student reading and math tests have also been introduced to measure whether students meet grade-level expectations; more recently, they have been used to gauge how well teachers perform.[14]

Regulations such as these create their own problems. For example, teacher-certification requirements can lead to undesirable barriers to entry in the labor market for teachers. In most states, for example, college professors and other professionals with Ph.D.s cannot teach in public elementary or high schools. And standardized student testing creates incentives for schools and teachers to "teach to the test" to achieve high rankings and increases in funding. As it turns out, students' test scores tend to be higher in wealthier school districts. The same holds true for graduation rates. Does this mean that the education in these districts is higher quality? Or do these quality metrics reflect the socioeconomic status of households in specific school districts? One piece of evidence that supports the latter explanation is that when low-income

· · · · · · ·

[13]Tamar Lewin, "Alternatives to Neighborhood School Are Vaster than Ever." *New York Times,* June 29, 2002.

[14]Jennifer Medina, "Should Student Test Scores Measure a Teacher's Value?" *New York Times,* January 22, 2008.

students are fed breakfast at school, their academic performance, according to these measures, improves dramatically.[15]

In reality, it is extremely difficult and costly to determine the quality of teachers and schools. Sometimes, the "value-added" of an education only becomes apparent after many years when graduates achieve financial and professional success. Still, economists have developed statistical value-added models that hundreds of school districts are now using to rank teachers. These models focus primarily on the change in students' test scores from the start to the end of a school year, rather than tracking longer-term indicators of student success.

Making Public Schools Compete

We've already discussed why quality issues rarely arise in private competitive markets: consumers choose to buy from suppliers that offer the degree of product quality they are willing and able to pay for. Is there a way that the competitive mechanism can be introduced to achieve the quality standards demanded in public education?

Some economists have suggested that the easiest way to introduce competition in public-school systems is to simply let students attend any school in, or across, local school districts. That is, expand the magnet school concept to all public schools in the region. Programs that permit city kids to enroll in suburban public schools have existed in the past, primarily as part of court-ordered school desegregation programs. Magnet schools and the practice of bussing students to better-quality suburban schools have expanded the educational options available to many urban households. Bussing has also increased the competition among schools when it comes to attracting students and the public funding that comes with these students. Recently, the Supreme Court of Missouri ruled that parents living in failing, unaccredited St. Louis city school districts have the right to enroll their children in neighboring suburban public schools and that the St. Louis Public School system was responsible for paying the out-of-district student tuition.[16] This ruling sets up a competitive situation between city and suburban public-school systems. Exactly how do public schools compete against each other for students if they are all free to the students? They must compete on nonprice dimensions such as course offerings, class size, safety, college acceptance rates, and so forth.

The possibility of expanding the competition between public schools to include private schools has been ferociously debated over the past several decades. Supporters of this option contend that public-education funds should flow to the schools that students enroll in regardless of whether they go to public *or* private schools inside or outside their school districts. The tax revenues that now go directly to local public-school districts would be converted into subsidy checks that parents could use at the schools of their choice, including their neighborhood public school. Supporters argue that this would revolutionize public-school education by introducing competition into the educational sector. Understandably, this has created a great deal of debate, especially within minority communities, whose children disproportionately attend lower-performing city schools. Some younger leaders in the African American community have cast school choice as a civil rights issue, arguing that it would eliminate the last barrier facing minorities by guaranteeing equal educational opportunities.[17]

· · · · · · ·

[15]"U.S. School Breakfast Program Lifts Test Scores." *New York Times*, June 22, 1988.

[16]Elisa Crouch, "Missouri Supreme Court Affirms Students' Right to Transfer From Failing Schools." *St. Louis Post Dispatch*, July 16, 2010.

[17]Jodi Wilgoren, "Young Blacks Turn to School Vouchers as Civil Rights Issue." *New York Times*, October 9, 2000.

Government subsidy checks-called vouchers-are not new: the federal food-stamp program distributes vouchers to low-income people, who use them to buy food at private grocery stores. And the federal government provides Pell grants and subsidized loans to college students who attend private colleges and universities, while at the same time, state governments provide funding directly to public universities in their state.

Many government agencies have successfully implemented voucher systems to finance social services that they had once directly provided. For example, over the past few decades, federal and local governments have stopped building and managing public-housing developments for low-income households. Instead, they now give these households rent-subsidy vouchers that can be spent in the private housing market.

The Benefits and Pitfalls of a Voucher System for Education

To better understand the benefits and pitfalls of a voucher system for education, we must first understand how tuition-based private schools currently operate when it comes to the admission process. If we take a look at these schools, we see that they don't usually admit students solely on the basis of their parents' willingness to pay. For example, many Catholic schools admit students even though their parents can't pay the full tuition. Tuition-based private schools often factor in nonprice considerations in their student selection process, such as the following:

- The student's academic record, talents, and achievements
- The student's contribution to diversity
- Whether the student's parents or grandparents are graduates of the school
- The prominence of the student's family in the community
- The wealth of the student's family
- The religion of the student's family

Because price (tuition) isn't used to "clear" the market, many tuition-based schools have waiting lists, just like the public magnet schools we discussed previously. This tells us that the price that these schools charge must be below the equilibrium price. At the equilibrium price, the quantity demanded would just equal the quantity supplied. Instead, there is excess demand for spots at these schools, as **Figure 13.2** illustrates.

Why don't these schools simply accept students based on their parents' willingness to pay—that is, those willing and able to pay the equilibrium price? The answer is that these schools have other goals they want to achieve, such as enhancing the school's reputation (which assures future demand for the school's services), increasing future donations, promoting certain religious beliefs, winning sports tournaments, and so on.

Certainly, accepting the most academically talented students—however measured—contributes to a school's academic reputation. This is sometimes referred to as the "smart in, smart out" enrollment strategy. This strategy may also reduce the cost of education because talented students tend to be self-motivated and to have fewer behavioral problems and fewer special needs.

What does this mean if a voucher system were instituted by the government? Highly sought after, tuition-based public and private schools might **cream-skim** the most attractive applicants. That is, they might selectively compete for the best public-school students, leaving higher cost, less-talented students behind.

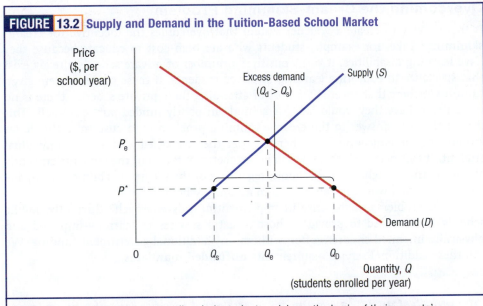

FIGURE 13.2 Supply and Demand in the Tuition-Based School Market

Tuition-based schools do not usually admit students solely on the basis of their parents' willingness and ability to pay. Because price (tuition) isn't used to "clear" the market, many of these schools have waiting lists. This tells us that the price that these schools charge (P^*) must be below equilibrium price (P_e). At P_e, the quantity demanded would just equal the quantity supplied. $Q_D - Q_S$ represents the excess demand that results in waiting lists.

CREAM-SKIMMING The process by which the "best" (usually defined as lowest cost or highest quality) are separated from the rest of their group and targeted for special treatment.

EXAMPLE Now that hospitals are paid by insurers according to each patient's diagnosis rather than the actual cost of treatment, hospitals have an incentive to cream-skim the healthiest patients in each diagnostic category and redirect the rest to other hospitals.

Opponents of magnet schools and voucher systems argue that both options encourage cream-skimming.[18,19] This is certainly a valid concern when public schools are required to meet federal and state mandates—to provide transportation or special-education services, for example—that magnet and private schools are not required to provide. Nevertheless, a preliminary study of the cream-skimming effect of private-school vouchers has demonstrated that while cream-skimming does occur, it has a negligible impact on the high-school graduation rates and college attendance of students who remain in the public-school system.[20]

• • • • • • •

[18]Tamar Levin, *op. cit.*

[19]Anemona Hartocollis, "School Voucher Experiment Will Be Extended and Expanded." *New York Times*, November 26, 1997.

[20]Joseph Altonji, Ching-I Huang, and Christopher Taber, "Estimating the Cream-Skimming Effect of Private School Vouchers on Public School Students." *NBER Working Paper* 16579, December, 2010.

Overcoming the Cream-Skimming Problem

Is there a way to create a voucher system that overcomes the incentive for cream-skimming? Take, for example, students who are high-cost to educate because they have learning disabilities. It turns out that a number of private schools already exist that specialize in educating learning-impaired students. If these students were given tuition vouchers that covered the cost of attending these private schools, there is no reason to believe they would be "left behind" in poorly funded public schools. This means that the answer to the cream-skimming problem is to customize the dollar amount of the educational voucher to cover the cost of educating each individual student. If this occurred, there would be competition for *all* of the students currently attending their neighborhood schools, regardless of their learning abilities or impairments. No child would be left behind in a failing school.

What problems might arise in implementing this approach? Currently, public schools are required to provide a host of extra services to learning-impaired and physically-impaired children, often without any additional government funding. We call these additional service requirements **unfunded mandates**.

UNFUNDED MANDATE A government directive that specifies services that are to be provided to specific groups without the funding necessary to meet this directive.

EXAMPLE Hospital emergency rooms are prohibited from turning away anyone whose life is in imminent danger, regardless of whether that person has insurance or can otherwise pay for the medical services.

EXAMPLE U.S. counties must provide a lawyer to individuals accused of committing a crime if they cannot afford their own attorney.

Unfunded mandates in the public-school system reduce the amount of money left over that can be devoted to the "average" student. In contrast, private schools tend to be exempt from most of these mandates. This may explain why the average expenditure per pupil in "failing" public schools often exceeds the average per pupil expenditure in elite, private schools. Converting to a student-specific voucher system would mean that each student's individual cost of education would have to be made explicit—tallied up, that is. This would put a price tag on the **cross-subsidies** that currently exist between public-school students.

CROSS-SUBSIDY The shifting of resources from one individual or group to another via a pricing or payment system that does not reflect the true opportunity cost of servicing each group.

EXAMPLE Picking up and delivering mail in rural areas is more costly than in urban areas. Nevertheless, everyone pays the same postal mailing rates. As a result, urban customers are cross-subsidizing rural customers.

EXAMPLE When government medical-insurance programs such as Medicare and Medicaid do not pay health-care providers enough to cover the cost of treating Medicare/Medicaid patients, providers cover the shortfall by charging privately-insured patients more.

By making the cross-subsidies in public-school systems explicit, taxpayers might reconsider all of the mandated services provided to high-cost students. When the airline industry was deregulated, the cross-subsidies built in to regulated airfares to subsidize air service to "underserved" cities such as Schenectady, New York, disappeared. As airlines began to compete on price, air service to many of these cities ended, was severely curtailed, or was replaced by lower-cost regional airline carriers. Even with direct government subsidies through the Essential Air Service Program, airlines continue to drop out of money-losing routes: in 2011 alone, Delta ended its flights in and out of 15 smaller markets.[21] This tells us that the direct subsidies are not nearly as great as the cross-subsidies that Delta received prior to the deregulation of airline routes and fares.

One group that has been consistently opposed to magnet schools and other forms of school choice is public-school teachers—especially those with seniority—who are represented by politically powerful public teachers' unions.[22,23] If parental demand for neighborhood schools fell in the face of new alternatives, so, too, would the demand for teachers in that school district. Although teachers could try to follow their students to other public-school districts or to private schools, their seniority would likely vanish along with their higher pay and benefits. Consequently, it is easy to understand why these teachers and their representatives would lobby against school choice reforms.

13.4 Investing in Other Types of Human Capital

Investing in education is only one way we can build human capital for ourselves and other members in our household. It turns out that improving our physical attributes—beauty, strength, body fitness, and so on—can also generate economic returns. Recent research studies have shown that people who are judged by others to be "above average" in terms of their attractiveness earn between 1 and 13 percent more than "average" looking people.[24] At the university level, professors who are rated by students as "better" looking tend to receive higher student evaluations, particularly when the instructor is male.[25] Attractive male lawyers appear to not only bill more hours but at a higher hourly rate.[26] And, in the advertising industry, better-looking executives disproportionately increase firm revenues. If it is true that better-looking employees earn higher returns in the labor market, then there is an incentive to invest in building one's "beauty capital."[27] This means that plastic surgery, cosmetics, hair transplants, and bodybuilding can yield payoffs that go far beyond vanity.

Researchers report similar findings when it comes to body fitness and obesity. One study found that an extra 65 pounds costs a white woman almost 7 percent

· · · · · · ·

[21]Kelly Yamanouchi, "Delta Wants Out of 15 Smaller Markets." *St. Louis Post-Dispatch,* July 16, 2011, p. A6.

[22]Julie Miller, "Schools, Choice and Tax Dollars." *New York Times,* January 1, 1996.

[23]Alison Mitchell, "McCain Attacks Unions and Vows Better Schools." *New York Times,* February 11, 2000.

[24]Jeff Biddle and Daniel Hamermesh, "Beauty and the Labor Market." *American Economic Review,* December, 1994.

[25]Daniel Hamermesh and Amy Parker, "Beauty in the Classroom." *Economics of Education Review,* 2004.

[26]Jeff Biddle and Daniel Hamermesh, "Beauty, Productivity and Discrimination: Lawyers' Looks and Lucre." *Journal of Labor Economics* (January, 1998).

[27]Gerard Pfann, Jeff Biddle, Daniel Hamermesh, and Ciska Bosman. "Business Success and Business' Beauty Capital." *Economic Letters,* 2000.

in wages.[28] This same study reports that obese nonwhite women pay a much stiffer wage penalty, while obese men appear to pay no penalty at all in the labor market. Another analysis estimated that obese women suffer a wage penalty of nearly 17 percent.[29] Much of the wage penalty for obesity seems to arise from the fact that obese women—regardless of their socioeconomic status—are less likely to earn a college degree.[30] Another contributing factor may be that employers recognize that obese people tend to incur higher medical costs, which can lead to higher employer-paid medical-insurance premiums. If this is indeed the explanation, then we would expect that smokers also earn lower wages, on average, than nonsmokers. This prediction has been confirmed by several studies, although the actual magnitude of the smokers' wage penalty is still unclear.[31]

Height also has a significant impact on people's earnings potential. One study estimated that an additional inch yields approximately $789 in additional pay each year.[32] While the underlying explanation for this phenomenon remains open to debate, recent research points to the impact of teenagers' heights on their participation in athletic and social activities, which has been linked to higher adult earnings streams. Because teenage and adult heights are closely correlated, this may explain the relationship between worker heights and worker pay.[33] Until recently, the only investment people could make to become taller was the purchase of shoe "lifts," a frequently used height-enhancer for movie stars. During the past two decades, however, endocrinologists have begun administering human growth hormone to young children experiencing growth issues, in part to circumvent the opportunity cost of short stature that arises during and after adolescence.

Because people have different initial endowments of human capital, we would expect them to invest differently to build their human capital "portfolio." For extraordinarily tall young men and women, investing in agility training may be an optimal way to improve their chances of becoming professional basketball players. Likewise, young people who sing well might earn a greater return from investing in voice lessons. The goal is to invest in those facets of one's human capital that will yield the greatest expected returns in the future.

SOLVED PROBLEM

Q Suppose that obesity becomes a protected employment class; that is, employers cannot discriminate against people based upon their weight in either hiring or pay practices. Using supply and demand curves, show the impact that this change in law would have on (1) the equilibrium price and quantity of gym memberships and (2) the equilibrium wage and employment of thin people. How do the returns to investments made in fitness change as a result of the change in the law?

· · · · · · ·

[28]Steven Lansburg, "Hey Gorgeous. Here's a Raise!" *Everyday Economics,* July, 2001.

[29]Susan Averett and Sanders Korenman, "The Economic Reality of the Beauty Myth." *The Journal of Human Resources* (Spring, 1996).

[30]Christy Glass, Steven Haas, and Eric Reither, "Heavy in School, Burdened for Life." *New York Times,* June 3, 2011, p. A19.

[31]Silke Anger and Michael Kvasnicka, "Biases in Estimates of the Smoking Wage Penalty," SFB 649 Discussion Papers SFB649DP2006-089 (Berlin, Germany: Humboldt University, 2006).

[32]Associated Press, "Want a Raise? Stand Tall." *MSNBC,* October 16, 2003.

[33]Nicola Persico, Andrew Postlewaite, and Dan Silverman, "Walk Tall: Height and Earnings." *The Economist,* April, 2002.

A

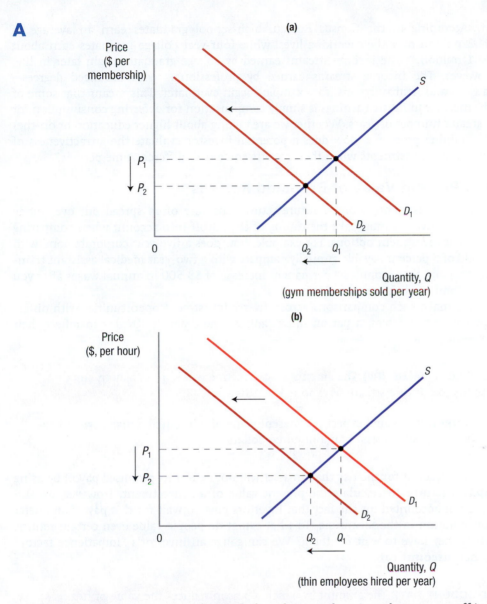

(a)

Price
($ per
membership)

P_1

P_2

Q_2 Q_1

Quantity, Q
(gym memberships sold per year)

(b)

Price
($, per hour)

P_1

P_2

Q_2 Q_1

Quantity, Q
(thin employees hired per year)

The return to investments in fitness declines because there is no longer a payoff in terms of higher wages and lower unemployment in the labor market.

13.5 Comparing the Stream of Returns for Alternative Investments

When we invest in our human capital, we typically incur two types of costs: implicit and explicit. Since you began college, for example, you have borne such explicit costs as tuition, the cost of your books, and so forth. Your implicit costs include the well-being you forgo from the leisure time you lose, the consumables that you could have purchased had you spent your time working instead, and the household-production activities that are sacrificed. A person will defer consumption to gain more education only if the expected return more than offsets all of these costs.

According to the Census Bureau, high-school graduates earn an average of $1.2 million over their working lives, while four-year college graduates earn about $2.1 million.[34] The income streams earned by college graduates begin later in life, however. The income streams earned by professionals with advanced degrees—lawyers and neurosurgeons, for example—begin even later. This means that some of the increase in future earnings is simply compensation for deferring consumption for a greater number of years. Whether we are talking about higher education or on-the-job training programs, how does a potential investor evaluate the attractiveness of alternative investments when their payoffs come over different time periods?

The Present Value of Expected Returns

Because investments promise future returns that are often spread out over many years, an investor must take the timing of the payoff into account when comparing different investment options. For example, how does a five-year corporate bond with a yield of 5 percent payable annually compare with a two-year medical assistant training program that promises a permanent increase of $3,500 in annual wages after you have completed the program?

To make such comparisons across diverse investment opportunities with different payoff timetables, a person must "adjust" these payoff streams to reflect their **present value**.

> **PRESENT VALUE (PV)** The amount that someone would pay *today* to buy the rights to a future stream of expected returns.

> **EXAMPLE** We would expect the present value of a hundred dollar payment received in a year is less than a hundred dollars.

We account for the risk that an asset will not deliver its promised payoff by using *expected* returns to calculate the present value of an investment. However, we still have not accounted for the fact that investors have to wait for this payoff and defer consumption in the meantime. To what extent do people value even certain returns less if they have to wait for them? We can gauge an investor's "impatience factor" by her **discount rate**.

> **DISCOUNT RATE** The amount by which a person reduces the value of future returns or events because they are not immediate. The lower the discount rate a person has, the greater the "patience" she demonstrates when it comes to waiting for a return to materialize. The discount rate is sometimes referred to as the "time value of money."

> **EXAMPLE** Let's say that your discount rate is 10 percent. This means that for every year you must wait for an investment to pay you back, you "discount" the eventual return by 10 percent. For example, you would only invest $100 in a one-year risk-free investment that pays $110 a year later.

---

[34]Jennifer Day and Eric Newburger, "The Big Payoff: Educational Attainment and Synthetic Estimates of Work-Life Earnings." Current Population Reports, Special Studies (Washington, DC: Commerce Dept., 2002), pp. 23–210.

EXAMPLE A local car dealership offers you a 24-month no-interest loan if you buy a new car. As a result, you will "discount" the price that you negotiate for the car to reflect the fact that you will not actually pay anything for two years. A dollar paid in two years is less valuable to you than a dollar paid today.

As we discussed earlier, the opportunity cost of deferring consumption is different for different people. This means that discount rates will vary as well: individuals with longer time horizons will tend to have a lower discount rate than those with shorter time horizons. Children are apt to only understand "now" and, therefore, have very high discount rates: the value they place on anything they have to wait for is small. In contrast, parents who treat their children as an extension of themselves have time horizons that go way beyond their own natural lives. This translates into a very low discount rate. Indeed, it turns out that parents with low discount rates tend to raise children with stronger cognitive skills.[35]

The higher a person's discount rate, the higher an investment's expected return must be to compensate him for deferring consumption. To be more precise, an investment's *after-tax* expected return must equal or exceed an investor's discount rate for him to be willing to defer consumption and make the investment.

Estimating the Discount Rate

Over time, people often reveal their individual discount rates through the investment choices they make. At any given time, however, economists, investment advisors, and project managers are frequently called upon to compare the present value of the returns of different investment opportunities. How can they do this if people have different discount rates?

Recall that the yields on U.S. Treasuries tell us the amount that an investor must be paid to defer consumption for a specified period of time. There is no risk premium built-in because Treasuries are considered to be risk-free. The market determines the return that these Treasuries pay. This return is the equilibrium "price" (interest rate) that equates the dollar amount of Treasuries sold (funds borrowed by the federal government) to the dollar amount of Treasuries bought (funds lent to the government). **Figure 13.3** illustrates this equilibrium. The supply curve for loanable funds to the government reflects the opportunity cost of buying Treasuries, which depends on the security's time to maturity and the investor's opportunity cost of deferring consumption that long. This means that the equilibrium price is the interest rate that must be offered to the marginal (last) investor to entice him to buy the last Treasury sold at any given maturity. This investor will be indifferent to consuming today or receiving the security's payoff at maturity. In other words, the equilibrium interest rate exactly equals the marginal investor's discount rate. Because the supply curve is upward sloping, we know that every other investor will have a lower opportunity cost of deferring consumption, and, therefore, have a lower discount rate than the marginal investor.

Predictably, the supply curve for loanable funds shifts left the longer investors must wait for their payoff because the opportunity cost of investing rises. This leads to higher equilibrium yields for Treasury securities with longer maturities. This is

[35]Mark Agee and Thomas Crocker, "Parents' Discount Rates and Intergenerational Transmission of Cognitive Skills." *Economica* 69 (2002), pp. 143–154.

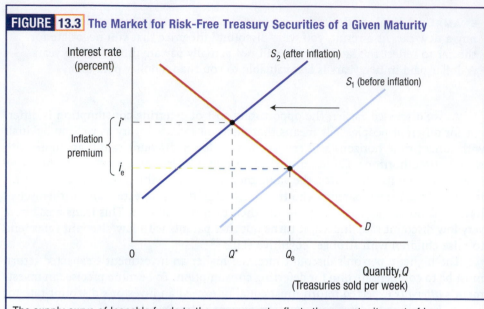

FIGURE 13.3 The Market for Risk-Free Treasury Securities of a Given Maturity

The supply curve of loanable funds to the government reflects the opportunity cost of buying Treasuries, which depends on their time to maturity and the opportunity cost of deferring consumption for that long. The equilibrium price (i_e) is the interest rate that must be offered to the marginal (last) investor to entice him to buy the last Treasury offered at any given maturity. When the risk of future inflation increases, investors expect the purchasing power of money to decline while they wait to be paid back. As a result, the opportunity cost of loaning funds to the government rises, causing the supply curve for Treasuries to shift left. This leads to a higher equilibrium interest rate (i^*) and a lower quantity of Treasuries purchased.

demonstrated in **Table 13.1**, which shows the yields for Treasuries of different maturity levels sold on March 15, 2011.

These equilibrium risk-free returns will be affected by the economic environment. When the risk of future inflation increases, for example, investors expect that the purchasing power of money will decline while they wait to be paid back. As a result, the opportunity cost of loaning funds to the government rises, causing a leftward shift in the supply curve of money in Figure 13.3. This leads to a higher equilibrium yield; people's discount rates have, in effect, increased due to inflationary expectations.

ECONOMIC FALLACY   When inflationary expectations increase, the amount of investment declines.

Uncertain. The mix of investments will certainly change because some assets "hold" their value and generate higher returns during periods of inflation. For this reason, the demand for gold and land tends to grow when inflationary expectations increase. In contrast, the demand for bonds, bank CDs, and other investments whose return is a fixed interest rate falls because this payoff will buy less in the future. To compete for investment dollars, these types of investments must raise their payoffs. Alternatively, they can build in protections for investors. For example, the U.S. government has introduced Treasuries with yields that vary with the inflation rate, which are called Treasury Inflation-Protected Securities (TIPS).

Table **13.1**	**Yields for Treasury Securities of Different Maturities**
	03/15/2011
1 month	0.07
3 month	0.10
6 month	0.14
1 year	0.23
2 year	0.63
5 year	2.00
7 year	2.68
10 year	3.33
20 year	4.21
30 year	4.47

Source: www.treasury.gov/resource-center/data-chart-center/interest-rates/Pages/TextView.aspx?data=yieldYear&year=2011

Calculating the Present Value of a Stream of Future Expected Returns

Suppose that you go to a bank and invest $100 today in a one-year, risk-free certificate of deposit (CD) that yields a 10 percent return in one year. We know from our previous discussion that this return must be equal to or greater than your discount rate or you wouldn't make the investment in the first place. If we use 10 percent as a conservative approximation of your annual discount rate, then we can say that the most you would pay for a CD that returns $110 in a year is $100. In other words, the *present value* (PV) of the CD is $100.

We define the *future value* (FV) of your one-year investment as

$$FV = \$100 \, (1 + 0.10) = PV \, (1 + r)$$

where r is the interest rate you are offered (and our approximation of your discount rate).

Rearranging the calculation, we get

$$PV = \$100 = FV \, / \, (1 + 0.10) = FV \, / \, (1 + r)$$

That is, the present value of the CD equals the future value discounted by 10 percent for the year you have to wait.

What if, instead, you invested $100 in a two-year bank CD that pays 10 percent per year but is paid out only at the end of two years? Then your investment after one year has passed and interest has been earned will earn another 10 percent interest in the second year. In other words,

$$FV = [\$100 \, (1 + 0.10)] \times (1 + 0.10) = PV \, (1 + 0.10)^2 = PV \, (1 + r)^2$$

We sometimes describe this result as the "miracle of compound interest." Every year, there is an increase in the base to which the interest rate is applied. In effect, interest is paid not only on the original investment but also on the interest that has been paid in previous years.

The investment's present value equals

$$PV = FV / (1 + 0.10)^2 = FV / (1 + r)^2$$

We can easily extend this analysis to five-year, ten-year, and longer CDs. The longer you must wait for your payoff, the greater the total return must be. This means that

$$FV = PV (1 + r)^t \quad \text{and} \quad PV = FV / (1 + r)^t$$

where t is the number of years you must wait for the payoff.

Some financial assets, such as corporate bonds, promise that you will get an annual return (R) each and every year in which you own the bond. How do we compute the present value of this stream of expected returns? Extending our earlier result, we get

$$PV = R_1 / (1 + r) + R_2 / (1 + r)^2 + R_3 / (1 + r)^3 + \cdots + R_t / (1 + r)^t$$

where R is the return expected in a particular year and t is the last year in which a payoff is made. Note that this computation allows for the possibility that the annual expected returns vary, which means that we can easily handle *unequal*, multiperiod investment returns. The present value is the maximum amount you would pay today to "own" this future stream of returns. As we can see, the present value will *increase* when the magnitude of the expected returns (R) increase and *decrease* the longer the wait for the payoff (t) and the higher the discount rate (r).

The payoff from investing in human capital tends to be uneven over a person's lifetime. Investments in education, for example, lead to higher wages, greater job satisfaction, a lower probability of unemployment, and enhanced job mobility throughout our lifetimes. During our retirement years, education continues to pay returns in terms of better health, greater mental acuity, and a generally higher level of consumption. Because the payoff stream generated by investments in human capital is uneven and multiperiod, we must use the last equation to calculate the present value of these investments.

The Net Present Value of Returns to Human Capital Accumulation

When it comes to financial capital such as bank CDs, we make our investment and then sit back and wait for the payoff to occur. In contrast, when it comes to human capital, we tend to invest in installments. That is, the cost of acquiring human capital is spread over time through a stream of investments. Consequently, we must not only discount the future stream of expected returns but also the future stream of the investment dollars we commit. Have you ever noticed that paying a bill in installments is always less painful than paying it upfront, in full? This is the reason that people are often willing to pay more for furniture, cars, and even vision-correction surgery if sellers offer them deferred payment plans. It also explains the popularity of student-loan programs, which delay tuition payment, sometimes far into the future. Anytime we can defer costs, our well-being increases. A dollar that we pay tomorrow is worth less to us than a dollar we have to pay today. This is just the mirror image of what we already know about investment returns: a dollar paid back to us tomorrow is worth less to us than a dollar paid to us today.

We can adapt our previous multiperiod return calculation to compute the present value of a stream of future investment costs:

$$PV = C_1 / [1 + r] + C_2 / [1 + r]^2 + C_3 / [1 + r]^3 + C_4 / [1 + r]^4$$
$$+ C_5 / [1 + r]^5 + \cdots + C_t / [1 + r]^t$$

where

C_t = investment cost incurred in year t.
r = discount rate.
t = last year in which investment cost is incurred.

After we have calculated the present value of our stream of investment dollars, we subtract it from the present value of our stream of expected returns. This gives us the **net present value** of an investment opportunity.

NET PRESENT VALUE The maximum amount an investor would pay today to acquire future capital based on the present value of the investment's stream of expected returns minus costs. In other words,

Net present value = PV of expected returns − PV of costs

EXAMPLE Suppose that you pay $20,000 in tuition for each of four years to obtain a college degree in engineering. You live at home, so there are no additional explicit costs (we ignore the implicit costs of attending college to simplify things). If you have qualified for a no-interest, no-payment loan that has to be paid in full upon graduation, and your discount rate is 10 percent, then the present value of your tuition bills equals $80,000 / $[1.10]^4$. This amount would be subtracted from the present value of the expected returns from an engineering degree to get the net present value of the degree.

We would actually get the same result if we computed the *net expected return* (expected return minus cost) for each time period and then found the present value of this stream of net returns. That is,

Net present value = PV [stream of (expected returns − costs) over time]

What is the present value of this stream of *net* returns? How will the choice of discount rate affect the end result? The discount rate that is used to compute net present value tends to have a big effect on the calculation and, therefore, our investment decisions. As you have already learned, this discount rate varies across people and across the life cycle. This helps explain why people with identical financial resources rarely invest in the same way and in the same amounts.

Table 13.2 presents data on the average wage of full-time male workers in the United States, by age, with and without a bachelor's degree. For simplicity, let's assume the average wage for 18- to 21-year-old college students is zero because they aren't working but instead are earning their undergraduate degrees. During these years, college students incur both explicit and implicit costs in the form of tuition and forgone wages.

As the table indicates, the net present value of a college degree based on a 5 percent discount rate would be $293,913. However, a 10 percent discount rate would yield $55,510, or roughly 80 percent less. Consequently, if a high-school graduate has a high discount rate (of say, 10 percent versus 5 percent), the net present value

Table 13.2 Computing the Net Present Value of Earning a Bachelor's Degree

Return to a College Education for a Male, 2007

Earnings are for full-time, year-round workers. Assumptions: College completed in four years, full-time student. Explicit costs: Public-university fees (annual) = $10,625.

Age	A College Profile	B High School Profile	C Net Benefits of College (A − B)	D [Assumes r = .05] PV (Net Benefits) PV (A − B) = PV (C)	E [Assumes r = .10] PV (Net Benefits)	
18	−10,625	25,153	−$35,778	−$34,074	−$32,525	1
19	−10,625	25,153	−$35,778	−$32,452	−$29,569	2
20	−10,625	25,153	−$35,778	−$30,906	−$26,881	3
21	−10,625	25,153	−$35,778	−$29,435	−$24,437	4
22	37,025	25,153	$11,872	$9,302	$7,372	5
23	37,025	25,153	$11,872	$8,859	$6,701	6
24	37,025	25,153	$11,872	$8,437	$6,092	7
25	55,310	34,197	$21,113	$14,290	$9,849	8
26	55,310	34,197	$21,113	$13,610	$8,954	9
27	55,310	34,197	$21,113	$12,962	$8,140	10
28	55,310	34,197	$21,113	$12,344	$7,400	11
29	55,310	34,197	$21,113	$11,757	$6,727	12
30	70,702	37,937	$32,765	$17,376	$9,491	13
31	70,702	37,937	$32,765	$16,549	$8,628	14
32	70,702	37,937	$32,765	$15,761	$7,844	15
33	70,702	37,937	$32,765	$15,010	$7,131	16
34	70,702	37,937	$32,765	$14,295	$6,482	17
35	80,582	47,182	$33,400	$13,878	$6,007	18
36	80,582	47,182	$33,400	$13,218	$5,461	19
37	80,582	47,182	$33,400	$12,588	$4,965	20
38	80,582	47,182	$33,400	$11,989	$4,513	21
39	80,582	47,182	$33,400	$11,418	$4,103	22
40	83,345	47,119	$36,226	$11,794	$4,046	23
41	83,345	47,119	$36,226	$11,233	$3,678	24
42	83,345	47,119	$36,226	$10,698	$3,344	25
43	83,345	47,119	$36,226	$10,188	$3,040	26
44	83,345	47,119	$36,226	$9,703	$2,763	27
45	86,607	45,952	$40,655	$10,371	$2,819	28
46	86,607	45,952	$40,655	$9,877	$2,563	29
47	86,607	45,952	$40,655	$9,407	$2,330	30
48	86,607	45,952	$40,655	$8,959	$2,118	31
49	86,607	45,952	$40,655	$8,532	$1,926	32
50	90,067	47,484	$42,583	$8,511	$1,833	33

	A	B	C	D	E	
			Net Benefits	**[Assumes *r* = .05]**		
	College	**High School**	**of College**	**PV (Net Benefits)**	**[Assumes *r* = .10]**	
Age	**Profile**	**Profile**	**(A − B)**	**PV (A − B) = PV (C)**	**PV (Net Benefits)**	
51	90,067	47,484	$42,583	$8,106	$1,667	34
52	90,067	47,484	$42,583	$7,720	$1,515	35
53	90,067	47,484	$42,583	$7,352	$1,378	36
54	90,067	47,484	$42,583	$7,002	$1,252	37
55	84,502	46,817	$37,685	$5,902	$1,008	38
56	84,502	46,817	$37,685	$5,621	$916	39
57	84,502	46,817	$37,685	$5,353	$833	40
58	84,502	46,817	$37,685	$5,098	$757	41
59	84,502	46,817	$37,685	$4,855	$688	42
60	82,161	44,769	$37,392	$4,588	$621	43
61	82,161	44,769	$37,392	$4,370	$564	44
62	82,161	44,769	$37,392	$4,162	$513	45
63	82,161	44,769	$37,392	$3,963	$466	46
64	82,161	44,769	$37,392	$3,775	$424	47
				$293,913	$55,510	
				NPV(0.05)	NPV(0.10)	

Data courtesy of Professor Anne Winkler.

of a college degree is comparatively low. In fact, it may be so low given his current wage opportunities that he decides to enter the labor force full-time with only his high-school diploma in hand.

ECONOMIC FALLACY   The higher a university's tuition is, the lower its net present value will be.

Uncertain. Leading business magazines rank colleges in terms of their "value" by comparing their tuitions to teacher-student ratios and other measures of educational "quality," but typically ignore the fact that degrees from different schools can yield different streams of earnings in the marketplace.

In the next chapter, we will discuss the benefits of getting a degree from Harvard University, for example, versus a state university, even when the quality of the education of the two schools is exactly the same! We call this phenomenon the "signaling" effect of the degree-granting institution's name.

Social versus Private Discount Rates

There are situations in which the discount rate that is used by individuals differs from the **social discount rate**.

SOCIAL DISCOUNT RATE The value that society places on future well-being versus current well-being.

> **EXAMPLE** When a society spends lots of money on its current population and pays for this by amassing a huge national debt, we can infer that this society has a much higher discount rate than if it paid for current consumption by taxing the current population.
>
> **EXAMPLE** During times of war, societies tend to have very high discount rates in the sense that they will use up all the capital they have—materials, equipment, and people—to be victorious.

The social discount rate reflects the extent to which we, as a society, consider the well-being of future generations beyond the current generation. Why is the social discount rate so important? It goes to the heart of such questions as how much of the world's current wealth should be invested in technologies that lessen air pollution and conceivably forestall adverse climate change for future generations. If we invest today in the development of new fuels, "smart" electricity-transmission grids, and more fuel-efficient cars, this will require us to reduce our current standard of living. Meanwhile, the bulk of the returns from these investments will likely come in the far future. Even if we knew with certainty what the costs and future returns are, what is the appropriate discount rate to use to calculate the net present value of such investments?

When private discount rates are applied to these types of investments, there is evidence that the resulting net present value is lower than is socially optimal. A good example of this is the uproar that the Environmental Protection Agency faced in 2006, when it proposed new emission standards for lawn mowers.[36] Despite evidence that lawn mowers generate a significant amount of smog, lawn-mower manufacturers rallied home owners and small lawn-care providers to defeat the new rules by drawing attention to the private costs that would be borne by current users.

If, in fact, the social discount rate is lower than private discount rates, then there "should" be more investment in environmental protection activities from society's point of view. In effect, the current generation is imposing a negative externality on future generations. The socially optimal amount of investment today—to internalize this future externality—depends crucially on the social discount rate that is applied.[37] The lower the social discount rate is, the more "weight" future generations have in the decision to reduce current well-being to achieve greater well-being.

Because legislators are elected and re-elected in two-, four-, or six-year cycles, they have an incentive to invest in government programs that generate immediate returns for today's voters, rather than for future generations that can't vote today. This explains why government programs that improve the current well-being of voters—such as cost-of-living increases for Social Security recipients—usually trump long-term investments in water-treatment and sewage facilities, schools, and other infrastructure. It also explains why politicians prefer to borrow money rather than tax their own constituents to finance programs that largely benefit these voters. Future generations will likely foot the bill for government expenditures made with borrowed money.

· · · · · · ·

[36]Felicity Barringer, "A Greener Way to Cut Grass Runs Afoul of a Powerful Lobby." *New York Times,* April 24, 2006.

[37]Hal Varian, "Recalculating the Cost of Global Climate Change." *New York Times,* December 14, 2006.

The Internal Rate of Return (IRR)

Suppose that a company decides to invest $1 million to lower its future production costs. The company is likely to have a number of investment options it can choose from (e.g., adopt new manufacturing technologies or build a factory that improves work flow). The stream of expected returns—in terms of future increases in profits—associated with each of these options is likely to be different. A simple way that some businesses choose between alternative investment opportunities is to look solely at the *payback period*—that is, the number of months or years it takes before an investment's returns cover the initial amount invested. However, this approach does not take into account variations in the *stream* of returns over time. For example, two investments could both pay back the initial investment in five years, but one might pay a level stream of returns over the entire period, while the other pays off in a lump sum at the very end of the five years.

A more sophisticated approach is to use the present value calculations we already outlined: after a discount rate is chosen, the present value of each alternative's stream of expected returns is calculated. The company would then choose the investment with the highest present value—as long as it is greater than $1 million. After all, the company wants to get back more money from the investment than it put in. The choice of the discount rate is critical though: for example, a high discount rate would "punish" an investment that pays off big, but way in the future, relative to an investment that pays off more modestly but in less time.

An alternative approach to making investment decisions is to compare the **internal rate of return** of each investment.

> **INTERNAL RATE OF RETURN (IRR)** The discount rate that results in a *zero* net present value for an investment's future stream of returns.

> **EXAMPLE** If you invest $1,000 in a five-year Treasury security that pays 2.50 percent a year, then the IRR would be 2.5 percent. Applying a 2.5 percent discount rate to the stream of returns yields a present value of $1,000, which means that the *net* present value (returns minus cost of investment) equals zero.

In other words, the IRR is the discount rate that makes an investor *just indifferent* to making an investment or not. In the case of a one-time $1 million investment, the IRR is the discount rate that results in a present value of $1 million for each investment option. Investments with greater payoffs made in a shorter period of time will require a higher discount rate to end up with a present value of $1 million. This means that a project with a higher IRR would be preferred to one with a lower IRR.

After the IRR is calculated for each of the proposed investment options, these alternatives can be ranked in terms of their IRR. For any given investment budget, a company would then simply move down this ranking until all of its investment dollars are spent. If, however, any or all of these IRRs are less than the returns that could be had by investing in opportunities external to the company, the business would do better to invest in these other alternatives. This is why the IRR methodology is a key concept when it comes to corporate strategic planning.

WHAT YOU SHOULD HAVE LEARNED FROM CHAPTER 13

■ That people are continually evaluating whether to consume all of their resources now or invest some of them to increase their future well-being.

■ That there are three classes of assets in which we can invest:
- Physical capital: buildings, land, and equipment.
- Financial capital: stock, bonds, and CDs.
- Human capital: education, sleep, our health, and so forth.

■ That to attract investors, assets that are higher risk, longer-term, or taxed at higher rates must offer higher expected returns.

■ That a person can "grow" his human capital by investing in his education, physical appearance, health, and social networks.

■ That investing in people's human capital generates positive externalities for their communities at large.

■ That the spillover benefits of education through high school may justify government intervention in the educational services market.

■ That there is a difference between government-financed/government-subsidized services and government-provided services.

■ That tuition-based schools typically set their tuitions below equilibrium and ration admission based on nonprice considerations.

■ That people have discount rates that vary with their time horizons. This discount rate determines the expected return required to entice a person to defer current consumption and instead invest to increase future well-being.

■ That the present value of an asset is its stream of future, after-tax returns discounted according to the amount of time an investor must wait for the return(s) to be paid out.

■ That the social discount rate reflects the relative importance society puts on its future well-being, including the well-being of future generations.

■ That internal rates of return are used primarily for capital budgeting purposes to prioritize projects and investments.

KEY TERMS

Consumption, p. 364

Investment, p. 364

Investment return, p. 366

Expected investment return, p. 367

Risk premium, p. 367

Time horizon, p. 369

Human capital, p. 370

Cream-skimming, p. 377

Unfunded mandate, p. 378

Cross-subsidy, p. 378

Present value (PV), p. 382

Discount rate, p. 382

Net present value, p. 387

Social discount rate, p. 389

Internal rate of return (IRR), p. 391

QUESTIONS AND PROBLEMS

1. Indicate how the following events will change (increase; decrease; no change) the present discounted value of an accountant's earning stream:
   a) elimination of mandatory retirement at age 65;
   b) introduction of a simplified flat income tax;
   c) increases in price inflation;
   d) introduction of tougher CPA standards for new accounting grads; and
   e) exercising daily.

2. A grape grower who converts his grapes into wine is an investor. How can this be if all he is doing is taking one consumption good (grapes) and converting it into a second consumption good (wine)? Explain your answer.

3. Once in a great while, we see the Treasury bond yield "curve" invert; that is, short-term Treasuries pay more than longer-term Treasuries. Offer an explanation for this phenomenon that does not violate the principles of investing discussed in this chapter.

4. You have $100 you want to invest and are offered two options at the bank: the first will pay you 10.3 percent interest compounded annually, while the second will offer you 10 percent compounded quarterly. Which is the better one-year investment?

5. Two couples are discussing their plans to start a family. Both are two-worker couples and expect that the lower-paid partner will stay home for two years with the new baby. One of these is a college graduate with a higher wage than the other, who has a high-school diploma. Which couple will have a child first? Explain your answer.

6. Suppose that the federal government introduces a program to provide each and every high-school graduate with a college education. What will happen to the net present value of a bachelor's degree? Explain your answer.

7. Explain how private discount rates differ across two countries, one of which has a 100 percent confiscatory estate tax (leaving nothing to be inherited), and another that has a 5 percent estate tax. How will these different tax systems impact the consumption/investment decisions of individuals?

8. Some states have usury laws which set the maximum amount of interest that can be charged on loans to individuals and businesses.
   a) Using supply and demand curves, show the impact of these laws on loanable funds.
   b) Show what happens when there is an increase in the inflation rate.
   c) Now show what happens to the quantity of loans made to riskier borrowers, for example, first-time home buyers or small businesses in blighted areas of town. Do you think usury laws are good for borrowers? Explain your answer.

9. What would happen to the rate of return from investing in beauty capital if health-insurance companies agreed to cover plastic-surgery procedures? Explain your answer.

10. Many states have imposed "term limits" on their state legislators. Explain how, if at all, this would change politicians' political discount rate in those states. Design a test of your prediction based on comparing states with and without term limits.

11. Suppose that the tuition and fees are $13,500 per year at a public university, and $33,700 per year at a private university. Explain why anyone would ever opt to attend a private university.

12. Treasury Inflation Protected Securities (TIPS) offer lower yields than traditional fixed-interest Treasuries with the same time to maturity. What factors would impact the magnitude of this "gap" in the yields of these two types of government investments? Explain your answer.

13. College is often viewed as a "recession" industry: full-time enrollments typically rise during recessionary times and fall during expansions. Using principles learned in this chapter, explain why this is the case, and identify situations that might run counter to this enrollment pattern.

14. We observe that people who live in countries experiencing hyperinflation tend to spend all of their current income on consumables. Why? What do you think happens to the supply of consumables during times of hyperinflation? Explain your answer.

15. What do you think happens, if anything, to the discount rate of teenagers when their weekly allowance is replaced by a monthly allowance? Explain your answer.

16. Why do you think that the interest rates that are charged for credit card balances, automobile loans, housing loans, and "payday" loans differ? Explain your answer.

17. People often get "residual" well-being from the fond memories they have of their past consumption activities. Baby boomers still talk about their Woodstock and hippie experiences 50 years later. Does this mean that these consumption activities are also investment activities? Explain your answer.

18. A die-hard St. Louis Cardinals fan placed a $50 bet in Las Vegas near the end of the baseball season that the Cardinals would win the 2011 National Baseball League's pennant, even though the team was 10+ games back at that time. In fact, the Cardinals did go on to win the NLB pennant (and the 2011 World Series) and the bet paid off $25,000. Is this sufficient information to conclude that the fan is a risk-preferring person? Why or why not? Explain your answer.

Human Capital in the Workplace

"A college degree is not a sign that one is a finished product but an indication a person is prepared for life."

Reverend Edward A. Malloy
Former President,
University of Notre Dame

You have learned that individuals and households must make choices as to whether they will consume all of their current resources or invest some to enhance their future well-being. Among the investment options are those, such as education, that build human capital. Researchers have found that educational attainment is strongly related to a person's lifetime earnings: high-school graduates make, on average, $200,000 more during their work lives than those without a high-school degree. College graduates make, on average, almost twice what high-school graduates make ($2.1 million versus $1.2 million). This translates into a present discounted value of $500,000 more in lifetime earnings. Moreover, the unemployment rates of college graduates tend to be substantially less than those of high-school graduates: at the start of 2011, for example, these rates were 4.7 percent versus 9.8 percent, respectively.

Why do education and other investments in human capital have such a significant impact on a person's labor market potential? In this chapter, we look at two explanations for this phenomenon: signaling and human-capital accumulation. We then continue on to discuss how these investments in human capital affect labor productivity, which, along with other factors, determines wage rates in the labor market. Finally, we address the growing concern about income inequality in the United States and examine various root causes, including the growing inequality in human-capital accumulation.

14.1 Signaling or Human-Capital Accumulation?

Economists have long debated why accumulating human-capital—especially earning a college degree—has such a significant impact on a person's earnings. After all, we know people who never graduated college but have still succeeded remarkably well in the labor market. Bill Gates and Oprah Winfrey come immediately to mind. And

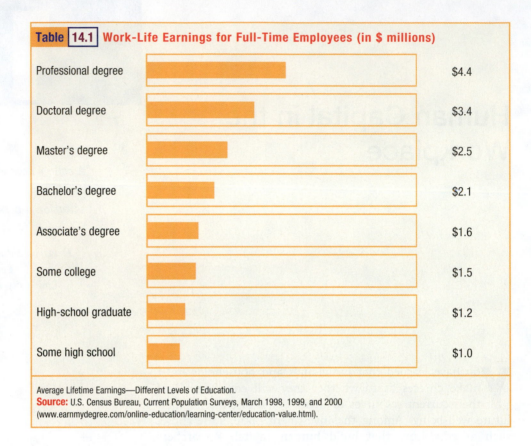

Table 14.1 Work-Life Earnings for Full-Time Employees (in $ millions)

Professional degree	$4.4
Doctoral degree	$3.4
Master's degree	$2.5
Bachelor's degree	$2.1
Associate's degree	$1.6
Some college	$1.5
High-school graduate	$1.2
Some high school	$1.0

Average Lifetime Earnings—Different Levels of Education.
Source: U.S. Census Bureau, Current Population Surveys, March 1998, 1999, and 2000
(www.earnmydegree.com/online-education/learning-center/education-value.html).

Paris Hilton, Hilary Swank, and Britney Spears didn't even complete high school. In other words, there are ways to accumulate human capital other than going to school.

Nevertheless, *on average*, a college graduate will do a lot better than a high-school graduate when it comes to employment stability and lifetime earnings. **Table 14.1** shows how people's lifetime earnings increase, on average, as they accumulate more education. A four-year college degree appears to pay off even for occupations that do not require a degree.[1] **Table 14.2** reports the annual salary differential associated with having a college degree for a number of jobs, including plumbers, hairdressers, and cashiers.

Does the relationship between educational attainment and lifetime earnings arise because college graduates gain highly valued, specific skills—an ability to do a statistical analysis or design a Web page, for example—or is there another, more subtle explanation?

The Role that Signaling Plays in the Labor Market

We know that gathering information about a good's quality is rarely costless. This is why travelers often rely on their favorite restaurant and hotel chains when they are away from home and must decide where to eat and sleep. Brand names provide

[1]David Leonhardt, "Even for Cashiers, College Pays Off." *New York Times*, June 26, 2011, p. 3.

Table 14.2	Difference in Median Salaries for College Graduates versus High-School Graduates in Various Occupations, 2009
Dishwasher	+83%
Child-care worker	+80%
Dental hygienist	+76%
Hairdresser	+69%
Cashier	+56%
Plumber	+39%
Waitress/waiter	+34%
Firefighter	+25%
Cook	+16%
Secretary	+13%
Casino worker	+3%

Source: David Leonhardt, *New York Times*, June 26, 2011, p. 3

consumers with a low-cost **signal** about the quality, breadth of services, and so forth that can be expected at a specific business location. People come to rely on signals such as these, even if they experience an occasional "lemon."

SIGNAL A characteristic of a group, such as brand name, that is easily observable and can be relied on to assess the quality of the group's individual members.

EXAMPLE People expect that every Whole Foods market will carry high-quality organic foods, fish, and meat.

EXAMPLE Many puppy buyers consider a puppy's breed as an indicator of its temperament: yorkies tend to be possessive, while golden retrievers aim to please.

EXAMPLE The average college student expects to receive lower grades in economics and math courses than in most other courses.

Consumers, employers, and even students rely on signals as a low-cost method for determining the quality or attributes of specific alternatives that they face. When it comes to the hiring process, employers often give priority to applicants with a particular "stock" of human capital, such as a college degree. What does a college degree signal to employers? Perhaps it signals that the applicant is likely to meet a deadline, be on time for a meeting, take direction, respect authority, solve complex problems, work independently, and so on. Quite likely, the employer has had previous, favorable experiences with college-educated employees and found that, *on average*, college graduates are more productive employees than nongraduates, at least in some employee positions.

Unlike educational attainment, other types of human capital that job applicants possess can often be evaluated directly. Aspiring actors and opera singers can be individually "sized up" in terms of their physical presence, gracefulness, and talent during the audition process (or during the 15 episodes of *American Idol*). In these situations, there is less need—in terms of saving on information costs—to rely on signals to assess the quality of an applicant. However, for job applicants whose talents are harder to gauge, signals become increasingly important.

If a college degree does, in fact, send a positive signal about productivity to employers, this will increase the demand for college graduates as well as their equilibrium pay. But just as travelers will occasionally find a lemon among their favorite chains, so, too, will employers occasionally find a lemon among the college graduates they have hired. New hires are evaluated in the workplace and terminated if they are found lacking. So a college degree might "get you in the door," but it will not keep you there. In fact, research has shown that the usefulness of educational signals declines as an employee's work experience grows because each employee's actual productivity can be directly observed through this work experience.[2]

Over time, a hiring signal such as a college degree can erode and no longer be a good predictor of an applicant group's labor productivity. When this happens, signals will be modified or replaced by more accurate signals. For example, college degrees from *particular* institutions or specific majors might be used as signals—rather than simply the college degree itself—leading to greater demand for a *subset* of college graduates. Many employers distinguish between campus-based bachelors' degree programs and online degrees, valuing the former as a more reliable signal of an employee's future success.[3] And there is little doubt that an advanced degree—an MBA or MA degree—has become the signal of choice for many employers.

Gender as a Signal in the Hiring Process

In past generations, a job applicant's gender was often used as a signal of long-term productivity: men were considered to be, on average, more productive based on the length of time they were likely to remain with a company. Many employers once viewed women—especially those who were married and of childbearing age—to be less reliable employees because, *on average*, they were more apt to leave the workforce due to family demands. In other words, women employees—as a group—were viewed as "quitters."[4] As a result, women were hired at lower wage rates and received fewer hours of on-the-job training.[5]

In recent decades, this "gender signal" has weakened significantly as a predictor of employee reliability and with good reason: the median number of years that female workers born between 1926 and 1945 were out of the labor force was ten years, as compared to *zero* years for female baby boomers born between 1945 and 1960.[6] This change in working women's behavior can be attributed, in part, to the substantial increase in the number of households in which women are the primary wage earners (for more detail, see Appendix 10A). Also, women have accumulated unprecedented amounts of human capital through greater educational attainment, which raises their opportunity cost of having children and leaving the labor force, even temporarily.

· · · · · · ·

[2]Dale Belman and John Heywood, "Sheepskin Effects By Cohort: Implications of Job Matching in a Signaling Model." *Oxford Economic Papers,* 49, no. 4 (1997).

[3]Alex Wellen, "Degrees of Acceptance." *New York Times,* July 30, 2006.

[4]Lalith Munasunghe and Alice Henriques, "Gender Gap in Wage Returns to Job Tenure and Experience." *Labour Economics,* 15, no. 6 (December, 2008).

[5]*Ibid.*

[6]Chad Newcomb, "Distribution of Zero-Earning Years by Gender and Cohort." Office of Policy, U.S. Social Security Administration (November 2000). Note 2000-2.

Gender has become even less of a factor in the hiring process in countries where both fathers and mothers are offered favorable family-leave benefits.[7] In Sweden, for example, men and women are both eligible for paid family leave, and men are required to take at least a portion of this leave. In contrast, the U.S. Family Medical Leave Act of 1993 requires only that employers grant 12 weeks of *unpaid* leave to either or both parents, making it far less common for higher-earning men to take leave than it is for lower-earning women.

To what extent do U.S. employers still consider gender in their hiring and promotion decisions, and in their wage offers? Some researchers believe that the 17–20 percent "wage gap" between women and men—which for the past few decades has not closed by much—shows that employers still expect there to be a difference in the average productivity of the two sexes. Others have found that this pay gap is most pronounced in the highest paid positions (referred to as the "glass ceiling" effect)[8] but that advanced degrees significantly reduce the gap.[9] Still other researchers have begun to examine whether it is motherhood, rather than gender, which explains the existing wage gap between men and women.[10] Finally, preliminary evidence suggests that women are less-aggressive negotiators when it comes to upping their pay.

Warren Farrell, a researcher who studies gender issues in the workplace, posed an interesting question related to the gender wage gap. He wondered why at least some employers wouldn't take advantage of the wage gap and hire only women, thereby reducing their labor expenses by an average of 17 percent (when compared to all-male firms). He found that much of the existing wage gap can be explained by the systematically different career choices that men and women make. Careers that pay more often entail frequent travel, longer hours, safety risks, and so forth. Women tend to make career choices that offer them more flexibility and a better balance between their work and family lives. This conclusion is consistent with Farrell's findings that a wage gap also exists between married and never married men: never-married men out-earn married men irrespective of whether the married men have children or not. In contrast, marriage alone appears to have an insignificant impact on women's wages, but childbearing and child-rearing activities substantially reduce women's earnings. Citing a St. Louis Federal Reserve analysis of the wages of men and women who have never been married nor had children, Farrell reports that these women earned, on average, 117 percent more than their male counterparts.[11]

SOLVED PROBLEM

Q During the past decade, the number of female college students has grown substantially relative to male students. In 2009, over 54 percent of college students were female.

· · · · · · · ·

[7]Elina Pylkkänen and Nina Smith, "The Impact of Family-Friendly Policies in Denmark and Sweden on Mothers' Career Interruptions Due to Childbirth." IZA Discussion Paper No. 1050, March 2004. Available at SSRN: http://ssrn.com/abstract=522282.

[8]Spyros Konstantopoulos and Amelie Constant, "The Gender Gap Reloaded: Are School Characteristics Linked to Labor Market Performance?" *Social Science Research,* 37, no. 2 (June, 2008).

[9]Mark Montgomery and Irene Powell, "Does an Advanced Degree Reduce the Gender Gap? Evidence from MBAs." *Industrial Relations,* 42 (July, 2003).

[10]Catalina Amuedo-Dorantes and Jean Kimmel, "The Motherhood Wage Gap for Women in the United States: The Importance of College and Fertility Delay." *Review of Economics and the Household,* 3, no. 1 (March, 2005).

[11]Liz Wolgemuth, "Why Some Women Skirt the Wage Gap." *U.S. News and World Report,* May 14, 2010.

Using supply and demand diagrams, show the impact of this trend on the gender wage gap when (1) employers value all college graduates the same regardless of their gender, and (2) employers pursue hiring and wage practices that favor male college graduates.

A (1) If the percentage of female college graduates grows, then a greater percentage of women will enjoy a college wage premium relative to men. This would narrow and possibly eliminate the existing gender wage gap. It could even lead to a situation where men, on average, earn less than women. Of course, this assumes that employers value female college graduates in the same way that they value male college graduates.

(2) What if this is not the case? If employers do not view female college graduates as good substitutes for male graduates, then the decrease in supply of male graduates will lead to a higher wage for them. Meanwhile, if the demand for female college graduates does not grow by at least the same rate as their supply, then the wages for these graduates will fall. In this situation, the gender gap between two the groups could actually increase.

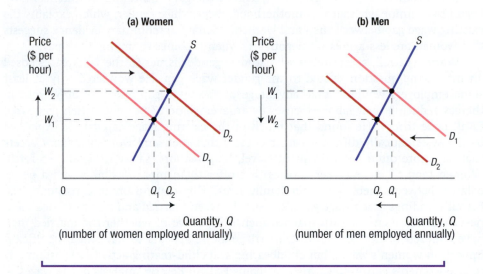

Signaling or Economic Discrimination?

Given the role that signals play in the hiring decision, we would expect that only those signals that accurately gauge group members' labor productivity will survive. Why, then, do some employers rely on "bad" signals to assess the productivity of different groups of job applicants?

So far, we have assumed that an employer's sole objective is to hire employees with the highest level of productivity: in other words, employees who will generate the greatest amount of output per dollar of wages paid. What if, instead, an employer chooses to hire people solely to make the workplace more enjoyable for her? What if, for example, she personally prefers employees who are funny or are snappy dressers or are male, regardless of their productivity? What if she categorically rejects applicants with visible tattoos, body piercings, or long hair? When hiring is based on *signals unrelated to productivity*, we refer to this as **economic discrimination**.

> **ECONOMIC DISCRIMINATION** A situation in which signals unrelated to quality or productivity are relied upon to assess the members of a group.

EXAMPLE Some employers will not hire job applicants with visible physical deformities, even if these do not interfere with the person's ability to get the job done.

EXAMPLE Airlines used to reject flight-attendant applicants who did not meet strict weight and height guidelines, despite the lack of a job performance rationale.

EXAMPLE Many parents refuse to let their daughters date someone with long hair or lots of tattoos, even though these characteristics are not necessarily indicative of that person's labor market potential or personal integrity.

Milton Friedman, a Nobel Laureate in economics, examined the employment discrimination that Jews, Catholics, and blacks suffered when they applied for industrial and professional positions in the United States and Europe.[12] Friedman concluded that employers eventually "pay" when they hire people to satisfy their own personal preferences instead of hiring based on worker productivity. Inevitably, these employers will turn away some of the most productive workers in the applicant pool. This, in turn, increases the discriminating employer's production costs and lowers his profits.

Employers who do not engage in discriminatory hiring practices will enjoy lower production costs and higher profits by hiring the most productive workers in the applicant pool, including those who have been discriminated against by other employers. These lower-cost firms may even drive companies that discriminate out of business. Based on this dynamic, Friedman concluded that competition will largely eliminate discrimination in hiring. This prediction was brought to the fore in 2008, when then presidential candidate Barack Obama was asked whether his race might hurt his campaign. He responded:

> "What I've found is that people here, they don't care what color you are . . . What they're trying to figure out is, who can deliver? It's just like the Pittsburgh Steelers. They don't care what color you are, they want to make sure you can make the plays."[13]

Friedman's prediction—that competition will ultimately eliminate employment discrimination—is subject to some caveats. We know from recent historical events that governments around the world have, at times, actively initiated and enforced laws that encourage discrimination in employment. The Nuremberg Laws in Nazi Germany prohibited Jews from holding government positions and from serving as doctors, lawyers, or journalists. And, prior to the passage of the U.S. Civil Rights Act in 1964, some Southern cities required employers to segregate their workplaces by race. Because duplicating work spaces and equipment for black workers tended to be cost prohibitive, these laws discouraged employers from hiring productive black workers even when they wanted to. Likewise, South Africa's apartheid laws "institutionalized" discrimination in the workplace. Currently, Saudi Arabian women are protesting a new fatwa (Islamic religious) ruling that prohibits them from cashier positions and other employment opportunities in which they would mix with men. When all employers are forced by law—whether enacted legislatively or through religious edict—to discriminate among job applicants, the ability of competition to eradicate discrimination in employment is greatly diminished.

· · · · · · ·

[12]Milton Friedman, "Capitalism and Discrimination." *Capitalism and Freedom* (Chicago: University of Chicago Press, 1962).

[13]Robert H. Frank, "When it Really Counts, Qualifications Trump Race." *New York Times,* November 16, 2008.

A College Degree's Contribution to Future Earnings

A college education increases a graduate's *specific* and *nonspecific* human capital. By **specific human capital**, we mean skills that are required for certain aspects of a production process.

> **SPECIFIC HUMAN CAPITAL** Human capital that imparts skills required for certain aspects of a production process.
>
> **EXAMPLE** Learning to write software in the computer language Java or C++ creates specific human capital.
>
> **EXAMPLE** Earning a commercial driver's license bestows specific human capital.
>
> **EXAMPLE** A training class that teaches you how to draw blood develops specific human capital.

The demand for these specific human-capital skills is often industry-specific. As employers' production processes change, their demand for specific skills will change too. For example, the manufacturing sector has ratcheted up its demand for college graduates who can manage and maintain assembly-line robotic systems.[14] And software developers require their programmers to be knowledgeable about Perl, ASP, and other programming languages in addition to Java and C++.

Nonspecific human capital imparts skills that are applicable to a whole host of production processes and are more "general" in nature.

> **NONSPECIFIC HUMAN CAPITAL** Human capital that imparts skills that are applicable to a broad range of production processes.
>
> **EXAMPLE** Learning to solve algebraic equations creates nonspecific human capital.
>
> **EXAMPLE** Engaging in physical strength training builds nonspecific human capital.
>
> **EXAMPLE** Becoming skilled at speed-reading bestows nonspecific human capital.

Nonspecific human capital corresponds to generic skills such as the ability to define and solve problems, access information from a variety of sources, work in teams, write in complete sentences, and interpret data. When students opt for a specific program of study such as economics or mechanical engineering, they are indirectly choosing the mix of specific and nonspecific skills they will acquire. Because these skills are valued differently by employers at any given point in time, college degrees and majors tend to differ in terms of the future wage streams they generate.

The variability of these wage streams may also differ over time. Movie directors, for example, have "bumpy" wage streams that reflect the completion of one film project and the search for a new one to embark upon. In contrast, public-school teachers and salaried nurses receive steadier, more reliable, wage streams. The less reliable a wage stream is, the higher the pay must be to compensate a person for the "lean times." Graduates whose majors or programs of study generate less reliable earning streams must be compensated for accepting this additional risk. This is no different from other investments: the higher the risk, the greater the expected return must be.

• • • • • • •

[14]Elizabeth Fowler, "Careers: Learning to Repair Robots." *New York Times*, February 18, 1981.

College graduates who bear an increased risk because they have acquired relatively more specific human capital will demand more pay—when they are paid—to compensate them for investing in these types of skills. Consider, for example, the "boom-and-bust" cycles that have long plagued aeronautical engineers. When they are working, they are paid fairly high salaries to compensate in part for those periods in which they are unemployed or underemployed, such as when NASA programs suffer significant budget cutbacks. Similarly, the livelihoods of petroleum engineers are at risk from oil reserve shutdowns and increased government regulation. Even accounting graduates face some risk because their relatively high income streams are sensitive to the complexity of government tax laws and financial-reporting requirements. The passage of a simplified income-tax system or the elimination of estate taxes could significantly reduce the demand for accounting services. Among lower-income filers, simplified tax filings and the introduction of tax software (e.g., TurboTax) have already reduced the demand for these services. And the growing outsourcing of accounting to India and elsewhere introduces yet another source of risk when it comes to the income streams of U.S. accountants.

By contrast, nonspecific human capital tends to be less susceptible to changes in the economic environment because employers, by and large, always are in the market for employees that have strong communication, problem-solving, quantitative, and interpersonal skills. This creates greater opportunity for people to move between industries as markets ebb and grow, thereby reducing the risk of unemployment. But in return for this lower risk of unemployment, graduates who have accumulated less-specific human capital tend to earn lower wages, on average, than graduates with more-specific human capital.

Even when the course of study or choice of major is the same, all college degrees are not created equal when it comes to the average earnings they command. For example, graduates of Harvard's Business School report higher incomes on average than graduates of other MBA programs. Is this because MBA degrees earned at highly selective schools such as Harvard signal higher-quality employee applicants? Or, is there a real difference in the human capital that different graduate programs build?

Finally, certain educational programs—for example, medical training in orthopedic surgery—entail several years of additional full-time study prior to entry into the job market. Each additional year of formal education represents a year of forgone earnings. Without the promise of a higher earnings stream down the line, it would be difficult to entice many people to invest ten years beyond college to become orthopedic surgeons. In 2008 and 2009, orthopedic surgeons earned an average of $481,000 per year. This compared with $173,000 for family medicine practitioners who spend seven years in training after college. How much of this earnings differential is due to the additional time spent in training is uncertain. However, it is clear that the amount of time spent in postgraduate study creates another opportunity cost that is likely to result in a higher future wage stream.

14.2 The Demand for Labor

To better understand the connection between people's education and the wages they earn, we must dig deeper into the factors that dictate an employer's willingness to pay—his demand—for different types of labor. You already learned in Chapter 6 about derived demand, which is the demand for an input into production. As you saw then, the demand for certain inputs is closely linked to demand for the output that is produced using these inputs. For example, the demand for horse-pulled buggies fell after the automobile was invented and mass-produced. At the same time, the demand for buggy whips and buggy-whip workers also fell. Likewise, the introduction of e-mail reduced the demand for "snail mail" and, as a result, mail carriers and couriers.

Sometimes the demand for an input can change even when there is no change in the demand for an output. As we will explain further, this can happen when there is a change in input prices or production technology.

The Marginal Product of Labor

Let's begin by assuming a competitive labor market in which each employer is a *price taker* or, more precisely, a *wage taker*. This means that when it comes to hiring, an employer can only "vote with her feet" and refuse to hire if the "going" wage rate is higher than her willingness to pay for an employee. This going wage rate is usually the market-determined, equilibrium wage. However, we already know that there are situations in which the going wage rate may diverge from equilibrium, even in the long run. This would be the case when the government imposes a minimum wage or other wage controls. Similarly, unions that exert wage-setting power in specific industries, such as U.S. automobile manufacturing, can keep wages above their equilibrium levels.

Assuming an employer faces a competitive labor market and a market-determined wage rate, how does she decide how much, if any, labor to hire? To complicate the problem, what if there are several "classes" of labor (skilled, unskilled, high-school graduates, college graduates, experienced, and inexperienced), each with its own market-determined wage rate?

The concept of marginal product will help us answer this question. **Marginal product** is the additional output produced when one more unit of a specific input, such as labor, is added to the production process, *everything else held constant*.

> **MARGINAL PRODUCT** The additional output produced when an additional unit of an input is added to the production process, everything else held constant.

> **EXAMPLE** A local gym added a new trainer, which increased the number of clients seen each day from 20 to 30. The marginal product of the new trainer is 10 clients a day.

> **EXAMPLE** A brick-making company added a person to its assembly line, which increased daily output from 5,000 bricks a day to 6,000 bricks a day. The marginal product of the new worker is 1,000 bricks a day.

For labor services, a "unit" of input is defined by the time period over which an employee is hired and paid—that is, hours, days, or years. A unit of labor input must also specify the type of worker that is being hired—skilled, unskilled, college-educated, and so forth. We know, for example, that the daily marginal product of a college graduate working in an accounting firm may be very different from the daily marginal product of a high-school graduate who is covering the reception desk at the same company.

To simplify our analysis, let's say that there are only two types of workers—college graduates and high-school graduates. For both groups, we'll assume that the marginal product of adding workers first increases and then at some point starts to diminish. (We will explain why this is a reasonable assumption later on.) The employment level at which this occurs is referred to as the point of **diminishing marginal returns**.

> **DIMINISHING MARGINAL RETURNS** A situation in which the addition of another unit of an input results in a lower marginal contribution to output than what was contributed by the preceding unit, all else remaining unchanged.

EXAMPLE Suppose that a road crew is assigned to repave a section of highway. At its disposal, the crew has a fixed amount of equipment consisting of bulldozers, backhoes, asphalt machines, shovels, and sweepers. The first six workers that arrive man the bulldozers and backhoes to remove the existing surface and regrade the roadway. The second group of six is responsible for pouring the new asphalt. The third group of six workers grabs shovels to fill nooks and crannies with tar and smooth out the bumps. The fourth group uses the sweepers to remove loose debris on the pavement. The fifth group that arrives washes down the new pavement to "set" the asphalt. The last group of six workers picks up refuse from the roadside. While all of these groups are productive, we could argue that diminishing marginal returns have certainly set in by the last group of workers.

Figure 14.1 illustrates the relationship between the number of high-school and college graduates employed and each worker's marginal product, assuming there is a point of diminishing marginal returns. Suppose these are representative marginal product curves for high-school and college graduates who work at ExpressScripts, a large pharmacy-benefit manager. The product that ExpressScripts sells is a filled prescription, delivered by mail to a patient. If college graduates are indeed more productive, their marginal product curve will be higher than the curve for high-school graduates at any given level of employment. In other words, holding all other inputs constant, each college graduate will contribute more to output than her high-school equivalent.

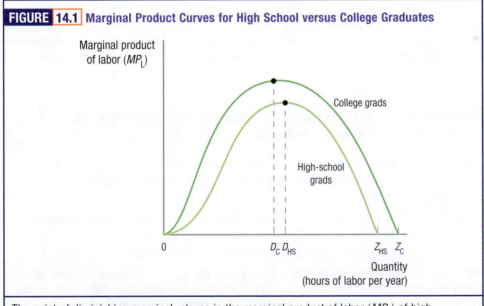

FIGURE 14.1 **Marginal Product Curves for High School versus College Graduates**

The point of diminishing marginal returns in the marginal product of labor (MP_L) of high-school and college-educated workers occurs at the employment levels D_{HS} and D_C, respectively. Assuming that college graduates are more productive, their marginal product curve will be higher than the curve for high-school graduates at any given level of employment. In other words, holding all other inputs constant, each college graduate will contribute more to output than her high-school equivalent. At Z_{HS} and Z_C, respectively, the marginal product of the last high-school and college-educated workers equals zero.

The accuracy of this depiction depends crucially on whether there are opportunities for workers to **specialize** in production.

SPECIALIZATION A situation in which a worker performs a subset of production tasks.

EXAMPLE At a local McDonald's, one worker specializes in handling drive-through customers, another is in charge of the inside front register, and a third is responsible for food preparation.

EXAMPLE In large universities, professors are responsible for in-class activities and writing exams, while teaching assistants specialize in leading breakout sessions and grading exams.

You might recall that we already introduced the concept of specialization when we talked about division of labor and comparative advantage within a household. In that case, we were interested in maximizing the household's production of goods and purchase of market-based consumables. In much the same way, we are now interested in how production tasks can be organized and assigned so that an employer's output is maximized for any given amount of labor used, holding all other inputs constant.

Division of Labor

To understand the connection between specialization and productivity, consider an accounting firm that opens with only one employee—the accountant herself. She must complete all kinds of tax returns, answer the telephone, send out bills, and so forth. When the practice is small, a one-person business may make sense. But as the demand for her services increases, this accountant is likely to hire more employees and assign certain tasks to them. This division of tasks among workers is called the **division of labor**.

DIVISION OF LABOR The process of delegating a specific subset of tasks in the production process to specific workers.

EXAMPLE At many universities, part-time professors are assigned to teach large lower-level classes, while tenured full-time faculty focus on upper-level and graduate courses.

EXAMPLE Within the U.S. Postal Service, there are mail carriers who deliver the mail and clerks who sort the mail to prepare it for delivery.

Let's step through the accountant's hiring process. As the demand for her services grows, the accountant will likely hire her first employee, which permits both of them to specialize in specific tasks and thereby increase their individual productivity. For example, one person might specialize in managing the firm's business office and clients, while the other focuses solely on preparing tax returns. The additional number of tax returns that can be completed in a set amount of time as a result of this specialization is part of the marginal product *attributed to the second employee*. But this isn't to say that the second person is any more productive than the first. Rather, it is because the second person is hired that gains from specialization can be had.

This means that part of the contribution to output attributed to the second person is really due to specialization.

This is an especially important point. If the marginal product of a third employee is higher than that of the second, and this were solely due to the third worker's superior skills, then why not hire the third person before you hire the second person? The answer is that the second and third workers are inherently interchangeable, but the gains from specialization that are enjoyed when each is added to the team are reflected in their marginal product.

Hiring more and more employees can generate even greater gains from specialization, at least up to a point. This means that each additional worker will have a higher marginal product than the one before. Some of these gains come from the fact that by specializing, workers develop an expertise in performing their tasks. They may even find more efficient ways to perform these duties. For example, an international reservations specialist at American Airlines may discover less time-consuming ways to search for available routes and fares after performing this service hundreds of times for customers.

At some point, however, if all other inputs into the production process remain unchanged, this will limit the additional output that can be had by continuing to add employees. For instance, if there is no growth in the accounting firm's work space, number of computers, desks, or telephones, this will slow down employees who require these tools to do their jobs. The fact that these other inputs are fixed essentially creates "congestion" in the workplace. At some point, the costs of this congestion will outweigh the gains from further specialization. When this occurs, we say that the *point of diminishing marginal returns* has been reached. In Figure 14.1, shown earlier, the corresponding levels of employment associated with the point of diminishing marginal returns for the two types of employees are designated by point D_C and point D_{HS}. Continuing to hire employees beyond these points will result in lower and lower marginal contributions to output. Nevertheless, the total output of the business will continue to grow with additional hiring, albeit at a slower rate than before, because each additional worker's contribution to output is still positive.

Is there ever a point at which the hiring of an additional employee can actually reduce output? Yes. In Figure 14.1, you can see that at employment levels designated by points Z_{HS} and Z_C, the last employee hired from both groups contributes zero additional output. Beyond these hiring levels, the marginal product of additional workers is *negative*. That is, the total output of the firm will actually fall if these workers are hired. This could occur because congestion is so great that adding any more workers interferes with the work that other employees are trying to accomplish. Once again, it is worth emphasizing that job applicants beyond these employment levels are not necessarily any less productive than those workers that have a positive marginal product. It is simply that congestion outweighs any further gains from specialization, thereby resulting in a negative marginal product for these job applicants.

Table 14.3 reports a hypothetical marginal product schedule for college graduates hired by an accounting firm. This schedule indicates that diminishing marginal returns to labor set in after the fifth employee is hired. This corresponds to D_C in Figure 14.1. The marginal product of college graduates turns negative after the tenth employee is hired, corresponding to Z_C.

Based solely on the concept of marginal product, what predictions can we make about an employer's hiring decisions? Hiring employees beyond points Z_{HS} and Z_C reduces the total output of the business, which would make no sense to an owner. It would only make sense if the business owner derives personal pleasure from adding to her employment rolls. Perhaps she wants to hire all of her grandchildren so that

Table 14.3	Marginal Product Schedule for College Graduates Employed in an Accounting Firm (Personal Income Tax Returns Prepared for $300 per Return)		
Units of Labor (Workers per Day)	Total Output (Tax Returns per Day)	Marginal Product of Labor (Number of Returns)	Value of Labor's Marginal Product per Day ($) ($300 × MP)
1	1	1	300
2	3	2	600
3	6	3	900
4	10	4	1,200
5	15	5	1,500
6	19	4	1,200
7	22	3	900
8	24	2	600
9	25	1	300
10	25	0	0
11	24	−1	−300

they get guaranteed paychecks, or she wants to be envied for being the largest employer in her town. In any event, an owner will "pay" for hiring beyond these points by incurring higher business costs than necessary. Also, she will suffer in terms of profitability, as long as her output market is competitive—that is, as long as she is a price taker when it comes to the output she sells.

Now that we know that hiring beyond points Z_{HS} and Z_C is highly unlikely, the question we are left with is whether or not an employer would hire beyond D_C and D_{HS}, the points of diminishing marginal returns. According to our earlier model of economic decision making, the employer will weigh the *marginal cost* of each additional hire versus the *marginal benefit*. The marginal cost of an additional hire is the amount this employee is paid, including the cost of health-insurance benefits, uniforms, training expenses, payroll taxes, and so forth. Going forward, we refer to this cost as the employee's wage per period of time worked. The marginal benefit is the employee's incremental contribution to output, or marginal product, weighted by the price that the employer can get for this output. In other words, the marginal benefit of hiring an employee is the additional revenue that this employee generates for his employer. We call this the **value** of the employee's **marginal product**.

VALUE OF THE MARGINAL PRODUCT (VMP) The market value of each worker's incremental contribution to output; the employee's marginal product weighted by the market price of this output.

EXAMPLE The head of the economics department is contemplating whether to hire a new full-time lecturer who would teach an additional 8 sections a year of introductory economics. Assuming 30 new students per section, each paying $600 for the course, the value of the lecturer's marginal product is $144,000 a year (8 × 30 × $600).

In Chapter 8, we talked about price-taking producers who can sell as much output as they want at the going market price, P_e. For these suppliers, the value of each employee's marginal contribution to output will equal his marginal product multiplied by P_e:

$$\textbf{Value of the marginal product} = P_e \times \text{marginal product}$$

The value of an employee's marginal product is sometimes called his *marginal revenue product*. It is the incremental contribution to revenue that an additional unit of an input, such as labor, generates, holding all other inputs constant. Table 14.3 shows the *VMP* for each college graduate applying for a position with our hypothetical accounting firm. These values assume that the equilibrium market price of an individual income tax return is $300. It should come as no surprise that the *VMP* starts to decline at the point of diminishing marginal returns, and that it turns negative when the marginal product of labor turns negative.

When a job applicant's *VMP* is greater than his wage, the *net benefit* of hiring him is positive. That is, the difference between the employee's contribution to revenue (marginal benefit) and his wage (marginal cost) is positive. If, instead, his *VMP* just equals the wage he would be paid, the net benefit of hiring this applicant equals zero. Inasmuch as the employer just covers all of her opportunity costs if she hires this person, she is indifferent to doing so. Finally, if the applicant's *VMP* is less than the wage he would earn, then the net benefit of hiring him is negative, and the employer will lose money if she hires this person.

We saw this hiring dynamic at work during the 2007 Great Recession, when a large number of highly skilled people—laid off from six-figure salaried positions—took pay cuts of as much as 50 percent to fill job vacancies at smaller companies. Small business owners were delighted to upgrade their workforce at no additional expense, courtesy of the bleak labor market.[15] The *VMP* of most displaced employees fell because the price of many goods and services declined in the face of weaker demand, thereby reducing the value of their work contributions.

The Hiring Decision

We have just seen that an employer's hiring decision is dictated by both the job-seeker's *VMP* and the market-determined wage rate. The *VMP* curve is shown in **Figure 14.2**. If you compare the *VMP* curve to the *MP* curves depicted in Figure 14.1, you will see that they look a lot alike. This is because a worker's *VMP* is simply his marginal product (*MP*) multiplied by the price (P_e) that the employer receives for each unit of output the employee contributes. When we multiply *MP* by P_e, a constant, the *MP* curve is simply scaled upward.

Suppose that the market wage rate for high-school graduates is $9 per hour ($W_{HS}$) and $20 per hour ($W_C$) for college graduates. If we superimpose these wage rates on each group's respective *VMP* curve in Figure 14.2, we can see exactly how many employees will be hired in each labor class. In our example, 35 high-school graduates and 28 college graduates will be employed each month. At this level and mix of employment, the *VMP* = *W* for the last of each type of worker hired. You might be wondering why the employer would hire more than 12 high-school students and 14 college students. At these two hiring levels, the *VMP*s also equal the wages for each type of worker.

....

[15]Michael Luo, "Overqualified? Yes, But Happy to Have a Job." *New York Times*, March 28, 2010.

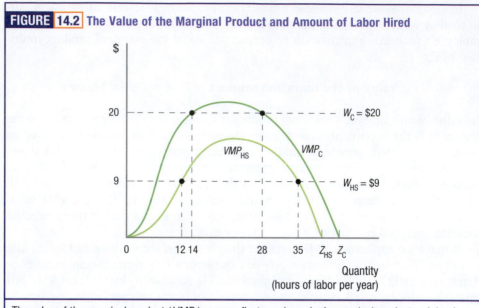

FIGURE 14.2 The Value of the Marginal Product and Amount of Labor Hired

The value of the marginal product (VMP_L) curve reflects each worker's marginal product weighted by the price that the employer receives for each unit of output. If the market wage rate for high-school graduates is \$9 per hour (W_{HS}) and \$20 per hour (W_C) for college graduates, then according to the *VMP* curves, 35 high-school graduates and 28 college graduates will be employed each month. At this level and mix of employment, the VMP_L equals *W* for the last of each type of worker hired. An employer would never stop hiring at 12 and 14, respectively, where the VMP_L also equals *W* because this is in the range of *increasing* marginal product. Consequently, hiring at these lower levels would *minimize*, rather than maximize, the net benefit an employer reaps from her workers.

To answer why the employer would do so, notice that 12 and 14 workers are in the range of *increasing* marginal product. Consequently, hiring at this level would *minimize*, rather than maximize, the employer's net returns from labor, because hiring beyond 12 and 14 workers, respectively, would yield *VMP*s that are greater than the market wage (marginal cost) for each group.

Suppose that a college graduate in an accounting firm earns \$38 per hour, or \$304 per eight-hour day. Returning to Table 14.3, we can see that the optimal number of college grads hired is eight: the ninth employee costs \$304 but only generates \$300 in additional revenue per day for the firm.

We can draw a number of conclusions directly from our analysis of the demand for labor:

- Increases in the wage rate will lead to a decline in the quantity of labor demanded, holding everything else constant. As **Figure 14.3** indicates, when the wage increases from W_1 to W_2, employers hire fewer workers. The last worker hired will have a *VMP* that is equal to the new, higher wage. This result is consistent with the Law of Demand: when the price of labor goes up, the quantity demanded decreases.

- When the market price of an output increases, the *VMP* curve ($P_e \times MP$) for inputs such as labor shifts upward. As **Figure 14.4** demonstrates, more labor will be hired at any given wage rate, assuming nothing else has changed. This translates into a rightward shift in the demand curve for labor.

- New technologies and educated workers can be complementary to one another; that is, technology can increase the worker productivity. When this

FIGURE 14.3 The Impact of a Wage Increase on Employment

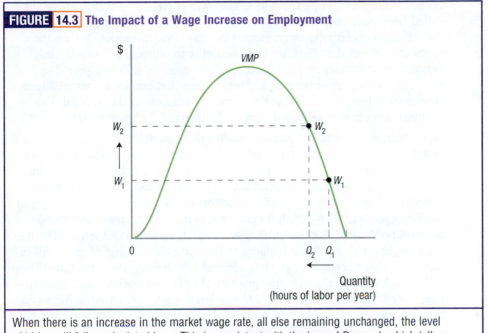

When there is an increase in the market wage rate, all else remaining unchanged, the level of hiring will fall, as depicted here. This is consistent with the Law of Demand, which tells us that when the price of a good or service increases, less will be demanded, all else remaining constant.

FIGURE 14.4 The Impact of an Increase in the Price of an Output on the Value of the Marginal Product and Employment

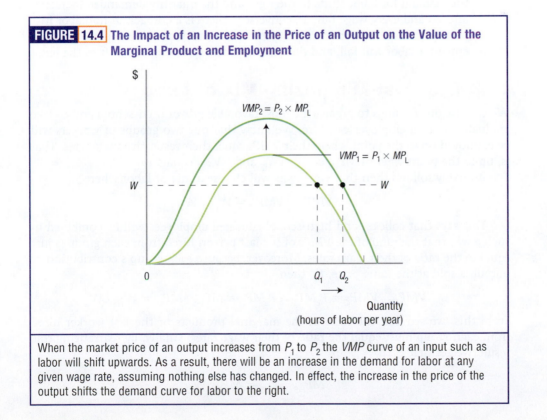

When the market price of an output increases from P_1 to P_2 the *VMP* curve of an input such as labor will shift upwards. As a result, there will be an increase in the demand for labor at any given wage rate, assuming nothing else has changed. In effect, the increase in the price of the output shifts the demand curve for labor to the right.

occurs, it leads to an upward shift in the *VMP* curve. These technologies are called *labor-enhancing* technologies. Computer-based technologies, for example, favor those workers who can creatively process newly accessible information to meet employer demands, such as the ability to estimate the relationship between interest rates and the number of automobiles sold in a year. The resulting increase in worker productivity means that employers are willing to hire more at the going wage rate, assuming nothing else has changed. This also translates into a rightward shift in the demand for these workers.

■ New technologies and less educated labor can be substitutes in that they fail to benefit from each other in terms of their productivity. When this is the case, the new technology replaces less-educated workers and is called *labor-saving* rather than labor-enhancing technology. These technologies tend to be most effective in replacing clerical and production-line workers who are engaged in simple, repetitive tasks. What, for example, is the incremental contribution to output of an additional cashier after a store has introduced self-checkout scanning technology? What happens to the marginal product of an unskilled factory worker after a company has adopted fully robotic assembly lines? These technologies reduce the marginal product of unskilled workers, which means that their *VMP* curve shifts down. At any given wage rate, fewer cashiers and assembly-line workers will be demanded. Unlike in Figure 14.4, there will be a leftward shift in the demand curve for these types of workers.

■ Increasing the employment of nonlabor inputs can improve labor productivity by easing congestion in the workplace. For example, a factory may decide to increase its use of electricity and other inputs to run a night shift. When this occurs, there will be a shift up in the *VMP* curve for labor. As a result, the demand for labor shifts to the right and the quantity demanded increases at each and every wage rate. If, conversely, there is a cutback in nonlabor inputs, perhaps due to shortages in chemical or precious metal inputs, the *VMP* curve for labor will fall, and the demand curve for labor will shift to the left.

14.3 The Cost-Minimizing Mix of Labor

We can use our findings to predict the most favorable *mix* of high-school and college graduates that an employer can hire. We know that our two groups of workers will be employed up to the point where their *VMP*s equal their respective wage rates. That is, up to the point where VMP_{HS} equals W_{HS} and VMP_C equals W_C.

It readily follows then that employers will choose a mix of labor where

$$VMP_{HS}/VMP_C = W_{HS}/W_C$$

This says that college- and high-school educated employees will be combined in such a way that the *ratio* of the *VMP*s of the last person hired from each group is just equal to the *ratio* of their wage rates. Moreover, because each group's contribution of output is sold at the same price, P_e, then

$$VMP_{HS}/VMP_C = P_eMP_{HS}/P_eMP_C = MP_{HS}/MP_C = W_{HS}/W_C$$

From this, we see that the ratio of the marginal products of the last worker hired from each group must equal the ratio of their wage rates. Finally, by rearranging this result, we get that

$$MP_{HS}/W_{HS} = MP_C/W_C$$

In other words, the last wage dollar spent on each type of labor generate the same contribution to output.

We can generalize this result to any set of inputs in the production process. If the producer combines inputs in such a way that the *very last dollar* spent on each input contributes the same amount of output, her **costs of production** will be **minimized**.

> **COST-MINIMIZING PRODUCTION** A situation where the very last dollar spent on each input generates the same amount of output.

EXAMPLE Suppose that each self-serve checkout scanner costs a supermarket $85,000 per year in maintenance and lease payments. The scanner can handle 50,000 customer transactions a year. A cashier, who costs the supermarket $47,000 a year in wages and benefits, can check out 25,000 customers a year. This means that the self-serve scanning system can process each transaction for $1.70, whereas the cashier's cost per transaction is $1.88. The supermarket could reduce its costs by leasing more scanners and reducing its number of cashiers (assuming that there is no difference in the transactions handled by cashiers and scanners).

14.4 Human Capital and Income Inequality

Now that you better understand the factors underlying the demand for labor, we can use these findings, along with our basic supply and demand model, to explore the sources of income inequality in the United States and around the world. We have seen that, all else equal, employers are willing to pay a higher wage if it is justified by higher worker productivity. To the extent that this productivity is related to human-capital accumulation, those with more human capital will tend, on average, to have greater earnings potential.

Beautiful, talented actresses tend to be in limited supply. In return for making movie studios a great deal of money, they receive hefty paychecks: Angelina Jolie earned more than $30 million in 2010 by generating almost $1 billion in movie revenues that year. The scarce human capital that these actresses bring to the job comes from their initial endowments (e.g., high cheekbones) and from the accumulation of additional human capital through investments in acting classes, plastic surgery, and grueling workouts to maintain their figures. Similarly, skilled and educated workers—when they are in limited supply—can also command higher wages than their unskilled and less-educated counterparts. To what extent do these differences in human capital explain the growing earnings gap among workers in the United States and contribute to the growing inequality in income?

Income Inequality in the United States

Table 14.4 reports the change in the distribution of total U.S. income across households, which have been categorized according to whether they are in the bottom 20 percent (first quintile), the next lowest 20 percent (second quintile), the middle 20 percent (third quintile), the next to highest 20 percent (fourth quintile), and finally, the top 20 percent (fifth quintile) of income recipients. The numbers show that in the span of a little more than 40 years (from 1967 to 2009), the share or fraction of total money income that went to the poorest 20 percent of U.S. households dropped from 4.0 percent to 3.4 percent, while the share received by the richest 20 percent of

Table 1	Share of Total U.S. Income Received by Quintiles and Top 5 Percent of Households* (1967–2009, selected years)						
Households Divided Into Quintiles (Fifths)	1967	1975	1979	1989	1999	2006	2009
Lowest fifth	4.0	4.4	4.1	3.8	3.6	3.4	3.4
Second fifth	10.8	10.5	10.2	9.5	8.9	8.6	8.6
Third fifth	17.3	17.1	16.8	15.8	14.9	14.5	14.6
Fourth fifth	24.2	24.8	24.6	24.0	23.2	22.9	23.2
Highest fifth	43.6	43.2	44.2	46.8	49.4	50.5	50.3
Highest 5 percent	17.2	15.9	16.9	18.9	21.5	22.3	21.5

Source: U.S. Census Bureau, Income in the United States: 2010, Table A-3.

*Income before taxes and government transfer payments (such as Social Security), excluding capital gains. Due to rounding, column sums may not equal 100 percent.

families rose from 43.6 percent to 50.3 percent. Much of the growth in the share of total income going to this top quintile actually went to the top 5 percent of households, whose share grew from 17.2 to 21.5 percent. While this trend does not bode well for income equality, it should be pointed out that the total income received grew in all of the quintiles during this period. And, this analysis does not reflect the distributional impact of income taxes paid or government income and in-kind transfer programs.

Based on these quintile numbers, it is clear that income inequality is growing dramatically in the United States, particularly when you look at the growth in the income share of the rich—the highest 5 and 20 percent of households. Still, Thomas Garrett, of the Federal Reserve Bank of St. Louis, sounds a cautionary note in drawing broad inferences based on this information:

> "For many households, [their] income changes over time which means that they often move to a higher income quintile over time. For example, nearly 58 percent of the households in the lowest income quintile in 1996 moved to a higher category by 2005. The reverse also happens: of those households that were in the top 1 percent in income in 1996, for example, more than 57 percent dropped to a lower income group by 2005."[16]

One obvious reason for the observed movement between quintiles is the aging of a household's wage earners. People's earnings are usually lower at the beginning of their work lives and drop down once again after they reach retirement age.

Inequality in Educational Attainment and Income Inequality

To what extent can the growth in income inequality be explained by inequalities in educational attainment? If we look at differences in the earned income of college graduates versus high-school graduates, we find that over time (1) the wages of college-educated workers have risen, on average; while (2) the wages of high-school graduates, on average, have fallen. Both of these effects clearly contribute to a growing inequality in the earnings of the two groups. The question that remains is what has caused the college premium to rise over time?

· · · · · · ·

[16]Thomas Garrett, "U.S. Income Inequality: It's Not So Bad." *Inside the Vault*. Federal Reserve Bank of St. Louis, Spring, 2010.

We know that the economic environment changed dramatically during the last decades of the twentieth century. The technological innovations during this period—desktop computing, online data retrieval, robotics, and so forth—were overwhelmingly labor-enhancing for college-educated workers, many of whom contributed to the development of technologies such as these. In other words, these innovations increased the marginal product of college-educated workers, justifying higher and higher wages. This phenomenon was most apparent in the late-1970s through the 1980s,[17] when the college wage premium grew from 45 percent of the average high-school graduate wage to over 70 percent. Researchers have estimated that during much of this period, the growth in supply of college-educated workers slowed to 2 percent per year. At the same time, demand for college-educated workers increased at a rate of approximately 3.46 percent per year, driven by technological advances. Based on these findings, the researchers concluded that "Overall, simple supply and demand . . . [did] a remarkable job explaining the long-run increase in the college wage premium."[18]

SOLVED PROBLEM

Q At the close of World War II, returning soldiers were offered college educations free of charge, paid for in full by the federal government through what was called the GI Bill. How, if at all, did the GI Bill affect income inequality in the United States? How did it affect high-school graduates who did not qualify for benefits under the bill?

A The GI Bill increased the supply of college graduates, thereby placing downward pressure on the wages of well-educated employees and professionals. This had the effect of reducing income inequality in the United States. At the same time, the GI Bill increased the demand for a college education, thereby pushing up tuition costs (which eventually led to the establishment of new colleges to serve the returning veterans). Those high-school graduates who were ineligible for GI Bill benefits faced higher tuition costs, leading some of them to forgo college. This, in turn, had the perverse effect of increasing income inequality in the United States.

During the same time period, other technologies arose that were distinctly labor-saving with respect to less-educated workers. The U.S. Postal Service, for example, replaced its hand-sorting mail operations with an automated, optical-scanning system. These kinds of technologies increasingly substituted for unskilled workers, thereby resulting in a leftward shift in the demand curve for unskilled labor and a decline in these employees' wage rates. As **Figure 14.5** shows, technological changes have clearly rewarded more-educated workers while penalizing less-educated workers.

Labor-saving technologies in unionized manufacturing sectors—such as automobile manufacturing—also put downward pressure on the wages of less-educated workers by undercutting the bargaining power of their labor unions. The mere availability of low-cost technology increased the *elasticity of demand* for unionized workers. As a result, unions that bargain hard nowadays for higher wages or richer benefit packages do so at the risk of losing jobs to these technologies in the long run. For example, in 1986, a private venture-capital firm bought the Safeway grocery chain and began to automate each store's production processes. Initially, many of these innovations were labor-enhancing, such as handheld scanners and bar-coding, thereby increasing

[17]David Leonhardt, "The New Inequality." *New York Times,* December 10, 2006.

[18]Claudia Goldin and Lawrence Katz. *The Race Between Education and Technology* (Cambridge, MA: Harvard University Press, 2008).

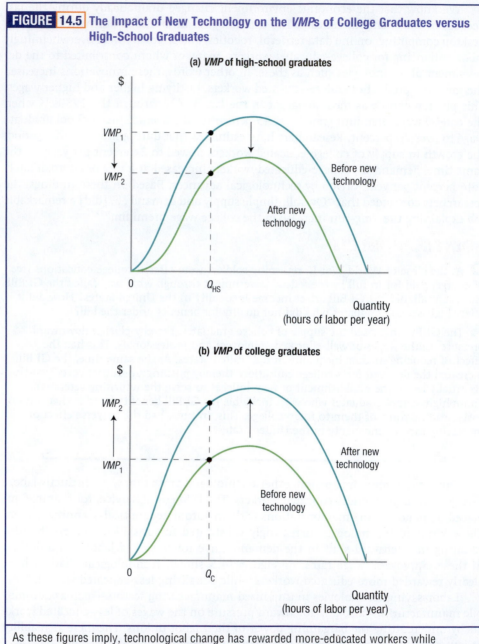

FIGURE 14.5 The Impact of New Technology on the *VMP*s of College Graduates versus High-School Graduates

As these figures imply, technological change has rewarded more-educated workers while penalizing less-educated workers. At any given wage rate, the demand for more-educated labor has increased, leading to a rightward shift in the demand for these workers. In contrast, at any given wage rate, the demand for less-educated labor has fallen, thereby resulting in a leftward shift in the demand curve for these workers. The end result is that there is an increase in wage inequality between the two groups as long as everything else remains unchanged.

worker productivity and justifying higher wages. However, after a number of highly contentious and long-running worker strikes in the late 1990s, Safeway and others in the retail food industry began introducing technologies that were labor-saving, such as self-serve scanner checkout systems. At the same time, "big box" self-serve retail food outlets continued to grow. From 1986 to 2002, Safeway's employment numbers dropped from 160,000 to 67,000, and the company began to shift to part-time workers. While some of this decline was clearly in response to Safeway's loss in market share to low-cost, nonunion competitors such as Walmart, there is little doubt that labor-saving technologies also contributed significantly to Safeway's drop in employment.

The Effect of Offshoring and Outsourcing on Income Inequality

Another major economic change that began in the latter part of the twentieth century and continues unabated was the expansion of global markets. Trade agreements have reduced trade barriers, and innovations in communications and transportation technologies have reduced the transaction costs of international trade. This has led to the **offshoring** of jobs abroad and the **outsourcing** of production to foreign companies with lower labor and nonlabor input costs.

OFFSHORING The movement of a company's production facilities overseas.

EXAMPLE Microsoft has a large campus in India where software is developed and tested.

EXAMPLE Many large accounting firms in New York City have set up operations in India to take advantage of the lower wage costs there.

OUTSOURCING The process of shifting business functions to nonemployees.

EXAMPLE Many organizations outsource the management and hosting of their Web sites to outside Web consultants or companies such as Go Daddy!

EXAMPLE Computer manufacturers in the United States often outsource the production of their motherboards to overseas producers.

The negative impact of offshoring on U.S. wage rates has been primarily borne by less-educated workers in the United States. Many labor-intensive companies have taken advantage of nonunion, low-wage labor pools in less-developed countries that are also exempt from costly U.S. workplace regulations and employee-benefit mandates.

In truth, jobs have been offshored to lower-wage locations throughout much of the history of the United States. For example, northeastern textile mills and other labor-intensive industries moved to the southern United States during the mid-1970s to take advantage of lower-cost (nonunion) unskilled labor. These relocations increased regional income inequality in the northeastern states because the demand for less-educated labor dropped there. Conversely, income inequality in the South declined as the demand curve for its less-educated workers shifted right, resulting in higher wages for lower-income households.

Global offshoring of manufacturing plants and the jobs that go with them is merely a continuation of this trend. Only now, the regions are defined on a global scale. Ironically, the same phenomenon of offshoring has begun to occur in countries such as India, to which U.S. companies have been offshoring jobs for several decades: Indian companies are now offshoring their own manufacturing plants to countries with lower labor costs.[19]

Pressures to offshore jobs have slowly begun to impact the U.S. college-educated labor market as well. Accounting and software-development positions are increasingly offshored to Indian subsidiaries of multinational corporations such as Microsoft and IBM. In this way, these companies can take advantage of lower-cost, yet highly skilled, workers who can tackle high-end technical projects.[20] Even Wall Street financial-services firms are relying upon greater numbers of low-cost, skilled technical analysts living in India.[21] To the extent that this trend continues, it will reduce the demand for college graduates in the United States, particularly those with a highly specific skill set. This, in turn, will depress the average wage rate for college graduates and, somewhat ironically, reduce the income inequality between people with and without college degrees. In other words, greater income equality can be achieved by making more-educated workers worse off. Of course, this presumes that new, high-paying employment opportunities will not emerge for these college graduates.

ECONOMIC FALLACY Offshoring has depressed the prevailing wages of American workers in both the college-educated and less-educated labor markets.

Uncertain. It is the combination of offshoring *and* the reluctance of American workers to relocate outside of the country to take advantage of well-paying job opportunities that has created the downward pressure on wages in the United States. Consider the fact that highly educated Americans, including professors and physicians, are increasingly taking advantage of lucrative work opportunities in wealthy nations such as Dubai (Jason DeParle, "Rising Breed of Migrant: Skilled and Welcome." *New York Times,* August 20, 2007). Software developers are likewise relocating to India (Amy Waldman, "A Young American Outsources Himself to India." *New York Times*, July 17, 2004). Indeed, some of the most competitive internships for MBA students are in India (Saritha Rai, "MBA Students Bypassing Wall Street for a Summer in India." *New York Times*, August 10, 2005).

The fact that Americans are "sticky" in terms of exiting local labor markets and moving into international labor markets makes them "captive" to the full effects of movements in global labor markets. Some of this stickiness may be the result of the limited language skills of Americans, although research shows that the stickiness exists even when there are foreign opportunities in countries in which English is commonly spoken.

In addition to offshoring, U.S. companies have expanded their outsourcing activities, shifting entire production processes to overseas companies. For example, pharmaceutical companies and medical-equipment manufacturers are outsourcing their clinical studies of new pharmaceuticals and devices to sites in India, Latin America, and other international locations. While this is in part due to the lower wages at these foreign sites,

· · · · · · ·

[19]Anand Giridharadas, "Outsourcing Works, So India Is Outsourcing Jobs." *New York Times,* September 25, 2007.

[20]Saritha Rai, "Microsoft Expands Operations in India." *New York Times,* November 16, 2004.

[21]Anand Giridharadas, "India's Edge Goes Beyond Outsourcing." *New York Times,* April 4, 2007.

it is also a reaction to the increasing regulatory costs imposed by the U.S. Food and Drug Administration (FDA) on clinical studies performed in the United States.

Advocates for offshoring and outsourcing argue that these activities reduce production costs and, consequently, the prices of goods that American consumers buy. Ultimately, living standards in the United States rise because households can now purchase more goods for the same amount of income. These advocates also claim that the U.S. economy will continue to increase its demand for U.S. workers in growth industries such as health care and civil engineering, as well as in the service sector of the economy. That said, radiology films are already being read offshore,[22] "transplant tourists" shop foreign destinations for their surgeries, and e-commerce has turned retailing into a global enterprise. Most labor market analysts contend that offshoring and outsourcing will continue to negatively affect those U.S. labor markets that are characterized by high wages, rapid growth, and portability of production.

Immigration and Income Inequality

Whereas offshoring and outsourcing export jobs overseas, immigration brings foreign workers to the United States. In effect, immigration is just the flip side of the same coin: workers search for their highest wage opportunities worldwide, while employers seek global opportunities to reduce their labor costs. In the United States, there has been tremendous attention paid to the impact that legal and illegal immigrants have on the demand for unskilled U.S. workers. Many people believe that immigrants drive down the wages of unskilled U.S. workers by shifting the supply curve of locally available workers to the right. This is illustrated by the supply and demand diagram in panel (a) of **Figure 14.6**. Notice that immigration into the United States leads

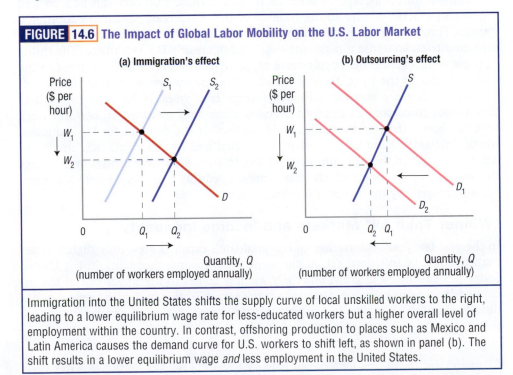

FIGURE 14.6 The Impact of Global Labor Mobility on the U.S. Labor Market

(a) Immigration's effect

(b) Outsourcing's effect

Immigration into the United States shifts the supply curve of local unskilled workers to the right, leading to a lower equilibrium wage rate for less-educated workers but a higher overall level of employment within the country. In contrast, offshoring production to places such as Mexico and Latin America causes the demand curve for U.S. workers to shift left, as shown in panel (b). The shift results in a lower equilibrium wage *and* less employment in the United States.

· · · · · · · ·

[22]Andrew Pollack, "Who's Reading Your X-ray?" *New York Times*, November 16, 2003.

to a lower equilibrium wage for less-educated workers but a higher overall level of employment within the country. In contrast, offshoring production to places such as Mexico and Latin America causes the demand curve for U.S.-based workers to shift to the left, as shown in panel (b). This results in a lower equilibrium wage and less employment in the United States.

In 2010, Arizona, Alabama, and a number of other border states passed strict new laws to reduce the number of illegal immigrants pouring in from Mexico and Central America. Ironically, this came at exactly the same time that illegal immigration was falling off, largely because of the relative improvement of economic conditions in Mexico.[23] The number of construction jobs in the United States— jobs that many unskilled illegal workers pursue—dropped precipitously at the start of the 2007 Great Recession. In contrast, the Mexican economy has delivered a whopping 45 percent increase in average family income since 2000. In addition, the 10-to-1 wage rate differential that existed between the United States and Mexico during the 1950s and 1960s declined to less than 4-to-1 in 2003, before the Great Recession hit and reduced this differential even further. The bottom line is that all else being equal, immigrant labor—just like labor *within* a country—gravitates to its highest valued use, as reflected in available wage opportunities, regardless of national borders.

At the same time that the immigration of unskilled workers from Mexico has slowed, the number of highly educated guest workers recruited to the United States by high-tech firms has been increasing. Currently, these companies compete for approximately 85,000 H-1B work visas a year that can be used to bring high-tech and other specialty employees—preferably those with master's or doctorate degrees—into the country for an average of three to six years. These numbers can add up and become significant relative to the number of U.S. holders of advanced educational degrees. Foreign employees here on work visas, along with legal residents from foreign countries, comprise almost one-third of Microsoft's U.S workforce. The influx of these workers shifts the supply curve of highly-educated employees located in the United States to the right, thereby reducing the equilibrium wage rate. This effect becomes even more pronounced when foreign employees' H-1B visas expire, and they return to corporate campuses overseas where they continue to perform work that has been offshored by U.S. multinationals.[24] If the demand for U.S.-educated workers falls, the earnings gap between educated and less-educated U.S. employees will fall as well. In the long run, whether immigration actually increases or decreases this wage gap depends on which group—the well-educated or less-educated—is more "disadvantaged" by the influx of foreign workers.

"Winner Take All" Markets and Income Inequality

In the past few years, the average college graduate's earnings grew only slightly faster than the rate of inflation. Yet, at the same time, income inequality in the United States has continued to grow, especially when it comes to the upper end of the income distribution. Evidence suggests that the source of this increased inequality has little to do with inequality in educational attainment. Rather, it can be traced to a

· · · · · · ·

[23]Damien Cave, "Better Lives for Mexicans Reduce the Allure of Heading North." *New York Times*, July 6, 2011, p. A1.

[24]Associated Press, "Quota Quickly Filled on Visas for High-Tech Guest Workers." *New York Times*, April 5, 2008.

growing divergence in the very top (1 percent) and the very bottom of the income distribution; in effect, the very rich are getting relatively richer and the very poor are getting relatively poorer.[25] Why has this occurred?

It turns out that over the past few decades, the very rich have experienced large earnings windfalls in markets that have been recently deregulated. This has been particularly true in the financial-services market, where it is not unusual for hedge-fund managers and other market traders to earn millions of dollars per year. These individuals tend to be a very tiny subset of the highly educated labor market, distinguished by their willingness to take risks in return for the promise of seemingly astronomical returns. Other risk takers—including those who have ridden the technology wave without college degrees—have likewise struck it rich through a mixture of ingenuity and loosely regulated capital markets. Bill Gates is the ultimate example of a college dropout who won big in the high-tech sector, exploiting the economies inherent in distributing computer operating and software systems.

Some economists see these as examples of the increasing pervasiveness of "winner take all" markets,[26] which arguably fuel the growth in income inequality. It remains to be seen whether this trend continues after the near-collapse of the U.S. financial sector in 2008, and the decline in "easy money" to finance high-risk ventures. From 2007 to 2009, the percent of total U.S. income attributable to the top 1 percent fell from 23 percent to 17 percent. And up through the end of 2010, many Wall Street employees were bemoaning their loss of bonuses.[27] Nevertheless, hedge-fund managers' bonuses rose 15 percent in 2009 and another 5 percent in 2010, while the median CEO compensation jumped 27 percent in 2010, largely recovering to prerecession levels. At the same time, the handful of owners of privately held Facebook saw their company's valuation soar to $50 billion. Inasmuch as unemployment rates barely budged during the same period from their 2007 Great Recession levels, we can infer that the "winner take all" phenomenon continues to contribute significantly to the growing inequality in U.S. incomes, especially at the very top end of the income distribution.

Does a Stagnant Minimum Wage Contribute to Income Inequality?

The poorest workers are disproportionately minimum-wage workers. Because the minimum wage has not grown at the same rate as the growth in income among working Americans as a whole, these workers have become poorer relative to other wage earners. During economic expansions, the wages paid to unskilled workers often exceed the minimum wage. However, in economic downturns, a reduction in the demand for goods and services produced by employers of minimum-wage workers results in a decline in output prices, which results in a drop in the value of the marginal product for these workers. This leads to a leftward shift in the demand curve for unskilled workers. In some cases, the new equilibrium wage will fall until it hits the minimum wage floor. In this case, a stagnant minimum wage (one the government hasn't adjusted for a long period of time) will contribute to income inequality because the floor on wages is lower than if the minimum wage had increased.

· · · · · · · ·

[25]Roger Lowenstein, "The Inequality Conundrum." *New York Times,* June 10, 2007.

[26]Michael Lind, "Why the Rich Get Richer." *New York Times,* September 24, 1995.

[27]Nelson D. Schwartz and Susanne Craig, "This Bonus Season on Wall Street, Many See Zeroes." *New York Times,* December 19, 2010.

However, if the minimum wage is raised, we already know that this will lead to higher unemployment (we don't know by how much) as long as it exceeds the equilibrium wage. So a higher minimum wage will reduce income inequality among wage earners but may increase it if we include those left without jobs because of the increase in the minimum wage.

14.5 Weighing the Factors that Contribute to Income Inequality

According to economists Claudia Goldin and Lawrence Katz, immigration explains only 10 percent of the wage gap that has persisted since 1950 between skilled and unskilled labor.[28] And, virtually every study of outsourcing has reported there is only a minimal impact on unskilled wages in the United States, although individual manufacturing sectors may be disproportionately affected. In one such study, economist Charles Schultze, the chairman of the Council of Economic Advisors during the Carter administration, found that between the end of 2000 and the end of 2003, no more than 215,000 U.S. jobs were lost to outsourcing, which was less than one-seventh of 1 percent of the total U.S. labor force at that time.

The consensus opinion of economists is that the accelerating rate of technological change since the 1950s has led to an enormous increase in the demand for creative, flexible workers who can handle "complex" jobs. More often than not, these are people who have completed college and, more recently, postgraduate study. Yet at the same time, Goldin and Katz point to "bottlenecks" in the educational system that have limited the rate of growth in the supply of college graduates, especially those with the skills necessary to benefit from technological advances. The end result is that demand has outpaced the supply of highly skilled workers, thereby increasing both the returns to a college education and the wage gap between educated and less-educated workers. As long as technological innovations continue to emerge at a breakneck pace, it appears that the only way that income inequality will diminish is by improving people's access to higher education and the higher wages it promises.

How likely is it that this prescription will be followed? Appendix 10A shows that changes in household composition have further aggravated the inequality in investment in children's human capital. Married couples—who tend to be more highly educated—have sufficient income to substitute away from household production in favor of market-based outputs for such tasks as meal preparation, thereby leaving them with a growing amount of time to invest in their children. In contrast, single-parent households lack both the money and time to make similar investments in their children. Given this disparity in building children's early human capital, it remains to be seen whether access to—and success in—higher education will become more equal in the future.

WHAT YOU SHOULD HAVE LEARNED FROM CHAPTER 14

- That educational attainment has a positive impact on lifetime earnings, which may be due to signaling or additional skills that have been gained through education.
- That a signal is a characteristic of a group that is easily observable and that is relied on to assess the quality of the group's members at low cost.

· · · · · · · ·

[28]Claudia Goldin and Lawrence Katz, *op. cit.*

■ That an employer may rely on a variety of signals in choosing between job applicants, including educational attainment and gender.

■ That economic discrimination results when employers rely on characteristics unrelated to productivity in their hiring decisions.

■ That a company that engages in economic discrimination will incur higher production costs and lower profitability than other suppliers, as long as labor and output markets are competitive.

■ That the derived demand for labor and other inputs into production depends on the demand for the output produced.

■ That an employer is willing to pay more for employees whose human capital translates directly into higher productivity.

■ That some investments in human capital result in higher wage rates to compensate for greater fluctuations in lifetime wage streams.

■ That the division of labor leads to specialization, which increases the marginal product of labor up to the point at which diminishing marginal returns set in.

■ That an employer will use inputs up to the point where the cost of doing so is equal to the value of the marginal product produced by the last unit used, holding all else constant.

■ That an employer will produce at minimum cost when the last dollar spent on each input generates the same contribution to output.

■ That technology, globalization, and deregulation have all contributed to growing income inequality in the United States.

KEY TERMS

Signal, p. 397

Economic discrimination, p. 400

Specific human capital, p. 402

Nonspecific human capital, p. 402

Marginal product, p. 404

Diminishing marginal returns, p. 404

Specialization, p. 406

Division of labor, p. 406

Value of the marginal product (*VMP*), p. 408

Cost-minimizing production, p. 413

Offshoring, p. 417

Outsourcing, p. 417

QUESTIONS AND PROBLEMS

1. Signaling theory is crucial to the ongoing debate about whether to use racial and ethnic "profiling" for national-security purposes in the United States, for example, at airport-screening sites. Do you think that these are good signals for improving airport security?

2. Explain whether the following actions of a potential employer would likely be the result of signaling or economic discrimination. The employer
   a) hires a male over a female applicant, assuming qualifications are the same;
   b) hires a married male over an unmarried male applicant, assuming qualifications are the same;
   c) hires a Protestant over a Catholic applicant, assuming qualifications are the same;
   d) hires a senior citizen over a teenage applicant, assuming qualifications are the same.

3. Assume that the U.S. strawberry market is in equilibrium. Demonstrate using market supply and demand curves

   a) the impact on equilibrium price and quantity in the U.S. strawberry market of increasing border patrols and thereby reducing the stream of illegal farm workers into the U.S.;

   b) the impact if Mexican strawberry producers can freely ship strawberries to the United States. What will happen in the long run to the U.S. strawberry industry?

4. Assume that there are two markets for labor: the market for high-school graduates (unskilled labor) and the market for college graduates (skilled labor). Using a set of supply and demand curves for each labor market, show the impact on the college wage premium of

   a) a state initiative that cuts back funding for public universities, leading to higher tuition fees;

   b) an outsourcing of unskilled manufacturing jobs to overseas locations;

   c) illegal immigration of "day" laborers into the United States;

   d) a recession, which reduces the opportunity cost of attending college; and

   e) a federal budget initiative to give "everyone" a college education through generous grants programs.

5. Suppose that a major Gulf Coast hurricane knocks out one-third of oil production in the United States.

   a) What is the impact on the price of domestic oil?

   b) How, if at all, does the marginal product of Gulf Coast oil-drilling workers change?

   c) Based on your answers to (a) and (b), can you predict what happens to the wages of these workers? Explain your answer.

   d) How would your answer to (c) change if you knew that the price of oil rose by 80 percent and the marginal product of the oil workers fell by one-third?

6. In the face of recent events, the U.S. military is grappling with a shortage of enlisted manpower (men and women). It is currently considering the following options to meet its recruitment requirements:

   a) raise the wage until the number of recruits voluntarily supplied just equals quantity demanded;

   b) keep the existing wage and draft the remaining recruits (i.e., demand that they serve at the going wage);

   c) follow policy (b) but allow those drafted to pay someone to take their place. Evaluate these three strategies using supply and demand analysis. For each proposal, address (a) who pays the wages for the recruits; (b) total wages paid to recruits; and (c) how effectively U.S. labor is deployed.

7. Suppose that a price ceiling is placed on the output of a particular industry. How does this affect the equilibrium wage and employment level for workers in this industry?

8. The federal government is hoping to stimulate economic growth by giving businesses a tax credit for investing in new plants and equipment. Will this necessarily reduce the nation's unemployment rate? Why or why not? Explain your answer.

9. Suppose that the demand for college-educated workers grows at only 2.6 percent per year in the first decades of the twenty-first century, as compared to 4.1 percent per year in the 1980s. If the growth in the supply of college-educated workers doesn't change, what prediction would you make about the college wage premium in 2010 versus 1985? Explain your answer.

10. Since the start of the 2007 Great Recession, the wage gap between women and men has fallen to an all-time low of 17 percent. Do you think this is because

women are doing better in the labor force or because men are doing worse in the labor force? Explain your answer.

11. The following table reports the net present value (*NPV*) of the lifetime earnings of college graduates by major. Why do you think that some majors are paid more than others? Do you think it makes economic "sense" that engineering majors will, on average, earn more than four times the lifetime earnings of education majors? Explain your answer.

	NPV
Engineering	$497,930
Computer science or information technology	$443,180
Business	$349,028
Science	$283,286
Liberal arts	$243,883
Social science	$210,080
Education	$108,461

12. Why is the distribution of people's lifetime incomes more equal than the income distribution in any one year? Explain your answer.

13. When the U.S. dollar gets weaker—in terms of purchasing power—relative to less-developed countries, would you predict outsourcing to increase, decrease, or remain at the same level as before the dollar weakened? Explain your answer.

14. One of the single greatest causes of unemployment among the poor is labor immobility. Jobs in one geographical area decline—due to changes in local employment conditions—but workers decide to stay put even though job vacancies exist elsewhere. To what extent do you believe that these workers should be "held harmless" and receive long-term government unemployment benefits? Explain your answer.

15. At one time, lawyers and paralegals generated an enormous amount of income by finding documents relevant to a lawsuit and reviewing their contents (a process called "discovery"). In the past few years, advances in artificial intelligence have led to the development of "e-discovery" software that can find and review documents at about 20 percent of the cost.[29]

    a) Using supply and demand curves, show how this impacts the labor market for lawyers and paralegals.
    b) Do you think that paralegals have specific or nonspecific human-capital skills? What about lawyers? Explain your answer.

· · · · · · ·

[29]John Markoff, "Armies of Expensive Lawyers Replaced by Cheaper Software." *New York Times,* March 5, 2011, p. A1.

PART 4

The Strategic Behavior of Firms: Surviving in the Marketplace

In Part 3, we discussed household-based and market-based production and the substitutions that can occur between one and the other. In Part 4, we examine the production decisions faced by a variety of organizations—households, private for-profit firms, nonprofit groups, and the government. We begin by introducing the decision process of organizations trying to minimize their costs and why this is a goal of all producers. The short- and long-run cost-minimizing mix of inputs into production is tied back to the findings at the end of Part 3 about how wages are determined.

After you have a better understanding of the cost conditions that producers face, we then look at the objectives that diverse types of organizations have and the constraints they face with respect to their sources of revenue, the types of goods they produce, and their ownership forms. We focus on the profit-maximizing output decisions of for-profit producers and develop the profit-maximizing "rule" using our marginal benefit-marginal cost framework. We also explore the response of perfectly competitive firms and markets to changes in the economic environment.

After we have completed our review of perfectly competitive markets, we move on to firms operating in imperfectly competitive markets. We carefully examine the profit-maximizing decision process for monopolies (markets with one supplier), oligopolies (markets with only a few suppliers), monopsonies (markets with one buyer), and monopolistically competitive firms (markets with many suppliers, each with its own "niche"). We also identify the barriers that keep potential competitors from entering markets. Finally, we once again apply game theory to better understand the interdependent behavior of household and market rivals. The concept of rivalry is important because it more clearly distinguishes competition between the few from competition between the many.

Minimizing the Costs of Production

"This film cost $31 million. With that kind of money I could have invaded some country."

Clint Eastwood,
actor and director

Whether we are talking about a household, an auto manufacturer, a nonprofit hospital, or a city trash-collection service, it seems reasonable to expect that these organizations would want to minimize their costs of production. The rationale for minimizing costs will likely differ depending on an organization's ultimate goals. If a household does not minimize its production costs, for example, there will be less output available to improve its members' well-being. In terms of its production possibilities frontier (PPF), this household would be *inside* its frontier if it wastes scarce resources by inefficiently producing its outputs—meals, money management, housecleaning, and so on.

Firms that compete in the marketplace continue to exist only if they can successfully adopt and maintain cost-minimizing production processes. As you have learned, a price-taking firm that incurs higher costs than its competitors can't simply raise its price above the market price and pass along these costs. If it tries to cover its higher costs this way, it will simply lose business as buyers vote with their feet and migrate to lower-cost firms that are charging the lower market price.

Nonprofit and government agencies can better achieve their objectives if they, too, minimize their costs of production. Nonprofit charities and hospitals can provide more services to more people if they minimize the cost of producing these services. The same is true of government agencies: your town's trash-collection division (assuming that these services are provided by your town) can provide more services per tax dollar—leaf-collection, recycling, and so forth—if it produces them in a cost-minimizing way. When government services are produced at minimum cost, elected officials can keep tax rates low and provide more services at any given tax rate.[1]

---

[1]Jean-Luc Migue and Gerard Belanger, "Toward a General Theory of Managerial Discretion." *Public Choice* (Spring, 1974).

In this chapter, we identify the types of costs that organizations face in the production process. By costs we mean *economic* costs, not just *accounting* costs. After this is done, we will examine the obstacles that producers face when it comes to actually achieving a cost-minimizing outcome. Even though cost minimization is a commonly shared goal, not every firm will be as successful as another. This is what allows some firms, such as Walmart, to become giants in their markets, while others—even one-time giants such as K-Mart and General Motors—have filed for bankruptcy.

15.1 Producer Costs in the Short Run

We begin our discussion with the results of the previous chapter where we showed that the optimal combination of inputs into the production process depends on their marginal products and their marginal costs, or input prices. To minimize the cost of producing a given amount of output, inputs must be combined in such a way that the very last dollar spent on each input results in the same contribution to output, holding all else unchanged. This means that if the cost of skilled labor is twice as much (say, $20 per hour) as unskilled labor ($10 per hour), then the optimal mix of skilled and unskilled labor is where the last skilled worker's contribution to output is *double* the contribution of the last unskilled worker hired.

Consider a firm that uses one type of physical capital (K) and two types of labor, skilled (LS) and unskilled (LU). To minimize its costs of production, it would combine these inputs in such a way that the last dollar spent on each input contributes the same additional amount of output. We can write this condition algebraically as

$$MP_K / P_K = MP_{LS} / P_{LS} = MP_{LU} / P_{LU}$$

where MP is the marginal product of the input, and P is the price of one unit of the input.

This cost-minimizing rule assumes that a producer can easily change the amount of each input used whenever an input's productivity or price changes. It also assumes that the marginal product of *each unit of each input* used can be accurately measured. In the real world, it turns out that one or both of these assumptions may be unrealistic.

To see the difficulty of actually applying our cost-minimizing rule, suppose that a radiologist cannot immediately adjust the number of specialized machines—three-dimensional ultrasound machines, for example—that she uses for medical imaging. It may be that these machines are on backorder for 12 to 15 months because the equipment manufacturer is facing a delay in getting parts. In a situation like this, the radiologist cannot immediately expand her services in the least-cost way, if this entails purchasing more machines. In the meantime, she will have to consider more costly ways to increase her output, whether this means paying employees to work overtime or adding an additional weekend shift. Because she is constrained in terms of one or more inputs, she is said to be operating in the short run. The short run is defined as the time period during which the level of at least one input is fixed and cannot be adjusted. For example, when demand for American cars fell at the start of the 2007 Great Recession, auto manufacturers could not immediately reduce their labor force because their employees were protected by union contracts. Similarly, when the state of Massachusetts passed a law guaranteeing health care to all of its residents, medical practices and hospitals could not expand right away to meet the resulting increase in demand because the number of licensed doctors in the state was limited.

This is the same short run we introduced in Chapter 7, when we talked about the short-run supply curve of individual producers and the market. In the short run, producers do not have the flexibility to fully minimize their production costs and, as a result, are less sensitive to changes in the market price. It should come as no surprise, therefore, that short-run costs will usually be higher than in the long run, when all of the inputs into production can be adjusted. For example, in the long run, a manufacturer can relocate outside of the United States to reduce his production costs after he has built or leased a foreign plant and received a license to operate in that county. Once again, this is the same long run we introduced in Chapter 7, when we talked about the more price sensitive long-run supply curve of individual producers and the market.

The actual number of days or months that a firm is forced to operate in a short run position depends on just how specialized an input used in production is, that is, how easy it is to expand or contract the use of that input. When it comes to expanding the number of licensed doctors in Massachusetts, for example, the short run may correspond to a lengthy amount of time, dictated in large part by the state's medical-licensing requirements. In contrast, most snow-removal providers can quickly adjust their use of labor and equipment to respond to seasonal changes in demand. It really does not take very long to purchase and attach a snow blade to the front of a truck. But if there is a winter in which unusually frequent and severe snowstorms occur, even this might not be the case.

Most, but not all, businesses have at least one input that cannot vary in the short run. We call these **fixed inputs**. Examples of fixed inputs include land and factory floor space that can't be quickly adjusted when there is a sudden change in demand for the firm's product.

FIXED INPUT An input whose quantity cannot vary in the short run.

EXAMPLE Wind and solar energy producers are limited in their ability to extend power to new customers because the distribution system they rely upon—the national electricity transmission grid—has a fixed capacity.

EXAMPLE The ability of hospital emergency rooms to respond to events that cause massive casualties is limited by their existing space and personnel.

In contrast, there are **variable inputs** that can be adjusted in the short run.

VARIABLE INPUT An input whose quantity can vary in the short run.

EXAMPLE Businesses can usually increase or decrease their use of electricity at any time.

EXAMPLE Most restaurants can recruit teenage dishwashers without virtually any delay.

EXAMPLE Universities can usually hire more part-time English instructors at the very start of a semester when class sections are oversubscribed.

We've already seen in the previous chapter that when a company varies its use of labor, the marginal product of workers first increases and then, at some point, starts to decline (assuming all other inputs remain unchanged). This result can be extended to all of the company's variable inputs. Because at least one input is fixed, the marginal product of labor and other variable inputs begins to diminish at some level of usage. This leads to diminishing marginal returns for each variable input.

By its very nature, the concept of diminishing marginal returns applies only in the short run. This is because in the long run, all input levels can be adjusted to eliminate the "bottlenecks" that lead to diminishing marginal returns. Manufacturers are frequently constrained in the short run by the size of their manufacturing plant. Take, for example, a pharmaceutical company that has just gotten approval by the U.S. Federal Drug Administration (FDA) for a new drug to fight AIDS. Because of the uncertainty about when, or even if, the FDA would grant approval, the company did not build a new manufacturing plant in advance of the drug's approval. In the short run, then, the company must produce the newly approved drug in its existing plant, along with other, previously approved drugs.

The company is constrained not only by the overall size of its plant but also by its number of assembly lines and quality-control stations. After it receives FDA approval for the new drug, the company will have to add higher-cost late-night and weekend shifts to produce the new drug if it wishes to maintain its production of older drugs. At some point, however, the marginal product of additional workers begins to diminish as the capacity of the plant is exhausted. If the company attempts to produce too many drugs using one plant, congestion on the factory floor begins to negatively impact worker productivity and quality. In the long run, these costs will most likely be reduced by expanding the plant or building a completely new facility.

Short-Run Costs

Cost-minimizing producers face two kinds of costs in the short run: the cost of their fixed inputs and the cost of their variable inputs. For any given level of fixed inputs, there will be a combination of variable inputs that minimizes the short-run cost of producing each level of output (q). (Recall that we use a small q to represent one firm's output and a large Q to represent the market's total output.)

Total fixed cost is the sum of the costs of the fixed inputs, such as the company's lease payments for its existing plant and manufacturing equipment.

TOTAL FIXED COST (TFC) The total cost of a firm's fixed inputs, which remains constant in the short run, even when output increases or decreases.

EXAMPLE Rent, the cost of leased machinery, the wages of workers under contract, and property taxes are all examples of fixed costs.

By their very nature, fixed costs do not change in the short run, even when output levels change. They must be paid regardless of the company's level of production and even when the firm has gone out of business. It's only in the long run that fixed costs go away.

The remaining short-run costs of production arise from the amount of variable inputs used. Variable inputs change when a firm's output level changes, which means that variable costs do, too. When we add together all of the variable inputs' costs, we get the firm's **total variable costs**.

TOTAL VARIABLE COST (TVC) The total cost of variable inputs, which increases when output rises and decreases when output falls.

EXAMPLE The cost of electricity, water, labor, and most disposable materials used in production are all variable costs.

We can add together the firm's total fixed costs and total variable costs to arrive at the firm's short-run total cost of production:

Total cost (TC) = Total fixed costs (TFC) + Total variable costs (TVC)

Figure 15.1 shows the relationship between TFC, TVC, and TC at each level of output.

The firm's total fixed costs (TFC) are represented by a horizontal line because they do not vary with the quantity produced. Based on our previous discussion, we know that it takes more variable inputs to produce more output; therefore, the firm's total variable costs (TVC) must grow along with output, resulting in an upward-sloping TVC curve. We also know that because of diminishing marginal returns, the TVC curve will start to slope sharply upward at the output level where diminishing returns set in (at point A in Figure 15.1). This is the case because the firm is forced to use a lot more variable inputs to expand production after diminishing marginal returns have set in.

In Figure 15.1, you may have noticed that the total cost (TC) curve looks identical to the total variable cost (TVC) curve, only shifted upward. This is because the total cost (TC) curve is equal to the total variable cost curve (TVC) plus the total fixed cost curve (TFC). The vertical distance between the TC and TVC curves is the company's fixed costs. This distance is the same no matter how much output is produced because total fixed costs do not vary with output level. For example, suppose a cell-phone company's fixed costs are $1 million a month to lease a portion of a communications satellite. Regardless of whether the company is handling 100 calls or 10,000 calls a day, its total costs (TC) will equal its total variable costs (TVC) plus the $1 million in total fixed costs (TFC).

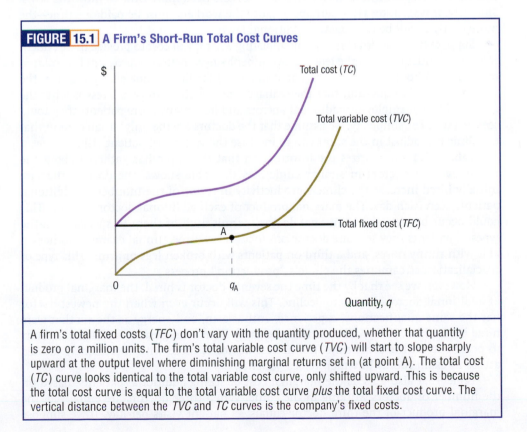

FIGURE 15.1 A Firm's Short-Run Total Cost Curves

A firm's total fixed costs (TFC) don't vary with the quantity produced, whether that quantity is zero or a million units. The firm's total variable cost curve (TVC) will start to slope sharply upward at the output level where diminishing marginal returns set in (at point A). The total cost (TC) curve looks identical to the total variable cost curve, only shifted upward. This is because the total cost curve is equal to the total variable cost curve *plus* the total fixed cost curve. The vertical distance between the TVC and TC curves is the company's fixed costs.

Marginal Cost

In the short run, the cost of producing one more unit of output depends solely on the cost of the additional variable inputs required to produce this unit. This is the only way a firm can expand output in the short run. This means that the firm's short-run **marginal cost** equals the increase in total variable costs (*TVC*) incurred to produce one more unit of output.

> **MARGINAL COST (SHORT RUN)** The short-run cost of producing one more unit of output; the increase in total variable costs incurred to produce an additional unit.

> **EXAMPLE** A plumbing company's marginal cost of providing an additional after-hours emergency call is higher than the marginal cost of providing an additional scheduled daytime call because of the need to pay employees overtime.

> **EXAMPLE** A dog walker's marginal cost of walking one more neighborhood dog (in terms of time and effort) is only $8, whereas the marginal cost of traveling across town to walk one more dog located there is higher: $12.

Consider a local lawn-mowing service where labor is the only variable input in the production of mowed lawns. In this situation, the marginal cost of producing one more mowed lawn—our unit of output—depends on both the workers' marginal product and their wage rate. The more productive the workers are, the less time it will take to mow an additional lawn. This means that the amount of additional wages that have to be paid will be less than if the workers need more time to mow the lawn. Similarly, if wage rates rise—perhaps because the workers must be paid overtime—the more costly it will be to mow the additional lawn.

Suppose that a health clinic is contemplating what it will cost to provide more patient services in anticipation of the federal government's new insurance program for children previously without insurance. The clinic's physical facility cannot be expanded in the short run. The key question that the managers of the clinic must address is what the cost would be of employing additional doctors and how many more patients they could see each day. For simplicity, we assume that the doctors are the only variable input that the clinic can adjust in the short run to increase the volume of patient visits.

Table 15.1 summarizes the information that the clinic has gathered about the productivity of doctors in similar clinics. As the table shows, the doctors that are initially hired increase the clinic's productivity in terms of the number of additional patients seen each day. The marginal product of each additional doctor is rising. This could occur because the additional doctors permit each of them to specialize in the types of patients they see: one doctor can focus on routine annual exams, another on kids with runny noses, and a third on patients with broken legs or arms. This type of specialization streamlines the clinic's "production" process.

However, we see that by the time the seventh doctor is hired, the marginal product of additional doctors begins to decline. This will occur even when the newest doctor has the same qualifications, experience, enthusiasm, and energy as the six that were hired before him. The problem is that the gains from even greater specialization start to peter out. At the same time, the newest doctor is faced with increasingly limited access to exam rooms in which to see patients.

Table 15.1 also tells us the marginal cost of seeing additional patients, based on the number of doctors working in the clinic. When three doctors are employed, the marginal product of the third doctor equals 39 patient visits per day. If we suppose

No. of Doctors	Total Patient Visits	Marginal Product (MP)	Average Product (AP)	Total Variable Costs (TVC)	Average Variable Cost (AVC)	Marginal Cost (MC)
1	24	24	24	$400	$16.66	$16.66
2	54	30	27	$800	$14.81	$13.33
3	93	39	31	$1200	$12.90	$10.26
4	136	43	34	$1600	$11.76	$9.30
5	185	49	37	$2000	$10.81	$8.16
6	235	50	39.16	$2400	$10.21	$8.00
7	280	45	40	$2800	$10.00	$8.89
8	324	44	40.5	$3200	$9.88	$9.09
9	365	41	40.55	$3600	$9.86	$9.76
10	400	35	40	$4000	$10.00	$11.43
11	422	22	38.36	$4400	$10.43	$18.18

Table 15.1 A Clinic's Productivity and Costs When the Number of Doctors Increases

that this doctor, along with the others, is paid $400 a day, the marginal cost incurred by the clinic for each of the 39 additional visits "produced" by adding the third doctor equals $400/39 or $10.26 per visit.

Now look at the marginal product of the 11th doctor hired. Table 15.1 indicates that this equals 22 visits per day. If she is also paid $400 a day, then the marginal cost of producing each of these additional 22 visits equals $400/22 = $18.18 per visit. We can compute the marginal cost for additional patient visits resulting from hiring the 4th through 10th doctors in a similar fashion, by dividing their wage ($400/day) by their marginal product.

What this tells us is that there is an *inverse* relationship between the marginal product of each additional doctor and the marginal cost of expanding the clinic's number of patient visits: the higher the doctor's marginal product, the lower the marginal cost of incremental patient visits, and vice versa. And there is a *direct* relationship between the wage paid each doctor and the marginal cost of production: the higher the wage, the higher the marginal cost of delivering patient visits.

Panel (a) in **Figure 15.2** shows the marginal product of each additional doctor, divided by the doctor's daily wage (W) of $400. The curve looks like a typical marginal product (MP) curve because each value on the MP curve is simply divided by the same constant, in this case, $400. You can see that diminishing marginal returns set in with the seventh doctor, as indicated in Table 15.1. As the table shows, the marginal product resulting from hiring the sixth doctor is 50 visits a day, whereas the marginal product of seventh doctor hired is just 45 patient visits a day.

In as much as the marginal cost of production in the short run is equal to the price of the variable input (in this case, the doctor) divided by its marginal product, we can take the curve in panel (a), which displays the marginal product of each doctor divided by the daily wage, and turn it upside down to get the marginal cost curve shown in panel (b). As Table 15.1 indicates, the marginal cost of production begins to increase when the seventh doctor is hired. As the table shows, the last visit supplied with six doctors working—the 235th clinic visit of the day—costs the clinic $8, whereas the 236th through 280th visits provided after hiring a seventh doctor cost $8.89.

What would happen if the doctors' compensation increased to $480 per day? Although the doctors' marginal product curve has not changed, we are now dividing

FIGURE 15.2 **The Relationship between the Marginal Product of a Variable Input, Its Price, and the Short-Run Marginal Cost of Production: Doctors and Patient Visits**

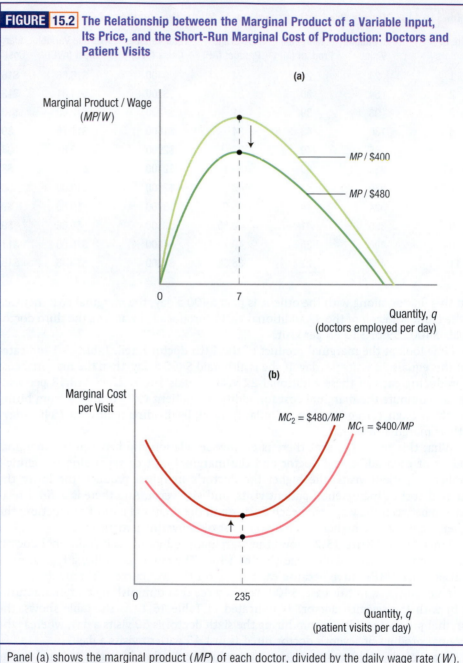

Panel (a) shows the marginal product (MP) of each doctor, divided by the daily wage rate (W). Diminishing marginal returns set in with the seventh doctor. At this point, the marginal cost of producing more patient visits begins to rise. This occurs at 235 visits per day in panel (b), the number of visits produced by the first six doctors together. If the doctors' compensation increases to $480 a day, the same MP curve will be divided by a higher wage, which shifts the curve in panel (a) down. As a result, the marginal cost of producing patient visits increases and the MC curve shifts up in panel (b).

each value on it by a higher wage. This means that the marginal cost of all of the patient visits must increase. The hiring of the third doctor, for example, still generates 39 additional patient visits each day, but the new marginal cost of these visits will equal $480 / 39 or $12.31 per visit. It is now 20 percent greater than what it was before ($12.31 / $10.26). Not coincidentally, this is the exact same percentage increase as the doctors' wage rate ($480/$400). This result is also shown in Figures 15.2a and 15.2b. Notice in panel (b) that the output level at which marginal cost begins to rise (235 visits) has not changed because the point at which diminishing marginal returns set in has not changed.

SOLVED PROBLEM

Q Suppose that Halo Company, a producer of halogen bulbs, has two assembly lines that it can switch between to produce its bulbs. The following equations exhibit the marginal costs of production for each line: $MC_{Line\ 1} = 0.0008q1$ and $MC_{Line\ 2} = 2 + 0.0004q2$. If Halo wants to minimize its marginal cost of production, (1) how much should it produce on each assembly line if it wants 2,000 units of output? (2) 4,000 units of output? (3) How should the firm allocate production across the two assembly lines?

A In general, output should be spread across the two assembly lines so that the last bulb produced on each line costs the same amount to produce. That is, where

$$MC_{Line\ 1} = MC_{Line\ 2}$$

When $q = 1,000$, $MC_{Line\ 1} = 0.8$ (or $.80 a bulb), and $MC_{Line\ 2} = 2.4$ (or $2.40 a bulb), so the firm should use the first assembly line to produce the first thousand bulbs.

When $q = 2,000$, $MC_{Line\ 1} = \$1.60$, and $MC_{Line\ 2} = \$2.4$, so the firm should use the first assembly line to produce the first and the second thousand bulbs (i.e., up to 2,000).

When $q = 3,000$, $MC_{Line\ 1} = \$2.4$, and $MC_{Line\ 2} = \$2.4$, so the firm can use either the first or second assembly line to produce bulbs $2,001 - 3,000$.

Assuming the firm uses the first assembly line to produce bulbs $2,001 - 3,000$, then when $q = 4000$, $MC_{Line\ 1} = 3.2$, and $MC_{Line\ 2} = 2.4$, so the firm should use the second assembly line to produce bulbs $3,001 - 4000$.

This method of allocating production between the two assembly lines will continue until the point where the MC of the very last bulb produced on each line is the same.

Another way to see this is as follows:

q	MC_{Line1}	MC_{Line2}
1000	0.8 (1)	2.4 (4)
2000	1.6 (2)	2.8 (5)
3000	2.4 (3)	3.2 (6)
4000	3.2 (7)	

To produce 7000 bulbs, 4000 will be made using the first assembly line and 3000 will be made using the second assembly line.

Average Costs

Often, it is difficult for a firm to accurately measure its marginal cost of producing an additional unit of output, especially when several variable inputs are involved. For this reason and others that we explore later on, producers are interested not only in the marginal cost of production but also in the average cost per unit produced. To compute the **average total cost** of production, we divide the firm's total costs by the number of units produced. Likewise, a firm's **average variable cost** can be computed by dividing total variable costs by the number of units produced; and **average fixed cost** will equal total fixed costs divided by the number of units produced.

AVERAGE TOTAL COST (ATC) Total cost divided by the number of units (q) produced.

AVERAGE VARIABLE COST (AVC) Total variable cost divided by the number of units (q) produced.

AVERAGE FIXED COST (AFC) Total fixed cost divided by the number of units (q) produced.

You have already seen that the firm's total cost is the sum of total variable and total fixed costs. Likewise, the firm's *average* total cost (*ATC*) equals the sum of its *average* variable cost (*AVC*) and *average* fixed cost (*AFC*). That is,

$$ATC = AFC + AVC$$

Figure 15.3 shows the relationship between these short-run average cost curves. You can see that the firm's average fixed cost (*AFC*) is constantly declining as the firm's output increases. This is because the firm's total fixed costs (*TFC*) don't change; however, the number of units of output over which these fixed costs are "spread" is growing. For example, when the $1 million fixed cost that Verizon incurs to lease a communications satellite is spread over larger and larger numbers of cell-phone calls, the fixed cost *per call* gets very, very small. While the *AFC* for one call is $1 million, the *AFC* for one million calls is $1.

The average variable cost (*AVC*) curve has a U-shape, much like the marginal cost (*MC*) curve. Why is this so? Take a look again at Table 15.1. Notice that at the same time that marginal product is rising, the **average product** of the doctors is also rising, but more slowly.

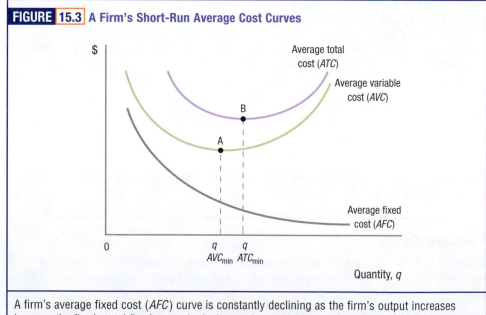

FIGURE 15.3 A Firm's Short-Run Average Cost Curves

A firm's average fixed cost (*AFC*) curve is constantly declining as the firm's output increases because the firm's total fixed costs don't change; however, the number of units of output over which these fixed costs are "spread" is growing. The average variable cost (*AVC*) curve begins to turn upward at a lower level of output (point A) than the level at which the average total cost (*ATC*) curve begins to turn up (point B) because the *AFC* curve continues to "pull it down."

AVERAGE PRODUCT (AP) Total output (q) divided by the amount of the variable input that is used in production.

For example, if we look at the average product of the first two doctors in our hypothetical clinic, we see that it is equal to 54/2, or 27 visits per day.

The *average* product of the doctors continues to rise beyond the point that diminishing marginal returns set in, that is, when the seventh doctor is hired. To understand why this is so, notice that the number of visits produced by hiring the eighth and ninth doctors is still higher than the average number of visits per doctor. This means that the average continues to rise. It is only when the tenth doctor is hired that her contribution to output (35 visits) is lower than the average of the first nine doctors (40.55 visits). At this point, the average product of the doctors as a group begins to decline. **Figure 15.4** depicts the relationship between the marginal and average product of the doctors.

Just as the marginal product of the doctors—along with their wage rate-determines the marginal cost of production, their average product and wage rate determine the average variable cost of production. Table 15.1 shows that the average number of visits completed by the first seven doctors hired is 40 visits per day. The total compensation per day of these doctors equals $2,800 ($400 per day × 7 doctors). This means that the *average variable cost* (AVC) of each visit is $10 ($2,800 in compensation per day / 280 patients per day).

Table 15.1 also reveals that the average variable cost of patient visits is inversely related to the average product of the doctors. This makes perfect sense: if, on average,

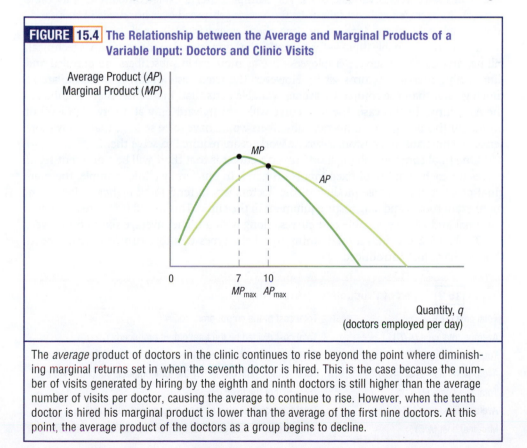

FIGURE 15.4 **The Relationship between the Average and Marginal Products of a Variable Input: Doctors and Clinic Visits**

The *average* product of doctors in the clinic continues to rise beyond the point where diminishing marginal returns set in when the seventh doctor is hired. This is the case because the number of visits generated by hiring by the eighth and ninth doctors is still higher than the average number of visits per doctor, causing the average to continue to rise. However, when the tenth doctor is hired his marginal product is lower than the average of the first nine doctors. At this point, the average product of the doctors as a group begins to decline.

doctors are more productive, then the average cost per patient visit will be lower than if the doctors are less productive. So, if the clinic's average product (*AP*) first *increases* and then *decreases*, its average variable cost (*AVC*) must first *decrease* and then *increase*. As a result, the average variable cost (*AVC*) curve will be U-shaped, just like the marginal cost (*MC*) curve. We also know that the bottom of the *AVC* curve occurs at a higher level of output than the bottom of the marginal cost (*MC*) curve because marginal product starts to fall before average product.

As Figure 15.3 shows, we can vertically "add" the average variable cost (*AVC*) to the average fixed cost (*AFC*) at each quantity level (q) to get the firm's average total cost (*ATC*) curve. It is important to recognize that the marginal cost (*MC*) curve cuts through the bottom of the average total cost (*ATC*) curve. This tells us that after the marginal cost of producing a unit of output is greater than the average total cost of production, it will begin to "pull" the firm's average total costs up.

Notice that the output level corresponding to the bottom of the *ATC* curve is greater than the level associated with the bottom of the *AVC* curve. Even though average variable cost (*AVC*) starts to rise when diminishing marginal returns set in, average fixed cost (*AFC*) continues to fall. (Recall that as quantity increases, the firm's fixed costs get spread over more and more units, so the *AFC* keeps on falling.) The *AFC* curve's fall "pulls down" the *ATC* curve. However, as average variable cost (*AVC*) continues to rise, it eventually more than offsets the decline in average fixed cost (*AFC*), resulting in an upturn in the average total cost (*ATC*) curve.

The point at which the *ATC* curve turns upward depends on the relative magnitude of a firm's fixed versus variable costs. For example, after a cable company lays its cable network, its average fixed cost falls as its fixed costs get spread over hundreds of thousands of new cable subscribers. At the same time, the average variable cost of the firm's relatively small amount of variable inputs—for example, the costs related to the company's technical, billing, and customer-service employees—rise as more cable subscribers are enrolled and diminishing marginal returns set in. However, the fixed costs of laying the cable are so much greater than the company's average variable costs that, in a sense, they "dominate" the *ATC* curve. In this case, the *ATC* curve will turn upward only at a very high level of output. At this point, the number of subscribers would have to be so large that many more service technicians and customer-service workers are required to serve them.

One final comment about short-run cost curves is that there will be a different set of curves for each quantity of fixed inputs on hand. In our family clinic example, the marginal product and average product of the doctors would tend to be higher if there were more exam rooms and diagnostic equipment in the clinic. This would translate into lower marginal and average variable cost curves, along with a higher average fixed cost curve.

Table 15.2 provides a brief summary of the types of short-run production costs that we have just introduced.

Table 15.2 Types of Production Costs	
Total cost (*TC*)	Total cost of the output produced
Average total cost (*ATC*)	Total cost divided by the total output produced: TC/q
Total variable cost (*TVC*)	Total cost of the variable inputs
Average variable cost (*AVC*)	Total variable cost divided by the total output produced: TVC/q
Total fixed cost (*TFC*)	Total cost of the fixed inputs
Average fixed cost (*AFC*)	Total fixed cost divided by total output produced: TFC/q
Marginal cost (*MC*)	The increase in total cost resulting from a one-unit increase in q

15.2 Shifts in Short-Run Cost Curves

As you discovered in our clinic example, an increase in the doctors' daily wage rate will cause the marginal cost (MC) curve of the clinic to shift upward. In other words, the cost of each incremental patient visit goes up. Similarly, the clinic's average variable cost (AVC) curve shifts upward, reflecting the increase in the price of the variable input (doctors). And, because the average total cost depends directly on the average variable cost, its curve, too, shifts upward by the same amount as the AVC curve. (Note that the relationship between these new cost curves remains the same: the new MC curve cuts through the bottoms of the new AVC and ATC curves.) The only cost curves that are unaffected are the total fixed and average fixed cost curves, which represent such fixed costs as rent and the cost of leased equipment, but not the cost of variable inputs such as the doctors.

We can generalize this result as follows: any increase in the price of a variable input will shift the short-run ATC, AVC, and MC curves upward. Conversely, any decrease in the price of a variable input will shift these curves down.

Consider a landscape business that uses a lot of minimum-wage workers. If the minimum wage is raised by federal or state law, the ATC, AVC, and MC curves of the landscaper will rise. The effect of this wage increase on the landscaper's costs of doing business is illustrated in **Figure 15.5**. In the short run, the landscaper is stuck with these higher costs of operating his business. Of course, in the long run, he may be able to reduce his labor costs by adjusting his fixed inputs (equipment) and thereby substituting labor-saving mowers that cover more ground, automatically collect clippings, and mulch leaves.

In addition to a change in the price of a variable input, there are other reasons that these three short-run cost curves can shift. Suppose that the government imposes

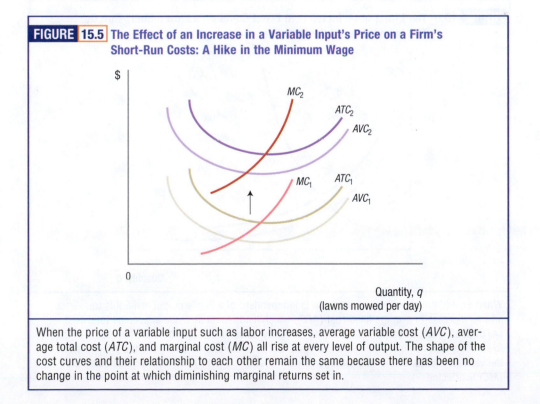

FIGURE 15.5 The Effect of an Increase in a Variable Input's Price on a Firm's Short-Run Costs: A Hike in the Minimum Wage

When the price of a variable input such as labor increases, average variable cost (AVC), average total cost (ATC), and marginal cost (MC) all rise at every level of output. The shape of the cost curves and their relationship to each other remain the same because there has been no change in the point at which diminishing marginal returns set in.

a $5 tax on the landscaper for each lawn he mows. This tax is a variable cost because the total amount of taxes paid changes with the producer's level of output (number of lawns mowed). The tax will lead to an upward shift in the same three curves—*ATC*, *AVC*, and *MC*. If the government chooses instead to subsidize the price of a variable input—for example, by offering a tax credit for using low-phosphate fertilizer—then there will be a downward shift in these three cost curves.

In some instances, only a company's fixed costs are affected by a change in the economic environment. When this is the case, only the average fixed and average total cost curves of the firm shift. For example, what if a city council imposes a new license fee on certain businesses operating within its limits, say, burglar-alarm companies? This fee has to be paid up front and does not vary with the number of homes that a company monitors in the city; it is a fixed cost. Or, what if the city increases its property tax rate for commercial buildings and requires owners to pay this increase in taxes regardless of whether the building is partially or fully leased—or even if it is 100 percent vacant. **Figure 15.6** shows what happens to a firm's short-run cost curves when there is an increase only in its fixed costs. You can see that only the *AFC* and *ATC* curves shift. Notice that there is no change in the marginal cost of production because there has been no change in the price or productivity of the *variable* inputs. For the same reason, there is no increase in the average variable cost (*AVC*) curve.

Technological innovations can also affect short-run cost curves, although they are likely to have the greatest impact in the long run, when all inputs (such as equipment) are variable. The most recent innovation in management methods is the use of computer software to improve coordination with input suppliers, thereby reducing inventory costs and production delays. For example, a fast-food restaurant might keep

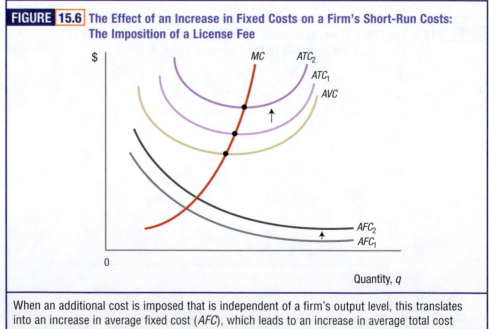

FIGURE 15.6 **The Effect of an Increase in Fixed Costs on a Firm's Short-Run Costs: The Imposition of a License Fee**

When an additional cost is imposed that is independent of a firm's output level, this translates into an increase in average fixed cost (*AFC*), which leads to an increase in average total cost (*ATC*) at all levels of output. License fees, property taxes, and lease costs are just some of the fixed costs that can increase in the short run. Because there is no change in the price of any of the variable inputs, neither the average variable cost curve (*AVC*) nor the marginal cost curve (*MC*) is affected.

a computerized record of the amount of frozen french fries it has on-site; its supplier, which also has access to this information, automatically schedules a delivery of french fries whenever the amount on hand falls below a certain level. This process is part of a broader set of management techniques, collectively referred to as **supply-chain management**.

> **SUPPLY-CHAIN MANAGEMENT** The process of managing the coordination between input suppliers and input users to achieve efficiencies and lower production costs.
>
> **EXAMPLE** By working with a few select growers, Walmart has improved the delivery schedule for perishable produce to each of its stores, thereby reducing the cost of unsold, rotten produce.
>
> **EXAMPLE** ExpressScripts, a large prescription-drug management company, automatically refills prescriptions at the end of each 30-day prescription period to streamline the ordering process and ensure that its customers don't run out of their medications.

Improvements in supply-chain management can reduce both the short-run and long-run costs of production by reducing inventory carrying costs as well as the potential costs of production shortages and delays.[2] Walmart, for example, announced at its 2009 annual shareholders' meeting that it had already achieved over $150 million in savings due to supply-chain management.

> **ECONOMIC FALLACY**   Because new firms can buy the latest equipment and are not burdened with older, less-economical equipment, they can underprice older firms. This explains why new entrants do better than existing firms in most markets.
>
> **False.** Both new and old firms have access to new, cost-saving technologies and equipment. The older firm will compare the total *variable* costs of production using the old equipment to the total costs of production using the new equipment to decide whether to scrap the old equipment. Remember that the old equipment is a sunk cost: it has to be paid off whether it is used or not. So if the *total* cost of introducing new equipment is less than the current variable costs of production, then the older firm will reduce its total costs of production by switching to the new equipment. Whether this cost comparison causes the older firm to switch equipment or not, its total cost of production will be no more than new entrants.

15.3 A Firm's Costs in the Long Run

Earlier, we characterized the long run as a period in which all inputs are variable. This means that a producer's costs can be truly minimized because the firm is able to vary the use of all of its inputs as its level of output changes. Given this flexibility, we would expect a firm's long-run costs to be lower than its short-run costs: the firm can now follow the cost-minimizing "rule" of hiring inputs until the last dollar spent

....

[2]Claudia Deutsch, "Weighing Demand and Figuring Supply." *New York Times,* December 16, 1996.

on each input yields the same contribution to output. (Appendix 15.1 provides a detailed discussion of the relationship between short-run and long-run cost curves.) One of the most important results to appreciate is that in the *long run*, the principle of diminishing marginal returns becomes irrelevant.

Why is this important? In the opening part of this chapter, we derived short-run cost curves by relying heavily on the existence of diminishing marginal returns. Diminishing marginal returns means that a firm's short-run marginal cost (*MC*) and average variable cost (*AVC*) curves eventually "turn upward," and that a company's average total cost (*ATC*) curve will, at some level of output, begin to rise as well. However, because a firm can expand all of its inputs in the long run, these inputs can be just as productive at any level of output. In the long run, there are no fixed inputs to "depress" the marginal product of a variable input such as labor.

If, in the long run, a firm can produce a higher level of output by simply scaling up its use of all of its inputs proportionately, it will end up with a long-run *average total cost* (*LRAC*) curve that is horizontal (flat) over a wide range of output. This is in marked contrast to the U-shaped short-run average total cost curve. When this occurs, the firm is said to exhibit **constant returns to scale**.

CONSTANT RETURNS TO SCALE A situation in which increasing all inputs proportionately yields the same proportionate increase in output and, therefore, the same long-run average cost per unit of output.

EXAMPLE Doubling all of the ingredients in a casserole recipe doubles the amount of the casserole produced. Assuming that input prices don't change, the cost per serving will not change.

What if, in the long run, a proportionate increase in inputs yields more than a proportionate increase in a firm's output? Say, for example, you double the amount of inputs you use in production, and you get triple the amount of output. This would lead to a decline in long-run average total cost when there is an increase in output. In this case, we say that the firm enjoys **increasing returns to scale** (sometimes referred to as *economies of scale*).

INCREASING RETURNS TO SCALE A situation in which increasing all inputs proportionately yields more than a proportionate increase in output, thereby resulting in a decline in the firm's long-run average total cost.

EXAMPLE Suppose that a small neighborhood restaurant rents an adjoining space when it becomes available, knocking out the wall between the two spaces to double its seating capacity. It staffs double the tables by doubling its number of employees. If this makes its service staff sufficiently more productive because they can now specialize in various tasks—such as setting and clearing tables and refilling drinks—then the restaurant's long-run average total cost per diner may actually decline.

Finally, it is possible, in the long run, that a proportionate increase in all inputs can yield less than a proportionate increase in output. This would be the case if a 50 percent increase in all inputs increases a firm's output by only 40 percent. When this occurs, the firm's long-run average total cost will increase as the quantity it produces increases, and we say that the firm's production process exhibits **decreasing returns to scale** (sometimes called diseconomies of scale).

> **DECREASING RETURNS TO SCALE** A situation in which increasing all inputs proportionately leads to less than a proportionate increase in output, resulting in an increase in the firm's long run average total cost.

EXAMPLE Harold, a discount shoe reseller, buys a huge warehouse when it becomes available to store large lots of shoes purchased from manufacturers during their end-of-season "close-out" sales. However, organizing and managing so many shoe brands, styles, and sizes requires more than a proportional increase in employees along with additional coordination mechanisms. As a result, the average cost of handling each pair of shoes actually goes up.

Many firms face *both* economies and diseconomies of scale in the long run, depending on their level of production. **Figure 15.7** illustrates a long-run average total cost curve that exhibits economies of scale at low levels of output and diseconomies of scale at high levels of output.

The smallest output level that achieves the lowest long-run average total cost (LRAC) is called the **minimum efficient scale** of production. This is indicated by output q with subscript 1 in Figure 15.7.

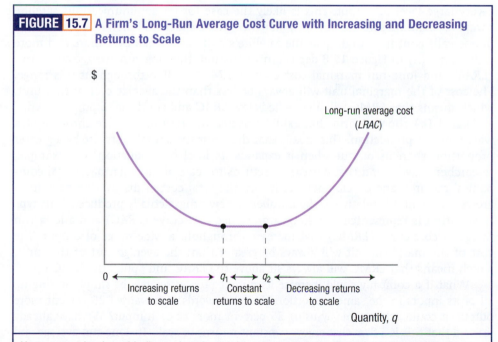

FIGURE 15.7 **A Firm's Long-Run Average Cost Curve with Increasing and Decreasing Returns to Scale**

Up to output level q_1, this firm enjoys increasing returns to scale, likely due to its exploitation of the gains from specialization and division of labor. Average total cost is at its minimum for the output levels between q_1 and q_2. The lowest output level at which average total cost is at a minimum is q_1, which is referred to as the *minimum efficient scale of production*. After decreasing returns to scale kick in beyond q_2, the firm's long-run average cost (LRAC) curve starts to turn upward, indicating that the average cost of producing each unit is increasing as the level of output continues to expand.

MINIMUM EFFICIENT SCALE OF PRODUCTION The lowest level of output that achieves the lowest long-run average total cost (*LRAC*).

Is the *LRAC* curve depicted in Figure 15.7 a reasonable approximation of reality? A company will enjoy falling average costs of production as its output level expands if it can take advantage of increasing productivity arising from specialization. Ford Motor Company was at the forefront of using customized assembly lines where workers could specialize in various aspects of production, such as installing windshields or bumpers. Nevertheless, at some point, a firm can get so large that it begins to suffer from internal coordination problems, which may lead to decreasing returns to scale. Of course, you might wonder why coordination problems would arise if all of a firm's inputs—including computer systems and management—can be increased in the long run. The source of the problem may be that the production process becomes too unwieldy to effectively manage because so much specialization occurs in large-scale production. The greater the decreasing returns to scale, the more likely it is that additional output will be supplied by new firms that operate at a lower output range where increasing returns to scale exist. Alternatively, as you may recall from Chapter 10, inputs can be combined through a series of market transactions if coordinating production within a firm becomes too costly. For example, Ford typically subcontracts the production of car seats and sound systems to outside suppliers.

There are instances where a producer may enjoy increasing returns to scale over a very large level of output. This is likely the case for telecommunications satellite companies: after a satellite has been launched, the average and marginal cost of cell-phone calls continues to drop as the satellite's costs are spread over more and more calls. Panel (a) in **Figure 15.8** depicts this situation: the long-run average cost curve (*LRAC*) and long-run marginal cost curve (*LRMC*) decline throughout this range. The cost of the marginal unit will always be less than the average cost of that unit, which means that *LRMC* will always lie below *LRAC* and continue to pull it down.

Panel (b) shows a firm that exhibits decreasing returns to scale throughout a wide range of production. This means that the company's total costs rise by a greater proportion than its output when it expands its level of production. For example, researchers have found that decreasing returns to scale plague pharmaceutical companies' research and development activities: the total cost of discovering new drugs grows exponentially relative to the number of new drugs actually produced. This type of situation is represented by a long-run average cost curve (*LRAC*) and a long-run marginal cost curve (*LRMC*) that increase throughout a wide range of output. The cost of the marginal unit will always be greater than the average cost of that unit, which means that *LRMC* will always sit above the *LRAC* and "pull" the *LRAC* up.

What if a company could increase its output proportionately by simply scaling up all of its inputs in the same proportion? In other words, if it wanted 25 percent more output, it could achieve this by using 25 percent more of each input? We have already learned that this is a firm that enjoys constant returns to scale. Its long-run average and marginal cost curves are depicted in panel (c): *LRAC* doesn't change—the cost of every unit produced is the same. As a result, the marginal cost of each unit is also the same and the *LRAC* and *LRMC* curves coincide. Finally, panel (d) shows the long-run cost curves of a firm that enjoys increasing returns to scale over a lower range of output and, as it expands, enters into a range of decreasing returns to scale. The *LRMC* curve lies below the *LRAC* curve, eventually turning up and finally intersecting the minimum of the *LRAC* curve, at which point the *LRAC* curve begins to be "pulled up" and turn ups as well.

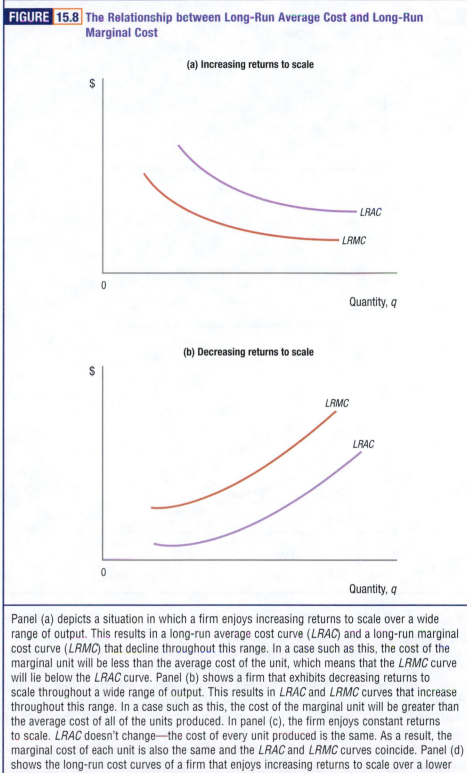

FIGURE 15.8 The Relationship between Long-Run Average Cost and Long-Run Marginal Cost

Panel (a) depicts a situation in which a firm enjoys increasing returns to scale over a wide range of output. This results in a long-run average cost curve (*LRAC*) and a long-run marginal cost curve (*LRMC*) that decline throughout this range. In a case such as this, the cost of the marginal unit will be less than the average cost of the unit, which means that the *LRMC* curve will lie below the *LRAC* curve. Panel (b) shows a firm that exhibits decreasing returns to scale throughout a wide range of output. This results in *LRAC* and *LRMC* curves that increase throughout this range. In a case such as this, the cost of the marginal unit will be greater than the average cost of all of the units produced. In panel (c), the firm enjoys constant returns to scale. *LRAC* doesn't change—the cost of every unit produced is the same. As a result, the marginal cost of each unit is also the same and the *LRAC* and *LRMC* curves coincide. Panel (d) shows the long-run cost curves of a firm that enjoys increasing returns to scale over a lower range of output and, as it expands, enters into a range of decreasing returns to scale. The *LRMC* curve lies below the *LRAC* curve, eventually turning up and finally intersecting the minimum of the *LRAC* curve, at which point the *LRAC* curve changes direction and begins to rise.

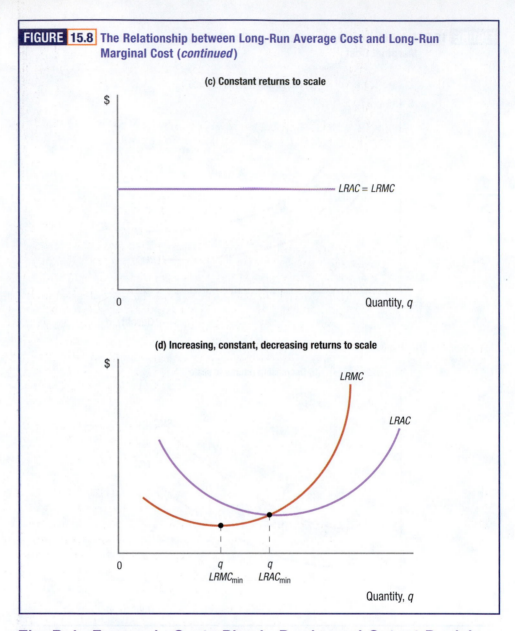

FIGURE 15.8 The Relationship between Long-Run Average Cost and Long-Run Marginal Cost (*continued*)

(c) Constant returns to scale

(d) Increasing, constant, decreasing returns to scale

The Role Economic Costs Play in Producers' Output Decisions

At the beginning of this chapter, you read about why it is in a producer's interest— whether nonprofit, governmental, or private for-profit—to minimize its costs of production. After a firm has figured out how to minimize its costs, it must decide on the "right" level of output to produce based on its corporate objectives. Just as other economic decision makers consider the marginal benefits and marginal costs of the alternatives they face, producers also focus on the marginal benefits and costs of producing at different output levels.

The marginal benefit realized from an additional unit of output depends on the objectives of the producer. For nonprofit health clinics, the marginal benefit of vaccinating an additional child against a new flu virus is the value placed on keeping the child healthy and reducing the risk that the virus will spread throughout the community.

A for-profit mortgage-lending firm, on the other hand, might assess the marginal benefit of making a new loan in terms of the organization's growth in market share. Whatever the producer's objectives, we will see in the next chapter that the cost concepts we have just developed play a significant role in deciding how much output an organization will produce.

SOLVED PROBLEM

Q The city council in Oceanside, California, is debating several options to raise more tax revenue. The two at the top of the list are (1) charge every existing business within city limits a $1,000 fee each year; or (2) place a 2 percent payroll tax on each business.

(a) Show the effect that these two alternatives would have on a firm's short-run cost curves.

(b) What would you predict would happen in the long run? Explain.

A The first proposal will shift *TFC, TC, AFC,* and *ATC* upward.

The second proposal will shift *TVC, TC, AVC,* and *ATC* upward.

In the long run, if the businesses in Oceanside are competing for the same customers as untaxed businesses that are close by but outside of Oceanside, the Oceanside businesses will no longer be able to compete as effectively at the equilibrium market price. They will consider the costs and benefits of shutting down and moving out of Oceanside to places that don't have the tax.

15.4 X-Inefficiency: Why Firms Don't Always Minimize Their Production Costs

The cost-curve structure that we have just developed is how economists conceptualize firm production costs. Like any model, it is an abstraction from reality. In the best of worlds, it is how firms *would* measure and monitor their costs of doing business. But, as we've noted, trying to accurately measure some of these costs is difficult. The end result, based on imperfect information about input productivity and production costs, is referred to as **X-inefficiency**.[3]

X-INEFFICIENCY Wasteful expenditures or inefficient production processes that increase the cost of production.

EXAMPLE Clothing retailers are often stuck with unsold inventory at the end of a fashion cycle because they have not managed their inventories in a cost-effective manner.

EXAMPLE Manufacturers that do not invest sufficiently in quality-control systems tend to have more product returns and warranty claims, which increase supply costs.

There are a number of reasons why firms may have less than ideal cost structures. Most commonly, X-inefficiency occurs because producers do not know what their actual costs of production are and what they would be if they were minimized. This situation is exacerbated when a company is producing multiple products and

[3]Harvey Leibenstein, "Allocative and X-Efficiency." *American Economic Review* 56 (1966).

different sizes of products. It can be very costly to figure out exactly what the marginal and average costs are for each product.

Some economists argue that in a world where information is costly, firms may actually be acting in a cost-minimizing way when they make decisions based on imperfect knowledge about their production costs. For example, before low-cost computing became widely available, supply-chain management was difficult; clothing retailers and suppliers may have found it too costly to better coordinate their orders at the start of each fashion cycle. And fast-food chains may have run out of french fries because it was too costly to more precisely coordinate deliveries with their food suppliers. In other words, the cost of the information and resulting coordination efforts to better manage inputs outweighed the savings from doing so.

Production inefficiencies can also occur when firms face external constraints that limit their ability to minimize their costs of production. Most often, these arise from government control over how inputs can be used in the production process.

Regulatory Impediments to Cost-Minimization

Certain laws and regulations can impinge on how a firm uses inputs in its production process. As a result, a company sometimes cannot employ its cost-minimizing mix of inputs. This is certainly the case when it comes to regulations that affect the use of labor. The Occupational Safety and Health Administration (OSHA), the Federal Labor Board (FLB), and other government agencies regulate the workplace environment and the hours employees can work. Such restrictions are likely to increase a firm's costs because they limit the ways in which labor can be used in the production process. Even though it can be argued that these restrictions improve worker safety, which is undoubtedly an important objective, we must still recognize that they result in higher production costs for companies that are subject to these regulations. Ultimately, these regulations put compliant producers at a competitive disadvantage relative to other suppliers who either break the rules or are not subject to them in the first place—for example, foreign producers.

Agricultural producers face government regulations that target pesticide use and fertilizer runoff. These regulations also constrain a farmer's input choices. The rationale for banning certain pesticides (such as DDT) is that they create negative externalities in the form of tainted ground and surface-water pollution. This may be a worthy reason for the ban, but it does not come without cost as long as DDT is a cost-minimizing input into production. The same holds true for regulations that limit offshore oil drilling and the burning of sulfur-laden coal. It may be that these regulations push a producer toward a *social* cost-minimizing mix of inputs rather than a *private* cost-minimizing mix. In any event, the cost of production must increase.

Regulations can also affect the mix of inputs used by regulated companies such as water utilities and cable companies. The prices that these companies can charge their customers are usually set so that the producer will earn a legally allowable rate of return (profit margin). This rate of return is based on the amount of plant and equipment that the utility has invested in. For example, regulators may permit a utility to charge enough to earn a profit equal to 6 percent of the value of its plant and equipment. As a result of these regulations, utilities and other similarly regulated firms have an incentive to use more capital and less labor in their production process—because more capital leads to higher prices and profit margins. (Economists call this regulatory-induced overcapitalization the *Averch-Johnson effect* of regulation.) While such behavior will increase the firm's profitability, it will, most likely, lead to a production process that is not cost-minimizing.

It also is possible for employees in an industry to collectively impose regulations that restrict a firm's use of labor and thereby increase production costs. Consider the case where unions dictate the number of employees a company must hire or the hours they can work each day. Unionized airline carriers, for example, face these types of personnel restrictions, whereas nonunionized competitors do not. As a result, a nonunionized company such as JetBlue Airlines enjoys a competitive advantage arising from its lower costs of production. To become more competitive, some unionized airlines, including Delta, United Airlines, and most recently American Airlines, have filed for bankruptcy protection, in part to renegotiate their union contracts and lower their labor costs. Other unionized carriers have introduced nonunionized subsidiaries to provide lower-cost short-hop air service.

Assessing Productivity: The Shirking Problem

To combine inputs in the most cost-effective way, producers must know each input's marginal product at each and every level of employment. As you will recall, the marginal and average products of a firm's variable inputs underlie the short-run marginal and average variable cost curves. In the long run, the marginal product of each input and the input's price determine the cost-minimizing combination of inputs to use for each and every output level. It turns out that accurately measuring the marginal product of each input becomes more and more costly as production processes increase in complexity.

Some production processes are not very complex. Take, for example, a company in which people each independently produce one good from start to finish. A cabinet maker who works alone is an example; another is a Starbucks barista who takes care of a customer from start to finish by taking the order and the money and preparing the drink. There are even some large companies that run this way. One of the best known is Lincoln Electric, a major welding corporation. Employees at Lincoln Electric are actually paid per piece they weld together. We call this type of production process "piecework" production.

In a world of piecework production, an owner of a company can easily assess the productivity of each employee by calculating the number of units of output she produces each hour or day. Consider our previous example of the doctor that "produces" patient visits: we can easily count the number of visits completed each day. As it turns out, so can insurance companies—some of which reimburse doctors based on the number of patient visits completed during a specific time period.

Measuring each employee's productivity becomes much more difficult when production requires teamwork. A good example of this is when teams of accountants come together to audit large corporate clients. Although members of the team may divide up the work, they still must interact when it comes to such activities as processing and validating financial data and cross-checking data entries. The output—a certified set of corporate books and tax returns—is the result of a team effort.

This type of production process makes it difficult to isolate each employee's marginal contribution to output. Because of this, there is an incentive for each team member to work a little less hard and enjoy more "on-the-job" leisure time—chatting on the telephone or surfing the Web, for example. We call this behavior **shirking**.

SHIRKING A decision to contribute less than one's maximum work effort to the production process.

EXAMPLE High-school and college teachers often assign group projects to promote team skills. Sometimes, however, one or more members of the team will shirk their responsibilities and contribute very little to the final product.

EXAMPLE Smokers will often sneak unauthorized smoking breaks, leaving nonsmokers to pick up the slack.

Shirkers "free ride" off of their teammates' work effort. Because the output is produced jointly by the team, it can be difficult to identify shirkers and "punish" them by lowering their wage or firing them. Compounding the shirking problem is the fact that every member of the team has the same incentive to shirk, which can have an exponential impact on the team's productivity and resulting production costs. For example, an accounting team from St. Louis that is sent to London to audit a client may take more time to complete the job, spending time instead in the city's pubs and sightseeing.

Now let's look again at Lincoln Electric. Would it surprise you to learn that Lincoln has an amazing efficiency record? Probably not if you consider the fact that when the company's workers slack off and produce fewer welded pieces, they get paid less.

Economists have done a great deal of research on shirking and whether economic incentives can be crafted to curtail this behavior. In summary, they have found that:

- The smaller a team is, the easier it is for teammates to apply peer pressure to keep each other from shirking.
- Companies can use incentives such as profit-sharing to encourage team members to monitor one another and potentially reduce the amount of shirking.
- Managers can be hired to supervise team production and potentially lessen the amount of shirking.

As a team grows larger, it becomes harder (more costly) for members to detect each other's shirking behavior. Even if an employer offers the team incentives such as profit sharing or bonuses when a project is completed early, team members still have an incentive to shirk if they cannot be identified and excluded from receiving the profit or bonus payments that their teammates generate. One proposal to reduce shirking is to empower team members to monitor each other and decide how the profits or bonuses will be distributed among themselves. This may not mean equal workloads for all team members, but it can lead to a more efficient allocation of rewards based on member productivity. However, such a strategy opens itself up to collusion between team members to deprive others of their "fair share" of the reward.

Managerial oversight of teams will reduce shirking only if the productivity of each team member can be assessed at a cost that is lower than the resulting cost-savings. While it is relatively easy to monitor certain aspects of labor productivity—for example, whether people come to work on time and appear to be busy—it can be quite difficult to accurately gauge each worker's actual contribution to output. In fact, focusing on these easily observable measures rather than on actual contributions to output can actually reduce productivity. Take, for example, an employee who must clock in by 8 A.M. but is most productive when he begins work at 10 A.M. You have probably watched movies and television shows such as *The Office* that ridicule managers who fixate on superficial measures of worker productivity.

Who Monitors the Managers?

One of the most interesting questions related to shirking is "who monitors the managers who are hired to discourage shirking?" After all, managers also have an incentive to shirk if no one oversees their work effort. This type of shirking can take many forms at the managerial level. While employees tend to shirk by using work time for personal activities such as surfing the Internet, managers may also shirk by taking two-hour lunches, leaving early to play a round of golf, managing their investment portfolios at work, or running up large corporate expense accounts.

A firm's owners are ultimately responsible for monitoring the managers they have hired. When a firm has only a few owners, such as the corner dry cleaner or deli, these owners have a strong incentive to invest scarce resources to closely monitor their managers. If the number of owners increases, however, each owner's individual return from investing time in monitoring management falls. Instead of the corner deli, now think of a sandwich shop with thousands of stockholders, such as Panera Bread Company. All of these owners benefit when there is less shirking, which will translate into increased profits and a higher stock price. But it is unlikely that any one of these owners will invest much time or money to monitor management. Like employees who work in teams, owners have an incentive to shirk and rely on other owners' monitoring activities. Owners who do invest resources to keep an eye on a firm's management bestow benefits on those owners who choose not to make this investment.

There are many examples of large stockholders who invest heavily to monitor management. In the 1990s, billionaire investor Kirk Kerkorian bought enough shares in Chrysler to become its biggest shareholder, accumulating a 10 percent ownership stake in the company.[4] As a dominant owner, he became actively involved in shaking up management and pursuing strategic changes within the company. He eventually initiated a failed hostile takeover of the firm's management, believing that he could wring substantial cost-savings from the company. Instead, Kerkorian and other shareholders enjoyed a huge windfall when Chrysler was sold to Daimler-Benz, which also thought it could increase Chrysler's profitability. As it turned out, the company was eventually put back on the selling block for less than half the original purchase price. At about the same time, Kerkorian acquired 120 million shares in Ford Motor Company, promising to be a "constructive agitator."

Kerkorian and other "takeover artists" such as Carl Icahn take huge investment positions in companies that they believe can be made more profitable by reducing production costs or selling off undervalued assets. The shirking behavior of existing managers is likely to diminish when there are potential managers sitting on the sidelines and agitating for more cost-effective production at the behest of large shareholders. Whether such a threat is credible or not depends on many factors. But it is interesting to see how often managers actively fight potential takeovers of their companies by adopting costly barriers. For example, a manager may push his company to take on a lot of debt or embark on an expensive expansion project to reduce the firm's potential profitability. This behavior is known as a "poison pill" strategy. "Golden parachutes" and other lucrative management payouts that trigger in the event of a takeover can also reduce the likelihood of a managerial shakeup. Finally, CEOs who are members of their own corporate Board of Directors can exert enormous influence on Board decisions about takeover and merger proposals, executive compensation, and so on.[5]

· · · · · · ·

[4]Micheline Maynard, "Kerkorian Offers $4.5 Billion for Chrysler." *New York Times*, April 6, 2007.

[5]Floyd Norris, "A $2.8 Billion Mistake by Steve Jobs." *New York Times*, December 29, 2006.

An interesting case in point was the 2008 takeover of Anheuser-Busch, the giant U.S. beer producer, by InBev, a Belgian company. While the CEO of AB—August Busch IV—lobbied his board of directors to pursue other strategic opportunities, his 70-year-old father—August Busch III—pressured these same directors to take the InBev deal. Both father and son held large ownership stakes in the company. Apparently, August Busch III believed that the value of his stake would be compromised in the future by his son's management style; indeed, August Busch IV had a reputation for hard-partying, indecisiveness, and detachment. Engineering the InBev takeover may have been the only way that August Busch III could assure that Anheuser-Busch would achieve its maximum valuation. InBev apparently agreed with this assessment, paying $70 a share—a total of $52 billion—despite the fact that AB's share price had languished at the $30–$40 level for several years.

ECONOMIC FALLACY   The greed of takeover artists destroys companies, drains the economy of jobs, and produces nothing, thereby reducing economic growth.

False. Takeover artists try to maximize their returns by investing in poorly performing companies and turning them around so that their profitability increases. Sometimes, it turns out that the best way to do this is to merge the company with another or to "spin off" profitable lines of business. It is true that jobs are likely to be lost as a result of these activities, but this is no different from the jobs lost when a firm cuts back output or adjusts its use of labor to become more cost efficient. By having a major shareholder or an entity that takes a company private, the shirking problem is substantially reduced. By pursuing their own self-interest, takeover artists help to ensure that scarce resources are put to their highest-valued use. This is a prerequisite for achieving the highest economic growth possible.

WHAT YOU SHOULD HAVE LEARNED FROM CHAPTER 15

- That regardless of their ultimate objectives, virtually all producing organizations strive to minimize their costs of production.

- That firms are constrained in the short run and can only adjust their output levels and production costs by changing their use of variable inputs.

- That because diminishing marginal returns set in, in the short run, the average and marginal costs of production must eventually rise as output levels increase.

- That in the short run, marginal cost and average total cost curves are U-shaped because of diminishing marginal returns.

- That in the long run, marginal cost and average total cost curves are not always U-shaped because the law of diminishing returns no longer applies.

- That firms do not always end up minimizing their costs because there are informational costs that limit their ability to assess costs of production.

- That regulatory policies can distort the mix of inputs used and lead to a production process that is not cost-minimizing.

- That team members have an incentive to shirk on their work effort if it is difficult for them to be identified and punished.

- That a major role of management is to monitor team production and deter shirking.

- That the threat of a company takeover can discipline existing management and result in lower costs of production.

KEY TERMS

Fixed input, p. 431

Variable input, p. 431

Total fixed costs (TFC), p. 432

Total variable costs (TVC), p. 432

Marginal cost (short run), p. 434

Average total cost (ATC), p. 438

Average variable cost (AVC), p. 438

Average fixed cost (AFC), p. 438

Average product, p. 439

Supply-chain management, p. 443

Constant returns to scale, p. 444

Economies of scale, p. 444

Diseconomies of scale, p. 445

Minimum efficient scale of production, p. 446

X-inefficiency, p. 449

Shirking, p. 451

QUESTIONS AND PROBLEMS

1. Indicate whether shirking will be greater or less in the following situations: (a) employees produce products on a piecework basis; (b) there are small teams required for production; (c) the company is owned by one individual; (d) the company is held by many small shareholders; (e) a large percent of corporate stock is held by a small number of pension funds; (f) employees all belong to the same church; (g) employees all live in the same neighborhood.

2. "A firm will never expand its use of variable inputs into the range of diminishing marginal returns." True or false. Explain your answer.

3. Suppose that you rent a car for $29.95 per day. The first 150 miles are free, but each additional mile thereafter costs 15 cents. You drive the car 200 miles. What is the fixed cost, the marginal cost, and the total cost of driving the car that day?

4. Consider a textile manufacturer located in India that ships all of its output to the United States. Do you think that this producer will measure her costs in rupees (India's currency) or in U.S. dollars? Explain your answer.

5. Forty years ago, several trains used the Union Railroad Station in St. Louis, Missouri, each day; ten years ago (and today), the station was used by one train per day traveling in each direction. In deciding whether to tear down its old large station and replace it with a smaller building, did the train station's owner, the Terminal Railroad Association, evaluate whether (a) the total cost of the old building was greater than the total cost of the new building; or (b) the variable cost of operating the old building was greater than the total cost of the new building; or (c) the variable cost of the old building was greater than the variable cost of the new building; or (d) the total cost of the old building was greater than the variable cost of the new building?

6. Suppose the employees of a certain firm join a labor union that demands the firm employ more workers than the conditions of cost minimization require. Show the impact this agreement would have on the short-run cost curves of the firm, assuming labor is its only variable input.

7. A student was asked to create an average total cost table for a firm where "increasing returns" prevail. This student constructed the following schedule for average total cost:

q	ATC
60	$15
70	$12
80	$8

Should the student receive an A or F for her work? Explain your answer.

8. The following table shows how the total product (*q*) produced by a farm varies when different amounts of labor (*L*) are applied to 10 acres of land.

   a) Fill in the average and marginal product of labor columns.
   b) With which unit of labor do diminishing returns set in?
   c) If labor were free, how many units of labor would be employed on this farm?
   d) If the price of *L* were six units of output per *L*, how many units of *L* would be employed on this farm if it were trying to maximize its profits?
   e) When 5 units of labor are being applied to 10 acres of land, what is the marginal product of *land*?

L	q	Average Product of L	Marginal Product of L
0	0		
1	5		
2	13		
3	23		
4	38		
5	50		
6	60		
7	68		
8	75		
9	81		
10	86		
11	89		
12	91		
13	92		
14	92		
15	91		
16	88		
17	84		

9. In 2004, the union representing supermarket workers ended its seven-month strike in California with an apparent victory—more benefits and higher pay for workers. Yet only three years later, when its contract was up again for renewal, the union was told that one-third of its membership would be laid off due to the introduction of self-serve checkout scanners.

   a) How does this example reflect the short-run versus long-run position of the supermarkets?

   b) Was it cost efficient to replace workers with self-serve scanners? Explain your answer.

10. Use the concept of diminishing marginal returns to explain why all prescription drugs cannot be manufactured in one pharmaceutical plant.

11. If government agencies care about minimizing their costs of production, how is it that the Air Force spent $2,000 for a toilet seat and five road workers are always assigned to fill a single small pothole?

12. Suppose that the government decides to impose a 2 percent payroll tax on employers to reduce the federal deficit. What do you think will happen to the amount of labor employed in the short run? In the long run?

13. Identify three fixed costs and three variable costs that a household incurs in the short run. Explain how adjusting one or more of the fixed inputs in the long run can reduce the costs of household production.

14. As a U.S. clothing manufacturer, you must decide how to allocate production of your goods across the manufacturing plants you have in Vietnam, China, Singapore, and Jordan. Your cost of goods will depend not only on the productivity of inputs in these countries but also on the exchange rate (because you pay for all of the plant's inputs in the local country's currency). Explain carefully how changes in the exchange rate can either reinforce or detract from the underlying productivity conditions in your decision process.

15. Restaurant servers are paid a very low hourly wage but have the potential to earn a lot from tips; clerical workers are paid an hourly wage with the potential of earning overtime pay; teachers are paid an annual salary with no overtime or tips; lawyers are paid a percent of their billable hours. Explain why the compensation plans for these workers differ, using the concept of shirking.

Appendix 15A An Isoquant Analysis of Cost Minimization

In Chapter 14, we saw that producers will minimize their costs of production when they use inputs up to the point where the value of the marginal product contributed by the last unit of each input is just equal to its price. This is consistent with the basic model of economic choice, which predicts that we consume goods and services up to the point where the net benefit (in this case, the value of an input's marginal product minus its input price) is equal to zero. Assuming that producers act as price-takers in both their input and output markets, then we know that the price of one unit of an input—say an hour of skilled labor—is the going market wage (W) and that the value of its marginal product is P_Q (MP_L) where P_Q is the market price for one unit of output, and MP_L is the marginal product generated by adding one more hour of skilled labor.

Economists have formalized this decision process to draw additional inferences about how producers respond to changes in input prices, output prices, and production technologies. This framework also permits us to analyze how the costs of production change in response to changes in the economic environment.

MAXIMIZING OUTPUT OR MINIMIZING PRODUCTION COSTS?

For many producers, their goal is to maximize the amount they can produce for a given amount of expenditures on inputs. This will be the case when a company has limited funds on hand to buy the necessary materials and cover payroll expenses.

A producer must *minimize* her costs of production if she is to *maximize* the level of output she can attain in the face of an expenditure constraint. Minimizing costs and maximizing output are really two sides of the same coin: both problems require that inputs be used in the same optimal way. For this reason, economists refer to the *duality relationship* that exists between these two "optimizing" problems—choosing an input mix that (1) minimizes the cost of producing a particular output level; and (2) maximizes the output level that can be achieved for any given expenditure level.

REPRESENTING COSTS USING ISOCOST LINES

Suppose that an apple grower is faced with an expenditure constraint of $150,000 a month, which can be spent on his two inputs into production, chemicals (C) and labor (L). (We know there are a number of other inputs the apple grower will need to buy each month, but for simplicity, we focus on a two-input production process. If we wanted to, we could extend this analysis to include additional inputs.) How much of the money should be spent on C versus L to maximize the grower's monthly output level?

The first half of **Table 15A.1** shows combinations of C and L that the grower can buy for $150,000 assuming that the price of a pound of dry chemicals is $50 and that the going wage rate is $20 an hour. The second half of the table shows the combinations of C and L that the grower can buy if he has $250,000 to spend on these inputs.

In **Figure 15A.1**, we graph these two sets of C and L combinations—the one for $150,000 in monthly expenditures and the other for $250,000 in monthly expenditures.

The resulting graphs are called **isocost lines** because every combination of inputs (C, L) on each line costs the grower the same amount. *Iso* means "same." In other words, each of the input bundles on the line to the left costs $150,000, and each of the bundles on the line to the right costs $250,000.

Table 15A.1	Combinations of Inputs That Can Be Purchased with a Monthly Expenditure Allowance
Expenditures = $150,000 per month	
Chemicals ($50 per pound)	Labor ($20 per hour)
3,000	0
2,000	2,500
1,000	5,000
500	6,250
0	7,500
Expenditures = $250,000 per month	
Chemicals ($50 per pound)	Labor ($20 per hour)
5,000	0
4,000	2,500
3,000	5,000
2,000	7,500
1,000	10,000
0	12,500

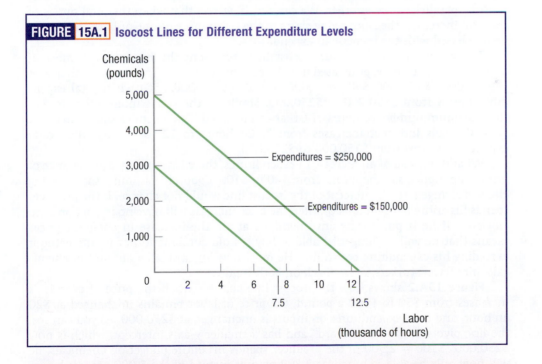

FIGURE 15A.1 Isocost Lines for Different Expenditure Levels

ISOCOST LINE Line that shows all combinations of inputs that cost the same. Lines to the right are comprised of input bundles that cost more; lines to the left are comprised of bundles that cost less.

Notice that these isocost lines are straight lines that are parallel to one another. Why is this the case? Recall that the slope of a line is "the change in rise (C) for a one unit change in run (L)." In the current context, this translates into the *trade-off* between chemicals and labor—that is, how many more hours of labor could be hired (ΔL, where Δ means "change in") if the producer cut back his purchases of chemicals by one pound (ΔC). The prices of the inputs dictate this trade-off, which means that it is completely independent of the producer's technology or production processes.

If one pound of C is $50, and the price of one hour of L is $20, we know that giving up one pound of C will "free up" $50 that can be used to purchase 2.5 more hours of labor than before. This trade-off doesn't change whether the producer reallocates his $150,000 outlay from a C, L combination of (3,000, 0) to (2,000, 2,500) or from (1,000, 5,000) to (500, 6,250). The trade-off remains constant: 1 pound of chemicals to 2.5 hours of labor. The slope of the graph (ΔC/ΔL) equals −1/2.5. Why is the slope of the isocost line negative? If the total amount spent on inputs is constant, then the only way to hire more workers is to give up pounds of chemicals, and vice versa. In other words, the numerator of the slope calculation must move in the opposite direction from the denominator of the calculation.

What about when the producer's monthly expenditures increase to $250,000? Because the prices of C and L haven't changed, the trade-off between C and L hasn't changed either. If the producer initially chooses the (C, L) combination (5,000, 0) and then decides to reallocate his spending to (4,000, 2,500) the next month, he has given up 1,000 pounds of chemicals to acquire 2,500 hours of labor. Once again, the trade-off between chemicals and labor is constant at 1:2.5, and the slope of the isocost line is −1/2.5. Because the slopes of the two isocost lines are the same, they must be parallel to one another. We can see, however, that when the total outlay of the firm increases, the isocost line shifts to the right: more of one or both inputs can be purchased with the increase in expenditures.

The *y*-axis intercepts of our isocost lines represent the maximum number of pounds of C that can be purchased if no labor is hired (L = 0). This intercept increases from 3,000 ($150,000/$50) to 5,000 pounds ($250,000/$50) when total expenditures grow from $150,000 to $250,000. Similarly, the *x*-axis intercepts represent the maximum number of hours of L that can be hired if no chemicals are purchased (C = 0). This intercept increases from 7,500 hours to 12,500 hours when total expenditures grow from $150,000 to $250,000.

What if, instead of an increase in expenditures, there is an increase in the price of one of the inputs, say chemicals, from $50 to $100 a pound? Assuming that nothing else has changed, the L intercept of the isocost line would not change. If the producer spends his entire budget on labor, then the price increase will have no impact on him. However, if he is purchasing any chemicals at all, the increase in chemical prices means that he will no longer be able to buy his old combination of inputs without exceeding his expenditure constraint. He must now buy a smaller amount of chemicals, hire fewer workers, or cut back on both inputs.

Figure 15A.2 shows how the isocost line changes when the price of chemicals increases from $50 to $100 a pound, the price of labor remains unchanged at $20 an hour, and total expenditures on inputs is unchanged at $250,000. As you can see, the line pivots or "rotates inward" and has a smaller *y*-axis intercept, which is now $250,000/$100 = 2,500. If the producer spends his entire budget on chemicals, he will now only be able to purchase 2,500 pounds instead of the 5,000 pounds before the price increase.

The slope of the isocost line also changes because the trade-off between labor and chemicals has changed. Now if the apple producer cuts back one pound of chemicals, he frees up $100 that can be used to purchase 5 hours of labor (not the 2.5 hours before the price increase). So the trade-off between labor and chemicals is now 1:5, and the slope of the isocost line decreases (in absolute value) from −1/2.5 to −1/5.

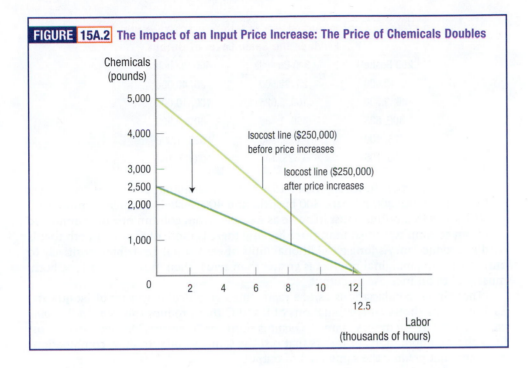

FIGURE 15A.2 The Impact of an Input Price Increase: The Price of Chemicals Doubles

Using the same approach, we can derive a new isocost line when the price of chemicals declines or the price of labor changes.

CHARACTERISTICS OF ISOCOST LINES

We can generalize our findings about isocost lines as follows:

- An isocost line shifts parallel to the right when total expenditures on inputs increase; it shifts parallel to the left when total expenditures on inputs decrease.

- An isocost line "pivots"—one intercept remaining unchanged—when the price of one input increases or decreases.

- Producers who face the same input prices and spend the same total amount on inputs will have the same isocost line.

REPRESENTING THE PRODUCTION PROCESS USING ISOQUANTS

Suppose, for example, that our apple producer is faced with the following **production function**, which shows the relationship between the amount of chemicals (C, in pounds) and labor (L, in hours) used each month and the resulting output (in bushels):

$$Q = .4C^{.5}L^{.5}$$

PRODUCTION FUNCTION A representation of the relationship between the amount of each input used in production and the amount of output generated.

The production function for apples tells us that the same number of bushels—say 200 bushels—can be produced by combining different amounts of chemicals and labor.

Table 15A.2	Combinations of Inputs (L, C) That Will Produce the Same Level of Output	
200 Bushels	300 Bushels	400 Bushels
25, 10,000	25, 22,500	25, 40,000
100, 2,500	100, 5,625	100, 10,000
400, 625	400, 1,406	400, 2,500
625, 400	625, 900	625, 1,600
2,500, 100	5,625, 100	10,000, 100

Using this production function, **Table 15A.2** shows combinations of the two inputs that would produce 200 bushels, 300 bushels, and 400 bushels of apples per month.

We know that output must increase as we move from column one to column two and from column two to column three because there is more of C or L or both that is used in production. As long as additional units of each input contribute positively to output (i.e., the marginal product is greater than zero), then more of C or L, or both, must lead to an increase in output.

These input combinations can be represented graphically by a set of **isoquants**. Each isoquant shows all combinations of L and C that produce the *same level of output*. Once again, *iso* means "same." *Quant* is short for "quantity." So, whereas isocost lines show combinations of inputs that *cost* the same, isoquants show combinations of inputs that *produce* the same level of output.

ISOQUANT A graph that shows all combinations of inputs that yield the same level of output.

There will be a different isoquant for each level of output. **Figure 15A.3** shows the isoquant corresponding to an output level of 300 bushels based on the data reported in Table 15A.2.

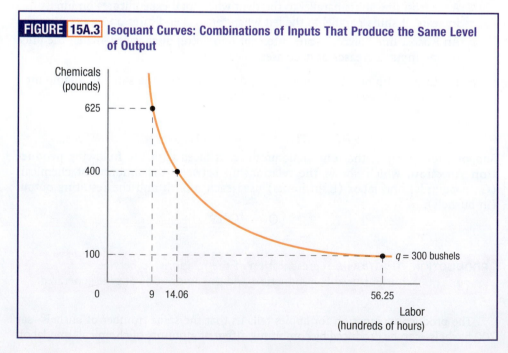

FIGURE 15A.3 Isoquant Curves: Combinations of Inputs That Produce the Same Level of Output

The first thing to notice is that this isoquant slopes downward. This has to be the case because if the grower uses more of one input, say C, then he must give up some L if the level of output is to remain unchanged. If he did not give up any L, he would end up producing more output because of the additional C used in production. This would move the producer to a higher isoquant.

The second thing to notice is that this isoquant is "convex to the origin." That is, it bows in to the origin of the graph. This tells us that the slope of the isoquant isn't constant. In other words, the trade-off between inputs required to produce the same amount of output is not constant. This must be the case if diminishing marginal returns set in for each input, such that the incremental output generated by additional units of one input declines.

Table 15A.2 illustrates diminishing marginal returns in action: to produce 200 bushels, the producer can use 25 hours of labor and 10,000 pounds of chemicals (25, 10,000) *or* give up 7,500 pounds of chemicals and add 75 hours of labor (100, 2,500). Or, he can give up an additional 1,875 pounds of chemicals and add 300 more hours of labor to produce the same level of output (400, 625). Notice that the trade-off between labor and chemicals is changing: it takes more and more labor to compensate for additional reductions in chemicals usage. This is because the marginal product of the last pound of chemicals that is given up is *rising* while the marginal product of each hour of labor added to the production process is *declining*. So the *trade-off* between labor and chemicals that just keeps the level of output constant changes as the input combination changes.

We know something more about this trade-off and, therefore, the slope of an isoquant. For every one-hour reduction in labor, the loss in output equals the marginal product generated by that last hour (MP_L). How many pounds of chemicals are required to compensate for this loss in output? This depends on the contribution to output that additional pounds of chemicals will generate—that is, each pound's marginal product (MP_C). Consequently, the trade-off between inputs that leaves output exactly the same is equal to the ratio of the marginal product of the two inputs, MP_L/MP_C. If, for example, a one-hour reduction in labor reduces output by 5 bushels, while an additional pound of chemicals yields 10 additional bushels, then .5 pounds of chemicals will just offset the one-hour reduction in labor: MP_L/MP_C equals 5/10 or 1/2.

We call the trade-off between inputs that holds output unchanged the **marginal rate of technical substitution**.

MARGINAL RATE OF TECHNICAL SUBSTITUTION (MRTS) The rate at which one input must be traded off for another to hold output constant; the ratio of the marginal products of the inputs.

Inasmuch as the slope of the isoquant tells us how much C is required when L changes (and vice versa) to remain on the same isoquant, the absolute value of the slope of the isoquant must equal to the MRTS. If diminishing marginal returns set in for each input, then the MRTS must decline (in absolute value) as we move down an isoquant and use more and more labor in lieu of chemicals: as the numerator (MP_L) gets smaller, the denominator (MP_C) gets bigger.

CHARACTERISTICS OF ISOQUANTS

We can generalize our findings about isoquants as follows:

- Isoquants are dictated by the production process and are, therefore, likely to differ across goods and industries.
- When there is an increase in the use of input X or Y, or both, a producer will move to the right to a "higher" isoquant, corresponding to a higher level of

output; when the use of X or Y, or both, decreases, a producer moves to the left to a "lower" isoquant, corresponding to a lower level of output.

- The slope of an isoquant is negative and decreases (in absolute value) as you move down the curve.
- The marginal rate of substitution between inputs X and Y is equal to the ratio of the marginal products of the two inputs.
- The slope of an isoquant (in absolute value) is equal to the marginal rate of technical substitution between inputs X and Y.

HOW ISOCOST LINES AND ISOQUANTS, TOGETHER, DETERMINE PRODUCTION DECISIONS

You may have noticed that the discussion about the apple grower's isocost lines ignored the production process—that is, how inputs C and L must be combined to produce bushels of apples. Conversely, the discussion about the production process ignored the price of inputs and the grower's expenditure constraints. Isocost lines reflect the trade-off between inputs *that the market dictates*, regardless of the production process, while isoquants reflect the trade-off between inputs that is *dictated by the production process*, irrespective of the input prices that the grower faces. To prove this to yourself, look again at Table 15A.2 and the input combinations that generate 200 bushels: they do not cost the same. Assuming that the price of one pound of C and one hour of L are $50 and $20, respectively, the input combination (25, 10,000) costs $201,250, whereas the combination (100, 2,500) costs $55,000, and combination (400, 625) costs $32,500.

To minimize the cost of production—and thereby maximize the quantity that can be produced for any given level of expenditure—the apple grower must take into account both the market-determined price of his inputs as well as his production technology. We represent this decision process by combining the producer's isocost lines and isoquants as shown in **Figure 15A.4**.

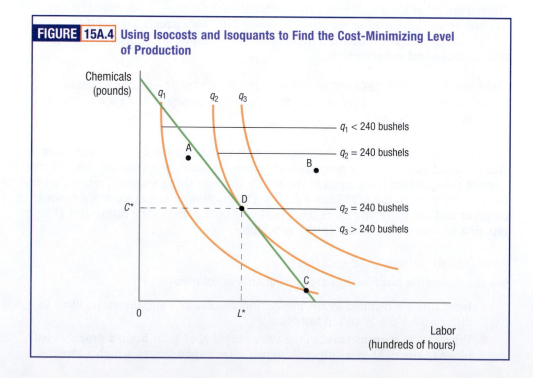

FIGURE 15A.4 Using Isocosts and Isoquants to Find the Cost-Minimizing Level of Production

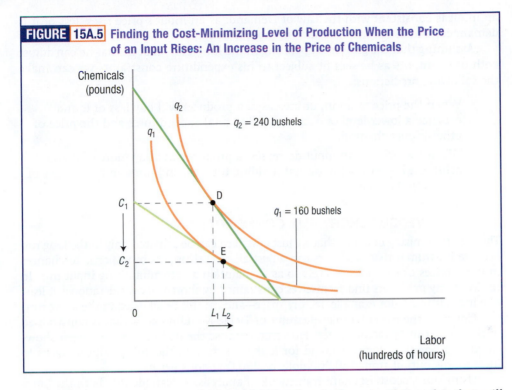

FIGURE 15A.5 Finding the Cost-Minimizing Level of Production When the Price of an Input Rises: An Increase in the Price of Chemicals

Given an expenditure level of $250,000, what is the mix of C and L that will maximize output?

Consider four possible input combinations, indicated by the letters A, B, C, and D in Figure 15A.4. Combination A lies inside the isocost line, which means that if the grower chooses this combination of inputs, there will be money left over. Because the purchase of more of either input translates into more output, the grower would be better off buying more C or L, or both, than buying input combination A.

Combination B lies outside of the isocost line, which means that the grower cannot afford to buy this combination of inputs. It is unattainable at this expenditure level. This leaves the grower to choose between combinations C and D, which lie on the isocost line: they are both affordable and exhaust his $250,000 budget. However, combination D lies on a higher isoquant than combination C, which means that it will deliver a higher level of output than input combination C.

Notice that at combination D, the isocost line is just *tangent to* an isoquant—that is, it is just touching the highest isoquant that can be reached. As the graph shows, this corresponds to a quantity of 240 bushels. This is the maximum output that can be attained with $250,000 worth of inputs. Another way to say this is that the cost of producing 240 bushels is minimized using input combination D.

Now consider what would happen to this result if the price of chemicals rose but total expenditures remained at the same level. **Figure 15A.5** shows that the isocost line pivots inward, so combination D is no longer attainable, nor is the isoquant associated with 240 bushels.

The best the grower can now do is to move to combination E and produce 160 bushels. Notice that the new isocost line is tangent to the isoquant at combination E and that this new input mix uses less chemicals and more labor than before. In fact, as long as the grower's isoquants are convex to the origin, he will always minimize his costs and maximize his output by using less of the input whose price has increased (and possibly less of other inputs as well). In other words, the producer's demand for an input is consistent with the Law of Demand: as an input's price rises, less of it is demanded, and as its price goes down, more is demanded.

Assuming that the grower is operating in the long-run—that is, that he can adjust both of his inputs as he sees fit subject to his expenditure constraint—we can make the following predictions:

■ When the price of an input increases, a producer will buy less of it and produce a lower level of output, holding total expenditures and the price of other inputs changed.

■ When the price of an input decreases, a producer will buy more of it and achieve a higher level of output, holding total expenditures and the prices of other inputs unchanged.

LONG-RUN VERSUS SHORT-RUN CONSIDERATIONS

The cost-minimizing outcome that we just described can be achieved only in the long run because it assumes that producers can adjust all of their inputs in response to changes in input prices or expenditure levels so as to maintain a cost-minimizing input mix. In reality, many producers find themselves constrained by short-run considerations: at least one input is fixed—for example, factory space—and cannot be adjusted in the short run.

Consider the case of a manufacturer of Tickle Me Elmo dolls that is constrained in the short run by factory space. However, because the doll has recently been show-cased in a popular movie, demand for it skyrockets, and the doll producer wants to increase his output from 120,000 dolls to 290,000 dolls per month.

Using our isocost/isoquant framework of analysis, we can identify both the long-run and short-run input mix that will produce 290,000 dolls per month at the lowest cost possible. **Figure 15A.6** shows that combination F (500 full-time employees and 100,000 square feet of factory space) is the lowest-cost input mix that will produce 290,000 dolls per month. Notice that this combination occurs at a tangency point

FIGURE 15A.6 **Cost-Minimizing Output Expansion in the Short Run versus the Long Run: Increasing the Number of Tickle Me Elmo Dolls**

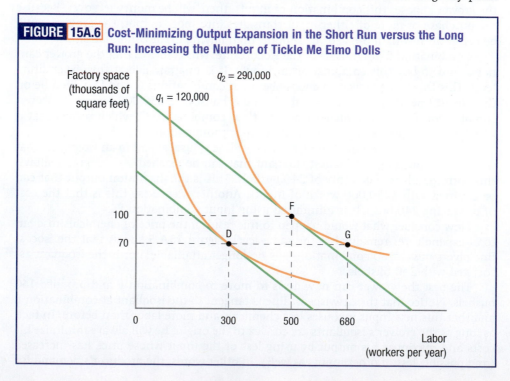

between the isocost line and isoquant corresponding to 290,000 dolls per month. There is no way to reallocate expenditures on inputs to further reduce the cost of producing this number of dolls.

Unfortunately, the producer is "stuck" at 70,000 square feet of space in the short run due to the choice of manufacturing space made when the output level was 120,000 dolls. Prior to the increase in demand, the producer was operating at point D, the lowest cost input mix for an output of 120,000 dolls. The lowest-cost input mix that is attainable in the short-run to produce 290,000 dolls is combination G (680, 70,000). As you can see, this combination is not at a tangency point between an isocost line and the isoquant for 290,000 dolls.

We know that the cost of combination G is greater than the cost of combination F because combination G lies on a higher isocost line than combination F, which means that the expenditure on combination G must be greater than what is needed to buy combination F. We can generalize this finding: even when costs are minimized in the short run, they can usually be reduced even further in the long run when all inputs are fully adjustable.

A MATHEMATICAL REPRESENTATION OF PRODUCER DECISION MAKING

We can express our isocost/isoquant analysis mathematically.

The Isocost Line

Given input prices P_X and P_Y for each unit of inputs X and Y, all of the combinations of X and Y that would just exhaust a producer's monthly expenditure limit (E) must meet the following expenditure constraint:

$$P_X X + P_Y Y = E \qquad (15A.1)$$

We can graph this relationship—with X and Y on the horizontal and vertical axes, respectively—using the following equation derived directly from equation 15A.1:

$$Y = E/P_Y - (P_X/P_Y) X \qquad (15A.2)$$

Equation 15A.2 is the equation for the isocost line. E/P_Y is the Y-intercept and E/P_X is the x-intercept. The y-intercept (E/P_Y) tells us how many units of Y could be purchased if no money is spent on input X, and the x-intercept (E/P_X) tells us how many units of X could be purchased if no money is spent on Y. The slope of the isocost equation ($-P_X/P_Y$) indicates the market's trade-off between Y and X: the higher the price of X and the lower the price of Y, the greater the number of units of Y that can be purchased when one unit of X is sacrificed. When E changes value in 15A.2, there is no change in the slope, which means that the isocost lines will always be parallel as long as the prices of the inputs don't change.

Isoquants

Consider the following production function:

$$q = f(X, Y) \qquad (15A.3)$$

Changes in output (q) are directly related to changes in the inputs X and Y, such that

$$\Delta q = MP_X (\Delta X) + MP_Y (\Delta Y) \qquad (15A.4)$$

Along an isoquant, Δq is equal to zero. As a result, along an isoquant

$$0 = MP_X (\Delta X) + MP_Y (\Delta Y) \qquad (15A.5)$$

and rearranging

$$MP_X / MP_Y = -\Delta Y / \Delta X = -\text{slope of isoquant} \tag{15A.6}$$

Conditions for Cost Minimization

As we demonstrated graphically, the cost-minimizing input mix will occur where the isocost line is tangent to an isoquant: at this point, the slopes of the two must be equal. This leads us to the following result:

$$P_X / P_Y = -MRTS_{X,Y} = MP_X / MP_Y \tag{15A.7}$$

This result is a necessary condition for cost minimization in production. The input mix that satisfies this condition is the long-run *equilibrium* input combination. Producers will not adjust their inputs any further after this equality is met as long as input prices, total expenditures, and the production process remain unchanged.

Rearranging equation 15A.7, we find that when production costs are minimized,

$$MP_X / P_X = MP_Y / P_Y \tag{15A.8}$$

This tells us that the cost of production is minimized (and the output generated from E is maximized) when the last *dollar* spent on each input generates the same contribution to output. What would happen if the marginal product of an input increases due to technological change—for example, labor becomes more productive due to the introduction of labor-enhancing technology? The condition in 15A.8 tells us that a producer would buy more of this input and less of other inputs whose marginal product had not changed. Conversely, if the marginal product of an input decreases due to technological change—as would occur for unskilled labor if labor-saving technology were introduced—then a producer would use less of this input and more of other inputs whose marginal products had not changed.

KEY TERMS

isocost lines, p. 458

production function, p. 461

isoquants, p. 462

marginal rate of technical substitution, p. 463

PRACTICE PROBLEMS

1. What would a house painter's isoquant curve look like if one of his inputs had a positive marginal product (labor) while the second input had a negative marginal product (smog)? Explain.

2. What would a producer's isoquant curve look like if she was choosing between two "perfect" complementary inputs that have to be used together in a specific combination—say painters and paintbrushes? Explain.

3. What does a straight-line isoquant "curve" tell you about a production process in terms of its two inputs, X and Y? Explain. If the isoquant curve is, in fact, a straight line, what would this mean in terms of finding the cost-minimizing bundle of inputs?

4. Could an isocost line ever be curved? Explain.

5. Why can an isoquant curve never intersect with another isoquant curve?

Appendix 15B Long-Run Cost Curves and Their Relationship to Short-Run Cost Curves

As you have learned, in the short run, a firm's cost curves reflect the fact that at least one input is *fixed* and cannot change as output levels change. Any expansion or contraction in the quantity produced in the short run can only occur as a result of changes in the level of *variable* inputs used. If there is at least one fixed input, variable inputs are subject to the diminishing marginal returns phenomenon, which leads to U-shaped marginal cost, average variable cost, and average total cost curves.

In contrast, all inputs are variable in the long run. As Appendix 15A demonstrated, we would expect that the cost of producing any given level of output in the long run will be less than, or equal to, its corresponding short-run production cost. It is only in the long run that producers are able to minimize their costs by altering all of their input levels; that is, by exploiting all production possibilities.

Because there are no fixed costs in the long run, the total and average fixed cost and variable cost curves disappear, and we are left with only the average total cost and marginal cost curves. What does this long-run average cost curve (LRAC) look like? In the long run, all inputs can be adjusted, so we are not constrained to the short-run U-shaped curve arising from diminishing marginal returns. In fact, it turns out that the LRAC curve can be horizontal, upward sloping, downward sloping, or U-shaped.

HORIZONTAL LONG-RUN AVERAGE COST (LRAC) CURVES

Suppose that a producer faces a production process where doubling his inputs would double his output, halving his inputs would halve his output, and so on. If this is the case, then the average cost of producing each unit of output would be *constant*. We say that such a production process exhibits *constant returns to scale*.

What does a long-run marginal cost curve (LRMC) that is associated with a horizontal LRAC curve look like? It turns out that this will also be horizontal and the same as the LRAC curve because the additional cost of producing another unit of output is the same as the cost of each unit that has already been produced. This follows directly from our constant returns to scale finding: the output can be expanded or contracted proportionately, and the cost per unit will remain unchanged.

Figure 15B.1 depicts the *LRAC and LRMC* curves for a constant returns-to-scale production process, along with the corresponding short-run cost curves. As you can see, the minimum of each short-run average total cost curve (SRAC) coincides with the LRAC curve.

This tells us that when one input is fixed, the minimum of the corresponding SRAC curve is both the short-run and long-run minimum cost of producing a particular level of output, say q_1. That is, this short-run input mix meets the cost-minimization conditions in the long run for q_1. Likewise, the minimum of another SRAC curve corresponding to a higher level of the fixed input is both the short-run and long-run minimum cost of producing a higher level of output, say q_2. Note that even when the LRAC and LRMC curves are horizontal, the short-run cost curves remain U-shaped.

UPWARD-SLOPING LONG-RUN AVERAGE COST (LRAC) CURVES

Suppose, instead, that a producer faced a production process where doubling his inputs *less than* doubles his output, halving his inputs leaves him with more than half of his output. The average cost of producing each unit of output *increases* as the quantity produced increases. **Figure 15B.2** shows the corresponding LRAC curve along with its

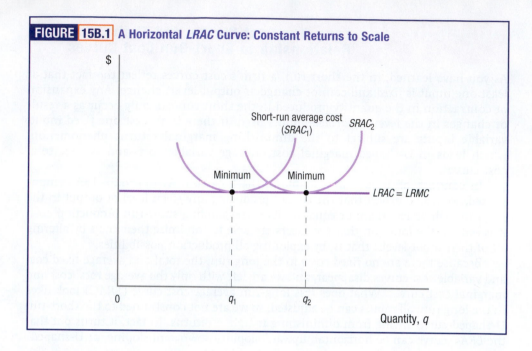

FIGURE 15B.1 A Horizontal *LRAC* Curve: Constant Returns to Scale

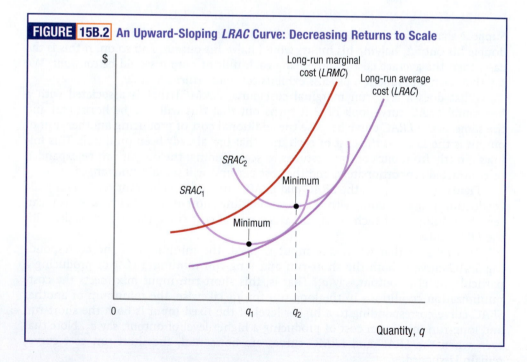

FIGURE 15B.2 An Upward-Sloping *LRAC* Curve: Decreasing Returns to Scale

LRMC curve. Because the *LRAC* is rising, this means that additional units of output cost more to produce than previous units. Essentially, the *LRMC* "pulls" the *LRAC* curve up and is always greater than the average cost of production.

Notice how the *SRAC* curves relate to the *LRAC* curve. The minimum of the $SRAC_1$ curve—which shows the output level where average costs are minimized using

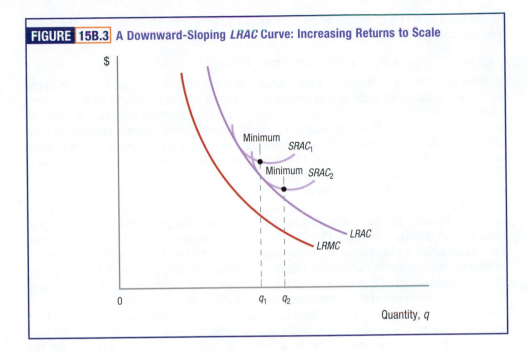

FIGURE 15B.3 A Downward-Sloping *LRAC* Curve: Increasing Returns to Scale

the amount of fixed inputs corresponding to the $SRAC_1$ curve—does not coincide with the minimum long-run average cost of producing that level of output. *Lower* levels of the fixed inputs will reduce average costs in the long run. This yields the short-run average cost curve $SRAC_2$.

DOWNWARD-SLOPING LONG-RUN AVERAGE COST (LRAC) CURVES

Now consider the case of a producer who faces a production process where doubling his inputs *more than* doubles his output, halving his inputs leaves him with less than half of his output. This producer's long-run average total cost of producing each unit of output *decreases* as the quantity produced increases. We say that such a production process exhibits *increasing returns to scale*. **Figure 15B.3** shows the corresponding *LRAC* curve, along with its *LRMC* curve. Because the long-run average cost is falling, this means that additional units of output cost less to produce than previous units. As a result, the *LRMC* curve "pulls" the *LRAC* curve down and is always lower than the long-run average cost of production, at least over the range of output corresponding to total market demand.

This type of *LRAC* curve is frequently associated with monopolies that can produce additional units of output at lower and lower cost. It looks much like the short-run average fixed cost curve, and with good reason. In the long run, a capital-intensive firm can increase its volume of customers and services for very little cost. For example, after the supplier of cable television programming has laid its cable, it can extend access to more and more customers at little additional cost to the company. As it spreads the cost of the cable network over greater numbers of customers, the average cost of the network per user falls.

Notice how the SRAC curves relate to the LRAC curve. The minimum of the $SRAC_1$ curve—which shows the output level where average costs are minimized using the amount of fixed inputs corresponding to the $SRAC_1$ curve—does not coincide with the minimum long-run average cost of producing that level of output. *Higher* levels of the fixed inputs will reduce average costs in the long run. This yields the short-run average cost curve $SRAC_2$.

U-SHAPED LONG-RUN AVERAGE COST (LRAC) CURVES

In the short run, we know that a firm's total cost curve will be U-shaped because of the diminishing marginal returns phenomenon. Is there a reason to believe that the firm's *LRAC* curve would also be U-shaped? Obviously, we need another rationale because all inputs are variable in the long run. Why might a production process exhibit increasing returns to scale at low levels of output and then grow to the point where it faces decreasing returns to scale? **Figure 15B.4** illustrates this situation. The *LRMC* curve is likewise U-shaped and cuts through the minimum of *LRAC* just as the marginal cost curve cuts through the minimum of the average total cost curve in the short run.

Economists have theorized that firms enjoy increasing returns to scale in the long run because of the specialization that arises when input levels expand to produce greater levels of output. Think about it: there is not much specialization that can occur when a custom car rehabber—like the one in the TV show *Pimp My Ride*—produces one custom car at a time. What if, instead, the firm produced 1,000 custom cars, all customized in the exact same way? It could then capitalize on the specialized skills of each member of the team: the welder would now only do welding, the painter only painting, and so on, rather than each performing a multitude of tasks. In fact, we might expect the welder to get better at what she does—in terms of productivity—as she finds ways to complete work in a more efficient way. The same is true for the painter and other workers.

Why wouldn't this specialization continue to generate increasing returns to scale for the company over greater levels of output? That is, why wouldn't the *LRAC* curve continue to fall?

The answer to this question is a little less clear-cut. Some economists argue that congestion sets in, but congestion requires that at least one input—say, factory space—is limited. This would put the firm back into a short-run position, not moving

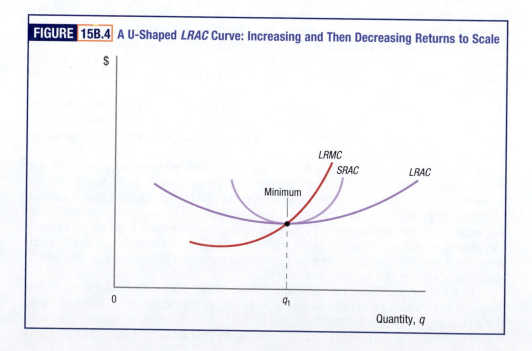

FIGURE 15B.4 A U-Shaped *LRAC* Curve: Increasing and Then Decreasing Returns to Scale

along its *LRAC* curve. The same problem arises when we explain the rising *LRAC* curve by pointing to limitations in coordination and communication capabilities as a firm grows "too" large.

CHARACTERISTICS OF LONG-RUN COST CURVES

The following conditions hold for long-run cost curves:

- Each *SRAC* curve is tangent to the *LRAC* curve at only one point. That is, each and every level of fixed inputs—which is reflected by each of the SRAC curves—corresponds to only one cost-minimizing level of production in the long run.

- When a production process exhibits constant returns to scale, the minimum of every *SRAC* curve is tangent to the *LRAC* curve. This means that the level of fixed inputs corresponding to the lowest average cost of production in the short run also minimizes the long-run average cost of production for that same level of output.

- When a production process exhibits increasing returns to scale, the minimum of each *SRAC* curve is always to the right of the point of tangency between the *LRAC* and the *SRAC* curves. This means that the level of fixed inputs corresponding to the lowest average cost of production in the short run must be increased to minimize the long-run average cost of production for that same level of output.

- When a production process exhibits decreasing returns to scale, the minimum of each *SRAC* curve is always to the left of the point of tangency between the *LRAC* and the *SRAC* curve. This means that the level of fixed inputs corresponding to the lowest average cost of production in the short run must be reduced to minimize the long-run average cost of production for that same level of output.

A MATHEMATICAL EXPOSITION OF RETURNS TO SCALE

In the case of *constant returns to scale*, we know that if we double the inputs used to produce q_1, we will get exactly double the output, q_2. What does this tell us about the average cost of production?

$$C(q_1) = P_X X + P_Y Y, \text{ where C is total cost, and } X \text{ and } Y \text{ represent input levels}$$
$$\text{for X and Y, respectively.}$$

$$C(q_2) = P_X(2X) + P_Y(2Y)$$

$$C(q_2) = 2[P_X X + P_Y Y]$$

$$C(q_2) = 2\,C(q_1)$$

$$C(q_2)/q_2 = 2\,C(q_1)/2q_1$$

$$ATC_{q_2} = ATC_{q_1}$$

When we *scale* inputs up by the same proportion, total output will increase by exactly the same proportion. Therefore, to double the output level, we would double the inputs used, which leads to the same, or *constant*, average cost of production. The average cost of production will remain *constant* as we *scale* the inputs up or down by the same proportion as total output increases or decreases.

In the case of *decreasing returns to scale,* we know that if we double the inputs used to produce q_1, we will get less than double the output, q_2. What does this tell us about the average cost of production?

$C(q_1) = P_X X + P_Y Y$, where C is total cost, and X and Y represent input levels for X and Y, respectively

$C(q_2) = P_X(2\lambda X) + P_Y(2\lambda Y)$, where λ is a factor > 1 by which all inputs must be scaled up to achieve double the output

$C(q_2) = 2\lambda [P_X X + P_Y Y]$

$C(q_2) = 2\lambda C(q_1)$

$C(q_2)/q_2 = 2\lambda C(q_1)/2q_1$

$ATC_{q_2} = \lambda ATC_{q_1}$, where $\lambda > 1$

When we *scale* inputs up by the same proportion, there will be a proportionately smaller increase in the level of output produced. This means that to double output, we will have to more than double the inputs used, which leads to an increase in the average cost of production.

In the case of *increasing returns to scale,* we know that if we double the inputs used to produce Q_1, we will get more than double the output, q_2. What does this tell us about the average cost of production?

$C(q_1) = P_X X + P_Y Y$, where C is total cost, and X and Y represent input levels of X and Y, respectively

$C(q_2) = P_X(2\lambda X) + P_Y(2\lambda Y)$, where λ is a factor < 1 by which inputs must be scaled up to achieve exactly double the input

$C(q_2) = 2\lambda [P_X X + P_Y Y]$

$C(q_2) = 2\lambda C(q_1)$

$C(q_2)/q_2 = 2\lambda C(q_1)/2q_1$

$ATC_{q_2} = \lambda ATC_{q_1}$, where $\lambda < 1$

When we *scale* inputs up by the same proportion, there will be a proportionately greater *increase* in the level of output produced. This means that to exactly double output, we would use less than double the level of inputs, which leads to a decrease in the average cost of production.

16

How a Firm Chooses the Right Level of Production

"In the end, all business operations can be reduced to three words: people, product, and profits."

Lee Iacocca, businessman, author, and former Chrysler CEO

In the previous chapter, you learned that producers—regardless of their ultimate objectives—will try to minimize their production costs. The question that remains is how much output a company should produce after it has figured out how to minimize its costs of production. The answer to this question *does* depend on the firm's objectives and the environment within which it operates.

Nonprofit charities and universities, for-profit companies, government agencies, and households tend to operate in different spheres of the economy. They produce different types of goods and are subject to different types of operational constraints. For example, nonprofit organizations such as the Salvation Army cannot distribute their net revenue (profits) to individuals; for-profit firms such as Safeway cannot set their own prices without regard to the competition; government agencies such as the Environmental Protection Agency (EPA) cannot spend their budgets to benefit private interests; and households cannot send their ten-year-old children into the labor force to supplement the family's income. It turns out that these producers differ in the kinds of goods they produce and the constraints they face because they play distinctive roles in the economy. This leads to different decision rules when it comes to determining the "right" amount of output to produce.

In this chapter, we will look at how different types of producers choose their scale of operation. We will explore why economists rely so heavily on competitive markets to deliver the "best" allocation of scarce resources. We will also consider the role of private nonprofit and government organizations in filling the void when markets do not exist or function effectively, and whether these institutions can assure an economically efficient allocation of resources in such situations.

16.1 Our Three-Sector Organization of Production

We have already discussed the important role that households play in the development of human capital and the provision of personal services. When we look beyond this sector, we find a myriad of other producing organizations that can be roughly sorted into three categories: for-profit organizations, nonprofit organizations, and government organizations.[1] Of course, there are "hybrid" organizations such as the U.S. Post Office. It is self-financed, but still owned by the federal government, which sets postal rates.

During the financial crisis that began in 2007, you probably heard about the mortgage companies Freddie Mac and Fannie Mae. Originally, these two organizations were created by the U.S. government to help low-income Americans get mortgages. Later, the two companies were spun off to private shareholders but continued to be regulated by the government and supervised by boards comprised of political appointees. Following the subprime mortgage meltdown in 2007, the federal government once again assumed partial ownership of Freddie Mac and Fannie Mae and, in return, infused hundreds of billions of dollars to stabilize the mortgage market.

Nonprofits, for-profits, and government organizations differ in important ways: in their formal missions, ownership structures, sources of revenue and investment capital, ability to transfer ownership, and goods they produce. We address each of these differences separately to see how they influence the production and output decisions of each type of producer.

Ownership Differences

Private nonprofit organizations such as the Salvation Army, the Nature Conservancy (a charitable conservation group that operates worldwide), and the Archdiocese of San Diego do not have owners in the traditional sense. Members or employees of such private, nonprofit groups cannot legally sell any of their assets and pocket the proceeds. Nor can they spend the revenues they generate for their private betterment. Likewise, government agencies do not have owners who can buy or sell the government's assets solely for their private enrichment. Privately held rights to assets and income that can be legally transferred are virtually unique to the household and the private, for-profit sector.

For-profit businesses owned by one individual or a handful of individuals are often referred to as *sole proprietorships* (one owner) and *private partnerships* (more than one owner). Think of a law firm with two lawyers who own and run the business, or the bicycle shop near campus where the bike mechanic is also the owner and bookkeeper. These owners produce goods and services—legal services, wills, bicycle repairs, and sales—for their companies. Perhaps more importantly, they bear the risks and enjoy the financial rewards that come with the success or failure of their businesses. For example, if a sole proprietorship or private partnership goes into debt, the owners are personally liable for this debt. (By declaring bankruptcy, they can sometimes get legal protection against the collection of some of these debts.) If, instead, the firm is wildly successful and makes a huge profit, the owners can claim this for themselves. We call these owners **residual claimant**s.

· · · · · · · ·

[1]Burton A. Weisbrod, "Toward a Theory of the Voluntary Nonprofit Sector in a Three-Sector Economy," in E. Phelps, ed., *Altruism, Morality, and Economic Theory* (New York: Russell Sage Foundation, 1975), pp. 171–195.

RESIDUAL CLAIMANT Owner that has the right to the net revenue, or profit, of a firm.

EXAMPLE The Mars family is the sole owner of Mars Corporation, the maker of Milky Way, Snickers, and other popular candy products. This has made the family one of the richest in the United States.

EXAMPLE Most small physician practices are owned by their doctors, who split up the practice's profits according to their ownership shares.

Contrast this type of firm with one that is owned by many people, all of whom own shares, or stakes, in the company. These firms are called *publicly held* corporations, whose ownership shares are typically bought and sold through stock exchanges such as the New York Stock Exchange or NASDAQ. In the United States, these shareholders range from individual investors to large pension plans that are looking to grow the value of their funds to maximize employees' future pensions. Like private partnerships and sole proprietorships, the owners of publicly held corporations—the shareholders—also are residual claimants who benefit when the company is profitable. After the firm's suppliers, employers, debt holders, and so forth are paid, the shareholders—at the discretion of the company's board of directors—may receive regular payments called *dividends*. Dividends are one way for publicly held firms to distribute their profits. Owners also benefit from increases in the price of their shares, which result from increases in the company's profitability.

Unlike sole proprietors and partners, however, shareholders of a publicly held corporation are not personally liable for the company's losses or debts. If the corporation goes bankrupt, a shareholder's liability is limited to what was originally paid for the shares. Consider what would have happened if you had bought 100 shares in the second-largest long-distance telephone company—WorldCom—at $60 a share in 2001, only to see the company go bankrupt in 2003. Your loss would have been your initial investment of $6,000. Although the value of your shares would have been wiped out, as a shareholder, you would not have been taken to court to pay any of the firm's outstanding bills.

Having a residual claimant is important to assuring that scarce resources are used effectively. Why? When people personally benefit from a productive activity and personally bear the cost of the resources used up in the process, they will try to make choices that maximize the return they get from these resources. They will consider not only near term returns but future returns as well. For example, for-profit companies that grow trees and own thousands of acres of forest land tend to schedule their harvesting and replanting activities to maximize the returns they get from their forest land far into the future.[2] To do otherwise would be irrational from an economic perspective.

Contrast this with the behavior of an employee of the U.S. Forestry Service or a legislator in Congress. Even if they have good intentions, neither has a personal stake in putting resources that their organizations control to their highest valued use now and in the future. A government forester does not have a financial incentive to invest the time and effort necessary to ensure that forest harvesting, burn off, and preservation activities take place to maximize the long-term return to the forest. Similarly, an

. . . .

[2]Vivian Marino, "For Some Investors, Money Grows on Trees." *New York Times*, May 27, 2007.

individual legislator would not personally benefit from transferring the administration of the federally funded national forestry service to the state level (unless it is to her own state), even if this turned out to be a more cost-effective way to manage our publicly owned forests.

This suggests that despite our prior assumption that government organizations have an incentive to produce in a cost-minimizing way, *individual* decision makers may not be similarly motivated. This in no way demeans what these officials may be trying to achieve; it simply recognizes that they face an entirely different set of incentives and constraints when it comes to choosing how to allocate the resources under their control. Government bureaucrats do not share in the savings when they are successful in reducing production costs, nor do they personally benefit from the higher returns that come from using resources more effectively. They may not even be employed in the same position when these savings or returns are realized. A similar argument can be made in the case of private nonprofit organizations that also function without residual claimants.

Different Sources of Revenue and Financial Capital

Private nonprofit organizations—such as homeless shelters and universities—receive revenue from a number of sources: donations, sales revenue from goods and services related to their missions, and grants from government agencies and private foundations. Those that have high capital requirements, such as hospitals that need CAT scanners and expensively equipped research laboratories, often finance these acquisitions through donations or by selling tax-free bonds.

Quite often, the prices of the goods and services that nonprofit firms sell are highly subsidized, either by other users or by donations or endowments. For example, there tends to be a big difference between the tuition that a university charges and what most students actually pay. Nonprofit universities are able to offer tuition subsidies to many students via financial-aid packages funded by government grants and loans, along with individual donations and private foundation grants. Some students do pay full "sticker price,"[3] which provides an additional source of revenue to cross-subsidize those who are unable to pay the full tuition. Pricey Ivy League universities such as Harvard and Yale, for example, do not offer merit scholarships but, instead, allocate all financial assistance based on financial need. This policy ensures that there will be a large number of "full pay" students to help subsidize those who cannot pay full price.

Government entities rely heavily on tax revenue to finance the goods and services they provide. National governments also sell bonds to borrow funds when their expenditures outpace tax collections. Often, these bonds are sold to other national governments. In fact, the Chinese government purchased more than $1 trillion in U.S. bonds from 2008 to 2009.[4] Under special circumstances, states, cities, and school districts also issue bonds to fund special projects. But only one funding mechanism is available exclusively to national governments: they can actually print money to pay their bills.

· · · · · · ·

[3]Burton A. Weisbrod, Jeffrey Ballou, and Evelyn Asch, *Mission and Money: Understanding the University* (New York: Cambridge University Press, 2008).

[4]Michael Wines, "China's Leader Says He Is Worried over U.S. Treasuries." *New York Times*, March 13, 2009.

In contrast, for-profit companies have much more limited sources of revenue and financial capital available to them. They receive sales revenue from the goods and services they supply to the market. An owner can also self-finance her company from personal savings, or, if need be, she may take out a bank loan for start-up or expansion funds. Publicly held companies can also raise financial capital by issuing corporate bonds or selling more ownership shares.

How does the source of a firm's revenue and financial capital affect its production decisions? Consider private nonprofit charities that are funded almost completely by donations. To increase the amount of donations they receive, charities usually apply to the Internal Revenue Service (IRS) for tax-exempt, public-charity recognition. This tax status means that donors' contributions are tax-deductible and that the charities themselves are exempt from paying taxes on the donations and sales revenue they collect. In return for these valuable benefits, the IRS prohibits tax-exempt groups from selling ownership shares, distributing profits, or selling assets to benefit any private interest. In effect, the IRS forbids nonprofit firms from having any residual claimants. The IRS also encourages nonprofit charitable organizations to provide free or highly subsidized services to people who cannot pay for them. If you've ever wondered, this is why local hospitals never turn away patients who come into their emergency rooms (most states also now have laws to this effect) and why city symphonies often offer free matinee concerts to children who otherwise wouldn't be able to experience a symphony.

Because government entities receive a large amount of their revenue through taxes, there is enormous pressure put on politicians to direct "pork" projects to voters back home. Whether we are talking about elected officials at the federal, state or local level, the goal is to bring back more dollars in projects than are collected in taxes from the politician's constituents. You've probably heard about recent efforts to limit the "earmarks" that U.S. Congress members direct to projects in their home districts. And because government organizations can impose taxes and provide subsidies, they are prime targets for interest groups that lobby for income transfers—in the form of entitlement programs, subsidies, protective regulations, and so on—at the expense of other groups. The end result is that the quantity of goods and services a government provides is unlikely to be determined by the community's willingness to pay.

Compare this to private, for-profit companies that compete for all of their sources of revenue. To generate sales revenue, they must be able to successfully compete against other suppliers in the market. To raise investment dollars, they must be able to obtain loans, float debt through bond offerings, or sell shares in the competitive capital markets they face. Consequently, for-profit firms must sell their output at the price dictated by the market and pay a return on borrowed financial capital that is also determined by the market. Both the market price and the cost of capital provide important signals to for-profit firms about the opportunity cost of resources used in production as well as the willingness of consumers to pay for the goods produced by these resources.

Differences in Output

Why do nonprofit, government and for-profit organizations differ so much in their ownership and sources of revenue and capital? Some economists have explained these differences by pointing out that there are systematic differences in the output produced by each sector of the economy. They argue that the comparative advantage of each type of organization depends on the degree to which the goods produced are consumed *privately* or *collectively*. A **private good** is used by one person and is not simultaneously available to others. Generally speaking, the more of a private good that one person has, the less someone else will have. Your home or apartment is an example of a private good; after you have purchased or rented it, it is no longer available to other people to purchase or rent.

PRIVATE GOOD A good whose use by one person prevents use by others.

EXAMPLE Food is a private good. Two people cannot both consume the same sandwich (although they could share different parts of the same sandwich).

EXAMPLE Your reserved seat at the upcoming NFL football game is a private good. No one else can sit in your seat while you are sitting in it.

When you buy a private good—such as a Porsche Boxster or a pair of athletic shoes—you acquire the right to access and control the use of that good and benefit from it. This means that you can exclude others from also receiving benefits from the good. We call this the right to **exclusivity**. If you do not purchase the good, you cannot benefit from it unless its owner allows you to do so.

EXCLUSIVITY The right of an owner of a good to exclude others from using it without permission.

EXAMPLE You control who can enter your home (except for police with a warrant).

EXAMPLE You decide who can and cannot drive a car that you have purchased.

The owners of private goods also have the right to voluntarily transfer partial or full ownership of the good to new owners.

It is relatively easy for for-profit firms to produce and sell private goods. The marketplace will see to it that goods are supplied to consumers with the highest willingness to pay. Every good is produced up to the point where the willingness to pay for the very last unit is just equal to the marginal cost of production.

In contrast to a private good, a **collective good** is one that can be consumed by more than one person at a time. A golf course, a symphony, and a lecture are all goods that can be consumed by many people at the same time. Also, one person's consumption of a collective good does not diminish another person's consumption, at least not until overcrowding occurs.

COLLECTIVE GOOD A good that can be consumed by more than one person at the same time.

EXAMPLE You and 250 other people can study in the library at the same time.

EXAMPLE At the same time that you are accessing the Internet, millions of others are doing the same thing.

Notice that we can both enjoy a lecture or the symphony at the same time, but we cannot occupy the same seat in the lecture or symphony hall; in this respect, each seat is a private good.

How should collective goods be provided? For example, how should producers of collective goods charge consumers for access, and how much should each consumer pay? If one person is willing to pay $100 to attend a lecture, and another is only willing to contribute $25, does it make sense to refuse admission to the second person? Does it make sense to turn anyone away from the lecture if there are empty seats available? How do producers decide how many symphonies to produce and lectures to offer? Will for-profit producers whose revenue depends solely on ticket sales sell the "optimal" number of tickets, that is, the quantity where the marginal benefit of the last ticket sold is just equal to its marginal cost? Will they choose the "right" number of performances and lectures from an economic perspective?

The more collective a good is, the more likely it is that nonprofit or government organizations will provide it. It's easy to understand why: too many people will understate their willingness to pay for a collective good, hoping that others will cover most of the production costs. For example, if people are asked how much they would pay to gain access to a new science museum, they are likely to understate the value of the benefits they would actually receive. It is in their interest to get other people to pay as much of the bill as possible. The end result is that there will be too little private money invested in establishing science museums, and some cities may even have to do without one. After all, who would be willing to build a museum if patrons aren't willing to pay enough to cover its cost? This is why the for-profit sector is unlikely to supply this kind of collective good.

Nonprofit science museums, hospitals, and symphonies can solicit donations and grants to cover this shortfall in investment and sales revenue. Just think about all of the "named" buildings, lobbies, and exhibits at your hospital or zoo. Nonprofit groups are also heavily subsidized by virtue of their tax-exempt status. These additional revenue sources allow them to supply more of a collective good than what would be justified solely by the amount that people offer to pay.

There is a subcategory of collective goods whose provision is especially problematic for *both* for-profit and nonprofit producers. The problem with these special collective goods is that it is prohibitively costly to exclude people from consuming them. We call these **public goods**.

PUBLIC GOOD A collective good that no one can be excluded from using.

EXAMPLE A country's national defense system cannot protect one citizen and, at the same time, exclude his neighbor.

EXAMPLE A program that improves air quality in Los Angeles cannot exclude any residents from enjoying the benefits that arise from cleaner air.

While providers of most collective goods, such as golf courses, can selectively exclude people if they don't pay anything, providers of public goods cannot exclude anyone from using them. This is why governments often end up financing public goods. By exercising its exclusive right to tax people, a government entity can forcibly collect revenue to fund the provision of public goods, regardless of what each person would voluntarily pay. As a result, taxpayers will sometimes pay for public goods that they may, in fact, value very little. Like it or not, your tax dollars help fund public goods such as nuclear warheads and climate-change initiatives.

16.2 Choosing the Optimal Level of Output

The differences that exist among for-profit, nonprofit, and government entities have a substantial impact on the amount of output each will produce. Let's look at why this is so.

Private Nonprofit Organizations

Many economists speculate that private nonprofit institutions such as hospitals and charities tend to act like *output* maximizers because there are no owners who would benefit from income that is not spent on production.[5] That is, these organizations spend their funds to maximize the amount of goods and services they produce. Consequently, they will produce to the point where their total costs of production just equal their total revenue, leaving them with zero economic profits. This still permits nonprofits to use more profitable "product lines" to subsidize less profitable ones. For example, Harvard University makes money on its undergraduate program, which is used to subsidize the school's money-losing graduate programs.[6]

Figure 16.1 shows the optimal level of production for a nonprofit, output-maximizing food pantry. (Note that we once again use q to represent a single producer's output and Q to represent total output in the market.) When the food pantry serves 1,000 meals per day, its total cost of production is just equal to the total daily revenue it receives from all sources. At any higher output level, the organization would incur losses. And, if it served fewer meals—between 500 and 999 per day—there would be residual profits (because total revenues exceed total cost in this range of output) that could have been used to supply more meals.

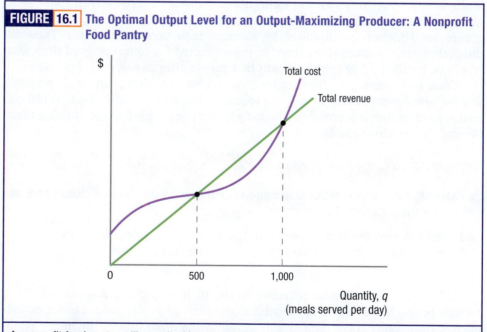

FIGURE 16.1 **The Optimal Output Level for an Output-Maximizing Producer: A Nonprofit Food Pantry**

A nonprofit food pantry will use all of its revenue to provide meals to those in need. As depicted, it will serve 1,000 meals per day. At this level, the total revenue collected from all of its sources just equals the total cost of the meals. Why wouldn't it serve 500 meals, where total revenue is also equal to total cost? If it did this, it would miss out on the net revenue that would be generated between 500 and 1,000 meals, which can then be used to provide more meals each day.

....

[5]Joseph Newhouse, "Toward a Theory of Nonprofit Institutions: An Economic Model of a Hospital." *American Economic Review*, 60, no. 1 (1970): 64–74.

[6]Estelle James, "Product Mix and Cost Disaggregation: A Reinterpretation of the Economics of Higher Education." *Journal of Human Resources* (Spring, 1978): 157–186.

A good example of a nonprofit that follows this decision rule is a local food pantry, which spends all of the revenue it receives—from government grants and donations—on its operations, including the purchase of food to distribute to people in need. If the food pantry is successful in meeting its objective—to feed as many people as possible—in a manner of speaking, it will be constantly "going broke."

Government Entities

Government entities operate a little like nonprofits. Some models of government behavior theorize that in the absence of residual claimants, bureaucrats have a strong incentive to spend every dollar of revenue they receive. Most models of government production also take into account the fact that elected officials strive to be reelected. This means that it is in their economic self-interest to respond to the will of the voters or, more precisely, to the will of at least 50 percent of the voters. We call this a **median voter model** of government decision making.[7]

> **MEDIAN VOTER MODEL** A behavioral model which predicts that elected officials, seeking to retain their positions, make decisions that benefit slightly more than 50 percent of their voters.

> **EXAMPLE** In 2009, U.S. Congressmen flew home to assess whether a majority of their voters would support President Obama's health-care reform bill.

> **EXAMPLE** In late 2010, Congress members polled voters in their home districts to gauge the amount of opposition to eliminating the mortgage-interest tax deduction.

Other models of government behavior take into account the roles that lobbyists, campaign funding, and interest groups play in determining which goods and services will be produced and at what levels.[8] These models predict that by tempting politicians with the promise of large campaign contributions, lobbyists can exert pressure on them to support the overproduction of a public good or even subsidize production of a private good. The construction industry, for example, has lobbied continuously over the past 50 years to have more and more government dollars committed to the expansion of the interstate-highway system, even into areas with low population densities and sparse commercial activities. At the local level, government agencies are often pressured into providing private goods such as garbage collection and leaf pickup. These services are often priced or taxed in such a way as to benefit voters at the expense of nonvoters. If you've wondered why cities so often rely on sales taxes to fund their services, it is precisely because a large share of these taxes comes from shoppers who live outside the city but shop within its limits.

Finally, there is evidence to show that government agencies struggle to grow their budget allotments over time. They do this by demonstrating that there is an unmet "need" for their output[9] or by expanding the range of goods and services they provide. In 1998, for example, the National Institutes of Health (NIH)

. . . .

[7]Anthony Downs, *An Economic Theory of Democracy* (New York: Harper Collins, 1957).

[8]James Buchanan and Gordon Tullock, *The Calculus of Consent* (Ann Arbor: University of Michigan Press, 1962).

[9]William Niskanen, Jr., *Bureaucracy and Representative Goods* (Chicago, IL: Aldine-Atherton, 1971).

successfully lobbied Congress for a new research center. The mission of this new center—the National Center for Complementary and Alternative Medicine—was to evaluate unconventional medical practices. By fiscal year 2008, this center alone accounted for more than $120 million in additional Congressional funding for the NIH.

16.3 A Profit-Maximizing Firm's Optimal Output Level

How do for-profit firms decide how much output to produce? We explained earlier that these types of producers have residual claimants that share in the firm's profits. Of course, whether an economic profit is actually made or not depends on whether total revenue exceeds the total economic cost of production. Total revenue, in turn, depends on the producer's sales volume (q) and the price at which each unit is sold.

Suppose that the firm is a price taker because it is too small to influence the market price for its product. In this situation, the firm can influence its revenue flow only by its choice of output level (q). This means that a for-profit firm that has minimized its costs of production and chosen an output level that maximizes its profits has no way to increase its profits any further.

In earlier chapters, we developed a model of individual decision making which argued that a person's well-being is maximized when she allocates her scarce resources to various activities up to the point where the marginal benefit received equals the marginal cost—that is, up to the point where the last unit of the good or activity yields *zero net benefit*. It turns out that a for-profit producer chooses the "right" level of output in much the same way. Just like individual decision makers, a for-profit firm will choose an output level where the marginal benefit of the last unit produced just equals its marginal cost.

What is the marginal benefit that a for-profit firm receives from producing each unit? If the only thing that the company cares about is profitability, then the benefit it gets from each unit sold is the revenue that this unit generates. The revenue generated by each incremental unit sold is called **marginal revenue**.

> **MARGINAL REVENUE (*MR*)** The contribution that each incremental unit of production makes to total revenue.

> **EXAMPLE** When Dunkin' Donuts sells a fancy doughnut, it earns $1.29 in additional sales revenue; this is the marginal revenue of each fancy doughnut sold.

> **EXAMPLE** AMC Movie Theaters receives $11.50 in marginal revenue for each adult it admits to an evening showing of a feature film.

The "right" level of output will be where the marginal cost (MC) of the last unit produced just equals its marginal revenue (MR). At this output level, a firm's *total net benefit* from production is maximized. While the net benefit of the last unit produced is equal to zero (i.e., $MR - MC = 0$), all units before this one generate a positive net benefit.

We actually know something more about the net benefits enjoyed by a producer. If marginal revenue is the increase in revenue resulting from selling each additional unit, and marginal cost is each additional unit's cost of production, then the net benefit derived from each unit equals the difference between the two. In other words, the net benefit generated by each unit is, in fact, the incremental **profit** that this unit contributes to the firm. When we add together each unit's contribution to profit (its net benefit), we get the firm's total **profit** (total net benefit) from production, that is, total revenue − total cost.

> **PROFIT** Total revenue minus total economic cost; the total net benefit of production.
>
> **EXAMPLE** A local home builder sold $8.2 million worth of homes in 2009. His total costs—including his own opportunity cost—equaled $8 million. This left him with $200,000 in economic profits.
>
> **EXAMPLE** A professional eBay trader bought $42,000 of goods to resell on eBay. His total sales revenue net of eBay listing and shipping fees amounted to $54,400. The opportunity cost of his time was $1,400, leaving him with $11,000 in economic profits.

When a firm's marginal cost is low relative to the marginal revenue it earns from producing another unit, the company will keep expanding its output. Because the marginal cost is less than the marginal revenue, the firm earns positive net benefits, or profits, from each and every additional unit. But at some point, the marginal cost of production begins to increase relative to marginal revenue. This might occur because the firm has to pay its workers overtime to keep cranking out more output or, more generally, because diminishing marginal returns to one or more of the variable inputs set in. It makes sense that after marginal cost rises sufficiently to exceed marginal revenue, the firm will stop producing any more output. After all, the firm doesn't want to produce units that cost more than the additional revenue they will garner. The **profit-maximizing output level**, then, is where the last unit's cost of production just equals the revenue it generates—that is, where marginal revenue equals marginal cost. (This is exactly the same answer we arrived at when we looked at the output level that will maximize a producer's total net benefit.) At this output level, profits have been maximized.

> **PROFIT-MAXIMIZING OUTPUT LEVEL** The level of output at which the marginal cost of the last unit produced just equals the marginal revenue received for it.
>
> **EXAMPLE** If Pizza King sells all of its large pizzas for $10 each, then it will make pizzas up to the point where the last pizza sold costs $10 to make.
>
> **EXAMPLE** If a local restaurant delivery service charges $14 for each delivery, it will make deliveries only to locales where the cost of delivering meals does not exceed $14.

In **Figure 16.2**, we see that Pizza King's profit-maximizing output level is 160 pizzas per day. The marginal revenue received for the 160th pizza ($10) is just equal to the marginal cost of producing it.

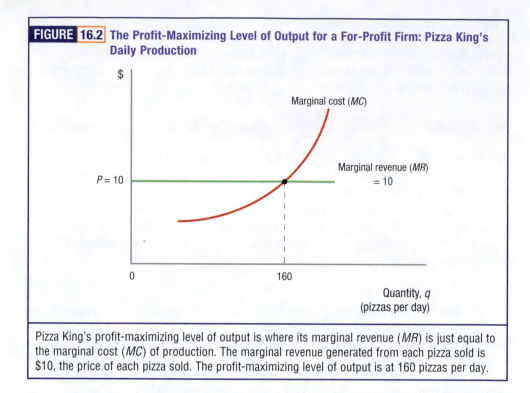

FIGURE 16.2 The Profit-Maximizing Level of Output for a For-Profit Firm: Pizza King's Daily Production

Pizza King's profit-maximizing level of output is where its marginal revenue (*MR*) is just equal to the marginal cost (*MC*) of production. The marginal revenue generated from each pizza sold is $10, the price of each pizza sold. The profit-maximizing level of output is at 160 pizzas per day.

Price-Taking Firms

We have spoken at great length about price-taking firms that are simply too small relative to the market to have any impact on market price. For example, a local dairy farmer who supplies milk to your grocery store cannot charge the grocer $25 a gallon and expect any sales when the going market price is only $2.50. A corollary to this is that the dairy farmer can sell as little or as much milk as he wants at $2.50 without having a noticeable effect on the going price of milk. This means the marginal revenue (*MR*) that the dairy farmer receives for each gallon of milk he produces is equal to $2.50, the market price.

Figure 16.3 shows that a price-taking dairy farmer will choose to produce 1,200 gallons of milk each week. This is the point where the marginal cost of producing the last (1,200th) gallon of output just equals $2.50. How do we really know that the firm's profits are maximized when it produces 1,200 gallons of milk? We can see this by subtracting the area under the marginal cost curve, which represents the total cost of producing 1,200 gallons, from the area under the price line, which equals total revenue ($2.50 × 1,200). This is equivalent to the area *between* the price line and the marginal cost (*MC*) curve, which is equivalent to the total net benefit.

We can generalize our result. A price-taking, for-profit firm will maximize its profits by producing up to the point where its marginal cost equals its marginal revenue, which in turn equals the market price, *P*:

$$MC = MR = P$$

The last unit produced and sold will not generate any economic profit because its marginal cost just equals the price (*P*) received for that unit. Beyond this point, additional output will *reduce* the firm's total profits because the marginal cost of

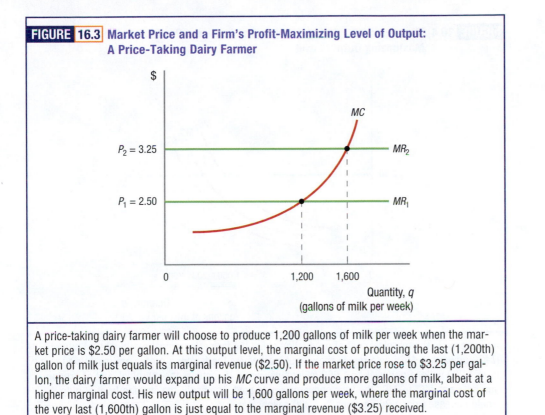

FIGURE 16.3 Market Price and a Firm's Profit-Maximizing Level of Output: A Price-Taking Dairy Farmer

A price-taking dairy farmer will choose to produce 1,200 gallons of milk per week when the market price is $2.50 per gallon. At this output level, the marginal cost of producing the last (1,200th) gallon of milk just equals its marginal revenue ($2.50). If the market price rose to $3.25 per gallon, the dairy farmer would expand up his *MC* curve and produce more gallons of milk, albeit at a higher marginal cost. His new output will be 1,600 gallons per week, where the marginal cost of the very last (1,600th) gallon is just equal to the marginal revenue ($3.25) received.

producing these units is greater than the price that they will sell for in the market. This is why our farmer would not want to expand output beyond 1,200 gallons a week.

Figure 16.3 also shows the farmer's response to an increase in the market price of milk, from $2.50 to $3.25. You can see that the profit-maximizing quantity also increases, from 1,200 gallons a week to 1,600 gallons a week (the price line intersects the *MC* curve at a higher level of output). To put this in a slightly different perspective, recall from Chapter 7 that supply curves slope upward: the supply of a good expands in response to an increase in market price. The converse is also true: a decline in market price will lead a firm to cut back its supply. This is the case because at a lower price, continuing to produce at the original level would mean that the marginal cost of the last unit produced now exceeds the revenue, or price, received from selling it.

It also is true that a change in the cost of producing a good will alter a firm's profit-maximizing output level. To see this, suppose that there is an increase in the dairy farmer's cost of producing each gallon of milk. Perhaps the cost of hay or feed has risen due to a drought.

This increase in production costs shifts the farmer's marginal cost curve upward to MC_2. **Figure 16.4** shows that the output level where profits are maximized falls from 1,200 gallons per week to 1,050 gallons per week. If, instead, production costs fell for some reason from MC_1 to MC_3, then the converse would be true. The profit-maximizing level of output would increase from 1,200 gallons per week to 1,300 gallons per week.

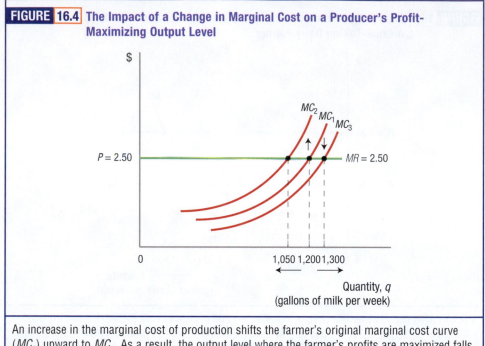

FIGURE 16.4 The Impact of a Change in Marginal Cost on a Producer's Profit-Maximizing Output Level

An increase in the marginal cost of production shifts the farmer's original marginal cost curve (MC_1) upward to MC_2. As a result, the output level where the farmer's profits are maximized falls from 1,200 gallons per week to 1,050 gallons per week. If, instead, the marginal cost of production fell from MC_1 to MC_3, then the converse would hold. The profit-maximizing level of output would increase from 1,200 gallons to 1,300 gallons per week.

16.4 Profit Maximization in the Short Run

We know from the previous chapter that a firm's costs of production will usually differ in the short run versus the long run. In the short run, many firms are stuck with their current production process—that is, the size of their plants, their computer systems, and so on. In the long run, however, firms can change their production process by building more plants, upgrading their technology, and so forth to lower their costs.

Consider the short-run profit-maximizing decision facing Cuppola, a small firm that sells bags of gourmet coffee in a competitive market. Operating in the short run, the company's production is constrained by its current space. Cuppola's cost structure—its short-run marginal cost curve (*MC*) and short-run average total cost curve (*ATC*) for each pound of coffee produced—is shown in **Figure 16.5**. The market price of coffee, $9 per pound, is also shown. Given its marginal cost of production and the price of coffee, Cuppola will produce and sell 110 pounds of coffee per day to maximize its profits. The 110th pound will be produced at a short-run marginal cost of $9, which is just equal to the going market price. Now the question is, how much profit will Cuppola earn each day?

In the previous chapter, we defined the *average* total cost per unit (in this case, pound of coffee) as total cost divided by the number of units (pounds) produced. If we know Cuppola's average total cost of producing 110 pounds of coffee and the revenue it gets from each pound, we can calculate Cuppola's *average profit* per pound. Based on the information in Figure 16.5, this equals the price per pound ($9) minus the average total cost per pound of the 110 pounds of coffee produced ($6). So the

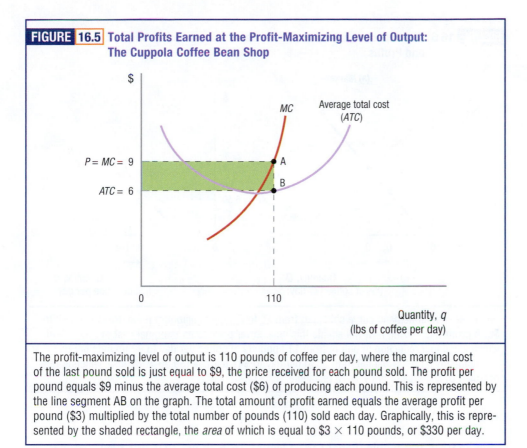

**FIGURE 16.5 Total Profits Earned at the Profit-Maximizing Level of Output:
The Cuppola Coffee Bean Shop**

The profit-maximizing level of output is 110 pounds of coffee per day, where the marginal cost
of the last pound sold is just equal to $9, the price received for each pound sold. The profit per
pound equals $9 minus the average total cost ($6) of producing each pound. This is represented by
the line segment AB on the graph. The total amount of profit earned equals the average profit per
pound ($3) multiplied by the total number of pounds (110) sold each day. Graphically, this is repre-
sented by the shaded rectangle, the *area* of which is equal to $3 × 110 pounds, or $330 per day.

average profit earned for each pound sold, which is sometimes referred to in the
business world as the company's "profit margin," is $3. The company's total profit,
then, is its average profit per pound multiplied by the total number of pounds sold:
$3 × 110, or $330 per day.

How can we show this in Figure 16.5? If we draw a horizontal line at $P = \$9$, it
will intersect the MC curve at 110 pounds, which is the profit-maximizing output.
Now, drop a line from this point of intersection (labeled A) to the ATC curve (labeled
B). At B, the average total cost of production is $6. The line segment AB represents
the average profit per pound ($9 − $6) earned by Cuppola. We know this must be
positive because at 110 pounds, the price per pound ($9) is higher than the average
total cost ($6) of production.

Now that we have shown graphically the average profit earned on each pound
of coffee, we can proceed to show graphically Cuppola's *total profits*. We do this by
drawing a horizontal line from point B ($6) on the ATC curve back to the vertical
price axis. The result is a rectangle, the height of which represents the per unit profit
($3), and the length of which represents the number of units produced (110 pounds).
From this information, we can calculate the *area* of this rectangle (which equals
its height multiplied by its length). This represents the total profit that Cuppola
earns: $3 × 110 = $330 per day.

What would happen to this firm's profit-maximizing output level and profitability if a health report came out that linked coffee drinking to higher rates of stomach
cancer? To answer this question, let's first consider the impact of this news on the

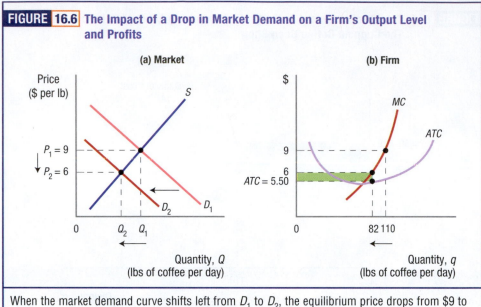

FIGURE 16.6 The Impact of a Drop in Market Demand on a Firm's Output Level and Profits

When the market demand curve shifts left from D_1 to D_2, the equilibrium price drops from $9 to $6. A profit-maximizing firm will equate this new, lower price to its marginal cost of production, which leads to a reduction in output from 110 pounds of coffee per day to 82 pounds per day. The company's profits will fall from $330 per day to $41 per day ($0.50 × 82 lbs), which is represented by the area of the shaded rectangle.

coffee market as a whole. Panel (a) of **Figure 16.6** shows that this news reduces demand for coffee in the market: the market demand curve shifts left, from D_1 to D_2. This eventually results in a drop in the equilibrium price of coffee from $9 to $6 a pound.

This decline in price has a direct impact on Cuppola's scale of operations. As panel (b) of Figure 16.6 demonstrates, the company's profit-maximizing output would fall from 110 pounds to 82 pounds a day in response to the lower price. Here, Cuppola's short-run marginal cost of producing the last (82nd) pound just equals $6, the new market price. While reducing its output to 82 pounds a day is the best way to protect its profitability in the face of a drop in market price, Cuppola's total profits will still fall. How do we know this? Following the company's reduction in output, we obtain a new profit rectangle—the shaded area—that reflects the firm's new, lower total profits after the health report appears. The new average total cost for each of the 82 pounds produced is $5.50 per pound. Figure 16.6b shows that the average profit per pound of coffee falls from $3 to $0.50 ($6 − $5.50), which means that total profits each day fall from $330 to $41 ($0.50 × 82). There is no other output level that will produce more profits in the face of the lower market price and Cuppola's short-run cost structure.

The bottom line is that when the demand for a product falls, firms in that market will suffer a decline in total profits, at least in the short run. All they can do to mitigate the impact of the drop in price is to cut back on their output to the point where the new, lower market price just covers the marginal cost of the last unit produced. Note also that this decline in output will translate into lower demand for variable inputs used in production, such as labor. This, in turn, means that some employees will be laid off or have their hours cut back.

The Shutdown Decision

What if the health report continues to place downward pressure on the demand for coffee, and its price drops to $5 a pound? Given its short-run costs of production, Cuppola will reduce its output to maximize its profits in the face of this lower price. **Figure 16.7** indicates that the optimal output will now be 43 pounds per day. This is the point—represented by point A—where the marginal cost of the last (43rd) pound produced just equals $5. Just as Cuppola's profit-maximizing level of output has changed, so has its profitability. In Figure 16.7, you can see that the average total cost of producing 43 pounds is $5. This means that the firm's per unit profit—price minus average total cost—is exactly equal to zero; no economic profits are now earned.

What should Cuppola's owner do? Maybe you think this owner should leave the business because it is not making any economic profit. However, take a closer look: the firm is covering all of its economic (opportunity) costs at $5 a pound. This means that the next-best opportunity to which each of the firm's inputs could be put—including the talents of the owner/entrepreneur—would generate a return no greater than the return earned in the current gourmet-coffee venture. So it makes no sense to leave the market when the market price is covering all of the opportunity costs of production.

But what happens if the price of coffee falls below $5, say to $4? In this situation, which is illustrated in **Figure 16.8**, the market price ($4 per pound) intersects the marginal cost curve at an output level equal to 28 pounds per day. At this output level, the average total cost of producing the 28 pounds of coffee is $5.50 per pound. Because this is greater than the price that each pound commands in the market, there

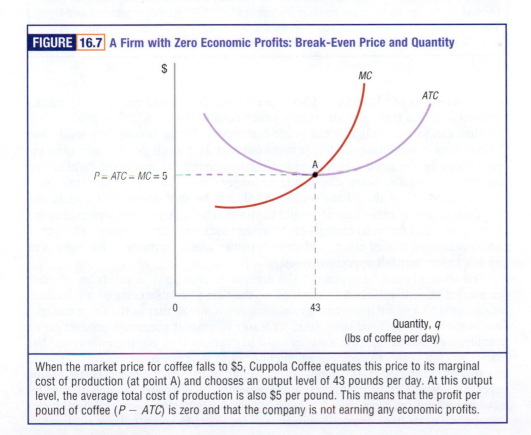

FIGURE 16.7 A Firm with Zero Economic Profits: Break-Even Price and Quantity

$P = ATC = MC = 5$

MC

ATC

A

0   43

Quantity, q
(lbs of coffee per day)

When the market price for coffee falls to $5, Cuppola Coffee equates this price to its marginal cost of production (at point A) and chooses an output level of 43 pounds per day. At this output level, the average total cost of production is also $5 per pound. This means that the profit per pound of coffee ($P - ATC$) is zero and that the company is not earning any economic profits.

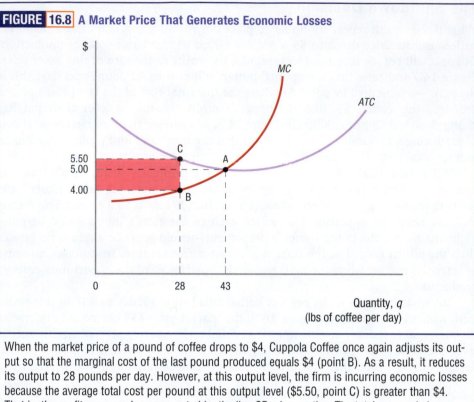

FIGURE 16.8 **A Market Price That Generates Economic Losses**

When the market price of a pound of coffee drops to $4, Cuppola Coffee once again adjusts its output so that the marginal cost of the last pound produced equals $4 (point B). As a result, it reduces its output to 28 pounds per day. However, at this output level, the firm is incurring economic losses because the average total cost per pound at this output level ($5.50, point C) is greater than $4. That is, the profit per pound—represented by the line CB—is negative. The total economic loss is −$42 per day (−$1.50 × 28 pounds). This corresponds to the area of the shaded rectangle.

is an average loss of $1.50($4 − $5.50) per pound. The shaded rectangle represents the total daily *loss* that Cuppola suffers, which equals −$42(−$1.50 × 28).

How can we reconcile that the profit-maximizing output is now 28 pounds, but the company is still losing money? It turns out that 28 pounds per day *minimizes the losses* borne by the firm, which is equivalent to maximizing its profits (which just happen to be negative here). Cuppola is no longer covering all of its economic costs of production. What should the owner do? Should he shut down the business immediately to avoid further losses? Should the inputs that Cuppola uses—including the owner's time and financial capital—be "released" back into the economy so that they can be redirected toward other productive activities where consumers' willingness to pay will cover their full opportunity cost?

The answer is that "it depends." The decision to shut down depends on whether the market price is sufficient to cover all of the firm's variable costs of production, which could be avoided altogether by shutting down. Recall that in the short run, the firm is stuck with its fixed costs (e.g., its lease) whether it continues production or not. Open or closed, Cuppola's owner must pay certain bills. So, the only costs that matter when it comes to deciding whether or not to shut down are the variable costs incurred by staying open. If Cuppola can cover all of its variable costs (coffee beans, paper cups, wages, trash pickup, etc.) and generate a few dollars to apply toward its lease and other fixed costs, then it is better off staying in business—at least until it can "escape" all of its fixed financial obligations—for example, until its lease runs out.

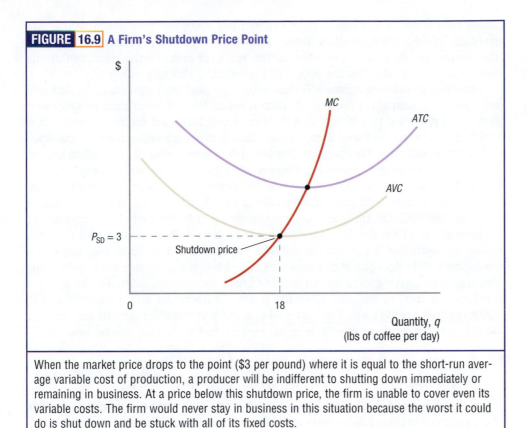

FIGURE 16.9 **A Firm's Shutdown Price Point**

When the market price drops to the point ($3 per pound) where it is equal to the short-run average variable cost of production, a producer will be indifferent to shutting down immediately or remaining in business. At a price below this shutdown price, the firm is unable to cover even its variable costs. The firm would never stay in business in this situation because the worst it could do is shut down and be stuck with all of its fixed costs.

Figure 16.9 shows the market price—$3—at which Cuppola's owner would be *indifferent* to operating in the short run or immediately shutting down. If it stays in business in the short run, Cuppola will produce 18 pounds of coffee per day. At this price—called the **shutdown price**—all of the firm's variable costs are being covered, but there is not even one dollar left that can be used to pay down any of the fixed costs.

> **SHUTDOWN PRICE** The market price that just covers a firm's variable costs of production. Below this price, a firm will minimize its losses by immediately halting production.

> **EXAMPLE** A fashion designer averages $340,000 in variable costs—the cost of materials, wages, and so on—to create each new dress line that she sells to the merchandisers that produce Tommy Hilfiger and La Coste clothing. In addition, she must pay $770,000 per year to lease production space and $4,600 to be a member of the Fashion Designers' Guild. If the designer receives less than $340,000 for each dress line, she will shut down business immediately. This is her shutdown price. At this price, the designer will just cover all of her variable costs but none of her fixed costs.

If the market price of coffee drops below Cuppola's $3 shutdown price, the company is better off shutting down immediately, because at this price it would no longer be able to cover all of its variable costs, let alone any of its fixed costs. By shutting down immediately, Cuppola avoids the losses arising from its variable costs that it cannot fully cover. It will still have to pay its fixed costs, but this would be the case regardless of whether Cuppola's output level is zero or some positive amount. In other words, the *maximum* losses that a firm will ever incur in the short run are its fixed costs, as long as it has the option of immediately shutting down.

However, sometimes a firm will choose to "ride out" an unprofitable period and keep operating, even when the price its output would fetch is lower than its shutdown price. Firms do this if they believe that their economic losses are temporary and that it would cost more to close and then reopen when prices once again rise. For example, road construction often has a negative impact on consumer demand for retailers located on or just off the existing roadway. However, after the construction is completed, the new road may actually favor these businesses by bringing more shoppers to the location. Retailers might make a different decision about shutting down in this instance versus one where the road construction will permanently divert traffic away from their stores.

Even when a firm decides that shutting down is in its best interest, this does not necessarily mean that it will exit the industry. For example, a producer may move to a new location if, by doing so, it can reduce costs and become profitable once again. This, of course, is the driving force for outsourcing production overseas. Or, a seller may opt to reduce her costs by shutting down her storefront operation and exclusively selling online through her Web site. Only after all of these cost-reducing options are explored will the supplier decide whether it is in her best interest to exit the market entirely.

16.5 The Short-Run Supply Curve of a Price-Taking Firm and the Market

As you have learned, the output level of a price-taking, profit-maximizing firm is where the market price it faces just equals the marginal cost of the last unit produced, *as long as this price is not lower than the firm's shutdown price.* At prices above the shutdown price, the firm will move up its marginal cost curve in response to increases in price, increasing its output level to the point where price always equals marginal cost. In effect, this portion of the firm's marginal cost curve reflects its supply response to changes in market price. In other words, it is the firm's individual supply curve.

Consider the supply curves of two gourmet-coffee companies—Cuppola and New Age Coffee—as shown in **Figure 16.10**. Suppose that these firms are the only two producers in the gourmet-coffee market. Assume further that they face different marginal costs of production, which lead to different short-run *MC* curves. Because of this, their short-run supply curves and shutdown prices will be different.

Nevertheless, Figure 16.10 shows that we can still *horizontally sum* the short-run supply curves of these two producers to derive a short-run supply curve for the entire market. This is exactly the same way we first derived a market supply curve from producers' individual supply curves in Chapter 7. What we didn't know then—but do now—is the range of prices over which each producer is willing to supply output to the market (at and above its shutdown price), exactly why the short-run supply curve of each firm must be upward sloping (diminishing marginal returns cause the short-run *MC* curve to slope upward), and why the short-run market supply curve must also slope upward (it is the horizontal sum of upward-sloping short-run *MC* curves).

Because the short-run market supply curve is simply the horizontal sum of each firm's marginal cost curve, any change in the economic environment that shifts these marginal cost curves will also shift the market supply curve in the same direction. For example, we discussed in Chapter 15 how an increase in the price of a variable input such as hay or feed would result in an upward shift in the *MC* curve for dairy farmers. This would lead to a corresponding shift left (up) in the short-run market

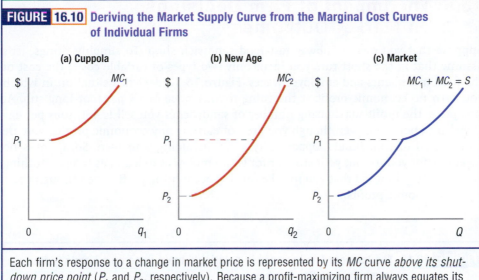

FIGURE 16.10 Deriving the Market Supply Curve from the Marginal Cost Curves of Individual Firms

Each firm's response to a change in market price is represented by its *MC* curve *above its shut-down price point* (P_1 and P_2, respectively). Because a profit-maximizing firm always equates its marginal cost of production to the market price, this segment of the *MC* curve tells us how its supply of output will vary with the market price. We can horizontally sum these individual supply curves to derive the market supply curve: at each and every price above each firm's shutdown price, we add together the quantity that each is willing to supply. Because Cuppola's shutdown price is P_1, it will not contribute to the market supply curve if the price drops below this level. New Age will supply coffee to the market until the market price drops below P_2.

supply curve for milk: less will be supplied at any given price. Similarly, an increase in the price of gasoline would cause the short-run MC curves of FedEx, UPS, and other competitors in the overnight-delivery market to shift upward. Consequently, the short-run market supply curve will shift left (up) as well. This result is depicted in **Figure 16.11**.

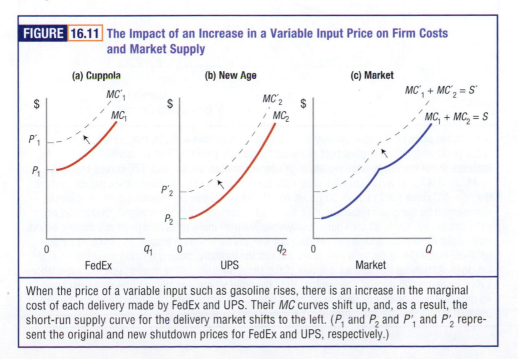

FIGURE 16.11 The Impact of an Increase in a Variable Input Price on Firm Costs and Market Supply

When the price of a variable input such as gasoline rises, there is an increase in the marginal cost of each delivery made by FedEx and UPS. Their *MC* curves shift up, and, as a result, the short-run supply curve for the delivery market shifts to the left. (P_1 and P_2 and P'_1 and P'_2 represent the original and new shutdown prices for FedEx and UPS, respectively.)

16.6 The Impact of Firm Decisions on Market Outcomes

Suppose that you own a Subway fast-food sandwich shop. To simplify things, let's assume that in the short run, you incur only two types of variable costs: the cost of the food ingredients and employee wages. **Figure 16.12** depicts a situation in which you earn no economic profit at the going market price of $5 per foot-long sub. At this price, the profit-maximizing number of sandwiches you sell is 480 subs per day (labeled as point A). Even though you are not earning any economic profits, you are covering all of your inputs' opportunity costs, including your own. So, there is no incentive for you to shut your store or for your employees to leave, as long as nothing changes. Keep in mind that you may be earning accounting profits even though there are no economic profits.

FIGURE 16.12 The Impact of an Increase in a Variable Input Price on a Firm's Output Level: Subway Sandwiches

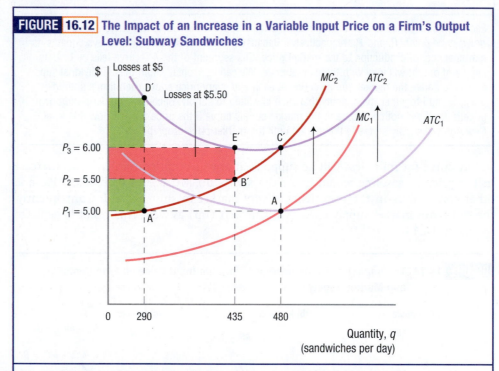

At a market price of $5, your Subway sandwich shop produces 480 sandwiches per day. This is the point where the marginal cost of the last sandwich produced just equals $5 (point A). An increase in the minimum wage results in an upward shift in the MC and ATC curves from MC_1 to MC_2 and ATC_1 to ATC_2. So, your shop cuts back its supply to 290 sandwiches per day, where the new MC curve (MC_2) equals $5 (point A'). At this point, you are incurring economic losses represented by the green rectangle. If all sandwich shops cut back their output, the market price will start to rise, say to $5.50. Your Subway shop will then move to its new profit-maximizing output level (point B') of 435 sandwiches per day, but will still be incurring losses, as indicated by the light-red rectangle. In the long run, firms will exit the industry, putting upward pressure on market price. Assuming that you are not one of the shops that leaves the market, you will experience a rise in the market price of sandwiches, until the point where you are just breaking even again. As depicted here, this price rises to $6 per sandwich, in which case, you operate at break-even point C', where you are again producing 480 sandwiches per day.

Responding to an Increase in the Price of a Variable Input

Typically, fast-food employers such as Subway owners hire minimum-wage workers. What if the federal government passes legislation that increases the minimum wage? How will this affect you and other fast-food providers? What about the fast-food market as a whole?

We see in Figure 16.12 that your original marginal cost (MC_1) curve and average total cost (ATC_1) curve rise to MC_2 and ATC_2 because these costs depend on the price of minimum-wage labor, one of your two variable inputs. In the short run, you can't substitute machines (a fixed input) for employees to offset this wage increase. At the going market price of $5 per sandwich, you will cut back your production to the point where the new marginal cost of producing the last sandwich is $5 (point A'). This occurs at a lower level of output—290 sandwiches per day. Perhaps you will do this by closing earlier in the evening or opening later in the day.

Figure 16.12 shows that you are now incurring losses as a result of the increase in minimum wage: the average loss per sandwich equals the new average cost of producing 290 sandwiches (point D') minus the price received for each sandwich, which is $5. (This is represented on the graph by the dotted line D'A'.) This makes sense because the market price hasn't changed, and you were just covering all of your costs before the wage increase. By cutting back on your output, the best you can do in the short run is minimize your losses.

We would expect other fast-food owners to also cut back on their output for the very same reason. How will these changes affect the market as a whole? We know that the total number of meals supplied at the market price of $5 falls due to the increase in minimum wage. Because each company's MC curve rises, the short-run market supply curve must shift to the left.

Suppose that this results in a new market price of $5.50. You and other fast-food providers will once again adjust your output levels, expanding to the point where the new marginal cost of the last meal sold just equals $5.50 (point B'). You will now produce and sell 435 sandwiches per day, assuming that $5.50 is above your *new* shutdown price. Typically, firms like yours will still be losing money (the average per unit loss equals the dotted line E'B'), but not as much as when the market price was $5 per sandwich. The price still hasn't gone up enough to cover the entire increase in average total cost resulting from the increase in the minimum wage. This is likely to be the case when consumers are price sensitive and readily substitute other types of fast food for sandwiches when sandwich prices begin to increase. (In other words, the demand curve for sandwiches is relatively flat.)

In the long run, you have more ways to deal with an increase in the minimum wage. One option is to purchase machines to replace at least some of your minimum wage employees. In fact, this is exactly what the fast-food industry has done over the past several decades as the minimum wage has risen. Many firms now use self-serve soda machines and computers to transmit customers' orders straight to the kitchen, thereby reducing the need for wait staff and counter workers.[10] If you and other fast-food shop owners can at least partially offset higher labor costs by integrating labor-saving technologies in the long run, then your marginal and average total cost curves will fall and the market supply curve will move back to the right, offsetting some, or all, of the impact of the increase in minimum wage. One result we can be sure of: in the long run, fewer minimum-wage workers will be employed in the

· · · · · · ·

[10]"Food Automation—Technology Can Help Kitchens Run Smoothly." *Franchise Times*, May 2007.

fast-food industry, just as we predicted in our earlier discussion of the minimum wage in Chapter 8.

If none of these long-run, cost-reducing strategies enable fast-food businesses such as yours to break even, companies will begin to exit the industry. Assuming that the market price is above the shutdown price, the timing of these shutdowns will depend on when individual firms can "escape" from their fixed costs. Because firms enter the market at different times, it should come as no surprise that they will leave at different times, even if they share the same cost structure. In response to the 2007 Great Recession, for example, hard-hit day spas with leases expiring in 2008 were more likely to exit the market than those with leases expiring in 2011. Some spas with earlier lease expiration dates remained in business because they were able to negotiate lower lease renewal rates early in the recession, thereby allowing them to once again break even.

Figure 16.13 illustrates what happens in the market when businesses exit: there will be a leftward shift in the short-run market supply curve because there are fewer suppliers and, therefore, fewer individual short-run supply curves to sum over. Exiting will continue until the market price of a sandwich increases to the point where the remaining suppliers can once again just break even and cover their total costs of production. As shown in Figure 16.12, the break-even price is $6 per sandwich. At this price, you will once again supply 480 sandwiches per day. Note that total market output is less than before the increase in minimum wage because firms have left, and there will be, a lower level of employment in the industry. At the break-even price of $6, there is no further incentive for firms to exit the market or adjust their output levels. At this point a **long-run market equilibrium** has been achieved.

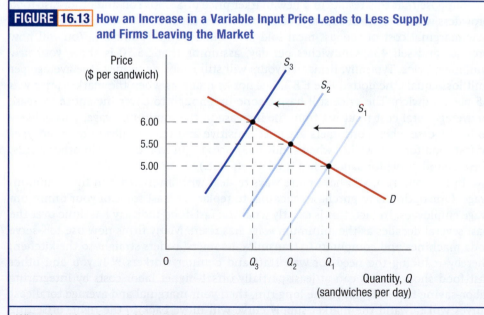

FIGURE 16.13 **How an Increase in a Variable Input Price Leads to Less Supply and Firms Leaving the Market**

When the price of a variable input rises, the short-run supply curve in the market shifts to the left, from S_1 to S_2. If existing firms are incurring economic losses at the new price of $5.50, some will begin to leave the market. The short-run supply curve in the market will again shift to the left, from S_2 to S_3, until the new equilibrium price of $6 is established. At this price, there will be no further exiting from the industry.

LONG-RUN MARKET EQUILIBRIUM A situation in which there is no incentive for firms to exit (or enter) a market or for existing firms to adjust their output levels.

Some companies can take advantage of another option when their variable costs rise: in the long run, they can relocate their production facilities to another country. When it comes to increases in the minimum wage, relocating outside of the United States reduces labor costs—foreign workers are not covered by the same minimum-wage laws in place at home. We would predict the same type of response when new workplace regulations related to worker safety or employee benefits are imposed that significantly increase the cost of labor. The pressure to outsource production increases anytime the government of a "home" country adopts new rules that impose substantial costs on businesses which can be avoided by relocating production facilities. These include environmental regulations that require manufacturing plants to dispose of their waste by-products in more costly ways than simply dumping them into the neighboring river. Just as you probably "shop" for the lowest prices you can find, firms will shop for the lowest input prices available, even if it means having to pull up stakes and, in the long run, relocate to another country.

Responding to a Reduction in the Price of a Variable Input

A similar analysis can be done to predict the impact of a *decrease* in the price of a variable input on short-run firm output levels, profits, market supply and market price, and, in the long run, firm entry into the market and equilibrium market price and quantity.

If, for example, the cost of food ingredients falls—perhaps due to better than average weather patterns and crop yields—then the cost of producing sandwiches would likewise fall. Suppose that these cost-savings translate into a dollar of savings for each sandwich produced and sold. Then the marginal cost curve would fall by $1 (along with a $1 fall in the average variable and total cost curves), and the profit-maximizing level of output would now be higher than before. If you were just breaking even before the cost reduction, you will now earn economic profits at the same market price as before. This makes sense because the cost of producing each sandwich has fallen by $1, while the price at which they are sold ($5) has not.

Assuming that all of the fast-food producers in the market enjoy a similar reduction in marginal costs, there will be a rightward shift in the short-run market supply curve, from S_1 to S_2 as illustrated in **Figure 16.14**. At each and every market price, you and your competitors have an incentive to supply more output to maximize the economic profits resulting from your lower costs of production.

However, as Figure 16.14 indicates, this increase in supply will lead to a fall in the market price of sandwiches, say to $4.50. You and your competitors will respond by reducing your output to the point where your new marginal cost for the last sandwich produced is just equal to $4.50 (not $5, like before). Still, your output level is higher than before the reduction in the cost of food ingredients and the fall in market price: this is represented by the expansion in market output from Q_1 to Q_2. And, economic profits are still earned because the price has not fallen by the full amount that average total cost has fallen ($1).

What happens in the long run? New entrepreneurs, attracted by these economic profits, will eventually enter the fast-food sandwich industry. Because the number of companies contributing to the short-run market supply curve increases, the market supply curve shifts to the right, from S_2 to S_3. The market price falls, and the equilibrium quantity increases from Q_2 to Q_3. Entry will only cease when the last firm that enters the

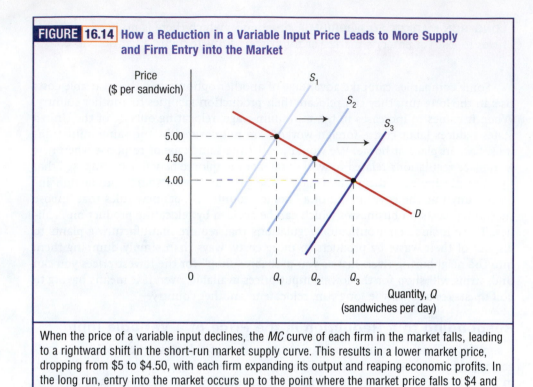

FIGURE 16.14 **How a Reduction in a Variable Input Price Leads to More Supply and Firm Entry into the Market**

When the price of a variable input declines, the *MC* curve of each firm in the market falls, leading to a rightward shift in the short-run market supply curve. This results in a lower market price, dropping from $5 to $4.50, with each firm expanding its output and reaping economic profits. In the long run, entry into the market occurs up to the point where the market price falls to $4 and all existing firms (original and new) are just breaking even once again.

market earns zero economic profits. This will be where all of the cost savings have been passed on to consumers—that is, where the market price has dropped to $4 per sandwich.

To summarize, in response to an *increase* in the price of a variable input (e.g., wage rates), an *existing* firm will do the following:

- Reduce its output to the point where its new, higher short-run marginal cost (MC_2) curve equals the market price *or* shut down if the market price does not cover the new (higher) average variable costs of production. (Recall from our earlier discussion that the decision to shut down depends on whether the market price is sufficient to cover all of the firm's variable costs of production—costs which could be avoided altogether by shutting down.)

- Assuming it hasn't already shut down, increase its output when the market price rises due to the initial cutbacks in quantity supplied by existing firms.

- In the long run, (1) exit the industry; (2) reduce costs by adjusting the level of its fixed inputs; or (3) adjust its output level to the point where its MC_2 curve equals the higher, break-even market price that results when other companies exit the market.

In response to a *reduction* in the price of a variable input (e.g., food ingredients), an *existing* firm will do the following:

- Increase its output to the point where the new (lower) marginal cost of the last unit produced is just equal to the market price.

- Subsequently cut back somewhat on this expansion in output as the market price falls due to the increase in market output.

■ In the long run, reduce its output to the point where the new (lower) marginal cost of the last unit produced equals the lower market price that results from new companies entering the market.

SOLVED PROBLEM

Q Suppose that the value of the U.S. dollar increases substantially relative to the euro. Recall that this means that 1 dollar can purchase more European goods, and that 1 euro can buy fewer U.S. goods.

(a) Using two graphs—one graph for a U.S. industry and another graph for an existing U.S. firm in that industry—show the short-run impact this stronger dollar will have on the industry and the firm if they import goods from Europe, such as ceramic tiles or upscale foreign cars (Mercedes and BMWs). Now show what happens to each (the industry and the firm) in the long run.

(b) Next, show what happens in the short run again using two graphs—one graph for the U.S. market and another graph for the U.S. industry—if they sell a great deal of their output, such as chemicals and agricultural products, to the European market. Now show what happens to each (the industry and the firm) in the long run under this scenario.

A

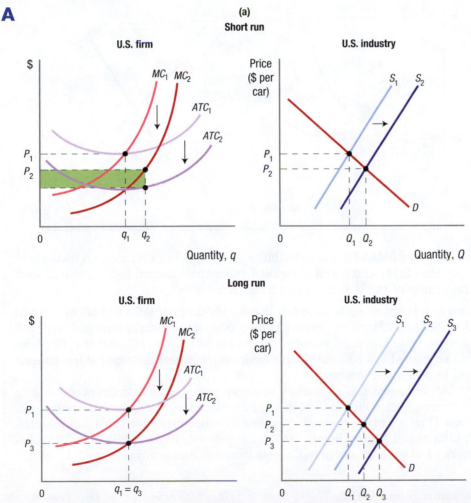

(a)
Short run

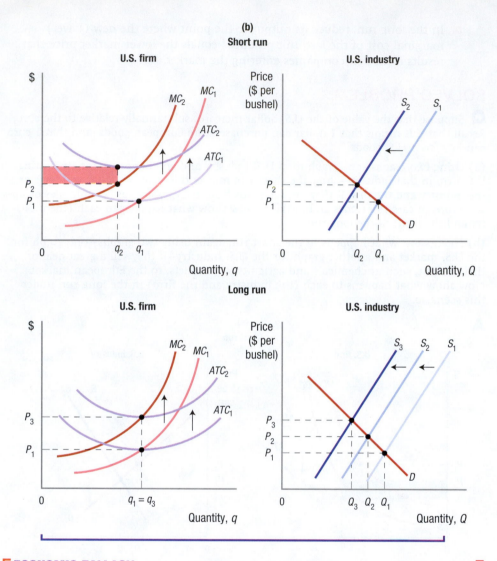

(b)
Short run

U.S. firm

U.S. industry

Long run

U.S. firm

U.S. industry

ECONOMIC FALLACY   The availability of cheap labor overseas, an increase in American labor costs, and the global movement toward free trade will spell the demise of the U.S. manufacturing sector.

False. It is important to recognize that a wide-range of skills and talents exist in the labor force. Firms that manufacture goods using primarily unskilled labor will likely move to low-wage locations around the world. This assumes that the firms can be assured of a politically stable environment where their capital investments will be adequately protected.

At the same time, a subset of American manufacturers has concentrated on producing high-value products that require skilled, educated workers. In fact, the United States remains the world's leading manufacturer by *value of goods produced*. It hit a record $1.6 trillion in 2007—nearly double its $811 billion in 1987. For every $1 of value produced in Chinese factories, Americans generate $2.50.[11]

· · · · · · ·

[11]Stephen Manning, "Does the United States Make Anything Anymore?" *St. Louis Post-Dispatch*, February 16, 2009.

In other words, U.S. manufacturing is increasingly reliant upon skilled employees at the expense of unskilled (and often unionized) workers. Also, the introduction of high-tech manufacturing processes into U.S. manufacturing has led to an enormous expansion in output even as the overall level of employment in manufacturing industries has fallen.

The Impact New Technology (Knowledge) Has on Firms and Markets

As you have learned, when the price of an input falls, new firms are tempted to enter the market in the long run. The same thing happens when cost-saving technologies are introduced.

Consider the retail banking industry in the 1960s. Virtually every bank was a "full-service" operation at that time. In addition to providing customer banking services at teller windows inside the bank, bank employees would manually process checks prior to sending them to a central clearinghouse. Back in those days, all payroll and Social Security checks had to be presented at the bank so that they could be deposited into the appropriate accounts. And most savings accounts came with a "passbook" in which deposits and interest payments were logged manually on a monthly or quarterly basis.

Suppose that these banks were just breaking even—no economic profits were being earned. As a result, there was no incentive for existing banks to exit the industry or change their level of output in terms of the number of accounts they serviced. Also, there were no economic profits to attract new banks into the market.

Fast-forward to a banking world that has been revolutionized by technological changes. ATMs permit deposits and withdrawals at any time of the day or night; paychecks and Social Security checks are automatically (electronically) deposited to the appropriate accounts; savings account statements are electronically generated and updated with the latest deposit and interest payments; checks are scanned, sorted, and processed electronically; and account holders can pay bills by electronically transferring money via the Internet. All of these technological innovations have led to a reduction in the number of employees that banks require for their daily operations, thereby reducing the variable costs of providing retail banking services to customers. What effect do you think this has had on individual banks and the retail banking industry as a whole?

Because these cost-saving technologies have led to a substantial downward shift in the marginal cost, average variable cost, and average total cost curves for retail banking services, existing banks have increased the number of accounts and transactions handled (just like when the price of a variable input falls). This goes a long way toward explaining why retail banks have grown enormously in size over the past three decades: technological innovations have "favored" bigger banks not only because of the decline in the marginal cost of providing banking services but also because the cost of electronic systems can be spread over larger and larger numbers of accounts and transactions. (It also may explain the push by banks during the 1980s and 1990s to deregulate the industry to permit them to expand their business across state lines.)

As the supply curve for banking services shifts to the right, we would expect service fees or prices to fall. While economic profits fall with the decline in the price of banking services, they are likely to remain positive even after the banking services market achieves a new short-run equilibrium. At this point, there is no further incentive for *existing* banks to adjust the quantity of services they supply.

What about in the long run? The fact that existing banks are earning economic profits tells us that at least some of the resources used in the banking sector are enjoying a return that is greater than their opportunity cost (the return they would receive if put to their next-best use). In the long run, this higher return will attract new resources into the retail banking industry, as long as there are no costly regulatory barriers to entry. Owners of financial capital will invest in new banks. Some of the newest bank owners have exploited recent technological innovations to create online only, branchless banks, where the only human contact comes through call centers.

As these new banks enter, the market supply curve shifts further to the right; this entry will continue until price drops to the point where the very last bank that enters earns zero economic profits. At this new market price, all of the banks—new entrants and older banks—will earn zero economic profit, as long as they share the same cost conditions. After this new equilibrium is achieved, all of the resources employed in the retail banking market will once again be paid exactly their opportunity cost.

The Role Economic Profits Play

The retail banking example suggests that economic profits play a crucial role in competitive markets: they signal to owners of resources *outside* the market that if they enter, the going price will cover their opportunity costs and then some. In other words, it makes sense for these additional resources to be attracted into the market and away from their next-best use. This very process tends to dissipate economic profits in the long run. But remember that this adjustment does not take place overnight. In some situations, such as in the case of outdoor refreshment stands, the adjustment process may take only a few weeks. However, for other industries, particularly those that have high start-up and overhead costs, the long run may take years to achieve.

There are instances, however, in which firms will continue to earn economic profits, even in the long run. This can happen if these firms have lower cost structures than new entrants. Perhaps some producers benefit from cost-saving technologies that new entrants don't have. Or, maybe the existing firms have developed international reputations, so they are able to spend less money marketing their products. Whatever the reason, the market price that is established when the last entrant earns zero economic profit will still generate long-run profits for lower-cost producers. **Figure 16.15** illustrates this situation. Here, the long-run competitive market price (P_e) leaves the last entrant in a zero economic profit position, as shown in panel (a). However, panel (b) shows that at this price, some of the previously existing firms still earn economic profits because they have lower average total costs of production. Their profits are indicated by the shaded rectangle.

Nonmarket Responses to Business Losses

Our discussion has focused thus far on how profit-maximizing companies respond to changes in their economic environment that leave them with short-run profits or losses. In reality, many companies that suffer losses—especially those that are large and have unionized workforces—will not exit the market quietly. Instead, they will seek legal and political remedies to mitigate their losses so that they can stay in business in the long run.

For example, companies that are "bleeding red ink" may do the following:

- Seek court protection under federal bankruptcy laws to renegotiate contracts with input suppliers and thereby lower their fixed or variable costs.

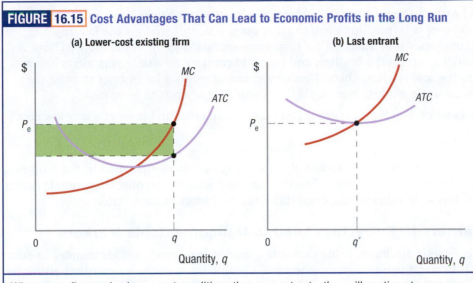

FIGURE 16.15 Cost Advantages That Can Lead to Economic Profits in the Long Run

When some firms enjoy lower cost conditions than new entrants, they will continue to earn economic profits, even in the long run. At the equilibrium market price, P_e, the last entrant is earning zero profits as panel (a) shows. Meanwhile, some of the previously existing firms—those with lower marginal and average total costs like the ones shown in panel (b)—are still earning economic profits, as indicated by the area of the shaded rectangle.

- Lobby for legislation or regulations that either increase the market price they receive for their output or reduce what they have to pay for their inputs.

- Lobby for favorable tax treatment, government subsidies, bailouts, and so on in an effort to shift some of their production costs to taxpayers or other producers.

In 2008 and 2009, the U.S. government heavily subsidized American companies bleeding billions of dollars in red ink due to the 2007 Great Recession. The biggest industry winners were companies in the investment-banking industry[12] and the automobile-manufacturing industry,[13] which were deemed to be "too big to fail." In fact, the government took ownership shares in many of the companies it helped, thereby transforming what were once private, for-profit firms into quasi-public companies. This, in turn, has led to government involvement in the setting of corporate salaries and bonus plans. Only time will tell whether these bailouts will be successful in reinvigorating companies so that they can return to their private, for-profit status.

16.7 Competition in the Long Run

In competitive markets, we tend to see firms entering and exiting over time. If the cost of doing so is relatively low, we call these markets **contestable**.

CONTESTABLE MARKET A market that, in the long run, a firm can enter or leave from at low cost.

· · · · · · · ·

[12]Stephen Labaton, "Obama Urged to Move Swiftly to Rescue Banks." *New York Times,* January 17, 2009.

[13]Stephen Labaton and David Herszenhorn, "White House Ready to Aid Auto Industry." *New York Times,* December 12, 2008.

EXAMPLE David, a college student, purchases pizzas before his dorm curfew and profits by reselling them to other dorm residents who get the late-night munchies. All of a sudden his roommate—attracted by all of the money David is making—enters the business and begins to compete by also buying pizzas before curfew and reselling them. Neither roommate incurs a lot of costs to enter the pizza-resale market. Nor would they incur a lot of costs to leave it.

EXAMPLE Vendors at outdoor flea markets can enter and leave at a very low cost.

For competitive markets to allocate scarce resources efficiently in the long run, they depend on the ability of firms to enter and leave in response to economic profits and losses. In other words, competitive markets must be contestable.

Barriers to Entry That Lead to Noncontestable Markets

If economic profits are being earned in a market, new producers are tempted to enter it. However, there are instances when it is prohibitively costly or legally impossible for new competitors to enter a market, even when existing firms are earning enormous profits. In such a case, we say that these potential entrants face **barriers to entry**.

BARRIERS TO ENTRY Impediments that substantially increase the cost of potential competitors entering a market.

EXAMPLE State governments issue licenses that permit individuals to legally practice medicine, law, massage therapy, and so forth. The more burdensome the requirements for getting a license are—in terms of educational requirements, apprenticeships, exams, and so on—the higher the cost is of entering into a licensed profession. These costs serve as barriers to entry, which discourage people from entering professions with licensing requirements.

EXAMPLE Taxicabs in New York City are licensed by the city. The total number of licenses available has been fixed by the city for many years. Although these licenses can be freely bought and sold, there is no way for additional cabdrivers to legally enter the market.

Barriers to entry prevent economic profits from being competed away in the long run. And, because of these barriers, the average cost of production and the market price remain higher than they would otherwise be in a contestable market. In the long run, more scarce resources are being used to produce each unit of output than if there were no barriers to entry. Meanwhile, the equilibrium quantity supplied is too low from the perspective of consumers' willingness to pay.

To illustrate this, consider the impact of barriers to entry on the market for physicians. Doctors must obtain separate licenses for each state in which they want to practice medicine. To obtain a license, doctors must have had at least five years of medical school training after college and a passing grade on a national medical exam. States that are more "desirable" in terms of lifestyle—such as Florida and California—have even more stringent licensure requirements.

Let's say that the market for doctors' services in the United States is in equilibrium and that no economic profits are being earned. Now suppose Congress passes a law that guarantees every American access to medical care. This leads to a rightward shift in the demand curve for physician services, as illustrated in **Figure 16.16**. The

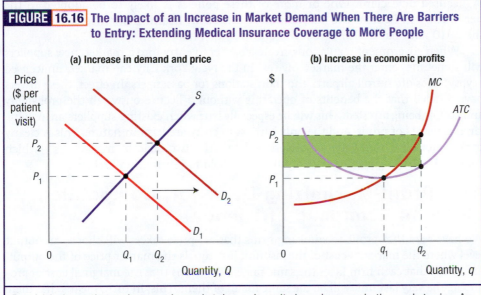

FIGURE 16.16 The Impact of an Increase in Market Demand When There Are Barriers to Entry: Extending Medical Insurance Coverage to More People

Panel (a) shows that an increase in market demand results in an increase in the market price. As a result, existing medical providers move up their MC curves and expand their output from q_1 to q_2 as shown in panel (b). This expansion accounts for the market's increase in output from Q_1 to Q_2. The existing practitioners are now making economic profits in the short run, as represented by the area of the shaded rectangle. If barriers to entry exist that can effectively block the entry of new practitioners into the medical-services market, then these profits will not be competed away, even in the long run.

result is an increase in market price and the quantity of services provided by existing medical practices. Doctors will now earn economic profits, which will attract new entrants—whether they are undergraduates thinking about going into medicine or foreign-trained doctors—into the market. However, the existing licensure requirements effectively prevent a great deal of entry, even in the long run. Depending on the rigidity of these barriers, none or only some of the short-run economic profits earned by physicians will be competed away in the long run.

This result is quite problematic for the federal government, which pays for over 50 percent of all physician services supplied in the United States through its publicly funded Medicare and Medicaid insurance programs. (Medicare covers people over 65; Medicaid covers the poor.) The increase in physician prices translates into large increases in the budgets of these programs, only to be compounded by the increase in the number of people now covered. While states have the ultimate right to establish physician-licensure requirements, the federal government can impose price ceilings on the amount it reimburses doctors through its insurance programs. These price ceilings would reduce the economic profits generated by the increase in demand for medical services. However, if these price caps are below the equilibrium price, we know that they will lead to excess demand, long waits for services, and, eventually, some type of rationing for the limited services that are made available.

To alleviate this situation, the federal government can fund the construction of new medical schools. Or, it can relax immigration restrictions for foreign-born and foreign-trained physicians, hoping that states will issue licenses to them after only a minimum amount of additional training. Another alternative is for Medicare and Medicaid to permit physician "extenders"—nurse practitioners, certified nurse anesthetists, and so on—to be reimbursed directly for services currently provided only by licensed physicians. One or more of these policies is likely to be adopted in the near future in light of the substantial expansion in health-insurance coverage that the 2010 national health-care law requires by 2014.[14]

When government regulations create a barrier to entry into a market, new suppliers will sometimes enter the market anyway. In the New York City cab market, unlicensed "gypsy" cabs often troll airports and train stations for passengers. In effect, these drivers have decided that the benefits of operating without a license outweigh the probability and cost of being arrested. This will be especially true when existing suppliers are reaping large amounts of profit, and the only barriers to entry are legal in nature. This is clearly the case for New York City taxi drivers: in late 2011, two taxicab "medallions"—which convey the legal right to operate a yellow cab—sold for $1 million each.[15]

16.8 Profit-Maximizing Behavior, Competition, and Economic Efficiency

We have seen that profit-maximizing firms that are price takers will choose an output level where the marginal cost of the last unit just equals the market price of the output. Assuming that each firm faces the same price, this means that the marginal cost of producing the very last unit will be the same for all of them. This, in turn, means that there is no way to reallocate production among existing firms to reduce the cost of the last unit supplied to the market. Therefore, the cost of producing the market's equilibrium quantity is minimized. Moreover, in the long run, all of the firms in a market operate at the minimum of their average total cost curves, earning zero economic profits. As a result, the average per unit cost of production is the same for all firms in the market, and there is no way to reduce the per unit (average) costs of production any further.

Recall, too, that the demand curve represents the willingness of consumers to pay for each and every unit of output. So when the market is in equilibrium, the willingness of buyers to pay for the very last unit purchased is just equal to its price, which in turn equals the marginal cost of producing this last unit. Economists call this an *efficient* market outcome. When there is **economic efficiency**, scarce resources are put to their highest-valued use, where "value" is determined by the willingness to pay for them. When resources are put to their highest-valued use, they can't be attracted away to alternative productive activities because the willingness to pay of consumers in these other markets is lower.

> **ECONOMIC EFFICIENCY** A situation in which scarce resources are put to their highest-valued use, where "value" is determined by the willingness to pay for them.

> **EXAMPLE** Suppose that a local bank is contemplating whether to loan money for a residential development or for a multiuse commercial center. The residential developer predicts he will earn a return of 6 percent on his project and is willing to offer the bank a 5 percent return on its money. The commercial center developer forecasts a 9 percent return on her project and offers the bank a 7 percent return on its investment. The bank will invest in the commercial project, where the willingness to pay for its investment dollars is greatest. This willingness to pay by the developer reflects the underlying willingness to pay of leaseholders in the center.

·······

[14]Robert Pear, "Shortage of Doctors an Obstacle to Obama Goals." *New York Times,* April 26, 2009.
[15]Michael Grynbaum, "Medallions to Run Cabs Hit $1 Million." *New York Times,* October 21, 2011.

As we have just seen, the willingness to pay of the party that gains access to a specific resource (e.g., investment dollars) outweighs the willingness to pay of the party that is denied access to this resource. This suggests that if resources were reallocated from their higher-valued use, someone will be made better off *and someone will be made worse off.* Why? Because the party with the lower willingness to pay is unwilling to adequately compensate the party with the higher willingness to pay to voluntarily forgo the scarce resource. In other words, reallocating resources from their economically efficient use means that those with a lower willingness to pay will benefit at the expense of those with a higher willingness to pay.

Consider the case of foreign clothing manufacturers who ship their products to the U.S. market and can sell them at a lower price than American producers because of their lower labor costs. As a result, American consumers will spend less for clothing and have more income left over to buy other goods that increase their well-being. By indirectly benefiting from lower-cost foreign labor, clothing purchasers are made better off without making other consumers worse off. Their increase in well-being does not come from redirecting scarce resources away from the production of goods and services that others are willing to pay more to consume.

What if American clothing manufacturers are successful in lobbying for a tariff on imported clothing? This would result in an *inefficient* use of labor in both the United States and abroad: the opportunity cost of using unskilled foreign labor in the garment industry is less than using American labor. U.S. consumers would be made worse off if they were forced to purchase only U.S.-made clothing. At the same time, U.S. garment workers and the owners of their companies are made better off.

Achieving an Efficient Market Outcome

In a rather amazing way, consumers and producers tend to bring about an efficient market outcome simply by reacting independently to price signals. This price-taking activity yields goods and services that, in the *long run*, are produced (1) at their lowest average total cost and (2) at a level where the opportunity cost of the last unit produced just equals the willingness to pay for it. The fact that millions of decision makers can act independently to achieve this efficient market outcome is what Adam Smith referred to as the "invisible hand in the marketplace."

Does this mean that prices will always be at their long-run equilibrium levels in a competitive market, or even be market-clearing for that matter? No. What it does mean is that there is a *tendency* for competitive markets to move toward their long-run equilibrium prices and quantities, as long as there are no external obstacles such as price controls or barriers to entry.

When markets don't move toward their short-run and long-run equilibrium outcomes, this is often a sign that resources are not being used in an economically efficient way. The question that economists then follow up with is, why not? The next two chapters offer additional insights into why markets don't always operate in an efficient way in the short run or the long run.

Should Economic Efficiency Be the Only Standard for Resource Allocation?

Economic efficiency is by no means the "be all and end all" when it comes to a society's goals. For example, we have shown that lower-cost clothing from abroad makes American clothing buyers better off. At the same time, American workers are displaced from their U.S. garment-industry jobs. Whether kind or not, economists treat labor inputs the same way they do all other scarce resources. If some U.S. garment workers and the firms that employ them are not low cost suppliers, then the pressure of competition will lead to unemployment and firm closures. For this reason, many economists oppose barriers to competition. Quotas and tariffs on foreign clothing sold in the United States might temporarily save some American jobs, but these come at the expense of U.S. consumers.

Would these consumers vote, if given the chance, to pay higher prices to protect American jobs? In fact, consumers vote everyday—with their feet and wallets—when they choose to purchase lower-priced products made overseas rather than goods labeled "made in America." In this way, the market has "spoken." Still, politicians and interest groups point to the inequities resulting from international trade as a rationale for erecting barriers to entry into domestic markets. Moreover, they regularly protest that "the rules of the game" are rigged against the United States to the extent that foreign governments heavily subsidize their export industries. Ironically, much of the rest of the world similarly complains about the large subsidies that the U.S. government gives to U.S. export industries such as agriculture and chemicals.

Chapter 19 focuses on the "fairness" of competitive market outcomes and addresses the potential role, as well as unintended consequences, of government policies that try to lessen the perceived inequities arising from competition.

SOLVED PROBLEM

Q Suppose that in an effort to reduce the demand for fossil fuels, the U.S. Congress introduces subsidies for the purchase and installation of solar panels in residential and commercial structures. Assume that the solar panel market is in long-run equilibrium. Using two graphs—one for the market and one for a typical price-taking solar panel producer—show the impact that the new subsidies will have on (a) the equilibrium price and quantity of solar panels sold in the market, and (b) an existing solar panel manufacturer's quantity and economic profits in the short run. Indicate what will happen in the long run (c) in the solar panel market, and (d) to an existing firm's quantity and profits.

A

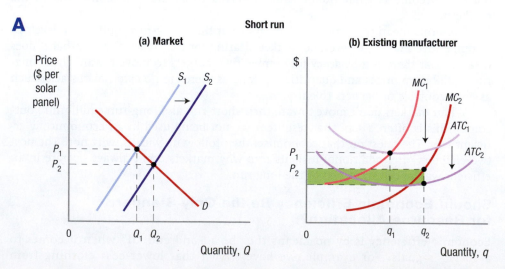

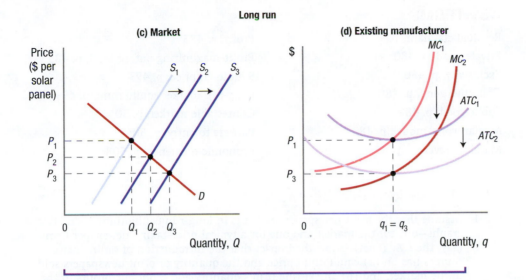

WHAT YOU SHOULD HAVE LEARNED FROM CHAPTER 16

■ That there are a variety of producing organizations that differ in their goals, as well as in their sources of revenue and capital.

■ That a for-profit firm will maximize its profits by choosing an output level where the marginal cost of the last unit produced is just equal to the marginal revenue received for this unit.

■ That a price-taking profit maximizer will choose an output level so that the marginal cost of the last unit produced is just equal to the market price at which the firm's output is sold.

■ That in the short run, firms will continue to operate as long as the market price is sufficient to cover their variable costs of production.

■ That the short-run supply curve in a market is equal to the horizontal sum of each firm's marginal cost curve above its shutdown price.

■ That in the long run, the market price must, at a minimum, cover all of a firm's long-run opportunity costs for it to stay in business.

■ That in the long run, if firms can enter or exit a market at low cost, the short-run economic profits or losses of existing producers will disappear.

■ That profits serve as a signal to attract new resources to a market so that output can be expanded at the lowest possible economic cost.

■ That the marginal cost of the last unit produced by each firm in a market is the same, which means that there is no way to reduce the cost of producing the market's equilibrium level of output.

■ That in the long run, as long as all firms face the same cost conditions, each firm in the market will choose an output level that corresponds to its minimum average total cost curve, such that the average cost of producing the equilibrium level of output will be minimized.

■ That competitive markets will allocate scarce resources efficiently only if there are no barriers to entry—that is, as long as markets are contestable.

■ That scarce resources are allocated in an economically efficient way when there is no way to reallocate them to make anyone better off without making someone else worse off.

KEY TERMS

Residual claimant, p. 477

Private good, p. 480

Exclusivity, p. 480

Collective good, p. 480

Public good, p. 481

Median voter model, p. 483

Marginal revenue, p. 484

Profit, p. 485

Profit-maximizing output level, p. 485

Shutdown price, p. 493

Long-run market equilibrium, p. 499

Contestable market, p. 505

Barriers to entry, p. 506

Economic efficiency, p. 508

QUESTIONS AND PROBLEMS

1. Assume that the print newspaper market is in long-run equilibrium. Using two graphs—one for the market and one for a typical price-taking newspaper firm (say, the *L.A. Times*)—show the impact that the introduction of online news sources has on (a) equilibrium price and the quantity of print newspapers sold in the market, and (b) an existing firm's quantity and economic profits in the short run. Indicate what will happen in the long run (c) in the print newspaper market; (d) to the existing firm's quantity and profits; and (e) to the print newspaper layout editors' labor market.

2. Suppose the government decides to levy a sales tax on a price-taking firm that is equal to a percent of the revenue collected by the firm. Using firm cost curves, show (a) the maximum tax the firm would be willing to pay without shutting down production in the short run, and (b) the impact of the tax, if any, on the level of the firm's output in the short run, assuming that it doesn't shut down.

3. "Nonprofit organizations are just for-profit companies that spend all of their profits on their mission. For example, a medical-research charity spends its profits on medical research." Do you agree or disagree with this statement? Explain your answer.

4. Suppose that the city of Houston imposes a tax per unit of output on its local ballpoint pen producer BIK. Using firm cost curves for BIK, show the impact that this tax will have on BIK in the short run and long run. (Hint: Untaxed ballpoint pen producers exist in other cities.)

5. The U.S. Consumer Safety Board is considering a regulation that would require automakers to increase the steel content of automobile frames from 42 percent to 54 percent. (a) Using two graphs—one for the U.S. steel market and one for a typical U.S. steel manufacturer—show the impact that this proposal would have on the (b) short-run and (c) long-run profitability of existing steel producers. (d) What do you think would happen to the amount of steel imported in the United States, given that there are high-cost environmental regulations currently in place for U.S. steel production? Explain your answer.

6. U.S.-based industries, such as steel, automobile, and agriculture, spend a lot of money lobbying the government to impose high tariffs or import quotas to block imports. Assume that the U.S. steel market is in long-run equilibrium and that high tariffs on imported steel are imposed. Explain how, if at all, your answer(s) in Question 5 would change in this situation.

7. Suppose that you are a government official who heads a large government agency, such as the Federal Drug Administration (FDA). Identify at least three decisions that you would make that would differ from those of a for-profit drug-licensing company if you are trying to (a) grow your annual congressional budget appropriation; (b) expedite approval of new drugs in response to pharmaceutical industry pressures; or (c) reduce Medicare insurance outlays on new and expensive drugs and medical treatments.

8. Assume that the market for chewing gum is in long-run equilibrium. Using two graphs—one for the market and one for a typical gum producer—trace through the impact of a federal law that prohibits smoking in all buildings and parking lots. (You can assume that the ban on smoking causes smokers to redirect their oral fixation to chewing gum.) What effect will the law have on:

   a) the equilibrium price and quantity of gum in the short run?
   b) the profitability of existing firms in the short run?
   c) How, if at all, would your answers to (a) and (b) change if you were instead considering the long run?
   d) How, if at all, would your answer to (c) change if new entrants into the chewing gum market cannot produce at the same low cost as existing producers?

9. Assume that the U.S. strawberry-production market is in long-run equilibrium. Using two graphs—one for the U.S. strawberry market and one for a typical U.S. strawberry grower—demonstrate the impact of increasing border patrols and thereby reducing the stream of low-cost Mexican farmworkers into the United States. What effect would this have on (a) the equilibrium price and quantity in the U.S. strawberry market; and (b) the profitability of existing U.S. strawberry producers? How, if at all, would your answers change if Mexican strawberry producers can freely export strawberries to the United States? If this occurs, what would happen in the long run to the U.S. strawberry industry? Explain your answer.

10. In an effort to fund a health-insurance program for the uninsured, Congress may impose a 1 percent payroll tax on employers. Labor, business, and consumer groups are all fighting this new tax, believing that they will be the ones to ultimately bear the burden of the tax.

   a) Show the cost curves of a typical accounting firm, assuming it is in long-run equilibrium.
   b) Carefully analyze the short-run effects of the tax on firm costs and output, assuming that labor is the only variable factor of production.
   c) Now show the short-run impact of the tax on equilibrium price and output in the accounting market. How does this equilibrium price and quantity change in the long run?
   d) Can you determine who bears the tax in the short run? In the long run? Explain your answers.

11. Suppose that the retail food industry in Miami is in long-run equilibrium. Assume further that the firms in this market—supermarkets—only use union labor. Using two graphs—one for the supermarket market and another for a typical supermarket—show what happens to equilibrium food prices when Walmart Supercenters (which sell groceries and do not employ union workers) are permitted to open in Miami. What will the impact be on a typical unionized supermarket? If you were a consultant to Piggly Wiggly, a unionized supermarket chain, what would your recommendation be? Explain your answers.

12. To combat teenage obesity, Congress has proposed a tax on sugared sodas and other sugared drinks.

   a) Using two graphs—one for the sugared soda market and another for a typical soda producer—show the short-run and long-run impact of this tax on existing producers and on market price and quantity.
   b) Again using two graphs, show the impact of the tax on an untaxed substitute good such as naturally flavored, unsweetened bottled water.
   c) Do you think that such a tax results in a more efficient allocation of resources? Why or why not?

13. Economists are proud of the fact that prices act as virtually costless signals to consumers and producers about how to allocate their scarce resources. In effect, prices "ration" these scarce resources in terms of what is produced, how

it is produced, and who benefits from these goods and services. Suppose you have been named president of a small island in the South Pacific. Propose an alternative way to allocate the island's scarce resources, and compare it to the price system in terms of costs of production, mix of goods and services produced, and who benefits from these goods and services. If you think that your system is preferable, explain why.

14. China has been loudly criticized by various U.S. and European industries (such as the rolled-steel and candle-making industries) for subsidizing Chinese producers to such an extent that they can "dump" their output in Western markets at prices that don't even cover the cost of raw materials used in production. Using three graphs—one for the U.S. candle market, one for a typical U.S. candle producer, and one for a Chinese candle producer—show the short-run and long-run impact of dumping in the candle market. Who "wins" and who "loses" from dumping? Is the outcome economically efficient? Why or why not?

15. There has been a recent uptick in the number of young people in France who are jumping barriers to ride the public Metro subway system without buying a ticket. They argue that free transportation should be a basic right for everyone. On occasion, some of these people are caught riding without a valid ticket and are fined. If more riders join this "Free Metro" movement, what do you think will happen to the way that the Metro system is financed? Specifically, where will the money come from to keep the trains running? Explain your answer.

16. Some local municipal governments provide trash collection for their residents; others license a number of private waste-collection companies that can then privately solicit business from these residents.

   a) Why do you think that both government and privately provided trash-collection services coexist across municipalities?

   b) Do you have any reason to expect that one delivery system would be less expensive than the other?

   c) Could you predict in advance what types of municipalities would opt for government-provided versus private-provided services? Explain your answer.

From Price Takers to Price Makers: Monopolies and Monopsonies

"Our freedom of choice in a competitive society rests on the fact that, if one person refuses to satisfy our wishes, we can turn to another. But if we face a monopolist we are at his mercy. And an authority directing the whole economic system would be the most powerful monopolist conceivable."

Friedrich Hayek, economist

So far, we have treated producers and consumers as price takers. In other words, we have built a predictive model of their behavior based on the assumption that they are too small relative to the size of their market to have an impact on price. This means that a single dairy farmer cannot have an effect on the market price of milk. Nor can you, as a purchaser at Starbucks and other coffee vendors, influence the market price of coffee. In such an atomistic world, all that buyers and sellers can do is decide how much, if any, of a good to buy or sell and who their trading partners will be.

While this is a workable and useful way of looking at how many firms and consumers behave, this model does not characterize all of the supplier and buyer relations that, in reality, exist. There *are* producers and consumers that have market "power"—power that gives them some control over the price of the goods they sell or buy. In the extreme case, if there is a single supplier, it can choose the sales price or quantity (not both, as you will see shortly) that maximizes the firm's profits. Similarly, situations exist in which there is only one buyer in the market, that can exploit its position when choosing the price or quantity of goods purchased so as to maximize its well-being or profitability.

In this chapter, we explore the process by which a single supplier or buyer decides how much to charge or pay for a product or how much to sell or buy. We continue to assume that a producer's objective is to maximize profits and that a buyer's objective is to maximize its economic well-being. Despite sharing the same objectives, a single supplier or buyer will make choices that are quite different from those of price-taking firms and consumers. For example, we will see that when there is a single supplier in a market, the profit-maximizing price tends to be higher, and the output level tends to be lower, than if the firm were operating as a price-taker in a competitive market. This is why most economists believe that competitive markets with many suppliers are preferable to those in which there is only a single supplier. We conclude this chapter with a discussion of government policies aimed at combating the abuses that can arise when a single seller or buyer exerts pricing power in a market. We also examine government activities that, in and of themselves, create and sustain this pricing power.

17.1 Monopolies in Action

When there is only one supplier in a market and the market is noncontestable—that is, additional producers cannot enter at low cost—we say that a **monopoly** exists.

MONOPOLY One supplier operating in a noncontestable market.

EXAMPLE Your local cable company is a monopoly when it comes to providing cable TV and cable Internet services in your neighborhood.

EXAMPLE Home owners must purchase their water from their local water utility, which is a monopoly.

EXAMPLE The U.S. government has a legal monopoly in the production of U.S. dollars and other currency.

The word "monopoly" comes from "mono," which means "one" in Latin, and "poly" which means entity.

The existence of a single supplier in a noncontestable market means that barriers to entry prevent new producers from entering that market even when the existing firm is earning substantial economic profits. The barriers can be legal or arise from the scarcity and control that a producer has over certain natural resources or technologies. A company is able to exercise pricing power only if it produces a good for which very few close substitutes exist. This means that consumers can't easily switch to other products in response to higher monopoly pricing.

The De Beers Story

Before we present a general model of the economic behavior of monopolists, we can learn a great deal about this behavior by simply observing how monopolies operate in the real world. Perhaps one of the most famous monopolized markets in recent history was the diamond market because, for the better part of the twentieth century, De Beers—a South African diamond-mining company—controlled the sale of between 85 and 90 percent of all rough diamonds mined worldwide.[1] While 85–90 percent is not exactly 100 percent, De Beers was widely viewed as the de facto price setter in the rough-diamond market.

From the late 1800s through the turn of the century, De Beers built its monopoly position in rough diamonds by buying up diamond mines in South Africa. At the same time, it created a syndicate of distribution partners to control the worldwide distribution and sale of its diamonds. This enabled the company to adjust the number of diamonds released to the market in response to changes in demand. In times of low demand, De Beers would simply hoard some of its diamonds (keep them in inventory) rather than sell them. In some periods when demand for diamonds was low, the company went so far as to buy up the supply of diamonds from mines it didn't own.

[1] Nicholas Stein, "The De Beers Story: A New Cut on an Old Monopoly." *Fortune*, February 19, 2001.

Because supply and demand together determine the market price, De Beers' ability to control supply meant that it could manipulate the price of diamonds.

The enormous economic profits earned by De Beers during the early to mid-twentieth century encouraged other companies to search for new sources of rough diamonds outside of South Africa. So much so that by the beginning of the twenty-first century, Australia's diamond mines became the largest suppliers of diamonds (as measured by carats) in the world. De Beers' ability to control the supply and distribution of diamonds worldwide—and, as a result, market price—was seriously undermined when Australian mine owners decided to offer their diamonds directly for sale in the diamond market rather than sell them exclusively to De Beers. De Beers' control was further eroded by a major discovery of rough diamonds in Canada. The end result was that De Beers' ability to control the flow of diamonds to the market through the purchase of "excess" supplies simply became cost-prohibitive.

Not only did De Beers lose its stranglehold over the production and distribution of diamonds, but, to make matters worse, the diamond industry came under scrutiny by antimonopoly government agencies in the United States and Europe. In 2004, the U.S. Justice Department indicted De Beers for "price fixing." To avoid prosecution and government-directed changes in its distribution system, De Beers chose instead to end direct sales to customers in the United States (De Beers diamonds can still be purchased through foreign resellers). In 2008, the European Union's anticompetitive commission insisted that De Beers stop hoarding diamonds to manipulate prices.

The 2007 Great Recession reduced the demand for wholesale polished diamonds from roughly $30 billion in 2007 to just $12 billion in 2009. No longer able to hoard its mined diamonds to control market supply and price, De Beers instead closed more than 90 percent of its mines in response to this severe downturn in demand.

Ironically, around the time that the EU banned De Beers' hoarding activities, the Russian diamond company Alrosa—which is 90 percent state-owned—began its own hoarding program to prop up its diamond prices. Because it has continued to mine diamonds rather than shut its mines during the recession, Alrosa has surpassed De Beers as the largest diamond producer in the world, to the tune of over 3 million carats per month.[2] This mining continues unabated in spite of unfavorable market conditions because the Russian government is apparently concerned that labor unrest would ensue if the mines were closed. Instead of closing its mines, the government is paying Alrosa to hoard diamonds after they are mined.

Whether De Beers' price-setting role in the diamond market has permanently ended remains to be seen. The company has a history of finding ways to protect and enhance its pricing power. In 2001, for example, De Beers purchased its first mines in Canada at a cost of more than $300 million. At about the same time, the company purchased 40 percent ownership in Australia's Argyle Mine, one of the world's largest rough-diamond producers.[3]

Other Attempts to Control Market Price

De Beers was successful in hoarding its own diamonds in the face of weak demand largely because diamonds are very small and, therefore, relatively inexpensive to store. The bulk

· · · · · · ·

[2]Andrew Kramer, "Russia Stockpiles Diamonds, Awaiting Return of Demand." *New York Times*, May 11, 2009.

[3]Jamey Keaton, "Cartel Out, Competition in at Diamond Leader." August 25, 2000. www.money.cnn.com.

of the hoarding costs are related to keeping them safe and secure, which tends to be a fixed cost that varies little with the number of diamonds hoarded. Of course, to the extent that the diamonds tie up financial capital, there is an additional opportunity cost.

It can be much more difficult to control the amount of other types of resources supplied to the market, especially when they are more plentiful, more geographically dispersed, or more costly to store. The Hunt brothers, a Texas clan, famously tried to "corner" the silver market in 1979 by buying and holding onto more than half of the world's deliverable silver.[4] Their behavior had the intended effect: the price of silver increased from just $9 an ounce in 1979 to over $50 an ounce in late 1980.

However, the Hunt brothers' pricing power in the silver market collapsed in the face of a falloff in demand and an increase in supply stimulated by the run up in silver prices that their buying spree had triggered. Ultimately, the price of silver fell from these highs, and the Hunt brothers were unable to pay back the loans they had taken out to purchase their silver hoard.

More recently, in 2006 and again in 2008, market watchers blamed "speculators" for running up the world price of oil to over $160 a barrel. Options traders allegedly did this by purchasing options (rights) to buy enormous amounts of oil in the future through the oil futures trading market.[5] They were accused of "cornering" the market in future oil at very low prices through the purchase of these options, which could then be resold at higher prices when the price of oil rose. By solely investing in options to buy, the oil itself was never actually purchased. Based on these allegations, U.S. legislators pushed to impose restrictions on futures trading in oil.[6] However, the political will for these reforms waned in the first quarter of 2009, when the price of oil fell to under $50 a barrel as a result of the falloff in world demand.[7]

The latest and arguably most successful attempt in recent years to corner the market in natural resources is China's growing control over the mining and sale of "rare earth elements."[8] China's mines account for more than 93 percent of the production of rare earths, which factor into the production of such things as green-energy technologies (including compact fluorescent bulbs), smart phones, and missiles. One of the reasons that China dominates global rare-earth production has been its willingness to tolerate highly polluting, low-cost mining. Within the past few years, China has substantially reduced its exports of these elements while, at the same time, it has been buying up rare-earth mines located in other parts of the world, including Australia and Africa. Most analysts believe that China's goal is not to increase the world prices of these rare earths but, rather, to require that producers who need these inputs relocate their manufacturing to China. As we have already discussed, governments often pursue goals other than profit maximization. In the case of rare earths, China is pursuing a strategy to gain low-cost access to cutting edge technologies developed by foreign producers who may be forced to operate in China.

The Longevity of Government-Granted Monopolies

Monopolies that are awarded by a government tend to be far more successful in terms of longevity. As early as the sixteenth century, monarchies in Western Europe gave

· · · · · · ·

[4]Financial Desk, "Cornering Markets Past, From Silver to Salad Oil." *New York Times,* July 13, 1989.

[5]Roger Lowenstein, "What's Really Wrong with the Price of Oil." *New York Times,* October 17, 2008.

[6]Diana B. Henriques, "Lawmakers Seek to Curb Speculators." *New York Times,* September 10, 2008.

[7]Paul Krugman, "The Oil Nonbubble." *New York Times,* May 12, 2008.

[8]Keith Bradsher, "China Seizes Rare Earth Mine Areas." *New York Times,* January 20, 2011.

specific companies monopoly control over brewing, mining, and trading activities. One such monopoly was the British East India Company, which was the only company that could import Indian products into England. In return for these grants of monopoly, the resulting profits were heavily taxed by the royal family to finance their personal needs as well as the country's court system, jails, and wars. Not only were these profits (and, hence, taxes) significantly greater than what would have occurred under competition, but it was also far easier for the royal family to tax a handful of monopolies than to collect taxes from numerous suppliers.

In contemporary times, the U.S. government has granted a monopoly to each of the 12 regional, privately owned Federal Reserve Banks to perform such functions as check clearing for the U.S. Treasury. Similarly, local governments have granted monopoly status to TV cable providers, water companies, and natural gas and electric utilities that provide services to their residents. Airport authorities often award monopoly rights to restaurant chains, bottled water and soda companies, and newspaper-stand vendors located inside the airport. In rare cases, we will see that some of these monopolies can actually improve upon competitive market outcomes.

ECONOMIC FALLACY   If there is only one bookstore on campus, it can act like a monopolist.

False. First of all, other than the cost of opening a store, there are no other barriers to entry into the retail book market. In fact, even these costs have been reduced considerably by the advent of eShopping: Amazon and other online vendors have moved aggressively into the college textbook market. These online book retailers, along with off-campus bookstores, effectively limit the campus bookstore's pricing power. It will only be able to capitalize on the "convenience" factor that we have discussed previously, if this is worth something to students. Where the campus bookstore *does* have monopoly pricing power is when books are purchased by students who receive financial aid and can simply debit their financial aid accounts rather than pay out-of-pocket for their books. Typically, these students are not allowed to shop for lower prices online or off-campus if they want their financial aid to cover the bill.

17.2 Can Monopolies Be Beneficial to an Economy?

The famous economist Joseph Schumpeter once argued that most product innovation comes from entrepreneurs who seek to "capture" economic profits by creating substitutes for monopolized goods.[9] He called this the process of **creative destruction**.

CREATIVE DESTRUCTION The process by which innovation undercuts monopoly pricing power and profitability.

EXAMPLE The introduction of the PC undercut the virtual monopoly that IBM had in the mainframe-computer market.

EXAMPLE The rise of digital photography undercut Polaroid's virtual monopoly in the instant photography market.

. . . .

[9]Joseph Schumpeter, *Capitalism, Socialism and Democracy* (New York: Harper & Brothers, 1942).

Recall that a monopoly can only exist if there are costly barriers to entry and no close substitutes. This suggests that competition will arise only if an entrepreneur is able to create a close substitute through innovation. This is why Schumpeter argued that monopolies—or more precisely, the profits they earn—stimulate innovation and benefit the economy in the long run. The possibility that the entrepreneur who creates the close substitute may herself become a monopolist is of little concern because Schumpeter would argue that she, too, would eventually fall prey to creative destruction brought about by other eager entrepreneurs waiting in the wings.

The Patent System, Monopoly, and Innovation

The patent system was introduced to protect ownership rights to intellectual property, a topic we first addressed in Chapter 4. Patents also promote the types of innovation that Schumpeter envisioned.

PATENT A legal protection of intellectual property rights that conveys exclusive control over an invention or process for a certain period of time.

EXAMPLE Monsanto holds numerous patents related to the production of its genetically altered crop seeds.

EXAMPLE In 1876, Alexander Graham Bell received patent #174465 for the telephone.

EXAMPLE In 2009, Bill Gates submitted five patent applications for technologies that aim to control the weather and, more specifically, halt hurricanes.

The purpose of a patent is to grant an inventor exclusive rights to his invention—including the sole right to profit from it—for a limited period of time. In return, the innovator agrees to make public the science and technology underlying the innovation. By granting these exclusive rights, the government erects legal barriers to prevent competitors from copying and selling the invention during the life of the patent without the inventor's express permission. The rationale behind patents is that even though they create monopolies in the short run, they give inventors the incentive to invest in innovation activities and make their findings public in the longer run. Otherwise, why would anyone spend years developing a device, like Thomas Edison did when he created the first long-lasting lightbulb?

To the extent that patent protection eliminates the threat of copycats, it greatly diminishes the return that an inventor would get from locking up his formula or burning his blueprints. It gives patent seekers the security they require to be willing to share detailed information about their devices in their patent applications, which is published and made available to the public. This, in turn, serves as a catalyst for additional investment in scientific activities to create close substitutes for the patented product. In other words, patents promote the creative destruction that Schumpeter described: entrepreneurs can build upon patented technology rather than "reinventing" it, thereby speeding up the cycle of creative destruction. This process has been particularly evident in the pharmaceutical industry, where first-generation drugs are sometimes competed out of existence by newer and better substitutes before their patents even run out.

It is up to patent examiners in the U.S. Patent and Trademark Office to evaluate applications for patent protection and to determine whether new products are sufficiently different from those protected by existing patents. In other words, an innovation can be a close, but not too close, substitute for a patented product. Often, a patent holder will pursue legal action to protect its monopoly position, alleging that a "new" invention actually infringes on an existing patent. MercExchange—a Virginia-based company—sued eBay, claiming that eBay had stolen its "Buy It Now" feature.[10] After seven years in court, eBay agreed to pay MercExchange $25 million in exchange for the three patents that were in dispute.

What Can Be Patented?

U.S. patent laws state that

> Whoever invents or discovers any new and useful process, machine, manufacture, or composition of matter, or any new and useful improvement thereof, may obtain a patent therefor, subject to the conditions and requirements of this title.

The interpretation of this law has been fraught with controversy, especially as it has been applied to software and biological innovations. In many cases, the U.S. Supreme Court has intervened to resolve contradictory federal court rulings. Even then, these Supreme Court decisions have sometimes contradicted themselves over time. The underlying issue appears to be how to distinguish "ideas" and "products of nature"—which are not patentable—from "inventions" and "devices" which are patentable.

In the 1970s, a debate arose as to whether computer algorithms could be patented; after all, weren't they simply the manifestation of abstract mathematical ideas? Owners of software programs had, up to this point, sought weaker protections through copyright and trademark laws. When the value of software skyrocketed with the revolution in personal computing, developers began to pursue patent protection for their products. By the 1980s, several court rulings had extended patent protection to computer software. This led giant software producers such as Microsoft to spend substantial sums of money to obtain patent protection for both groundbreaking and run-of-the-mill software applications.[11]

More recently, patent fights have centered on whether or not biological material can be patented. In 1989, Amgen, a U.S. company, claimed the first U.S. patent covering "biological materials and the genetic engineering processes used to produce a natural occurring protein in the human body."[12] In the late 1990s, the University of Wisconsin Research Foundation was awarded a patent for embryonic stem cells that its faculty had developed. Since that time, the university has granted licenses to other researchers to use the cells. Still, the patent eligibility of stem cells continues to be challenged in court. Of primary concern is whether extending patent protection to biological materials, genetic sequences, and so on will eventually create a tangle of overlapping patents that becomes prohibitively costly for a researcher to negotiate. If this happens, the resulting transaction costs and uncertainty about patent infringement may themselves create barriers to entry, thereby slowing genetic innovation.[13]

The ability to patent a single gene has been challenged in federal court. The basic question is whether a company that "isolates and purifies" a gene has significantly

· · · · · · ·

[10]Associated Press, "eBay Settles Patent Dispute Over 'Buy It Now' Feature." *New York Times*, February 29, 2008.

[11]Randall Stross, "Why Bill Gates Wants 3,000 New Patents." *New York Times*, July 31, 2005.

[12]Lawrence M. Fisher, "Amgen Beats Japanese on Protein Patent." *New York Times*, March 9, 1989.

[13]Karl Bergman and Gregory D. Graff, "The Global Stem Cell Patent Landscape: Implications for Efficient Technology Transfer and Commercial Development." *Nature Biotechnology,* 25 (2007): 419–424.

altered it in such a way that it is no longer a "product of nature." In March, 2010, a federal court judge in New York revoked a number of patents that had been granted in the 1990s to Myriad, a company that had isolated the BRCA gene, which is used to test whether a woman is at high risk for breast cancer. Patients, clinicians, and researchers all argued that revoking this patent would substantially reduce the cost of BRCA gene testing (from the then-current $3,000 per test that Myriad charged) and that patients would be able to get independent confirmation of test results from other vendors.[14]

Of course, the question could also be asked about the impact of Myriad's loss of patent protection on the willingness of other companies to invest in future projects to isolate genes that can predict the risk of other diseases, such as multiple sclerosis. These ongoing debates reflect the inherent conflict in granting monopoly protection in the short run to generate more innovation in the long run. The costs and benefits of this trade-off are likely to vary depending on the innovation in question.

In 2010, the U.S. Supreme Court weighed in on the question of what can be patented in a ruling that instructed lower-court judges to be more flexible in determining whether *methods*, rather than objects, are eligible for patent protection.[15] The case involved patent protection for a method of hedging weather-related risks when buying and selling fuel. This opinion is sure to provide additional incentives for innovation in a wide variety of production processes, such as inventory control, medical diagnostics, and robotic artificial intelligence.

17.3 How a Monopoly Maximizes Its Profits

A monopolist, unlike a price-taking firm, can choose *either* the total output supplied to the market *or* the price at which this output is sold—but not both—because the law of demand still applies, *even when a monopoly exists*. The higher the price of a good, the less of it will be sold, even when a company is the sole market supplier. This means that if a monopolist chooses its sales price, the market's demand curve will determine the quantity of the good that is sold. Alternatively—as in the De Beers case—a monopolist can choose the quantity it will supply to the market, but then the demand curve will determine the price at which it will sell. This is why monopolists are so often engaged in gathering up-to-date data about the demand for their product. To maximize profits, a monopolist must know the price–quantity combinations that consumer demand will support at any given point in time.

How does a monopolist choose the output level or price that will maximize its profits? The first thing to emphasize is that just like a price-taking firm, a monopolist will maximize profits by choosing an output level where the marginal revenue gained from the very last unit sold is just equal to its marginal cost of production. In other words, the basic marginal benefit and marginal cost framework still holds, even for a monopolist.

However, one of the key differences between a monopolist and a price-taking firm is that when a monopolist wants to sell more output, it must move down the market demand curve and charge a lower price for the product. This is something that De Beers understood all too well and why it was so focused on controlling the flow of diamonds to the market. To better appreciate De Beers' decision process, we

......

[14]John Schwartz, "Cancer Patients Challenge the Patenting of a Gene." *New York Times,* May 12, 2009.
[15]Bilski v. Kappos, 08-964, U.S. Supreme Court.

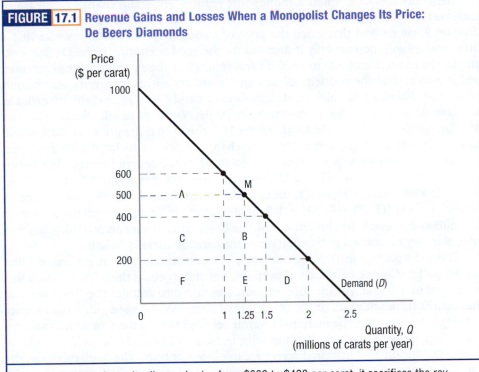

FIGURE 17.1 Revenue Gains and Losses When a Monopolist Changes Its Price: De Beers Diamonds

When De Beers reduces its diamond price from $600 to $400 per carat, it sacrifices the revenue represented by area A. However, it gains the revenue represented by areas B and E, which results from selling 0.5 million more carats. This equals $400 × 0.5 million, or $200 million, which just offsets the lost revenue (area A). This means that De Beers receives the same total revenue whether it sells 1 million or 1.5 million carats. It turns out that this price/quantity change brackets the midpoint (M) of the demand (D) curve, where the demand is unitary elastic. (More precisely, the arc elasticity as we move from $600 to $400 is one.). But if De Beers continues to cut the price, say from $400 to $200, its lost revenue (areas B plus C) will be greater than the amount gained by selling yet another 0.5 million carats: the lost revenue equals $200 × 1.5 million carats, or $300 million, while the added revenue is area D, which only equals $200 × 0.5 million, or $100 million.

depict the global demand for diamonds in **Figure 17.1**. For simplicity's sake, we treat De Beers as a monopolist controlling 100 percent of the diamond market.

At $600 per carat, suppose that 1 million carats can be sold annually in the worldwide diamond market. If De Beers wants to sell a larger quantity, say 1.5 million carats, it will have to drop the price to $400 per carat for *all of the diamonds* it sells. This means that it will have to give up area A in revenue in return for areas B and E in additional revenue. We can compute the value of these areas in the De Beers example. Area A equals $200 multiplied by 1 million carats; De Beers gives up $200 million in revenue to sell more diamonds because all carats will now be sold for $400 per carat instead of $600. By lowering the price, De Beers will gain areas B and E in revenue, which equal $400 multiplied by 0.5 million carats, or $200 million. In other words, the increase in output from 1 million to 1.5 million carats does not change De Beers' total revenue! At a price of $600 dollars per carat, De Beers will sell 1 million carats for a total of $600 million in revenue. At a price of $400 per carat, the company will sell 1.5 million carats, also for $600 million in revenue.

Generally speaking, when a monopolist reduces price, the change (increase or decrease) in revenue will depend solely on the elasticity of demand for the good. In Chapter 9, we showed that when the price of a good drops, the total revenue that a firm receives will increase only if demand for the good is elastic. In the De Beers example, the move from $600 to $400 a carat resulted in the same amount of revenue, which means that the elasticity of demand is *unitary* within this price and output range. But also recall that along a straight-line demand curve, price elasticity varies as we move up or down. What if, for example, De Beers wanted to sell another 0.5 million diamonds, or 2 million in total? Figure 17.1 shows that the price per carat would have to drop to $200 (remember that the change in price associated with any given change in quantity must be the same along a straight-line demand curve). As a result, De Beers would gain area D in additional revenue—$200 multiplied by 0.5 million carats, or $100 million. However, the company would have to sacrifice areas B and C, or $300 million (($400 − $200) × 1.5 million carats) in revenue to sell the additional 0.5 million diamonds. Total revenue *falls* due to the price reduction, meaning that the price elasticity of demand in this portion of the demand curve is *inelastic*.

This example tells us that the marginal, or incremental, revenue generated when a monopolist sells one more unit of output is not simply equal the price at which this additional unit is sold. The monopolist must also take into account the "lost" revenue that results from selling *all* of the other units (carats) of the good (diamonds) more cheaply. Consequently, the marginal revenue received from selling an additional unit is *less than* the price at which that unit sells; in fact, it can even be negative. This is reflected graphically by a marginal revenue curve that lies below the demand curve, the curve that determines the market-clearing price at which all of the units will be sold.

When the market demand curve is a downward-sloping straight line, we know something more about how the monopolist's marginal revenue curve relates to its demand curve. As we demonstrated in the De Beers example, when the market price of a good falls, and we move down the demand curve, demand becomes increasingly inelastic. This is exactly what we showed in Chapter 9: consumer demand is elastic above the demand curve's midpoint, point M; unitary elastic exactly at M; and below M, the price elasticity of demand is less than one—that is, demand is inelastic. When De Beers dropped its price from $600 to $400, the quantity demanded increased, but the total revenue the company earned stayed the same. However, when it dropped its price further, from $400 to $200 a carat, the quantity demanded continued to increase, but *total revenue* actually fell. The marginal revenue that De Beers received when it lowered its price from $400 to $200 was *negative*! A monopolist will always lose revenue when it produces beyond the midpoint of the demand curve, something that it would clearly want to avoid doing.

Figure 17.2 shows a straight-line demand (*D*) curve and its corresponding *MR* curve for our De Beers example. At 1.25 million carats, the *MR* curve crosses into negative territory. This makes sense because we already saw that beyond this output level, total revenue will fall, meaning that the marginal revenue must be negative. It also makes sense that this is the quantity corresponding to the midpoint (point M) of the demand curve, which is where demand is unitary elastic. At any higher output level or lower price, the marginal revenue is negative because demand is inelastic.

If we draw in the monopolist's marginal cost (*MC*) curve, we see that the profit-maximizing quantity is 1 million carats, where the marginal cost of the last diamond supplied just equals the marginal revenue received for it.

Note that the process of finding the profit-maximizing level of output is the same regardless of whether a firm is a monopolist or a price taker operating in a

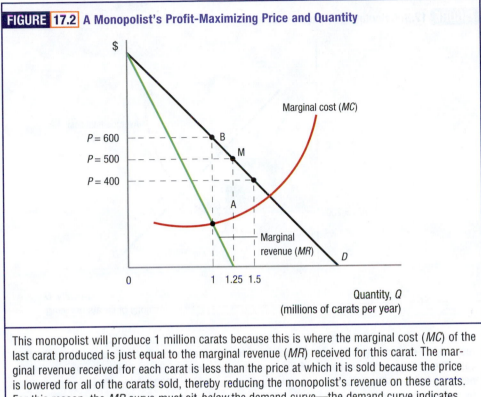

FIGURE 17.2 A Monopolist's Profit-Maximizing Price and Quantity

This monopolist will produce 1 million carats because this is where the marginal cost (*MC*) of the last carat produced is just equal to the marginal revenue (*MR*) received for this carat. The marginal revenue received for each carat is less than the price at which it is sold because the price is lowered for all of the carats sold, thereby reducing the monopolist's revenue on these carats. For this reason, the *MR* curve must sit *below* the demand curve—the demand curve indicates the price at which the total carats supplied are sold. Reading up the demand curve at the profit-maximizing level of output—1 million carats—we see that the market-clearing price is $600.

competitive market. Both types of firms will produce to the point where the marginal cost of supplying the last unit is just equal to the marginal revenue this unit generates. The difference is that for the price taker, the marginal revenue received for each additional unit sold equals the going market price. In contrast, the marginal revenue received by the monopolist is less than the price at which the additional unit is sold. That is, the point at which marginal revenue equals marginal cost lies *below* the demand curve because a monopolist must reduce the price on all of its units of output to sell an additional unit. Consequently, the monopolist's marginal revenue will be lower than the price it receives for the last unit sold.

After a monopolist's profit-maximizing quantity is chosen, the market's demand curve will determine the market-clearing price. We know that the profit-maximizing output in this case is 1 million carats. How do we find the price? Reading up to the demand curve at 1 million, we see that it occurs at point B, or $600. This is the price that consumers are willing to pay for the very last (1 millionth) diamond that the monopolist supplies to the market.

We can determine the monopolist's economic profits by following the same procedure we used for price-taking firms. **Figure 17.3** illustrates this approach.

We calculate the difference between the price received for each diamond and the average total cost (*ATC*) of producing each of these diamonds, which at 1 million units equals $200. This is designated by point C. This tells us the average profit per carat, which is $400 ($600 − $200). The final step is to calculate the company's

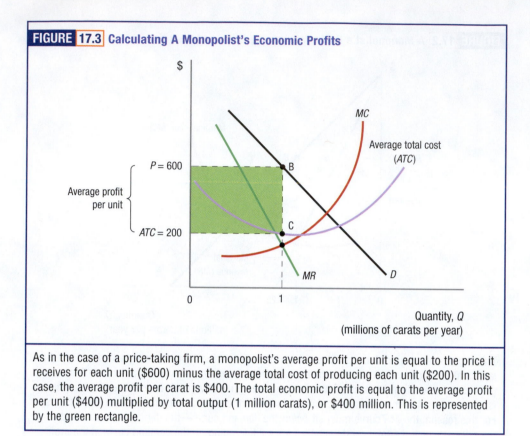

FIGURE 17.3 **Calculating A Monopolist's Economic Profits**

As in the case of a price-taking firm, a monopolist's average profit per unit is equal to the price it receives for each unit ($600) minus the average total cost of producing each unit ($200). In this case, the average profit per carat is $400. The total economic profit is equal to the average profit per unit ($400) multiplied by total output (1 million carats), or $400 million. This is represented by the green rectangle.

total profits by multiplying the average profit per carat ($400) by the total number of carats sold (1 million). This yields $400 million in profits. Notice how the green-shaded area in Figure 17.3 is rectangular shaped. The height of the rectangle represents the average profit the monopolist earns per carat, while the length represents the total number of carats sold. Multiplying the height and length of the rectangle, we get the area of the rectangle, which provides a graphic representation of the monopolist's economic profits.

There is no reason to believe that these profits will be competed away in the long run as long as barriers to entry prevent this from happening. As you will recall, the presence of these barriers was a necessary precondition for a monopoly to exist in the first place. Nevertheless, as the De Beers example demonstrates, monopoly profits may eventually erode if close substitutes—such as diamonds from mines outside of South Africa—come into existence.

ECONOMIC FALLACY   A monopolist will charge the highest price possible for its product.

False. A monopolist will charge a price that maximizes its profits, taking into account the demand curve that it faces. After it decides how much output to supply to the market, the demand curve will determine the market-clearing price so that the quantity supplied is just equal to the quantity demanded.

The decision process that we have just discussed applies to a monopolist that charges the same price for all of the units of output it sells. We call this a **simple monopoly**.

SIMPLE MONOPOLY A monopoly that charges the same price for all of the units of output supplied to the market.

EXAMPLE The U.S. postal service charges the same price for all of its first-class stamps.

EXAMPLE The only shoeshine stand in the airport charges the same price for all of the shoes it shines.

Why can't a monopolist sell its output at different prices? Why can't the monopolist charge consumers who are willing to pay more a higher price? After all, the demand curve it faces is downward sloping, which means that some consumers are willing to pay a much higher price for the good compared to other buyers. If our monopolist could do this—charge different consumers different prices—then it wouldn't have to lower the price of all of the units it supplies each time it wants to sell one more unit.

One problem with such a pricing scheme is that often it is difficult (and costly) to determine which consumers are willing to pay a higher price. But even if this could be overcome, there's another reason it's unusual for monopolists to sell their output at different prices: people who are charged a lower price will become instant "competitors" to the monopolist in the sense that they can resell their lower-priced purchases to consumers who are being charged a higher price by the monopolist.

This is why book publishers that sell surplus books at lower prices to discount resellers heavily mark the spines and ends of these books with black ink to keep them from competing against new, pristine copies. Sometimes paperback publishers even rip off the covers of novels to prevent their resale to customers willing to pay full price for new titles. Likewise, airline companies—which often have significant pricing power when it comes to less-heavily traveled routes—have always prohibited buyers of low-priced tickets from reselling them to other travelers. Nowadays, the U.S. Department of Homeland Security enforces this airline policy by requiring that the name on a ticket matches the person who actually flies.

17.4 A Price-Discriminating Monopolist

Under special circumstances—such as those existing in the airline industry—a monopolist can charge different customers different prices. The most important prerequisite is that customers are unable to resell the good between themselves at low cost. A good example is electricity provided by your local electric utility. Most electric companies charge higher prices for electricity used during peak daylight hours and lower prices for electricity used during off-peak nighttime hours. Unless a consumer has some means of storing electricity, there is no way for the person to purchase cheap electricity during off-peak hours and resell it for a profit to daytime users.

Another example is an oil producer that has a monopoly and charges a different price for home heating oil in the northeastern United States than in the southwestern United States. During winter months, you would expect that consumers located in the northeast are willing to pay more for heating oil than consumers located in the southwest. The monopolist is able to charge these two consumer groups different prices because it is too expensive for consumers in Albuquerque to resell heating oil to home owners in Boston.

When a monopolist sells its output at different prices, it is engaging in **price discrimination**.

> **PRICE DISCRIMINATION** A situation in which a producer sells units of its output at different prices despite the absence of any cost differences in supplying this output.

> **EXAMPLE** Disney World charges Florida residents a lower admission fee than visitors who come from out-of-state.

> **EXAMPLE** Movie theater chains often offer ticket discounts to senior citizens and students.

We sometimes notice sellers charging different prices to different groups of customers in markets that are not dominated by monopolists. Restaurants such as the International House of Pancakes or Denny's might offer a seniors' menu with lower-priced entrees. Yet we know that there are lots of local restaurants that compete with IHOP and Denny's. If you look closely, the entrees available to senior citizens tend to be more limited and smaller than those served to other customers. The same is true for the items and prices on a children's menu. So the fact of the matter is that IHOP and Denny's are really not charging different prices for the very same good. If they did, servers would have to "card" their patrons before they were permitted to order from the reduced-price menus.

In situations where different groups of consumers are charged different prices, more often than not, the supplier is providing different goods or services to each group. When it comes to movie theaters, for example, no senior or student discounts are permitted during the first weeks of a movie's run. Beyond this period, showings are priced lower because the opportunity cost of offering these tickets at a discount has dropped—there would be empty seats that would not be filled otherwise.

Different Types of Price Discrimination

A monopolist can engage in different types of price discrimination depending on market conditions. The most profitable type of price discrimination occurs when a monopolist is able to charge *each and every* consumer their full willingness to pay for *each and every* unit of output. This type of pricing system is called "consumer surplus skimming" or **first-degree price discrimination**.

> **FIRST-DEGREE PRICE DISCRIMINATION** A pricing scheme that charges each and every consumer his full willingness to pay for each and every unit sold.

> **EXAMPLE** At the "name your price" Web site, Priceline, individual buyers will bid up to their willingness to pay to purchase airline flights and hotel rooms.

> **EXAMPLE** A medical-device manufacturer will often sell doctors the same equipment at different prices. These prices usually vary with the size of the doctor's medical practice, which is a good indicator of a doctor's willingness to pay for the device.

A good example of first-degree price discrimination is eBay's bidding process for buying a good or service. A bidder will offer up to his willingness to pay to obtain the product in question. In effect, this bidder is willing to relinquish his total consumer surplus, if necessary, to "seal the deal." Whether or not he has to pay this full amount will depend, in part, on the amount of competition that exists among suppliers of the good. For example, the seller of a limited edition 1970 Rolling Stones poster is in a better position to squeeze the entire consumer surplus from the winning bidder than the seller of an open edition Rolling Stones record cover.

A first-degree price-discriminating monopolist attempts to capture the entire consumer surplus from buyers in the market. Why would a consumer be willing to still purchase a good if he has to hand over his entire consumer surplus? Recall that at this point, he is *indifferent* to whether he makes the purchase or not—he is willing and able to offer up to this amount for the good. At any higher price, however, the net benefit received from the purchase would be negative, and the consumer's well-being would therefore decline if he made the purchase, so he will move on to his next-best spending opportunity.

Figure 17.4 illustrates the market outcome for a first-degree price-discriminating monopolist. This type of monopolist charges a different price for each and every unit sold, thereby extracting each buyer's total willingness to pay for each unit sold. Of course, this assumes that the monopolist can accurately assess and collect the willingness to pay for each unit without incurring high transactions costs. By pricing in this

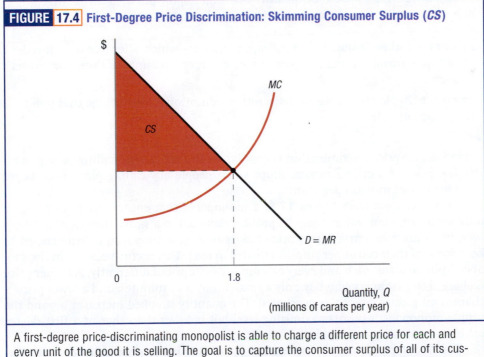

FIGURE 17.4 **First-Degree Price Discrimination: Skimming Consumer Surplus (*CS*)**

A first-degree price-discriminating monopolist is able to charge a different price for each and every unit of the good it is selling. The goal is to capture the consumer surplus of all of its customers (represented by red triangle *CS*). When units are priced differently, the monopolist does not have to drop its price on all of its output to sell an additional unit. The monopolist will sell this unit at the price that consumers are willing to pay for it. As a result, the marginal revenue the monopolist gets for each additional unit is represented by the demand (*D*) curve, which shows the willingness of consumers to pay for each incremental unit. The profit-maximizing output, which in this case is 1.8 million carats, will again be where *MR* equals *MC*.

way, the monopolist attempts to capture all of the consumer surplus of its customers. This additional revenue is represented by the red triangle.

A crucial characteristic of first-degree price discrimination is that the monopolist does not have to reduce the price on all of the units sold in order to sell additional units of the good. It can charge the highest prices for the first units sold and then, as it progressively moves down the demand curve, charge a lower and lower price as the willingness to pay falls. In this special situation, the monopolist's *MR* curve is *exactly equal* to the market demand curve it faces; that is, the marginal revenue received for each unit is exactly equal to the price at which it sells that unit. As Figure 17.4 illustrates, the profit-maximizing output level for a first-degree price-discriminating monopolist is 1.8 million carats—that is, where the *D* curve intersects the *MC* curve. At this point, the price received for the last unit sold—which equals its marginal revenue—is just equal to the marginal cost of producing this unit. The output, as well as total profits, will be greater for a price-discriminating monopolist than for a simple monopolist who can charge only one price for each and every unit of output.

A less "precise" type of price discrimination—called **second-degree price discrimination**—occurs when a monopolist gives customers a price "schedule" with prices that vary according to the amount of the good they purchase. The more a buyer purchases, the less he pays per unit.

SECOND-DEGREE PRICE DISCRIMINATION A monopoly pricing scheme that offers buyers discounts based on the quantity they purchase.

EXAMPLE Airline frequent-flyer mileage programs—which offer free or reduced-price trips—provide an indirect way to give quantity discounts to flyers that travel frequently.

EXAMPLE Apple offers volume discounts to educational institutions that purchase apps in bulk.

Second-degree price discrimination is popular among cell-phone calling-plan providers. The price of a calling minute drops when people buy calling plans with larger amounts of call minutes per month.

As you can see from **Figure 17.5**, a monopolist that engages in second-degree price discrimination will increase its profits compared to a simple monopolist. However, in contrast to a first-degree price-discriminating monopolist, consumers get to keep some of their consumer surplus (shaded in red). This occurs because, in the case of cell-phone plans, each and every call minute isn't priced differently. A higher price is charged to customers who buy only a small number of minutes, and a lower price is charged on greater quantities purchased. The quantity supplied increases beyond the simple monopolist's profit-maximizing level but is lower than that of a first-degree price-discriminating monopolist.

The final type of price discrimination is called **third-degree price discrimination**. Here, the monopolist separates groups of consumers into submarkets and sets the price in each submarket according to its elasticity of demand.

THIRD-DEGREE PRICE DISCRIMINATION A monopoly pricing scheme that charges groups of buyers differently based on their price elasticity of demand.

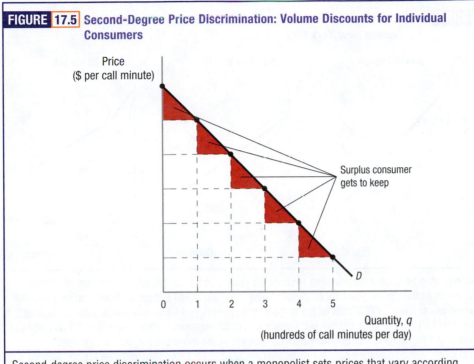

FIGURE 17.5 **Second-Degree Price Discrimination: Volume Discounts for Individual Consumers**

Second-degree price discrimination occurs when a monopolist sets prices that vary according to the amount of the good purchased. The more a buyer purchases, the less he pays for each additional unit purchased. This pricing scheme is also referred to as "block pricing" because the seller charges different prices for different ranges, or blocks, of output. The key to success is that the monopolist is able to differentiate among consumers based on the quantity of output they purchase. Because the price changes for "blocks" of purchases rather than for each and every unit, consumers get to keep some of their consumer surplus.

EXAMPLE Airlines find ways to charge business travelers higher airfares than leisure travelers.

EXAMPLE Movie theater chains charge weekend evening moviegoers more than weekday matinee patrons.

EXAMPLE Hospitals negotiate bigger discounts with insurance companies for elective outpatient services than they do for organ-transplant services.

Third-degree price discrimination is a very common form of price discrimination used by all kinds of companies, including airlines, art galleries, and gasoline stations. Have you ever noticed that the gasoline sold on toll roads is much more expensive than the gasoline sold after exiting the road? Or that the Burger King and Pizza Hut prices are much higher inside security checkpoints at an airport than across the street from the airport? Or that the price of an airline ticket purchased a couple of days before departure is usually substantially higher than one bought 21 days in advance? In these situations and others like them, consumers who pay the higher prices exhibit a much lower price elasticity of demand because it is costly, or very inconvenient, for them to take advantage of lower-priced opportunities.

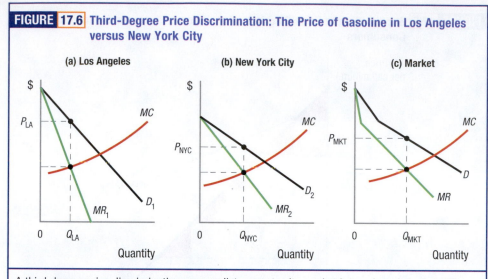

FIGURE 17.6 Third-Degree Price Discrimination: The Price of Gasoline in Los Angeles versus New York City

A third-degree price discriminating monopolist separates its market into submarkets that differ in terms of their price elasticity of demand. The monopolist will supply each submarket up to the point where the marginal cost of the last unit produced is just equal to the marginal revenue of the last unit sold in each submarket. Consumers in the less price-elastic submarket, Los Angeles, will pay a higher price for gasoline than consumers in the more price-elastic submarket, New York City. For this pricing scheme to be successful, it must be cost-prohibitive for consumers in the lower-priced submarket to resell the good to consumers in the higher-priced submarket.

Figure 17.6 depicts two submarkets for the same product where each subset of consumers exhibits a different price elasticity of demand, for example, gasoline consumers in Los Angeles versus New York City. In Los Angeles, there are few good transportation substitutes for the automobile. In contrast, there are so many good transportation options in New York City that relatively few people even own a car. In any event, we know that the price elasticity of demand for a product is higher (in absolute value) when good substitutes are available.

How does a price-discriminating monopolist take advantage of these different price elasticities and prevent buyers from reselling gasoline? If the marginal cost of supplying gasoline to both submarkets is the same, then the monopolist will supply gasoline to each one up to the point where the marginal revenue received for the last gallon sold in each submarket is just equal to its marginal cost of production. After these quantities are set, the demand curve in each submarket will determine that market's price of gasoline. As panels (a) and (b) of Figure 17.6 indicate, the price will be higher in the less price-elastic submarket (Los Angeles) and lower in the more price-elastic submarket (New York City). This result will maximize the monopolist's total economic profits from the two markets. This type of price-discriminating scheme is sustainable because it is cost-prohibitive for consumers to buy gasoline in the lower-priced New York City submarket and resell it in Los Angeles where the price is higher.

Cost-Justified Price Differentials

It is important to distinguish between price-discrimination schemes that monopolists pursue and situations where price differentials exist because the marginal cost of supplying different consumers is not the same. We know, for example, that computer manufacturers such as Dell operate in a highly competitive market, which means that they do not have the monopoly power required to engage in price discrimination. Yet, we observe that when Dell supplies laptops to large corporations and universities, it usually charges far less per laptop than when it supplies a laptop to a single retail customer. The reason for this price difference is that the marginal cost of supplying 1,000 standardized laptops to one buyer is lower than the marginal cost of supplying 1,000 customized laptops to 1,000 retail customers. As we will see later in this chapter, this "marginal cost" justification for price differences is a common defense that companies offer when they are accused of illegal price discrimination schemes (i.e., those that aim solely to capture more consumer surplus).

17.5 Natural Monopolies

Have you ever wondered why you and a friend of yours—who lives just over the line in another city or county—have different cable TV providers? You might be particularly aware of this if he is being charged a lot less a month than you, and you find out that you cannot switch to his provider. This situation arises because local governments typically award only one operating license to a cable TV company per geographic area to provide services to its residents. This, in turn, creates local monopolies in the cable TV market.

Why would a government do something like this, knowing that monopolies tend to produce less and charge more than companies in a competitive market? Why don't these governments encourage many cable TV companies to vie for your business? One answer is that the cable TV industry—along with the wired telephone, electricity, sewage, and water industries—tend to be highly capital-intensive. In other words, it costs a lot of money to lay networks of pipes, wires, and cables. As a result, these companies enjoy long-run average costs of production that fall over large ranges of output. In Chapter 15, we first introduced these types of firms and said that they exhibit *increasing returns to scale* in the long run.

We call this type of firm a **natural monopoly** because the very nature of its cost structure means that one firm can supply the market at a lower resource cost in the long run than multiple producers.

NATURAL MONOPOLY A firm whose long-run *MC* and *ATC* curves fall continuously throughout the full range of market demand.

EXAMPLE Water, gas, and electric utilities; telephone and cable services; and sewage-treatment plants all enjoy falling marginal and average costs for wide ranges of output.

Given these cost conditions, one large firm would come to dominate even a once-competitive market solely because its marginal cost of additional units of production would fall below that of smaller firms. Given this eventual outcome, it would be very costly to permit this type of competition to "play out" because that would require redundant capital investments—for example, multiple TV cable systems or gas utility lines connected to every house in the neighborhood.

Figure 17.7 illustrates the long-run cost structure of a natural monopoly, where the long-run average cost of production (*LRAC*) falls continuously as output expands. This is likely to occur when a firm has very high capital costs, such as the costs associated with launching a communications satellite or building an underwater

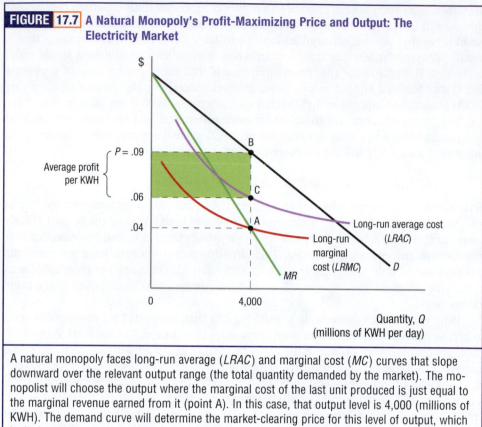

FIGURE 17.7 A Natural Monopoly's Profit-Maximizing Price and Output: The Electricity Market

A natural monopoly faces long-run average (*LRAC*) and marginal cost (*MC*) curves that slope downward over the relevant output range (the total quantity demanded by the market). The monopolist will choose the output where the marginal cost of the last unit produced is just equal to the marginal revenue earned from it (point A). In this case, that output level is 4,000 (millions of KWH). The demand curve will determine the market-clearing price for this level of output, which is designated by point B and is $.09 per KWH. Point C shows the average total cost (*LRAC*) per unit, which is $.06 per KWH. The average profit per KWH is $.09 – $.06, or $.03 per KWH. The green-shaded rectangle represents the total economic profit earned by the natural monopoly in the long run.

fiber-optics network. The cost of this capital per unit of production falls as more and more output is produced. We can also draw in the natural monopoly's long-run marginal cost (*LRMC*) curve. As we discussed in Chapter 15, the *LRMC* curve must lie below the *LRAC* curve for the average to be continuously falling.

A natural monopolist would follow the usual profit-maximizing rule and choose to produce where the marginal cost of the last unit is just equal to the marginal revenue earned from it. In Figure 17.7, which shows the price and output for a natural monopolist in the electricity market, the intersection between marginal revenue and marginal cost occurs at point A, leading to a profit-maximizing output level of 4,000 (millions of KWH). The demand (*D*) curve will determine the market-clearing price, which in this case is $0.09 per KWH. The long-run average cost per unit at this level of output is $0.06 (designated by point C). The per-unit profit is therefore $0.03 per KWH ($0.09 − $0.06). The firm's total profits equal $0.03 per KWH multiplied by 4,000 (millions of KWH) or $120 million. This is represented graphically by the green-shaded rectangle.

What would happen if a local government let firms bid for the right to become the city's only provider of electricity services? Bidders would bid up to the amount they are willing to pay for the license. This in turn would equal the monopoly profits they expect to earn if they were granted the monopoly. In effect, the bidding process would transfer virtually all of the monopoly profits to the local government. When this occurs, a monopoly license can be a financially winning proposition for local governments. Taxpayers, too, would win if the bulk of electricity users were buyers other than themselves—for example, local commercial industries that are stuck paying the monopoly price.

If a local government's sole goal is to maximize its "take" from awarding a company a monopoly, then this would be the end of the story. But the truth is that governments are likely to also be concerned about the possibility that an unregulated natural monopoly will supply too little output to the market. After all, cities and counties don't want rolling blackouts or backed-up sewage in residents' homes because too little electricity or inadequate sewage-treatment services are provided. **Figure 17.8** shows that at the monopoly output level of 4,000 (millions of KWH), consumers' willingness to pay for an additional KWH of electricity is $0.09 per kilowatt-hour (point B), which is greater than the $0.04 per KWH marginal cost of production (point A). It is only at an output level of 6,000 (millions of KWH) that consumers'

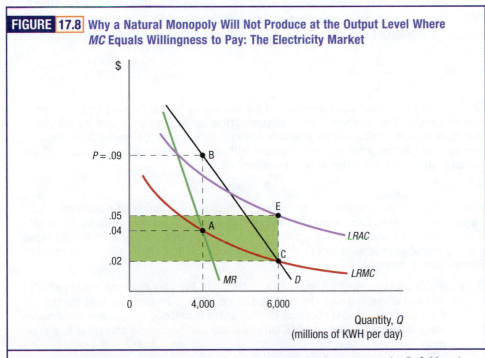

FIGURE 17.8 **Why a Natural Monopoly Will Not Produce at the Output Level Where *MC* Equals Willingness to Pay: The Electricity Market**

This natural monopolist's profit-maximizing price and output level occurs at point B: $.09 and 4,000 (million KWH). If the government required the monopolist to supply output up to the point where the marginal cost of the last KWH produced is just equal to the willingness to pay for it (point C), the firm would have to increase its output to 6,000 (million KWH). However, at this level of output, the monopoly is incurring losses: the average cost per KWH is $.05, designated by point E, but the price per KWH (determined by the demand curve) is just $.02, which is designated by point C. The resulting loss is $.05 – $.02 or $.03 per KWH. Total economic losses are represented by the green rectangle. The monopoly would go out of business unless regulators allowed it to collect enough additional revenue to at least break even.

willingness to pay, $0.02 per KWH, is equal to marginal cost (point C). However, if a simple monopolist charges what the market will "bear" at this higher output level, it will end up with a price of $0.02 per KWH, which is substantially *below* its average cost of production at this output level—$0.05 per kilowatt-hour (point E). As a result, the natural monopolist would suffer losses equal to the green-shaded area.

For this very reason, local governments have gotten into the business of setting the prices that natural monopolies can charge their customers. Their goal is to assure a level of output that is greater than what an unregulated monopoly would supply while, at the same time, permitting these companies to cover all of their costs of production. As we first discussed in Chapter 15, regulators often set prices that guarantee the natural monopoly a profit that is a percent (say, 12 percent) of its capital investment—that is, the money it has invested in hardware, facilities, and so on. The problem with this method of price setting is that it tends to encourage natural monopolies to spend more money on plants and equipment than they otherwise would. For example, they might lay more pipelines and fiber-optic cables than the cost-minimizing mode of production would dictate.[16]

Competitors cannot legally enter a market that has been awarded to a licensed, natural monopolist. However, there are many instances in which unregulated producers of substitute goods emerge and eventually erode the regulated monopolist's market dominance. A good example is the unregulated satellite dish TV industry, which now competes against regulated cable TV providers. The profits earned by regulated companies must be sufficiently attractive for such substitutes to arise.

SOLVED PROBLEM

Q Suppose a company has been granted the monopoly to sell naming rights to the stars in the sky. The company's costs of production are negligible so that its marginal cost curve is zero at all levels of production. (a) If this is a simple monopolist that charges only one price for its product, what will its profit-maximizing output be if the demand curve for the market is be represented by

$$P = 64 - 4Q$$

where P is the price charged per star named, and Q is the number of named stars purchased per month by consumers? (b) What is the price that corresponds to this level of output? (c) What is the price elasticity of demand at this level of output? (d) How, if at all, would your answer to (a) change if we were talking about a first-degree price-discriminating monopolist?

A   a. It will want to produce where $MR = MC = 0$. We can draw the monopolist's demand curve by using the equation given. (The X-intercept equals 16; the Y-intercept equals 64.) Because the MR curve is twice as steep when the demand curve is a straight-line, the MR curve will cut the horizontal axis (that is, equal zero) at $Q = 8$. Therefore, the profit-maximizing output is $Q = 8$, where $MR = 0$.

b. At $Q = 8$, the equilibrium price would equal $64 - 4(8) = \$32$ per star.

c. The price elasticity of demand equals -1 (unitary) at this level of output because marginal revenue equals zero at the midpoint of the demand curve.

· · · · · · ·

[16]Stratford Douglas, Thomas A. Garrett, and Russell M. Rhine, "Disallowances and Overcapitalization in the U.S. Electric Utility Industry." *Federal Reserve Bank of St. Louis Review* (January/February, 2009).

d. If the monopolist could perfectly price discriminate, it would produce 16 units of output. At this output level, the price of the last star sold is just equal to the marginal cost of supplying it, which in this case is zero.

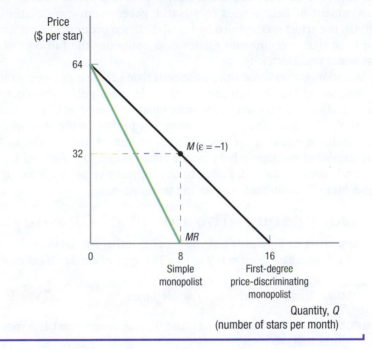

Publicly Owned Monopolies

Sometimes a local government will own a natural monopoly rather than granting monopoly rights to a privately owned company. For example, smaller cities often own their water and electric utilities outright rather than relying upon regulated private providers. We call these companies **public monopolies**.

> **PUBLIC MONOPOLY** A monopoly owned by a government entity.
>
> **EXAMPLE** A small city government owns the water and electric utility providers in that city.
>
> **EXAMPLE** Smaller cities often own the paramedic and ambulance company that serves their residents.

Public monopolies employ city workers, and customers are charged a user fee based on their level of consumption of the good or service. Sometimes the public monopoly is financed in full or in part through local tax assessments. A good deal of empirical research has been conducted on the cost-efficiency of regulated private utilities versus publicly owned monopolies. Most of these studies have concluded that private, regulated utilities incur substantially lower costs of production and distribution than their publicly owned counterparts.[17] Nevertheless, public monopolies may

[17]Susan K. Feigenbaum and Ronald Teeples, "Private versus Public Water Delivery: A Hedonic Approach." *Review of Economics and Statistics* (1983).

help a municipality achieve objectives other than cost minimization, such as employing local residents or subsidizing purchases by the elderly or poor. Goals such as these can be very important to the general public. Bolivia provides such an example: when the government of Bolivia tried to privatize government-owned utilities during the late 1990s, the effort was stymied by massive citizen protests against private investors who insisted that everyone—no matter how poor—pay the full cost of basic services such as water and electricity.

Public monopolies sometimes exist even when there is no economic rationale for them. The state of New Hampshire, for example, has a public monopoly in the supply of liquor: all liquor purchased in the state must be bought at a government retail outlet. The goal, of course, is to generate monopoly profits for the state while, at the same time, allegedly monitoring the sale of liquor to minors and drunks. In Denmark, the 60-year gambling monopoly held by the state-owned Danske Spel Corporation has only recently come to an end, falling to the competitive pressures brought by unregulated gambling Web sites such as online poker rooms.

17.6 Monopsony: The Power of One Buyer

Just as some markets have only a single supplier, other markets may have only a single buyer who can purchase from many sellers. This type of market is called a **monopsony**.

MONOPSONY A market with only a single buyer.

EXAMPLE Within the United States, the federal government is a monopsonist in the jet fighter market.

EXAMPLE Canada's publicly funded health-care system is the only buyer of medical services in Canada.

The same elements that sustain a monopolist also apply to a monopsonist; that is, there must be significant barriers to entry, but now they must exist on the buyer's side of the market. New buyers cannot enter the market at low cost, and suppliers cannot easily move to other markets to escape the monopsonist's pricing power.

Most often, economic models of monopsony have been used to predict the hiring behavior of a single employer in a specific labor market. The classic example is a mining or logging "company town," where all of the miners or loggers are employed by one local company. To the extent that it is costly for workers to relocate away from these towns, they are "sitting ducks" when it comes to the wages and work conditions they must endure. Company towns are common around the world. Toyota City in Japan is home to virtually all of Toyota Motor Company's 72,000 Japan-based employees and accounts for most of the employment in the city.[18] During the 2007 Great Recession, many foreign workers living in Toyota City left after losing their jobs, but native Japanese workers have remained, awaiting a rebound in the automobile industry.

In the early twentieth century, Standard Oil was a monopsonist when it came to the purchase of oil from Appalachian oil producers. Its market power came from the fact that Standard Oil owned the only pipeline connecting Appalachia's oil fields to

· · · · · · ·

[18]Martin Fackler, "Toyota's Troubles Slam Japan's Motor City." *New York Times,* April 29, 2009.

the rest of the country. Using lengthy and expensive legal maneuvering, Standard Oil effectively blocked other oil companies from laying pipelines. As a result, it was the sole buyer of oil in the region. It turns out that because of this, the amount of oil that Standard Oil bought was less than what would have been purchased in aggregate had there been numerous buyers in the market.

How Much Will a Monopsonist Buy?

Why was this the case? Keep in mind that a monopsonist is no longer a price taker when it is the only buyer in the market. It faces an upward-sloping supply curve, which shows all of the quantity that will be supplied to the market at each and every price. Unless he can price discriminate, a monopsonist is only able to increase its purchases by offering a higher price—that is, by moving up the market's supply curve. In a one-price market, this translates into paying more for each and every unit of the good the monopsonist buys. In the Standard Oil example, this meant that to purchase more oil from its Appalachian suppliers, the company had to pay a higher price for all of the oil that it purchased.

You may recall that a monopolist faces a similar situation. If it wants to sell more output, it must move down the market demand curve and reduce the price of all of the units it sells (assuming it cannot price discriminate). This is the reason why the marginal revenue that a monopolist receives for each additional unit of output sold is less than the price at which this unit is sold. Similarly, when a monopsonist increases its purchases, it must move up the market supply curve and pay a higher price not only for each additional unit purchased but also for all of the units bought. This means that the marginal cost of buying an additional unit will be greater than the price that is actually paid for this unit. We call this the monopsonist's **marginal factor cost**, or marginal outlay.

> **MARGINAL FACTOR COST (MFC)** A monopsonist's cost of purchasing an additional unit of the good or service for which it is the sole buyer.

> **EXAMPLE** In small rural towns, McDonald's is sometimes the only employer of local teens. In such cases, any expansion in hiring requires an increase in the wage rates for all of the teens working for the local fast-food outlet.

To better understand this situation, consider **Table 17.1**, which is a hypothetical supply schedule for Appalachian oil producers in the early 1900s. Output is measured in "cubic meters" (1 cubic meter equals approximately 265 gallons). As we can see from the data, these producers were willing to supply more oil when the price of oil increased, which is consistent with an upward-sloping market supply curve. This makes sense because oil producers would be willing to tap oil located deeper under the earth's surface if the price justified the additional expense of drilling it out of the ground.

If Standard Oil was forced to pay the same price for each and every cubic meter of oil purchased, then the marginal cost of buying additional oil would be greater than the price actually paid for the last cubic meter bought. Its marginal factor cost is computed and reported in Table 17.1.

How would the marginal factor cost figure into Standard Oil's decision about how much oil to purchase? In **Figure 17.9**, we graph both the supply (*S*) curve and

Table 17.1	A Monopsonist's Cost of Buying		
	A hypothetical example		
Qty of Oil Purchased (thousands of cubic meters)	Price ($ per cubic meter)	Total Expenditure ($ in thousands)	Marginal Factor Cost (*MFC*) ($ per cubic meter)
1	1.50	1.50	1.50
2	1.75	3.50	2.00
3	2.00	6.00	2.50
4	2.25	9.00	3.00
5	2.50	12.50	3.50
6	2.75	16.50	4.00

FIGURE 17.9   Market Equilibrium in the Presence of a Monopsony: The Case of Standard Oil

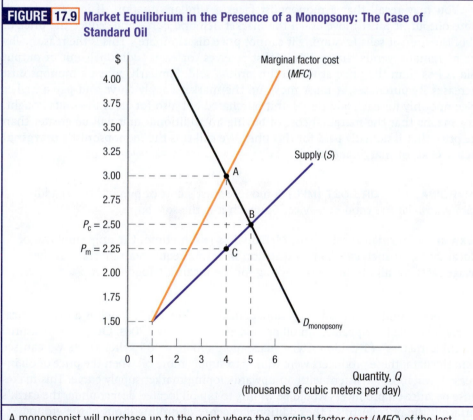

A monopsonist will purchase up to the point where the marginal factor cost (*MFC*) of the last unit purchased is just equal to its willingness to pay for it (represented by the monopolist's demand curve). In this case, the monopolist will purchase 4,000 cubic meters, and its *MFC* will equal $3.00 (point A). The supply (*S*) curve determines the market-clearing price for this level of purchases; reading down to the *S* curve, we see that this is $2.25 (point C). Notice that the quantity that the monopsonist purchases (4,000 cubic meters) is lower than the 5,000 cubic meters that would be purchased in a competitive market, which is where the *S* and *D* curves intersect (point B). The price the monopsonist pays is lower as well: the market-clearing price in a competitive market is $2.50, also shown by point B.

marginal factor cost (*MFC*) curve for Appalachian oil, based on the numbers in Table 17.1.

If we introduce Standard Oil's demand (*D*) curve (which represents its willingness to pay) into Figure 17.9, we see that the optimal amount of oil purchased by Standard Oil is 4,000 cubic meters per day. This is the quantity at which Standard Oil's willingness to pay is just equal to $3.00, the MFC of the last unit of oil purchased. It is indicated by point A. The supply (*S*) curve determines the market-clearing price for this quantity; reading down to the *S* curve we see that this is $2.25 (point C). Why doesn't Standard Oil have to pay $3.00? As shown, $3.00 is Standard Oil's cost (MFC) of buying another thousand cubic meters of oil in as much as it now has to offer a higher price for all of the oil it purchases. Although the MFC helps determine the amount of oil the firm will buy, it has nothing to do with the price per cubic meter that is ultimately paid—this is determined by the *S* curve. Notice too that Standard Oil's daily purchase is substantially less than the amount of oil that would have been bought if the market demand was comprised of many price-taking buyers. Had this been the case, the equilibrium output would have been 5,000 cubic meters per day and the market-clearing price would be $2.50, where market supply equals market demand (point B).

It is unclear whether Standard Oil actually paid all of its Appalachian oil producers the same price for their oil. If it was able to price discriminate between suppliers, it would have purchased more than 4,000 cubic meters per day. For Standard Oil to price discriminate, there could be no reselling of oil between the oil producers. Otherwise, the seller that was offered a higher price for his supply would have an incentive to purchase oil from lower-paid oil producers and re-sell it to Standard Oil at this higher price. This, in effect, would have resulted in multiple buyers of oil, thereby counteracting Standard Oil's original monopsony power.

The Government as Monopsonist

At first glance, monopsonies appear to be far less common than monopolies, which may explain why they tend to receive far less scrutiny by economists and regulators. Although private monopsonies are relatively rare, government entities often act like monopsonists.

For example, the U.S. government—in partnership with state governments—purchases more than 55 percent of all health-care services in the United States through government-financed health-insurance programs. While 55 percent is not 100 percent, the federal government has gained monopsony pricing power in health-care services by encouraging private insurers to adopt the same fee schedules used by the government to reimburse hospitals and physicians. The hotly debated Patient Protection and Affordable Care Act (ObamaCare), passed in 2010, expands government health-insurance programs to cover uninsured people and subsidizes the purchase of private insurance plans by poor or ill individuals. Given the potential budgetary impact of these initiatives, it is likely that the government will further exploit its monopsony pricing power in the physician, hospital, medical technology, and pharmaceutical drug markets.

Unlike private monopsonists, governments can attempt to impose price controls rather than move up a supply curve and pay the higher price required to entice suppliers to provide more services voluntarily. However, we already saw in Chapter 8 that price ceilings tend to lead to supply shortages. They can only work if the government can somehow "persuade" suppliers to provide a sufficient level of services at these below-equilibrium prices. For this very reason, Canada prohibits most Canadian doctors and hospitals from offering medical services that are paid for privately. It does not want these providers to leave the price-controlled government health-care system for unregulated private markets where prices are dictated by patients' willingness to pay and the opportunity cost of supply. In response, many Canadian physicians have moved to the United States and set up practice there—even if it means additional training to meet licensure requirements. And Canadian patients have turned to U.S. medical providers in the face of supply shortages, privately paying full price for hip replacements, MRIs, and other medical services with long waitlists in Canada.

17.7 Monopolistic Competition

Even in markets with numerous suppliers, we sometimes find producers that have some degree of pricing power. For example, Coke and Pepsi are able to price their products higher than supermarket and "second-tier" soft drink brands such as Shasta and Vess. And, Clorox bleach is priced higher than generics such as Safeway bleach. In these types of situations, competition does not necessarily result in a one-price market. We call this type of competition **monopolistic competition**.

MONOPOLISTIC COMPETITION A market in which many firms sell differentiated products—from the consumers' point-of-view—and where there are no barriers to entry.

EXAMPLE Burger King, McDonald's, and Wendy's compete in the market for fast-food hamburgers.

EXAMPLE Nike, Adidas, Converse, Avia, Reebok, Skechers, and New Balance compete in the market for athletic shoes.

EXAMPLE Yale, Princeton, Harvard, MIT, and Northwestern are among the universities that compete in the "most highly selective" category of the college market.

How is it that firms which sell "similar" products in the "same" market can exert pricing power in the face of multiple competitors? As we've discussed before, brand names can convey information to consumers, information that shapes their opinions about the quality and superiority of particular products. These brand names help companies distinguish their products from others in the same market, thereby creating **product differentiation** in terms of consumer perceptions.

PRODUCT DIFFERENTIATION Features of a product that consumers rely on to distinguish it from otherwise similar products.

EXAMPLE Wendy's has square hamburgers; its major competitors do not.

EXAMPLE Michael Jordan has a line of Nike—not Reebok or Adidas—athletic shoes.

EXAMPLE Harvard and Princeton are members of the Ivy League, while MIT and Northwestern are not.

Product differentiation is often achieved through advertising and other forms of product promotion. Advertising is used to convey the unique qualities of a good or service, sometimes relying on testimonials from everyday people and celebrities. The Marlboro Man made Marlboro cigarettes the choice of "rugged" independent men, while thin, fashionable models featured in Virginia Slims cigarettes ads targeted young, stylish women. Celebrity endorsements are meant to create an image of the buyer of a particular product, such as when Snoop Dogg appeared in a Hilfiger logo rugby shirt on the TV program *Saturday Night Live.* And product placements by Coke and other companies in popular movies indelibly link the movies and their stars to the goods in question.

Sometimes the packaging of a product can differentiate it from competitors, such as Wheaties cereal boxes featuring the faces of Olympic gold-medal winners. Even seemingly unrelated themes such as the gecko in Geico insurance ads or the duck in AFLAC disability insurance commercials can distinguish a brand from others in the market. This type of marketing repeats the brand name over and over so that potential customers will remember it should they ever be in the market for insurance services.

Product differentiation has the effect of reducing a good's price elasticity of demand; as a result, the demand curve facing a monopolistically competitive firm slopes downward to a certain extent rather than being horizontal like that of a price taker. In contrast to a price taker, a monopolistically competitive firm creates some "stickiness" in customer demand by creating product loyalty: when the firm raises its price, all of its buyers do not leave for lower-priced competitors. Some buyers are willing to pay additional money for a specific brand over and above what they would pay for substitutes in the market.

Figure 17.10 depicts just such a demand (*D*) curve for Coca-Cola. Because the *D* curve facing Coca-Cola is not horizontal, the company has some pricing power and can reap economic profits. In panel (a), we see that the giant soft drink company reaps an average of $0.10 profit for each of the 1.4 billion servings it supplies per day; this amounts to $140 million in total profits per day. This outcome looks a lot like the pure monopoly outcome, except that a firm under monopolistic competition tends to have a much flatter *D* curve because there are similar products available that can serve as substitutes if the company tries to raise its price too high.

Can Coca-Cola sustain these profits in the long run? Because there are no barriers to entry into monopolistically competitive markets, we would expect new competitors to be attracted into the soft-drink market by Coca-Cola's profitability. Panel (b) shows what would occur if these entrants were successful in siphoning off enough of Coca-Cola's demand so that there are no longer any excess profits. As the quantity of Coke demanded at each and every price drops, Coca-Cola's *D* curve would shift left to the point where it is just tangent to the *LRAC* cost curve (point A). As you can see, this zero-profit output level occurs to the left of the minimum of the *LRAC* curve, which is where a firm in a competitive market would operate in the long run (represented by point B). Point A is Coca-Cola's long-run equilibrium because even when entry into the market competes away excess profits, it does not eliminate the brand loyalty of at least some Coke drinkers. And it is this loyalty that underlies Coca-Cola's pricing power.

Of course, entrants may be unable to compete away all of Coca-Cola's profits if there are sufficient numbers of loyal Coke drinkers who do not think that a good substitute exists. Perhaps Coke has a formula that is difficult to replicate. Whatever the reason for this strong brand loyalty, it may preserve at least some of Coca-Cola's profits even in the long run.

FIGURE 17.10 **Monopolistic Competition: Coca-Cola's Pricing Power in the Short Run and Long Run**

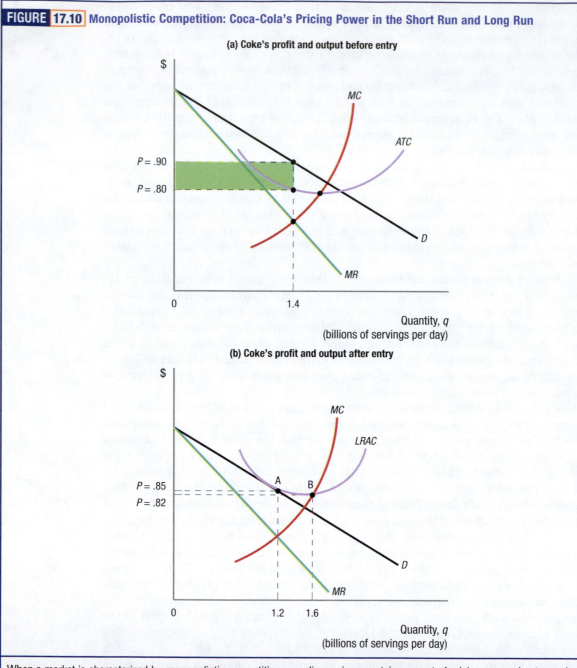

(a) Coke's profit and output before entry

(b) Coke's profit and output after entry

When a market is characterized by monopolistic competition, suppliers enjoy a certain amount of pricing power due to product differentiation. As a result, the prices they charge will vary according to the price elasticity of the demand that they face. The lower the price elasticity of demand (in absolute value), the less substitutable other products are from a consumer's perspective. The green rectangle in panel (a) represents the economic profits Coke earns due to this pricing power.

Panel (b) shows what would occur if new entrants into the soft drink market were successful in siphoning off enough of Coca-Cola's demand so that there were no longer any excess profits. These new entrants would reduce the quantity of Coke demanded at each and every price. As a result, Coca-Cola's demand (*D*) curve would shift left to the point where it is just tangent to the long-run average total cost (*LRAC*) curve (point A). However, this zero-profit output level occurs to the left of the minimum of the *LRAC* curve, where a firm in a competitive market would operate (point B). Coke's price of $.85 will therefore be higher than the competitive price ($.82), and the company's output of 1.2 billion servings a day will be lower than the output resulting from a competitive soft-drink market (1.6 billion servings a day).

17.8 The Problem with Monopolies and Pricing Power

From an economic standpoint, three major problems arise from the existence of monopolies. The first is that too little output is produced by a simple monopolist, as compared to the amount supplied by competitive markets. Competitive firms will, in aggregate, produce output up to the point where the willingness to pay for the last unit sold is just equal to its marginal cost of production—that is, where the market demand and supply curves intersect. By contrast, simple monopolists will only produce to the point where the marginal revenue (MR) generated by the last unit sold is equal to its marginal cost. Because marginal revenue is less than price (recall that the MR curve lies below the market demand curve), consumers' willingness to pay for the last unit sold exceeds its marginal cost of production. Consumers are willing to compensate the monopolist for more output, but it won't produce more because it will have to charge less for all of the units it sells. And, because a simple monopoly produces too little output based on consumers' willingness to pay, it also employs too few inputs in the production process.

When a monopolist can price discriminate, it will move closer to the competitive level of output. Earlier, Figure 17.4 showed that first-degree price discrimination will result in a monopoly output level corresponding to the point where the marginal cost of producing the last unit just equals consumers' willingness to pay for it—the same output level as that of a competitive market.

A second problem associated with monopolies is that they do not produce at the minimum of their average cost curve, even in the long run. This means that the scarce resources used up in producing each unit of output will not be minimized. In contrast, recall that in the long run, competitive price-taking firms will all produce at the minimum of their average cost curves (assuming they have the same cost conditions).

Finally, monopolies are undesirable from an economic standpoint because their prices don't reflect the true opportunity cost of supplying additional units of output. As a result, the price signals that consumers face are "distorted." From a resource-allocation point of view, there will be too little consumption of monopolized goods relative to (substitute) goods produced in competitive markets. For example, if a prescription cough syrup is priced higher than its marginal cost of production because it is a patented drug, consumers will purchase less of it and more of the lower-priced, weaker over-the-counter remedy, even though they would prefer to buy the prescription drug if it was priced at marginal cost.

This distortion in price signals is exacerbated in the presence of third-degree price discrimination. Groups of consumers are charged different prices for the monopolized good according to their elasticity of demand, even though the marginal cost of production is the same for all of the groups. We know that this pricing behavior causes market inefficiencies because consumers charged a lower price would be made better off if they could resell to members in higher-priced groups if the opportunity arose. Leisure passengers would be willing to resell their airline tickets to business travelers who are charged a higher fare; Florida residents would be willing to resell their discounted Disney World entry passes to out-of-state tourists who are charged a higher entry price. This tells us that there are unexploited gains from trade: that is, trades exist that would make some consumers better off without making others worse off. Whenever voluntary trade is blocked by legal or market barriers, we know that the market outcome is not as economically efficient as it could be.

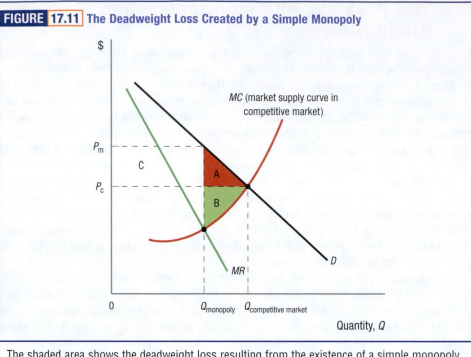

FIGURE 17.11 The Deadweight Loss Created by a Simple Monopoly

The shaded area shows the deadweight loss resulting from the existence of a simple monopoly. Both consumer surplus (area A) and producer surplus (area B) are lost because of the shortfall in production. Area C represents consumer surplus that is transferred to the monopolist—this is a wealth transfer that has no impact on the consumer's willingness to trade with the monopolist.

The Deadweight Loss from Monopoly

As you may recall, we first introduced the concept of deadweight loss when we discussed government taxation in Chapter 12. Another situation where deadweight losses arise is in the case of a monopoly. The shaded area in **Figure 17.11** shows the deadweight loss resulting from monopoly pricing and output. Both consumer surplus (area A) and producer surplus (area B) are lost because of the shortfall in production. Area C represents the amount of consumer surplus that is converted into monopoly profits.

Notice that we haven't argued that monopoly profits, in and of themselves, are a problem from an economic standpoint. Certainly, these profits represent a transfer of wealth from consumers to the monopolist. However, these transfers do not affect the allocation of resources in the economy. After all, consumers are willing to give up their entire consumer surplus if necessary to make a trade. In other words, the exchanges that occur between consumers and monopolists are still voluntary.

There is one important exception to the assertion that monopoly profits are "just" a transfer of wealth between buyers and sellers. This exception relates to (potential) monopolists who spend scarce resources to gain or protect their monopoly. For example, think about all the money that U.S. Steel has spent over the years trying to convince politicians that they should impose high tariffs that effectively block foreign steel imports, or consider the amount of money that pharmaceutical companies have spent lobbying Congress to extend the length of drug patents. These are examples of *rent-seeking* activities, where scarce resources are spent to capture future monopoly profits, which we first discussed in Chapter 4.[19]

How much would a potential monopolist be willing to spend in such rent-seeking activities? The upward limit would be the amount of monopoly profits it expects to gain over time weighted by the probability of obtaining the government's grant of monopoly. These resources could instead be used to produce goods and services valued by consumers. When a potential monopoly engages in rent-seeking activities, the economic loss resulting from the subsequent monopoly will be substantially greater than the deadweight loss illustrated in Figure 17.11. This loss must include the amount of real resources used up in rent-seeking activities. In other words, the monopolist's subsequent profits can no longer be viewed as simply an income transfer from consumers to the monopolist.

17.9 Government Strategies to Prevent Monopoly: Antitrust Law

Many countries have enacted laws that prohibit firms from engaging in what are deemed to be monopolizing activities. These laws do not outlaw monopolies but only those "anticompetitive" actions that are likely to increase a company's pricing power. Among the activities that governments monitor are companies' pricing schemes, mergers and acquisitions.

In the late nineteenth century, the U.S. government passed the Sherman Act, followed almost 25 years later by the Clayton Act. These are referred to as "antitrust" laws for historical reasons. Prior to the introduction of the Sherman Act, owners of large companies such as Standard Oil placed their ownership shares "in the trust" of a handful of nonowners to conceal plans to consolidate their industries. Because antitrust laws are federal statutes, they apply only to those companies that sell products across state lines. However, many states have adopted their own anticompetitive statutes for companies that sell solely within their state. Over the past 50 years, the European Union has also adopted antitrust laws that are largely the same as U.S. statutes.

We noted at the outset of this chapter that U.S. antitrust enforcers indicted De Beers for price fixing, thereby leading to De Beers' withdrawal from the U.S. diamond market. Antitrust action was also taken almost a century before against Standard Oil in response to its stranglehold over the Appalachian oil reserves and other aspects of its production and distribution systems. In fact, virtually every oil company in the United States that arose during the first part of the twentieth century had its start in the court-ordered breakup of Standard Oil in 1913. Ironically, some of these very companies have consolidated once again in the past few decades.

Of late, high-tech companies—such as Microsoft, Apple, and Intel—have received a great deal of attention from antitrust regulators in the United States and Europe. The reason for this growing focus may have to do with certain aspects of high-tech production that favor "bigness" and market dominance. These include patented intellectual property such as computer operating systems and smart-phone software, the high fixed cost of innovation, and the relatively low marginal cost of production.

Without a doubt, the most contentious, long-running antitrust investigation in recent times involved Microsoft. In the 1990s, the government accused Microsoft of trying to monopolize the PC software market by providing users with a bundle of

· · · · · · ·

[19]Tullock, G. "The Welfare Costs of Tariffs, Monopolies and Theft." *Western Economic Journal*, 5 (1967): 224–232.

software applications tied to its then-popular operating system, MS-DOS. In response to this government complaint, Microsoft agreed that it would no longer bundle software programs together with its operating system but reserved the right to exploit the interrelated capabilities of its operating system and its Web browser, Internet Explorer.

In 1998, the U.S. government again filed an antitrust complaint against Microsoft, claiming that it had engaged in anticompetitive activities by bundling its Web browser together with its new Windows operating system. The software giant was also accused of requiring PC manufacturers to install the browser when they installed Windows or risk losing their license to install Windows at all. Finally, Microsoft's licensing practices pertaining to its operating system and browser were considered anticompetitive because PC makers only had to renew these licenses once a year and, in the interim, could load the software onto additional machines at no cost. In 1999, the court found that Microsoft had indeed engaged in monopolizing activities by tying its browser to its operating system and strong-arming PC makers to install both.

The final issue that the court addressed was the appropriate remedy for Microsoft's monopolizing efforts. In 2000, the court ruled that Microsoft should be broken up into two companies—one focusing solely on the development of operating systems and the second on software applications, including browsers. Microsoft appealed this ruling and nearly four years later, it won a substantial victory—the original remedy was discarded and replaced by the far weaker requirement that Microsoft make public its operating system interface, thereby reducing the barriers facing independent software and browser developers.

More recently, the European Union has imposed a $1.45 billion fine on Intel for "abusing" its dominant position in the microchip market.[20] The chipmaker—which controls over 80 percent of the global market in microprocessors—was accused of offering illegal financial inducements to PC manufacturers in the form of loyalty rebates, which were reduced considerably if competitors' microprocessors were also purchased. The ruling made clear that "the fact that Intel had such a large market share is not a problem in itself."[21] Rather, it was Intel's anticompetitive activities that harmed both EU consumers—through higher end-user prices—and Intel competitors such as Advanced Micro Devices (AMD), which brought the complaint against Intel to the EU antitrust agency in the first place.

Economists differ greatly in their perspectives on government antitrust activities and remedies. Most would agree that "size alone is not an offense" and that antitrust regulators must guard against protecting competitors rather than competition. Did U.S. regulators prosecute Microsoft in 1998 for the anticompetitive effects of bundling Internet Explorer with its operating system or to protect Netscape, a competing browser company? When, in 2009, the European Union forced the computer chipmaker Intel to end its rebates to computer makers who bought fewer chips from competing companies, was this designed to protect the rival chipmaker AMD, which had brought the complaint to the EU regulators? In both cases, the regulators had to convince the courts that they weren't merely protecting competitors such as Netscape and AMD, but had a legitimate purpose for taking action against Microsoft and Intel. Sometimes it is cost-effective for certain goods to be bundled together for sale: new cars and GPS systems (but not bullet-proof windows); laptops and LCD

[20]Charles Forelle and Don Clark, "Intel Fine Jolts Tech Sector." *Wall Street Journal*, May 14, 2009.

[21]Neelie Kroes, European Commissioner for Competition Policy, "Commission takes antitrust action against Intel: Introductory remarks." Press conference, Brussels, May 13, 2009.

screens (but not external speakers or most software). How easy is it to distinguish between pricing or bundling strategies that reflect cost efficiencies and those that are aimed solely at monopolizing a market? The difficulties inherent in applying antitrust laws to improve market outcomes is perhaps best evidenced by the fact that several prominent MIT economics professors testified as expert witnesses against each other in the Microsoft case!

WHAT YOU SHOULD HAVE LEARNED FROM CHAPTER 17

■ That a monopoly arises and is sustainable only if there are barriers to entry into the market.

■ That governments sometimes grant monopolies to increase the tax revenues they receive from those monopolies.

■ That to stimulate investment in intellectual property, governments have adopted patent and copyright systems to protect the ownership rights to this property; this often results in monopoly.

■ That just like price-taking firms, a monopolist will maximize its profits by choosing an output level where marginal cost equals marginal revenue for the last unit produced.

■ That because a monopoly faces a downward sloping demand curve, the monopolist must consider the revenue it will lose by reducing its price in order to sell more output.

■ That the marginal revenue generated by each additional unit of output sold by a monopolist is less than the price at which the unit is sold.

■ That a monopolist will produce less output than if price-taking firms supplied the market.

■ That a price-discriminating monopolist will increase its output beyond that of a simple monopolist as long as it can prevent the resale of its product from one customer to another.

■ That depending on market conditions, there are three different strategies a monopolist can adopt to discriminate between consumers when it comes to price.

■ That natural monopolies arise because of the nature of the cost structures of some industries.

■ That natural monopolies are typically regulated by local governments or taken over completely as public monopolies.

■ That single demanders, called monopsonists, can exist in certain markets.

■ That monopsonists will purchase too little of a good because they must take into account that the purchase price will rise as the monopsonist buys more—that is, the monopsonist must move up the market supply curve to buy more output.

■ That companies engage in advertising and other activities to differentiate their products from close substitutes in order to achieve some pricing power—we call this monopolistic competition.

■ That economists are generally not very worried about the economic profits earned by monopolists but, instead, are more concerned about the shortfall in output resulting from monopolies.

■ That a firm will spend scarce resources on rent-seeking activities to gain a license for a monopoly, which is an inefficient use of resources from an economic standpoint.

■ That antitrust laws prohibit anticompetitive "monopolizing" activities, not the actual existence of monopolies.

KEY TERMS

QUESTIONS AND PROBLEMS

1. A single buyer in a market (a monopsonist) faces an upward-sloping supply curve given by $P = 40 + 10Q$. Graph the supply curve and the curve representing the marginal factor cost of buying an additional unit. Which is relevant to the buyer's decision making?

2. Suppose that due to prohibitively high import tariffs, U.S. steelmakers have a virtual monopoly in their home (U.S.) market. Show how they (together) would set price in this home market if (a) they do not export steel; (b) they export steel to the world market, where they face a given world price (i.e., where they are price takers).

3. (1) Many major airlines have employee travel cards that permit employees to fly "space available" (i.e., no reservations allowed) at substantial discounts. (2) Local theaters often have a half-price "rush hour show." (3) Restaurants often offer special senior citizen menus and discounts. (4) Airline tickets are typically less if purchased for a Saturday night stay and 14 days in advance.
   a) Which of these practices constitute price discrimination? Explain your answer.
   b) In which of these cases do you think that price discrimination is sustainable? Why?

4. Contrast the short-run and long-run impact of a per unit tax on a competitive industry versus a monopoly. Under which scenario (competition or monopoly) will consumers bear the greatest share of the tax?

5. Suppose that the government placed a price ceiling on a monopolist. Will this have the same impact on the quantity produced as it would if the market were competitive? Explain your answer.

6. True, False, or Uncertain. As with a competitive firm, a monopoly's short-run supply curve will be the portion of its marginal cost curve that sits above its average variable cost curve. Explain your answer.

7. Explain why the marginal cost curve can never intersect the marginal revenue curve in the inelastic portion of a monopolist's demand curve.

8. You have been hired by a monopolist to confirm whether it is producing at the profit-maximizing level of output. You observe that it is collecting $12,000 in revenue by selling 2,000 units of output. Furthermore, its average total cost is $5.20, which is 80 cents below its marginal cost. Should the company change its level of output? Why or why not?

9. Another monopoly client is charging $12 per unit of output and selling 4,000 units of output. Its marginal cost of production is $6 a unit and marginal revenue is two-thirds of its price. Should the company change its level of output? Why or why not?

10. In the 1960s, one of the rationales offered for regulating the airfares and routes of airlines (or creating a public airline monopoly like Air France) was that the industry was a natural monopoly. Do you think that this was a reasonable

justification for regulation? If so, what changed that justified deregulation of fares and routes in the late 1980s? Explain your answer.

11. In 1949, the American Can Company—a producer of can-closing equipment—was prohibited by the U.S. government from continuing its practice of leasing its equipment and requiring lessees to also buy all of their cans from them. This business arrangement is called "tying" or "bundling." Why do you think that American Can adopted this business practice? Why did federal antitrust regulators fight to end it? Explain your answer.

12. Suppose that a major movie theater chain is about to debut a highly anticipated film. It faces two sets of demand curves—one for tickets in New York City and the other for tickets in a "sleepy" suburb upstate about 90 miles away. If the demand curves for tickets for opening night (where Q is in thousands) are

$$P = 22 - 6\,Q \text{ NYC}$$

$$P = 16 - 4\,Q \text{ suburb}$$

and the MC of exhibiting the film is $4 per ticket holder in both markets,

a) How many tickets will the movie chain sell in each theater location?
b) At what price(s)?
c) What must the movie chain assume about urban moviegoers to adopt this type of pricing scheme?

13. Economists sometimes talk about a "second-best world" in which a market is dominated by one seller (monopolist) and one buyer (monopsonist). This is called a *bilateral monopoly*. Show this situation graphically by superimposing the market diagram for a monopolist onto the market diagram for a monopsonist. Can you determine how much output will be produced and sold in this market, and at what price? What do you think may be important in determining this outcome?

14. Instead of rewarding innovation through a patent system, which creates monopolies, some economists suggest that the government should subsidize research and development and/or give cash "prizes" to successful innovators. Discuss how this alternative reward system differs from the patent system in terms of (a) how the "value" of the innovation is assessed, and (b) who funds the payoff that the inventor receives.

15. Using a diagram for a typical monopsonist, indicate the deadweight loss that results from having just one buyer in a market.

16. Medicare, the federal medical insurance program for the over-65 population, is the predominant purchaser of medical services in the United States. It pays urban teaching hospitals a higher amount than rural hospitals for the same service (for example, hip replacement surgery). Explain whether such a price-discriminating monopsonist ends up closer to the competitive outcome than a "simple" monopsonist.

Oligopolies: The Strategic Behavior of Rivals

"Our strategy is one of preventing war by making it self-evident to our enemies that they're going to get their clocks cleaned if they start one."

General John W. Vessey, former U.S. Army and Chairman of the Joint Chiefs of Staff

So far in this book, we have explored three types of profit-maximizing firms that lie along the competitive spectrum:

- The price-taking firm that must accept the prevailing price in the marketplace
- The price-setting monopoly that can set the price in the marketplace
- The monopolistically competitive firm that has some control over the price it can charge

Price-taking firms and monopolists lie at the opposite ends of the spectrum in terms of their pricing behavior. Monopolistically competitive firms fall somewhere in between but are typically closer to the price-taking end because their markets contain many firms, and no barriers to entry exist.

There is yet another type of profit-maximizing firm that cannot be classified as either perfectly competitive or as a monopoly. An *oligopolist* is a producer that operates in a market in which there are only a small number of firms, and entry is costly. This type of market is called an **oligopoly**, where *oligos* is Greek for "few" and *poly* means "entity." In contrast, you will recall that the *mono* in monopoly means "one."

OLIGOPOLY A market comprised of only a few sellers, with high barriers to entry.

EXAMPLE The military and passenger aircraft-manufacturing industry is an oligopoly.

EXAMPLE The pharmacy-benefit management (PBM) industry is an oligopoly.

EXAMPLE The U.S. cellular communications industry is an oligopoly.

Oligopolists are interdependent when it comes to making pricing and output decisions. This is not only because they face the same market demand curve but also because one firm's pricing decisions usually set off strategic responses by rivals in the market. The airline industry provides a good example of this kind of behavior. When one airline raises or lowers its fare on a particular route, rival airlines tend to quickly do the same. The same thing happens when a gasoline station on one corner of an intersection raises or lowers its price—other stations in close proximity usually follow suit.

The term "rival" suggests that a person, firm, or group knows its opponents and vies with them for some type of prize. Examples include the baseball rivalry between the Boston Red Sox and the New York Yankees for the World Series Championship; the rivalry between the Republican and Democratic parties for control of Congress; and the rivalry between smart phone manufacturers for dominance in the cellular-communications market. A similar type of rivalry sometimes arises between parents who may think it necessary to compete for their children's affection and loyalty.

The strategies that rivals adopt to win the "prize" they seek depend on the assumptions they make about how their competitors will react to their own behavior. In some sense, it is like a video game or game of chess: to be strategic, a player's moves will depend on what she thinks the other player will do in the next round and in the rounds ahead. We will soon see that this also holds true for firms that are seeking to maximize their profits in the face of only a handful of rival producers.

Rivals may attempt to influence their opponents' behavior by sending misleading signals. It is not uncommon for oligopolists to try to bluff one another by issuing press releases announcing anticipated stock buybacks, acquisition targets, and even future retail locations. This is no different from the misleading signals that poker players project to bluff their opponents into folding.

Rivals may also "cheat" on implicit or explicit agreements they have made with one another. Consider the parent who agrees privately to let his son stay out after curfew after having presented a united front with his spouse about how important it is to enforce curfews. Clearly, the parent who secretly acquiesces earns lots of "brownie points" with his son, leaving the other parent to shoulder the costs of enforcing curfew rules. In a similar fashion, oligopolists may cheat on agreements about prices or production levels if they think they can earn greater profits and get away with it.

18.1 Incorporating Rivals into the Profit-Maximizing Decision Process: A Game Theory Approach

Ultimate Electronics was a national retail chain that sold big-screen TVs and video equipment. It proudly advertised that it "shopped its competitors" (such as Best Buy and Walmart) and set its prices to meet or beat the competition. The interesting question is why Ultimate adopted this pricing policy. Was it to attract more customers by ensuring its prices were the lowest, or was it to signal to its rivals that they would not benefit from lowering their own prices? Clearly, Ultimate recognized the mutual interdependence that existed between it and rival retail chains selling similar electronic products. This is exactly the type of situation in which a company's very survival can be at risk if it does not accurately forecast and adapt to its rivals' behavior.

The Cournot Model

Economists have paid a great deal of attention to the assumptions, or *conjectures*, that rivals make about each other and how these are incorporated into their decision-making process. In the mid-nineteenth century, the French economist Augustin

Cournot attempted to explicitly model these assumptions to predict what the eventual equilibrium price and output would be in a market with only two profit-maximizing rivals. These rivals are called *duopolists*, where *duo* means "two" in Greek. They compete in a **duopoly** market.

DUOPOLY A market comprised of only two firms, with high barriers to entry.

EXAMPLE Airbus and Boeing are currently the only producers of large, wide body commercial passenger aircraft in the world.[1]

EXAMPLE Intel and Advanced Micro Devices (AMD) are duopolists that share the microprocessor market.

EXAMPLE Until 1992, the comic book industry was a duopoly comprised of Marvel and D.C. Comics.[2]

Cournot suggested that each rival would take the other's current output level as a given and would then choose its own profit-maximizing output. To be more precise, Cournot proposed that a duopolist would subtract its rival's output from total market demand at each and every price. Then, based on this remaining market demand, it would choose its own profit-maximizing output level.

Consider the example of the rental-car market depicted in **Figure 18.1**. This shows a situation in which a duopolist in the car-rental business (Hertz) assumes

FIGURE 18.1 **A Cournot Duopoly: Hertz's Initial Output Decision**

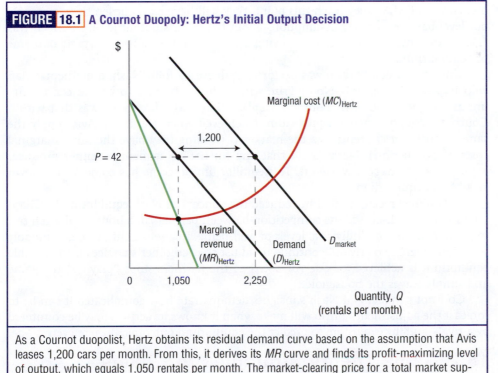

As a Cournot duopolist, Hertz obtains its residual demand curve based on the assumption that Avis leases 1,200 cars per month. From this, it derives its *MR* curve and finds its profit-maximizing level of output, which equals 1,050 rentals per month. The market-clearing price for a total market supply of 1,050 Hertz rentals plus 1,200 Avis rentals per month (2,250 total rentals) is $42 per rental.

· · · · · · · ·

[1]Daniel Solon, "Bumpy Ride Ahead for Air Industries." *New York Times*, July 18, 2010.

[2]Alain Anderton, *Economics,* 3rd ed. (London: Pearson Education, 2000).

that its rival (Avis) will supply 1,200 car rentals each month at its Boston–Logan airport location.

Based on this assumption, Hertz subtracts the 1,200 car rentals from the Logan airport market demand (D) curve to calculate the quantity demanded that remains unfilled at each price. Then, Hertz derives its marginal revenue (MR) curve based on this adjusted or "residual" demand curve. Acting as a monopolist for this residual segment of the market, Hertz will maximize its profits by choosing the output level where its marginal cost equals its (residual) marginal revenue. According to Figure 18.1, Hertz will maximize its profits by supplying 1,050 car rentals per month.

The price at which Hertz supplies these cars must take into consideration the quantity that Avis supplies to the market. In Figure 18.1, the equilibrium price is equal to $42 a day, the market-clearing price when the *total* quantity supplied by both duopolists to the market equals 2,250 car rentals per month. Note that because consumers can still choose between the two suppliers, there can be only one rental price in the market (for a particular type of car and terms of rental). If there *were* more than one price, all of the consumers would migrate to the lower-priced supplier.

What if you were the manager of the Avis location at Logan airport? Would you just sit back and let Hertz "take" nearly half the market? This is the fundamental problem with the Cournot duopoly model: it is unrealistic to believe that Avis would not respond to Hertz's output decision by readjusting its own output level. In other words, the Cournot model will not achieve a "one-shot" stable outcome. Each rival will react to the other's decisions by adjusting its own output levels until such time as they both reach the point where there is no incentive to make any further adjustments. If and when they reach this point, they will have each chosen their own output level based on correct assumptions about the other's output level. In effect, this "game" of moving, reacting, and moving again, will have achieved a stable outcome or "equilibrium."

This type of equilibrium was explored in-depth by John Nash, a mathematician who is probably the only Nobel Prize winner in Economics to be the central figure in a popular movie (*A Beautiful Mind*). What Nash discovered was that within Cournot's duopoly model, equilibrium is achieved when Hertz and Avis supply the same quantity of car rentals to the market (assuming they have the same marginal costs of production). Nash found that any further adjustment by either producer would make them *both* worse off. This equilibrium outcome has come to be known as a "Nash equilibrium."

As you may recall, we first introduced the concept of Nash equilibrium in Chapter 11 when we discussed the competition between partners in a household, each trying to maximize their individual levels of well-being. In a sense, this, too, is a duopoly situation where two "rivals" continue to adjust to each other's choices until a stable equilibrium is achieved, or one (or both) of the partners stops "playing" the game and simply leaves the household.

Cournot's model and Nash's insights demonstrate how complicated it can be to forecast the adjustments a firm will make when it knows its actions may be countered by a rival—and, by extension, to predict the equilibrium outcome, if there even is one.

18.2 Game Theory Strategies for Rivals

In the century that has passed since Cournot, economists and mathematicians have continued to struggle with the question of how a small number of rivals react to one another when making decisions. Working together, mathematician John von Neumann (considered the greatest mathematician of the twentieth century) and economist Oscar Morgenstern created a whole new way of portraying this interdependent behavior. Their framework of analysis is called **game theory**.[3]

GAME THEORY A model of decision making that portrays the set of strategies that each rival can choose from and uses this information to predict how each will respond to one another.

EXAMPLE A large pharmaceutical company that currently dominates the asthma-medication market must assess the probability that its primary rival will pursue a costly direct-to-consumer TV campaign for its own new asthma drug rather than increase its sales force to call upon doctors who prescribe such medications. Subject to this assessment, the company will decide which strategy will maximize its own profits.

EXAMPLE An economics textbook company must assess the strategy that a rival company will adopt when it comes to scheduling the release of new introductory economic books before it adopts a schedule for releasing its own textbooks.

Game theory considers all of the strategies available to each rival and predicts the choices that will be made, whether we are talking about political, household, or even military decisions. (Recall the quote by General John Vessey at the beginning of this chapter, if you don't think this is true.) It does this by providing a framework that captures all of the possible strategies available to each rival, as well as the payoffs that result from each combination of decisions that the rivals make. This information is conveniently represented in a **payoff matrix**.

PAYOFF MATRIX A chart with rows and columns representing the strategies available to each rival; the intersection of each row and column reveals the payoff to each rival for the combination of strategies that the two rivals choose.

EXAMPLE The payoff matrix in **Table 18.1** shows the additional profits that two cigarette companies—R.J. Reynolds (Camel) and Philip Morris (Marlboro)—would earn depending on each one's advertising strategy. Each company can choose between two options: advertise or don't advertise. Each cell in the payoff matrix indicates the additional profits to be had by each company given the strategies that both rivals follow.

Table 18.1 Tobacco Companies' Advertising Strategies

Payoff Matrix
(additional profits per year, in millions of dollars)

		R.J. Reynolds	
		Do Not Advertise	Advertise
Philip Morris	**Do Not Advertise**	R.J. Reynolds: $300 Philip Morris: $300	R.J. Reynolds: $400 Philip Morris: −$50
	Advertise	R.J. Reynolds: −$50 Philip Morris: $400	R.J. Reynolds: $100 Philip Morris: $100

[3]John von Neumann and Oscar Morgenstern, *Theory of Games and Economic Behavior* (Princeton, NJ: Princeton University Press, 1944).

In the upper-left cell, we see that both companies add $300 million to their bottom lines by not advertising. This makes sense because by not advertising, they both save themselves a costly advertising war. But, assuming that the rivals do not share their strategies with each other, this is not likely to be the outcome. Why not? If R.J. Reynolds advertises and Philip Morris does not, R.J. Reynolds will earn an additional $400 million while Philip Morris will lose $50 million in profits due to its loss in market share (reported in the upper-right cell). The reverse occurs if Philip Morris decides to advertise but R.J. Reynolds opts not to (as reported in the bottom-left cell). Given these payoffs, both companies will choose to advertise, and each will realize an additional $100 million in profits (reported in the lower-right cell).

What makes this outcome seemingly illogical is that the profitability of both companies would be higher if neither advertised. Nevertheless, this type of outcome tends to arise in real-world situations just like this. For example, during the Cold War between the United States and the former Soviet Union, both spent hundreds of billions of dollars building up nuclear arsenals when both would have been better off if neither did so.

Why do rivals make such apparently perverse decisions? The answer is that each rival will assume the worst-case scenario about the other's choices; that is, each assumes that the other will choose the strategy that inflicts the most harm. In the cigarette-advertising example, both companies assume that the other will choose the strategy—advertising—that hurts their own profitability the most. Based on this assumption, each company will adopt the strategy that maximizes profits. In other words, each rival follows the strategy that offers it the greatest protection *no matter what the other company chooses to do.* In this case, each firm is made better off by advertising whether its rival advertises or not. A strategy that is the best choice regardless of what one's rival does is called a **dominant strategy**.

DOMINANT STRATEGY The strategy that is the best choice regardless of what a rival decides to do.

The payoff matrix in Table 18.1 is an excellent example of one of the first types of matrices used in game-theory analysis. It represents a situation called the **prisoners' dilemma**, in which the dominant strategy of each rival leads them *both* to a second-best outcome—that is, an outcome that does not maximize either rival's payoff.

PRISONERS' DILEMMA A game where each rival has a dominant strategy that leads to a second-best outcome for all of the rivals.

The name given to this game may seem odd—what do prisoners have to do with cigarette makers' advertising decisions? In fact, the relationship is quite close. Consider two criminals who, acting together, burglarize a 24-hour grocery mart. Suppose they are apprehended based on circumstantial evidence and are placed in separate interrogation cells. Each is told that if he is the first to confess, the district attorney will "go easy" in terms of a sentencing recommendation (think of your favorite *Law and Order* or *CSI* episode). If both confess, they will receive a slightly lighter sentence than if one doesn't confess while the other does. The district attorney offers this deal because if they both confess, the expense of a trial can be avoided.

Table 18.2 shows the payoff matrix facing the two suspects, Bonnie and Clyde. Bonnie quickly assesses the situation and realizes that if Clyde confesses, she is better off confessing, too: she'll get six years rather than ten years. If he doesn't confess,

Table **18.2**	A Prisoners' Dilemma Payoff Matrix		
		Bonnie	
		Do Not Confess	Confess
Clyde	Do Not Confess	Bonnie: 4 years Clyde:　4 years	Bonnie: 2 years Clyde: 10 years
	Confess	Bonnie: 10 years Clyde:　2 years	Bonnie: 6 years Clyde:　6 years

then she is even better off confessing because she will receive a two-year rather than four-year sentence. Clyde faces the same alternatives. The dominant strategy for both criminals is to confess and take the lesser sentence. This is the same outcome that will occur if each suspect assumes that the other will act in the most harmful way possible, by confessing. The end result is that both go to prison for six years, rather than the four years they would have gotten if *neither* had confessed.

Of course, if the two suspects could have talked to one another before choosing a strategy, they might have been able to strike a mutually agreeable, enforceable deal such that neither would confess. Similarly, if the two cigarette companies could get together and strike an enforceable agreement that neither would advertise, both would be better off. As our payoff matrices make clear, these types of agreements would *have to be* enforceable because each rival has an incentive to cheat on the deal and be made better off. Such cheating, if detected, would lead us back to the prisoners' dilemma outcome.

Given these incentives to cheat, it is noteworthy that cigarette producers have managed to reduce their advertising expenditures over time. Was this the result of a secret agreement struck by the companies? Hardly. In 1971, Congress banned TV and radio ads for tobacco products. Other countries around the world, including England, Canada, and Malaysia, have since done the same. The effect of banning the advertising—effectively moving companies to the top-left cell of the payoff matrix in Table 18.1—has been to increase the profits of tobacco companies. Sometimes the unintended consequence of well-meaning government policies is to actually help rivals achieve their most profitable payoffs by providing the necessary enforcement mechanism.

More recently, a group of the largest pharmaceutical companies agreed "voluntarily"—in response to the threat of regulation—to eliminate all physician gift programs, which had included free pens, meals, drug samples, and conference support. It is too early to know whether smaller companies, which are usually more difficult to monitor, will cheat on this agreement and thereby undermine its continuation. Congress is also considering a ban on direct-to-consumer advertising of prescription drugs. If the tobacco industry's experience is a good predictor, these changes may well have the same unintended consequence of increasing pharmaceutical industry profits.

Can Rivals Ever Learn?

Assuming that there is no communication between rivals, an intriguing question arises: Will a rival ever learn from its own choices and those of its rivals so that it eventually makes better decisions? Can Bonnie and Clyde "learn" not to confess if they are arrested often enough? This type of learning can only occur if rivals replay the "game" over and over so that they can better understand each other's payoff possibilities and how inclined each is to cheat.

The Ultimate Electronics example is a good one to highlight this dynamic: if Best Buy does not cut its prices, neither will a rival such as Ultimate. For the strategy to work, however, Ultimate must follow through on its threat to cut prices if Best Buy does—even if this results in lower profits or even losses. By lowering its prices when necessary, Ultimate is making the investment necessary to assure the cooperation of its rivals. It is signaling that its threat to match prices is *credible*, that is, believable.

After Best Buy realizes that Ultimate isn't bluffing, it will "learn" that there is no advantage to lowering its prices. In this way, the two firms "escape" from the second-best outcome that a prisoners' dilemma so often achieves. Given what you now know about game theory, you probably wouldn't be surprised to learn that in the face of Ultimate's threat, Best Buy turned to nonprice strategies to beat Ultimate in the electronic-goods market. It has, for example, created a Geek Squad to provide installation and repair services and technical support to buyers to attract more business from its rivals.

SOLVED PROBLEM

Suppose two gas stations sit on opposite corners of an intersection. They will both make greater profits if they can charge higher prices for their gasoline. Assume that the cost of gasoline is $2 per gallon for both sellers, and that if they charge the same price per gallon, they will evenly split the total sales at the intersection. Also assume that if one of them charges a higher price, it will lose all of its sales; if it charges less, it will gain all of the sales. The following table shows the payoff matrix if the two gasoline stations are choosing between two prices: $2.49 per gallon and $2.39 per gallon.

		QuikTrip's Price	
		$2.39	**$2.49**
Phillips 66's Price	**$2.39**	Phillips 66: $5,000 QuikTrip: $5,000	Phillips 66: $10,000 QuikTrip: $0
	$2.49	Phillips 66: $0 QuikTrip: $10,000	Phillips 66: $9,000 QuikTrip: $9,000

Q What is the dominant pricing strategy for each gasoline station?

A The price each station will charge will be $2.39 per gallon. Each station will earn a lower profit than if both were to charge $2.49 per gallon. This is an example of a prisoners' dilemma outcome. Why does this occur? If the first station charges $2.49, then the second station is better off charging $2.39; if the first station charges $2.39, then the second station is again better off charging $2.39. This, then, is the dominant strategy for each of the two gas stations. What if the two gas stations made a tacit agreement that when one raised its price, the other would as well, knowing that if it didn't, the other station would immediately lower its price again. In this type of "repeat" playing of the game, both stations recognize their interdependence and the ways in which they can enforce a cooperative outcome. Still, there are subtle ways to cheat, such as offering free or discounted car washes with each fill-up.

18.3 Cooperation between Multiple Rivals

Oligopolists can differ in size, cost structure, and product quality and still be interdependent. For example, the oil-producing countries of the world have different types of oil reserves, in terms of quality, quantity, and costs of extraction. Yet the amount of oil one country sells on the world market can have a substantial impact on the prices and profits of other oil-producing nations.

The same is true for airline companies. In early 2008, United Airlines announced that it would charge fliers $25 for checking a second bag on all of its routes, waiting to see if other airline companies would follow suit. Within a matter of weeks, all of the major airlines, with the exception of Southwest Airlines and a couple of other no-frill airlines, had adopted the same policy.[4] Had UAL's rivals decided not to follow suit, UAL would have likely rescinded its checked baggage fee.

More recently, Bank of America announced that it would levy a $5 per month debit card fee. Initially, it appeared that rival banks, such as Regions, Chase, and SunTrust, would follow suit. However, the public outcry that resulted convinced these rivals to abandon their plans to follow Bank of America's lead, and Bank of America was left alone to deal with a public-relations nightmare. It wasn't long before Bank of America announced that it had "heard" its customers and was withdrawing the proposed debit card fee.[5]

Having a small group of rivals permits "players" to keep an eye on each other and adjust prices accordingly. At the same time, as long as prices are above their competitive level, each firm has an incentive to undercut its rivals to gain market share and greater profits, as long as this can be accomplished undetected and without any others following suit. Once again, we are back to our prisoners' dilemma game: enforcement mechanisms must exist that discourage one rival from cheating on the others. As we have explained, a popular enforcement tool used by rival airlines is one in which airlines match each other's prices when fares are discounted on particular travel routes—exactly the same threat used by Ultimate Electronics against Best Buy.

If one or more rivals fail to fall in line in reaction to this disciplinary threat, price wars can occur. These hurt all of the suppliers but benefit consumers. This is precisely what happened in the late 1990s when the three largest publicly traded laser vision-correction companies began an unrelenting price war to increase their own market share. Within a decade, one company had ceased operations, and the remaining two were on the brink of bankruptcy because their heavily discounted prices could not cover their production costs.

Oligopolists can benefit by cooperating on matters other than price or production levels. For example, Silicon Valley companies Google, Apple, and Genetech have allegedly agreed to an unwritten hiring rule not to poach (hire) each other's employees.[6] However, this implicit understanding appears to be ignored when an employee "superstar" is willing to jump companies. Moreover, because smaller tech start-ups are not partners to this agreement, they frequently raid larger, well-established companies for experienced employees. In fact, this is the situation in which Google currently finds itself: its star employees are being lured away by Facebook, Twitter, and other, newer players in Silicon Valley. Ironically, Google itself was the "new kid on

[4]Martha White, "Airlines to Charge for Second Bag." *New York Times,* April 22, 2008.

[5]Tara Siegel Bernard, "In Retreat, Bank of America Cancels Debit Card Fee." *New York Times*, November 1, 2011.

[6]Miguel Helft, "Unwritten Code Rules Silicon Valley Hiring." *New York Times*, June 4, 2009.

the block" only a decade or so ago, poaching employees from Apple, Yahoo!, and Hewlett-Packard.

It should come as no surprise that many companies attempt to block key employees from moving to rival firms by adding noncompete restrictions to their employment contracts. That is, to be hired in the first place, employees have to agree that they will not go to work for a competitor for a certain amount of time after they resign their current positions. To the extent that the legal system can be used to prevent poaching, unenforceable "understandings" between rivals are unnecessary. However, noncompete clauses are not always enforced: state and federal court rulings have varied depending on an employee's occupation, industry, and region of the country in which the employee works. Some courts have ruled that noncompetes are illegal because they are restraints on trade.

Cartels

You have learned that a monopolist can set the price or quantity of the goods and services it sells to reap monopoly profits. Oligopolists can achieve the same level of profitability if they band together and act in unison, effectively acting like a monopoly. When they band together in this way, they form what is called a **cartel**.

> **CARTEL** A group of cooperating oligopolists that jointly set price or output levels to achieve monopoly profits.

> **EXAMPLE** The Organization of Petroleum Exporting Countries (OPEC) is a global cartel of 12 countries whose governments control oil production and distribution.

> **EXAMPLE** In 2011, the European Commission found Unilever, Proctor and Gamble, and the German company Henkel guilty of forming a cartel to set the prices of laundry detergent in eight European countries.

In most countries, there are laws that prohibit firms from forming cartels and engaging in "price fixing" activities. However, OPEC is a perfectly legal entity because cartel members aren't firms but countries, and international laws prevent one country from applying its antitrust laws to another.

The ideal outcome for a cartel would be if it could act like a monopolist that has several production sites, where each site is, in fact, a cartel member. The monopoly output level would be produced at the lowest cost sites, and the total profits generated by the cartel would equal that of a multiplant monopolist. To see, this, consider **Figure 18.2**, which shows the marginal cost curves for the Qatar and Kuwaiti state oil producers.

Let's assume for simplicity that these are the only two oil producers in OPEC. (The analysis can be extended to include additional cartel members.) If Qatar and Kuwait collude to maximize their total *joint* profits, then more oil will be produced by Qatar—the lower-cost producer—than by Kuwait. Oil production will be allocated between the two countries so that the last barrel produced by each has the same marginal cost of production and generates the same marginal revenue. In Figure 18.2, this condition is met when Kuwait is producing 2.6 million barrels per day, and Qatar is producing 4.3 million barrels per day. Reading up to the market demand curve, we find that the market-clearing price for a total market supply of 6.9 million barrels per day is $32 per barrel.

FIGURE 18.2 **Allocating Production in a Cartel: The Case of Oil Producers Kuwait and Qatar**

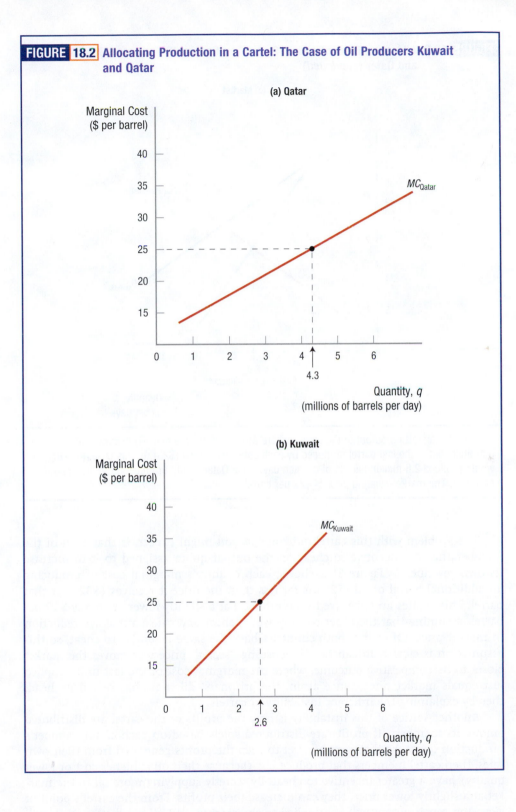

(a) Qatar

(b) Kuwait

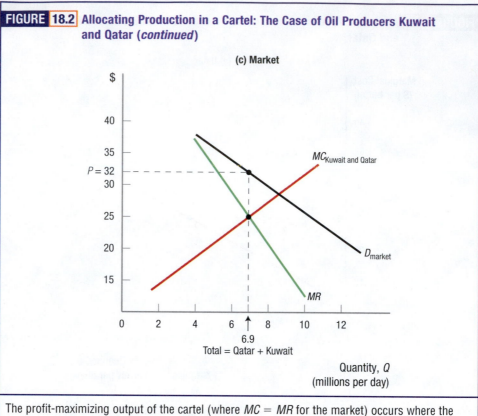

FIGURE 18.2 Allocating Production in a Cartel: The Case of Oil Producers Kuwait and Qatar (*continued*)

(c) Market

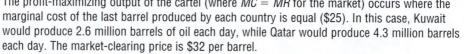

The profit-maximizing output of the cartel (where $MC = MR$ for the market) occurs where the marginal cost of the last barrel produced by each country is equal ($25). In this case, Kuwait would produce 2.6 million barrels of oil each day, while Qatar would produce 4.3 million barrels each day. The market-clearing price is $32 per barrel.

The problem with this cartel outcome, as you might expect, is that each of the members has an incentive to cheat on the output quota assigned to it to increase its own revenue. As Figure 18.2 shows, each country's marginal cost of producing an additional barrel of oil ($25) is far less than the price it receives ($32) for that barrel. This creates an incentive to sell more oil at a slightly lower price, say $30 per barrel, assuming that the other country won't cheat and cause a massive reduction in market price. Of course, both countries have the same incentive to cheat, so this assumption is clearly unrealistic. The ensuing "secret" price war moves the market closer to its competitive outcome, where the marginal cost of the last unit supplied just equals market price. Once again, the prisoners' dilemma has reared its head, thereby explaining the inherent instability of cartels.

Another source of this instability is how the profits of the cartel are distributed among its members. If profits are distributed solely based on each cartel member's production quota, so that members get to keep the profits generated from their own sales, then cartel members that produce less (because their oil is higher cost or lower quality) have a greater incentive to cheat. By secretly supplying more oil to the market at a slightly lower price, they can increase their profits. From the cartel's point of view, too much output will be supplied to the market, and oil production costs will not be minimized.

How can the cartel enforce its production quotas? If a cartel member cheats, the other members can punish it by increasing their output, too. Of course, this presumes that the cartel can accurately detect cheating and that its members are willing to sacrifice short-term profits to inflict pain on cheaters (just like Ultimate Electronics). The faster a cheater can be caught, the smaller the gains from cheating will be and, therefore, the lower the probability will be that cheating will occur in the first place.

In most cartels, there is one dominant member. In the OPEC cartel, Saudi Arabia is the biggest "player" in terms of oil reserves and production. Using its dominant position, Saudi Arabia has served as the cartel's "enforcer" by adjusting its output levels to punish cheaters.[7] For example, in the 1980s, Saudi Arabia flooded the market with oil to discipline OPEC-member Kuwait, which had just discovered a large oil reserve and had quickly erected numerous oil wells to extract more oil.

Saudi Arabia's response to Kuwait is just what game theory would have predicted. Researchers have found that when a prisoners' dilemma game is repeated over and over, a strategy of cooperation arises, especially when cheaters are harshly treated. When one member of the cartel does cheat, other members often cheat in the same way to retaliate. This "do unto others" strategy of revenge is called a **tit-for-tat strategy**.

TIT-FOR-TAT STRATEGY A strategy whereby a rival inflicts harm on another rival in exactly the same way as that rival inflicted harm in the previous round of the "game."

EXAMPLE It has been reported that during World War I, enemy German and British troops, living in horrible conditions in trenches, made an unspoken pact not to shell each other unless one side fired first. Only infrequently did one side fire, which was met with immediate retaliation.

EXAMPLE Household partners sometimes adopt a tit-for-tat strategy: if one leaves her dishes in the sink, the other does, too. If one partner leaves dirty clothes strewn all over, the other does as well. The purpose is to punish these types of noncooperative behaviors.

Tit-for-tat was exactly the strategy adopted by General Vessey in response to the war-mongering activities of enemies of the United States. A tit-for-tat strategy can be very effective in enforcing an implicit pact, especially when violators are forgiven *after* the retaliation has taken place. However, it can fail when it turns into a spiral of escalation, as in some well-known family feuds (the Hatfields and McCoys) and military conflagrations (North Korea versus South Korea).

When it comes to the OPEC cartel, Saudi Arabia faces the difficult challenge of keeping the cartel intact and monopoly profits flowing. One of the problems it faces is external: major oil reserves have been discovered over the past several decades in Alaska, the North Sea, and Canada. Because OPEC has been relatively successful in keeping oil prices high, there is an incentive for these higher-cost competitors to enter the market—competitors who might not be inclined to cooperate with the cartel.

In addition to threats from oil producers outside the cartel, Saudi Arabia must cope with energy substitutes that become increasingly cost-justified when the price

· · · · · · ·

[7]James Griffin and Weiwen Xiong, "The Incentive to Cheat: An Empirical Analysis of OPEC." *The Journal of Law and Economics*, 40 (October, 1997).

of OPEC oil rises.[8] Renewable wind energy is an example: when the price of oil rose to almost $150 a barrel in mid-2008, investments in wind farms grew substantially. Then again, these investments in alternative energy sources fell precipitously when oil once again dropped below $50 a barrel in early 2009.[9]

The bottom line is that cartel members find it difficult to sustain a cooperative outcome for a long period of time. Even when cartels are able to effectively enforce their prices or total output levels, there are other ways for their members to cheat. One way is for a member to compete on nonprice dimensions, such as offering customers easy credit terms, discounted delivery fees, "freebies" with their purchases, and so on. Practices such as these can quickly erode cooperation within a cartel and its subsequent profitability.

SOLVED PROBLEM

Q Suppose that three major beer producers form a cartel and that their total costs of production are as shown in the following table (marginal costs are shown in parentheses).

Units of Output	Firm 1	Firm 2	Firm 3
(thousands of cans)		(total cost)	
0	$200	$250	$150
1	250 (50)	350 (100)	220 (70)
2	350 (100)	500 (150)	320 (100)
3	500 (150)	800 (300)	470 (150)
4	800 (300)	1,200 (400)	770 (300)
5	1,200 (400)	1,600 (400)	1,170 (400)

If the cartel decides to produce 11 thousand cans of beer each month, (a) how should the output be distributed between the three companies to minimize the cartel's costs? (b) If this is the profit-maximizing level of output, what is the marginal revenue the cartel is receiving for the last thousand cans of beer sold? (c) How would your answer change if the profit-maximizing output level rose to 15 thousand cans?

A   a. The production should be distributed so that the marginal cost of the last unit produced by each firm is the same. The marginal cost for each unit for each company is provided in parentheses in the total cost table. The lowest cost way to produce 11 units is for Firm 1 to produce 4 units, Firm 2 to produce 3 units, and Firm 3 to produce 4 units. (4 + 3 + 4 = 11). The marginal cost of the last unit each produces is $300.

   b. At the profit-maximizing output level, $MC = MR$, so we know that the marginal revenue equals $300 as well.

   c. At 15 units, the three firms would each produce the same amount—5 units of output each (5 + 5 + 5 = 15). At this level, the marginal cost of the last unit produced by each firm is $400.

The Ivy League University Cartel

While OPEC is probably the most famous cartel in the world, others have formed that have been considerably more successful over longer periods of time. One such cartel was formed by the eight U.S. colleges and universities that comprise the "Ivy League."

·······

[8]Kenneth Stier, "In an Oil Squeeze, Attention to the Alternatives." *New York Times,* September 22, 2005.

[9]Tom Wright, "Winds Shift for Renewable Energy as Oil Price Sinks, Money Gets Tight." *Wall Street Journal,* October 10, 2008.

In the late 1990s, these institutions were accused by the U.S. Department of Justice of engaging in price-fixing behavior when it came to what they charged students.[10] For more than 40 years, they allegedly did so by consulting with each other before setting tuition increases and by sharing information on the financial-aid packages they intended to offer newly accepted students. Also, they held annual meetings—along with 15 other prestigious schools—to discuss the financial-aid applications of thousands of students that had been accepted to more than one school in the group. The goal of the meeting was to agree on a uniform financial-aid offer for each of these students.

Another product of this cooperation was the understanding that all of the Ivies would offer only needs-based financial aid, thereby preventing awards based on academic merit or other exceptional student talents. This understanding virtually guaranteed that applicants accepted by more than one of the colleges would be offered the same financial-aid package by all of the Ivy institutions to which they were accepted.

The stability of this cartel was assured not only by the College Board's formula for determining needs-based financial aid and the resulting uniformity in award offers but also by the ability of the cartel members to monitor where each student eventually went to college. If any one school consistently enrolled a larger proportion of students who were accepted by more than one of the colleges, this was at least circumstantial evidence that cheating had occurred through more generous financial-aid offers.

In 1991, the Ivies agreed to the Justice Department's demand that they stop consulting one another on tuition and financial-aid matters. At the same time, the schools insisted that they had the right to offer solely needs-based financial aid and that they would all continue this policy. Nearly 20 years later, they remain unanimously committed to their needs-based financial-aid policies, thereby squelching competition for students through more generous financial awards. However, "public Ivies" (such as the public-university flagship campuses in North Carolina, Michigan, Indiana, California, Texas, Florida, Illinois, and Wisconsin) and many non-Ivy private institutions have engaged in fierce competition for students through both needs-based and merit scholarship offers, especially since the start of the 2008 recession.[11] How this will impact the Ivies, if at all, remains to be seen.

Nonprice Competition in Oligopoly Markets

So far, we have talked about the price-fixing nature of cartels and the difficulty they face in maintaining price compliance among members. Even when members of the cartel adhere to the price that is fixed, it turns out that nonprice competition can still erode the cartel's monopoly profits. A good example of this took place in the regulated airline industry, whose prices were set by the Civil Aeronautics Board (CAB), a federal government agency. No matter which airline offered a flight from New York to Los Angeles on Saturday morning, the fare was the same. In effect, the government was an external enforcer of cartel pricing.

If the airlines could not compete in terms of prices, did this mean that there was no competition in the airline industry? In reality, a huge amount of competition arose in nonprice dimensions of the airline services that each carrier provided its passengers. Airlines competed on the quality of the meals served, the convenience of flight departure and arrival times, the comfort of the airplane seats, and so on. These

· · · · · · ·

[10]Anthony DePalma, "Ivy Universities Deny Price-Fixing But Agree to Avoid It in the Future." *New York Times,* May 23, 1991.

[11]Lynn O'Shaughnessy, "How Rich Kids Get College Aid," March 16, 2009. www.moneywatch.com.

competitive activities raised the marginal cost of providing service, thereby eroding much of the economic profit that existed due to regulated prices that were set above their competitive levels.

Even in the deregulated oligopoly airline industry, there are carriers that continue to compete in nonprice dimensions. In early 2011, American Airlines tried to revise its arrangement with online travel sites Expedia and Orbitz to make it more difficult for travelers to compare its airfares to those of other carriers. Its goal was to distinguish itself on dimensions other than price and thereby create a "premium" brand.[12] This was exactly the antithesis of what the Web sites wanted to do, which was to make price comparisons as simple as possible for travelers and, indirectly, promote price competition among the carriers. While the dispute was eventually resolved, the end result was to give American more control over the prices and schedules that are now displayed by the online travel sites.

Nonprice competition between rivals in oligopoly markets can take many forms, including free deliveries and installation, extended after-sale service and warranties, freebies or heavily discounted goods provided with the cartel good, more convenient hours of operation, more liberal return policies, and so on. These activities can undercut collusive price agreements, particularly when they are costly for other cartel members to detect.

From an economic standpoint, what's "wrong" with nonprice competition beyond the basic problems arising from oligopoly pricing (prices that are too high) and output levels that are too low? Nonprice competition is a form of "bundling" in that it combines goods and services and sells them as a package: airline tickets and fine dining in the sky, barrels of oil and free shipping, and so on. The practice of bundling is not, in and of itself, a concern. Apple sells iPhones bundled together with operating software; new GM cars are sold together with the OnStar communications system. As long as the price of the bundle is no greater than the sum of the consumer's willingness to pay for each product separately, then the consumer is made no worse off from bundling. However, we would expect that at least some consumers would prefer that the goods be unbundled so that if they don't want one of the goods, they don't have to buy it. They can instead spend their money on something else. A good example of bundling that can reduce consumer well-being is the packaging of channels by cable TV providers: many viewers would prefer to buy only the channels they actually watch rather than pay more for all of the channels in the package.

Even when goods in oligopoly markets are bundled with a "free" good or service, this good or service is not really free when it comes to the scarce resources used up to produce it. If a consumer's willingness to pay for the free good is lower than its opportunity cost of production, then from an economic standpoint, the "free" good should not be produced in the first place, irrespective of the price that consumers ultimately pay for it.

Nevertheless, consumers are still made better off when there is nonprice competition in an oligopoly market because as long as there is a cartel agreement in force, the oligopoly price will not be pushed down to the competitive level through price competition. Therefore, as long as the goods and services that are bundled with the cartel good give consumers any well-being at all, they are made better off by nonprice competition versus no competition at all.

End Games

As you have just learned, a cooperative outcome between rivals is fragile, especially in the absence of external enforcement mechanisms. What happens, for example,

- - - - - - -

[12]Liam Denning, "American's Dogfight with Expedia." *Wall Street Journal,* January 4, 2011, p. C10.

when a rival is convinced that the "game" is about to end and no longer worries about retaliation? We often talk about "end game" strategies in the context of warring nations: for example, the United States ended its World War II war "game" by dropping atomic bombs on major population centers in Japan. Before this occurred, both countries abided by the generally accepted international war protocol that protected civilian populations from knowingly being targeted. The United States didn't worry about retaliation for breaching this "understanding" because Japan did not have nuclear capabilities. In effect, the U.S. cheated on this agreement and brought about an abrupt end to the war.

Another example hits literally "closer to home." Previously, we discussed the incentive that each partner in a household has to use pooled resources to enhance his own well-being, rather than the overall well-being of the household. This leads to rivalrous behavior. Over time, these partners usually reach a cooperative outcome when it comes to how much is spent to improve the private well-being of each partner, for example, how much is spent on each other's education or wardrobe.

However, the partners will only continue to cooperate with one another if they view the relationship as an ongoing one ("'til death do us part"). Now consider the possibility that one partner wants to exit the household and prepares for the "end game." He might squirrel away household money in untraceable bank accounts or invest heavily in his own human capital by going back to school or joining a gym. This partner acts in a noncooperative way because he knows that a divorce—which the other partner does not know about—is fast approaching and that it will end the rivalry over the distribution of joint resources once and for all.

18.4 Tacit Pricing Agreements

Because most countries prohibit collusion and price-fixing, oligopolists will often engage in unwritten—even unspoken—understandings whereby each firm informally follows a strategy that jointly maximizes everyone's profits. We call these "tacit" agreements, where tacit means "understood without being stated."

Price Leadership

The most common type of tacit agreement is where one producer—the **price leader**—consistently sets price, and all other rivals follow suit.

> **PRICE LEADER** A firm that consistently sets prices that rivals subsequently adopt.

> **EXAMPLE** In the 1990s, Kraft General Foods was the price leader in the bulk cheese market.[13]

> **EXAMPLE** In the 1920s and 1930s, when Reynolds Co. (the maker of Camel and Winston cigarettes) set its prices, these prices were immediately adopted by its competitors Liggett and Myers (the maker of Chesterfield and L&M cigarettes) and American Tobacco (the maker of Lucky Strike and Pall Mall cigarettes).

A price leader does not have the power to force its rivals to follow its lead but simply "passes along" information to rivals through its pricing decisions. The price leader may

· · · · · · ·

[13]Willard Mueller, et al., "Price Leadership on the National Cheese Exchange." *Review of Industrial Organization*, 12, no. 2 (April, 1997).

be the largest firm in the industry or a smaller firm that has a knack for accurately forecasting future market conditions. This latter type of price leader is called a "barometric" firm because, like a barometer, it accurately assesses the market "climate."

Often, a firm becomes the price leader in its market because it has superior cost conditions, whether in terms of production or distribution. Walmart has become a price leader for many products in the geographic markets within which it operates. Its rivals often have no choice but to adopt the same prices that Walmart charges for identical goods. It is interesting to note that when Walmart enters new markets, it often promises to not only match its competitors' advertised prices, but to charge 5 percent less. In contrast, in more mature markets, Walmart promises only to match the advertised prices of competitors.

Immediately following the U.S. Airline Deregulation Act in 1978, which permitted airlines to set their own fares, American Airlines assumed the informal role of price leader in the industry. It publicized fare changes and then waited to see if other carriers followed its lead. If they didn't, then the new fares didn't "stick," and American would quickly back off of them. In October of 1992, American's CEO, Robert Crandall, lamented that "American has tried to provide some price leadership in its industry but it hasn't worked, so we are back into the death by a thousand cuts."[14] But Crandall's announcement was probably just a ruse—a bluff designed to discourage regulators from cracking down on its practice of price announcements. American Airlines' position as price leader in the airline industry has diminished over time, especially as smaller airlines have merged and challenged American's dominance. For example, in response to United Airlines' announcement that it would charge $25 for a second checked bag, American followed and then announced a $15 fee for the *first* checked bag as well. It waited for weeks to implement the policy until United and U.S. Air announced that they would adopt the same luggage fees.[15]

For many years, Citibank set its prime rate (the interest rate banks charge their best corporate customers), and its rivals in the commercial banking industry in New York followed suit. Sometimes, this price leadership position rotated between the four largest banks in New York.[16] In contrast, a relatively small bank, Southwest Bank, was the price leader in the St. Louis commercial lending market—it was always the first to reset its prime rate in response to a change in the Federal Reserve Bank's bank lending rates. This was before the banking industry was deregulated in 1999, leading to an explosive growth in interstate banking institutions. As a result, the largest banks in the country became price leaders nationwide. At the same time, smaller commercial banks have entered the market and have grown by undercutting the loan rates offered by the largest banks.

Rivals that follow the market's price leader treat the price that has been set as the marginal revenue they will receive for each unit of output sold. Like any other profit maximizer, they will produce up to the point where the marginal cost of the last unit produced is just equal to its marginal revenue. In this way, they act like price-taking competitive firms. The difference, however, is that the price that the price leader sets is typically above average total cost, thereby generating profits for the price followers.

· · · · · · ·

[14]Steven Morrison and Clifford Winston, *The Evolution of the Airline Industry* (Washington, D.C.: Brookings Institution, 1995) p. 71.

[15]Micheline Maynard, "Like American, More Airlines Add Fees for Checking Luggage." *New York Times,* June 13, 2008.

[16]David Alhadeff, *Monopoly and Competition in Banking* (Manchester, NH: Ayer Publishing, 1980) p. 129.

The price leader will choose its own profit-maximizing output level based on the assumption that this is the way that its rivals will act. It does so by taking into account the total amount of output that the price followers will supply at each and every price. This permits the price leader to derive the *residual* demand at each of these prices. Unlike the Cournot duopolists, the price leader has already taken into account that price followers will change their output levels when the market price changes. Consequently, the price leader won't have to worry about readjusting its output level in response to the output decisions made by its price followers.

The interesting question that arises is why low-cost price leaders such as Walmart don't push smaller, higher-cost rivals out of the market altogether by simply cutting their own prices. Some economists believe that price followers provide "cover" for these price leaders when it comes to antitrust scrutiny. By "permitting" smaller rivals to coexist, a dominant firm can argue that entry barriers are low and that there is sufficient competition. More likely, companies like Walmart are unwilling to lower their prices enough on their items to win 100 percent of the market—at this point, they would likely suffer negative marginal revenue. They may do so for short periods of time to "discipline" price followers who decide to set their own, lower prices, but it is far too costly to do this in the longer run, especially when there are no barriers to entry into the market.

Entry-Limit Pricing

Suppose that barriers to entry are relatively low in a market with only a few firms, but that these existing companies enjoy lower costs of production than potential entrants. If all the firms in this market tacitly agree to adopt a high price—say, one that a monopoly would charge—to generate higher profits, this will entice firms with higher costs to enter the market. What if, instead, the existing firms agree to a lower price, one that generates less economic profit but effectively deters the entry of higher-cost producers? We call this strategy **entry-limit pricing**.

> **ENTRY-LIMIT PRICING** A tacit pricing strategy adopted by existing rivals to set a price lower than the monopoly price to deter higher-cost producers from entering the market.

In effect, entry-limit pricing is a pricing strategy that signals to potential entrants that they would be foolhardy to enter the market because their higher costs would not be covered at the going price. Although this may be successful in deterring entry into the market, entry-limit pricing means that existing producers must sacrifice profits in the short run in the hopes of increasing their long-run profits. The problem with this approach is that potential entrants will always be at the ready should existing firms ever raise their prices to earn higher profits.

18.5 Spotting Collusive Activity in Markets With Small Numbers of Firms

Antitrust regulators monitor various markets for signs of collusive behavior such as price fixing and tacit price agreements. Their goal is to promote competitive pricing and output levels. Oligopolies, like monopolies, result in prices that are, even in the long run, above the marginal and average costs of production. When this occurs, there will be too little output supplied and purchased in the market as well as deadweight loss. As with monopolies, oligopolies lead to an economically inefficient market outcome.

Regulators know that collusion is most likely to occur in markets that have only a few suppliers and high entry barriers. But how, exactly, do they go about identifying those industries and firms that deserve closer scrutiny? And if an agreement between suppliers to collude is unspoken, how can regulators prove there even is one?

The question of how many firms it takes to guarantee a competitive market is a tricky one. We know that even when there is only one bakery in town, it can't act as a monopolist as long as substitutes exist—such as the bakery department in the local supermarket—and entry barriers are low. We also know that systematic changes in demand or in the costs of production cause prices to move in the same way for all of the suppliers in a competitive market, absent any collusion whatsoever.

How do regulators uncover collusive schemes? First, they must identify which suppliers actually compete in the same market, whether that market is defined geographically or by product characteristics. This, in itself, is no easy task, inasmuch as rivals may not compete in exactly the same geographic or product market precisely because they have entered into a collusive agreement to divide the market in the first place.

When competitors in the same market can be identified, the next step is to evaluate whether the number of suppliers is small enough to permit collusion. Finally, regulators must confirm that high barriers to entry exist; that is, that the market is not contestable. Because this process is difficult, regulators often adopt "rules of thumb" to measure the competitiveness of various industries. Notice that there is a subtle substitution of "industry" for "market" competition. This simply reflects the insurmountable difficulties in delineating markets according to our conceptual definition.

In addition to the number of firms in an industry, regulators are often interested in whether an industry is dominated by a handful of large companies. One measure they use to gauge dominance is the industry's **concentration ratio**.

CONCENTRATION RATIO Share of an industry that is attributable to its largest 4, 8, or 16 firms.

To calculate a concentration ratio, companies in an industry are ranked by size, which can be measured in terms of total employment, total assets, total sales, or total wages paid during a certain period of time. The sizes of the top 4 (or 8 or 16) firms are then added together. This total is compared to the size of the entire industry to arrive at the share of the market accounted for by the top 4 (or 8 or 16) firms. If, for example, there is only one firm in an industry—with annual sales of, say, $58.6 million—the industry's concentration ratio would be 1 ($58.6 / $58.6). If there are 4 firms in an industry with total sales of $196.4 million, the industry's 4-firm concentration ratio would also be 1 ($196.4 / $196.4). The 4-firm concentration ratio can differ from 1 only when there are more than 4 firms in an industry. If, for example, there were 50 equal-sized firms in an industry—each accounting for one-fiftieth of industry sales—then each would control 2 percent of the market. The 4-firm concentration ratio would therefore be 8 percent (2 + 2 + 2 + 2), and the 8-firm concentration ratio would be double that (16 percent).

The left-hand column of **Table 18.3** contains the 2002 concentration ratios for various manufacturing industries, as reported by the U.S. Department of Commerce, Bureau of the Census. The Department of Commerce calculates these concentration ratios for both broadly defined industry categories (e.g., chemical manufacturing) and narrowly defined industry subcategories (e.g., soap and other detergent products). With rare exception, we see that the concentration ratio increases substantially the narrower the industry definition is; there are fewer manufacturers of soaps and other detergents, for example, than there are chemical manufacturers. The critical question that antitrust

Table 18.3 Four-Firm and Eight-Firm Concentration Ratios versus the Herfindahl Index: Select Industries

Industry	Four-Firm CR (%)	Eight-Firm CR (%)	Herfindahl Index
Food Manufacturing	16.8	25.4	118.7
Animal Food Manufacturing	29.8	40.9	364.9
Dog and Cat Food Manufacturing	64.2	81.3	1845.4
Beverage and Bottled Water Manufacturing	42.6	58.3	709.5
Beverage Manufacturing	39.5	53.2	511.8
Bottled Water Manufacturing	62.6	76.7	1409.2
Chemical Manufacturing	13.7	21.8	99.9
Basic Chemical Manufacturing	22.3	34.2	216.7
Soap and Detergent Manufacturing	60.6	72.4	2006.2
Machinery Manufacturing	14.4	19.4	71.3
Agricultural Construction and Mining Machinery Manufacturing	36.4	44.9	521.2
Farm Machinery Manufacturing	57.6	64.7	1656.8
Computer and Electronics Manufacturing	18	25.7	135
Electronic Computer Manufacturing	75.5	89.2	2662.4
Computer Storage Device Manufacturing	65.6	79.3	1725.8

Source: "Sector 31: Manufacturing: Subject Series—Concentration Ratios: Share of Value Added Accounted for by the 4, 8, 20, and 50 Largest Companies for Industries: 2002." U.S. Census Bureau, May 23, 2006.

regulators must address is whether any chemical manufacturer could, at low cost, enter the soap market if there were economic profits to be had—for example, if the existing soap manufacturers colluded to generate economic profits. If the answer is yes, then the soap market is much more competitive than its concentration ratio would suggest, and the fruits of any collusive agreements would likely dissipate in the long run.

Concentration ratios are, at best, imperfect measures of market competition. One reason is that they are based on industries rather than markets. Another is that they don't account for differences in barriers to entry into specific industries. And, they typically exclude foreign companies that export goods to the United States and compete with domestic producers. For example, Toyota automobiles manufactured in Japan and sold in the United States are not included in the computation of the concentration ratio for the U.S. automobile industry. This means that the concentration ratio *understates* the degree of price competition in the auto market. Likewise, the industry definitions that are used to define markets often exclude substitutes that are produced in other industries. The movie-rental industry might include Blockbuster, Hollywood Video, Netflix, and Pay-per-View but exclude movies that can be downloaded from the Web.

Still another limitation of concentration ratios is that, as we just saw, whether there is one firm or four in an industry, the concentration ratio will be identical: 1. Yet most economists would agree that having four firms rather than one would add to the competitiveness of a market. To fully capture the entire size distribution of firms in an industry, an alternative measure that has come into favor is the **Herfindahl Index**.

HERFINDAHL INDEX A measure that captures the entire size distribution of firms in an industry.

This index is computed by adding together the *square* of each and every firm's share of the industry, with shares measured the same way as in the concentration ratio computation. If an industry has only one firm—a monopoly—then the firm controls 100 percent of the industry output, and its corresponding Herfindahl Index equals 100^2 or 10,000. This is the highest value that the Herfindahl Index can take on. If, instead, there are 100 firms in an industry, each accounting for 1 percent share of total sales revenue, then the Herfindahl Index would equal the sum of $(1)^2 + (1)^2 + \cdots + (1)^2 = 100$. The value of the Herfindahl Index decreases when the number of firms in an industry increases, and when firm sizes become more equal.

The Herfindahl Index is heavily relied upon by U.S. antitrust regulators to assess the anticompetitive impact of proposed mergers and acquisitions. The right-hand column of Table 18.3 reports the index for various industries, based on the size distribution of their top 50 firms. As you can see, the values of the concentration ratios and the Herfindahl Index are fairly consistent when it comes to a simple ranking of industries. There are some inconsistencies between the two, though. For example, according to the Herfindahl Index, the soap-manufacturing industry (2006.2) is more concentrated, and by inference less competitive, than the dog and cat food-manufacturing industry (1845.4). However, using the 4-firm concentration ratio would yield exactly the opposite result: the dog and cat food industry is more concentrated (64.2 percent) than the soap industry (60.6 percent).

ECONOMIC FALLACY   Oligopolies, collusive agreements, and cartels exist solely on the supply side of a market.

False. Just as we saw that there can be a monopolist (one seller) and monopsonist (one buyer), we can also have a market in which there are only a few dominant buyers, which we call an *oligopsony* (a few buyers). These buyers can put downward pressure on the prices they pay, as long as there are many price-taking suppliers. For example, a small number of large buyers in the fast-food industry (in particular, McDonald's and KFC) account for a substantial share of chicken purchases made in the United States. Their dominance allows them to negotiate lower prices from their poultry suppliers. A similar situation exists in the music-recording business. Because there are only a handful of major recording companies left in the world, a musician must deal with one of these studios if she wants to get her music widely distributed.

Would an oligopsonist ever have an incentive to cheat and pay more for its purchases? The answer is, yes. One possible reason it might cheat would be to ensure that it would be the first in line to receive delivery during periods when the supply of a product is tight.

Blocking Mergers to Limit Oligopoly Pricing Power

In late August 2011, AT&T and T-Mobile—the second and fourth largest wireless carriers, respectively—announced a $39 billion merger deal that would create a company with nearly 130 million subscribers, easily surpassing the first-largest carrier, Verizon Wireless. Currently, the top four wireless carriers account for over 90 percent of the market. United States antitrust regulators at the Department of Justice (DOJ), along with wireless competitor Sprint, have separately filed court suits to block the proposed merger, expressing fears that the merger would create a wireless duopoly that would hurt consumers. AT&T has responded that if the merger is not approved, T-Mobile will eventually fail anyway because it has no capacity to develop the next generation of 4G services for smart phone users. In fact, AT&T contends that its primary interest in T-Mobile is not to gain pricing power but to keep up with network demand in densely populated areas. T-Mobile's spectrum and cell-phone towers would give AT&T a low-cost way to add more capacity to its network without waiting for the government to auction additional spectrum.

Despite AT&T's arguments in favor of the merger, the DOJ filed suit against the merger. Deputy Attorney General James M. Cole stated in the filing that

> [T-Mobile USA is important as an] independent, low priced rival…in particular …places important competitive pressure on its three larger rivals, particularly in terms of pricing….Unless this acquisition is enjoined, customers of mobile wireless telecommunications services likely will face higher prices, less product variety and innovation, and poorer quality services due to reduced incentives to invest than would exist absent the merger.[17]

Whether there is any way that AT&T can salvage the deal by spinning off parts of its current operations into independent, competitive entities remains to be seen. But clearly, this is just the most recent salvo in the merger wars that have become increasingly frequent in high-tech industries that enjoy favorable economies of scale in production or distribution.

18.6 Summarizing Differences in Market Structures

At the start of this chapter, we suggested that markets can be arranged on a spectrum in terms of their degree of competitiveness. At one end is the price-making monopolist; at the other is the price-taking competitor. Monopolistically competitive markets sit in-between, but closer to the price-taking end because there are a number of firms and few barriers to entry. Where would we place an oligopoly along this spectrum?

If there are costly barriers to entry and only a handful of firms, we would expect these markets to look more like monopolies—in terms of both price and quantity levels—*for at least a short period of time.* How short this period is depends on the stability of collusive price-fixing arrangements, which depends on both internal and external market forces. **Figure 18.3** shows the relationship between different market structures and the degree of market competition that would be expected.

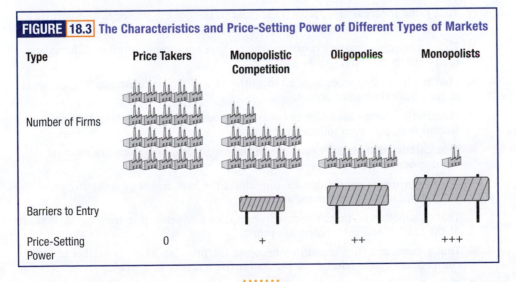

FIGURE 18.3 The Characteristics and Price-Setting Power of Different Types of Markets

Type	Price Takers	Monopolistic Competition	Oligopolies	Monopolists
Number of Firms				
Barriers to Entry				
Price-Setting Power	0	+	++	+++

ECONOMIC FALLACY   You can get a good idea of the amount of competition there is in an industry by its number of suppliers.

Uncertain. The answer depends on whether or not the market has barriers to entry. As we have already explained, the key factor contributing to the competitiveness of a market is the cost of entry. When entering a market is virtually costless, existing firms cannot maintain market prices that generate economic profits in the long run. If the companies attempted to do so—through collusion, for example—new firms would be attracted by these profits and would enter the market. Their additional supply would eventually depress the market price. This would continue until a competitive market outcome is reached with respect to equilibrium output and price. So when there are low barriers to entry, the number of existing firms tells us little about the amount of competition between them.

However, if there *are* costly barriers to entry—perhaps due to government regulations that require firms to have licenses—then the number of firms that currently exist in a market takes on more importance when it comes to assessing the market's competitiveness. In this case, it is probably reasonable to assume that fewer suppliers will lead to less competition. By contrast, the greater the number of firms and the more equal their size, the less probable it is that these firms will be able to collude and set the price above its competitive level.

WHAT YOU SHOULD HAVE LEARNED FROM CHAPTER 18

- That when there are only a few firms in a market and barriers to entry are high, rivals will recognize their mutual interdependence when making profit-maximizing decisions.

- That a dominant strategy is one that a rival will choose regardless of what the opponent chooses to do.

- That when cooperation is absent, rivals will often achieve an outcome that does not maximize their joint well-being or profitability.

- That cooperation can occur among rivals if there are repetitive interactions that permit them to learn about each other's strategies and potential payoffs.

- That game theory is an approach designed to predict the strategies and payoffs facing rivals given those of their opponents.

- That an oligopoly market is one in which there are a small number of firms and high barriers to entry.

- That rivals in oligopolies have an incentive to make tacit (unspoken) agreements to maximize their joint profits.

- That rivals have an incentive to cheat on agreements, leading them back to a second-best, prisoners' dilemma outcome.

- That cartels are inherently unstable in the long run unless there are external enforcement mechanisms.

- That government regulations are sometimes the best means of enforcing price and output agreements among rivals.

- That oligopolists will often engage in nonprice competition to increase their share of the market and their economic profits.

- That a dominant firm sometimes becomes the price leader in its market to limit competition and maximize the profits for the industry as a whole.

- That oligopolists sometimes set prices below their profit-maximizing levels to keep higher-cost companies from entering the market.

■ That government antitrust regulators consider an industry's concentration ratio and Herfindahl Index to assess its competitiveness.

■ That the extent to which firms can control prices or output in their market will depend on various market characteristics, including the number of existing firms and the presence of costly barriers to entry.

KEY TERMS

Oligopoly, p. 553

Duopoly, p. 555

Game theory, p. 557

Payoff matrix, p. 557

Dominant strategy, p. 558

Prisoners' dilemma, p. 558

Cartel, p. 562

Tit-for-tat strategy, p. 565

Price leader, p. 569

Entry-limit pricing, p. 571

Concentration ratio, p. 572

Herfindahl Index, p. 573

QUESTIONS AND PROBLEMS

1. Some cartels have been known to survive and operate effectively for long periods of time; others have fallen apart in relatively short order. Economists believe they know something about the various conditions that determine the effectiveness and life expectancy of a cartel. Explain carefully how each of the following factors would impact the longevity of a cartel:

    a) The prices members charge for their products are easily monitored.
    b) The quantities members deliver to customers are easily monitored.
    c) Members produce a single, homogeneous product.
    d) The demand for the product comes from a stable group of "repeat," loyal customers.
    e) No barriers to entry exist in the market.
    f) The government regulates the price and quality of a product.

2. A common complaint in business is "cutthroat competition" (also known as predatory pricing) where a competitor supposedly cuts price below its rivals' costs to drive them out of business. Under what conditions, if any, would this be a credible threat that antitrust regulators would have to worry about? Explain your answer.

3. In the early decades of the airline industry, the CAB (Civil Aeronautics Board) set the fares for all airline routes and assigned these routes to the airlines. The routes with the greatest demand—for example, New York City to Los Angeles— were given to several airlines. Given that their prices were fixed and enforced by the federal government, can you conclude that there was no competition between airlines for passengers on these shared routes? Explain your answer.

4. The beer industry is comprised of a small number of large, international brewers. Over the past decade or two, many local microbreweries have entered the market. Do you think that this has increased competition and lowered prices in the beer market? Explain your answer.

5. The following table is a payoff matrix for the two major league baseball teams in Southern California: the L.A. Dodgers and the Anaheim Angels. It indicates the payoff to each team resulting from its decision to broadcast or blackout at-home games on local TV. Suppose that both would be better off if the games were blacked out because that would increase their "take" at the gate, and local broadcast rights are not particularly lucrative. However, if one team *does* broadcast its games locally, then the other will be made worse off if it does not broadcast as well (because people will stay home to watch the team with the broadcasted games rather than go to the other team's stadium).

		L.A. Dodgers Broadcast Policy	
		Broadcast	Don't Broadcast
Anaheim Angels Broadcast Policy	**Broadcast**	Angels: $6 Dodgers: $8	Angels: $10 Dodgers: $6
	Don't Broadcast	Angels: $2 Dodgers: $12	Angels: $8 Dodgers: $10

a) What is the dominant strategy that each team will select? Will this lead to the highest payoff possible to each team?

b) The baseball league has established a rule that prohibits local broadcasts of games unless the game is sold out. How does this affect the outcome of the "broadcast/no broadcast" game? Explain your answer.

6. Sunkist, Inc. is a not-for-profit marketing cooperative that processes and markets the collective output of more than 6,000 citrus growers in California and Arizona. It is the largest supplier of lemon juice in the United States. In the United States, agricultural cooperatives whose membership is restricted to agricultural producers (versus processors, for example) are exempt from antitrust regulation. To what extent do you think that Sunkist and other "umbrella sales" organizations exercise pricing power in their respective markets? In the case of Sunkist, would your answer change at all if you were told that Mexico and Argentina have vastly expanded their lemon groves during the past decade? Explain your answer.

7. Using a game-theory approach and the concept of repeat games, can you explain why more American League batters get "beaned" by pitchers than National League batters? (Hint: The American League permits designated hitters who often substitute for the teams' pitchers.)

8. Employees—who are suppliers of labor—will sometimes collude with each other to call in sick or walk off their jobs if they are not given a raise or enhanced benefits. This often occurs in workplaces—such as the automobile industry—where there are hundreds, if not thousands, of workers. How is it that collusive activities between workers can be successful when so many (potential) suppliers of labor exist? Explain your answer.

9. Most government agencies solicit bids for contracts to provide goods and services to government entities. Examples include food services for the U.S. military, transportation services for government employees, and military equipment and supplies. Bidders usually make their proposals via sealed bids, which are opened all at once. The lowest bidder receives the contract (no rebidding is permitted), and all of the bids are then made public. Does this type of bidding process promote or inhibit collusion among bidders? Explain your answer.

10. The largest automakers in the United States are often the biggest buyers of new tires each year. However, during the 2007 Great Recession, tire manufacturers sold more tires directly to car owners than to the automakers. Do you think that the tire manufacturers were better off or worse off in terms of the prices they charged during the recession? Explain your answer.

11. Using a prisoners' dilemma game-theory framework, show why it is always the dominant strategy for a professional baseball player to take performance-enhancing steroids. How, if at all, would your analysis change if there was mandatory drug testing before every game?

12. Using game theory and the concept of repeat games, explain why parents punish their oldest children more for engaging in risky behaviors (drinking, speeding, etc.) than their younger children when they reach the same age.

13. Firms competing in the "big box super retailer" sector of the economy exhibit a great deal of interdependence in decision making. For example, Walmart expanded its grocery offerings to fresh fruits, vegetables, frozen foods, and milk products. For cost reasons, Target did not follow suit. When the Great Recession hit in 2007, Walmart's store traffic and profitability increased—much of this attributed to its expanded grocery offerings—at the same time that Target's declined. The end result: Target substantially expanded its fresh grocery offerings in 2009.[18]

   Given this information, create a payoff matrix that shows the returns to Walmart and Target of each deciding whether or not to enter the grocery market (you can make up the actual numbers). What must be true about the relationship between the values in each of the four cells of the matrix? Explain your answer.

14. Until 1992, there were only two comic book publishers—D.C. Comics and Marvel Comics. In 1992, Image Comics was created by a group of former Marvel artists. By 1994, Image accounted for 25 percent of the market, Marvel held 40 percent of the market, and D.C. represented 30 percent of the market.

    a) Calculate the four-firm concentration ratio and the Herfindahl Index for the comic book market in 1994 based on this information.

    b) Why do you think that there were only two comic book companies for so many years? Do you think there were barriers to entry and, if so, what were they?

    c) Comic books all sold for the same price, irrespective of the publishing company. Is this evidence of collusion and price fixing? Why or why not?

    d) How, if at all, did comic book companies compete when they all charged the same price? Explain.

• • • • • • •

[18]Associated Press, "Target Pushes Basics to Reverse Sales Slide." *New York Times*, May 26, 2009.

PART 5

Winners and Losers in a Competitive World: Are Free Markets Unfair?

Chapter 19, the concluding chapter of this book, focuses on the income and wealth effects that arise as by-products of competitive markets and their response to changes in the economic environment. While well-functioning markets tend to allocate scarce resources to their highest valued use, every shift in supply or demand results in individual winners and losers whose own resources increase or decrease in value. How do people perceive competitive markets in terms of their inherent fairness? Does having "skin in the game"—by owning private property, for example— affect this perception? What kinds of policies do governments enact to try to counteract some of the economic "pain" inflicted by market adjustments?

Here we draw an important distinction between maximizing the total economic "pie" and the piece that each individual receives. How is it that some people can be made worse off when trade occurs, despite the fact that market exchanges are voluntary and result in a bigger economic pie overall? How, for example, can labor-market dislocations lead to economic growth while negatively affecting wage rates and employment levels?

We explore some of the unintended consequences of government attempts to redistribute income, including the impact of these policies on the well-being of low-income households. We also look at the flip side—that is, the way in which government redistribution efforts are sometimes "captured" and transformed into thinly veiled "corporate welfare" programs that redistribute income to higher-income rather than lower-income individuals. We conclude with a discussion of efforts to alleviate global poverty by redistributing income from richer to poorer nations and how these programs have fared in terms of achieving their goals.

The Personal Cost of Maximizing the Economic Pie

"No society can surely be flourishing and happy, of which the far greater part of the members are poor and miserable."

Adam Smith, moral philosopher and pioneer in the study of political economy

Throughout this book, we have demonstrated that a competitive market tends to allocate scarce resources efficiently. When markets work well, they are very good at maximizing the total economic pie created from the scarce amount of resources a society has on hand. At the same time, we have acknowledged that market failure does exist and, in these situations, government intervention can sometimes improve upon market outcomes.

During the past several decades, there has been a notable shift in the landscape of national economies. In the 1980s, the Soviet Union broke apart; up to that point, it had a government-directed or **command economy**. This breakup led to the emergence of several independent nation states striving to develop market-based economies.

COMMAND ECONOMY An economic system wherein a society's means of production are predominantly controlled and deployed by the government.

EXAMPLE After the Cuban Revolution in 1959, Fidel Castro nationalized the ownership of land, businesses, and other private property in Cuba. From that point forward, until very recently, the Cuban government directed virtually all economic activity within the country.

EXAMPLE North Korea is a centrally planned command economy that deploys its resources based on a series of government-imposed economic plans. After the Korean War ended in 1953, the earliest plans gave highest priority to postwar reconstruction and the development of industries such as chemicals and metals.

Meanwhile, the rapid economic growth of China, a nation that has relied heavily on government control of its economy, has been stoked by the introduction of market-based reforms. In 2002, Milton Friedman, a Nobel Laureate in Economics and a champion of private, competitive markets, wrote an updated preface to his famous book *Capitalism and Freedom*. In it, Friedman cheered the movement of the former Soviet Union, along with Central and Eastern European countries, away from centralized government planning and toward market-based systems as a means of allocating their scarce resources. These events fueled Friedman's optimism that the "climate of opinion" had shifted decidedly in favor of **capitalism**.

CAPITALISM An economic system wherein the means of production are predominantly owned and controlled by private producers.

EXAMPLE The oil-producing industry in the United States is capitalist in nature, while its counterparts in Kuwait and Saudi Arabia—where the government owns these industries—are not.

EXAMPLE One proposal to offset some of the enormous national debt of the United States is for it to privatize (sell off) government-owned assets such as islands, airstrips, and lands, thereby handing over ownership and control to private interests operating in the capitalist economy.[1]

Prior to the 2007 Great Recession, there was growing sentiment worldwide in support of free-market systems and against economies controlled by fiat (government rules and directives). Much of this sentiment can be attributed to the worldwide economic growth that free markets fueled during the 1980s and 1990s. Chicago economist and Nobel Laureate Gary Becker estimated that the world's economic pie, as measured by gross domestic product (GDP), increased by over 145 percent, or 3.4 percent a year, between 1980 and 2004. This period corresponds roughly to the rise in global financial markets, deregulation of transport and other industries, and the worldwide emergence of free trade agreements. All of these trends promoted an increase in market-based exchange and a reduction in government control of production and allocation of resources.

If free markets are so successful in improving our economic condition, why have we experienced rising skepticism about the virtues of capitalism in the past few years? In fact, we have seen substantial retrenchment from the movement toward capitalism not only in socialist-leaning countries such as Venezuela—where oil-service firms and gold mines have recently been taken over by the government—but in highly advanced capitalist countries such as the United States. During the 2008 financial crisis, for example, the U.S. government seized control of the country's two largest mortgage-finance companies, Fannie Mae and Freddie Mac. It promptly infused billions of federal dollars into both firms and instituted government oversight of their daily operations, including the salary and bonuses paid to corporate executives. At the same time, the government loaned auto companies, banks, and Wall Street firms with billions of taxpayers' dollars because they were deemed "too big to fail" and extended government guarantees to many other struggling for-profit ventures.

We often see this reaction during times of great economic distress. The Great Depression, for example, provided the impetus for the creation of the Securities and Exchange Commission (SEC) and the Federal Deposit Insurance Corporation (FDIC) to rein in financial-market abuses. Since the 2007 financial crisis and economic downturn, it is not uncommon to hear political pundits, TV talk-show hosts, and

---

[1] Edward Wyatt, "Cash-Short, U.S. Weighs Asset Sales." *New York Times*, September 29, 2011.

even some economists claim that the economic catastrophe resulted from an over-reliance on free markets. The president of France, Nicolas Sarkozy, has gone so far as to proclaim that unregulated capitalism is "finished."

In light of the severity of the 2007 economic downturn, many public-policy experts and government leaders have argued that market activities require an increased amount of government oversight and control to ensure that such dire conditions never happen again. The United States, along with its European counterparts, has introduced sweeping regulatory reforms in the financial and banking sectors. The possibility of reregulating other previously deregulated markets, such as the airline industry, has also come under consideration. And, renewed political pressure for protectionist trade policies—import tariffs and quotas—is building worldwide. In the United States, there has been a move to exert greater government control over the health-care sector, which accounts for more than 16 percent of the nation's economy. In 2009, the U.S. government passed the Patient Protection and Affordable Care Act (health-care reform), thereby assuming primary responsibility for restructuring and regulating private health-insurance companies, employer health-care coverage, and medical providers. One of the government's new duties, for example, is to monitor private health-insurance company premium increases and to demand that any that are greater than 10 percent per annum be "sufficiently justified" to government regulators.

These types of public policies reflect an unwillingness to rely solely on market forces to determine how society's scarce resources are allocated. Still, a vast majority of Americans and their counterparts in wealthier countries remain optimistic about free-market systems. In late 2009, a poll was conducted which reported that only 13 percent of Americans and 29 percent of Spaniards and Italians considered free-market capitalism to be "fundamentally flawed."[2]

If, in fact, markets do such a good job in directing an economy's scarce resources, what is it that government intervention seeks to achieve? Recall that in free markets, trade occurs only when both parties are made better off, or at least neither is made worse off. This does not mean, however, that such trades can't hurt other parties. For example, consumers search for the lowest-cost producers of a good of a given quality, thereby pushing higher-cost producers out of business and their employees out of their jobs. While this competitive process leads to a bigger economic pie, some parties will end up with a smaller piece of this pie. If, instead, we decide to use up scarce resources to enable high-cost producers to remain in business, we will end up with a smaller economic pie overall, which will require some pieces to be smaller.

In this final chapter, we explore the virtues and limitations of capitalism when it comes to addressing societal concerns beyond economic efficiency, such as income inequality. At the same time, we address the unintended consequences that can arise when governments intervene in the workings of markets to resolve these social concerns. You will also come to appreciate the difficulties that arise when governments try to soften the "pain" of market adjustments or pursue income-redistribution activities. Reining in the adverse outcomes of capitalism can be costly in terms of a country's economic wealth, precisely because people will continue to pursue opportunities that enhance their own personal well-being. It is in this context that you are likely to better understand why capitalism has so often survived and triumphed over other economic systems. And why harnessing, rather than weakening, the forces of capitalism may be the most effective way to achieve a society's goals.

·······

[2] *The Economist*, July 24, 2010, p. 54.

19.1 Perceptions of the "Fairness" of Market Economies

Would a change in property rights—in your favor—affect the faith you have that markets work well and are "fair"? In the 1980s, a large group of families settled on land outside of Buenos Aires that they believed was owned by the government. As it turned out, the land was the property of 13 private owners. And, as you might expect, these owners took legal action to evict the squatters from their land. By 1998, the government had bought out nine of the private landowners and had given title to that land to two-thirds of the squatter families that resided there.

Researchers were interested in finding out whether the attitudes of the squatters toward markets and private ownership of assets changed when they themselves became landowners. To answer this question, the researchers compared the attitudes of families that had received title to their land to those of squatters who were still living on land that was in dispute.[3] One of the key questions asked was whether the family believed that it could be economically successful on its own or whether this could happen only with the external support of a large group (e.g., the government). The researchers found that families who held title to their land were much more likely to answer that they could be successful on their own compared to those families that still did not own the land they lived on.

This study suggests that having "skin in the game" through the ownership of private property affects people's attitudes about relying on government to ensure their economic success. This finding is consistent with other studies which have shown that when people receive ownership shares in state-owned businesses that are privatized, they tend to view markets more favorably. From these findings, we surmise that a fall in the value of privately held assets as a result of changing market conditions will diminish a person's pro-market sentiments.

Another implication of this body of research is that when private property rights are absent or are compromised by weak enforcement, corruption, or crime, there will be less faith in the market system and greater reliance on the government to control the economic process. The irony here is that much of the corruption present in a society typically stems from the government sector itself, which feeds this corruption through its control over scarce resources.

Winners and Losers in the "Great Recession"

Unlike any time since the Great Depression, the 2007 Great Recession has had a dramatic impact on the value of the core asset many people hold: their homes. For the U.S. population as a whole, home ownership grew to almost 70 percent prior to the onset of the recession. By the beginning of 2007, almost half of low-income families in the United States "owned" their homes. Collectively, these low-income families had built up a median value of $81,000 in equity in their homes. (Equity is the difference between a home's market value and its outstanding mortgage balance.) At the same time, these home owners tended to have very little in the way of "liquid" savings. Of low-income families who owned homes, those few who even had bank accounts had an average savings balance of $1,100, and fewer than one in four had an IRA or 401(k) retirement savings account.

•••••••

[3]Rafael Di Tella, Sebastian Galiani, and Ernesto Schargrodsky, "The Formation of Beliefs: Evidence from the Allocation of Land Titles to Squatter." *Quarterly Journal of Economics* (February, 2007).

Table 19.1 Housing Price Declines from Their Peak (through June, 2011)	
Las Vegas	−59.2%
Phoenix	−55.7%
Miami	−50.3%
Detroit	−48.5%
Tampa	−45.8%
San Francisco	−38.2%
Los Angeles	−38.1%
San Diego	−37.9%
Minneapolis	−34.4%
Chicago	−31.4%
Seattle	−28.5%
Washington, D.C.	−26.9%
Portland	−26.0%
Atlanta	−23.6%
New York City	−22.8%
Cleveland	−18.5%
Charlotte	−16.1%
Boston	−15.3%
Dallas	−8.2%
Denver	−5.1%

Source: S&P/Case-Shiller Home Price Indices: www.standardandpoors.com/indices/sp-case-shiller-home-price-indices

The real-estate market collapse that began in early 2007 wiped out a great deal of home owners' equity both in the United States and elsewhere. As **Table 19.1** shows, some U.S. cities suffered housing price declines of over 50 percent from their peak values in 2006 up through November, 2009. This severe downturn in housing prices had a massive impact not only on lower-income people's wealth holdings but also on the wealth of the middle class. According to one housing market analyst,[4]

> [The value of] household real estate fell from $23 trillion in 2006 to $16.5 trillion at the end of 2009. The bursting of the housing bubble has wiped out the middle class. Baby boomers are not nearly as wealthy as they believed; they must slash spending and save for the future. 51 million home owners have a meager $1 trillion [equaling $20,000 per home owner] in home equity. We're a nation of paupers.

The real-estate market collapse precipitated a crisis in the banking and financial sectors of the economy. Many financial institutions that had loaned money to home buyers were now stuck with mortgages on their books that had unpaid balances greater than the depressed value of the corresponding houses (these are often referred to as "underwater mortgages"). Also, the recession created thousands of newly unemployed home owners unable to afford their monthly mortgage payment. Add to this the thousands more who purchased their houses only because they could qualify for

· · · · · · ·

[4]Mike Whitney, "Decade of Declining Home Prices Ahead." August 2, 2010. www.globalresearch.ca.

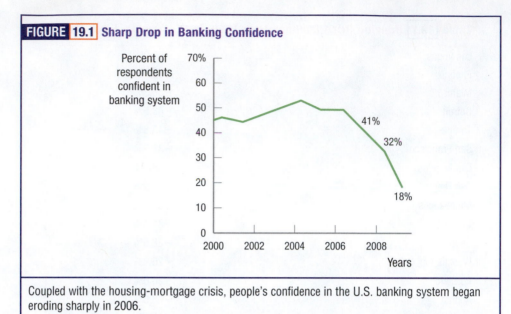

FIGURE 19.1 Sharp Drop in Banking Confidence

Coupled with the housing-mortgage crisis, people's confidence in the U.S. banking system began eroding sharply in 2006.

Source: Dennis Jacobe, "Americans Confidence in Banks Hits New Low." Gallup, April 23, 2009. www.gallup.com/poll/117841/americans-confidence-banks-hits-new-low.aspx.

low "teaser" mortgage rates and assumed wrongly that their homes would appreciate sufficiently to cover the eventual increase in interest rates. The subsequent wave of foreclosures left banks such as Bank of America with lots of houses on their balance sheets in place of once-profitable mortgages. Not surprisingly, the urgent call for more government intervention in the banking and financial sectors was bolstered by a sharp drop in consumer confidence in these institutions.

As you can see in **Figure 19.1**, people's confidence in the U.S. banking system began to erode in late 2006 and sank as the recession and housing woes spread through 2010. What had begun as a minor "adjustment" in the housing market due to lower demand (resulting from a decline in credit-worthy buyers due to the recession) now threatened to undermine global credit markets.

Figure 19.2 shows a supply-and-demand diagram for housing, like the one you saw in Chapter 8. It shows the housing market's adjustment to a fall in demand. Over time, there will be a drop in both housing prices and the quantity of housing supplied, as the market reaches a new equilibrium. What we don't see is the chaos that can accompany the move from one equilibrium position to another. For example, our supply-and-demand diagram does not capture the personal upheaval that accompanies a person's loss of his home or drop in home equity associated with the lower equilibrium price. Nor does the diagram capture the losses investors suffered when banks, brokerage houses, and home builders declared bankruptcy. In other words, our supply-and-demand analysis ignores the *wealth transfers* that typically occur when markets adjust to changes in the economic environment. We have focused only on predicting the direction of the market-clearing price and the new equilibrium output: Will equilibrium price eventually go up or down? Will quantity rise or fall? Will the scarce resources used up in this market increase or decrease?

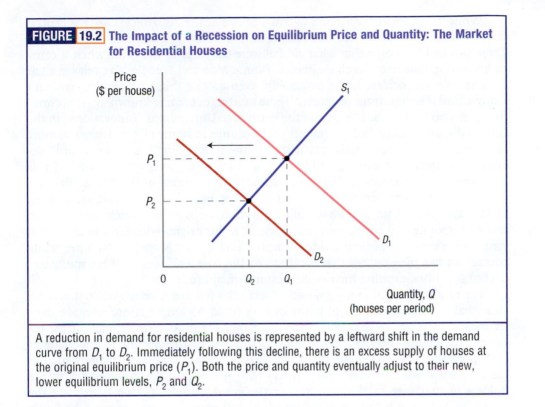

FIGURE **19.2** **The Impact of a Recession on Equilibrium Price and Quantity: The Market for Residential Houses**

A reduction in demand for residential houses is represented by a leftward shift in the demand curve from D_1 to D_2. Immediately following this decline, there is an excess supply of houses at the original equilibrium price (P_1). Both the price and quantity eventually adjust to their new, lower equilibrium levels, P_2 and Q_2.

Is there a fatal flaw in our supply-and-demand framework because it omits these wealth effects? No. It provides us with a useful way to help predict the impact of changes in the economic environment on prices, quantities and employment as the market adjusts over time. As this adjustment occurs, we know that there will be *both* winners and losers in the market. For example, at the very same time that owners lose equity in their homes due to the decline in housing prices, new buyers with a lower willingness or ability to pay are now able to purchase homes for the very first time.

It is not surprising that the wrenching experiences created by the bursting of the real-estate "bubble" have led to questions about whether markets "work." Did market failure lead to the 2007 Great Recession? In reality, a number of analysts warned far in advance of the imminent collapse in housing prices because they were rising too fast and at unsustainable levels. Several free-market advocates warned of impending doom as Fannie Mae and Freddie Mac exploited their government backing to borrow at will, with only a tiny amount of reserves set aside to protect them from volatility in housing prices.

Using supply-and-demand analysis, several analysts accurately predicted what would eventually happen: in an era of "cheap money," it became less costly to borrow, leading to an increase in the demand for housing. And as expectations of higher future housing prices set in, demand increased even more, fueled by housing speculators like those featured on the TV program, *Flip This House.*

Did the market "fail" because it did not rein in the "bubble" in housing prices? The fact is that what happened in the housing market happens in every market when demand increases: the quantity of housing supplied rose and prices increased to allocate this supply to those with the highest willingness to pay. Housing prices increased most in markets with the greatest increase in demand or smallest supply response.

While disagreement continues over the causes of the 2007 recession, the central question about whether there was market failure remains at the core of the debate. There can be little doubt that what *did* fail were the rules of the game when it came to borrowing money to purchase homes. Fannie Mae and Freddie Mac relaxed their lending rules to increase home ownership, even among those people who couldn't really afford their mortgage payments. These mortgages became known as "subprime" mortgages because of the riskiness of the borrowers. Unregulated "innovations" in the financial market magnified the impact of the plunge in home prices. A large number of investors—both individuals and institutions—invested in "mortgage-backed" securities comprised of bundles of high-risk and low-risk mortgages. Because of this bundling, most investors could not easily assess the riskiness of these securities as a whole, relying instead on the risk ratings assigned by independent companies such as Moody's. These companies had built their reputations on accurately assessing the risk of corporate and government bond issues. In hindsight, whether due to human error or the existence of financial incentives, it is clear that Moody's and other rating companies assigned ratings that understated the true riskiness of these mortgage-backed securities, creating increased investor demand for them.

The market value of mortgage-backed securities fell precipitously when it became clear that a growing number of home owners could no longer afford to make their mortgage payments, or they held underwater mortgages. As a result, many large investors (including some brokerage houses) suffered a large decline in the value of their portfolios. Compounding this problem was the fact that large insurers such as the American International Group (AIG) had offered insurance protection to the holders of mortgage-backed securities in the event of default—that is, in case the securities could not be resold or redeemed. As it turned out, these insurers had only a sliver of the necessary reserves in hand, having relied in good faith on the ratings companies. Unlike life-insurance companies and other types of insurers, AIG was not required by law to keep a certain amount of reserves on hand. Fearing that AIG was "too big to fail" and that its bankruptcy might trigger a financial crisis of international proportions, the federal government quickly infused capital into AIG, just as it had done for Fannie Mae and Freddie Mac.

Should the U.S. government have bailed out brokerage houses, banks, and large insurers such as AIG? Would the financial sector have come to a screeching halt leading to an economic meltdown as some argued at the time? Would bank failures have ensued and undermined confidence in the banking industry, thereby leading to a crisis in money markets? These were the types of concerns that led the U.S. government to intervene and bring companies that were deemed "too big to fail" back from the brink of bankruptcy.

19.2 Winners and Losers as the Economic Pie Grows

There will always be winners and losers when there is a change in the price of assets such as housing. We have already mentioned one group of winners: the first-time home buyers who were able to purchase homes after the price bubble burst. In the world of finance, investors such as Michael Burry correctly forecast the collapse of the subprime mortgage market and benefitted from investment strategies that bet against the mortgage-backed securities market. As $10 billion investment funds collapsed, other investment groups "swooped in for the leftovers."[5]

• • • • • • •

[5]Jenny Anderson, "Winners amid Gloom and Doom." *New York Times,* March 9, 2007.

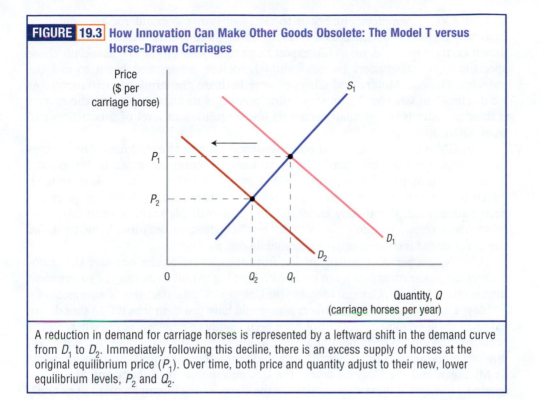

FIGURE 19.3 **How Innovation Can Make Other Goods Obsolete: The Model T versus Horse-Drawn Carriages**

A reduction in demand for carriage horses is represented by a leftward shift in the demand curve from D_1 to D_2. Immediately following this decline, there is an excess supply of horses at the original equilibrium price (P_1). Over time, both price and quantity adjust to their new, lower equilibrium levels, P_2 and Q_2.

There will be winners and losers whenever economic conditions redirect resources toward certain markets and away from others. Consider the introduction of the original Model T Ford in 1909. By adopting innovative, cost-saving assembly-line production techniques, Henry Ford was able to sell the Model T for $850 (a little less than the average $923 annual wage of nonfarm workers). In 1915, the price dropped further to $440. The Model T became the first affordable "horseless carriage" for the working class. Prior to this, most people relied on horse-drawn carriages for transportation. Even though not everyone could afford to run out and buy a new Model T, **Figure 19.3** shows the impact of the horseless carriage on the market for carriage horses.

As you can see, the introduction of the Model T resulted in a fall in both the equilibrium price and quantity of carriage horses. Due to the drop in market price, horse breeders, livery stables, and specialists such as blacksmiths suffered financially. Over time, these markets contracted, and suppliers exited from them. From an economic perspective, these responses to the introduction of the Model T ensured that resources were redirected—not by the government but by market forces—toward their highest-valued uses. The economic pie expanded because the growing use of automobiles allowed for the more efficient transportation of goods and services. The invention also gave rise to a large automobile industry that led to the employment of millions of people. Nevertheless, blacksmiths and others put out of business saw their piece of the economic pie shrink. This outcome emphasizes an important point: the economic pie can grow and, at the same time, some people can be made worse off.

Now fast-forward to the 2007 Great Recession. As we have already discussed, many home owners lost a substantial amount of their wealth when their home equity evaporated, credit markets were tightening, the price of gasoline was skyrocketing, and, in 2008, unemployment began to rise. Consumer demand for automobiles—especially for SUVs—declined as a result of all of these events. Just as in the horse-drawn carriage example, we would expect there to be auto producers, especially those specializing in gas-guzzlers (versus hybrids), to lose money and begin to exit the industry. General Motors and Chrysler were both on the brink of bankruptcy. As we discussed in Chapter 15, money-losing producers must begin to exit the market if their industry is to eventually reach its lower equilibrium level of production and manufacturing capacity.

But GM didn't ultimately go out of business, as you already know. The government infused it with taxpayers' money to keep the company alive. In return, the government took partial ownership of GM (sharing it with the autoworkers' union), which was one of the first times in recent U.S. history that a private company has been nationalized. We already know that the economic pie shrinks when labor and other scarce resources aren't put to their "best" (highest-valued) use. Why, then, did the government intervene to save automobile companies?

Clearly, the personal "pain" arising from the closure of one or more U.S. automakers led government leaders to consider a "too big to fail" rationale for government intervention. In 2007, General Motors—the largest U.S. manufacturer of automobiles—employed more than 100,000 workers who would have lost their jobs if GM shut down. Many of these employees would not have been readily re-employable elsewhere in the economy and almost certainly not at their union-negotiated wage rates. Allowing GM and other automakers to fail would have also put a huge strain on local governments in Michigan and the Midwest where the U.S. automobile-manufacturing industry is located. How would these states cope with the skyrocketing unemployment of not only the auto manufacturers but of their parts suppliers as well?

Should government intervene to save specific companies or industries when they are somehow deemed to be "too big to fail"? Who determines the exact definition of "too big"? Why, for example, did the government permit Lehman Brothers—a large investment house—to fail, while it loaned government funds to competitors such as Goldman Sachs? Was it fair to let tens of thousands of small businesses fail because of the falloff in demand for their goods and services caused by the recession? Did the bailouts that did occur make economic sense? That is, were the bailouts less costly to society than the months and years of unemployment that might ensue if the companies went bankrupt? Because economic policies are fashioned by elected politicians and their appointees, it is often difficult to distinguish political motivations—such as helping particular interest groups—from economically rational motivations.

19.3 Labor Market Dislocations

In Chapter 14, we showed how the introduction of cost-saving technologies allows us to do more with our scarce resources, thereby expanding the economic pie. More than half of the productivity gains in the U.S. economy since the mid-1990s have been attributed to information technologies that have made workers more productive. This also appears to be the case in Australia, Canada, Norway, and India.[6] College professors can now produce their own manuscripts and exams without the need for clerical assistance, courtesy of the PC. Lawyers can do their own legal research using online databases rather than relying on paralegals and other support staff. When technology

[6]Yoshihito Saito, "The Contribution of Information Technology to Productivity Growth—An International Comparison." *Working Papers, Bank of Japan.* March, 2001.

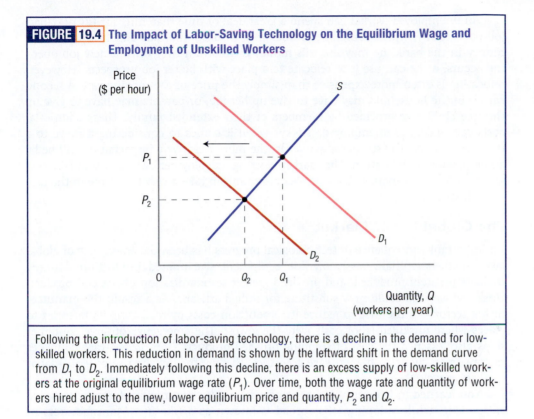

FIGURE 19.4 The Impact of Labor-Saving Technology on the Equilibrium Wage and Employment of Unskilled Workers

Following the introduction of labor-saving technology, there is a decline in the demand for low-skilled workers. This reduction in demand is shown by the leftward shift in the demand curve from D_1 to D_2. Immediately following this decline, there is an excess supply of low-skilled workers at the original equilibrium wage rate (P_1). Over time, both the wage rate and quantity of workers hired adjust to the new, lower equilibrium price and quantity, P_2 and Q_2.

increases labor productivity, it can lead to higher wages. Why? Because all else the same, employers are willing to pay more for employees who are more productive, that is, those who have a higher marginal product.

While technological advances can enhance the productivity of certain groups of employees, they often displace other types of workers. **Figure 19.4** shows a supply-and-demand diagram for unskilled workers, much like the ones we saw in Chapter 14. It illustrates the impact of labor-saving technologies on the demand for these workers. For example, the demand for secretaries with superb shorthand skills fell dramatically with the introduction of electronic dictation and, later, the PC. More recently, online banking has reduced the demand for bank tellers, and manufacturing robotics have led to a decline in the demand for less educated assembly-line workers.

Workers such as these will likely have to improve their skills by going back to school or receiving on-the-job training to work with robotic equipment. Until this occurs, there will be a sustained period of unemployment arising from the "mismatch" between the kinds of skills employers require and those found among the unemployed.[7] In fact, employers have argued that the stubbornly high rate of unemployment since the 2007 recession is largely due to their inability to find the "right people with the right skills." For example, nearly half of the job openings posted in St. Louis during the first quarter of 2011 were in the computer, sales, and health-care fields, which did not match the skill set of the area's unemployed job seekers.[8]

· · · · · · ·

[7]Motoko Rich, "Factory Jobs Return, But Employers Find Skill Shortage." *New York Times,* July 1, 2010.

[8]David Nicklaus, "Companies Say They Can't Find Workers with Skills They Need." *St. Louis Post-Dispatch,* September 4, 2011, p. E1.

An unemployed worker can spend a great deal of time searching for his next-best job opportunity, which sometimes comes with a substantial pay cut. If a person has money in the bank, he may use this money to tide him over until a new job opening occurs, or he can use it to relocate to a place with better job prospects. However, relocating is often more expensive than simply the price of the moving van. A second earner in the household may have to give up her job, or parents may have to give up the free child care provided by members of their extended family. These additional costs can make the unemployed "sticky" when it comes to considering a move to a new community. The stickier a worker is, the more negatively impacted he will be by an employment dislocation. The market-clearing redeployment of labor that is necessary to bring labor markets back into equilibrium can take a very long time in the face of such stickiness.

The Global Labor Market

An important consequence of technological progress has been the emergence of global labor markets. Initially, assembly-line equipment streamlined production, lowered the cost per item produced, and provided greater standardization of the end product. Unskilled workers could now substitute for skilled artisans. As a result, the manufacturing sector was the first to reduce its production costs by relocating its factories to places where unskilled-labor costs were the lowest. The emergence of large container ships also lessened the cost of shipping finished products from lower-wage countries to consumers living in higher-wage countries, thereby fueling the rise of global labor markets as well.

You learned in Chapter 14 that relocating production facilities abroad is called *outsourcing,* while shipping jobs abroad is known as *offshoring.* Manufacturers in higher-wage countries outsource to locations where wages are lower, where there is little or no union presence to drive up wages, and where payroll taxes and the cost of government mandates (such has employee health insurance) and regulations (such as workplace safety requirements) are minimal. Factors such as these also influence business decisions to relocate *within* a country, say, from New York to Texas.

It's been estimated that approximately 2 million manufacturing jobs in the United States have been offshored since 1983.[9] To put this number in context, there are about 130 million nonfarm workers in the United States. This suggests that relative to the *total* U.S. labor force, the loss of manufacturing jobs due to offshoring amounts to a small percentage (about 1.5 percent). However, because the U.S. manufacturing sector is highly unionized, this job loss has meant the elimination of many higher-paying, benefit-rich positions that had been held by less educated workers. Some labor-market gurus have even forecast the demise of the middle class as a result of these particular types of job losses.

Advances in IT and data-transmission technologies have contributed to the offshoring of "white collar" service jobs as well. Sharon Otterman summarizes the situation for the United States:

> Advances in technology and low-cost telecommunications now mean that a computer programmer, data entry specialist, or help-desk operator answering calls for a U.S. company can work as easily from India or the Philippines as from Iowa—and save parent companies some 30 percent to 70 percent in

· · · · · · ·

[9]Sharon Otterman, "Trade: Outsourcing Jobs." Backgrounder, *Council on Foreign Relations,* February 20, 2004. http://www.cfr.org/pakistan/trade-outsourcing-jobs/p7749.

costs, analysts say. This has led to considerable anxiety in some segments of the U.S. workforce that feel vulnerable to competition from well-educated workers abroad willing to work for, in some cases, one-tenth of the wages paid to Americans.[10]

Otterman reports that "Forrester Research estimates that 400,000 service jobs have been sent offshore since 2000, with jobs leaving at a rate of 12,000 to 15,000 per month. Moreover, the McKinsey Global Institute predicts that white-collar offshoring will increase at a rate of 30 percent to 40 percent over the next five years. By 2015, Forrester predicts, roughly 3.3 million service jobs will have moved offshore, including 1.7 million 'back office' jobs such as payroll processing and accounting, and 473,000 jobs in the information technology industry."

This trend in offshoring has even begun to impact professional occupations. The legal profession in the United States has begun to offshore its legal "grunt work" to employees in India,[11] a practice adopted several years ago by the accounting industry. European countries such as Germany and France have looked to the well-educated, multilingual labor forces in Eastern and Central Europe for professional offshoring opportunities.[12] For example, the Czech Republic is rapidly becoming a center for accounting and data services for higher-wage European countries: Czech employees earn about a quarter of the wages of their counterparts in Western Europe.

Americans are clearly alarmed about the job losses in the United States resulting from offshoring. However, little attention has been paid to foreign businesses that offshore jobs *to* the United States. These firms establish production facilities in the United States to take advantage of its abundant supply of highly skilled and educated workers. For similar reasons, some U.S. firms have stopped offshoring their jobs: they have found it too costly to control the quality of the goods and services produced by lower-paid, unskilled foreign workers. For example, a technical-support call center for computer back-up firm Carbonite will go online this summer in Lewiston, Maine. By the end of this year, 150 jobs that had been located in India will be shifted there, with another 100 jobs expected to be added next year. Carbonite made the decision to "reshore" these jobs to avoid the enormous training costs it was incurring at its call center in New Delhi, India, where the employee turnover rate was 100 percent or more each year. In contrast, its Boston center had a turnover rate in the single digits.[13]

Nonetheless, the outsourcing of production and offshoring of jobs will continue to occur when there are gains from trade to be had. Whether the company is a shirt-maker in Vermont or a chemical company in Germany, each will seek to produce goods to minimize production costs, as long as the quality of the goods is not compromised. By permitting people and countries to pursue their comparative advantage, the *global* economic pie grows. This generates economic benefits for lower-wage countries and workers, as well as for consumers in higher-wage countries who can purchase goods and services at a lower price. Countries that lose jobs to offshoring must seek to replace them with jobs for which they have a global comparative advantage.

· · · · · · ·

[10]Ibid.

[11]Heather Timmons, "Outsourcing to India Draws Western Lawyers." *New York Times*, August 4, 2010.

[12]John Tagliabue, "The Eastern Bloc of Outsourcing." *New York Times,* April 19, 2007.

[13]Chris Isidore, "Made in USA: Overseas Jobs Come Home." *CnnMoney,* June 17, 2011. http://money.cnn.com/2011/06/17/news/economy/made_in_usa/index.htm.

Sometimes, a worker's comparative advantage cannot be exploited unless she is willing to leave her home country. Many well-educated U.S. citizens have skills that are in high demand worldwide. For example, a large number of recent U.S. college graduates have taken white-collar management positions in China, where the unemployment rate is only 4 percent in the country's urban areas.[14] They have found that Chinese companies are eager to recruit native English speakers to help them succeed in American markets. Similarly, the most promising places for American lawyers to build their careers in the coming decades include Dubai, Abu Dhabi, Qatar, and Hong Kong. Prior to the 2007 Great Recession, it was difficult for U.S.-based law firms to recruit lawyers for permanent positions in these countries. Over the past few years, however, there has been a flood of applicants.[15]

Alan Greenspan, the former chairman of the U.S. Federal Reserve Board, has argued against protectionist policies to stem the offshoring of jobs. According to Greenspan, "We can be confident that new jobs will replace old ones as they always have, but not without a high degree of pain for those caught in the job-losing segment of America's massive job-turnover process."[16] It is this "pain" that he refers to—the income and wealth transfers that occur when labor markets adjust to changes in the economic environment—that is ignored in our economic analysis of competitive markets.

19.4 Can Government Ease the Pain of Capitalism?

In every society, there are people whose human capital has little value in the marketplace. These people may be relatively unproductive in the labor market because they are elderly, sick, or severely disabled. And we can't forget about children, who are either too young to have cultivated labor-market skills or are barred from the labor force by child-labor laws. Most of us would agree that these people are entitled to food, clean water, and shelter. The question is who should ensure that people receive an adequate amount of these basic goods and services?[17] We call these basic goods and services **entitlements**.

ENTITLEMENT A legal right to a certain set of goods and services.

EXAMPLE In the United States, a person accused of a crime is entitled to an attorney.

EXAMPLE In the United States, a person who has a life-threatening condition is entitled to receive care at an emergency room.

EXAMPLE In France and Finland, workers are entitled to 30 days of vacation and holidays.

When people speak about "entitlements" they are usually talking about benefits that everyone "should" have a right to under the law. These entitlements may go well beyond food, clean water, and shelter. As countries become wealthier, entitlements tend to expand, often into the areas of education and medical care.

· · · · · · ·

[14]Hannah Seligson, "Shut Out at Home, American Graduates Finding Jobs in China." *New York Times,* August 10, 2009.

[15]John Bringardener, "Lawyers Wanted: Abroad, That Is." *New York Times,* November 21, 2008.

[16]Otterman, *op cit.*

[17]Jim Yardley, "India Asks, Should Food Be a Right for the Poor?" *New York Times,* August 8, 2010.

Meeting Nutritional Entitlements

When it comes to meeting basic food requirements, the U.S. Department of Agriculture reports that nearly one in four children in the United States currently lives in a "food insecure household," that is, a household "where the members are unable to consistently access the adequate amount of nutritious food necessary for a healthy life." **Table 19.2** reports, by the state, the level of food insecurity for children in 2009.

We do not know how much of this food insecurity arises because adult members of a household decide to spend their scarce resources on things other than healthy,

Table	19.2	The States of Child Hunger

	Child "food insecurity" in 2009, by state					
Rank		Rate	Children in food insecure households	Rank	Rate	Children in food insecure households
1	D.C.	32.3	36,870	27	Colo.	22.7	271,660
2	Ore.	29.2	252,510	28	Kan.	22.6	158,040
3	Ariz.	28.8	482,340	28	Wis.	22.6	297,870
4	Ark.	28.6	200,290	30	N.Y.	22.4	1,006,390
5	Tex.	28.2	1,871,660	31	La.	22.1	246,720
6	Ga.	27.9	702,520	32	W.Va.	22.0	85,200
7	Miss.	27.7	211,340	33	Mont.	21.8	48,000
7	Nev.	27.7	182,710	34	Alaska	21.2	38,090
9	S.C.	27.6	292,840	35	Pa.	20.9	588,370
10	Fla.	27.5	1,116,260	36	Hawaii	20.8	60,250
11	Calif.	27.3	2,580,080	37	Neb.	20.7	92,360
11	N.C.	27.3	603,250	37	Utah	20.7	170,760
11	N.M	27.3	137,720	37	Vt.	20.7	27,160
14	Tenn.	26.9	396,470	40	Iowa	20.6	146,000
15	Okla.	26.7	240,740	40	Wyo.	20.6	25,940
16	Ala.	26.6	299,390	42	Del.	19.7	40,520
17	Ohio	26.5	731,040	43	S.D.	19.6	38,440
18	Mich.	25.4	618,910	44	N.J.	19.0	394,240
19	Mo.	24.8	354,520	45	Conn.	18.9	155,560
20	Wash.	24.7	382,860	46	Minn.	18.3	231,100
21	Me.	24.6	68,950	47	Mass.	18.1	262,650
22	Ind.	24.5	388,640	48	Md.	17.8	242,910
23	Ky.	24.1	243,920	49	Va.	17.6	321,490
24	R.I.	23.7	55,390	50	N.H.	15.6	46,400
25	Idaho	23.4	95,150	51	N.D.	12.7	18,270
26	Ill.	23.3	745,310		**U.S.**	**23.2**	**17,197,000**

Source: "Map The Meal Gap," Feeding America, ConAgra Foods Foundation

nutritious food for their family. What we do know is that the rate of food insecurity, which measures the food budget shortfall for families with children, has risen with the 2007 Great Recession. The ConAgra Foundation reports that regions with higher unemployment rates have higher food-insecurity rates, all else equal. Specifically, a 1 percentage point increase in the unemployment rate results, on average, in a 0.78 percentage point increase in the food-insecurity rate.

How should society respond to these unmet food needs? If the government is given this responsibility, which policies are more, and which are less, compatible with a market-based economy?

One way that state and federal agencies alleviate hunger is to give away bags of flour or pounds of cheese that they have stockpiled through their agricultural support programs. As you saw in Chapter 8, these stockpiling activities exert upward pressure on the prices of agricultural products, which can itself contribute to food insecurity. More often, the government gives food stamps—vouchers that can be used in lieu of money to purchase food—to people who meet certain eligibility requirements. Researchers have demonstrated that food security "begins to deteriorate in the six months prior to receiving SNAP (food stamp) benefits and to improve shortly after."[18]

In the United States, the familiar multicolored food-stamp coupons have recently been phased out and replaced by EBT (Electronic Balance Transfer) cards, which work like bank debit cards at the grocery store. The impetus for the EBT card system was to end the trafficking in food stamps, wherein food-stamp recipients sold their stamps at a discount—usually around 50 percent—to other food buyers and spent the cash on such nonfood items as children's shoes and cigarettes. Clearly, voucher systems create gains from trade: at least some voucher recipients get greater well-being from goods and services that can be purchased with the cash received by selling the vouchers at their going black-market price.

When there are large numbers of people requiring food assistance, governments may provide subsidies to producers or retailers that will expand output and reduce market prices. In Egypt and many other countries, bread prices are subsidized so that poor families—over 45 percent of the population—can make ends meet. The foodstuffs that are subsidized, along with the magnitude of the subsidies, are determined by the government. The success of these targeted market interventions depends on the government's ability to manage supply and demand effectively to avert any shortages and surpluses. The global recession that began in 2007 has eroded the amount of government aid that is available for these subsidies, increasing the risk of popular uprisings and riots. To counteract this potential threat to his regime, Iranian President Mahmoud Ahmadinejad has introduced a subsidy of $40 per household to offset the sizable cuts in government oil and food subsidies. Analysts maintain that this has created a massive redistribution of income from the country's wealthiest classes to Iran's middle class.[19]

Another avenue for assuring that people have their basic needs met is to supplement their incomes through cash transfers so that more food and other entitlements can be purchased in the market. According to the World Bank, *conditional cash-transfer* (CCT) programs—which give cash payments to poor families that achieve certain nutritional, health, and educational standards for their children—are the fastest

[18]Mark Nord and Anna Marie Golla, "Does SNAP Decrease Food Insecurity?" *USDA Economic Research Report,* no. 85 (October 2009).

[19]Steve LeVine, "Why Ahmadinejad Isn't on His Way Out." *Foreign Policy,* September 15, 2011.

growing part of the global safety-net. The Bank itself loaned $2.4 billion in 2009 to countries wanting to start or expand their CCT programs.[20] More than 30 countries, many in Latin America, now have sizable CCT programs, which have proven to be a major force in overcoming malnutrition in children.

ECONOMIC FALLACY   Providing everyone with the same opportunities will lead to a more equal income distribution.

Uncertain. If there are significant differences in people's initial endowments—in terms of their health, natural talents, beauty, height, and so on—then making opportunities accessible equally to all will not necessarily lead to a more equal income distribution. Instead, it is likely to lead to an income distribution that mirrors the way in which these initial endowments are distributed within the population. To counteract this outcome, society must be willing to invest in people's human capital to offset differences in their initial endowments.

CCT programs tend to be among the most "market-friendly" entitlement programs because they permit people to prioritize their own food and nonfood needs: whereas U.S. food stamps prohibit the purchase of children's shoes and school supplies, most CCT programs permit recipients to purchase a wide range of goods and services in the market. In effect, a CCT program allows people to express their willingness to pay in the market by giving them an ability to pay.

Just as a variety of mechanisms are available to meet a population's basic food requirements, different programs have been adopted to meet housing, medical, and educational entitlements. Why doesn't every country adopt the same support or safety-net programs? Often, the policy that a government implements is influenced by interest groups whose members "win" when a particular type of program is adopted. Farmers, for example, strongly prefer programs such as food stamps, which directly increase people's food purchases, rather than cash-transfer programs that increase the overall purchasing power of households but do not solely target food purchases. Farmers' groups and trade associations invest a lot of their scarce resources lobbying the U.S. Congress to ensure that the food-stamp program remains the primary vehicle for alleviating hunger in the United States. The agriculture lobby has been tremendously successful in this regard: in 2010, the U.S. government spent more than $73 billion on food stamps for almost 40 million recipients. Nonprofit food banks, in cooperation with various corporations, provided an additional $7 billion or so to meet community food needs.

By and large, economists agree that entitlement programs should be designed to be the least distorting with respect to market prices. The reason is that for both producers and consumers, market prices signal the opportunity cost of one good versus another; distorting these signals leads to choices that inefficiently allocate society's limited resources. For example, we provide a medical safety net by prohibiting emergency rooms from turning away uninsured sick patients, while, at the same time, we offer only limited incentives for these patients to see a health-care provider for preventative care. As a result, we have seen too many scarce resources devoted to expensive ER care and too little to preventive care.

In a similar vein, economists tend to support the idea that the financing mechanisms used to fund entitlement programs should be those that distort market prices

. . . .

[20]"Conditional Cash Transfers." The World Bank. http://go.worldbank.org/BWUC1CMXM0.

the least. When employer-paid payroll taxes are used to finance health insurance for the uninsured, for example, they increase the opportunity cost of hiring labor relative to investing in untaxed machinery and technology. Moreover, when payroll taxes are specific to a country or state, they encourage the offshoring of jobs and outsourcing of production.

The "Right" Bundle of Entitlements

While many people—including free-market economists—agree that civilized societies are obligated to meet their population's basic human needs, disagreement arises over which needs are basic and which are not. Should food-stamp recipients be limited to the purchase of hamburger, or should they be allowed to purchase steaks as well? This is not simply an academic question: New York City recently asked the federal government for permission to prohibit recipients from using their food stamps to purchase soda and other sugary foods.[21] Should the homeless receive housing assistance only if they move into public housing, or should they be able to rent privately owned apartments? Do governments have an obligation to provide financial, educational, or medical assistance to illegal immigrants who have been working in the United States and paying taxes?

Philosophers and ethicists are often consulted when communities attempt to establish guidelines for how their scarce resources should be (re)distributed. The prominent use of the word "should" that accompanies these types of discussions is a tipoff that we have left the positive economics domain and moved on to normative questions. For example, is it fair to give scarce kidneys to transplant candidates with the highest willingness to pay (which is what a market would do), to those who are the sickest, or to those who are the youngest? Is it fair to deny a liver transplant to a former alcoholic in favor of a nondrinker who played no role in destroying her own liver? If the market is not used to ration scarce kidneys and livers, other rationing rules must be established.

One of the most intriguing approaches to establishing these rules was proposed by John Rawls.[22] Rawls suggested that socially just rules for distributing scarce resources such as kidneys would be rules that members of a society would adopt before anyone knew "his place in society, his class position or social status . . . [or] his fortune in the distribution of natural assets and abilities, his intelligence, strength, and the like." Rawls argued that behind this "veil of ignorance," people would create rules that help those at the bottom of the income distribution. After all, no one knows whether or not they will actually be one of these people. Rawls concluded that in such a scenario, the adopted rules would maximize the well-being of the worst-off people in society. This is sometimes called a *maximin* rule of social justice because it *max*imizes the *min*imum well-being of everyone in the community.

Of course, in reality, many people do know something about their future socioeconomic status. Their parents' educational attainment and wealth holdings, their own current health status, and their initial human capital endowments foretell their future standing in the community and economic system. This may explain why nations with a high degree of variability in the socioeconomic status of their citizens (the United States and Mexico, for example) are less apt to adopt generous Rawlesian rules to protect their worst-off members as compared to nations in which citizens are relatively equal in terms of their socioeconomic status (Iceland, for example).

• • • • • • •

[21]Anemona Hartocollis, "New York Asks to Bar Use of Food Stamps to Buy Sodas." *New York Times,* October 6, 2010.

[22]John Rawls, *A Theory of Justice* (Cambridge, MA: Harvard University Press, 1971).

Compensating Losers at the Expense of Winners

Assuming that there is a social consensus about meeting the basic needs of people at the lowest end of the income distribution, is there a similar consensus about easing the pain inflicted by competitive forces? We know that market adjustments must be ongoing if scarce resources are to be allocated efficiently and the economic pie is to continue to grow. The fact that the total economic pie grows tells us that those who "win" as a result of a market adjustment could, conceivably, compensate the "losers," and both they and society would still be better off.

Let's assume that we can identify all of the winners and losers from a particular market upheaval. Does it make sense to tax the winners and redistribute these tax receipts to the losers? How high should these taxes be? Will the economic pie be smaller if they are too high? And, if so, are we willing to incur this cost in our pursuit of fairness?

It would not be surprising if our willingness to require winners to compensate losers depends on who the winners and losers actually are. For example, how do you feel about compensating New York textile workers for the loss of their $52.50 per hour union jobs when the winners are Egyptian seamstresses who work in these newly off-shored jobs and earn the equivalent of $10.25 a day—just enough to feed their children for a week? And, do you want to tax a single mother living in Chicago who earns minimum wage and "wins" because she can now buy Egyptian-made clothing for her children at one-fifth the price of American-made clothing?

Of course, when we read about the enormous profits amassed by oil companies at the same time that gasoline prices rise to $3.95 per gallon, we are likely to be much less sympathetic toward these companies when Congress proposes a massive earnings tax on these "winnings." The same might be said about foreclosure specialists who make a fortune by buying homes at depressed prices from unemployed home owners only to flip them for a tidy profit. The bottom line is that it is unlikely there will be a consensus about which market winners should be taxed (and, if so, at what rate) and which market losers should be compensated.

Even if we could come to some agreement about this, we must grapple with the secondary economic effects resulting from these government-directed wealth transfers. Consider a proposal to tax U.S. oil companies on the "windfall" profits they earn when OPEC cuts back supply and causes the world price of oil to rise. This may seem like a fair thing to do, especially in light of the generous tax incentives the United States gives for oil exploration. However, we know the role that profits play in an economy: they signal that there is a need for additional producers and capital in a market. The introduction of a windfall profits tax on the U.S. oil industry would likely lead to fewer new entrants into the oil industry, less domestic production, and, in the long run, higher oil prices. In fact, a Congressional Research Service study reports that the U.S. windfall profits tax that was placed on domestic oil producers during in the 1980s resulted in a 3 to 6 percent decline in domestic production.[23] The end result for the U.S. economy as a whole: an economic pie that is somewhat smaller, although how much smaller is hard to quantify.

Consider what would happen if a profits tax is imposed on home-foreclosure specialists who make speculative investments in the currently depressed housing market, hoping to buy low and eventually sell high. Taxing any potential profits that might be

· · · · · · ·

[23]Salvatore Lazzari, "The Windfall Profit Tax on Crude Oil: Overview of the Issues." *CRS Report* 90-442E, Congressional Research Service (September 12, 1990).

realized will dampen the willingness of these specialists to assume the risk of purchasing distressed properties. This, in turn, will reduce the demand for the homes about to be foreclosed on, thereby hampering a housing-market recovery and higher housing prices. Of course, if the government decided to also subsidize the investment losses that the speculators might suffer, then this would be an offsetting factor that would encourage risk taking. (The U.S. income tax system actually provides such a subsidy by permitting taxpayers to offset their investment gains with their investment losses.)

Suppose you decide that the next big technology wave will be interactive television, where viewers can be virtually beamed into TV game shows as contestants. You quit your job and work 70 hours per week for a year to develop this technology, while living off your savings. Your opportunity cost is not only your forgone wages and the interest on the savings you spend but also the value of your leisure time. Let's say that by the end of the year, you will either be a very big winner—selling your prototype for $1 billion to a giant media firm such as Viacom—or have a worthless piece of junk on your hands.

If a 50 percent tax is imposed on your winnings, you will pay $500 million in taxes if you are successful. What if instead your invention turns out to be a hunk of junk? Your primary investment—your time—is an implicit cost, which means that there is no way to take advantage of any tax relief for explicit losses. If there is a tax on gains and no relief on losses, what happens to your willingness to assume the risk inherent in developing your idea? To put this question in perspective, imagine that this person was Bill Gates approximately 40 years ago. How do you think a 50 percent tax on winnings would have influenced his decision to drop out of college and instead invest his time tinkering in a garage with his buddy Paul Allen?

SOLVED PROBLEM

Q To raise additional tax revenue, President Obama proposed that the tax deduction for charitable donations be eliminated. He argued that people would continue to give to these causes anyway. The additional tax revenue would be used to expand government safety-net programs. Some economists have argued that his proposal would rob charities that also help provide a safety net—such as the Salvation Army—of more money than the government would receive in additional tax dollars. As evidence, they point out that the estimated *price elasticity of giving* is −1.2. Given this information, do you think that the plan makes sense?

A Just like with any other price elasticity, the price elasticity of giving tells you the percentage change in the amount given for a 1 percent change in the price of giving. What is the price of giving? Say that your parents are in the 40 percent tax bracket (federal and state). Then the real price to them of giving away $100 to charity—if it is deductible—is $60 (the other $40 would have gone to taxes if the donation had not been made). If the price elasticity of giving is *elastic*—greater than 1 in absolute terms—then this means that when the price goes up, the amount of giving will fall by a greater percentage. So if the price of giving goes from 60 percent to 100 percent—that is, your parent's donation is no longer deductible—then giving will fall by a greater percentage than

$$\% \text{ change in price} = (100 - 60)/60 = .66 = 66\%$$

In fact, if the price elasticity of giving equals −1.2, then the amount given will fall by

$$-1.2(66\%) = -79.2\%$$

This tells us that the additional amount of taxes collected by the government will be less than the amount by which people cut back on their donations. There will be fewer total dollars—public plus private—to support safety-net programs. So if the goal is to maximize the funding for these programs, then the proposal does not make sense.

Does Redistributing Income Spur Job Growth?

Some economists claim that redistributing income is necessary if there is to be adequate demand for all of the goods and services that an economy's labor force produces. Robert Reich, an economic advisor to former President Bill Clinton, argues that the best way to escape from the 2007 Great Recession is to adopt policies that reduce economic inequality.[24] He points to studies of individual tax returns that show a sharp increase in the share of total income accounted for by the top 1 percent of earners in the United States. While the top 1 percent of tax filers accounted for 9 percent of total income in the 1970s, they accounted for over 23 percent by 2007. Reich concludes that because "the rich spend a much smaller proportion of their incomes than the rest of us . . . when they get a disproportionate share of total income, the economy is robbed of the demand it needs to keep growing and creating jobs."

Is this a valid argument for income redistribution? We know that even the very wealthy do not throw away their money. They use it to pursue both consumption and investment opportunities. When the investment is made locally or nationally, it will finance local and national economic growth. Investors directly—and indirectly through their savings—fund construction projects, the acquisition of new business equipment, and the expansion of businesses, all of which create jobs.

Reich also argues that wealthy Americans often pursue international investment opportunities that will not improve economic conditions in the United States. However, we know that a country's demand for goods and services comes not only from its own residents but from demanders worldwide. As other countries become wealthier through global investment, more international students come to the United States for graduate study, for example, thereby increasing the demand for college professors and the number of available teaching jobs. Does it really matter where this increased demand for higher education comes from if the sole goal is to generate more U.S. jobs?

It is likely that the increasing income inequality among U.S. earners mirrors a growing inequality in their marketable skills. This, in turn, reflects the growing inequality in household investment in children, discussed in Chapter 10. This trend in inequality has been exacerbated by the decline in organized labor's bargaining power, which tends to prop up unskilled wage rates above their free-market levels. If these explanations for the growing degree of income inequality are true, then a simple redistribution of income will not be a long-term solution. Rather, the "playing field" must be leveled in terms of investing in people's human capital—their education, language skills, health, safety, and nutrition—so that they can be competitive in the global labor market.

Regressive Redistribution Policies: Redistributing to the Rich

While most people assume that government redistribution policies take income from the rich and give it to the poor, there have been few studies that have actually tested this assumption. Even policies that are targeted to alleviating food insecurity among the poor—such as the SNAP (food stamp) program—may actually end up, on net, redistributing income to the rich.

How can this be, you might ask? Consider the fact that the SNAP program increases the demand for foodstuffs, thereby increasing prices and the profitability of existing agribusiness corporations such as ConAgra. These companies are owned by stockholders who come primarily from the richest classes in society: in 2007, the wealthiest 5 percent of Americans owned almost 70 percent of all of the outstanding common stock

[24]Robert B. Reich, "How to End the Great Recession." *New York Times*, September 3, 2010, p. A19.

in the United States, either directly or through their pension funds.[25] This means that the increase in profits generated by the SNAP program results in higher stock prices that benefit only a small percentage of the population. Moreover, any gains that these stockholders enjoy due to this run-up in stock prices are taxed at a capital gains rate that is far less than the tax rate for wages. Add to this that the higher food prices hurt the working poor and middle-class families that are not eligible for food stamps. You quickly begin to realize that the *net* effect of the SNAP program may be to make some of the rich richer, hurt the middle class, while helping the poorest families in society.

Even in the case of cash-transfer programs, economist Dwight Lee reports that

> Of the more than $500 billion a year spent [in the United States] on public assistance and social insurance programs, 75 percent—more than $400 billion a year—gets distributed regardless of need. Social Security payments shift approximately $270 billion of income a year to the elderly regardless of their wealth, and on average the elderly possess about twice the net worth per family as does the general population.[26]

In addition to safety-net programs that may enrich the rich at the same time they help the poor, there are "corporate welfare" programs—such as agricultural price supports and protectionist trade policies—that redistribute income to businesses by raising consumer prices. Analysts estimate that direct and indirect subsidies to corporations amount to upwards of $125 billion per year. Some of these subsidies may be economically justified as a way to promote corporate activities that generate positive externalities—such as subsidizing a corporation's development of the next-generation of medical lasers or computer software that protects against hackers. Nevertheless, critics argue that the bulk of corporate welfare goes to Fortune 500 companies solely as political payback. Perhaps it isn't surprising, then, that Lee concludes "the most important factor in determining the pattern of redistribution appears to be political power, not need."

19.5 Alleviating World Poverty

World poverty exists for the very same reasons that it exists in rich countries. A poor or developing country may lack the necessary investment—in people, infrastructure, and so on—to have a comparative advantage when it comes to competing in the global economy. It may also remain poor because of the lack of important natural resources such as water.

Government Foreign-Aid Programs

Wealthier countries have long provided large amounts of direct and indirect aid to developing countries. The motivations for doing so are multifaceted; suffice it to say that, according to our economic model, these activities must increase a country's well-being for it to persist. Perhaps this increase in well-being arises from purely noble motives to reduce suffering worldwide; or perhaps it stems from a desire to stabilize "friendly" regimes to protect access to scarce resources, such as oil; or it may be aimed at preserving a geopolitical advantage, such as access to the Suez Canal, which links the West to the East and is an important oil-shipping route.

Whatever the underlying reason, 22 of the richest nations endorsed a 1970 United Nations resolution that required each of them to contribute 0.7 percent of gross

· · · · · · ·

[25]Sylvia Allegretto, "The State of American Workers' Wealth, 2011." *Economic Policy Institute Briefing Paper*, #292 (March 23, 2011).

[26]Dwight R. Lee, "Redistribution of Income." *The Concise Encyclopedia of Economics* (1st ed.). www.econlib.org/library/Enc1/RedistributionofIncome.html.

national income (GNI) annually to Official Development Assistance (ODA) for less well-developed countries. Despite billions of dollars in ODA contributions since 1970, no country has ever met this funding commitment due to its sheer enormity. While the United States is the single largest contributor to ODA—giving $28.7 billion in 2009—it ranks at the bottom of donor countries in terms of percent of GNI donated (0.2 percent of GNI).[27] These numbers, however, understate some countries' foreign development assistance because they do not include direct loans and the cancellation of some of these loans later in time. In 2011, for example, after the ouster of then-President Hosni Mubarak, Egypt requested that the U.S. government forgive $3.6 billion in loans—in effect, wipe them off the books. With the support of President Obama, the United States agreed to forgive $1 billion of the debt in each of the three following years.

Originally, ODA was designed to provide poorer nations with grants and loans at exceedingly favorable terms. Because this type of aid is the least distorting in terms of prices in either the donor or recipient countries, it has long been heralded as the purest form of income redistribution between countries. This is much like the earned income credit in the United States and the CCT programs described previously, which give additional income to those who qualify. The aid is not tied to the consumption of specific goods, services, or government infrastructure purchases.

Nevertheless, the cancellation of loans by richer countries has introduced "distortions" in the loan market, specifically when it comes to the risk perceptions of recipient countries. Some of these countries, well aware of the possibility of loan forgiveness in the future, have accepted loans and not only failed to repay them but also failed to make the required interest payments on these borrowed funds. If and when these loans are forgiven, the accrued interest payments are likely to be forgiven as well.

Because foreign grants and loans are typically distributed by the recipient nation's government agencies, opportunities arise for corrupt foreign officials to divert funds into their own pockets, while leaving their populations impoverished. Through unorthodox accounting practices and other covert methods, these "kleptocrats" have siphoned off hundreds of billions of dollars in foreign aid to pay for luxurious lifestyles, bribe powerful warlords, finance international terrorism, and fatten private bank accounts in rich countries. Economist Dambiso Moyo, who has written about foreign aid to Africa, says that[28]

> Over the past 60 years at least $1 trillion of development-related aid has been transferred from rich countries to Africa. Yet real per capita income today is lower than it was in the 1970s, and more than 50 percent of the population—over 350 million people—live on less than a dollar a day, a figure that has nearly doubled in two decades . . . the African Union, an organization of African nations, estimated that corruption was costing the continent $150 billion a year. With few or no strings attached, it has been all too easy for the funds to be used for anything, save the developmental purpose for which they were intended.
>
> [This] evidence overwhelmingly demonstrates that aid to Africa has made the poor poorer, and the growth slower.

Corrupt government officials not only siphon off international aid, but they impose substantial costs on private companies that are considering whether to invest in their country. The greater the amount of corruption, the lower the probability that private foreign investment will take place, thereby slowing a country's economic

- - - - - - -

[27]Nergis Gulasan, "Official Development Assistance: The Status of Commitments, Projections for 2010 and Preliminary 2009 Figures." Office of Development Studies, U.N. Development Programme. April, 2010. www.undp.org/developmentstudies/docs/oda_april_2010.pdf.

[28]Dambiso Moyo, "Why Foreign Aid Is Hurting Africa." *Wall Street Journal,* March 21, 2009.

growth rate. Corruption can also affect the way in which a country's internal resources are allocated. For example, the government of the Democratic Republic of Congo (with a corruption rank of 154 and index of 2.2) is spending a good deal of the country's resources on the extraction of valuable minerals such as copper and cobalt—with most of the proceeds going into the pockets of government officials. In contrast, the amount of internal resources devoted to agricultural production has fallen markedly, to the point where many children and adults go without even one substantial meal a day.[29]

A number of watchdog groups monitor political corruption; in fact, Transparency International annually ranks virtually every country in the world in terms of their "corruption perception index." This index defines corruption as "the abuse of public office for private gain" and measures the degree to which corruption is perceived to exist among a country's public officials and politicians. A subset of the 2009 list is reported in **Table 19.3**. The scores range from ten (no corruption) to zero (highly corrupt). Transparency International considers countries with an index below 5.0 to have a serious corruption problem.

Tied Foreign Aid

ODA programs have evolved considerably since 1970. "Untied" assistance has been increasingly replaced by "tied" aid. Tied aid includes subsidies for specific goods and services exported from richer countries to less well-developed countries, food assistance that "dumps" agricultural surpluses of wealthier countries, and debt forgiveness for loans previously used to purchase goods and services from wealthier nations. The actual composition of this aid is influenced considerably by interest groups that seek to increase worldwide demand for their goods and services through government foreign-aid policies. As much as half of ODA today is estimated to be "phantom aid" that ignores the real need of less well-developed countries, which is long-term capital investment.

Some observers have argued that when richer nations export highly subsidized or even free goods to developing countries, they push unsubsidized native producers out of business. In effect, "tied" programs *do* change relative prices in both the donor and recipient countries, thereby distorting individual choices about consumption and investment. The same thing happens when richer countries subsidize machinery and technology to build infrastructure such as dams and sewage plants in poorer countries. Because of these subsidies, more capital-intensive methods are used in production, which inevitably increases the unemployment rate among native, low-wage, unskilled workers.

Can Capitalism Help Developing Countries?

At first glance, you might think that it is capitalism that perverts well-intentioned government foreign-aid programs. In fact, as we have just discussed, the success of these programs is compromised by individuals and interest groups that are able to harness the power of governments for their own private benefit.

Is it possible that capitalism can actually be successful in alleviating poverty in the poorest of nations? In 2006, economics professor Muhammed Yunus won the Nobel

· · · · · · ·

[29]Adam Nossiter, "For Congo Children, Food Today Means None Tomorrow." New York Times, January 2, 2012.

Peace Prize for his pioneering work in introducing *microcredit* in his native country of Bangladesh. Microcredit refers to the relatively new practice of lending small amounts of money ($25–$200) to small businesses and entrepreneurs in less well-developed nations. Yunus argued that these loans are a fundamental right of the poor. Vinod Khosla, a billionaire venture capitalist and co-founder of Sun Microsystems,

Table	19.3	Corruption Perception Index, 2009			
Rank	Country/Territory	CPI 2009 Score The CPI score indicates the perceived level of public-sector corruption in a country/territory	Rank	Country/Territory	CPI 2009 Score The CPI score indicates the perceived level of public-sector corruption in a country/territory
1	New Zealand	9.4	89	Rwanda	3.3
2	Denmark	9.3	97	Liberia	3.1
3	Singapore	9.2	99	Zambia	3.0
5	Switzerland	9.0	106	Argentina	2.9
12	Hong Kong	8.2	111	Egypt	2.8
14	Germany	8.0	120	Vietnam	2.7
16	Austria	7.9	126	Syria	2.6
17	Japan	7.7	130	Lebanon	2.5
19	United States	7.5	130	Libya	2.5
22	Qatar	7.0	130	Nigeria	2.5
24	France	6.9	130	Uganda	2.5
25	Chile	6.7	139	Pakistan	2.4
32	Israel	6.1	139	Philippines	2.4
35	Puerto Rico	5.8	146	Ecuador	2.2
37	Botswana	5.6	146	Kenya	2.2
43	Costa Rica	5.3	146	Russia	2.2
49	Jordan	5.0	146	Ukraine	2.2
52	Czech Republic	4.9	146	Zimbabwe	2.2
55	South Africa	4.7	154	Yemen	2.1
61	Cuba	4.4	158	Cambodia	2.0
63	Saudi Arabia	4.3	158	Central African Republic	2.0
65	Tunisia	4.2	162	Democratic Republic of Congo	1.9
66	Kuwait	4.1	162	Venezuela	1.9
71	Romania	3.8	168	Haiti	1.8
75	Brazil	3.7	168	Iran	1.8
75	Peru	3.7	176	Iraq	1.5
79	China	3.6	176	Sudan	1.5
84	Guatemala	3.4	179	Afghanistan	1.3
84	India	3.4	180	Somalia	1.1
89	Mexico	3.3			

Source: Transparency International, www.transparency.org

has made a substantial commitment to alleviating poverty in his native country by investing in a company that offers microloans to poor women in India.[30]

Nonprofit organizations from around the world have also entered the micro-credit market. Funded through donations from the international community, these nonprofits offer small, low-interest loans to impoverished families to support entrepreneurial ventures and self-employment opportunities. Armed with loans of as little as $25—to purchase a goat or cow, for example—many of these fledgling entrepreneurs have demonstrated the ability to pull themselves and their families out of poverty and eventually repay their loans. Lenders increase the odds of success by providing financial services such as bank accounts and requiring borrowers to attend regular meetings to improve their money-management and entrepreneurial skills.

At the same time that nonprofit groups have expanded their microcredit activities in poorer countries, commercial lenders have moved into the market in pursuit of profits. For example, in the absence of legal limits on interest rates and weak government oversight, for-profit microcredit banks in Mexico impose annual interest rates on borrowers that typically range from 50 percent to 120 percent. These seemingly exorbitant interest rates may accurately reflect the riskiness of the borrowers in terms of the probability that they will default on their loans. For this very reason, nonprofit microlenders—whose contributors do not require a return on their donations—are able to offer lower or no-interest microloans that have a greater potential for lifting families out of poverty.

Why does microcredit appear to work when government loans of a grander scale have such a dismal record? First and foremost, the size of these loans, along with the fact that they are given directly to the fledgling entrepreneur, insulate them from the corruptive reach of government officials. Also, there is ongoing oversight by the lending institutions, which monitor the financial health of the venture, the resulting impact on the household, and the likelihood that the loan will be repaid. Finally, the loans are not made by foreign governments that tend to be more interested in increasing the demand for their own producers' goods than in improving living standards in less well-developed countries.

While microcredit lenders can offer the poor the financial capital that would otherwise not be available to them in commercial credit markets, they are certainly not a panacea when it comes to eliminating world poverty. As we have previously acknowledged, there will always be members of society—in both economically advanced and less well-developed countries—whose human capital prevents them from achieving even a subsistence living from the free market. The question remains—how can a safety net be efficiently and effectively maintained to sustain these individuals?

19.6 Conclusion

Like other people, economists differ when it comes to choosing between policies aimed at alleviating the "pain" created by a free-market economy. Whether a proposed policy attempts to remedy poverty through the introduction of cash transfers or the expansion of preschool opportunities, economists are at the forefront when it comes to identifying the incentives that these policies create and predicting the impact on consumer and producer behavior. In addition, economists are often called on to estimate the cost of the policy, who will bear the burden, and who will enjoy the benefits, and its impact on economic growth, the size of the economic pie, and the

· · · · · · ·

[30]Vikas Bajaj, "In Capitalism, Sun's Co-Founder Sees a Pathway to Help the Poor." *New York Times,* October 6, 2010, p. B1.

> **PARETO OPTIMALITY** An allocation of scarce resources that cannot be altered to make anyone better off without making someone worse off.

> **EXAMPLE** Some minimum-wage workers would voluntarily accept a lower wage in return for employer-provided health insurance. By prohibiting this trade to take place, the government creates a situation that is not Pareto optimal: employees could be made better off without any loss in employer well-being.

> **EXAMPLE** The government sets the reimbursement rates for medical care provided to patients covered by the Medicare insurance program for the elderly. There may be some patients who are willing to supplement the government's payment for additional services—for example, an extra night in the hospital after surgery—but this is not allowed. By prohibiting this trade to take place, the government creates a situation that is not Pareto optimal: patients could be made better off without any loss in the well-being of medical providers.

distribution of income. Economists spend a lot of time estimating the magnitude of these effects so that decision makers can more accurately weigh the costs and benefits of one alternative versus another.

Economists also have a comparative advantage when it comes to understanding the conditions under which scarce resources will be allocated to maximize economic well-being. Striving to achieve economic efficiency requires that resources be used in such a way that no one can be made better off without making someone worse off. This allocation of resources is referred to as the **Pareto optimal** outcome (named after the famous Italian economist Vilfredo Pareto).

We have seen throughout this course that voluntary trade takes place when at least one party to the trade is made better off, and neither is made worse off. As long as there are trades to be made, we have not reached a Pareto optimal outcome. It is only after all voluntary trade has taken place that a Pareto optimal resource allocation has been attained.

When it comes to redistributing income and assets from one person to another, the person who receives the income is made better off at the expense of the person who gives up the income. By definition, someone is made worse off to make someone else better off. This, then, goes beyond the more limited goal of achieving a Pareto optimal, or economically efficient, allocation of resources.

Economists struggle with the question of how to weigh one person's well-being against another's to create a robust measure of a society's overall well-being. Over the years, they have done a better job of developing indexes that measure a nation's economic well-being along the four following dimensions: (1) total consumption of goods, services, and leisure; (2) amount of wealth (human, physical, and financial capital) accumulation; (3) degree of income inequality; and (4) degree of economic insecurity arising from job loss, disability, and so on.[31] In terms of the latter measure, you might recall from the very beginning of this book that financial security—irrespective of the actual level of income—appears to be a major contributor to people's sense of well-being.

· · · · · · · ·

[31]Lars Osberg and Andrew Sharpe, "The Index of Economic Well-Being." *Challenge*, 53, no. 4 (July, 2010): 25–42.

The debate continues over how to weight each of these four indicators of well-being to achieve a single measure of a country's overall economic well-being. To complicate matters, there are still other measures of a nation's well-being—such as infant mortality, population life expectancy, air and water quality—that are not reflected in these four indicators. The ultimate goal is to agree on one or more measures that can be monitored over time to ensure that economic well-being actually increases as the economy grows, and can be used to evaluate the goodness of alternative government policy proposals aimed at improving on market outcomes. The value judgments required to accomplish this Herculean task will inevitably embody individual and social preferences as well as the preferences of political decision makers.

ECONOMIC FALLACY   By boycotting Hershey's—which allegedly purchases cocoa beans from suppliers in Ghana and the Ivory Coast who put children as young as five years old to work—you can help end child labor in the cocoa industry and improve the well-being of these children.

Uncertain. If a large company like Hershey's terminates its contracts with companies in Ghana and the Ivory Coast that exploit children, then jobs there will be lost and the economic well-being of the former workers and their families will fall. Moreover, the cost of producing chocolate would rise, thereby reducing the quantity of cocoa beans demanded and produced in the long run, which could adversely affect these countries. In addition, other chocolate producers would have an incentive to undercut Hershey's prices by continuing to purchase lower-cost cocoa beans from suppliers that exploit child workers. It isn't clear whether all of the consumers of chocolate in wealthier countries would care enough to be willing to pay the higher price for Hershey's chocolate and refrain from buying lower-priced chocolate from companies that continue to rely on suppliers that use child labor.

In contrast, those workers who continue to be employed in the cocoa bean industry in Ghana and the Ivory Coast will enjoy higher wages and better work conditions largely because children are no longer competitors in the labor force. Given the poverty rates in these nations, parents would probably search for other work opportunities for their young children to earn more income for the family. Clearly, as long as the income from child labor is necessary for families to meet their subsistence needs, children will continue to be put to work in these countries.

As the dichotomy between the "haves" and "have-nots" becomes a rallying cry for some individuals and politicians in the aftermath of the 2007 Great Recession, support for a free-market economic system remains remarkably strong. In a December, 2011 Gallup poll, 41 percent of those polled agreed that the United States was increasingly a society of "haves" and "have-nots." At the same time, however, 58 percent of these respondents saw themselves as one of the "haves," down somewhat from the economic heyday of the late 1990s when 67 percent saw themselves as "haves."[32] When asked whether "the fact that some people in the United States are rich and others are poor represents a problem that needs to be fixed or is an acceptable part of our economic system," 52 percent of Gallup poll respondents agreed that

. . . .

[32]Lymari Morales,"Fewer Americans See U.S. Divided into "Haves and "Have-Nots." December 15, 2011. www.gallup.com/poll/151556.

this was an acceptable part of our economic system (up from 45 percent in 1998). The Gallup organization summarized its findings as follows:

> More Americans say it is important that the federal government enact policies that grow the economy and increase equality of opportunity than say the same about reducing the income and wealth gap between the rich and the poor.[33]

This majority perspective may go a long way towards explaining why a market-based economic system—which favors economic growth and the allocation of resources to their highest valued use—remains the system of choice for countries such as the United States which apparently place a higher value on equality of economic opportunity rather than actual economic success.

WHAT YOU SHOULD HAVE LEARNED FROM CHAPTER 19

■ That support for government intervention to soften the blow of market adjustments is most prevalent when there are large shocks to the economy, such as during the Great Depression and the Great Recession.

■ That there are both winners and losers whenever a market adjustment occurs.

■ That when the economic pie grows, everyone is not necessarily made better off.

■ That companies outsource production activities and offshore jobs overseas to take advantage of these foreign locations and thereby reduce their production costs.

■ That economic analysis tends to ignore the pain inflicted by wealth transfers that result from changes in market prices.

■ That government bailouts and other market interventions often distort people's consumption and investment decisions.

■ That society has goals other than economic efficiency, such as reducing income inequality, which it may pursue in spite of the smaller economic pie that results.

■ That efforts to alleviate world poverty have been thwarted by corruption and the political power of interest groups.

■ That the forces of capitalism may be harnessed through microcredit loan markets that provide the capital to turn poor women and their families into entrepreneurs.

■ That economic efficiency maximizes the total economic pie but does not consider the impact of making someone better off by making someone worse off—that is, by forcibly redistributing income from one person to another.

KEY TERMS

Command economy, p. 583

Capitalism, p. 584

Entitlement, p. 596

Pareto optimality, p. 609

QUESTIONS AND PROBLEMS

1. Berkeley (CA) Cares, a nonprofit charity, established one of the first programs in the United States to encourage people to give vouchers instead of money to local panhandlers. These vouchers, worth 25 cents each, could be redeemed for food, clothing personal-hygiene products, laundry services, and bus tokens. People

. . . .

[33]Frank Newport, "Americans Prioritize Economy Over Reducing Wealth Gap." December 16, 2011. www.gallup.com/poll/151568.

would purchase these vouchers at participating stores to give to panhandlers when approached for money. The program has since been replicated in a number of cities, including New Haven (CT) and Boston (MA).

a) From a panhandler's own perspective, is he better off receiving a voucher or a quarter?

b) From a donor's own perspective, is she better off giving a voucher or a quarter?

c) Do you think that the amount of donations will be the same under either scheme? Explain your answers.

2. Studies have shown that when the government gets heavily involved in redistributing income to people at the bottom of the income distribution, the amount of private charity given for the same purpose drops. In effect, the government's activities *crowd out* private initiatives. Which institution—government or private charity—do you think is better suited to alleviate poverty in a country? In a local community? Be sure to explain what you mean by "better" in your answer.

3. Do you think that the availability of unemployment benefits affects the amount of time an unemployed person spends searching for a new job? If so, how? What other factors do you think have an impact on the search process? Explain your answers.

4. In the United States, many government entitlement programs establish eligibility standards based on earning thresholds established by the U.S. Department of Health and Human Services. As the following table shows, the department's 2009–2010 guidelines established a cutoff, based on pretax cash income, below which individuals and households are considered poor. The cutoff varies with the size of the household.

Number of People in Household	Poverty Guideline (Cutoff)
1	$10,830
2	$14,570
3	$18,310
4	$22,050
5	$25,790
6	$29,530

a) Why do you think that the cutoff for a household with two people is only 35 percent more than the cutoff for a household comprised of only one person?

b) Do you think that the value of government assistance programs (such as welfare and Social Security payments) a household receives should be included in evaluating its poverty status? Explain your answer.

5. There are several ways governments can reduce the costs that people incur as a result of market adjustments. A government can (1) provide a safety net that guarantees people's basic needs are met; (2) require people to buy insurance in the event of an adverse market outcome—for example, unemployment insurance; (3) limit the types and amount of risk that a person can take in the market—for example, prohibit certain types of speculative investments. Will each of these approaches have the same impact on the allocation of scarce resources in society? Why or why not? Explain your answer.

6. Suppose the government is faced with a budget crisis and must choose whether to cut funds from a program that supplements the income of the elderly or from a program that supplements the income of families below the poverty line with young children. Is there any positive (versus normative) economic analysis you could offer legislators to help them make this difficult decision? Explain your answer.

7. One of the ways in which global poverty can be alleviated is by outsourcing production from richer countries to less-developed countries. Another way is for wealthier countries to donate foreign aid to less-developed nations. A third approach is to let foreigners from poor countries work in richer countries and send some of their earnings back home to their families.

   a) Who actually "pays" to alleviate global poverty under each of these three approaches?
   b) From an economic perspective, which approach do you think would most efficiently reduce global poverty?
   c) Which approach do you think is most politically palatable from the perspective of wealthier nations? From the perspective of less-developed countries? Explain your answers.

8. In the United States, a very strong relationship exists between poverty and health status: poorer people tend to be unhealthier, and unhealthier people tend to be poorer. Explain why this is the case.

9. Suppose you decide to major in engineering and subsequently experience "a boom or a bust" in your earnings. Sometimes you are flush with job offers and high-wage opportunities, and at other times you are out of work. Your best friend majors in elementary education and faces a steady, if lower, flow of earnings over her work life. Do you think it is "fair" for you to collect unemployment benefits during your "bust" periods if they are paid by taxpayers like your friend's wages are? Explain your answer.

10. If a family receives $145 in food stamps each month to purchase food, will the family end up spending $145 more on food each month? Why or why not. Explain your answer.

11. Using the Rawlsian concept of justice, explain why there are richer government entitlement programs in Norway and Iceland than in the United States (Hint: Is there any reason to believe that behind the veil of ignorance, you will see your eventual position in society differently if you are Icelandic versus American?)

12. Costa Rica runs a trade deficit with its trading partner, the United States. This means that Costa Ricans buy more goods from U.S. suppliers than Americans purchase from Costa Rican suppliers. The U.S. government and some major U.S. corporations buy empty bottles from the Costa Rican government that are filled with the "purer" air of the Costa Rican rainforests. One explanation for this seemingly odd behavior is that it reduces the trade deficit. At least a portion of the revenues received for bottled air is dedicated to providing small incentives for private landholders in Costa Rica to pursue environmentally friendly land management. Do you think this is an economically efficient way to provide support to Costa Rica, or do you think that giving foreign-aid grants (targeted to environmental protection if desired) is preferable? Explain your answer. Why do you think that empty bottles of air are bought and sold in the marketplace?

13. The Kyoto Agreement, which the United States has not signed, requires that wealthier countries reduce their air pollution emissions by a far higher percentage than less well-developed countries. The rationale given is that the standard of living in wealthier countries is far higher than in developing countries, so their populations should bear more of the cost of reducing air pollution. For example, it would be less "painful" for Americans to pay the extra $1,000 for an automobile with 30 percent less harmful emissions than it would be for the people of Bangladesh to reduce air pollutants by this same amount. Do you think that it makes sense to distribute the financial burden of reducing air pollution in this way? What will happen to manufacturing jobs in the United States if U.S. manufacturing plants are required to bear the brunt of reducing global air pollution? Explain your answer.

14. Richer countries often try to improve the welfare of children and "exploited" workers in less well-developed countries by urging their governments to enforce child-labor and minimum-wage laws. Do you think this is a good idea or not? Explain your answer.

15. Carl Icahn, an infamous corporate "raider," wants to buy Commercial Metals Company and combine parts of it with various metal recycling businesses that he already owns. He has offered to buy shares from Commercial Metals shareholders at $15 per share, which amounts to a 31 percent premium over the company's current stock price of $11.45.

    a) Why do you think that Icahn offered stockholders a price so much higher than the going share price?

    b) Should government regulators let Icahn buy this company, even though it is clear that it will be broken apart and employees will lose their jobs? Explain your answer.

16. Morissa is a 16 year old triplet. She argues that "fairness" means that she should be given the same opportunities and material goods as her two brothers. Her parents argue that "fairness" means "to each according to their needs." Which perspective more closely parallels your notions about "fairness." Explain your answer.

17. Teachers often disagree when it comes to their grading philosophies. Some contend that the fair way to grade is to put significant weight on the effort put in by a student. Others say that fairness requires that grades be based largely on objective measures of academic performance such as exam and assignment grades. Still others believe that grades should reflect the "value-added" (that is, change in academic performance) of students from the beginning to the end of the grading period. Discuss the merits and pitfalls of each of these views, including the incentives they create for individual student behavior.

GLOSSARY

absolute advantage The ability to produce more output than other producers using the same amount of resources.

accounting costs Explicit costs, or monetary outlays, incurred in the course of doing business.

accounting profit Total revenue less total accounting cost.

antitrust policies Government regulations and laws that are aimed at deterring the creation of monopolies as well as the exertion of monopoly and oligopoly pricing power, thereby promoting market competition.

arc elasticity of demand The price elasticity of demand calculated using the midpoint method.

average fixed cost (AFC) Total fixed cost divided by the number of units (q) produced.

average product (AP) Total output (q) divided by the amount of a variable input that is used.

average total cost (ATC) Total cost divided by the number of units (q) produced.

average variable cost (AVC) Total variable cost divided by the number of units (q) produced.

barriers to entry Impediments that substantially increase the cost of potential competitors entering a market.

barter The direct exchange of a good or service for another with no money changing hands.

budget constraint A line comprised of all bundles of goods that a person can afford at a given set of prices and income.

budget share The fraction of income spent on a particular good or category of goods.

calorie-income elasticity Percentage change in calories consumed during a specified time period resulting from a percentage change in income, all else remaining the same.

capitalism An economic system wherein the means of production are predominantly owned and controlled by private producers.

cartel A group of cooperating oligopolists that jointly set price or output levels to achieve monopoly profits.

ceteris paribus A Latin phrase meaning "holding all else unchanged." Assuming this condition allows us to analyze the impact of one change, and one change alone, in the economic environment that affects a decision maker's choices.

Coase Theorem Regardless of which party is given the property rights to a scarce resource that is creating an externality, the same socially optimal use of that resource will result as long as all parties to the externality can negotiate with each other at low cost.

collective good A good that can be consumed by more than one person at the same time.

command economy An economic system wherein a society's means of production are predominantly controlled and deployed by the government.

common property right A right that bestows shared control over a scarce resource to a group of people or entities.

comparative advantage The ability to produce a particular good at a lower opportunity cost than other producers.

complementary goods Goods that are usually consumed with one another.

concentration ratio Share of an industry that is attributable to its largest 4, 8, or 16 firms.

constant returns to scale A situation in which increasing all inputs proportionately yields the same proportionate increase in output and, therefore, the same long-run average cost per unit of output.

consumer surplus The difference between a person's willingness to pay for a unit of a good and the amount that is actually paid.

consumption Activities that create immediate well-being and that use up resources in the process.

contestable market A market that, in the long run, a firm can enter or leave from at low cost.

cooperative outcome An allocation of resources that is based on a voluntary, enforceable agreement about how the resulting net benefits will be shared.

corruption perception index A measure of the extent to which there is abuse of public office for private gain in a country.

cost-minimizing production A situation where the very last dollar spent on each input generates the same amount of output.

cream-skimming The process by which the "best" (usually defined as lowest cost or highest quality) are separated from the rest of their group and targeted for special treatment.

creative destruction The process by which innovation undercuts monopoly pricing power and profitability.

cross-price elasticity of demand The percentage change in the quantity of a good demanded in response to a percentage change in the price of another good.

cross-subsidy The shifting of resources from one individual or group to another via a pricing or payment system that does not reflect the true opportunity cost of servicing each group.

deadweight loss The reduction in consumer and producer well-being—beyond the amount of taxes paid to the government—when a tax is imposed.

decreasing returns to scale A situation in which increasing all inputs proportionately leads to less than a proportionate increase in output, resulting in an increase in the firm's long run average total cost.

demand Quantity demanded at *each and every* price, assuming that all else remains unchanged.

demand curve A graphical representation of a demand schedule. The demand curve plots various price–quantity combinations that a buyer is willing to accept.

demand schedule A table that shows the quantity demanded at each and every price.

derived demand The demand for an input, which is dependent upon the demand for the good that it is used to produce.

diminishing marginal benefit A situation in which the economic benefit generated from an additional unit of a good or activity is less than the benefit derived from the preceding unit.

diminishing marginal returns A situation in which the addition of another unit of an input results in a lower marginal contribution to output than what was contributed by the preceding unit, all else remaining unchanged.

discount rate The amount by which a person reduces the value of future returns or events because they are not immediate. The lower the discount rate a person has, the greater the "patience" she demonstrates when it comes to waiting for a return to materialize. The

discount rate is sometimes referred to as the "time value of money."

disequilibrium A situation in which the quantity demanded of a good does not equal the quantity supplied.

division of labor Concentration of a worker's full work effort on a subtask that contributes to the production of a specific good or service.

divorce-threat bargaining model A behavioral model in which household resources are allocated so that each member receives at least as much well-being as what could be obtained by leaving the household.

dominant strategy The strategy that is the best choice regardless of what a rival decides to do.

duopoly A market comprised of only two firms, with high barriers to entry.

economic "bad" A product, activity, or service whose consumption reduces well-being.

economic benefit The satisfaction, happiness, or sense of well-being created when a person allocates a scarce resource to a particular use.

economic cost Opportunity cost.

economic discrimination A situation in which signals unrelated to quality are relied upon to assess the members of a group.

economic efficiency A situation in which scarce resources are put to their highest-valued use, where "value" is determined by the willingness to pay for them.

economic environment Prices, wages, income, laws, and social norms that serve as external constraints on the choices we make; external factors that dictate the trade-offs we face.

economic "good" Any scarce resource, product, service, or other source of well-being.

economic profit Total revenue less total economic cost.

economic rationality People make choices that they believe will advance their own well-being.

eminent domain The right of the government to take private property for public use.

Engel's curve A grapxh that shows the relationship between income and the quantity of a good purchased.

entitlement A legal right to a certain set of goods and services.

entry-limit pricing A tacit pricing strategy adopted by existing rivals to set a price lower than the monopoly price to deter higher-cost producers from entering the market.

equilibrium price The price at which the quantity demanded is exactly equal to the quantity supplied; the market-clearing price.

equilibrium quantity The quantity bought and sold at the equilibrium price.

exchange rate The price of one country's currency in terms of another nation's currency.

exclusivity The right of an owner of a good to exclude others from using it without permission.

expected investment return An investment's return weighted by the probability that it will actually materialize.

explicit cost The monetary cost of a choice.

firm An organization that internally manages and coordinates inputs in the production process, rather than relying on prices and market exchange to perform these functions.

first-degree price discrimination A pricing scheme that charges each and every consumer his full willingness to pay for each and every unit sold.

fixed input An input whose quantity cannot vary in the short run.

food insecurity The inability to consistently access adequate amounts of food to meet basic nutritional requirements.

game theory A model of decision making that portays the set of strategies that each rival can choose from and uses this information to predict how each will respond to one another.

habits Routine choices that are made in lieu of actively weighing the costs and benefits of each alternative.

Herfindahl Index A measure that captures the entire size distribution of firms in an industry.

human capital The stock of personal characteristics that contribute to the market value of a person's labor and consumption opportunities. These include health status, intelligence, work ethic, educational attainment, strength, beauty, reputation, and social networks.

imperfect information Limited or erroneous knowledge about the economic cost or benefit of an alternative.

implicit cost The nonmonetary cost of a choice.

income elastic good A situation in which the quantity of a good purchased increases more, percentage-wise, than the corresponding percentage increase in income; and, conversely, where the quantity of a good purchased decreases more, percentagewise, than the corresponding percentage decrease in income.

income elasticity of demand The percentage change in the quantity of a good purchases in response to a percentage change in income, holding everything else constant.

Income inelastic good A situation in which the quantity of a good purchased decreases less, percentage-wise, than the corresponding percentage decrease in income; and, conversely,

where the quantity of the good purchased increases less, percentagewise, than the corresponding percentage increase in income.

increasing returns to scale A situation in which increasing all inputs proportionately yields more than a proportionate increase in output, thereby resulting in a decline in the firm's long-run average total cost.

indifference A situation in which the net benefit of a particular decision is zero and, as a result, a decision maker doesn't care about the choice that is made.

indifference curve A curve that shows all bundles of goods that yield the same level of well-being.

inferior good A good that a person is willing to pay less for as her income increases, and more for when her income declines.

input price The price of one unit of an input used in production.

intellectual property rights Control over the use of ideas and products arising from a person's creativity.

intelligent mistakes Errors in decision making that we learn from.

internal rate of return (IRR) The discount rate that results in a zero net present value for an investment's future stream of returns.

investment Current resources that are allocated for the purpose of building an accumulation or stock of capital to potentially increase your future well-being.

investment return The percentage change in the value of an investment over a given period of time.

isocost line Line that shows all combinations of inputs that cost the same. Lines to the right are comprised of input bundles that cost more; lines to the left are comprised of bundles that cost less.

isoquant A graph that shows all combinations of inputs that yield the same level of output.

labor union An organization comprised of workers who act in concert to improve their wages, benefits and working conditions.

law of demand The price of a good and the quantity demanded are inversely related. When price rises, the quantity demanded falls, and when price falls, the quantity demanded rises, assuming that nothing else has changed.

law of supply When a good's price increases, suppliers are willing to offer more units for sale, all other things held constant. Conversely, when the price falls, suppliers cut back on the number of units they are willing to sell.

long run The length of time over which a decision maker can fully respond to changes in the economic environment. Suppliers can adjust all inputs into production and output supplied to the market and consumers can fully adjust the quantity they demand.

long-run market equilibrium A situation in which there is no incentive for firms to exit (or enter) a market or for existing firms to adjust their output levels.

macroeconomics The study of economy-wide events, such as economic growth, inflation, and business cycles.

manager An individual that monitors inputs into production, focusing on those that have the greatest potential for shirking.

marginal analysis A thought process that compares the net benefit of allocating each additional unit of a scarce resource to one alternative versus another.

marginal benefit (MB) The increase in economic benefit, that results when an additional unit of a scarce resource is spent on a particular activity.

marginal benefit curve A graphic representation of the incremental benefit received from consuming an additional unit of a good.

marginal cost (MC) The increase in economic cost that results from consuming or producing an additional unit of a good or service.

marginal cost (short run) The short-run cost of producing one more unit of output; the increase in total variable costs incurred to produce an additional unit.

marginal cost curve A graphic representation of the incremental cost incurred to consume or produce an additional unit of an economic good or service.

marginal factor cost (MFC) A monopsony's cost of purchasing an additional unit of the good or service for which it is the sole buyer.

marginal product The additional output produced when an additional unit of one input is added to the production process, everything else held constant.

marginal rate of substitution (MRS) The rate at which a consumer is willing to trade off one good for another and remain indifferent.

marginal rate of technical substitution (MRTS) The rate at which one input must be traded off for another to hold output constant; the ratio of the marginal products of the inputs.

marginal rate of transformation (MRT) The rate at which two outputs can be traded off for one another. It is the *opportunity cost* of producing one more unit of one good in terms of forgone units of the other good.

marginal revenue (MR) The contribution that each incremental unit of production makes to total revenue.

marginal willingness to pay The maximum willingness to pay for each additional unit of a good.

market A place or circumstance in which buyers and sellers meet, either directly or through representatives, to voluntarily exchange goods and services.

market bubble A run-up in the price of an asset that is eventually followed by a crash in its price.

market-clearing price The price at which the quantity demanded just equals the quantity supplied.

market demand curve A graphical representation of the relationship between a good's price and the total quantity demanded in the market, at each and every price.

market period The length of time during which a decision maker is unable to respond at all to changes in the economic environment. Consumers cannot adjust the quantity they demand and suppliers and cannot adjust the quantity supplied to the market.

market supply The total number of units of a good supplied at each and every price by all producers in a market during a specific period of time.

market supply curve A graphical representation of the total number of units of a good supplied by all producers in a market during a specific period of time.

median voter model A behavioral model which predicts that elected officials, seeking to retain their positions, make decisions that benefit slightly more than 50 percent of their voters.

microeconomics The study of how individuals, households, and producing organizations make decisions to maximize their own well-being.

midpoint method A method that calculates percentage changes using the midpoint of the starting and ending values as the base.

minimum efficient scale of production The lowest level of output that achieves the lowest long-run average total cost (*LRAC*).

monopolistic competition A market in which many firms sell differentiated products—from the consumers' point-of-view—and where there are no barriers to entry.

monopoly One supplier operating in a noncontestable market.

monopsony A market with only a single buyer.

movement along the demand curve Increase or decrease in quantity demanded when only the price of the good changes.

Nash bargaining solution A bargaining outcome such that there is no way to reallocate resources to make someone better off without making someone else worse off; an outcome that is on the utility possibilities frontier.

natural monopoly A firm whose long-run *MC* and *ATC* curves fall continuously throughout the full range of market demand.

negative externality A situation in which a decision maker's choices impose economic costs on others.

net benefit The difference between the economic benefit and the opportunity cost of an alternative.

net marginal benefit The economic benefit from an additional unit of a good or service minus the economic cost of this unit.

net present value The maximum amount an investor would pay today for an asset based on the present value of the investment's stream of expected returns minus costs.

noncooperative outcome The allocation of resources that results in the absence of an enforceable agreement about how the gains from trade will be shared.

nonprice competition A firm's efforts to increase sales without lowering price by enhancing product quality, providing additional services or offering other enticements to buyers, most commonly pursued when price is above market equilibrium due to oligopoly restrictions or government regulation.

nonprofit firm A firm with no residual claimants that is legally prohibited from distributing its net revenue to privately benefit individuals or other entities.

nonspecific human capital Human capital that imparts skills that are applicable to a broad range of production processes.

normal good A good that a person is willing to pay more for as her income increases and less for when her income declines.

normative analysis Evaluation of economic decision making that is based on a person's values, religious beliefs, and opinions.

offshoring The movement of a company's production facilities overseas.

oligopoly A market comprised of only a few sellers, with high barriers to entry.

one-price market A market in which each and every unit of the good trades at the same price.

open economy An economy that has few, if any, costly barriers preventing trade from taking place.

opportunity cost The economic benefit given up when one option is chosen over another. The economic benefit you miss out on from your next-best opportunity because of the choice you have made.

outsourcing The process of shifting business functions to nonemployees.

Pareto optimality An allocation of scarce resources that cannot be altered to make anyone better off without making someone worse off.

partnership A firm with two or more owners, all of whom are personally responsible for the company's debts.

patent A legal protection of intellectual property rights that conveys exclusive control over an invention or process for a certain period of time.

payoff matrix A chart with rows and columns representing the strategies available to each rival; the intersection of each row and column reveals the payoff to each rival for each combination of strategies that the rivals choose.

perfectly income inelastic good A situation in which the quantity of a good purchased remains unchanged when there is an increase or decrease in income.

perfectly price elastic demand A situation in which the quantity demanded is so sensitive that it goes to zero when the price increases by only an infinitesimal amount.

perfectly price inelastic demand A situation in which the quantity of a good demanded is totally unresponsive to a change in its price. A good whose demand curve is vertical.

physical capital Land and other natural resources, machinery, and technology.

positive analysis Evaluation of economic decision making that is based on facts and theories, leading to testable implications and validation.

positive externality A situation in which a decision maker's choices generate economic benefits for others.

preferences Tastes; basis upon which alternative opportunities are ranked.

present value (PV) The amount that would be paid *today* to buy the rights to a future stream of expected returns.

price ceiling The maximum price that can legally be charged for a good.

price controls Prices set by a government authority rather than by the market.

price discrimination A situation in which a producer sells units of its output at different prices despite the absence of any cost differences in supplying this output.

price elastic demand A situation in which the percentage change in quantity demanded is greater than the percentage change in price.

price elasticity of demand The percentage change in the quantity of a good demanded in response to a percentage change in its price.

price elasticity of supply The percentage change in the quantity of a good supplied in response to a percentage change in its price.

price floor The minimum price that can be legally charged for a good.

price inelastic demand A situation in which the percentage change in the quantity demanded is less than the percentage change in price.

price leader A firm that consistently sets prices that rivals subsequently adopt.

price taker A potential buyer or seller who takes price as "given" and can only quantity-adjust in response to this price.

price wedge Difference in the price paid to suppliers and the net price actually paid by consumers.

pricing power The ability of an existing firm or group of firms to influence market price due to the existence of barriers to entry.

principle of increasing marginal cost The opportunity cost of consuming or producing additional units of a good begins to increase at some point.

prisoners' dilemma A game where each rival has a dominant strategy that ultimately leads to a second-best outcome for all of the rivals.

private benefit The economic benefit or well-being that a decision maker enjoys from a choice she has made.

private cost The economic cost or loss in well-being that a decision maker that a person bears from a choice he has made.

private good A good whose use by one person prevents use by others.

private property right A right that bestows exclusive control over a scarce resource to one person or entity.

producer surplus The difference between a supplier's marginal cost of producing each unit of output and the price received for that unit.

product differentiation Features of a product that consumers rely on to distinguish it from otherwise similar products.

production function A representation of the relationship between the amount of each input used in production and the amount of output generated.

production possibilities frontier (PPF) A graph that shows the maximum combination of outputs that can be produced from a given amount of scarce resources during a specified period of time.

profit Total revenue minus total economic cost; the total net benefit of production.

profit-maximizing output level The level of output at which the marginal cost of the last unit produced just equals the marginal revenue received for it.

progressive tax A tax that accounts for a larger percentage of income as income rises.

property right Legal or social right to control and use a scarce resource in a particular way.

proportional tax A tax that collects the same percentage of income from taxpayers, regardless of their income level.

proprietorship A firm with a single owner who is personally liable for all of the company's debts.

public good A collective good that no one can be excluded from using.

public monopoly A monopoly owned by a government entity.

publicly held corporation A firm whose owners hold shares of stock that can be traded in stock markets and who are not personally liable for the company's debts.

quantity demanded The number of units of a good that a person is willing and able to buy at a specific price.

rationing The process by which scarce goods and services are allocated among members of a society. Markets ration through the price mechanism, according to people's willingness to pay.

regressive tax A tax that accounts for a lower share of income as income rises.

relative price The ratio of the price of one good to the price of another good.

rent-seeking Interest group activities that seek to increase members' private economic well-being through the creation or reallocation of property rights, and the passage of economically favorable legislation.

reservation price Willingness to pay; the maximum amount that a person is willing and able to pay for each unit of a good.

residual claimant Owner that has the right to the net revenue, or profit, of a firm.

risk premium The additional return that must be given to induce a decision maker to engage in a risky activity such as a risky investment.

scarcity The condition we find ourselves in when only limited resources are available to meet our unlimited wants.

second-degree price discrimination A monopoly pricing scheme that offers buyers discounts based on the quantity they purchase.

shift in demand curve A movement of the demand curve to the left or right. This movement reflects the change in quantity demanded at each and every price due to a change in something other than the good's price.

shirking A decision to contribute less than one's maximum work effort to the production process.

shortage/excess demand A situation in which the quantity demanded exceeds the quantity supplied.

short run The length of time during which a decision maker is only partially able to respond to changes in the economic environment. Consumers can only partially adjust quantity demanded and suppliers are able to only partially adjust input levels and the quantity supplied to the market.

shutdown price The market price that just covers a firm's variable costs of production. Below this price, a firm will minimize its losses by immediately halting production.

signal A characteristic of a group, such as brand name, that is easily observable and is relied on to assess the quality of the group's individual members.

simple monopoly A monopoly that charges the same price for all of the units of output supplied to the market.

social benefit The total economic benefit enjoyed by everyone as a result of an individual's choice.

social cost The total economic cost borne by everyone as a result of an individual's choice.

social discount rate The value that society places on future well-being versus current well-being.

specialization Circumstance in which a person (or country) engages in a limited range of productive activities.

specific human capital Human capital that imparts skills required for certain aspects of a production process.

substitute goods Goods that are related in such a way that an increase in the price of one increases demand for the other; conversely, a decrease in the price of one decreases demand for the other.

sunk costs Costs that cannot be recouped if you walk away from a prior decision.

supply curve A graphic representation of a supplier's supply schedule. The supply curve plots various price–quantity combinations that an individual producer is willing to accept.

supply-chain management The process of managing the coordination between input suppliers and input buyers to achieve efficiencies and lower production costs.

supply schedule A table that shows various prices of a good and the number of units a producer is willing to sell at each price during a specific time period.

surplus/excess supply A situation in which quantity supplied exceeds quantity demanded.

switching costs The monetary costs, as well as psychological and time costs, incurred when a person changes brands, providers, or products.

tacit price agreement Unwritten and often unspoken cooperation between rivals to coordinate price or output levels so as to increase profits.

tariff A tax placed on imported goods.

tax credit An amount of money "credited" against a person's tax liability. When this results in a negative tax liability, a cash payment is made in the form of a tax refund.

tax incidence The way in which the burden of a tax is shared between consumers and suppliers.

third-degree price discrimination A monopoly pricing scheme that charges groups of buyers differently based on their price elasticity of demand.

threat point The minimum level of well-being that a person must receive to join and remain in a household.

tied foreign aid Foreign aid that comes in the form of subsidies for specific goods exported by the donor country.

time horizon The time period that people consider when making economic decisions.

tit-for-tat strategy A strategy whereby a rival inflicts harm on another rival in exactly the same way as that rival inflicted harm in the previous round of the "game."

total cost (TC) The total opportunity cost (implicit plus explicit costs) of resources used up in production. The sum of total variable and total fixed costs in the short-run.

total fixed cost (TFC) The total cost of a firm's fixed inputs, which remains constant in the short run, even when output increases or decreases.

total variable cost (TVC) The total cost of variable inputs, which increases when output rises and decreases when output falls.

trade-offs Opportunities we pass up when we make one choice versus another choice.

transaction costs Costs incurred in trading goods and services, including search and information costs, bargaining costs, payment costs, and enforcement costs.

transitory income Short-term or one-time increases or decreases in income.

unfunded mandate A government directive that specifies services that are to be provided to specific groups without the funding necessary to meet this directive.

unitary income elasticity A situation in which the quantity of a good purchases grows or declines at the same rate as any change in income, all else remaining unchanged. Unitary income elastic goods account for a fixed budget share at all levels of income.

unitary model of the household A predictive model which assumes that household members jointly pursue a commonly held set of objectives.

unitary price elastic demand A situation in which the percentage change in quantity demanded is exactly equal to the percentage change in its price.

utility Economic benefit or well-being.

value of the marginal product (VMP) The market value of each worker's incremental contribution to output; the employee's marginal product weighted by the market price of this output.

variable input An input whose quantity can vary in the short run.

wage The price at which labor services are supplied.

well-being A person's happiness, benefit, pleasure, or contentment.

willingness to pay The maximum amount of money a person is willing and able to pay for each unit of a good.

X-inefficiency Wasteful expenditures or inefficient production processes that increase the cost of production.